Jacqueline du Pré

Jacqueline du Pré

HER LIFE, HER MUSIC, HER LEGEND

ELIZABETH WILSON

Arcade Publishing · New York

Arcade Publishing books may be purchased in bulk at special discounts for sales promotion, corporate gifts, fund-raising, or educational purposes. Special editions can also be created to specifications. For details, contact the Special Sales Department, Arcade Publishing, 307 West 36th Street, 11th Floor, New York, NY 10018 or arcade@skyhorsepublishing.com.

Arcade Publishing® is a registered trademark of Skyhorse Publishing, Inc.®, a Delaware corporation.

Visit our website at www.arcadepub.com.

10 9 8 7 6 5 4 3 2

Library of Congress Cataloging-in-Publication Data is available on file.

ISBN: 978-1-61145-825-1

Printed in Canada

Contents

Illustrations

Jacqueline, Itzhak Perlman and Arthur Rubinstein playing trios, New York, 1970[9]
Jacqueline with Daniel Barenboim on the day her illness was made public, 1973[14]
Jacqueline and Daniel with her OBE, 1976[14]
Jacqueline and Harry Blech at a Haydn-Mozart Society Members' evening[15]
Jacqueline and Daniel after a rehearsal of Peter and the Wolf, London, 1978[12]

[1] © Angela Heskitt
[2] © EMI/Gérard Neuvecelle
[3] © Ana Chumachenko
[4] © Bob Martin/Collection des Archives Audiovisuelles de la Principauté de Monaco
[5] © BBC Picture Archive
[6] © EMI
[7] © EMI/David Farrell
[8] © Zamira Benthall
[9] © Courtesy of Daniel Barenboim
[10] © Eugenia Zukerman
[11] © EMI/Reg Wilson
[12] © Clive Barda/The Performing Arts Library
[13] © Tom Shanahan
[14] © PA News
[15] © Courtesy of the London Mozart Players

Acknowledgements

I wish to thank the innumerable people whose help and active contribution has made this book possible.

First and foremost, I wish to express my gratitude to Daniel Barenboim who trusted me to undertake the task, and who gave me support and encouragement in every way, initially by providing me with contacts and information, then sharing his memories of Jacqueline, granting me his fascinating insights into music and performance, and finally in reading through the manuscript, making corrections, suggestions, and giving judicious advice. He was careful never to impose himself, thereby allowing me to feel free to write about things as I saw them.

For the rest, my work has been facilitated by the generous collaboration and help of Jacqueline's many friends and colleagues — a mark of Jacqueline's own generous spirit. Only two or three people refused my request for an interview, preferring to keep their memories to themselves.

In most cases I was fortunate to be able to conduct interviews in person, and did so in Italy, Great Britain, the USA, Berlin and Paris. In other instances there was no choice but to do an interview by telephone. In certain cases, people submitted a written memoir or contribution in the form of written answers to my questions.

Sadly, I was denied access to the family archive, since during the period of my research Jacqueline's sister and brother, Hilary Finzi and Piers du Pré were engaged in writing their own book of family memoirs, published in October 1997. However, I wish to thank them for granting me one formal interview which enabled me to check some facts about Jacqueline's early years.

I wish to thank most warmly those musicians who knew and played with Jacqueline du Pré and who shared their memories with me: Vladimir Ashkenazy, Quin Ballardie, Harry Blech, Pierre Boulez, Ana Chumachenko, Maggie Cowan, Lamar Crowson, Diana Cummings,

Herbert Downes, Lawrence Foster, Rodney Friend, José Luis García, Richard Goode, Antony Hopkins, Stephen Kovacevich, Anita Lasker, Alberto Lysy, Oscar Lysy, Hugh Maguire, George Malcolm, Zubin Mehta, Yehudi Menuhin, Joanna Milholland, Itzhak Perlman, Arnold Steinhardt, Peter Thomas, Fou Ts'ong, John Williams, and Pinchas Zukerman.

My deep gratitude to Jacqueline's teachers: principally to William Pleeth, also to Mstislav Rostropovich.

Cellists are wonderful colleagues, and I wish to thank the following whose eagerness to help me in this project was undoubtedly a reflection of their enduring love and high esteem for Jacqueline du Pré: Sandy Bailey, Lowri Blake, Ottomar Borwitsky, Robert Cohen, the late Joan Dickson, David Geringas, Karine Georgian, Natalia Gutman, Andrea Hess, Tim Hugh, Stephen Isserlis, Ralph Kirshbaum, Misha Maisky, Boris Pergamenshchikov, Melissa Phelps, Anna Shuttleworth, Raphael Sommer, Jeanine Tétard, Maud Martin-Tortelier, Gill Thoday, Jenny Ward-Clarke, Moray Welsh, and Yo-Yo Ma.

I wish also to thank Jacqueline's many friends and acquaintances who agreed to talk to me and share their reminiscences: John Amis, Peter Andry, Lady Barbirolli, Clive and Rosie Barda, Charles Beare, Kate Beare, Y. Beinisch, Zamira Benthall, Susan Bradshaw, Alison Brown, Joanna David, Jeremy Dale-Roberts, the late Peter Diamand, Madeleine Dinkel, Howard Ferguson, Rabbi Albert Friedlander, Cynthia Friend, Lady Groves, Suvi Grubb, Penelope Lee, Guthrie Luke, Lotte Klemperer, Teddy Kollek, Susie Maguire, Christopher Nupen, Jan Pleeth, Oleg Prokofiev, Diana Rix, Stuart Robinson, Jill Severs, Jeremy Siepman, Clive Smart, Sonia Sommerville, Sylvia Southcombe, Ursula Strebi, Sir Ian and Lady Stoutzker, Mona Thomas, Mrs Jeremy Thorpe, Charles Wadsworth, Eleanor Warren, James and Elaine Wolfenssohn, and Eugenia Zukerman.

I would further like to thank:

(i) Jacqueline's agents at different times and in different parts of the world: Hans Adler, Terry Harrison, Sir Ian Hunter, Harold Shaw, and the late Wilfrid Stiff. In particular I was given invaluable help by Diana Rix, who allowed me to consult the Harold Holt office files and diaries. I would also particularly like to thank the Tillett Trust for allowing me access to their archives.

(ii) Jacqueline's doctors Dr Len Selby and Dr Leo Lange, the late Dr Adam Limentani, and her nurse Ruth Ann Cannings.

(iii) Jacqueline's godparents Lord Harewood and Mrs Isména Holland.

(iv) Patsy James, Mary May, Margot Pacey, and Ronald Smith, for helping me acquire information about Iris du Pré's musical background.

(v) Commonweal Lodge, Croydon High School, Queen's College, The Guildhall School of Music and Drama, The Paris Conservatoire, Cynthia Gosnell, Doreen Ashdown, Queen's College, Jacqueline's schoolmates Andrea Barron, Parthenope Bion and Freddie Collarbone (née Beeston) for helping establish facts and sharing reminiscences about Jacqueline's schooling.

(vi) Paolo Donati, Maria Fontecedro, Dr Maria Majno, Bob Martin, Franco Scala, Valery Voskoboinikov for information about Jacqueline's musical activities in Italy.

(vii) Lyudmila Kovnatskaya for checking information about concerts in Russia.

(viii) the writers Robert Baldock and William Wordsworth for suggestions and invaluable advice.

My particular thanks to Madeleine Dinkel, Guthrie Luke, Rodney and Cynthia Friend, and Maggie Cowan for allowing me to see and quote from Jacqueline du Pré's private letters. Also to Valerie Beale of the Musicians Benevolent Fund, who allowed me to see and use a letter of Jacqueline's written to the Suggia Trust.

At EMI I would like to thank Roger Lewis and also the most helpful assistants at the Archive Department in Hayes. I am particularly indebted to Charles Rodier, not only for granting permission to quote from documents in the archive, but for his encouragement and help throughout.

I am most grateful to the following institutions for enabling me to have access to information about du Pré's broadcasting and television engagements and to listen to tapes: the archives of BBC Radio and BBC Television, Danish Radio, Granada Television, The National Sound Archive, the New York Philharmonic, the RAI in Rome and Turin, and Swedish Broadcasting (where I am grateful in particular to Dorette Leygraf and Tage Olhagen).

In addition I am indebted to the Arts Council of Great Britain, the British Council, The Musician's Benevolent Fund, Norman Webb of the Jacqueline du Pré Memorial Fund, Sylvia Lawry of the International Federation of Multiple Sclerosis Societies and St Hilda's College, Oxford, for providing me with much useful information.

My thanks to the archives of orchestras worldwide:

(i) in Great Britain: the BBC Symphony Orchestra, the CBSO, the Hallé Orchestra, the London Symphony Orchestra, the London Philharmonic Orchestra, the Philharmonia Orchestra, the Royal Liverpool Philharmonic, the Northern Sinfonia, the Royal Philharmonic Orchestra, and the Scottish National Orchestra.

(ii) in Europe: the Danish Radio Orchestra, the Residentie Orkest, the Hague, L'Orchestra Filarmonica della Scala, L'Orchestra di Santa Cecilia, Rome, L'Orchestre de Paris, the Berliner Philharmonisches Orchester, the Deutches Symphonie Orchester, Berlin, the Israel Philharmonic Orchestra, the Oslo Philharmonic, and the Swedish Radio Orchestra.

(iii) in the southern hemisphere: the ABC Document Archives and the Sydney NZBCO (a particular thank you to archivist Joy Tonks).

(iv) in North America: the Boston Symphony Orchestra, the Chicago Symphony Orchestra (and in particular to Frank Villella, the archives assistant), the Cleveland Orchestra, the Dallas Symphony Orchestra, the Denver Symphony Orchestra, the Detroit Symphony Orchestra, the Honolulu Symphony, the Kansas City, the Los Angeles Philharmonic Association, the Minnesota Orchestral Association, the Montreal Symphony Orchestra, the New York Philharmonic Orchestra, the Oklahoma City Philharmonic Orchestra, the Philadelphia Orchestra, the San Francisco Symphony Orchestra, the Toronto Symphony Orchestra, and the Vancouver Symphony Orchestra.

I am most grateful for some invaluable help about the dates and programmes of Jackie's concerts from the following archives: the National Trust Concerts, the Royal Albert Hall, London, the South Bank Centre, and Gino Francesconi of the Carnegie Hall, New York, and the Festivals of Bath, Cheltenham, City of London, Edinburgh, Chester, Norwich, and Lucerne.

I wish to thank the following for the use of photographs from their private collections: Daniel Barenboim, Eugenia Zukerman, Ana Chumachenko. Also to Clive Barda, Fritz Curzon, the Press Association, the BBC Photo Archive, and the State Archive of the Principality of Monaco for use of Bob Martin's photos.

My work has been eased by invaluable help from two excellent research assistants, initially from Anna Wilson and then over the next four years from Rosie Chambers. Rosie was indefatigable in gathering information, organising the material, setting up contacts and gaining access to archives, proving to have far more persistence that I did. I am most grateful to my editor Elsbeth Lindner for all her comments, suggestions and corrections. I would also like to thank all those at Weidenfeld & Nicolson who helped bring this book into being, in particular Ion Trewin and Ian Pindar.

I was sustained throughout my task by the patience and support of my family and friends. I thank them all, but particularly Catherine Wilson, Francesco Candido and Christine Anderson, all of whom read the manuscript through and made many useful suggestions and comments. I would also like to thank Ann Wilson and Eilis Cranitch for their help.

Finally my apologies to any person whom I may have inadvertently overlooked while attempting to recall and record the enormous amount of help I have received from so many people all over the world.

Preface

The idea of this book had its genesis in the months after Jacqueline du Pré's death. It was following the Memorial Thanksgiving Concert at Westminster Hall given in January 1988 by her husband Daniel Barenboim and many other musicians who had been du Pré's close associates that Daniel asked me if I would be prepared to write Jackie's biography. I was very touched that he should think of me, but my immediate reaction was to refuse. I did not feel up to the task and had as yet little experience of writing. But Daniel encouraged me to give his proposal unhurried consideration. From his point of view my qualifications to write about Jackie were that I was a cellist and had known and heard her in her playing days – I first met her in 1965. He generously added that I had his trust and that I had always had Jackie's. It was this last phrase of Barenboim's which gave me the strength to accept the challenge and start work some five years later.

Jacqueline du Pré was a much-loved figure. During her lifetime she was fêted in the press, first for her incomparable artistry, and later for her courage and fortitude in the face of terrible affliction. Since her death in October 1987 interest in her has not abated: two biographies have appeared, as well as articles, plays based on her life, a further documentary film, let alone a projected feature film based on her sister's and brother's recent book of memoirs. More importantly her memory has been sustained by the discovery of further recordings, allowing EMI to issue as a fiftieth-birthday tribute du Pré's versions of the Lalo Cello Concerto and Richard Strauss's *Don Quixote*.

Unravelling the reality from the legend is a particularly hard job in the case of Jacqueline du Pré. Over the last ten years, the mythical aura around her name has not dimmed. The story of a young woman endowed with extraordinary gifts and then cruelly cut down in her prime retains the force of Greek Tragedy, imposing the idea of an almost pre-ordained destiny. So much so, that fiction seems to invade the reminiscence material available to us, while the very mention of her

I

name evokes eulogies and laments. One might well ask if there is any need for more to be written about her.

Yet it seemed to me that no book has as yet seriously examined Jacqueline du Pré's considerable musical achievement. Neither have the sources of her talent or the influences that she exerted on musicians and cellists ever been systematically studied. As those who knew her will testify, Jackie herself was very modest about the extent of her achievements. While researching this biography I was continually surprised to learn of the scope of her activity. She packed so much music-making into a very short time, and had a far wider range of repertoire and musical knowledge than she is usually credited with.

Although the music-making is the main theme of this book, in Jackie's case it is wellnigh impossible to separate music from her personal life. Her artistry was unified with her personality to an unusual extent, and, until illness imposed silence on her music-making, speaking through the cello was her preferred means of communication.

Having enjoyed a friendship with Jackie for more than twenty years gave me certain advantages as a biographer. But it was nevertheless easy to allow my memories to be clouded by hindsight. Sometimes I had to – at least temporarily – lay aside my personal feelings and judgements, in order to give an objective viewpoint. It was important initially to disassociate myself from the harrowing images of Jackie's final illness, so as to recapture the feeling of exhilarating adventure that was so much part of her youthful personality. In all I have tried to take a fresh stance so as to re-establish Jackie's experiences and feelings in relation to the time she lived through them and to supply the context and background of her accomplishments.

It has been an enormous pleasure whilst researching the book to have the opportunity to talk and reminisce about Jackie with so many people. Yet I have found still greater pleasure from immersing myself in du Pré's recordings, and living closely with her marvellous artistry. Apart from the issued recordings, I was lucky to discover several concert performances preserved in radio archives around the world. In Great Britain, we are fortunate in having the National Sound Archive in Exhibition Road, London, which has a splendid collection of radio tapes, extremely helpful staff and good listening facilities available to the general public.

The recordings are undoubtedly the most valuable and lasting of

Jacqueline du Pré's legacy. We are well served by EMI's catalogue of audio recordings and Christopher Nupen's documentary films, which are available on video.

I have decided not to include a discography for two main reasons. First, because I have dealt in detail with most of the recordings in the text. Secondly, catalogue numbers of commercially recorded discs tend to quickly go out of date, as re-issues and new couplings are released and others withdrawn. But readers who wish to further their enjoyment of du Pré's artistry will find that all of the EMI recordings discussed are today available on CD. There is no reason to believe that this situation will change, as du Pré's unique qualities will continue to appeal to a new generation of music lovers. The only EMI recorded works which are currently unavailable are Beethoven's clarinet Trio Op. 11 and the Piano Trio in E flat WoO 38, which were omitted when the complete Barenboim/Zukerman/du Pré Beethoven Trios were reissued on CD.

Being that rare bird, a magnificent British string-player, it was natural that du Pré's performances were frequently recorded by the BBC. Indeed, she started her recording career in the Radio 3 studios. Throughout her playing career her concerts were often transmitted directly (not only in Britain, but in other countries). Disappointingly, the tapes of many of these radio broadcasts are not to be found in the radio archives, some seem to have been lost altogether. In certain cases they have been preserved by chance as non professional tapes recorded off the air; often these are of scarce quality.

Enthusiasts of du Pré's playing can further their pleasure by making an appointment at the National Sound Archive, where many of the BBC radio recordings mentioned in the text are available to listen to. These include such rarities as a 1962 studio recording of Jacques Ibert's Concerto for Cello and Winds, the Schumann Cello concerto with Tortelier's cadenza from a concert in December 1962, Priaulx Rainier's Concerto from the 1964 Proms, as well as several concert performances of the Elgar Concerto – the earliest with Norman Del Mar from a performance in October 1962.

In addition to EMI's catalogue, there are two further CDs on the market: the 1970 version of the Elgar Concerto from a concert in Philadelphia issued by CBS, the 1979 recording of Prokofiev's Peter and the Wolf with du Pré as narrator issued by Deutsche Grammophon. In addition, in some countries du Pré's performance of Alexander

Goehr's Romanza from a concert in October 1968 is available on CD on the Intaglio label.

Du Pré, although remembered chiefly as a musician, left a further legacy in her concern to help the cause of research. During her lifetime, through her compassion, her humour and her enormous dignity, she held out a beacon of hope to sufferers of chronic illness and multiple sclerosis in particular. Her name and influence live on in various Trusts and Institutions.

The first of these, the Jacqueline du Pré Research Fund of the IFMSS (International Federation of Multiple Sclerosis Societies), was founded with Jacqueline's participation in 1979 by Daniel Barenboim and James Wolfensohn. Encouraged by Barenboim's unstinting generosity and example, the concerts given by star performers in support of the Fund over the ensuing years have ensured its high profile. In April 1987, just a few months before du Pré's death, the IFMSS set up the Du Pré Fellowship which provides an annual award of $20,000 for the training of a research worker. Although Jackie realised that she would never benefit from the findings of research, it meant something to her to know that the use of her name might contribute to the relief of other MS patients.

Shortly after her death, the Jacqueline du Pré Memorial Award was founded to finance a young cellist in a course of study, to help towards the purchase of an instrument or to fund a concert. The first award was made in 1988. In November 1988 the Jacqueline du Pré Memorial Fund was launched in London with a double purpose. The proceeds were to be divided between the Appeal Fund for the construction of the new concert hall complex at St Hilda's, Oxford, and a Trust administered by the Musician's Benevolent Fund, whose aim was to help musicians suffering from degenerative and chronic diseases stay in their own homes as long as possible and finance beds in nursing homes. The Memorial Fund achieved both aims, having collected donations nearing a total of just under £3 million.

Thus, the most tangible monument to du Pré's influence exists in the new Jacqueline du Pré Music Building by St Hilda's College which was opened in September 1995. Apart from a concert hall seating 200 people, it incorporates practice rooms and rehearsal halls, and provides recording facilities. The project was conceived in 1985, shortly after du Pré had been elected Fellow of St Hilda's College, and she was able to give it her approval and blessing.

After the Memorial Fund was wound up a further living tribute to du Pré was instituted in 1996 by the Fund's ex-director Norman Webb in the form of an annual Memorial Concert at London's Wigmore Hall held on or near 1 March, the anniversary of du Pré's own debut in that hall. The proceeds of ticket sales and donations are given to a charity connected with either music or medicine.

In recent years a cello competition bearing du Pré's name was inaugurated in England, initially sponsored by EMI. I have also discovered that in Italy, a country where du Pré was admired and loved during her lifetime, a music school has been named after her in Bologna, while a young group of musicians in Naples have founded the Jacqueline du Pré Piano Quartet.

I hope that, while concentrating on du Pré the musician, my biography will also serve to put the rest of her life into perspective. Naturally no book can ever replace Jacqueline's own voice which lives on in the audio and video recordings.

Elizabeth Wilson
Giaveno, Italy
June 1998

I

The Birth of Talent

'The musical talent may well show itself earliest of any; for music is something innate and internal, which needs little nourishment from without, and no experience drawn from life.'

Johann Wolfgang von Goethe*

The phenomenon of a child prodigy is always a source of wonder. It is impossible to explain the extraordinary childhood abilities of a genius such as Mozart without speculating (as did Goethe) that his talent was divinely invested. In Mozart's case, the early gift proved to be the precursor of the inspired works of his maturity. But too often we are dazzled by a precocious outward display of virtuosity; when the prodigy grows up, he disappoints our early hopes. A young musician is only likely to attain a great destiny if his creative gift is welded to an unerring intuition and is enriched by a capacity for profound emotion.

The violinist Yehudi Menuhin, whose gifts were apparent at a very early age, described the strange imbalance between the prodigy's inner world of passion and restricted life experience: 'I was a child, I knew so much, I felt so many emotions, but I had never made their acquaintance! I felt the tragedy in life, I felt abandon, exuberance, exaltation, but hadn't met these feelings in the outer world.'[1] Menuhin, speaking with the wisdom of hindsight, saw this emotional precociousness almost as a limitation of his early performances. His development as an artist meant connecting these intuited emotions with real-life experiences, a difficult process of catching up with oneself in adolescence.

Jacqueline du Pré only began to perform publicly at the age of sixteen – a late start in comparison with most prodigies. Nevertheless, her musical genius was evident at a very early age and its special nature was defined by her rich emotional inner world, rather than her precocious virtuosity. Her mother, Iris du Pré, recalled that when the

* Eckermann, *Conversations with Goethe*, entry for 14 February 1831.

four-year-old Jackie was first given a cello to play – it was a full-sized 'whopper' – she exclaimed in delight, 'Oh Mummy, I do so love my cello.' Iris recalled her astonishment at 'the enormous wealth of feeling'[2] behind these childish words, which prompted her to foresee for her daughter a lifelong commitment to music and the cello. It is to Iris's credit that, while instantly recognising Jackie's special gifts, she saw to it that they were protected, carefully nurtured and only gradually exposed to the light.

Indeed, du Pré's relatively late appearance on the concert scene was partly due to an accident of birth. The English have always shown considerable distaste for pushing a very young musician into the public arena. In contrast to Menuhin's successful concert career as a child, the English pianist and harpsichordist George Malcolm remembers that he was deliberately held back from performing. While his parents and teachers recognised his musical potential at a very young age, they had no wish to imitate what they saw as the flagrant child exploitation of the boy Menuhin, his exact contemporary.[3]

This aversion of the English to exhibitionist display was at odds with the European tradition of stimulating performing talent at an early age. As Iris du Pré enjoyed recounting, it was probably for this reason that the veteran cellist Pablo Casals assumed that the fifteen-year-old girl who had just given an extraordinarily vital performance of the Saint-Saëns A minor Cello Concerto at his Zermatt master class could not be English.

'Oh, but I am,' she told him when challenged.

'But what is your name?' – Surely no English person could display such intense feeling and uninhibited passion in their music-making.

'Jacqueline du Pré.'

Casals just roared with laughter, convinced that he had proved his point.[4]

The name du Pré, however, derives from the Channel Islands, which had links with England from the middle of the eleventh century when they separated from Normandy. Although geographically closer to France – and indeed, until relatively recently predominantly French-speaking – the Channel Islands looked to England politically and culturally. Jackie used to take pride in saying that her father, Derek du Pré had never left the island of Jersey before the age of twenty, and when he did depart he was the first of many generations to do so. Like so many family legends, this was not strictly speaking true, as he was born in Portsmouth and spent some of his childhood holidays in England. But for all that, Derek du Pré considered himself a Jersey man and transmitted to his daughter something of an islander's proud, independent spirit.

Jacqueline's musical talent was inherited through the maternal line. Her mother, Iris Greep was a professional pianist who, in other circumstances, might have become a soloist in her own right. But more important, she possessed a remarkable gift as a children's music teacher and she had the sensitivity to recognise the unique nature of Jackie's talent – namely the deeply felt inner passion which illuminated her attitude to music from the earliest age, whether it was in her lisping of nursery rhymes, or singing of Christmas carols, or in her immediate identification with the sound of the cello.

Born in 1914, Iris Greep came from a humble Devon family. Her father, William Greep, was a ship's joiner in the Devonport dockyard and his musical activities were limited to singing in music-hall productions. Her mother, Maud Greep (née Mitchell), realised that Iris was exceptionally bright and bought her seven-year-old daughter a piano as a means of stimulating her outside school. Iris proved to have real musical talent and was soon winning prizes at local music festivals. Later she won a scholarship to Devonport High School where, apart from doing well academically, she enjoyed extra-scholastic activities such as swimming and drama. In the meantime she was making such remarkable progress on the piano that a year before leaving school she went to London to take her performing diploma. Iris made a good impression on the adjudicators at the Royal Academy of Music (two of them would become her teachers), gained her LRAM and returned home determined to become a professional musician. The following year, at the age of eighteen, she applied for a place at the London School of Dalcroze Eurhythmics. Through winning a scholarship, Iris now had the financial means to leave home.

Established in 1913 by Percy Ingham, the London School of Eurhythmics was closely associated with Émile Jaques-Dalcroze, who had created his method with the aim of basing musical education on rhythm as a means of expression, whereby the co-ordination of bodily movement and music help to fuse the integration of body and mind. Although his system was originally conceived for musicians, Dalcroze stated that 'its chief value lies in the fact that it trains the powers of perception and of expression in the individual and renders easier the externalisation of natural emotions'.

The Dalcroze method became a way of life for its practitioners. As Bernard Shaw put it, Dalcrozians 'walk to music, play to music, think to music, obey drill commands that would bewilder a guardsman to music, live to music, get so clear-headed about music that they can move their several limbs each in a different metre until they become living magazines of cross-rhythms and, what is more, make music for others to do all these things'.[5]

Apart from the evident importance of Dalcroze's system in children's education, it had an enormous influence in its day on dancers and actors, and was incorporated into theatre and dance by such diverse figures as Greville Barker, Isadora Duncan and Marie Rambert. Rambert in turn used a synthesis of Dalcrozian eurhythmics and classical ballet in her work with the Diaghilev company, and specifically helped Nijinsky to choreograph the rhythmically complex score of Stravinsky's *Sacre du printemps*.

Hence, when Iris Greep gained the certificate from the London School of Eurhythmics in 1935, she had become a committed Dalcrozian and remained involved with the method for the rest of her life. She was listed as an outside lecturer of the Dalcroze Society's Training Centre from 1949 until 1963 and in 1953 was elected to a commission, headed by Ernest Read, responsible for amending the syllabus of the Training Centre.

A year before she acquired the Dalcroze certificate Iris enrolled at the Royal Academy of Music as a first-study pianist with Eric Grant. Initially she chose viola as her second study, but very soon she had abandoned this instrument for composition and harmony lessons with Theodore Holland.

From 1935 onwards her fees were largely met by scholarships – she was the recipient of the Bach and Beethoven Scholarship and the William Stokes Bursary, and during the following four years she won a number of prizes for harmony, composition and piano. Additionally she supported herself through teaching piano and eurhythmics.

Iris gained her ARCM certificate in 1937, but she continued her studies until the outbreak of the war, while starting to play and teach professionally. Eric Grant had a high enough opinion of her to nominate her as his deputy and in 1940 she was appointed sub-professor of harmony at the RAM.

While in London, Iris lodged with Mary May, a fellow Dalcrozian, who described her then as 'about five foot seven tall, broad-shouldered and sturdy, good-looking with auburn hair'. Mary grew very fond of Iris and through her mother provided her with important contacts, including a wealthy patroness of the Arts, Violet Becker, who financed her London début recital. Mary's mother also introduced her to the German concert pianist Egon Petri.

According to Mary, Iris appeared to be 'entirely unversed in the art of living. She never knew that if you opened a door you should close it. Once I found the bath water coming down the stairs – we had to teach her about living in a house.' She found Iris's parents to be simple but warm-hearted – her father once attended a party at the house, but he was a 'shy man who felt quite out of place in London'.[6]

If Iris had arrived in London with few social graces, she quickly learnt to adapt to new situations and to appreciate the novelties and excitement of city life. Here she was especially fortunate in having teachers who not only transmitted professional skills, but also watched over the overall development of their students' personalities.

Iris's piano teacher Eric Grant was a highly civilised musician, if somewhat academic in his approach. His pupils remember that he was not interested in virtuosity for its own sake, rather he instilled deeply felt musical values – although some claimed that he did so at the expense of their technique. But Grant was as intent on enlarging his students' cultural horizons as training their fingers. Urbane, witty and with an eye for the girls, he enjoyed introducing his pupils to life outside the walls of the Academy, taking them to concerts at the Queen's Hall and acquainting them with the gastronomic delights of Soho. Not surprisingly, they were devoted to him.

Theodore Holland was likewise a teacher whose influence extended far beyond the walls of the teaching room. As a young man he had studied composition and violin at the Royal Academy of Music in London, then at the Berlin Hochschule, where his teacher, Joachim, did much to influence Holland's musical tastes. In 1927 Holland was appointed Professor at the Royal Academy of Music. A man of great dignity, he gained considerable prestige in London's musical circles, becoming a member of the Royal Philharmonic Society and of other public bodies.

Holland's music, light, well-crafted and full of idiosyncratic charm, had its day in the pre-war years when his vaudeville-like stage works gained popularity. Later his Edwardian 'salon' style gave way to composition of a more serious and astringent character. *Ellingham Marshes*, an impressionistic orchestral evocation of Holland's favourite Suffolk landscape, achieved considerable success at the time.

But by the mid-1930s Holland's works were no longer much performed. Margot Pacey, a friend of Iris who likewise studied composition with Holland, recalled his disappointment at being overtaken by more modern trends. 'I remember, to my cost, that suddenly everybody at the Academy was talking about Schoenberg and wouldn't listen to anything else.'[7]

This, however, was not the prevalent tendency. Another of Holland's composition students, the pianist Ronald Smith, claimed, 'Only a coterie of people in London knew about the avant-garde, and Schoenberg was considered very *outré*. Sibelius was the big name in those days. Theo Holland knew what he liked and he couldn't stomach Sibelius – "my dear boy, when these dreadful tunes appear, one has to leave the room." In his aesthetic he went as far as accepting early Stravinsky.'[8]

But Holland never used his influence to further performances of his own music. Rather, he wielded his power on behalf of the younger generation and encouraged his students to be daring. Ronald Smith recalled: 'Theo's favourite word was "cracked" – which meant music with some twist to it. He told me that once while adjudicating at the Academy a very bad composer had presented some work. The other adjudicators dismissed his score, but Holland found something in it. "It's cracked," he said "but it's got something." The composer in question turned out to be Benjamin Britten.'[9]

Holland helped Iris to develop a working compositional technique, although she remained one of his less adventurous students. After she had left the Academy she continued to consult him, both about professional and private matters. Ronald Smith recalls an occasion soon after the beginning of the war when Iris came to Holland's class clutching a batch of scores. Smith was particularly impressed by one of them, a ballet entitled *Cherry Stones*, which was later staged in London and achieved some measure of success. Around this time Iris also wrote a children's opera. This was to be the area that attracted her most; she wrote for – and with – children for the rest of her life.

At the Academy, Iris's loyalties were divided between composition and piano. Margot Pacey, who greatly admired her talents, perceived that 'Iris was on the same level as a pianist and composer, winning compositional prizes and playing concerts. But she never got a chance to get going in either field because of the outbreak of the war.'[10]

Nevertheless, the opportunity to go to Poland in 1938 to study with Egon Petri at his summer courses in Zakopane indicated that Iris entertained hopes of pursuing a career as a concert pianist. Together with Artur Schnabel, Petri was one of the great names in piano teaching in the pre-war years. Petri had been a favourite pupil of Busoni, and was noted for his performances of Liszt and Bach – particularly in his own and Busoni's transcriptions. Evidently Iris studied this repertoire with him – music that did not enter into Theodore Holland's aesthetic.

Iris's trip to Poland was momentous in more ways than one. A young Englishman, Derek du Pré, had come with his accordion on a walking holiday to the Polish Carpathians. On arrival at Zakopane, he sought out the young Englishwoman who was staying in a villa on the outskirts of the town. For the rest of his holiday Derek was caught up with Iris. They walked in the Tatrai mountains, listened to and played for folk musicians and fell in love in this romantic setting. On returning to London Derek wrote up his holiday impressions, asking Iris to contribute a chapter about Ukrainian folk music, with some annotated folk songs. Entitled *When Poland Smiled*, this somewhat innocuous travelogue was privately published with charming illustrations by Hector Whistler. It seems incredible that it contains no reference to the troubled political situation of 1938.

Mary May recalls that Iris had immediately set her heart on marriage. When she brought Derek to the house, May discovered him to be 'a well-educated, well-mannered gentleman'. Derek du Pré came from a prosperous family who owned a successful perfume-making business. He attended a good local secondary school, Victoria College, and at the age of eighteen started working for Lloyds Bank in St Helier. Two years later he was transferred to London, where he worked for the rest of his life. In 1937 he left banking for a new job as assistant editor of *The Accountant*.

By the time he had met Iris, Derek was already thirty and ready to settle down. Tall and handsome, with piercing blue eyes, he was a naturally shy man. Whether it was due to his reticence in the courtship or to Iris's ambition to have time to start her own career, the couple only decided to marry two years later. It seemed obvious to friends from the start that whatever Iris lacked in her social background she more than made up for with strength of character and talent. And it was she who was to become the dominant force in the marriage.

In accordance with the severe wartime conditions, Iris and Derek got married with a minimum of ceremony at Kensington Register Office on 25 July 1940. In any case, Derek's family had been cut off from all contact with him since the recent German occupation of the Channel Islands; neither were Iris's parents able to attend the wedding. Isména Holland recalled Iris telling her that they started married life with no possessions, in unfurnished lodgings sitting on packing cases, possibly in the company of a Jersey cow, an apocryphal wedding gift from Derek's friends and relatives.

In July 1941 Derek enlisted. While he was doing his military training, first in Lockerbie, then at Sandhurst, Iris continued her professional life as a pianist, teaching and giving concerts and broadcasts, mostly outside London. She played frequently with the outstanding viola player Winifred Copperwheat, with whom she gave a first performance of a work by Theodore Holland and for whom she herself wrote a sonata. With the birth of her children these activities were necessarily curtailed.

The du Pré's first child, Hilary, was born in April 1942, shortly before Derek received his commission as a captain in the Coldstream Guards Regiment. Two years later he was transferred to Oxford and it was there that their second daughter, Jacqueline Mary, was born on 26 January 1945. She was baptised in the autumn of 1945 at the Chapel of Worcester College, where Derek was a member of the senior common room. The child's chosen godparents, Isména Holland and Lord Lascelles (the future Earl of Harewood) were to play important roles at various stages of her life.

Derek du Pré had got to know George Lascelles at an Officer Cadet Training Unit course in 1942. Lord Harewood remembers that, 'Quite a lot of the fun that I had at that rather dreary stage of my life was with Derek. We used to bicycle from Sandhurst some distance to go and see Iris in hospital, just after Hilary was born. It was then that Derek asked me if I would be godfather to a second child, if they ever had another – to which I agreed.'

While Lascelles saw active fighting in Italy, Derek spent the war years in Britain, having been seconded to Intelligence. He never told his family that during this period he had worked for MI5. Lord Harewood recalled: 'When I came back to England in May 1945, Derek got in touch with me, and told me that he and Iris had just had another daughter. I saw Jackie for the first time at the christening in October that year, when I carried her – with some difficulty – to the font. She was a big and rapidly growing girl.'"

Jacqueline's godmother, Isména Holland, the wife of Iris's teacher Theodore, was born in Germany of an English father and a German mother, and had inherited a fortune in her own right. After the First World War Isména came to England, aged seventeen. When she married Theodore some years later it came as a surprise to his friends and colleagues – Isména was nearly thirty years his junior and much nearer in age to his students. Theodore's health had been seriously undermined by the shell-shock he suffered during the First World War and Isména devoted herself wholly to her husband's welfare.

In her spare time she took up weaving and calligraphy, copying her husband's scores with a meticulous hand. The couple had decided against having children because of the inherent genetic risks due to their being first cousins. But they extended warm hospitality to students, friends and colleagues alike at their beautiful Kensington house in Elton Road, where they often held music parties and concerts.

Although on the surface Isména Holland seemed an austere and somewhat forbidding character, she understood – and practised – the values of loyalty and supportive friendship. Hence it was a natural step for both Margot Pacey and Iris to ask her to become godmother to their daughters. Isména took her duties more than seriously, proving an extremely generous benefactor, as well as a source of wisdom and advice.

The du Pré family moved again to St Albans when Derek was demobilised and went back to his pre-war job in London as assistant editor (then editor) of *The Accountant*. In 1948, shortly after the birth of their son Piers, the du Prés moved again to a larger house at 14 Bridle Way, Purley, twenty miles south of London, within easy commuting distance of the city. It was to be the family home for the next ten years.

2

Early Musical Discoveries

A child prodigy is a child who knows as much when it is a child
as it does when it grows up.

Will Rogers

Before the advent of television, radio dominated every British household. Almost all British children who grew up in the late forties and early fifties remember some favourite programme – whether it was the *Goon Show*, Joyce Grenfell on *Children's Hour*, or listening to the Grand National or following the test match.

The du Pré family were also avid Third Programme listeners. Hilary recalls among her first memories hearing her mother's piano recitals broadcast on the 'wireless' and with childish incredulity 'wondering how they could possibly get both the piano and Mum inside it'.[1]

So it was that one day, while listening to a *Children's Hour* radio programme dedicated to instruments of the orchestra, Jackie first heard the sound of the cello. Without hesitation the four-year-old declared to her mother, 'That is the sound I want to make.'

Iris lost little time in procuring a cello for her daughter to try out. A first full-size instrument was brought to the house by Mrs Garfield Howe, the pianist Denis Matthews's mother-in-law. There is a photograph of the four-year-old Jackie, picturing her masterfully grappling with the bulky instrument. The extraordinary intensity of expression on the child's face shows that she was determined to get a sound that existed in her own mind. The young Jackie already seemed to demonstrate a marked purposefulness of action.

Mrs Howe came to the house every Saturday to give lessons to Hilary on the violin and Jackie on the cello. Two other children, Margaret and Winifred Beeston, came along to make up a string quartet. Mrs Howe was, according to Hilary, a 'wonderful, rather fat lady' and she appeared to have a remarkable capacity to teach the rudiments of just about any instrument. For the following three months she helped Jackie along

16

with the cello, until it became obvious that a more advanced level of teaching was required. Hilary recalled, 'The one thing that stays in my mind from these classes was that Jackie always picked everything up so quickly. Whatever Mrs Howe said, Jackie could do straight away. And so the classes quickly became unbalanced because Jackie was always way ahead of the rest of us.'[2]

The du Pré household was always filled with children coming for piano lessons and to participate in Eurhythmic groups with Iris. Both Jackie and Hilary joined in these. The Eurhythmic training not only stimulated their musical development through clapping rhythms, singing and movement, but their whole physical co-ordination. Hilary had started learning the piano and was proving to be very gifted. Her violin studies came to nothing, as she rebelled against the fiddle's squeaky high register. She concentrated on the piano, but later took up the flute and became equally skilled in both instruments. Jackie, with her unusually receptive ear, was soon imitating Hilary. Although she never had any formal training Jackie picked up the rudiments of piano playing with remarkable ease and could have become an excellent pianist.

Iris made music come alive for her pupils, explaining the mood of a piece in vivid characterisation, or depicting it visually. She had the ability to make each pupil identify with the innate sound of his or her chosen instrument. This meant not simply searching for the notes or playing exact pitches and rhythms, but learning to reproduce the sound you heard in your imagination.[3] In other words, development of the inner ear was fundamental to the learning process.

From the start, it was Iris's enthusiasm that spurred Jackie on. Iris knew of the imaginative work of the cellist Mira Henderson, who had composed tunes and songs for her beginner pupils. Using Henderson's work as a model and in response to Jackie's obvious passion for the cello, Iris started writing little pieces of music with easy tunes and words, all beautifully illustrated – she was also an excellent draughtsman. Composed in the evening while the children were asleep, these musical offerings were then slipped under Jackie's pillow. On awakening, Jackie would leap out of bed and immediately try out the new piece before getting dressed. Iris introduced new difficulties unobtrusively, in progressive order, starting with basic rhythms and open strings, thereby combining an element of fun with a not too daunting challenge.

Jackie was thrilled to have her very own music to play and later in life she would talk about her mother's pieces with touching pride. Iris could not have devised a better way to stimulate her child's receptive imagination. Later, these pieces were published as a collection entitled *Songs for My Cello and Me*.

In the summer of 1950 Iris consulted Isména Holland about a professional cello teacher for Jackie; it was to be the first of many times that she turned to the child's godmother for guidance and practical help. Isména suggested an audition with Herbert Walenn, the director and founder of the London Cello School. Walenn was suitably impressed by the talent and the fierce concentration of the neatly turned-out five-year-old blonde child. He promised to keep an eye on Jackie, while delegating Alison Dalrymple to teach her.

For the next few years a weekly trip was undertaken by Jackie and Iris to 34 Nottingham Place, where the London Cello School had its premises. After her lesson with Dalrymple, Jackie would go to sit on Walenn's knee and have a chat with him. On one occasion she remarked that his chiming clock was out of tune – Walenn was amused and impressed by this further evidence of an exceptionally good ear.

Herbert Walenn had studied with Hugo Becker at the Frankfurt Hochschule, and made a playing career as a soloist and as a member of the Kruse String Quartet. But it was as a teacher that he left his mark. Although he taught professionally at the Royal Academy, he adopted a policy unusual in those times of training children and encouraging amateurs. In order to realise his ideas, Walenn founded the London Cello School in 1919. Here he instituted regular concerts, including group performances with up to a hundred cellists participating.

The majority of London's cellists went to Walenn in their early years, including John Barbirolli, Dougie Cameron and William Pleeth. Among his most distinguished female pupils was the young Zara Nelsova, a Canadian of Russian origin, who studied with him from the age of twelve. Casals wrote his *Sardana for Sixteen Cellos* for Walenn's School and Theodore Holland was another composer who wrote a piece for massed cellos at Walenn's behest.

In her book *The Great Cellists* Margaret Campbell maintains that Walenn taught little technique and was thoroughly unorthodox in his methods.[4] But another of his pupils, Eleanor Warren, remembered that 'Walenn really made us practise, and made us do a lot of technique, scales and studies. And unlike so many teachers, he heard us do our scales and studies. I believe that there were rows with Bill Pleeth when he refused to play studies. Walenn played the piano quite well and accompanied us. But it went to a certain level and no further. Basically he passed on to us everything that Hugo Becker had taught him.'[5]

Alison Dalrymple had come to London from her native South Africa and had studied with Walenn. She soon gained a reputation in London as an excellent children's teacher. Dalrymple was able to teach the basics of technique without destroying the fun of playing and, as Pleeth was to note, she gave her pupils a good basic position in both hands. Jackie responded well to her vivacious manner and relaxed approach.

Dalrymple's teaching was backed up by close supervision at home; one cannot underestimate Iris's influence on Jackie's musical development. Most important, Iris knew how to maintain the fragile balance between allowing her daughter's natural intuition and spontaneity a free rein and ensuring that she gained sufficient cellistic prowess to express herself in the music.

The London Cello School encouraged all its pupils to perform and concerts were held at Queen Mary Hall in Great Russell Street. Jackie was six when she first played in a demonstration concert of Dalrymple's pupils. She was obviously already regarded as the star pupil and performed three pieces. One of them, Schubert's 'Wiegenlied', remained in her repertoire as an encore throughout her performing career. On that occasion Iris accompanied Jackie; she remained her permanent accompanist for another ten years or so.

Eleanor Warren, a cellist who later became a BBC producer, remembers the occasion well. Dalrymple had invited her to come and hear her most outstanding young pupil:

> It turned out to be Jackie. Hilary also played on this occasion. Both girls were very neatly dressed – Jackie in pink and Hilary in green. I talked to Jackie and found her to be terribly polite and nicely brought-up. But the moment she started playing, you could tell that she was special. Her playing had wonderful concentration, real sound and this power of communication that was so characteristic of her performances later on. She was totally involved in what she was doing. I thought at the time 'these are two very talented children'. However, Jackie was definitely the greater personality and already able to hold the stage.[6]

Jackie always performed the music by heart; she possessed a wonderful ear and an extraordinary musical memory, two necessary assets to quick learning. Already at this early age the act of performance came as second nature to her and whenever she played she would claim attention, however informal the occasion. Everyone who heard her was impressed by the intensity of her concentration, the inner power of expression as well as her own great joy in music-making. Even as a small girl, Jackie's single most striking gift was an innate ability to communicate.

Some twenty years later, Jackie spoke to her friend Eugenia Zukerman about that first public performance: 'She told me it was as if until that moment she had in front of her a brick wall which blocked her communication with the outside world. But the moment Jackie started to play for an audience, that brick wall vanished and she felt able to speak at last. It was a sensation that never left her when she performed.'

Jackie's godmother Isména Holland confirmed her goddaughter's love of the stage: 'Even when she was little she was totally unafraid of performing – she positively enjoyed it. It was completely natural with her, so you never thought about it – she played when she wanted to play. Hilary, despite being very talented, was never quite as natural and was not a performer to that extent. Later this provoked trouble between them.'[7]

The problems that arose between the sisters were in part due to Hilary's understandable envy of her younger sister's greater success as a performer. It was hard for her to be continually compared unfavourably with Jackie. Perhaps Iris was not sufficiently aware of the damage that these comparisons did to her elder daughter's confidence.

The situation was aggravated when Jackie and Hilary started competing in local music festivals. Although Hilary always did very well, she did not do as well as her younger sister. These festivals were a notable feature of English musical life, where children had the opportunity to meet like-minded spirits and to measure their talents against those of their peers. Jackie's prize certificates testify to the rounds of London suburbia – Coulsden and Purley, Bromley, Redhill, Reigate, Wimbledon. This music circuit assumed the same sort of significance as pony shows and gymkhanas did for 'horsy' children.

Certainly, competition held no terrors for Jackie and she swept up all available prizes. At the very first festival where the seven-year-old Jackie played, a judge saw her skipping light-heartedly down the corridor. He knowingly remarked, 'One can see that this little girl has just finished playing.' But he was wrong – the joy was the joy of anticipation.[8] Iris remembered that Jackie's natural charm affected everybody in the audience; after she had performed her pieces she would jump down from the stage to sit on her father's knee. Unlike the majority of children who were nervous of performing, Jackie actively enjoyed it.

Naturally, she became the most talked-about child on the festival circuit. For the violinist Diana Cummings, Jackie was very much part of her childhood and adolescence.

> We appeared at the same festivals and competed in the same competitions, despite the fact that I was four years older than her. Iris, an encouraging and friendly figure, if also somewhat intimidating, was always present to accompany her daughters. She looked the country type, dressed in brogues and tweeds, but she always saw to it that Jackie and Hilary were very neatly turned out. There was a certain aura around Jackie as a child – here she was doing lots of hours of special practice, while the rest of us just had to fit it in around school.[9]

Notwithstanding Jackie's obvious gifts and her success at local competitions, the du Pré family kept a low profile. While Jackie breathed music as her natural atmosphere from her earliest days, Iris and Derek made every effort to ensure that their daughter did not perceive herself as a child prodigy or 'musical freak'. Iris possessed that quality essential to a good teacher of being able to encourage without any apparent coercion. Her ex-pupils remember her as strict but kind, creating the right sort of expectations, whereby 'if you did not work you felt you were letting her down'.[10] At home, Iris evolved an automatic routine for practising, regarding school and other activities as subservient to music. In fact, Hilary and Jackie soon learnt to practise on their own without any help, something that never ceased to amaze their school friends. The only problem for Iris was to restrain her very keen daughters from starting their practice too early in the morning.

Iris was a strong guiding influence in both Hilary's and Jackie's lives, investing an enormous amount of time and effort in helping them. Indeed, the environment she cultivated at home was so exclusively geared to music that Derek and Piers, the less musically oriented members of the family, received scant attention from her. Derek enjoyed a good singsong and playing his accordion, but could not read music. Inevitably he communicated more with his son, stimulating the boy's interest in adventure stories, aeroplanes and boats. Piers largely opted out from anything to do with music, but eventually found his niche when he became a pilot.

From Jackie's point of view, her mother's devotion to music and her close relationship to her elder sister contributed to a sense of security throughout her childhood. This was seriously disturbed only once, when as a four-year-old she was taken to hospital to have her tonsils out. As Hilary recalled the events, Iris did not think to explain to Jackie that she was going to have an operation and would be away from home for a week. It was apparently hospital policy not to allow visits from family to children. Left on her own in hospital, Jackie felt totally abandoned and was unable to forgive such apparent treachery on her mother's part. It is hard to credit the truth of such a story, or to believe the insensitivity and severity of the hospital regulations, or that Iris had been unable to overrule them. Even in the late 1940s a routine operation to remove tonsils rarely necessitated more than a night or two in hospital; but even a short separation would have been enough to traumatise a small child.

The du Prés were a private, close-knit family and, when not over-involved in intensive musical activity, they enjoyed relaxing together. Holidays were spent in the countryside, usually with the grandparents in Devon and Jersey. It was here that Derek du Pré came into his own as an energetic outdoor man, whose intimate knowledge of the hidden coves and coastline of his native Jersey gave the children a taste of excitement and wonder. His interest in geology naturally influenced family expeditions on Dartmoor and elsewhere. For the children, rock collecting was a *de rigueur* activity, later somewhat resented.

One of Jackie's childhood friends, Winifred (Freddie) Beeston, shared some of the du Prés' expeditions to Jersey and Dartmoor. As she recalled, 'Uncle Derek was a real Jersey man. He knew the tides, he would take us shrimp fishing in places that were only accessible at low tide. Jackie loved swimming and walking was a big thing in the family. Uncle Derek was extremely fit, and I had to run to keep up with him and Auntie Iris.'[11]

Freddie Beeston had got to know Jackie at school when she was five years old. Through their friendship she started having piano lessons with Iris. It was at Iris's instigation that she also took up the violin, although on hearing Jackie play the cello Freddie immediately clamoured to change to that instrument. She followed Jackie to the London

Cello School. Because of their shared interests, the two girls became inseparable. After her piano lesson Freddie would stay on at the house to play. As she recalled, even then the cello dominated Jackie's life: 'It was natural for us to go upstairs to her room and get out the cello. Although we were very little, we were able to exchange ideas. I thus became Jackie's first "cello" friend.'

In addition, they enjoyed fooling around on the piano, inventing stories and improvising. Freddie remembered: 'Jackie would sing – she had a great voice. When she was about eight or nine she could play anything by ear and she was terrific at making things up. By that stage Auntie Iris had written quite a lot of music for the children. If I played something on the piano, Jackie would add a bottom voice, improvising around what I was doing, adding the harmony and so on.'

The two children also indulged in tomboy activities outdoors, climbing trees and playing Cowboys and Indians. They detested 'girl's stuff' – dolls and stuffed animals. Freddie admired Jackie's strong but gentle disposition. 'She would never hurt anyone or get cross. She wasn't dominating and even if in our relationship she was the leader, she knew how to give and take.'

It was firmly impressed on family and friends that Jackie's hands were precious and games had to be restricted accordingly. Jackie's maternal grandmother Maud and her sister Em – known to the children simply as 'auntie' – came up from Devon to stay and were frequently left in charge of the children. They were reassuring figures of whom Jackie grew extremely fond. Freddie remembers a horrifying occasion when, while playing on the swings in the garden, Jackie caught a left-hand finger in the ropes and squashed it badly. 'Jackie was in terrible pain and became quite hysterical, and her granny, who was looking after us that day, was terribly concerned that it would be the end of her cello playing. We were only about six or seven at the time, but that incident shows how important the cello was for her.'[12] Even as a little girl, Jackie was so attached to the cello that it always came with her on holiday. She once burst into tears on a walk on Dartmoor, because she so missed her cello – she hadn't played it since yesterday, she complained. Jackie did not like her cello playing to be taken anything less than very seriously. While holidaying in Jersey she was left one day to practise in the care of her uncle Val, Derek's clergyman brother, while the rest of the family went down to the beach. Jackie asked for an 'A' on the piano, so she could tune her cello. Uncle Val unthinkingly struck the first key to hand, but did not deceive Jackie, who stormed out of the house to complain to her mother.

Although the cello always came first in her life, Jackie inherited a strong feeling for nature and a great love of the sea. Towards the end of her life she related an anecdote describing an early bid for independence. As a three-year-old she had run away from home on her tricycle. When she was found, her parents asked her where she thought she was going. 'To the sea, to the sea,' she replied unhesitatingly.[13] Whether or not this was an apocryphal story, it indicated Jackie's later vision of herself as a rebel, as well as demonstrating her lifelong love of the elements. When in later years people described her as 'a child of nature', this was apt, not only because of her extraordinary spontaneity, but because of an almost primordial attachment to the natural world. Thus, even when she was involved with her performing career, walking and the outdoors were to provide an escape valve as well as a source of joy.

3

Recognition

For sensuous appreciation of beauty and flights of imagination there was little space or time once you were in the school system. That section of the brain which deals with such impressions must have been, and is to a large extent, undeveloped in our people.

Dora Russell, *The Tamarisk Tree**

In 1950 Jackie started attending Commonweal Lodge School in Purley, which catered for children aged five to eighteen years. Although ex-pupils remember it as having a happy atmosphere, it was not a school to promote either academic interests or such disciplines as art and music. One might say that its philosophy reflected the limitations of genteel suburbia, or as an ex-alumni described it, 'Commonweal was a school which turned young girls into well-groomed young ladies' – something of that English anachronism, a miniature ladies' college.

Doreen Ashdown, the School Secretary at Commonweal Lodge at the time, remembers Jackie as a happy and cheerful child who, like her sister Hilary, got on well with the rest of her class-mates. She described her as having a smiling face, with clear, cornflower-blue eyes, framed by short blonde hair.[1]

Jackie's best friend Freddie Beeston started school at the same time. During breaks from lessons they ran and skipped with the rest of the girls. As Freddie recalled, Jackie won all the running races: 'It came easily to her, having such long legs. Our three-legged race was famous because Jackie and I were the tallest and shortest in the class respectively – she would carry me along.'

According to Hilary, Jackie was not happy at Commonweal Lodge, or at any of her subsequent schools, and demanded to be taken away.[2] Jackie might have seemed shy and quiet to outsiders, but she was also

* Vol. I, Virago, London, 1977, p. 23.

a wilful child and soon learnt to get her own way with her mother. By using the argument that staying at home meant more time to study music, Jackie quickly found the right tactical approach to gain Iris's sympathy. Perhaps without intending to discriminate between her children, Iris did start to focus more of her attention on her middle daughter. Her lenient attitude towards Jackie's skipping school must often have seemed unfair to Hilary and Piers.

From the school's point of view, the time given to music took a heavy toll on Jackie's school work. She had to leave early at least twice a week to get to her cello lessons in central London. Miss Bray, the headmistress of Commonweal Lodge, took a dim view of such irregularities and suggested to the du Pré parents that Jackie should be transferred to Croydon High School.

The move was justified since Miss Bolwell, the headmistress, was sympathetic towards the individual needs of a highly gifted child and gave Jackie permission to take time off school for her cello lessons. In fact, Jackie's move to her new school in September 1953 coincided with Herbert Walenn's death and the subsequent closure of the London Cello School. But she continued private lessons with Alison Dalrymple in London.

Croydon High School had a reputation as one of the best in the area, with high academic standards. It was classified as a direct grant school (also known as a Public State School Trust), combining a fee-paying junior school and a senior school where forty per cent of the pupils were state-assisted. The school was divided into three sections – the primary section (up to nine), the nine to eleven year section and the High School for the eleven- to eighteen-year-olds, each housed in a separate building. As was usual at the time, uniform was obligatory – a navy-blue skirt, white blouse, green tie, brown shoes, and a hat with a brim and an oak-leaf badge pinned to its ribbon – an outfit that was 'altogether drab and unflattering' as an ex-pupil, Parthenope Bion, recalled.[3]

The change of school meant separation from Hilary, who was to remain at Commonweal Lodge for the rest of her schooldays. Jackie's new friends at Croydon High – among them Rebecca Saintonge and Andrea Barron as well as Parthenope – found her to be a very lovable, ordinary and unsophisticated child from a rather dull, conventional background. As Andrea recalled, Jackie did not manifest any signs of her outstanding talent in the normal course of school routine.[4] This was no doubt because almost all her musical activity happened outside school.

The du Pré parents did little to encourage their children to extend the limits of their world. When Iris organised parties for birthdays and special occasions, school friends were invited to the house, but Jackie seldom reciprocated their visits. Parthenope Bion recalled that several class-mates, Jackie included, were forbidden by their parents to visit her home, since her father's profession – he was the well-known psychiatrist Wilfred Bion, pioneer of group therapy – was viewed with disapproval. This speaks volumes for the cultural climate in suburban England, where psychiatry was an unknown – and consequently totally suspect – science. For his part, Dr Bion regarded Iris du Pré as a narrow-minded person, whose 'niceness' was somewhat spurious.

It was not until Jackie's school friends had the chance to hear her play that they became aware of just how remarkable her gifts were. In Parthenope's words,

> Even at that young age she was a completely different person when she played the cello – fiercely concentrated and passionate. You could say that underneath it all Jackie had a communication problem with every-body when she wasn't playing, although at the time it wouldn't have been defined as a problem. Outwardly she was a very nice, rather chubby, well-brought-up large 'little girl'. But as with many creative people, she interiorised her emotions and her real life operated on another plane.

Her more observant friends noted an incipient strain of melancholy underneath Jackie's sunny exterior. It was as if she absented herself from her surroundings, retreating into her private world. But Jackie came into her own with her ability to entertain her friends at the piano. Parthenope recalled: 'In the junior school there was a refectory in the basement and we would all traipse down to meals in Indian file. While waiting, we would sit cross-legged on the floor and people would be asked to sing something, recite a poem or play the piano, which was used for morning prayers. We always asked Jackie to play "The Whirligig", a piece composed by Mrs du Pré. It stretches my imagination to think that she had no instruction on the piano, because she played very well.' Another favourite request were the songs from the film *Hans Christian Andersen*, made popular by Danny Kaye.

In fact, Croydon High School could boast an extremely good music teacher, Phyllis Hunt, who took the school choir and gave piano lessons.

She had recently come back from a sabbatical year studying in Vienna and was a good enough accompanist to play with such names as the distinguished viola player William Primrose. Young and energetic, Hunt was instrumental in making Croydon High School a venue for public concerts in the days before Fairfield Hall was opened. Among those who came to perform at the school were the horn player Dennis Brain, the percussion player James Blades, and the pianist Fou Ts'ong. Fully aware of the exceptional nature of Jackie's musical gifts, Hunt became an ally and ensured that she always performed something on the cello at school concerts.

In the meantime it was becoming apparent that Jackie was reaching the limits of what could be learnt from Alison Dalrymple and needed the stimulus of a new cello teacher. Iris was aware of the importance of finding exactly the right person to guide the ten-year-old Jackie at this next, most vital stage of her development. In approaching William Pleeth, she made an inspired choice. Pleeth was a natural and sensitive musician, and a wonderful communicator. He had already gained a reputation as a fine teacher, although, because of his busy performing schedule, he only taught at student level.

Iris's one concern was whether he would accept such a young pupil. As a first step she had taken Jackie to hear the Amadeus Quartet in the Schubert C major Quintet, with Pleeth playing the second cello part. The achingly eloquent second movement had reduced the young child to floods of tears. In the spring of 1955 Iris rang Pleeth and a meeting was arranged. Later Jackie recalled her vivid memory of

> standing on William Pleeth's doorstep for the very first time. I was ten years old. As I pressed the doorbell I felt nervous and yet strangely elated. We had never met before, although I had heard him play at a concert and been deeply moved. Now that I was actually face to face, I wondered what sort of a man he would be. Wonderful, like his playing? Or remote and aloof – very much the great artist – who would not have time or interest in his new child pupil? I need not have worried. His warm, welcoming personality soon put all my doubts at rest, and in that first hour we managed to explore a lot of musical territory, and a lot about ourselves.[5]

Stimulated by her new teacher, Jackie felt increasingly committed to the cello, with the inevitable result that she started to fall behind in her school work. She was academically bright and in her first years at

Croydon High School she was able to keep up with her class without too much effort. She showed an aptitude for English Literature, but spelling and grammar proved to be weak points; despite her gift for mimicry, Jackie found the sounds and structures of foreign languages difficult.

At home, she complained that she felt a misfit and was teased and even bullied by the other children. Those of her former class-mates whom I interviewed do not recall such bullying; rather, they remarked on her reticence and her seeming unwillingness to engage in the discussions and arguments that they enjoyed. In any case, music took up almost all her time outside school hours, so she had little opportunity to socialise or develop stimulating friendships with her peers.

All in all, Croydon High School probably did as well for Jackie as any other school would have done at the time. As Parthenope Bion pointed out, the problem lay in the school system itself, which tended to stifle creativity: 'Jackie suffered from the English school "heartiness", which is not compatible with an artistic sensibility.'[6]

In the meantime, Pleeth was so impressed by Jackie's remarkable progress on the cello that after a year of study with him he suggested she should compete for the Suggia Gift award, open to cellists up to the age of twenty-one. By winning the award when she was only eleven, Jackie's talents were publicly recognised, implying a full-scale commitment to music. Jackie's general education was now officially regarded as subordinate to music and this in itself set her yet further apart from her contemporaries at school.

Apart from recognition, the award of the Suggia Gift provided the means to pay for Jackie's cello lessons over the next six years. It was eminently suitable that her musical education should be financed by the posthumous generosity of Guilhermina Suggia. The Portuguese cellist became one of the first women to achieve international recognition in a previously male-dominated profession. Her haughty and dramatic image has been immortalised for us in Augustus John's portrait, which now hangs in the Tate Gallery. Draped in the luxuriant folds of her wine-coloured dress, the cellist sits with head thrown back, chin jutting defiantly. Her right arm stretches out regally, if not quite in accordance with the rules of good bowing technique. As Robert Baldock comments in his biography of Casals, '[the painting] dealt conclusively with the suggestion that the cello was not an elegant instrument for women.'[7]

In view of the growing number of female virtuosi of the instrument today it is extraordinary to think that until relatively recently women were discouraged from playing the cello at all because of the unladylike posture it required. At best, they were allowed to play 'side-saddle', with their legs squeezed together at the left of the instrument, a pose guaranteed to make the player uncomfortable and tense. In recent history Paul Tortelier recorded that his first (female) teacher adopted this position.

Born of Portuguese–Italian parentage, Suggia made her début aged seven in her native town of Porto. She was ten years old when she first played for Casals in 1898, but her close association with him came eight years later when, after a brief period of study with Klengel she arrived on his doorstep in Paris and became not only his favourite student, but his companion and lover. For five years their domestic and musical lives were inextricably linked. Eugene Goossens claimed that the two cellists were near equals, and remembered an occasion when Casals and Suggia took their cellos behind screens at a party in a private London house and asked the assembled company to guess which of them was playing – a task in which most people failed.[8] Gerald Moore, who accompanied Suggia on many occasions, recalled that she '... gave an impression of boldness, romance and colour. She persuaded you her playing was passionate and intense, but the reverse was the case: it was calculated, correct and classical.'[9]

Casals and Suggia performed concerts together and premièred the Hungarian composer Emanuel Moor's Concerto for Two Cellos, written specially for them. Donald Tovey, another composer whom Casals promoted and admired, proved to be the unwitting cause of the final split between the couple at Casals' Spanish retreat at San Salvador. After the break-up of their relationship Suggia moved to London, which remained her principal base until before the Second World War. She was to perform more in England than in any other country.

England also happened to be a country where women cellists flourished. A contemporary of Suggia's – and no less flamboyant a personality – was Beatrice Harrison, who championed the works of contemporary British composers. She is also remembered, somewhat eccentrically, for recording Rimsky-Korsakov's *Chanson Hindu* in duet with a nightingale in her country garden and for her extravagant wardrobe – she never wore the same dress twice at a concert.

Harrison premièred Delius's Cello Sonata and the Double Concerto (which she played with her violinist sister May), and made the first recording of the Elgar concerto with the composer conducting. Delius also dedicated his Cello Concerto to her. Despite her achievements, Harrison found to her cost that female cellists were still regarded with some incredulity. She was reputedly the butt of one of Thomas Beecham's cruder jokes. Unhappy with the sound she was producing, Beecham is said to have upbraided the unfortunate lady: 'Madam, you hold between your legs an instrument that could give pleasure to thousands, and all you do is sit there and scratch it.'

England produced other fine female cellists in the succeeding generations: Thelma Reiss, Helen Just, Antonia Butler, Joan Dickson, Florence Hooten, Eileen Croxford, Amaryllis Fleming, Anna Shuttleworth and Olga Hegedus all achieved some measure of success as players and teachers, and had a notable influence on cello playing in England in the post-war years. Nevertheless, none of them, Suggia included, could compare as players or boast the achievements of Jacqueline du Pré in her heyday.

Soon after she transferred her home to England, Suggia was courted by a rich and well-connected Englishman (the owner of *Country Life* magazine) who reputedly presented her with a Stradivarius cello and a Scottish island. On breaking off her engagement to him, she returned the latter but kept the cello – the Strad was more useful to her and it was also a better investment. It was this instrument that she bequeathed to the Royal Academy, with the proviso that the income from its sale should be put into a Trust to provide funds to enable aspiring young cellists to study.

The Suggia Gift was established in 1956, two years after her death, and the first auditions took place at the Royal Academy on 25 July that year. The distinguished panel of five judges included Ivor Newton, Lionel Tertis and the chairman of the jury, John Barbirolli. The balance of numbers between players and auditioners was precise – only five cellists competed that first year. Theoretically, each applicant was to play for twelve minutes, but as Evelyn Barbirolli noted, 'Very often an impromptu cello lesson from John Barbirolli to a startled child (in the form of questions and advice) held up the proceedings.'[10]

William Pleeth's letter of recommendation certainly must have raised the expectations of the panel: '[Jacqueline du Pré] is the most outstanding cellistic and musical talent that I have met so far, to which she adds incredible maturity of mind. I am of the opinion that she will have a great career.'

At this first audition Jackie performed pieces by Vivaldi, Saint-Saëns and Boccherini. John Barbirolli recognised Jackie as the winner from the moment she started playing. Yet his audition notes show a sense of fairness and are a reflection of his insistence on professional standards:

Vivaldi: Certainly talented. Nice tone. Good intonation.

'The Swan' (Saint-Saëns): Very immature musically. Not very imaginative.

Boccherini: More advanced technically than musically. Feel that she should now really get down to her cello.[11]

In giving the award to an eleven-year-old, the panel chose to make a committed investment in a talent that was developing rather than formed, a policy it was to pursue in future years as well. Jackie was offered £175 a year to pay for her lessons, with the proviso that she must do four hours' practice a day. This stipulation was defined in the regulations of the Gift, and had to be agreed by Jackie's parents in consultation with Pleeth and the new headmistress of Croydon High School, Miss Margaret Adams. She arranged to create a special schedule for Jackie, who had just entered the senior section of the High School, allowing her to keep on the minimum number of subjects, and to drop games and needlework in favour of German – a concession to the cosmopolitan nature of an itinerant musician's life.

Pleeth remembers that 'Iris did consult me about Jackie's schooling. It is a great gamble to decide to withdraw a child (even partially) from school, but I didn't think it was with Jackie, as I had never doubted for a moment that she would go on to be a cellist. I may have been biased in that the same thing happened to me at the age of thirteen. But I supported Iris in this. Occasionally I would talk to Jackie and was satisfied that she was being educated to a considerable point and that her brain was being sufficiently stimulated.'[12]

More than anything, this dilemma reflected the predicament of parents of specially talented children in those days. The du Pré's rightly felt that Jackie must be given the best opportunities to develop her special talent. It is unlikely that they could have afforded the kind of private tutoring that young prodigies in the past (such as Yehudi Menuhin) tended to be given; on the other hand, the prodigies in question were earning their keep (and often maintaining their families) as they performed all over the world – a choice that the du Prés had never considered. In any case, private tuition would not have solved Jackie's sense of isolation from her peers.

In Russia (and later in the Eastern-block countries), the creation of specialist musical schools went as far back as the 1930s, and provided an integrated system of general education and specialised training. However, the hothouse atmosphere and the rigidity of such systems can – at worst – produce a conveyer-belt production of standardised virtuosi and carries the risk that a creative individuality could be destroyed. Although Yehudi Menuhin used the Russian specialist music school as a model when he founded his school in England in 1963, he also tried to ensure that each individual pupil could flourish in an all-round way. With the subsequent creation of other specialist music schools in Britain, today's parent has a larger choice of possibilities to ensure that a musically precocious child receives a balanced education.

The whole question of Jackie's schooling – or lack of it – became more aggravated as time went on. There existed a body of opinion that she was being over-protected and under-educated, and another that the unimaginative British school system would ruin her. Effectively, as her time at school was reduced to the minimum, Jackie found herself isolated from her age group, and came to feel socially gauche and inadequate in everything outside music. In retrospect, she would remark with a certain amount of bitterness that the opportunity of a general education had been denied her, often saying, 'Nobody asked me whether I wanted to go to school or not.' She may not have realised that she gained in recompense an autonomy of thought and creative imagination.

4

Studies With Pleeth

Is it 'I' that draws the bow, or is it the bow that draws me into
the state of highest tension? ... For as soon as I take the bow
and shoot everything becomes so clear and straightforward and
so ridiculously simple...

Eugen Herrigel, *Zen in the Art of Archery*

Jackie's new cello teacher, William Pleeth, was born in London in 1916
of Polish–Jewish ancestry. He had started playing the cello at the age
of seven and made such rapid progress that, aged thirteen, he was
awarded a scholarship to study with Julius Klengel in Leipzig.

As Pleeth recalled, 'Klengel was musically as dry as dust, but he had
a fantastic Paganini technique. He had a sincerity and innocence that
was a hallmark of the German School at the time. His greatest strength
lay in the flexibility of his teaching, which allowed you to discover your
own personality. Hence all his last pupils turned out very differently –
and Feuermann, Piatigorsky and myself were among them.'[1]

Pleeth is adamant that whatever he may have gained from his teachers, the larger part of his musical development depended on 'environment' – going to concerts, absorbing music and learning from the
qualities of different performers. 'I stopped going to school at the age
of thirteen and three years later I had my last cello lesson. Although I
had an intuitive cellistic talent, I was also very conscious of what
technique was about and later I was able to take it to pieces. For me,
cello playing and conscious thought were married together.'

At the age of fifteen Pleeth gave his orchestral début, playing Haydn's
D major Concerto at the Leipzig Gewandhaus. Two years later he
returned to England and started his professional career. Jackie would
often remark that Pleeth never fulfilled his formidable gifts as a performer because he did not have the ambition to push himself. Nevertheless, during the first twenty years of his playing career he not only
played the great 'war-horses', but learnt and played many new concertos.
Given the minimal amounts of allocated rehearsal with British orches-

tras (most particularly when making broadcasts) Pleeth became increasingly dissatisfied with the life of a soloist.

Thus it was that in the 1950s and 1960s William Pleeth decided to devote his energies to teaching and to chamber music. He was appointed Professor at the Guildhall, founded the Allegri Quartet with the violinist Eli Goren and was a member of the Melos Ensemble. Anyone who has heard the recordings of Haydn and Mozart made on the old Westminster label by the original Allegri Quartet will know how much vitality and expressive diversity Pleeth brings to the bass line. Peter Thomas, at one time second violin in the quartet, remembered that Pleeth acted as a perfect foil for Goren, so that the other two players could fit in easily like the filling of a sandwich.[2] Goren meant it as a compliment when he said that no other cellist could 'drive a quartet so well from below'; he was constantly amazed at the variety of strokes Pleeth could impart to a simple bass line.

When Jackie came to Pleeth in 1955, he already had gained a reputation as a gifted and inspiring teacher at student level. Although it was against his policy to teach children, Pleeth immediately realised that he must make an exception for Jackie. He recalled her playing at her first audition as

> ... beautifully clean and straightforward with good rhythm. She sounded like she looked – completely untainted. Her playing had none of the knowingly 'clever clever' aspect of a self-conscious prodigy. You weren't bamboozled by the flair or any rubbish overlay. I chatted with Jackie and got simple answers. It was clear to me that there was something remarkable in her talent waiting to be revealed. I was confident that in working together we would climb and climb.[3]

Pleeth gave credit to Alison Dalrymple for giving Jackie a good basic technique, while allowing her musicality and natural simplicity to flourish. 'Dalrymple had never imposed herself and this meant that there was no untangling of weeds for me to do. Rather, I had a clean bit of ground to cultivate.'

From the time she started lessons with Pleeth, Jackie's progress accelerated dramatically. At the beginning, they moved at a steady pace, but within two years Pleeth felt he could increase the pressure. 'It was like letting the horse off the reins, she was able to gallop away, depending on how much rein you gave her. The speed of her progress was phenomenal.'

With her extraordinary ability to assimilate the essence of music, as well as to memorise the notes, learning was never a grind. From the start, Pleeth had been impressed by Jackie's quick intuitive grasp of musical structure. The more he got to know her, the more he was amazed at the speed with which she learnt and brought a piece to a high level of performance.

By the time she was eleven Jackie was studying repertoire concertos like the Lalo. It was the first movement of this piece that she performed when she played with orchestra at the age of twelve, at a concert with the Guildhall School's student orchestra conducted by Norman Del Mar. When Jackie was thirteen, Pleeth set her the Elgar concerto and the first of Piatti's *Twelve Caprices*. He recalled:

> Jackie got two lessons a week from me then – one at my home on a Saturday and the other at the Guildhall on a Wednesday. At the Wednesday lesson I told her to get the Elgar – she will have got the music on a Thursday afternoon and will have started work then. She turned up for her Saturday morning lesson with the Piatti Caprice and the whole of the first movement and half of the second of the Elgar from memory – quite a feat. And she played them superbly. Soon afterwards we came to the other big concertos – the Haydn D major, Bloch's *Schelomo*, the Dvořák and Schumann. But the Elgar was her first big concerto. Although she was thrilled, she was very quiet and undemonstrative about it.

During her six years with Pleeth, Jackie covered a very large and catholic repertoire, from baroque sonatas and transcriptions, Bach suites to contemporary pieces such as Shostakovich's first concerto (newly written in 1959) and Benjamin Britten's sonata of 1961. Iris made herself available to come to lessons to accompany her and Pleeth found her presence very useful, lending the right kind of musical support. But he admits that had there been more time, he would have liked to introduce Jackie to more chamber music and to have had other pianists come in for lessons.

Pleeth encouraged Jackie to play a limited number of concerts before exposing her to a professional début. She loved performing and the occasional concert provided her with useful experience. For this reason, he agreed to her making early public appearances on BBC television, in programmes which featured highly talented children. BBC radio broadcasts, on the other hand, were a highly serious matter for which one had to audition. Television only made provisos about a child's age, rather than its professional status – the minimum age for TV presentation was twelve.

As the elder of the two du Pré sisters, Hilary was the first to be 'talent-spotted' and given television exposure. Her initial performances were on the piano, although in her teens she gradually transferred her allegiance to the flute. Jackie first appeared on television at a Young People's Concert recorded in Cardiff on 10 January 1958 – a couple of weeks before her thirteenth birthday – where she played the opening movement of the Lalo concerto with the BBC Welsh Orchestra and Stanford Robinson.

Later that year, on 28 April, Jackie and Hilary appeared together in the TV studios, performing one movement from Mozart's Flute Quartet with the violinist Diana Cummings and the viola player Ian White. Later they were to play the complete work in a music club concert. The BBC gave the group the name of the Artemis Quartet, although nobody remembers why. Their performance provided a cultural interlude in an arbitrary hotchpotch of instruction and entertainment ranging from Jeremy Hooker 'introducing Hedgehog', to enlightenment on campfire cookery.

Hilary recalled that on that occasion Prince Charles and Princess Anne were guests in the television studio.[4] Jackie used to enjoy telling the story of how the young Prince asked if he might have a go on her cello. To her dismay, he tried to mount it like a horse and she reprimanded him firmly. Several years later, Prince Charles heard her play the Haydn C major Concerto at the Festival Hall and was so moved by her playing that he decided to take up the cello himself.

The Artemis Quartet made one more appearance on television, although this time with a second violin (Sidney Mann) substituting the flute – when they played a short arrangement from Handel's *Water Music* and the Purcell *Fantasia Upon One Note*, where Stan Unwin (better known in his guise as 'Uncle Stan') handled the long sustained C in the second viola part.

Pleeth saw to it that Jackie developed her performing skills without exerting unnecessary pressure, ensuring that she had specific and achievable goals. Similarly, in the normal day-to-day course of study Pleeth believed in stimulating his pupils' musical rather than instrumental interests, without over-stretching their limits. His approach to solving technical problems through the music was such a natural part of his teaching that Jackie grew up with the impression that she had never studied technique. And, with a child as receptive as Jackie, Pleeth was able to impart technique in what he defines as 'an integrated way of life with the instrument'. Pleeth recalled that 'Jackie learnt to overcome instrumental difficulties without being aware she was doing so. I never had to spell things out.'

Pleeth's assertion that technique starts with 'Mother Nature' meant finding the right solutions for each particular physique and for every pair of hands. In Jackie's case, Pleeth identified a possible problem in her left hand. 'Her first and second fingers were more or less the same length, which can be awkward on the cello. We had to find a way round, keeping the second finger very rounded, especially when going into higher positions. But Jackie was never even aware that this was a problem.'

A further difficulty arose later, this time in the right hand. When playing with enormous force of passion Jackie tended to exert too much pressure and force the sound. As Pleeth saw it,

> Her problem lay in the explosiveness of her temperament – sometimes she used herself too much physically. She would squeeze the bow until the tension became too great. This meant that her thumb, which was very long, tended to cave in and slip off the nut of the bow. At this point you have to recognise that you have reached a limit; you cannot make holes in the bow, so you have to find an escape route. In the end Jackie learnt to deal with this by putting her little finger behind the bow stick, which allowed the thumb to relax in compensation.

Since he held that technique is so closely allied to musical expression, Pleeth believed in imparting technical skills in the course of studying repertoire pieces.

> As a teacher I try and smell out what type of discipline each individual pupil needs. I don't believe in doing scales just for the sake of discipline. Scales are part of music – not a narrow study. A finger stroke can differ in so many ways, just as a bow stroke can. The *touché* which is so much talked about by pianists is also something very necessary to string players. Certain conservatoire-trained cellists are turned out playing with machine-gun fingers – but to my mind these aren't strong fingers – they don't know how to dance and do different steps. A hundred scales can have a hundred different sentiments.

Pleeth derided the idea of automatic repetition in practising, or what he terms 'thoughtless grinding away'. He taught Jackie to avoid any kind of mechanical practice. Similarly, rather than have her wade through sterile repetitive exercises such as Ševčík, Cossman and Feuillard studies (the cellists' somewhat inferior version of Dr Gradus ad Parnassum), he would set Jackie studies such as the Piatti *Caprices*, where the technique is embodied in the music and even the passage work benefits from a singing cantabile. He felt it was important that his pupils never divided the pieces they studied into 'second-rate' material and 'proper' music from the mainstream repertoire.

The cellist Robert Cohen later emulated Jackie's experience and studied with Pleeth between the ages of ten and sixteen. He recalled that: 'With Pleeth there was never any question of just learning the notes and playing in tune as in many conventional schools of teaching.' Cohen had been warned by many people that he would not learn technique with Bill Pleeth.

> But this showed a basic misunderstanding of how Pleeth taught. He started from the precept that technique exists to fulfil the musical end. You must live through a process of discovery where you teach yourself to adapt your technique constantly. To my mind the emphasis on technique was much greater because it was there all the time. But you were always aiming to a point – how to produce this particular sound or to reproduce that particular emotion or effect. He did not talk in terms of bow changes or finger contact, because these techniques are all so subtle and sophisticated that he taught them only within the musical context.

In fact, if Pleeth felt it was relevant to a particular problem, he might set his pupils a scale, or one of the more arid Ševčík or Feuillard studies. But as Cohen pointed out, 'With Pleeth, every exercise had a specific aim and we never played a study just in one way. He might say, "... Don't do the printed bowing, let's do it this way," or "... Play it now at double speed with half bows ..." or "... Play it all with separate bows." This made it more interesting for him, and it made us more flexible.' Flexibility meant accepting that there were many ways of approaching a problem. Pleeth liked to stimulate thought and discussion with his pupils, thereby teaching them to think for themselves. Pleeth's motto was 'search and find', whereby every pupil was made to question his musical intentions. However many suggestions he might make himself, he always left the pupil to draw his or her own conclusions.

In cellistic terms, this meant never playing anything with just one set of bowings or fingerings. As Cohen remembers, 'Pleeth could suggest at least six fingerings for any given passage, not just for the sake of it, but he would make you find them yourself. In standard convention there exists the idea that the cello dictates the sound you make, that the A string makes a brighter sound than the D, for instance. But Pleeth taught us to control the bow and the vibrato so that you can achieve the same effects on the A and D strings.'⁵

Cohen termed Pleeth's approach to music as both logical and organic. 'He would talk about the physics of music – the rebound time in a rallantando or accelerando, of a ball bouncing quicker, of the process of natural gravity. And he spoke of how you achieve a response. If you throw a ball in a certain way, with a short, sharp action, you get that kind of response, but if you want distance, then you have a different sweep of motion.'

In Pleeth's view, the pupil had to be master of the whole musical process, which meant knowing how to feel, initiate and fulfil the musical impulse. At the same time he has to exercise objectivity. According to Cohen,

> Pleeth taught us that when playing you need to control the musical impulse in an almost schizophrenic way, feeling the music and being detached from it simultaneously. If you slip too much from one or the other state you are immediately in trouble, as you are in danger of actually giving out something that is different from what you intended. When somebody got terribly wrapped up in themselves Bill would come out with his favourite phrase: 'Now, dear, play that again and look out of the window.' Of course a consummate artist like Jackie had this ability of allowing the ear to go to the other side of the room while playing.

This ability to be objective, while remaining totally involved in the music, implied a canny awareness on Jackie's part, which does not coincide with the commonly accepted view of her being a basically intuitive and impulsive performer. When Pleeth talked of the astounding 'endlessness' of Jackie's temperament, he meant two things: her capacity for continuous and never-ending development and her willingness to appear to give her all in music, while always maintaining something in reserve. 'Jackie knew how to create the illusion of getting more and more dramatic, while all the time being conscious of building this process. She learnt how to hold back automatically, like a rocket which blasts off, then sends another rocket and another one after that. This ability to feed the music with passion from her endless reserves was, to my mind a spiritual process. She learnt to concede that the instrument has its limits and cannot be forced beyond them.'[6]

Pleeth taught Jackie during her most formative years and launched her into the world. During these seven years of study, and indeed throughout the rest of her life, he remained an influential figure; it was no wonder that she referred to him jokingly as her 'cello daddy'. Jackie recognised that Pleeth was capable of side-stepping his personal feelings, and always remained an unbiased and unmanipulative teacher. He stuck to an absolute policy of never using his influence to promote his pupils in the way that some ambitious teachers do and for this reason he discouraged the idea of using big international competitions as a means of making their name. He was happy to advise students about programming and when to begin their débuts, although he disliked getting involved in their careers. But in the case of such pupils as du Pré and Cohen he never worried, as he knew that they were well able to stand on their own merits.

Just as there exists the right teacher for each individual, so there also exists the ideal pupil for every teacher. Pleeth and du Pré were ideally suited from this point of view. Jackie's musical personality unfolded and grew from strength to strength under Pleeth's guidance. He was always able to stimulate her interest in the cello and never had to use coercion to make her practise. And it is to Pleeth's lasting credit that he allowed Jackie to retain what he termed 'her musical innocence', realising that the special and unique appeal of her talent lay in her natural communicative powers and in her endless reserves of passion. Even when she had become a fully fledged concert artist on the international circuit, Jackie was still able to allow her listeners that rare privilege of sharing the insights of her unspoilt natural intuition.

5

Emerging Into The
Public Eye

Es bildet ein Talent sich in der Stille,
Sich ein Charakter in dem Strom der Welt.

Talent develops in quiet places, character in the full current of
human life.

Johann Wolfgang von Goethe, Torquato Tasso

Towards the end of 1958, Derek du Pré was offered a new job. The
position of Secretary of the Institute of Costs and Works Accountants
suited him and his family ideally, since it came with a perk, an upstairs
flat at 63 Portland Place in the heart of London, a stone's throw from
Regent's Park and conveniently close to the Royal Academy of Music,
where Hilary had just enrolled.

There was one disadvantage about having a flat on the premises,
namely its proximity to other offices in the building. This necessitated
having a top-floor room sound-proofed so that Jackie could practise
without causing disturbance. Pleeth recalls this as a worrying problem,
because sound-proofing kills vibration, making a string instrument
sound dry and dead. He marvelled at Jackie's ability to continue to
produce sound as if she were playing in a normal acoustic. She retained
a healthy sense of proportion and got on with practice undiscouraged.
Jackie's one complaint, however, was having to keep the windows
closed; particularly on humid summer days, she found the heat and
stuffy atmosphere to be almost unbearable.

The move to London took place in November 1958. While the new
flat was being redecorated and adjusted to the family's needs, Isména
Holland helped out by inviting the du Prés to stay for several weeks in
her house in Kensington. Mrs Holland was generous in her hospitality
and tolerated this invasion of her space with equanimity. She recalled
that to give the family their privacy she decided to sup on her own;
apart from anything else, she found Iris's cooking to be very plain.

Jackie had already been a frequent visitor to her house in Elton Road. Mrs Holland remembered,

> When the family still lived in Purley, Iris would drive her up to London and, if there was time to kill between music lessons she would deposit Jackie at my house in Kensington. Jackie used to go upstairs into my studio and practise away like mad on her own. She had an enormous capacity to concentrate and never stopped to fool around. She was quite serious about it all. I remember trying to teach her some German when she was resting, but we didn't get very far, as she wasn't really interested. She was a funny child, very self-contained.[1]

Shortly after the move to London, and nearly a year after her television début Jackie was invited to appear again on TV. On 2 January 1959 she performed the last movement of Haydn's D major Concerto with Stanford Robinson conducting the Royal Philharmonic Orchestra before a studio audience. Two other young soloists, the violinists Peter Thomas and Diana Cummings, appeared in the same programme playing the first movement of Bach's Double Concerto. Diana already knew Jackie from the local music festivals circuit, but Peter was hearing her for the first time. He was bowled over by Jackie's stupendous cello playing, but felt too much in awe of her to approach her then. Six months her junior, he saw himself as a normal thirteen-year-old, with a talent for the violin; unlike Jackie he was nothing of a prodigy.

Jackie, for her part, was sufficiently impressed by Peter to write him a letter suggesting he should come round for some music-making. Soon he was a regular visit at Portland Place and became friendly with all her family. Peter described the du Prés as country people at heart, who enjoyed the simple pleasures of life.

> We would go for walks in Regent's Park – something Jackie loved. Then they would make tea and we talked a lot around the table. Later we went to the flicks together. There was a naïvety about the family, which meant that they would never question whether or not Jackie should go to school. Derek totally submitted to Iris and was quite a restricted personality. He seemed not to know how to handle Jackie and in any case he left it all to Iris.[2]

Peter had a great admiration for Iris, finding her to be unspoilt, direct and straightforward: 'Despite her adherence to social conventions, she was in many ways a free spirit and was able to convey her sense of freedom to both her daughters. They were unfettered by formal education – in Jackie's case the ability to dismiss rules was most important in her music-making. Her beauty lay in the fact that she was totally unspoilt – like a bird – one cannot imagine anyone having more freedom.'

In contrast to her capable and immensely energetic mother, Jackie appeared to be quite low-key and passive in everyday life. She needed a lot of rest. As Peter recalled, 'Although she had the capacity to be lively, she appeared quite placid. When she played the cello she was transformed and had extraordinary energy. But in general it was Iris who gave the impression of strength and energy, not Jackie.'

For Jackie, this friendship became extremely important, reflecting her desperate need for company of her own age. She was especially pleased to have a boy as a friend, although too shy to consider Peter a 'boy-friend'. Naturally, their friendship centred around their music-making together. According to Peter, 'We played a lot – Jackie dragged me through things like the Rolla Duos – which she perfected in no time at all. If she got keen on something she really went for it straight away. She assimilated things terribly quickly. This quick ear and wonderful memory were very impressive, as was the large scale of her playing.' As Peter observed, Jackie always played as if projecting in a big hall with an intensity and sense of unhurried time that are signs of a great performing artist.

Once Jackie suggested trying out the Brahms Double Concerto. A few days after acquiring the score she and Peter met. As he remembered, 'I discovered that Jackie had learnt the first movement from memory, whereas I had only looked at the first page or so. She also played fantastically well. I felt a bit out of my depth at that point.'

They also played unaccompanied Bach for each other and Jackie would share her thoughts on the music with Peter: 'Her approach was very emotional, very noble, dramatic and big. It had nothing to do with the so-called "authentic" style, although it had that purity of line which Pleeth had instilled in her, whatever the little extravagances she indulged in on the way.'

Iris welcomed Jackie's friendship with Peter, as it led to a rare opportunity for music-making with somebody of her own age. Unlike her contemporaries, Jackie never joined youth orchestras or participated in holiday music courses. Iris considered that general music standards in Britain were too low for her daughter. Perhaps from a musician's point of view Jackie would have been wasting time at such courses, but she did lose out on a chance of socialising with other teenagers who shared her interests.

At home, Jackie and Peter read through some Haydn trios with Hilary at the piano. Pleeth encouraged the young musicians and suggested they put a programme together, with Hilary playing flute and her Academy friend Christina Mason as the pianist. He then arranged a concert for them at Horsham Music Club, which took place on 10 June 1960. Peter and Jackie performed a Rolla Duo – from memory at Jackie's insistence – and Hilary played the Poulenc Flute Sonata with Christina. To complete the programme Peter and Jackie were joined by Christina in a performance of Beethoven's C minor Piano Trio Op. 1 No. 3.

Six months later Peter's parents arranged another chamber music concert at Rainham Primary School, where they taught. This time Hilary, Peter and Jackie each played short solo pieces and the main item in the programme was Mendelssohn's D minor Trio – with Peter's sister Judith replacing Christina as the pianist.

As Peter recalled, 'Although we were not in any sense Jackie's equals, it was fun for her to have someone of her age to play with.' Jackie might have been in a class of her own, but her companions were highly talented, and Hilary and Christina were already students at the Royal Academy. According to Peter, Hilary played with the same big style as Jackie. 'As a pianist she was a very direct communicator. But her flute playing was even more extraordinary. Hilary had amazing body language and moved far more than Jackie did – she was a real snake charmer.'

As it was, Jackie's uninhibited body movements in her cello playing already provoked comment; some people objected to them as a distracting mannerism. But Jackie's physical approach to performance was completely natural to her. As Casals later remarked when defending Jackie against criticism, 'But I like it. She moves with the music.' Peter remembered that, in contrast to her daughters, Iris remained quite still when performing, perhaps because piano playing does not lend itself so much to movement.

Jackie reciprocated Peter's visits to his family's home in Essex and before long the two families became friendly. Peter's mother, Mona Thomas, reminisced about the carefree times they all spent together. 'Life was great fun and uncomplicated for Jackie – she was such a happy, cheerful and radiant person, with a great sense of joy and humour. We sometimes went for walks along the creeks of Essex, and Jackie and Peter would bury one another in the snow in the garden.'³

Years later, Jackie described her childish love of snow and the wintry elements: 'I remember the search for the single, magically designed snowflake, or of flinging myself into the snow loving its texture, the cold against one's skin and the fun of constructing hard snowballs to throw at random to watch their passage through the air and then their splintering rebound on their chosen target.' These words, written when she was wheelchair-bound, were a kind of poetic recollection of the innocent fun she had with Peter in the distant years of her adolescence.⁴

Mona recalled her surprise when, on the occasion of her first visit to their home, the fourteen-year-old Jackie turned up accompanied by Iris. Already at the age of ten, the Thomas children were allowed to travel up to London unaccompanied to attend music lessons and visit friends. Jackie, on the other hand, rarely went anywhere without her mother. Yet while Iris ferried Jackie back and forth between school and music lessons, and attended to her every need, she left Piers and Hilary to fend far more for themselves. At the age of fifteen Hilary had been travelling up to the Royal Academy from Purley on public transport. Similarly, after the family moved to London, the thirteen-year-old Piers had to find his own way to school in Hampstead on the underground.

It is arguable that Iris over-protected Jackie so as to create the best possible conditions for the development of her musical talent; she did so, no doubt, with the best of intentions. A certain passivity in Jackie's character meant that she readily accepted her mother's protective role. But in addition, at this stage in her life Jackie identified very strongly with Iris, and was heavily reliant on her support and companionship.

Although initially surprised by Iris's constant presence near Jackie, Mona Thomas soon perceived that it was necessary to both of them. It had not been easy for Iris to deny her considerable gifts as a pianist and it was evident that in recompense she gained some satisfaction from dedicating her life to Jackie's extraordinary talent.

On her part, Iris often tried to persuade Mona to let Peter leave school so as to devote more time to violin playing.⁵ Jackie probably added her voice to Iris's; she certainly believed that Peter was not being sufficiently stretched in his violin studies. She therefore tried to convince him to change violin teachers and as a first step in her mission she took him to listen in to her lessons with Bill Pleeth. Peter found this new world of expression a revelation and, on Jackie's advice, began studying with Eli Goren, the leader of the Allegri Quartet in which Pleeth played. Goren's approach to music-making was similar to Pleeth's and Peter found him to be an inspirational teacher. However, unlike Jackie, Peter saw nothing wrong with school; he enjoyed the company of his class-mates and the opportunity to play football and other sports.

Although formal education was assuming a diminishing importance in Jackie's life, the move to London necessitated a change of school. The du Prés discovered that the prestigious girls' school, Queen's College, was within walking distance of Portland Place. They applied for a place for Jackie to start a restricted course of study of English, French and German in January 1959. In her letter of reference Mrs Holland described her goddaughter as a 'most sensible girl and endowed with exceptional musical talent and powers of concentration'. In addition, she spoke of her 'most delightful character and excellent manners'.[6]

More to the point, Miss M. C. Tatham, assistant Musical Director of the Arts Council (trustees of the Suggia Gift) sent a supporting letter to the principal of Queen's explaining that the 'advisers to the Gift have every hope that this child will develop into an international artist'.[7] She referred to the stipulated condition of four hours' daily practice and emphasised the priority of cello lessons over school subjects. Due to Pleeth's busy schedule, these lessons could never be arranged at the same time or on the same day.

In fact, Queen's College was a school which embraced the philosophy of the individual and had created the category of 'non-compounder' – meaning a part-time student. The principal, Miss Kynaston, accepted Jackie as a non-compounder on the proviso that the standard of her work would enable her to fit into the classes.

Yet despite the initial goodwill on both sides, the year that Jackie spent at Queen's proved unsatisfactory from both her point of view and the school's. At the awkward age of barely fourteen she had to insert herself into a group of girls who had already formed their friendships and who were altogether more sophisticated in everything, from their dress-sense and academic know-how to being *au fait* with the outside world. Jackie was still dressed by her mother in circular skirts and white knee socks which other girls of her age would not have been seen dead in. Her knowledge of the world outside the four walls of the family home was minimal.

Probably it was inevitable that Jackie should feel a misfit and, with her innate sense of modesty, she made little mention of her special gift, hiding her light under a bushel. The teachers were demanding in their own disciplines – as good teachers should be – and were unwilling to make concessions. From the start she came into conflict with the French teacher, Madame Blondeau, who regarded her poor knowledge of the language as 'shocking' and deplored the fact that Jackie appeared never to reflect before writing. Jacqueline always claimed that her schooldays were unhappy and referred to the day that she left school as a golden one.[8] In an interview given some ten years later, she confided that 'I was one of those children other children can't stand. They used to form gangs and chant horrid things. I always felt that in the cello I had some gorgeous secret and I guarded it jealously. It was the one thing that I didn't tell the other children about.'[9] Whether or not Jackie was the butt of such horrible taunting, and whether these incidents occurred at Croydon High School or at Queen's College, we cannot know. But the fact that Jackie recounted these stories proves that she felt unaccepted at school, if not an actual scapegoat.

Yet from the evidence that I have gathered from her contemporaries everything points to the fact that Jackie was well liked at school. Jennifer Cass, a class-mate at Queen's, described her as 'a friendly, jolly girl who fitted in well'. Nevertheless, it would appear that Jackie never formed any real friendship at school. Indeed, her sister Hilary recalled that even as a small child Jackie got on better with adults than with children and found it difficult to express herself in words.[10]

Throughout the year that Jackie spent at Queen's College Iris acted as a shield for her daughter – ultimately, perhaps, to her detriment. Just before the end of the Lent term Iris wrote the first of many letters excusing her daughter's poor attendance and her inability to prepare her homework. A few weeks later Iris explained in a long letter that Jackie had been left low after two attacks of flu, but 'as a result of a ten-day walking holiday on Dartmoor at the beginning of the holiday, she is feeling well again'. She was now busy practising for a Saturday morning children's concert at the Festival Hall, where she was to play the Lalo concerto with Ernest Read and the Royal Philharmonic. In view of all this Iris had thus decided that it was 'unwise' to spend time on French holiday prep and particularly asked that these circumstances be explained to the French teacher.[11]

The excuses continued during the summer term – Jackie was 'musically' extremely busy during this time, with three concertos and a Bach suite to prepare. Iris asked for indulgence when her daughter was unable to finish her preparation. It was evident that Jackie was struggling, since the girls in her class were already well ahead of her and 'in French she has been almost completely at sea'. In a letter of 24 May Iris made the first mention of her intention to withdraw her daughter from school on her fifteenth birthday (the following January) to have private coaching, fifteen being the legal school-leaving age in Great Britain at the time.

All this left the principal perplexed, since Jackie's timetable involved a minimal eight periods a week and three hours of preparation. Furthermore, Iris was willing to take Jackie back and forth from school, making sure that any gap between lessons was utilised for cello practice at home. It was difficult to believe that Jackie lacked sufficient time for her music.

Miss Kynaston replied to Iris's last communication with a terse note, and expressed her anxieties more fully in two letters, one to Miss Tatham at the Arts Council who acted as secretary of the Suggia Gift and the other to Mr Philip Wayne, one of the Suggia Gift trustees. Here she explained that Mrs du Pré was 'playing up' and had been unable to give satisfactory explanations for Jacqueline's poor attendance, which she regarded as tantamount to evasion. Miss Kynaston was also worried about the legality of a situation where a minimum of school hours was not being respected. She emphasised that Jacqueline 'has good intelligence, and should I am certain have some general education if she is to develop fully'.

It is interesting to note that Miss Tatham disclaimed responsibility for this state of affairs in her reply to Miss Kynaston: 'Our interest is in Jacqueline's musical progress – as a recipient of the Suggia – and arrangements for her general education remain in the hands of her parents.' She concluded that the advisers would not wish to modify their stipulation in regard to her practice time. However, later she did approach Pleeth asking if he would try to accommodate Jackie's cello lessons so that they did not clash with school hours.

A more perceptive and helpful reaction came from Philip Wayne. He defended Miss Kynaston's views to Miss Tatham, explaining that Jacqueline had started to make progress at Queen's and 'is well liked there, a circumstance that may well help to banish her initial unhappiness'. While recognising her total devotion to the cello, he emphasised the necessity of a wider view, in particular of stimulating her literary interests. Indeed, 'of a recent batch of literary essays, hers, I was told was the best.' Mr Wayne felt that it would be wrong for Jackie to leave Queen's and to have private tuition, since it would be hard to find a good tutor. 'Jacqueline needs the company of girls of her own age and to learn to fit in with people who are not ministers to her music and to her personal problems. I think that she is well worth all the trouble taken, and she will be the smaller musician if she misses the chance of a larger education.'[12]

Mr Wayne was impressed with Jackie when he talked to her, realising that she was 'intelligent enough to see in a flash that the significance of music comes from the resources of the mind'. She herself told him that she did not wish to be 'a horse in blinkers'. (A few weeks later she was to confess to him that she felt 'inept' at school.) He concluded his appeal to Miss Tatham by saying that in all this he believed that Jackie could 'to a great extent decide for herself'.[13]

However it would appear that decisions were taken on her behalf and that neither Iris nor Pleeth held with the usefulness of school education as a background to the development of an extraordinary musical talent. Certainly, this is made abundantly clear when Iris wrote towards the end of the summer term that homework seemed unimportant to her since Jackie would not be doing examinations. Indeed, Jackie was to leave school without a single qualification in terms of GCE exams.

These attitudes were in sharp contrast to those of Mona and Stanley Thomas, the parents of Jackie's friend Peter. Being schoolteachers, they advocated the benefits of an all-round education and were not to be persuaded by Iris that their son should be taken away from school. As opposed to Jackie, Peter gained his five GCSE equivalents before leaving school at fifteen. Only then did he start his full-time music studies. In retrospect he felt that this solution was the right one for him and also could have been right for Jackie. In Peter's opinion, 'Jackie would have been a great artist, whether or not she had gone to school. And studying under Pleeth, she would have become a fantastic cellist anyway, although her career might have started three years later. Personally I think that for her the chief benefit of school would have been to allow her to acquire social skills rather than formal education. At the time she certainly did feel left out of things.'

Evidently this sense of social unease is something commonly

encountered in a prodigy growing out of childhood into adolescence. Yehudi Menuhin admitted that it was so in his case. 'One vital experience I missed was the opportunity of, as it were, measuring myself, in the living moment, alongside other children. Instead, I was a law unto myself and my family, which was rather isolating – and frightening, because not until a long time afterwards did I feel at ease with people of my own age.'[14] Fortunately, as she grew into womanhood in her late teens, Jackie was able to catch up with her social skills very successfully.

The autumn term of 1959 was Jackie's last at school. It appeared to the staff at Queen's that she was settling down. As a gesture in the right direction, Miss Kynaston allowed Jackie to change French teachers halfway through the term. Her new teacher, Miss Dulcet, was recommended by the principal as being 'much gentler' and better able to understand Jackie's position. But neither Jackie nor Iris expended the necessary effort to make her attendance at school worthwhile or enjoyable.

Whatever Jackie's sense of failure might have been at school, this was more than fully compensated for by her success outside it. In October, Iris wrote to Miss Kynaston with more apologies for absences and explaining that on 27 October Jackie will 'receive three prizes at the annual Guildhall School of Music prize-giving to be held at Mansion House. The Lord Mayor presents the awards,' she concluded on a note of pride.

On 17 December 1959, the last day of the school term, Iris penned her final letter to Miss Kynaston with another apology for Jackie's absence. She went on to inform her, '... This may come as a surprise to you, but after much thought my husband and I have decided that it would be better for Jackie to leave school and have private coaching only.' Iris must have been aware that this last-minute announcement would hardly surprise Miss Kynaston. She had already told her the previous summer that she was thinking of taking Jackie away from school on or before her fifteenth birthday. At the time, Miss Kynaston had tried to force the du Prés into a decision, explaining that she could fill Jackie's place with a full-time student. Informing the school of Jackie's departure at the eleventh hour implied that Iris had wanted to keep her options open. But it may well also have been a sign of a somewhat guilty conscience, since Iris was allowing her ambition for Jackie's career to take precedence over her daughter's need for a wider education.

Jackie appears to have avoided participating in discussions about her general education. Because of her passive nature she opted for collusion rather than confrontation on the issue. In any case, as far as she was concerned, there was little to recommend school to her, although later she did admit to having enjoyed maths and English. As her godfather Lord Harewood observed, while Jackie may not have gained much book knowledge at school, she did already have an understanding of something that was far richer and more profound than anything most of us ever learn at school or afterwards.[15] Indeed, through music Jackie possessed a rich emotional world, which went a long way to compensate for her lack of friendships or intellectual stimulation.

In later life, though, she would recount an anecdote which demonstrated her feeling of isolation. When asked what she wanted for her birthday, the ten-year-old Jackie replied, 'A friend.' Nevertheless, one could also argue that her dedication to music allowed her a form of escapism from certain realities of the outside world with which she could not cope.

By her early twenties Jackie had formulated the following views on the matter: 'Looking back, I suppose that it might seem that I had a restricted life, but I never thought so. I still don't. I didn't have friends of my own age, but I didn't miss them. I got so much more out of music … To have been able to love something so intensely since I was small is tremendous. No one who has not experienced it can know just what it means to have a private world of your own to go into, to be quite by yourself whenever you need it.'[16]

But later still, when illness had prevented her playing the cello, her private world of music did not provide her with enough sustenance. Jackie would complain bitterly that she had been given little choice in the matter of her own schooling and that now, when she needed it, she had no general education to fall back on.

6

Wigmore Hall Début

But the cellist
Leaning over his labours, his eyes closed,
Is engaged in that study, blocking out, for the moment,
Audience, hall, and a great part of himself
In what, not wrongly, might be called research,
Or the most private kind of honesty.

Anthony Hecht, '*Dichtung und Wahrheit**

Removing Jackie from the school system on the eve of her fifteenth birthday was a sign of complete confidence in her destiny as a concert cellist on the part of her family and music teachers. And it was a confidence that was amply justified by her exceptional musical development.

Although she had enrolled as a student at the Guildhall School of Music in 1955, Jackie's connection with the school was limited to her lessons with Pleeth; she did not attend other lectures or courses there, neither did she participate in orchestras or chamber music lessons. But she did sweep up all the available prizes, notably in 1959 the Silver Jubilee Commemoration Challenge Cup and, the following year, the Guildhall's Gold Medal for the outstanding instrumental student of the 1960 graduation.

In general, Pleeth did not like his pupils to participate in competitions, since he held that the competitive instinct was incompatible with true artistic endeavour. But every now and then he deviated from his ruling principle if he thought that a student needed a particular stimulus. In the spring of 1960 he suggested to Iris that Jackie should enter for the prestigious Queen's Prize, which was open to British instrumentalists under the age of thirty. Pleeth felt that Jackie was ready to pit herself against the best students and young performing artists. She would gain limited public exposure without the pressure of a public

* *Millions of Strange Shadows*, OUP, Oxford, 1977, p. 10.

53

début, which implied a commitment to a concert career. Iris willingly agreed to Jackie's participation, in the knowledge that if she won the prize it would bring prestige and useful contacts.

The auditions for the Queen's Prize were held in June 1960 at the Royal College of Music and were open to the public. The fifteen-year-old Jackie played a forty-minute programme, which included Bruch's *Kol Nidrei* and Bach's D minor Suite for Unaccompanied Cello. She already possessed in abundance that communicative artistry which holds audiences in its sway. Pleeth found himself sitting next to her father in the hall:

> There beside me was this sweet, simple man half asleep. Each time Jackie finished a piece, the audience went wild with enthusiasm. Then Derek would turn to me and ask, 'Is she all right?' I thought to myself that this was the understatement of the year, it was quite staggering that he seemingly had no judgement in the matter. But he just trusted that she was all right, and displayed a lovely modesty and unpretentiousness, which essentially was a good influence to have around.[1]

It was here that Yehudi Menuhin, as chairman of the jury, first heard Jackie play. He immediately identified her as a pupil of Bill Pleeth's in the expressive freedom of her performance. 'To this day I can recall the elation she brought me ... with the excitement of her own joy and intoxication with the music.'[2]

Menuhin was to become an important figure in Jackie's life in the next few years and he showed his genuine appreciation of her artistry by inviting her to play with him. A couple of years later he brought Jackie to the attention of Peter Andry, then head of the HMV section of EMI, who immediately decided to record her.

In the meantime, Jackie's progress was reviewed once a year by the panel of the Suggia Gift. John Barbirolli, who was to become one of du Pré's greatest champions and supporters, invariably headed the panel of judges. He remained objective and exacting in his assessments, as demonstrated by his audition notes of July 1958: 'Certainly fulfilling her promise and would definitely recommend continuation of financial assistance. But on what lines? Needs developing in terms of real beauty of sound, poetry, imagination and warmth. Vitality she has plenty.'[3]

Just after she won the Queen's Prize, Jackie played her annual audition for the Suggia Trust. This year, she was applying for additional funds, which would enable her (accompanied by her mother) to participate in

Pablo Casals's annual master classes at the Zermatt Summer School.

Casals was a living legend and at the age of eighty-three he was as wholly committed to music as ever. He had been a great instrumental innovator and by virtue of his enormous artistry had given the cello a musical prominence it had never previously enjoyed. In the last decades of his life, Casals seldom performed as soloist, preferring to play chamber music, and to share his insights about music through conducting and teaching. In fact, his rehearsals with the festival orchestras, which were formed for his benefit with talented and highly motivated musicians, became the most important means for him to communicate his interpretative wisdom. In effect, his teaching and performing were born of the same principles, whereby music had to be illuminated by the inner spiritual impulse, to communicate emotion and joy. As David Blum has written, 'For Casals the formulation of feeling and the interpretation of music emanated from a single source and flowed together in a single stream.'[4]

Casals had not held a teaching position since the early 1920s when he gave regular master classes at the École Normale in Paris, of which, together with his trio partners, Jacques Thibaud and Alfred Cortot, he was artistic director. After the war, he occasionally taught privately at his home in Prades, where he lived in self-imposed retirement in protest against the fascist victory of Franco.

In 1952 he accepted an invitation to give master classes at the Zermatt Summer Academy. Here he relished the clean air and mountain scenery, and was glad of the opportunity to teach a specialised literature to small classes, and occasionally to make chamber music with trusted colleagues such as Sándor Végh and Mieczyslaw Horszowski.

Pleeth recalled that Jackie had mixed feelings about going to Zermatt. She was thrilled to be travelling abroad for the first time in her life, but hesitant about submitting to instruction with the legendary cellist: 'It was as though she was such a compelling player, she just wanted to do the playing. You could say that she wasn't a good listener, which is the narrow side of someone who is so much a player. It wasn't conceit in her case, it was a compulsion.'

Once she arrived, Jackie, with her horror of flattery and posturing, was quick to decide what it was she disliked about master classes – namely the sycophantic attitude of those in the Master's entourage. She once told me how, to her fury, some adoring old lady had taken her music and written on it every word that Casals had uttered during her lesson – from his musical comments to irrelevant remarks about the weather. Altogether she was not comfortable with the aura of saintliness that surrounded Casals. As Pleeth said, 'She could see through the atmosphere of didactic bombast and pooh-poohed it.' It would have been unnatural if Casals did not have a very strong sense of his import-ance. But such as it was, his didacticism was born of his own deep convictions about music, rather than from personal vanity.

In August 1960 Casals's master classes were devoted to the study of cello concertos – the previous two courses had been given over to Bach suites and Beethoven sonatas. The participants were told in advance when and what to play in the classes, which were open to outside listeners. Consequently there might be as many as fifty or sixty people attending, which most participants found quite nerve-racking.

But, as fellow cellist Jenny Ward-Clarke remembered, Jackie always rose to the occasion and gave a real performance. There was a dis-crepancy between her girlish looks and her mature artistry. 'Jackie still looked very much the schoolgirl, with short-cropped hair,' Jenny recalled. 'She seemed quite unsophisticated, gauche-looking, and was not dressed at all in a feminine way.'

Casals had a fine perception of his students and knew how much to demand of each one. The only thing he could not tolerate was mon-otony of spirit. As such, he lost patience with an Englishman who was as placid as Jackie was passionate and remonstrated with him: 'Life, life where are you . . .? You, a young man, play like an old man. I am eighty-three, but I am younger than you.'

Jenny vividly remembered Jackie's first appearance at Casals's class, playing the Saint-Saëns concerto:

> She stunned everybody there with her enormous exuberance. There was this beautiful freshness in her playing and even if it was sometimes slightly over the top, one completely accepted it. Her mother played for her. Casals just sat and beamed at her. He said very little. One doubts if he would have wanted to change anything in her playing, rather valuing it for its natural spontaneity. She had a wonderful ability to change moods and be capricious. Altogether her playing had enormous personality and was already characterised by a special romantic and poetic quality.[5]

In general Casals spoke little, and what he said was down to earth and simple. Jenny summed up the experience in these words: 'You learnt simply from being in Casals's presence, from the extraordinary spirit and vitality in the man and in his playing.'

In fact, Jackie only had three lessons with Casals. Undoubtedly she too was affected by his personality and by the amazing spirit of this legendary figure. But there was a certain scepticism – or 'bolshiness' as she herself defined it in later years – that characterised her attitude to Casals and other high-powered teachers, which in part was born from her defensive loyalty to her own teacher, Pleeth.

It is impossible to assess how much she learnt from Casals directly. But some four years later, in an article entitled 'Reflections' written for the Robert Mayer Saturday Morning Children's Concerts, she referred specifically to Casals's description of the Saint-Saëns concerto as 'a storm interrupted by passages of great calm and peace'.[6] Such an apparently simple phrase may not contain any portentous revelations, but it might well have remained in her memory as an associative poetic stimulus.

Jackie will undoubtedly have been aware that Casals at the age of eighteen, had played the concerto with Saint-Saëns himself. Indeed Saint-Saëns had apparently told Casals that his Cello Concerto was inspired by Beethoven's *Pastoral* Symphony. The opening of the first movement represented a storm and he likened the first cello entry to lightning, an effect he achieved through the enunciated attack (or accent) on the first note. When the opening theme is heard in D major in the development, 'we begin to see blue in the sky'. The second movement was likened to a peasant's dance, again invoking Beethoven.[7]

There was a ringing significance in the fact that Jackie was selected to play the Saint-Saëns concerto at the final students' concert on the eve of Casals's departure from Zermatt. Many will have seen the inspired performance of a fifteen-year-old in front of the aged Master as a sign of continuity, linking the young girl with the legendary figures of the past.

Once back in London, Jackie fulfilled the necessary courtesies and wrote to thank the Suggia Trust. In her letter of 17 September she spoke of the great musical experience of hearing Casals play and teach. 'I feel that his teaching has helped tremendously to clarify my personal thoughts and feelings about the concertos that were discussed,' she noted. Perhaps the atmosphere in some of the other classes at Zermatt was more conducive to friendly exchange. In particular, Jackie referred to Sándor Végh's chamber music lessons as 'thrilling'. She explained in her letter that '[Végh] spoke of the necessity of complete relaxation when playing. I found this most interesting as it happens to be a great theory of Mr Pleeth's.'

Her letter continued to recite the pleasures of Zermatt – the excitement of meeting so many foreigners and the wonderful excursions she had made with her new friends into the magnificent scenery of the Swiss Alps. 'The mountains were superb,' the young Jackie enthused, 'and twice we saw the Alpine glow, which is an experience I shall never forget.'[8]

Overall, the course served as an opportunity for Jackie to widen her range of musical contacts and to reaffirm her conviction that Pleeth was the right teacher for her. Together with him, she now could take stock of her position before the new academic year began.

With Jackie's recent success of the award of the Queen's Prize, and the overwhelmingly strong impression that she had made on such musical luminaries as Menuhin and Casals, Pleeth believed that the time had come to launch her on a concert career and suggested that she should prepare for her official London début some time in the coming spring.

As her godmother Isména Holland observed, Pleeth had always been cautious about allowing Jackie to be exposed too soon. He was worried that a successful début could lead to exploitation. But in her early teens Jackie herself desperately wanted to start performing. Isména recalled: 'She used to get angry with me and Iris – "Why can't I play to people?" she would say. She felt held back, as if she were doing all this study for nothing. I never actually had any say in when she should start her career. Then, when she was just sixteen, Pleeth thought it was time to let her go.'[9]

For Jackie the whole point of playing the cello lay in performing for people. She greatly looked forward to her official public début, without thinking too hard about the implications. In accordance with long-established tradition, the Wigmore Hall was chosen as the venue. A date was set for 1 March 1961 – five weeks after her sixteenth birthday.

Some weeks prior to the concert, Jackie received a Stradivarius cello as a gift from her godmother. Mrs Holland had provided her goddaughter with all her instruments and even extended her generosity to Hilary, buying her a silver Boehm flute. When Jackie first went to Pleeth for lessons he had recommended that she should have a better cello. Once again, Mrs Holland intervened and acquired for her the first in a series of good Italian instruments. Jackie played in succession on a Guarnerius (a $\frac{7}{8}$ size), a Ruggieri, then a Tecchler of 1696. Now that she was ready to embark on a public career, Pleeth strongly advocated that she needed an outstanding instrument.

It is not for nothing that old Italian instruments have acquired a unique reputation for their beautiful sound quality and their ability to project in soft playing as well as in loud. Their high prices reflect the enormous demand for them, which automatically excludes the majority of aspiring young instrumentalists from acquiring them without some form of subsidy.

While the Suggia Trust had given Jackie public support and prestige, her private benefactor acted with self-effacing generosity. Isména Holland recalled the circumstances that led to the acquisition of Jackie's first Strad:

> I was on the committee of the Courtauld Trust, which was run by Jean Courtauld, a great friend of mine and incidentally a relation of my husband's. The composer Howard Ferguson was also a committee member. I put forward a proposal to the committee, saying, 'I know a very good young cellist, who is clearly a great talent. She needs a suitable instrument.' They agreed to set up a fund for British artists and got hold of £2000. Eventually a very nice Strad was found and I paid the balance anonymously. I never wanted to get into the limelight myself. It was exactly what Jackie wanted at the time and she received it just in time for her Wigmore début recital.

The balance, it would seem, was over £3000.

There was an element of fairy-tale surprise for Jackie, when she was called to the London dealers, W. E. Hill & Sons, and given a choice of two instruments to play. She was not told anything about either of them – one was a Guarnerius, the other an early-period Stradivarius. (On the other hand, she did know who her benefactor was.) Jackie unhesitatingly chose the Strad.

Jackie loved this wide-girthed instrument, with its dark and rich nutty tone. In 1964 she recounted the history of the instrument in an article entitled 'Reflections'.

> In 1673 when Stradivarius the great instrument maker was twenty-nine years old, he was putting the finishing touches to a new cello – a cello destined to cross many seas and to pass through the hands of people in many different walks of life.
>
> Like many early Italian instruments, this cello after leaving Stra-

divarius's workshop, spent some time in a monastery. [...] That this cello was used by monks in religious processions is proved by a hole which is now refilled, in its back. Through it the monk secured a looped cord which he slung round his neck: he was then free to pace in slow procession playing the instrument suspended on his portly front. [...] When and how it finally crossed the seas and arrived in England is wrapped in mystery. In 1961, 288 years after this cello was made, it came into my hands.[10]

Armed with the very best tools of her trade, Jackie was ready to go out into the world. Pleeth understood better than anyone that such a highly publicised début recital implied a sort of public crusade – a responsible commitment to a soloist's career. In the light of this he issued Jackie with a stern warning that she should initially be very selective about accepting concert dates, and should leave herself plenty of time for study and reflection. But through putting the management of this recital into the hands of the concert agents Ibbs and Tillett, Pleeth also must have foreseen that the temptation to exploit public success while it was fresh and immediate would be very great.

For this important occasion Iris relinquished her post as duo partner to Ernest Lush, an experienced recitalist and accompanist. Jackie's programme, chosen in consultation with Pleeth, made no concessions to her tender age. It was devised on the premise that she would win her spurs through performing music of different styles and periods, where a serious musical perception was more relevant than virtuoso flamboyance. She was to open with Handel's G minor Sonata (Slater's arrangement of an oboe concerto), followed by Brahms E minor and Debussy Sonatas in the first half. The second half continued with Bach's C minor Suite for Unaccompanied Cello and, to finish on a lighter note, de Falla's attractive *Suite Populaire Espagnole* (in Maurice Maréchal's transcription).

For the evening of 1 March 1961 the Wigmore Hall was sold out and even the gallery, normally closed off to the public, was chock-a-block full. Jackie's reputation had preceded her and Mrs Tillett, the doyenne of London concert agents, saw to it that the audience included many influential names, representatives of London orchestras and concert societies, BBC producers and a bevy of critics. Isména Holland, among others, helped round up friends and musicians – including Ronald Smith and Howard Ferguson. Word had got around in London musical circles that this would be an exceptional event.

All of those I have spoken to who were present at this concert have a vivid memory of music-making that came from the heart, that was joyously communicative and pure in line. A typical reaction was that of the distinguished composer Howard Ferguson: 'I was bowled over, not only by Jackie's astonishingly mature technique, but even more by her innate musicality and the warmth and sheer joy of her playing.'[11]

Equally impressive were Jackie's authoritative control and complete self-possession. These qualities were immediately in evidence when, just a couple of bars into the Handel Sonata, her A string started to slip; in those days, like her teacher Pleeth, Jackie used pure uncovered gut strings, which have a greater tendency to lose pitch and slip than covered gut or metal ones. Initially she tried to compensate for the lowering of pitch by moving her left hand higher up the fingerboard. But realising that the string was unravelling itself totally, she stopped and went off-stage to re-string it.

Some artists in her position might have been unnerved by such initial bad luck, but Jackie used those few moments off-stage for quiet reflection. As Jenny Ward-Clarke recalled, 'the audience was horrified, but Jackie was completely unfazed and started again calmly. Her response was so completely natural that she won everybody over to her side, so the recital went forward without a hitch. She gave the impression of one with total command. It was wonderful seeing somebody play straight from the heart, exactly as she felt, with no complications.'

Jackie's friend Peter Thomas remembered that he was far more nervous about the concert than she was. Looking back now, he can reaffirm his impressions of those years:

At the Wigmore Jackie already had the whole range of musical qualities. Maybe there are cellists today who play better than she did in the technical sense, but I can't think of anybody who communicated so naturally – maybe Rostropovich at his best, or Casals in his heyday. With the others there was always a cello in between them and the listener; Jackie was able to get right to the music and this is a quality of the very great. From this point of view the recordings, marvellous as they are, do not represent her at her best. The communication with the audience at her concerts was quite breath-taking and left everybody spellbound.[12]

Another young musician, the violinist José Luis García, was particularly impressed by her playing of the de Falla *Popular Songs*. 'This was remarkable to me because, as a Spaniard, I was of the opinion that non-Spaniards found it very difficult to play Spanish music. Normally nationality doesn't come into it when we talk about German, French or English music. But Jackie had the ability to identify with anything she played and her de Falla was quite marvellous.'[13]

There were some who qualified their praise with minor criticisms. Doubts – such as Jenny Ward-Clarke's in regard to Jackie's sound – tended to be quite subjective. 'She had a very lovely singing sound quality, but sometimes I felt it lacked a deep core. You couldn't call it superficial, but there was something I would describe in it as almost too easygoing.'[14]

It seldom happens that a young artist is bestowed such unanimous praise by the national press – the critics' main reservations concerned the lack of projection in the outer movements of the Brahms Sonata. The finale in particular poses notorious problems of balance between the two instruments which has given rise to many anecdotes unflattering to cellists. Brahms himself is said to have drowned out the cellist Joseph Gänsbacher at the first reading through of the sonata. Gänsbacher protested he could not hear himself. 'Consider yourself lucky!' Brahms is reputed to have rejoined, as he let the piano rage on.

On the other hand du Pré earned nothing but superlatives for her playing of Bach, and Bach interpretation is hallowed ground for cellists. *The Times* critic declared that her account of the C minor Suite 'thrilled the blood with its depth and intuitive eloquence'. *Musical Opinion* also had the highest praise: 'The clarity of articulation and luminous phrasing were *per se* a source of unstinted admiration.' She had presented a Bach solo suite, 'for once, not as a dry academic exercise ... but as living music. It is not an exaggeration to say that such playing reminded us forcibly of Casals in his prime.'

Writing in the *Daily Telegraph*, Martin Cooper, perhaps the most perceptive of the critics in attendance, remarked on some of du Pré's salient qualities, in particular her innate sense of rhythm: 'Her ability to carry through a phrase to its very end and the gravity and poise of her line-drawing were already remarkable in the finale of the Handel Sonata. Her instinctive rubato in the trio of Brahms's E minor Sonata only emphasised the vigorous strength of her rhythms in general.' He concluded: 'Here is a young player whose technical accomplishments have not prevented from being wholly committed to whatever she plays – and this is one of the first essentials of a great player.'

7
Widening Horizons

For what has he whose will sees clear
To do with doubt and faith and fear,
Swift hope and slow despondencies?
                    A. C. Swinburne, 'The Prelude'

The enormous success of Jackie's Wigmore Hall début had been the logical outcome of a singular investment of time and energy in her talent. Emmy Tillett, with her long experience in concert management, recognised the unique nature of Jackie's critical success and lost no time in inviting her on to the Ibbs and Tillett roster. 'Ibbs' was something of an institution and in those days was at the height of its fame. As the longest established concert agency in London, it practically controlled the national music club circuit within Britain. Mrs Tillett, the director of Ibbs and herself something of a legend in London musical circles, was quick to realise that Jackie could become one of the brightest stars on her lists.

For Jackie, achieving overnight fame was both an exhilarating and bewildering experience, which spelt big changes in her life. Instant celebrity can often bring with it a multitude of dangers and temptations. But in her apparent lack of concern for the trappings of fame, Jackie proved herself to be completely devoid of that pushy competitiveness which motivates many young artists. Her natural innocence and unworldliness remained untouched, perhaps for the reason that she had lived for so long in the protective cocoon of her family. Iris and Derek had assiduously fostered a sense of normality at home and this served to deflect the glare of public attention.

It fell on Iris to establish the balance between protecting Jackie and encouraging her to go out into the world. Not only did she have to deal with all the practicalities of Jackie's day-to-day existence, but she soon found herself catering to her daughter's blossoming professional career, to the exclusion of almost everything else. Iris's ambitions for Jackie were based on a realistic perception of her exceptional gifts. But in trying to create the most favourable conditions for her to fulfil her artistic talent and responsibilities, she was perhaps too protective. In the words of Iris's friend Margot Pacey, 'At the age of sixteen and seventeen Jackie was still totally unversed in the practicalities of everyday living. She couldn't boil an egg or sew on a button. Everything was done for her – she was treated like royalty at home.' Margot maintained that Hilary and Piers had had a much more normal upbringing. 'I think there was friction between Jackie and Hilary, and I felt sorry for Hilary because she was a very talented musician, but all the floodlights were on Jackie. Possibly Iris didn't nurture her elder daughter enough.'[1]

Isména Holland remembered a certain amount of sisterly rivalry; Jackie would sometimes break down in tears over some small unkindness on Hilary's part. But as with Jackie's tears and complaints 'about Mummy' that Bill Pleeth had to deal with occasionally during cello lessons, her unhappiness tended to be seen as a passing phase of normal adolescence. If Hilary felt neglected by Iris and resented the attention accorded to her 'marvellous sister', then on her side Jackie admitted to feeling jealous of her sister's GCE success at school.[2]

In fact Jackie was faced with the deeper problem of having to reconcile the contrasts of ordinary home existence and the heady elation of public success. It was hard to accept that in forging ahead with her music she was destined for a solitary path, which meant depriving herself of a general education and the company of her contemporaries.

After she had left Queen's College, Jackie's schooldays were formally over. Iris was well aware that she not only needed to extend her general education, but that she lacked a wide musical perspective, being quite ignorant of music outside the mainstream cello repertoire. Iris asked Antony Hopkins, pianist, composer and broadcaster, if he would be prepared to take Jackie under his wing and give her some guidance in general musicianship.

Hopkins had first heard of Jackie from the Secretary of the Royal Society, who wished to persuade him to perform a recital with a brilliant young girl cellist. He agreed somewhat reluctantly, but his initial scepticism vanished when he realised that this was not just an ordinary gifted sixteen-year-old, but a major talent.

Hopkins recalled Jackie's first visit to his home at Brook Green. 'We sat down and talked quite a bit about music. I found that her actual knowledge was naïve and incomplete. She was a born interpreter and Pleeth had been more interested in teaching her the cello than in talking about what she was actually going to play. When somebody has a stunning natural gift, a teacher is delighted to exploit it. In any case, why should a cello teacher talk to his pupils about symphonies?'

To start with, Hopkins set Jackie a musical quiz.

> I played the exposition of a Beethoven sonata, where there was a surprise over the page. I told Jackie that I'd give her half a crown if she could tell me what the next note would be. And she was able to – it was a D flat (in the little C minor Sonata Op. 10 – it goes into G flat in the development). I thought this was quite cute of her. However with hindsight, I am not sure that she didn't know this sonata already, considering that Iris taught the piano and lots of music went on in the house. But either way it was obvious that Jackie did have an extraordinary intuitive insight into music.[3]

In fact, during this period Iris had virtually given up teaching to devote her energies to launching Jackie in her professional career. It is perhaps surprising that she herself did not do more to widen Jackie's musical horizons through taking her to concerts, encouraging her to listen to records, or even playing through the symphonic repertoire with her in four-hand arrangements. On the other hand, there were so many demands on Iris's time and she had little practical support from Derek, who was busy with his own work from early morning until late in the evenings.

Although Jackie had been removed from school with the excuse that she would continue her education privately, this did not happen straight away. By the autumn of 1960 the need to find a sympathetic tutor was becoming pressing. The right person turned up in the form of Lady Joan Clwyd, who taught English and General Studies at sixth-form level at Queen's Gate School and also coached students privately for university entrance. The introduction to the Clwyd family had come about through the violinist Sybil Eaton, who had arranged for Jackie to play an informal recital at her studio home as a try-out prior to her Wigmore début. Joan and her husband Lord Clwyd (also known as Trevor Roberts) were present on this occasion and were deeply impressed by Jackie's astonishing musicality. Iris and Derek expressed their anxieties about their daughter's situation to the Clwyds. Joan agreed to work with Jackie, but rather than give her conventional coaching, she saw her brief as providing the sort of background that a great artist needs.

Just before her sixteenth birthday, Jackie started going for weekly sessions to the Clwyds' house at the top of Campden Hill Square. Joan's daughter, now known as Alison Brown, recalled that Jackie quickly came to love and trust her mother, who was a marvellous all-round teacher with a great communicative gift. 'Although originally deputed as a tutor, I think that Mother rapidly became a valued confidante. She discussed everything under the sun with Jackie, but what she felt was most needed was advice on lifemanship – from the practicalities of moving around London on the Underground, an unknown world until then for Jackie, to handling the emotions of adolescence.'

The Clwyd family were enthusiastic amateur musicians; Joan was more than proficient on the violin and viola, Alison also played the violin, although less well, and had a lovely singing voice. Lord Clwyd, a cultured and well-read man, was a very fine amateur pianist and had been a pupil of Harold Craxton. Jackie often joined in the music-making in the Clwyds' large drawing-room with its two Steinway pianos.

Alison recalled:

> I actually first heard Jackie when we played chamber music at home – her energy and power were extremely exciting, and it made the rest of us feel rhythmically slack, however hard we tried to emulate her. But it was with my father that Jackie loved playing most. He was a very good chamber musician and he greatly enjoyed accompanying her. He never treated her as if she were grand or special and this was something she really valued. They developed this naturally bawdy relationship, where she could be quite provocative and he would tease her outrageously.

Jackie's relationship with Alison was based on instant empathy. Alison was a few years older and had just gone up to Cambridge University. 'I fell in love with Jackie when I first saw her,' Alison recalled. 'I loved the way she played with her voice – the way she talked and put on her affected accents – she was a great mimic. She wanted me as a friend – she was gauche, but so was I – despite my being older than her. But she had this beautiful inner authority of a wise and powerful soul, which made me feel like a kid in her presence.'

For her part, Joan encouraged Jackie to read widely and introduced her to a great range of English literature from Shakespeare through to the nineteenth-century novelists. (When Jackie later claimed that she knew no literature, it was not strictly speaking true.) But most important, Joan tried to give her a confidence in the real world, of which she seemed painfully ignorant.

The Clwyd family introduced Jackie not only to fresh disciplines and concepts, but to a wide circle of friends, old and young. Alison recalled Jackie's delight in every new experience. 'I remember the enormous pleasure she got when one of father's friends, Sir Noel Hutton, a consultant at Guy's Hospital, invited her for a spin in his red sports car. She adored every minute of it.'

While Jackie revelled in her new freedom and enjoyed her new friends, she could not help comparing them with her own family and drawing certain conclusions. As Alison Brown put it,

> It became clear to us that her home life was very claustrophobic and that she had been closeted by her very well-meaning parents. The family presented a strict veneer of respectability. Charming as they were, her parents left an impression of uprightness and earnestness. Jackie had moved realms away from them in her intuitive, imaginative depths and in the intensity with which she lived life. She was bursting at the seams and needed an outlet. Hilary and Piers seemed extremely nebulous in her life, they never came with her and she never talked about them. At the end of the day, I always remain amazed that she emerged relatively unscathed from such a seemingly restrictive conventional background.

In the meantime, the du Pré family was faced with further radical change through Hilary's new friendship with Christopher Finzi. Christopher (usually known as Kiffer) came from a family which inhabited a world that was far more intellectually stimulating than the du Prés'. Kiffer had studied cello at the Royal Academy, but soon realised that he was not cut out for a career as a cellist. His father, Gerald Finzi, had gained a reputation not only as a fine composer, but as an erudite man with an enormous range of interests, which included the cultivation of apples on his farm in Ashmansworth in the Hampshire downs. Gerald's wife, Joy Finzi, was a sculptor and artist and, like her husband, she devoted her time and energy to championing English composers, artists and poets. With this aim, Gerald Finzi had founded a small orchestra, called the Newbury String Players, in 1940. Although the orchestra was formed largely of amateurs, it had a lasting influence for its role in performing new works by British composers, and its unusual policy of promoting concerts in schools and small venues in the west of England. After his father's death in 1959, Christopher inherited the estate at

Ashmansworth and took over as conductor of the Newbury String Players.

Friends remember that Kiffer was the first to take the du Pré girls out to restaurants and the cinema, and caused eyebrows to be raised at home when he delivered them back late in the evening. Kiffer took a certain pleasure in teasing Derek and Iris who, with their natural innocence and shyness about the outside world, could not hide their anxiety that Hilary was being exposed to the wrong kind of influences.

Kiffer was good for Hilary in more ways than one, not least in helping to restore her sorely shaken confidence. Hilary's experience at the Royal Academy of Music had not been a happy one, since her flute teacher had unwittingly undermined her innate intuitive abilities. While Jackie was progressing by leaps and bounds, she seemed to be losing ground. Similarly Piers, who had recently taken up the clarinet, felt unable to be allowed to enjoy music at his own unambitious level. Not only did he resent the implied comparison with his brilliant sister by his music teachers at the Junior Guildhall, but he felt that he got short shrift from his mother; in fact, taking up the clarinet had been a way to gain Iris's attention. Jackie's affection for her siblings was always in evidence in her light-hearted teasing, but she developed very different relationships with each of them. Her bond with Hilary had been cemented at an early age by their common interests, whereas she felt protective towards Piers and later did much to encourage him to emerge from the restrictions of their family background.

Six months after Jackie's Wigmore Hall début, Hilary married Kiffer Finzi and they settled down to family life at Church Farm, Ashmansworth. The first of their four children, Theresa, was born in early April 1963. Jackie was aware that Hilary had in some way sacrificed her musical talent in her hurry to leave home and set up a family. In contrast, Jackie came to regard herself more of a 'modern' woman, who was free to pursue her profession in music and to enjoy a liberated life. Yet she was always to hanker after the sort of family home that Hilary established.

Not that music played an unimportant role in the young Finzi household but, connected as it was to the Newbury String Players, it held out for amateur values (in the best sense of the word) and was 'anti-career' in orientation. Shortly after their marriage, Kiffer decided to get Jackie down to play in the Newbury Players, so as to further her experience of orchestral playing; she had already performed in concert with the Bath Festival Orchestra at Menuhin's suggestion.

The cellist Jenny Ward-Clarke had grown up near Newbury and had known the Finzi family since she was a child. The Newbury String Players had formed an important part of her musical education in her early years and she started to play in the orchestra while a student. Jenny recalled the excitement caused by Jackie's first appearance in the orchestra. 'You can imagine what a sensation it was, particularly among the older lady players – whom we surreptitiously nicknamed the "Newbury Fruits". Jackie seemed to take up a lot of space, and played very loudly and flamboyantly. But the old lady I sat next to was absolutely thrilled.'

Hilary remembered that Jackie's cello soon drowned out the rest of the orchestra. Not only did she play loudly, but with such conviction that she carried the rest of the cello section with her, oblivious of the conductor's beat. Hilary also recounted how Jackie, seated as number two cello on the front desk, would play all passages marked solo with tremendous verve and expression. Unversed as she was in orchestral conventions, she afterwards expressed surprise that the section leader – whose prerogative it is to play all solos – was also 'tagging along'. But as Hilary recalled, 'for Jackie solo meant *me*.'[4]

Through Kiffer, Jackie was introduced to Jean Gibson, who worked with musicians on bodily awareness, helping them to sort out the physical aches and pains caused by professional use and abuse. Kiffer's younger brother Nigel was Jean Gibson's assistant. Gibson worked with Jackie for a year and soon was helping all the members of the du Pré family. She recalls Jackie as a sixteen-year-old being very much under her mother's thumb. In fact, Gibson felt that Jackie really did not need her assistance, given her naturally 'floppy' body tone and awareness, which helped her to channel her physical energy to maximum effect into her cello playing. Gibson did recall, however that Jackie complained on more than one occasion of a funny feeling in the right-hand index finger. At the time she never attached much significance to what seemed a minor complaint, although years later she did wonder whether it was an early symptom of the illness that was to strike her down in her prime.[5]

For Jackie, other sorties into 'alternative' education over the next two or three years included fencing, swimming and attending philosophy classes with Peter Thomas (these classes, which they had seen advertised on the London Underground, turned out to be rather disappointing and were soon discontinued). At the behest of Yehudi Menuhin, Jackie also took up yoga, working for some time with Iyengar, Menuhin's own teacher and guru from Poona.

In all the efforts to widen her horizons, Jackie herself played a passive role, accepting suggestions, whether they came from Iris or Yehudi Menuhin. Her inability to take the initiative reflects her lack of confidence in herself, and evidently this was not confined to her extra-musical activities. While she had always loved performing, she was now for the first time having to accept the responsibility of being a successful artist managed by a professional agent and as such, being a commodity that largely belonged to the public.

Pleeth had strongly advised Ibbs and Tillett (who also acted as his agents) that they should not 'pile on the concerts', but allow Jackie to play enough to enable her to grow on the platform, while leaving her time for other things. But within days of her Wigmore Hall début requests were pouring in for concerts at home and abroad. It was decided that for the immediate future she should play no more than a dozen or so carefully selected concerts a season. Only quality engagements were accepted. Indeed, Jackie's concert dates for the following season were ones that many an older artist would have coveted.

For Iris, this meant gradually having to relinquish a role that she particularly enjoyed, that of piano accompanist. This severing of the musical umbilical cord was a slow but necessary process of evolution. Jackie continued to play recitals with her mother for another fifteen months after her Wigmore début – they performed in Bath, Oxted and Cheltenham, as well as in Holland. But she also played the odd date with pianists such as Ernest Lush and Antony Hopkins, while Ibbs and Tillett encouraged duo-partnerships with two of their artists – George Malcolm, with whom Jackie started playing in 1962, and later with Stephen Bishop.

It was during this time that Jackie established a close connection with Yehudi Menuhin, who had first heard her play at the Queen's Prize competition. On the strength of his impressions then, he invited Jackie to play trios with him and his pianist sister Hephzibah, and also presented her at one of the first National Trust concerts at Osterley Park, outside London. Menuhin recalled that, now 'sedately' in their forties, he and his sister realised that it was Jackie and no longer they who represented the younger generation: '[...] this passionate and gifted young sprig probably felt, exactly as we had, that mixture of adventure and the unknown adding itself to the sheer joy of playing. [...] We had a lovely time together, the rehearsals were minimal for we found we shared the same language.'⁶

In his capacity as artistic director of the Bath Festival, Menuhin invited Jackie to the 1961 festival to play more chamber music and to play in the orchestra. The violinist, Rodney Friend remembered meeting Jackie at this time:

> In the early sixties I played in Menuhin's Bath Festival Orchestra – it was a star-studded orchestra which met for rehearsals at Lady Crossfield's house in Highgate. It was there that I first saw Jackie in the summer of 1961 – she was sitting in the second stand of cellos. As a young lad, I was stage-struck by everybody in those days. Jackie had recently played her Wigmore début and had made a name for herself. Later that week she played in another concert at the festival where the Schubert C major Quintet (with two cellos) was performed with Yehudi and Gaspar Cassadó. My first impression of hearing her play Schubert with Menuhin was that she completely held her own in the company of the greatest players. Perhaps, as such, it was not a memorable performance of the Quintet – there were elements in it I didn't like. But it was obvious that Jackie was quite exceptional and that she would go off on a tangent by herself.

It was at Bath that Yehudi's daughter Zamira and her pianist husband Fou Ts'ong first met Jackie. Zamira recalled Jackie as

> gawky, short-haired and tall; she appeared very gauche and shy. She was much under the influence of her mother, who was very sweet, but rather possessive and over-cushioned her. Jackie was a wonderful musician even then, and my father adored her and had enormous admiration for her. He loved her no-nonsense attitude towards music – she was so natural and completely un-prima-donna-ish. It wasn't as if she didn't know how wonderfully she played or what she looked like – she did. But these factors didn't assume any paramount importance for her.

Menuhin himself defined the special quality of Jackie's playing as follows: 'She always communicated a sense of passion, of intense emotion, for she lived as few other artists I know, with a metabolism which seemed to carry a heartbeat faster than most of us mortals.'⁷

Menuhin was indirectly responsible for another important introduction – to Alberto Lysy, the Argentinian violinist who, after gaining a prize at the prestigious Queen Elisabeth Competition in Brussels, had effectively become Menuhin's first pupil. Lysy, through a connection of his Italian wife, found the ideal setting for a chamber music course in Sermoneta, a hilltop town crowned by a large castle near Latina, eighty kilometres south of Rome. In the first years, the participants lived in the beautiful surroundings of the Oasis of Ninfa down the road from Sermoneta. Its park, rich with exotic and rare plants, was designed at the end of the last century by two Englishwomen on the site of the medieval ruins of a castle and monastic settlements. With the cold waters of a mountain stream flowing through them, the Ninfa Gardens are undoubtedly, to quote Yehudi Menuhin, 'one of the magical places of the world'.[8]

Here, Lysy invited talented students and budding young professionals to get together for a month and play chamber music. The musicians also performed in a small chamber orchestra which Lysy conducted – a precursor of his Camerata at Gstaad.

Alberto recalled receiving a letter early in 1961 from Derek du Pré (no doubt written at Iris's instigation) asking if Jackie could attend the Sermoneta courses. Thus it was that she travelled to Italy for the first time in June 1961, accompanied by her father. She returned – on her own – for three consecutive summers. In the summer of 1963 Iris, Derek and Piers joined Jackie there for a holiday. Lysy recalls Jackie bathing with her father in the icy stream of the Ninfa Oasis and Derek standing beaming in the Gardens, clad toga-like in his towel after taking his bathe.

For Jackie, everything was new and fun, whether it was her first glass of wine or a first play-through of a Beethoven quartet. She joined in all the musical activities with the greatest enthusiasm. Lysy once asked her if she would like to conduct the small orchestra: 'Initially Jackie thought she couldn't do it – "But I've never done any conducting," she reiterated. But it took only a little encouragement from me for her to accept the challenge and she went off to study her score like mad. She enjoyed it all so much.'[9]

Concerts were held outside in the Ninfa Gardens and in the Sermoneta castle keep, and also in the surrounding villages. In fact, the castle had not opened its gates to the ordinary citizens of Sermoneta for years and years. Lysy persuaded the current owner, an Englishman who had married into the Gaetani family, to put on concerts in the large inner courtyard and to encourage the ordinary townspeople to attend them. And gradually they started coming – tradesmen, shop-keepers, bartenders, the women of the village, all people who had never before been exposed to classical music. Lysy recalls the special atmosphere of these early pioneering concerts. Jackie was dubbed by the locals as '*quella inglese forte*' ('*forte*' in this instance referred to her robust build and height) and she became their undisputed favourite among the players. These concerts were also carried to the surrounding villages, an idea which the musicians developed spontaneously. The flautist Elaine Schaffer, Alberto Lysy and Jackie were some of the course musicians who performed at these improvised occasions. In Lysy's recollection, Jackie loved nothing better than playing in the village piazzas for people who had no knowledge of music and no pre-conceptions about performance, but who showed an immediate and warm appreciation of its beauty.

Lysy remembers Jackie's playing at sixteen already demonstrating those features characteristic of her mature artistry:

When she was young she was like a volcano. Her playing had enormous power and she had the complete range of colours in her sound, with the most beautiful pianissimos. Later she may have acquired more finesse and poise. But in those days she had that extraordinary magic, something that you hear in the young Menuhin's playing. She always played with such heart, with what Casals used to call 'the truth of the heart' – Casals talked of the truth of the heart and the truth of the head but insisted that of the two truths, the former was 'truer'.

Interestingly enough, while most musicians remember Jackie's playing at this time as being classically pure and contained, with direct-ness, warmth and simplicity of line, there comes a first mention of distracting mannerisms from no less an authority than John Barbirolli.

Although he was du Pré's consistent supporter, Barbirolli was a strict judge and had no hesitation about expressing criticism. In his notes at the Suggia Gift audition of 7 July 1961 he had written: 'Her mannerisms in the first movement [are] very distracting and frankly rather unpleasant. The second movement however had many very good qual-ities, especially in one so young. Debussy Sonata – There is no gain-saying her great talent musically and instrumentally, but she needs really first-rate musical guidance in the next two years, say – years which can be vital for her.'[10]

Guidance, in the meantime, came as before from Pleeth, whom

Jackie went on seeing for lessons twice a week when possible. For over a year after her Wigmore début he not only worked on enlarging her concert repertoire, but offered her judicious advice. This continuing rapport contributed greatly to the stability of her outlook.

For a variety of reasons Jackie was fortunate to live in London and start her professional life there. Her meteoric career owed much simply to being in the right place at the right time. London in the early 1960s held an unrivalled position as a European musical capital and had become the world centre of the recording industry. Young musicians gravitated to London from as far afield as South America and China, and in the early 1960s there was an influx of *émigré* musicians from Eastern Europe. One might say that the conservative element in the British amateur tradition, with its genuine love and enthusiasm for music, was much enriched by a new cosmopolitan perspective.

And London was also the focus of the 'Swinging Sixties', with the emergence of the Beatles and the other sixties cult groups dominating the world pop scene, and influencing everything from fashion to social issues and people's attitudes to sex and drugs. Of course, in terms of popular appeal, there was no equivalent of Beatlemania in classical music. But the directness and vitality of communication found in the best pop groups, as well as their ability to speak meaningfully to a large young audience and to exploit new mediums such as recording and television, did have vast repercussions on the classical scene.

All these factors contributed to a change of attitude towards music-making in England; on the one hand there was more informality, and on the other a more rigorous professionalism became evident at all levels of musical life. Hitherto, top-class British instrumentalists had been a rare breed, particularly among string players. Not surprisingly, the London public immediately took du Pré to its heart, recognising that with her combination of radiant communication and outstanding musicianship she was a match for anyone. Du Pré not only became a favourite of the ordinary British music-lover, but was championed no less by discerning experts.

Hans Keller, a brilliant and influential writer and speaker on music, had been present at Jackie's début in his capacity as a BBC radio producer. He immediately recognised her for what she already was – England's best string player. Through his championship she came to the attention of William Glock, controller of Radio Three and artistic director of the Proms, and in addition director of Dartington Summer

School. Keller's recommendation was also highly respected outside the BBC – Lord Harewood remembers inviting Jackie to the 1962 Edinburgh Festival on the strength of it.

The BBC, in the early 1960s, monopolised broadcasting in Britain and therefore was in a unique position to influence the public's musical tastes. It also had substantially more spending power than it does today and as such, was a force to be reckoned with. The Third Programme invested in a policy of promoting young artists through directly transmitted concerts, thereby ensuring the dissemination of their names nation-wide. The BBC were in part responsible for creating the image of Jacqueline du Pré as a sort of national prestige symbol, like the tennis champion Christine Truman, with whom she was often compared. All the more so after her stunning performances of the Elgar concerto, when Jackie was hailed as a young British musician dedicated to British music.

At Hans Keller's instigation Jackie was invited into the BBC recording studios immediately after her Wigmore début.[11] (Keller never tired of quoting his own amazement when Derek du Pré, unsure whether his daughter deserved this mark of attention, asked him 'Are you sure she's really good enough?')[12] Jackie made her first radio recording on 22 March 1961 with Ernest Lush, performing the Handel Sonata and de Falla pieces that she had played at the Wigmore, and adding Mendelssohn's *Song Without Words*. Her fee was set at ten guineas. In the next two broadcasts, made a couple of months later, she was accompanied by her mother who, incidentally, received a fee that was well under half her daughter's.

Between December 1961 and January 1962 Jackie was invited to perform the first three Bach Suites for Unaccompanied Cello at the newly instituted BBC Thursday Invitation Concerts – one suite in each concert, in a programme shared with other artists. These concerts were free to the public and were broadcast live.

Furthermore, at Keller's suggestion she learnt the delightful Concerto for Cello and Winds by Jacques Ibert and recorded it in the BBC studios on 11 January 1962 with the Michael Krein Orchestra. Later that month she made her 'adult' TV début playing a short studio recital with her mother. Excerpts from this filmed recording have survived through inclusion in Christopher Nupen's later documentary about Jackie. They included a performance of the 'Intermezzo' from *Goyescas* by Granados, and 'Jota' from de Falla's *Suite Populaire*.

The agent Basil Douglas, who ran the National Trust Concerts, had been particularly impressed by Jackie's performance of unaccompanied Bach at the BBC Invitation Concerts. Wishing to help her extend her experience, he suggested that she might like to play some baroque music with harpsichord and put her in touch with the young harpsichordist Jill Severs. Jackie and Jill met, got on well together and agreed to play some concerts together. Douglas organised their first appearance for July 1962 at one of the National Trust properties, Fenton House in Hampstead. Jackie and Jill decided on a programme of an unaccompanied Bach suite, some solo harpsichord pieces, as well as their joint offering of Vivaldi's E minor Sonata and the Bach D major Gamba Sonata.

Most conveniently, Jill and her husband Maurice Cochrane lived in the gardener's cottage. Jill recalled how 'Iris used to bring Jackie over and leave her to rehearse with me. She was still very much a little girl rather than a teenager and seemed to live in her own world.' Jackie's musical relationship with Jill soon developed into a warm friendship with her family. In their home she was introduced to new adult pleasures, such as drinking sherry and being taken for spins in Maurice's MG sports car. As the years went by and she became busier, Jackie would still drop in at the Garden Cottage behind Fenton House to chat with Jill and Maurice, or to play with their young children, delighting them with gifts and her amazing ability to whistle in a double-noted trill.

Jill was always struck by the transformation that occurred when Jackie sat down to play the cello. 'There was a wonderful dichotomy between this wide-eyed, innocent, unwordly child and the passionate musician. The minute she put her bow on the string something magical happened. It was almost as if she became a vehicle to convey something from outside herself.' Jill observed that Jackie had a similar wild and passionate rapport with the natural world. 'Sometimes she would get up and tear around the garden like an ungainly colt – tall and gangly with short hair. She still hadn't reached her full height. Then, around the age of eighteen, she suddenly blossomed into a woman.'

Jackie had never played with harpsichord before – partly because of the existing prejudice that the cello went well with the piano, whereas it was the viola da gamba that suited the harpsichord. (The gamba, a member of the viol family, was favoured over the 'common' cello during the baroque period.) For instance, George Malcolm, who was a harpsichordist as well as a pianist, preferred to perform the Bach 'gamba' sonatas on the piano with Jackie, although he did once, as an exception, play them on the harpsichord at a concert in Westminster Abbey.

Jill helped Jackie to hear the gamba sonatas as trio-sonatas, where the three voices (two on the keyboard and one on the cello) have equal parts. Pleeth welcomed the new partnership and dropped in on rehearsals a few times to give encouragement and when necessary make suggestions.

Jackie quickly grasped the idea of using spoken articulation rather than sustained strength in playing the Bach gamba sonatas. As Jill pointed out, 'With the harpsichord, the effect of dynamic contrast is achieved through the intensity of touch and quality of sound, through shaping the phrases with articulation and rubato. Even if the whole range of the harpsichord is small and contained, you can still be strong by releasing resonance – and, unlike the piano, you can never be aggressive.'[13] The harpsichord's sound, produced by plucking rather than hammering the strings, actually seems very loud and resonant close by. But it is no match for the piano in terms of massive projecting strength and a string player has to adapt accordingly.

For Jackie adapting did not mean compromise. She always maintained her intense vitality of expression, while responding with flexibility to her partner's playing. She was playing on uncovered gut strings at the time which made for a good blend of sound with the harpsichord. One hears the mellow quality of gut – as well as the slight rasp and roughness – in her existing BBC recordings of the first and second Unaccompanied Suites, which were later reissued as CDs.

To judge by these recordings, du Pré's interpretation of Bach's music stems more from an abstract idea of an immutable eternity than an understanding of the dance origins of the suite. Jackie invested her performances with a nobility of spirit, transcending the here and now. She favoured a large projecting style and a singing, sustained sound, perhaps at the expense of the vital rhythmic elements derived from speech and movement. Her predilection for slow, majestic tempi (the sarabandes move in 6/8 rather than 3/4) is certainly out of step with today's fashions in 'authentic' Bach interpretation.

Much as she enjoyed playing with her new friend, this experience with Jill Severs was a diversion from the main thrust of Jackie's growing career. By December 1961 she had given her last concerts with Peter Thomas and her sister Hilary. There was a definite feeling that she was outclassing her former chamber music partners and even the most talented of her contemporaries.

Until now, Jackie had regarded her cello playing as something spontaneous and natural; she could certainly never accept that a musician's quality might be measured by the size of his fees or the prestige of his engagements. Jackie was never a snob about her music-making and was always happy to participate in private chamber music sessions with friends who were amateurs. Nevertheless, she herself was becoming aware of the firm division between music-making for fun and performing professional engagements for a paying public. It took another three or four years before she was able to establish her ideal of playing in both areas with musicians of the highest standard, who shared her enthusiasm and spontaneous enjoyment of music.

8

Orchestral Début

> ... the artist appeals to that part of our being which is not
> dependent on wisdom: to that in us which is a gift and not an
> acquisition – and, therefore, more permanently enduring.
> Joseph Conrad, Preface to *The Nigger of the Narcissus*

At the tender age of seventeen, it was natural that Jackie should have
mixed feelings about committing herself so early to the life of a professional musician. But with the enormous public acclaim and the
rapturous reviews she had received after her Wigmore Hall recital, it
was difficult to stop the momentum of her career. This implied an
imminent solo début with orchestra as the next step for Jackie's investiture as a concert artist. Ibbs and Tillett had no lack of offers from
leading British orchestras wishing to present the young Jacqueline du
Pré in London. For Emmy Tillett it was only a matter of choosing the
right time and the best offer. Her decision to put Jackie's concerto
début in the hands of the BBC was governed by the obvious advantage
of an accompanying live radio broadcast, which would ensure the
widest possible audience.

Ibbs and Tillett entered into negotiation with the BBC Symphony
Orchestra in the spring of 1961. The BBC SO's initial offer of a London
concert in the autumn of that year was declined, since it was felt that
Jackie did not have enough time to prepare. Nevertheless, a date was
accepted with the same orchestra only a few months later, where du
Pré was booked to perform the Elgar concerto under Rudolf Schwartz
at the Royal Festival Hall on 21 March 1962. An internal BBC memorandum signed by Leonard Isaacs shows that Pleeth's support was
sought and gained for the idea of offering her an out-of-town concert
with a regional orchestra as a try-out date in the autumn of 1961.

The choice of the Elgar Cello Concerto was well considered – it was
the first big concerto Jackie had studied at the age of thirteen. She had
performed it once already with the Ernest Read Senior Orchestra at the
Albert Hall in December 1959. Pleeth knew how closely she identified

with it, and that she already possessed an astonishing understanding of Elgar's music. Jackie was not only well prepared but intensely eager in anticipation of her Festival Hall concert. And it was awaited no less eagerly in London musical circles, as news of her remarkable talent circulated.

Mona Thomas, who was present with her family to hear Jackie's début, recalled the atmosphere of expectancy in the audience: 'Jackie looked young and modest as she came on to the stage, but immediately looked magnificent when she sat behind the cello. She swayed with the music and communicated her delight with full, noble and extremely warm big tone.'

The critics were equally impressed by Jackie's uninhibited joy in making music and no less by her ease of authority. 'It seems almost incredible that last night was her first appearance in a concerto, so confident was her attack and so whole-hearted the way in which she threw herself into every one of the solo part's many moods – exultant, wistful, mercurial, noble,' wrote the critic of the *Daily Telegraph*. 'Indeed, if her interpretation had a fault it was that it missed Elgar's characteristic vein of understatement; the work's autumnal ambiguities faded in the light of such uncompromising ardour.'

Percy Carter, writing in the *Daily Mail*, praised Jackie's playing for uniting technical command with a profound expressive range. 'To me, it was affecting that this late Elgar work, with its hints of autumn, should be presented to us by a girl in springtime.'

Those who attended the concert were inspired by a feeling of wonder at a unique discovery. Jackie's insights into the complex world of Elgar's late music displayed a maturity and depth of vision extraordinary for her youth, and she was to be largely responsible for a re-evaluation of this concerto as one of the great repertoire pieces, on a footing with the Dvořák and the Schumann concertos. The BBC immediately invited du Pré to repeat the Elgar concerto, first at the Chester Festival in June, then at the Proms in August of that year.

Emmy Tillett, having won the BBC over to her side as a powerful champion of du Pré's talents, now worked on the press. Naturally, the growing interest in this rising star of British music was reflected in radio interviews and newspaper articles about the young Jacqueline. A few days after her concerto début the *Daily Express* published a long feature article, in which Jackie was portrayed as devoting every spare moment away from the cello to cultural pursuits. Readers were informed that du Pré read poetry, biography and the classic authors – the Brontës, Jane Austen and Trollope. She was quoted as follows: 'I walk in the park, or go to concerts ... Boy-friend? not really, though I have several friends who happen to be boys. [...] I love Beethoven, Bach, Brahms. I have favourites among recent composers too – I admire Bartók – but the very new stuff I don't like. ... The same with pop music, I've never really listened to it. ... I don't dance. When I go out it's the theatre or a concert, rarely the pictures.'

As the journalist commented, 'It seems the life of a purist, hardly touched by the outside world. Her happiest times are the holidays on Dartmoor, "stone-hunting" with parents, 19-year-old sister and 13-year-old brother. ... She's just not interested in clothes. The money she receives from her performances goes straight into the bank.'

This somewhat two-dimensional image of the perfect all-rounded child prodigy-cum-family girl may have communicated the truth on one level. But the picture largely represented how others, notably Iris and Derek, wished to present Jackie to the world. It gave no hint of her rich inner world, of the conflict of seething doubts and passions, and her increasing need to grow wings that would lift her beyond the confines of her background. One might add that ironically, within a few years, shopping for clothes was to be one of Jackie's favourite activities, when she developed a stylish dress sense, emancipated from the drab 'little girl' clothes her mother chose for her.

As her friends and family recalled, Jackie underwent a period of depression in the wake of both her recital and concerto débuts, which manifested itself in lethargy and a lack of interest in life. Undoubtedly she needed time to digest the momentous events of these last two years before making a decision to follow a full-time career as a cellist. As she told her friend Freddie Beeston, 'I don't know whether I want to be committed to the world.'[2] Jackie still felt the need to explore other avenues and, apart from anything else, she longed for the more normal opportunities of student life. Perhaps, like many of us at that age, she was not certain exactly what it was she did want – even though her enormous gifts so clearly pointed her in one direction. But it was crucially important that any choice regarding her commitment to the cello should be of her own making.

At home, her parents and friends tended to explain her misgivings as a passing adolescent phase. Adopting the old adage that distraction is the best medicine, they encouraged Jackie to take up all kinds of activities and to look for new mentors. Pleeth instinctively understood that Jackie would need time on her own to explore her feelings and face her doubts. He had warned Jackie and Iris of the dangers of over-exposure. 'I remember saying to her when she was seventeen, "I would be happy to see you put away the cello and stop performing for six months or a year. Give yourself time to think about music and study, have a rest and practise; don't live just for the cello." '³

In Pleeth's opinion an artist needs to extend his experience by opening himself up to new influences, even if this process involves some demo-lition as well as construction. As Peter Thomas put it: 'Pleeth's big input was during the seven years he taught Jackie – and he covered more or less the entire cello repertoire with her. Then, when she was around seventeen, she started changing in all sorts of ways. She became more extravagant and she lost this beautifully schooled approach. But this was inevitable – her playing represented for her a catching up with life. It was then that Pleeth lost her.'⁴

In fact, Jackie did take Pleeth's advice to heart and just before her seventeenth birthday she agreed to take some months away from concertising the following autumn. Both Pleeth and Iris felt it was a good idea for her to discover more about the outside world of cello-playing. Iris was of the opinion that Jackie would benefit from having lessons from a cellist with a big international name, which meant going abroad. Jackie herself hoped that she would find a mentor who could impart technical skills and also help to overcome her personal doubts.

But Jackie's repeated statement that she wished 'to acquire technique' must be regarded with some caution. In fact, her intuition was grounded in such a sure confidence that it allowed her to be open to other influences, to absorb them and make them her own, or to discard them as she wished. Although she may not have been able to articulate her ideas at the time, when she talked of putting her technique to the test, Jackie did not perceive the concept of technique in its purely mechanical aspect, but saw it as an inseparable part of her art. What doubts she had arose from her growing awareness, which now made her question how she played the cello. She started to realise that she had never made a conscious study of technique for itself and had little to fall back on.

At one stage she approached Christopher Bunting, a teacher who had developed a systematic approach to cello playing. Bunting had been a pupil of Maurice Eisenberg and Casals, and had formulated his ideas on technique with conscious meticulousness. He reputedly had declared that du Pré possessed no technique, but this claim would have provoked Jackie's curiosity rather than antagonism. While Bunting had an enormous respect for her talent and enjoyed working with her, Jackie found it difficult to accept his analytical approach and her contact was limited to a few lessons.

On 10 December 1961, at the instigation of Pleeth and Mieczyslaw Horszowski (whom she had met at Zermatt), Jackie wrote to Pablo Casals asking for private lessons the following autumn. But Casals only taught in master classes and for many years had refused all private pupils. Consequently he turned down her request. At the age of eighty-six Casals had effectively become a living legend. He held no teaching position and preferred to convey his musical insights through example, performing and conducting at the chamber music festivals which were built around him.

Instead, in the early 1960s the cello 'scene' in Europe was dominated by the French School, whose most illustrious representatives, Pierre Fournier, André Navarra, Maurice Gendron and Paul Tortelier, were all dedicated to teaching as well as performing. True, in the late 1950s another great virtuoso of the instrument and important musical personality made a great impact on Western audiences. This was Mstislav Rostropovich, who, together with a handful of other Soviet performers such as Oistrakh and Richter, proved that the famed Russian School had lost none of its excellence, notwithstanding the years of isolation from the West under Stalin's rule.

In fact, at the age of fourteen Jackie achieved a meeting with Rostropovich through the good offices of her godfather, Lord Harewood. Rostropovich heard her play the Debussy Sonata with her mother at Harewood's London house in Orme Square and was suitably impressed. He proceeded to put her through her paces, devising a set of increasingly difficult technical exercises, until he discovered the limits of her possibilities. Such an experience might have served to underline the fact that Jackie had bypassed technique as an aim in itself while studying with Pleeth.

Whether or not Rostropovich was considered at the time as a possible teacher, it was virtually impossible to go from the West to study in the Soviet Union in those days. Apart from a handful of exceptions, cultural exchange at student level was non-existent. Other older representatives of the Russian School such as Raya Gorbusova and Gregor Piatigorsky had emigrated to the United States from Russia in the 1920s. By the early 1960s Piatigorsky had acquired a great reputation as a teacher in Los Angeles. Temperamentally and artistically he might have proved the person best able to help Jackie, but evidently he was not considered as a suitable candidate to teach her. Perhaps California seemed just as inaccessible as Moscow.

It seemed a logical step to turn to Paul Tortelier, who was well-known as a player and teacher in Britain. An ideal opportunity for Jackie to meet him presented itself in August of that year, when Tortelier was due to give master classes at Dartington Summer School. It was decided to enrol Jackie in these classes and, assuming that the experience went well, to send her to Paris in the autumn of 1962, where she would continue her studies with Tortelier on a formal footing.

On 12 July 1962 Jackie played for the Suggia Gift panel for the last time and put in a request for financial assistance to allow her six months' study abroad. Barbirolli expressed the opinion that a period of study in Paris with Tortelier would be beneficial. On a personal note he jotted down, 'Had a little talk with her and was delighted to find how unspoilt she has remained.'⁵

In the meantime, Jackie was doing the round of some of Britain's most prestigious summer festivals, performing at those of Chester, the City of London, Cheltenham and Edinburgh. She also returned to Italy for the second time to take part in Alberto Lysy's chamber music course at Sermoneta. An important new dimension to her blossoming career involved an important recording contract. Again, she had Menuhin to thank for an introduction to Peter Andry, head of the HMV division of EMI. Andry invited Jackie to make a first-recital record during the summer of 1962.

On 6 July she performed what turned out to be her last public recital with Iris at the Cheltenham Festival. Their programme consisted of sonatas by Beethoven (the A major Op.69), Debussy and Edmund Rubbra – the last work was written for and dedicated to William and Maggie Pleeth. The reviews were mixed and one critic claimed that the variable quality of the performances was due to Iris's 'inadequate accompaniment'.

It was during the Cheltenham Festival that the composer Alexander Goehr remembered meeting Jackie for the first time.

> I used to go and stay in the very beautiful house of some music-loving friends, a Birmingham industrialist and his wife, who lived near

Cheltenham. I already knew of Jackie, since Hans Keller had recommended her playing to me and I had heard her performances on the BBC. Pleeth had brought Jackie to the house when she was playing at the festival. Despite her precocious artistry Jackie was really only a schoolgirl at the time. Somewhat to my surprise on arrival at the house, I saw a lady standing on her head on the lawn. This turned out to be a kind of minder-type lady, who was looking after Jackie. I felt that Jackie was in a sense being oppressed by those guardians and 'spiritual aids' of talented children who take it upon themselves to solve the difficult problem as to what you do with a girl who is both astonishingly gifted and on the other hand very naïve.

It was around this time that the guitarist John Williams also got to know Jackie; he had been invited to participate in her first EMI recital recording in July 1962. (They performed de Falla's 'Jota' arranged for cello and guitar.) John immediately identified Jackie's special qualities: 'She was not only musical, but musically open, her whole playing was totally uncontrived and spontaneous.' But like many others who had contact with her at this time, he saw the beginnings of a dilemma. 'There was in her a "lost" kind of feeling, as if she were in a world that she didn't quite understand herself. And there was nobody among her friends and family who was equipped to help her understand it.'[6]

Part of the problem for Jackie lay in the fact that as she matured artistically, she outgrew her family circle. However much her parents and siblings might have tried, it was increasingly difficult for them to understand the nature of Jackie's extraordinary creativity. As John pointed out, 'Even if her mother was a fine musician, there's an enormous difference in being a musician in the way Jackie was and just being a fine musician. Recognising that you have an exceptionally gifted child whom you want to help is still not the same as understanding the child.'[7]

The film-maker Christopher Nupen was sharing a flat with John Williams at the time and retains a vivid image of Jackie arriving to rehearse with John: 'She was tall, she was statuesque, she moved vigorously with a sort of curious energy and yet I could see shyness in her. So there were two contradictory things in the actual image – the confidence of the stride, and the modesty and shyness of the spirit in it.' Nupen has commented more than once on the seemingly contradictory element in Jackie's playing, which made it both totally natural and constantly surprising. He clearly perceived this contradiction stemming from Jackie's innate shyness in combination with her musical confidence. Yet few people who heard Jackie perform would have suspected that shyness or self-doubt could be part of her make-up. She played with total assurance.

During this period Jackie was consolidating the repertoire she had studied with Pleeth. On 19 July she gave her first performance of Boccherini's Concerto in B flat (in the Grützmacher edition) at the First City of London Festival in Merchant Taylors Hall with the Philomusica of London and Gordon Thorne. But her growing reputation was largely based on the extraordinary performance of the Elgar Cello Concerto at her début with orchestra. She performed it again at the opening concert of the Chester Festival on 28 June with the BBC Northern SO in Chester Cathedral. The conductor, Sir Adrian Boult, was one of the most sympathetic accompanists among British conductors and a committed Elgarian. The critic of the *Chester Observer* declared that du Pré 'is the most outstanding cellist of the decade to come from Britain'. He was full of praise for the maturity and accomplishment of her performance, and noted that she was already 'recognised as the outstanding British interpreter of this work ... One is left in complete wonderment.' Naturally Boult, as an illustrious son of Chester, was given credit for splendidly matching the soloist's accomplishment.

But it was at the Proms that Jackie reinforced her success with the Elgar. The Albert Hall Promenade concerts, with their long tradition, had a special appeal to young audiences. Intrigued by a soloist who was younger than most of her listeners, public expectations for Jackie's début on 14 August 1962 with Sir Malcolm Sargent conducting the BBC SO were unusually high. Mona Thomas recalled that

The queue outside the Albert Hall was one of the longest I'd ever seen. [...] Having heard Jackie from the age of twelve onwards, I always maintained that she was the cellist with the most thrilling sound – and I have heard the great ones, like Casals, Tortelier and Rostropovich. One remembers the warm and noble tone, the brushwork of the bow and the shaping of each phrase as 'a living line', as used by the great painters. On this occasion Jackie looked magnificent and was rapturously received. Afterwards, we were the only friends backstage in the Green Room and we felt very privileged. Malcolm Sargent came in to congratulate her warmly. Until that time Jackie did not have a large number of 'followers', but at future concerts we could not get near her after concerts without waiting in long queues.[8]

Jackie soon earned for herself a place in the history of the Proms. By popular demand she returned four seasons in succession to perform the Elgar concerto – each time with Malcolm Sargent. It was, of course, an enormous compliment to du Pré that the normally arrogant Sargent was so impressed by her musicianship. Nicknamed 'Flash Harry', Sargent enjoyed a vast popularity with the public, particularly the promenaders. A great showman, sporting a red carnation in his buttonhole, he seemed the epitome of the English gentleman. His strength lay in his conducting of choral music and particularly of English music (although he did not go further than Vaughan Williams and Walton in his repertoire). His high estimation of du Pré is confirmed by the fact that he insisted on having her as his soloist on the occasion of his seventieth birthday celebration concert at the Proms in 1965 and that he proposed her as soloist to record the Delius concerto.

The achievement was all the more remarkable since the cello had never been particularly popular as a solo instrument. Its status inferior to that of the violin and the piano was partly due to its much more limited repertoire. This position started to change in the post-war years thanks to the creation of an extensive new repertoire and to the charismatic musical personalities of such instrumental geniuses as Casals, Tortelier, Rostropovich and du Pré.

So it was that from the age of seventeen du Pré was to be irrevocably associated with the Elgar concerto. Not only did Jackie perform the work throughout Britain, but she acted as ambassador for Elgar abroad. It was the concerto that she played most often and which she recorded with enormous success. The composer Jeremy Dale-Roberts recalled the 'amazing public impact round her in those orchestral concerts in London – one almost stopped listening to the music-making, her Elgar had become a sort of ritual'.[9] In the exuberant cultural climate of London in the early sixties perhaps these Promenade concerts were the closest thing in classical music to the Beatlemania that swept England in the mid-sixties.

Immediately after her Prom concert Jackie went down to Dartington to play for Tortelier. The Dartington Summer School had been founded in 1948 by William Glock with the aim of providing higher education for British music students, affording them opportunities to get to know the best European musicians and exposing them to contemporary music, in particular the European avant-garde.

In the early years Dartington was unique in what it had to offer. As John Amis, then secretary of the summer school, remembers: 'In those days nobody knew much of the standard chamber music repertoire, let alone contemporary music. For instance, most of Haydn's quartets and Schubert's piano sonatas and four-hand music were unknown territory. Through inviting people like Schnabel, Nadia Boulanger and Pierre Fournier to teach at the School, Glock opened up new horizons for students and made it possible for them to pursue these contacts abroad.'

Just as in his capacity of Controller of Music at the BBC Glock revolutionised British musical life in the 1960s through his imaginative planning, so he made Dartington Summer School buzz with ideas. It became a place where people of different ages and cultures could have meaningful exchanges, and where amateur as well as professional musicians were welcomed. In the early sixties Dartington was in its heyday, attracting musicians from all over the country, who enjoyed not only the high level of inspiration, but the relaxed atmosphere and beautiful surroundings of the old Hall, the park and the wonderful Devon countryside.

As usual, a rich and varied programme was on offer during the four weeks of the 1962 summer school. Such luminaries as Norbert Brainin, Yehudi Menuhin, Vlado Perlemuter, Paul Tortelier, William Pleeth, Julian Bream and Gervase de Peyer were on the instrumental teaching staff, and lectures were given by Hans Keller and Wilfried Mellers. The compositional faculty included Luciano Berio, Luigi Nono, Nicholas Maw and Peter Maxwell-Davies – representatives of the avant-garde, who looked on the British compositional establishment as totally *passé*. John Amis recalled that when Benjamin Britten arrived to give a recital with Peter Pears that August, it was suggested that he should be introduced to Luigi Nono: 'Britten was enthusiastic. But then I asked Nono: "Gigi, would you like to meet Britten?" He answered, "Most certainly not." Britten was definitely "out".'[10] In fact the compositional and interpretative arts had become largely separate entities at Dartington, so that Jackie, like most of the other instrumentalists, was probably largely unaware of the presence of the European compositional avant-garde!

Jackie arrived in Dartington fresh from her triumphant Prom début, riding on the crest of the wave. She anticipated her first contact with Tortelier with excitement and a certain anxiety. It was soon apparent that she completely outshone the other participants of the master class. Tortelier himself was struck by du Pré's radiance and enthusiasm. He recalled

> I never met a more ardent young musician. One night after a recital I had given [with Ernest Lush], she asked if I would help her with Bloch's *Schelomo*. 'Why not?' I replied. 'But when?' 'Why not now?' she replied. As there had been a dinner after the concert, it was already past midnight. I protested that people were sleeping. 'We needn't worry about that,' she persisted; 'there's a room where we can work without disturbing anyone.' I thought it strange to give a lesson at the dead of night, but when she begged like that you couldn't resist. She began to play and I to explain, and in our enthusiasm the lesson lasted a good two hours, so that at two thirty we were still playing and discussing *Schelomo*. When I returned to my home in Paris, [my wife] Maud told me that one night she dreamt that I had been unfaithful to her. This was most extraordinary, because the dream had occurred on the very night I had given Jacqueline her lesson.[11]

Another work she played for Tortelier was the Debussy sonata with George Malcolm, one of Dartington's directors. Malcolm was impressed by Jackie's total confidence when playing in the class; she appeared to be very little in awe of the great *maître*. Not unnaturally, she was chosen to play at the public Friday night student concerts with George Malcolm. This already set her apart from other students, since Malcolm appeared in only one other duo recital, namely with Yehudi Menuhin.

During the next couple of years Malcolm played with Jackie at several of these Dartington late-night concerts. He vividly remembered one particular occasion when they played Bach's G major Gamba Sonata: 'At our final rehearsal in the hall, Jackie took a very slow, calm tempo in the opening 12/8 adagio. Somewhat bewildered, I stopped and said, "Jackie, you're not actually going to play it as slowly as that at the concert, are you ...?" "Oh yes, I think I will," she answered unperturbed. And she did, and it was quite perfect. She had that marvellous sense of which tempo would work at a concert, understanding its relation to the hall's acoustic and atmosphere.'

Jackie's certainty in her understanding of tempo was evident again to George Malcolm when he heard her play the Elgar concerto at one of her Prom performances. 'Sargent started at a tempo that was slightly faster than she wanted to play it. Within the first bar of her solo entry she dragged the music back to her tempo and he had to follow. I don't think he liked it. I remember that at the end she beckoned the orchestra to stand up and that really annoyed him, since that of course is the conductor's prerogative. He showed a visible sign of annoyance.'

George Malcolm found Jackie to be an ideal duo partner, secure and confident, and above all very responsive. 'Even if I made more suggestions than she did, most of the time I was just accepting her playing, because it was so remarkable and so right.' At the same time he remarked on that imbalance commonly found in prodigies between a very highly developed intelligence in one field and an almost infantile quality elsewhere in their personality. Malcolm's experience as Director of Music at Westminster Cathedral Choir School proved very useful in establishing contact with Jackie. 'We had a very youthful, teasing kind of friendship. I treated her somewhat like the young choristers and if I was rude to her she ended up throwing cushions at me.'

Malcolm took on the role of benign teacher in their partnership without ever being didactic. On one occasion, just as they were going on-stage to play the Bach D major Gamba Sonata, he turned to du Pré and said, 'You know Jackie, in the first allegro movement I have the tune, your part is subordinate to mine.' Du Pré hadn't noticed it before and as she was playing she conceded that he was right.

The duo she founded with George Malcolm lasted from 1962 to 1964, at which point she started playing with Stephen Bishop. Apart from the two summers at Dartington, du Pré and Malcolm played important recitals at Westminster Abbey and the Royal Festival Hall. They performed their last recital together in August 1965 at the Lucerne Festival.

To those who heard her at Dartington, Jackie appeared totally at home behind her cello. Her private doubts were not evident, and she is chiefly remembered as radiant, sunny and confident, although in social situations she could be awkward and shy. John Amis recalled:

Every Friday night at Dartington we had parties for the artists and students. At one of these I saw Jackie looking utterly miserable. I went up to her and asked if she was all right. 'I hate parties,' she answered. So I said, 'Would you like to play?' I had a piano score of Bloch's *Schelomo* with me, which I had taken with the intention of playing through with her since I adore that piece. So we found a room and we sloshed away at it. It was the only time I felt I had contact with her. Otherwise I never got through to her. But she seemed to have contact with everybody else at Dartington and she was loved by one and all.

At the same time Jackie's fame set her at a distance from her fellow students, many of whom felt in awe of her.

However, fortunately for Jackie there was an opportunity to reveal her doubts to a sympathetic and perceptive colleague, namely the cellist Joan Dickson, who was at the time Professor of Cello at the Royal Scottish Academy of Music. Joan coincided with Jackie at Dartington for two summers, but most vividly remembered their first candid discussion.

I was already in bed – it was two in the morning when Jackie came to my room. She had just performed at a Friday night concert with George Malcolm – they played the Beethoven A major Sonata [Op.69] and the Brahms F major [Op.99]. She asked what I thought of her playing and I asked her if she really wanted to know. She replied, 'Yes, I do, because everybody always just tells me everything I do is marvellous.' I remarked that I didn't always like the way she handled the cello when she was playing loudly. She seemed to hurl herself at the instrument. In the Beethoven A major Sonata the fortes sounded very aggressive, which to my mind didn't suit the music. I told her that forte doesn't just mean you should play as loudly as you can – sometimes it can be very rich, other times tense and sometimes cold. For her, forte seemed to mean a red rag to a bull – go for it for all you're worth, to see how much sound you can get. I thought that she would get more sound if she used less of her energy and more of the cello's. I told her, 'You're actually using it to get rid of some of your own internal aggressions.' I then tried to show her how you could get a forte without working nearly so hard, for instance, by playing with a slower bow nearer the bridge.

One of the specific things I commented on were the pizzicato notes at the opening of the slow movement in the Brahms F major. I told her, 'they sound so aggressive, as if you were trying to rip the C string off the peg ...' 'Oh, I think that opening is very aggressive,' she replied. 'Well that's funny,' I said, 'because when you took over with the bow in the fifth bar it was one of the most beautiful bits of playing in the whole concert, full of poignancy and anguish. After all, you were taking over the tune that the piano plays in the first four bars.' Jackie went very silent for a minute, then she said, 'You know I'm going to tell you something and you'll think I'm awful, but I hadn't noticed that the piano had the tune at the opening.' I thought it was both courageous and very honest of her to say this. It made me realise that Pleeth hadn't always heard her with piano – and that there isn't time to talk about everything at lessons.

It must have been a great relief for Jackie that in Joan she had found someone with whom to discuss her cellistic problems.

Jackie told me that for the first time in her life some of her instinctive movements – like shifting – weren't always working. She was in a real state because she couldn't play the opening of the Beethoven A major Sonata in tune; this was only because she had started to worry about it. In fact, she was growing up and questioning her intuition. She complained to me, 'When I was younger I just heard a note and went there, and I never stopped to think how. Now I think to myself – where is the note, what do I do with my arm and hand to get there? And things go wrong.'

Joan Dickson recognised that the mainspring of Jackie's musicality was her marvellous intuition. But she was perturbed by the apparent lack of conscious knowledge to back it up. Joan pointed out,

Intuition springs from a subconscious layer, but you can't develop at this level, you must do so on a conscious layer, where information gets stored and then filters through to the subconscious. As my teacher Enrico Mainardi once said, intuition is the most important thing a musician can have, but if your intuition is right you should always be able to find something in the score to justify it. Jackie lacked this kind of information in her training. I believe that it ought to be taught even before it is needed, so that when young musicians reach the age when they start to have fears and worries – and this is a different age for each of us – they have some concrete understanding of the way the music and the instrument function.

Joan admired Jackie's innate musicality, her poetic expressivity and her instinctive use of rubato. 'But at the time there was something wild inside her, which she would find increasingly difficult to control. Her rubato in those early stages was marvellous, but to my mind it soon began to get exaggerated.'

Despite the age difference between the two cellists, in many ways they had an equal relationship. Once, after Joan played a recital at Dartington, the tables were turned: 'I asked Jackie for some criticism and she told me that I didn't use my left hand expressively enough. She said, "You know, every time I put a finger down, I feel as if I was putting sound into the fingerboard." It was a completely new idea to me and I subsequently changed my technique radically because of her remark.'

The Dartington experience served its purpose in allowing Jackie to discover a congenial social context, where all her companions were likewise involved with music. And the success of her initial contact with Tortelier boded well for the future.

But before starting at the Paris Conservatoire term in October, Jackie still had some important engagements to fulfil. The first of these, on 3 September, was a shared BBC Invitation Concert at the Edinburgh Festival, where she performed the Brahms F major Sonata Op.99 with Ernest Lush. Desmond Shawe-Taylor, writing in the *Sunday Times*, spoke of her 'disappointingly forced performance' and issued a warning: 'This brilliant child needs to watch the quality of her tone, especially in the higher register; she also needs some sort of bandeau for her mop of fair hair, which swings constantly to and fro with the distracting abandon of a Betjeman tennis girl.'

In the CD issued from the BBC recording we have a document of her performance, which serves as a testimony to Jackie's interpretation. While there is evidence of a rough edge to her sound in loud passages (perhaps due to the uncovered gut A string she used in those days), there is no sense of her struggling. One does perhaps see what Joan Dickson meant about her rather over-violent pizzicato opening of the second movement. The volcanic impetuosity of the first movement is tremendously exciting and while du Pré drives the music forward, she never does so at the expense of the overall structure. Already she has an uncanny ability to judge exactly how much weight and intensity each note needs to 'feed the phrase' (a favourite expression of hers in later years when teaching) and knows how to spin out her rubatos. One might cite as an example her playing of the pizzicato notes that lead back to the recapitulation of the opening theme in the second movement, which govern the placing of the chords in the piano part. The whole sonata is played with the assurance of a seasoned artist, although to my mind the last two movements are less successful than the first two.

Yet this performance is a far cry from the gloriously spacious account of the same work in her later EMI recording with Daniel Barenboim. One can only be amazed as to how much Jackie went on to develop in terms of finesse, colouring and sustained beauty of sound and acutely heard phrasing, without losing a whit of the driving force of her enormous temperament.

The day after this concert, while still in Edinburgh, she recorded one of Schumann's *Fantasie stücke* for BBC TV's *Tonight*. Back in London, she made a BBC radio recording at the end of September of cello duets by Couperin and Defesch with her teacher William Pleeth. From this session, Couperin's Treizième Concert *Les Goûts-réunis* has been preserved and issued on CD in a delightful performance of give and take between pupil and master, where it is difficult to distinguish between them in their use of instrumental colour or in the humour, gaiety and touching eloquence of their playing.[12]

Before her departure for Paris in late October 1962, Jackie performed the Elgar concerto twice; in Stavanger, Norway, where she represented English music in a 'Gateway to Britain' celebration, then at the Royal Festival Hall with Norman Del Mar conducting the BBC SO. The London concert, held on 24 October, was given in honour of the United Nations – founded in the same year as Jackie was born – and was transmitted directly throughout Europe.

Again, a BBC recording of this concert has been preserved, the first of five archive performances of the Elgar concerto. The recording demonstrates that du Pré's interpretation of the piece was already formulated in all essentials and can be seen as a blueprint for her EMI recording with Barbirolli. What she was to gain in the intervening years was enormous finesse of colour, far greater dynamic range and an incredible imaginative understanding of the function of rubato. Certainly this recording gives us an idea of Jackie's dynamic natural talent and her surety of approach, qualities which had excited Tortelier at Dartington.

When Jackie arrived in Paris, she had the highest hopes of her study period. Tortelier expected her to stay for the full seven months' course until the end of June and assumed that she would play for (and win) the prestigious end-of-year Premier Prix. He also expected her to cancel all professional engagements during this period. This, however, was not part of her plan.

Already, in the summer of 1962, the press had reported Jacqueline du Pré's imminent 'five-month period of study' in Paris starting in the autumn. Iris had written to the BBC in early July explaining that her daughter could accept no further engagements from October for the following six months and would be available again for bookings from March 1963. In fact, Ibbs and Tillett had set up an extended recital tour in the south-west of England for Jackie and Iris starting in late March. No doubt Iris did not want to cancel these engagements. Ibbs had also accepted an engagement in December for Jackie to play the Schumann concerto at the Festival Hall.

One wonders why the du Prés failed to discuss these important practicalities with Tortelier when they met at Dartington. On the one hand apparently both Iris and Jackie did not inform Tortelier about her contracted concert engagements, or of her limited period of availability for study. On his part, Tortelier did not explain the teaching system at the Paris Conservatoire. Jackie arrived in Paris assuming that she would be able to have private tuition with Tortelier, not realising that the Conservatoire regulations stipulated instrumental teaching in master classes exclusively. Tortelier was actually forbidden to give individual lessons to Conservatoire students. The outcome of all this meant that when Jackie arrived in Paris there existed two unfortunate misunderstandings between teacher and student, which subsequently were never resolved.

9

Paris Interlude

One must, of course, master technique; at the same time one must not be enslaved by it.

Pablo Casals*

Technique is the whole Man.

Igor Stravinsky†

Tortelier was a player of enormous charisma, and one who had achieved his prowess through hard work, endless technical analysis and an open mind to all questions of cello playing. Born in 1914, he was a pupil of Louis Feuillard and Gerard Hekking at the Paris Conservatoire where, at the age of sixteen, he won the coveted first prize. Formally he had no more training on the cello, but furthered his musical development studying harmony and composition with Jean Gallon at the same Conservatoire, while earning his money playing at brasseries and cafés.

When he was twenty-one he became first cellist of the Monte Carlo Orchestra where, two years later, he played Richard Strauss's *Don Quixote* with the composer conducting – a work with which he was to remain closely associated. Tortelier furthered his orchestral career in Boston before the war, playing under Koussevitzky, and accepted his last orchestral position as leader of the Orchestre de la Société des Concerts du Conservatoire, which started its activities under Charles Munch after the liberation of France.

With this baggage of musical experience behind him, it was not until after the end of the war in 1945 that he embarked on a full-time career as a soloist. By then he was over thirty; in contrast, du Pré's playing days were already over before she reached that age.

Tortelier was a passionate admirer of Casals and spent the summers of 1950 to 1953 at the Prades Festival, where he profited from close

* Pablo Casals, *Joys and Sorrows*, Albert E. Kahn (ed.), Macdonald, London, 1970, p. 76.
† Igor Stravinsky and Robert Craft, *Conversations with Stravinsky*, Faber & Faber, London, 1959, p. 26.

musical contact with the Master. In the first year dedicated to the music of Bach, he agreed to play in the festival orchestra out of deference to Casals.

Casals's influence on Tortelier as a cellistic innovator was particularly evident in his use of the left hand. Previously, cellists held the left-hand fingers grouped closely together, causing the finger which was pressing the string to make the note to be inhibited by the others. Casals advocated a left-hand usage where each finger had an autonomy similar to a pianist's, thereby allowing more ease in stretching and shifting, and giving the vibrato greater diversity. But more than anything it was through his ideas of articulation that he revolutionised cello technique. A strong hitting articulation of the left-hand fingers was designed to set the string into vibration and the singing cantabile line was subordinated to the overall structure of the speaking phrase. Daniel Barenboim has described Casals's influence on him as making him play the piano as if he were a string player, saying that this mirrored the way Casals adopted pianistic articulation on the cello.[1]

In fact, beauty of sound was never important as a means in itself; Casals preferred expressive rhetoric to bel canto singing. Tortelier describes Casals's sonority as being indefinable: 'it was something spiritual – one never thought that Casals was playing the cello; he was playing music.'[2]

Casals regarded the problem of precise intonation as 'a matter of conscience. You hear when a note is false in the same way you feel when you do something wrong.'[3] Tortelier adopted Casals's use of 'expressive' intonation, the sharpening or flattening of notes according to their harmonic function. Casals based his theories of intonation on the 'gravitational attraction' of intervals, indicating the first, fourth and fifth degrees of the scale as points of repose to which other notes are drawn.[4] Tortelier describes this process as both subtle and vitalising. However, he never had to explain this system to du Pré, since she used expressive intonation in a completely natural and intuitive way.

Tortelier also admired Casals's rubato, which he termed 'the intuitive awareness of the relativity of notes in every direction: vertical, horizontal, diagonal'.[5] All in all, one could describe Casals as the first modern cellist, who set new standards of excellence. Previously, cellists sought indulgence for their technical deficiencies, claiming that the instrument was too difficult to master.

Before taking up a post at the Paris Conservatoire, Tortelier and his family spent the year of 1955–6 in Israel, living on a kibbutz at Ma'ab-aroth near Haifa. Tortelier not only was an idealist by philosophy, but he attempted to carry out his beliefs in practical life. He was much attracted by the idea of a community with no social differences and the pioneering spirit of the kibbutzim. He and his wife felt a deep affinity for Jews, a race with a great culture, and a passionate and intimate feeling for music.

In 1957 Tortelier was called in to replace the indisposed Piatigorsky at the inauguration of the Frederick Mann auditorium in Tel Aviv. He played that most Jewish of concertos, Bloch's *Schelomo* which, as he wrote '... transcends a purely personal message; it seems to express Israel's longing for a lost temple. The phrases ... rise from out of the past like a distant wail.'[6] The other two soloists and the conductor at that inaugural concert, Arthur Rubinstein, Isaac Stern and Leonard Bernstein, were not only amazed, but ashamed to discover that the only one of them to understand Ben Gurion's inaugural speech was the sole non-Jew among them. Tortelier knew Hebrew well enough to act as their translator![7]

Later in life, du Pré claimed to have been little influenced by Tortelier. Undoubtedly she was initially fascinated by his ebullient personality, and by the clarity and brilliance of his cello playing. Perhaps at the time she was unaware that they had in common a musicians' affinity with Jews. Of course, in later days du Pré went one step further, when at the time of her marriage to Daniel Barenboim she became a convert to Judaism and declared her intention of bringing up their children in a kibbutz.

Tortelier was to become one of the most highly regarded teachers in Europe. In 1958 he was appointed Professor at the Paris Conservatoire, where he taught for ten years, leaving after a disagreement with the Conservatoire directors. He then became Professor at the Essen Hoch-schule in Germany and finally returned to France to teach at the Nice Conservatoire. It was in Britain that he popularised the concept of the public master class through the medium of television, where his char-isma and his great articulacy (speaking in perfect English with an endearing French accent) won him and the cello new audiences.

Tortelier went much further than his own teachers, Feuillard and Hekking, and indeed than his idol Casals, in evolving his ideas on cello technique. His innovations particularly concerned the left hand, where he developed an almost pianistic technique, involving the use of the hand at right angles to the fingerboard, playing on it as if it were a piano keyboard turned sideways. This allowed for use of the little finger in high positions, where in conventional playing it is hardly ever used. He also adopted a more flexible use of the thumb, allowing it at times to rest under the fingerboard, (usually, when not playing it rests on the strings) and also sometimes passing it under the fingers as in pianistic usage.

Another of Tortelier's innovations was the invention of a curved spike or end-piece, which gave the cello a higher, almost horizontal position. He demonstrated that with the table and 'f' holes no longer facing downwards, the instrument was able to vibrate more freely, thereby achieving greater sound projection. For cellists with long arms it was not difficult to adapt to this new position – in fact, it simplified playing in high positions, while making it somewhat awkward to play in the first positions. Rostropovich, on his first try-out of the curved end-pin, jokingly remarked to Tortelier: 'You and I of course don't use first position.' Jokes aside, the fact remains that the first 'base' position is essential. Certainly the Tortelier spike put short-armed cellists (including his wife Maud, herself an excellent cellist) at a disadvantage.

Jackie made use of the patented Tortelier spike for several years. If the prototype was strong, the marketed version, made out of three separate pieces, was not. (It was also an awkward encumbrance, since it seldom fitted into standard-size cello cases.) To her cost, Jackie, with her forceful temperament, discovered that the middle section – a hollow wooden cylinder – tended to shatter when subjected to the kind of pressure she exerted. It took several years before she eventually reverted (with evident relief) to the standard straight metal spike, having in the meantime crushed a few Tortelier end-pins on the way. One can catch a glimpse of her using this end-pin in several photographs and in Christopher Nupen's film *Jacqueline*. Rostropovich adopted his own stronger version of the 'bent spike', having it fashioned out of one piece of metal.

It was with tales of his new pupil's prowess that Tortelier heralded Jackie's arrival in Paris. As Jeanine Tétard, a Tortelier student in the Conservatoire class at the time, recalled: 'Tortelier spoke to us at the beginning of the year of a new and quite extraordinary pupil. We must come and listen to her – " *Venez venez*" ...'[8] This feeling of excitement is confirmed by Raphael Sommer, the excellent Israeli cellist who had started his studies with Tortelier in Israel and became his most devoted pupil and disciple. 'When Jackie came to Paris it was a big noise; she created quite a stir in the class.'[9]

Jackie settled down to live with a French family and made her way into the Conservatoire in rue de Madrid on the Métro. It was her first experience away from home. Despite the fact that she had an excellent ear and was a fantastically good mimic, she was not a naturally good linguist and her knowledge of French never went beyond super-ficialities. She did not feel comfortable with the competitive atmosphere of the Paris Conservatoire and its class system, which seemed heavily orientated to success in the end-of-year prize competition. This sense of competition was as keenly felt by the professorial staff as the students. Tortelier would have been greatly pleased if Jackie, as his pupil, played for the prestigious 'Premier Prix', which undoubtedly she would have won. But she herself had little interest in such symbolic honours.

In Paris, the class system meant performing in front of an audience. Jackie observed that Tortelier (perhaps unintentionally) often humili-ated his pupils in public and she found this tendency to play to the gallery distasteful. These sentiments were borne out by another English cellist, Jenny Ward-Clarke, who studied with Tortelier in Paris at an earlier date:

> I hated the whole atmosphere of the Conservatoire Class, where com-petition was rife. Although Tortelier did give some marvellous lessons, he could be very unkind and he put his students down. Being twenty-one years old, I was older than all the French students, but not so well trained technically. While they could play virtuoso throw-away pieces with great ease, I was musically more serious-minded. By the end of the year I felt thoroughly crushed. Yet on the few occasions that I had private lessons with him I found Tortelier to be wonderful.[10]

Tortelier gave master classes twice a week at the Conservatoire. His wife, Maud Martin-Tortelier, acted as his assistant, and was a thorough and patient teacher. She exerted a calming influence on the students, who sometimes found the inspired Master too harsh in his criticisms, and over-demanding.

Maud remembered working with Jackie specifically on Beethoven's A major Sonata and was impressed by how open she was to suggestions. She compared Jackie with Jeanne d'Arc, with her short-cropped blonde hair, her statuesque height and her enormous floppy jumpers draped on her like a suit of armour (although never seeming to impede her movements).[11] The Viking image persisted in Tortelier's reminiscence of Jackie as a Wagnerian heroine and of her playing of the opening of the D major Beethoven Sonata Op.102 No.2 as the arrival of Siegfried, sword in hand.[12]

For Tortelier, the art of teaching meant conveying his style to his students, who accordingly had also to adopt his techniques. '[A student] must make a choice. If he keeps his technique, he keeps his style,' Tortelier claimed.[13] This principle of teaching was in du Pré's case doomed to failure, insofar as her ideas about musical style were too firmly rooted in her powerful intuition. For her, technique meant a creative ability to transfer musical ideas into sound and as such, she had it in abundance.

Tortelier's analytical and logical approach to the workings of instrumental technique and to the function of music did not coincide with Jackie's understanding of cello playing. Raphael Sommer recalled that this led to conflict between them: 'Tortelier was a demanding man and most things had to be done the way he wanted them – bowings, fingerings and phrasing. He explained everything very clearly and logically, but he did not encourage or respect the individual's way of thinking.' The conflict was all the greater because on one level du Pré had set herself the goal of studying pure technique with Tortelier.

Sommer admired Jackie's marvellous way of getting around all problems through her musicality. 'I wouldn't say that she had a perfect technique or that she didn't have problems. She had never studied technique in the way the rest of us students had, bringing by heart to lessons the study repertoire (Ševčík, Feuillard etc.), the concertos of Romberg, Davydov, Goltermann. The systematic method characteristic of the French School was alien to Jackie.'

If Tortelier regarded something as a technical problem, he would suggest ways of focusing on it. Sommer recalled: 'He might tell Jackie, "Your spicatto isn't working very well here, I suggest that you bring to the next lesson such and such a Popper study." But somehow it never happened, Jackie evaded set tasks and would bring something else to the lesson, and Tortelier would forget about it.'

However real her initial intentions were to study technique, Jackie avoided both the craft work that was a strong point of the French School and the study repertoire, preferring 'real' music in the form of the big romantic concertos. She brought to the classes those of Dvořák, Schumann, Bloch's *Schelomo* and Saint-Saëns.

In a later interview she recalled that at her first lesson with Tortelier at Dartington she had learnt a lot about the fingers and joints. But, she felt 'at the Paris Conservatoire in a master class, it wasn't quite the same. There was an audience and I felt I did not gain as much.'[14] Jackie found that she could not help giving a performance when she had a public, even if it only consisted of the other class students.

A month after her arrival in Paris, Jackie wrote home complaining that the master class created a barrier between her and Tortelier. 'Had I known that private lessons were impossible at the Conservatoire, I would not have joined. At the moment I feel utterly depressed and miserable since what seemed to be my salvation now turns out to be the opposite. I had to tell you because it's too much to keep to myself.'[15]

Other problems arose from her having to carry out concert engagements interspersed during the months of study. Jackie herself complained that since she had to prepare the Schumann concerto for a London concert early in December, she could not concentrate on technique, which she wanted to study 'cold'.

In fact, Tortelier was trying to impose changes, particularly in Jackie's left-hand technique, since he had noticed a weakness in her third and fourth fingers. He attributed the problem to the sloped angle of her hand and insisted that she adopted a perpendicular position of hand to fingerboard. He also suggested that she should change from gut to steel strings. Pressing the strings down now required far greater effort and tension. 'After practising a scale, my fingers ache with the strain,' Jackie lamented in another letter to her mother.[16]

Prior to her Royal Festival Hall performance, Jackie studied the Schumann concerto in detail with Tortelier. He suggested that she should learn his cadenza for the finale. There is actually no specific indication that a cadenza should be played, but Schumann suggests this option by placing a fermato sign before the coda. However, it became a cellistic tradition to add the cadenza in the late nineteenth–early twentieth century, a tradition which nowadays has been almost entirely abandoned.

Sommer remembered, 'Jackie really liked Tortelier's cadenza. Despite the tremendous technical difficulties, she played it beautifully – and this, without having systematically studied scales, studies and Goltermann concertos like the rest of us.'

At the end of November du Pré was flown back to London at the BBC's expense to perform the Schumann concerto at the Royal Festival

Hall on 2 December 1962. Jean Martinon was the conductor with the BBC SO. It was Jackie's first public performance of this most enigmatic of cello concertos and, in deference to Tortelier, she included his cadenza.

Once again, a BBC recording of the concerto has been preserved. Unlike the Elgar, her interpretation of the Schumann Cello Concerto was to develop considerably and gain in maturity over the next few years. It would seem that on this occasion Jackie was guided by the impetuous pianist Artur Schnabel's precept 'Safety Last' – and sometimes her risk-taking was not successful. Naturally, her playing exuded a wonderful youthful freshness and she produced a rich, beautiful sound, although seldom reaching the softer ranges of dynamic. A few years later the quality of extrovert wildness in her youthful interpretation was replaced by a magical poetry and intense inner feeling.

In this 1962 performance some of her best playing is actually in the Tortelier cadenza, a technically brilliant piece, utilising all the themes of the concerto, but which, to my mind, is overlong and ends too abruptly, destroying the initial magic of the wonderful G minor section of the beginning of the coda.

While back at home for the Christmas holidays, Jackie enlisted Iris's help to try and persuade Tortelier that he should give her private lessons, even if it would involve leaving the Conservatoire course. In a letter written on New Year's Eve, Iris explained that Jackie needed to get the most out of her time with him as 'there are probably no more than two years in which her studies can take precedence over her professional engagements'.[17]

As it was, Tortelier's suggestions sometimes seemed quite contradictory. Having asked Jackie to give up all her concert dates, he then invited her to take over one of his engagements in Berlin in early March, again to play the Schumann concerto. Iris informed him that Jackie would have to decline the invitation, as she had already refused other concerto engagements in the spring. Back in Paris in early January, Jackie was able to discuss the matter with Tortelier directly. As she explained in a letter to Iris, Tortelier had phoned her after a lesson. 'He apologised for making me play *Schelomo* to pupils in class. He realised that the moment he gives me an emotional piece to play I start forcing again and revert to bad habits. He said that I must do no concerts for at least six months and must cancel the Schumann [concerto] and the West of England tour. He wants me to work on Bach, Haydn and scales, allowing me to play no louder than mezzo-forte.'¹⁸

In fact, the other students were much impressed by Jackie's inspired performance of *Schelomo*. Sommer remembered her interpretation vividly.

> It was magnificent, but different from Tortelier's. He tried to alter her sentiments and explained to her certain Jewish characteristics – although in her own way she played it very 'Jewishly'. He talked of the significance of the quarter-tones, why a glissando should be used here and not there – always backing his ideas with a firm theoretical and harmonic basis. Jackie just poured her sentiments out and for him it was perhaps a bit too exaggerated.

Tortelier revealed his theories about glissandos in his later televised master classes. He regarded the exact placing of a slide as a question of taste, something he equated with gastronomic principles. 'You have no taste if you don't notice that the fish is off or that you are drinking beer in a can previously opened. And glissandos can be done all too easily in bad taste.' He recommended that most slides are done on to strong beats, and a 'singing shift' should be used as a way of emphasising a note. Many year later he was to cite du Pré's playing of the second subject in the first movement of the Dvořák concerto as an example of good taste and the right choice of glissando. Similarly, with the use of rubato in longer phrases Tortelier was insistent that the centre of a tempo should be retained, thereby creating the necessary equilibrium. 'It is indulgence when you lose this centre and indulgence means you love yourself more than the music.' (One suspects that Tortelier did regard du Pré's playing as being occasionally over-indulgent.)

If Tortelier could say to some of his students, 'Don't think – do things by enthusiasm,' in du Pré's case this exhortation was unnecessary. Rather, he attempted to rein in the uncontrolled element in Jackie's playing, and to introduce restraint, logic and organisation into her way of thinking about music. As Sommer recalled, 'With two such strong personalities clashes were inevitable. In fighting the uncontrolled element of spontaneity in her playing, Tortelier did so in ways that seemed to us somewhat harsh and cruel. I was amazed that Jackie swallowed quite a lot of criticism and always kept her cool. Her philosophical English sense of humour stood her in good stead. However, while she never reacted in the class, I knew that she would get upset afterwards.'

In another of her letters to Iris, Jackie commented,

It is interesting that after Uncle Bill's [Pleeth] lessons I felt physically exhausted and that after Tortelier's I feel mentally exhausted. I have never seen such merciless driving after a point on which he is convinced and I have never tried so hard to try and fulfil what anybody says. His quickly passing flashes of humour are an immense and longed-for relief! But this is only because I am not used to pitching concentration at such a high and consistent level. [. . .] There is no mercy in his convictions.[19]

At this stage Jackie had overcome her initial shyness and started asking Tortelier insistently for private lessons. Although he secretly disobeyed the Conservatoire rules and gave her the occasional lesson at his home, this issue remained an area of conflict between them.

No doubt from Tortelier's point of view Jackie was difficult to teach in any case. In later years he confessed that he did not know how Pleeth had done it! But if he found her resistance inexplicable, he was equally impressed by the amazing speed with which she would latch on to new ideas. In a master class televised in the 1980s he recalled du Pré's immediate response to his fingering suggestion for a passage in the first movement of the Dvořák concerto. 'An iron second finger leads in this passage . . . Jacqueline got the fingering immediately; like an eagle she swooped on it and had grasped it before she knew what I wanted her to do, before I had time to show her.'[20]

Tortelier used his capacity for technical analysis to support his spontaneity and his enormous imagination. But his spirit of innovation could be confusing as well as inspiring to his students and despite the fact that he believed in a systematic technical training he was not a consistent teacher. Continually being distracted by new enthusiasms, he tended to jump from one idea to another, seldom following any of them through. He was incapable of adhering to a system, in the way that a teacher like André Navarra did. As Sommer admits,

Ultimately there were few people who could follow Tortelier. Every week he would come with some new idea. He had little patience for those who did not want or were unable to follow his every suggestion immediately. For us in the class it was already a struggle to learn the repertoire and play the notes in tune. And here came the *maître* offering us visions of a new world. However much one wished to follow him in his quest we hadn't got sufficient instrumental prowess. We would go home and sweat blood to incorporate his new idea in our playing, only to come back the week after and find that he had made another new discovery, forgotten about the previous one and would ask you what idiot had told you to work exclusively on his forgotten 'new' idea. To make matters more confusing, here was this Jacqueline who just played everything with apparently no system whatsoever. It was quite mind-blowing for the other students.

One student who was able to follow Tortelier and assimilated and totally identified with his style of playing was the Finnish cellist, Arto Noras. He coincided with Jackie in Paris and inevitably comparisons were made between the two of them, although by nature they approached the instrument and music from opposite points of view. Maud Tortelier recalled that this spirit of competition was actually very beneficial to them both. Noras won the end-of-year Premier Prix and went on to make a distinguished international career.

Whereas students like Noras and Sommer accepted Tortelier's discipline without question, Jackie did not see the need for it. In any case, she was never one to observe rules and regulations. She already had definite views of how most pieces should go and although she could instantly assimilate new suggestions if they appealed to her, she could equally well resist them, remaining true to her own convictions.

Raphael Sommer came to the conclusion that Jackie's very naturalness was quite irritating to Tortelier: 'He had had to work very hard to build up his technique. He was not a natural – in this way he was the complete opposite of Jackie. She had everything, magnificent intonation, splendid sound, range of colour and spontaneity of expression.'

In the spring of 1963 Tortelier arranged for Jackie to perform the Schumann concerto with a student orchestra in the Salle Fauré of the Conservatoire. Maud Tortelier writes of Jackie's 'superb' interpretation and Jeanine Tétard also remembered her glorious playing of the concerto as a highlight of the year. A few days later Jackie played the date that Tortelier had passed on to her, performing the same concerto in Berlin with the Berlin Radio Orchestra on 5 March.

Just before these concerts, matters came to a head over private lessons. Once again, Jackie had asked for more individual lessons outside the classes. As Maud Tortelier remembers, her husband gave his final refusal with great regret, as he could not be seen to contravene the

Conservatoire regulations in private. This refusal influenced Jackie's decision to cut short her studies at the Paris Conservatoire and return home – she certainly wasn't bothered about the Premier Prix.

Nevertheless, Jackie's relationship with Tortelier and his family remained friendly, all the more so since it was agreed that his thirteen-year-old daughter Maria de la Pau would replace Iris in Jackie's forth-coming recital tour of the West Country at the end of March. Iris must have been disappointed to relinquish her accompanist's role, since she had looked forward to these concerts and had always regarded them as a valid reason to interrupt Jackie's studies in Paris. Possibly Iris agreed to step down for Maria as a gesture to please Tortelier. More probably this change of accompanist had been suggested by Ibbs and Tillett, who also had Tortelier on their lists. Maria de la Pau was a talented pianist and there was a special public appeal in seeing two young girls perform together. As a tribute to her French mentor, Jackie decided to include Fauré's G minor Sonata in their programme, a work she never performed again. A telegram sent on 25 March from Bridgwater by Miss Lereculey of Ibbs and Tillett to the Tortelier parents expressed delight at the enormous success of their concerts: '*Jacqueline beaucoup plus grand et eloquent, Pau adorable – pianiste premier ordre.*' Having fulfilled these engagements, Jackie did not return to Paris.

Many years later Tortelier admitted privately to Sommer that he had completely failed with Jackie. He realised that with her enormous force of personality it was necessary to accept what she did, even if it went contrary to his way of thinking. Jackie for her part showed little long-term effects of Tortelier's influence, although she admitted that she had incorporated some of his ideas about left-hand technique, particularly the use of the thumb, into her playing. Naturally she adapted these uses to her own needs.

Sommer is perhaps correct in saying that even if Tortelier's advice about technique went in one ear and out of the other, he was one of the few cellists around who had a sufficiently strong personality to help Jackie. His human personality, his love of philosophical questing and eager curiosity, must surely have rubbed off on her in some way.

Later Jackie usually spoke about her Paris experience in very negative terms. How much this was due to retrospective colouring and how much to her personal feelings of adolescent insecurity at the time is difficult to establish. It would be unfair to lay all the blame on Tortelier for her unhappiness at the time, beyond saying that as teacher and pupil they were incompatible personalities.

Whatever the mutual disappointments, in retrospect Tortelier spoke of du Pré with warmth and generosity, comparing her with the marvellous French violinist Ginette Neveu. He never took credit for teaching her anything – this he allocated firmly to Pleeth.[21] He wrote apropos of her period of study with him: 'It was very brave of her to do this because she was already a brilliant instrumentalist.'[22] She remained for him a phenomenon who 'stands out not only for the radiance of her playing, but for her personal radiance as well'.[23]

10

Overcoming Doubts

... Doubt wisely; in strange way
To stand inquiring right, is not to stray;
To sleepe, or runne wrong is ...

John Donne, 'Satyre III'

Jackie's accounts of her early return from Paris differed. But essentially her disappointment lay in her discovery that Tortelier was unable to provide solutions to her instrumental problems. Neither had he been able to expunge her fundamental doubts about pursuing a full-time career as a cellist. In the aftermath of her studies with him she fell into a depression, undergoing a crisis of confidence.

Back home, Jackie only played a limited number of concert engagements; evidently her agents had expected her to take the rest of the season off to complete her studies. Often her concerts assumed a semi-private character, such as those she played with her friend Jill Severs. Her depressed state perhaps accounted for occasional moments of lack of concentration during her performances. Once she had an unaccountable memory lapse in the first movement of the E minor Vivaldi Sonata. Jackie apologised to the audience and started again, but it was only at her fourth attempt that she overcame it and was able to play on.

Jackie may have been reluctant to play concerts, but she still loved playing for fun. She resumed her contact with Antony Hopkins and the intended scholastic element of her sessions with him soon gave way to playing. 'Although I am a very limited pianist, Jackie must have enjoyed herself, otherwise she wouldn't have kept on coming,' recalled Hopkins. 'We met in the evenings and ploughed through the cello and piano repertoire movement by movement. I remember her at one in the morning wrapping herself around the cello saying, "I can't play another note, I'm absolutely exhausted." I had more stamina, probably because I put less effort into playing – her colossal energy also went into the choreography!'

Hopkins recalled that over the time he knew her, Jackie always displayed an unstinted enthusiasm for music. Once when he invited her to play the Schumann concerto with him in November 1965 with the Norwich Philharmonic Jackie volunteered to join the back desk of the cellos for the second half of the concert. 'We were to perform Borodin's *Polovtsian Dances*, and Jackie was dying to play this rousing music,' Hopkins recalled. 'The orchestral players were thrilled that she wanted to join in with them after her glorious rendering of the Schumann. It was my one and only experience of a "rear-engined" cello section!'

In the meantime Hopkins invited Jackie to participate in an educational series about music to be presented by Granada TV. He had devised a form of lecture-recital suitable for children with a minimal knowledge of music, where he explained in simple terms the form and the salient instrumental features of chosen works. In a programme dedicated to Beethoven that was transmitted in May 1963, he and Jackie illustrated the A major Cello Sonata Op.69, interrupting the explanations about the music with performed excerpts from the first movement. They ended the programme with a complete performance of the finale and the short preceding adagio.

These were not, of course, ideal performing conditions; nevertheless this filmed recording gives us a unique opportunity to judge how Jackie played at the time. Dressed in a very plain and unflattering outfit of shirt and circular skirt, she exhibits a sense of awkwardness with herself, until the moment she starts to play. Then she comes alive, and conveys an exhilaration in the beauty and nobility of the music through tossings of the head and the odd private but ecstatic smile.

Antony Hopkins remembered that the schoolchildren did not know what to make of such a direct emotional expression of the music. 'At the time there were criticisms from teachers that Jackie threw herself about too much, making kids in the class laugh. In fact, this aspect of her physical, almost choreographic playing was one of her great appeals to an audience. She transmitted the feeling that she was totally uninhibited in her approach to the instrument. But I can imagine that for children who knew nothing about the cello or about Beethoven sonatas, it would seem funny."

As Hopkins noted, this is a typically English inhibition. Jackie's childhood friend Freddie Beeston remembers that she had to defend Jackie from such unfair and uninformed criticism on the part of her contemporaries at music college. Freddie found this sniggering at Jackie's physical, almost sensual performing manner both stupid and distasteful, and was very anxious that Jackie did not realise what was being said about her, knowing that she would have been mortified.[2]

Unfortunately, at that time such a display of unselfconscious joy and passion by a teenage girl was often misunderstood through ignorance. In fact, it was partly thanks to Jackie's free and unfettered spirit that the stiff aura of formality surrounding concert artists was debunked. Nowadays, the fact that many cellists (especially female ones) feel free to play with uninhibited physical movement is in itself a mark of her influence.

This early Granada TV programme with Antony Hopkins shows Jackie in complete mastery of the music and the cello. Her sound is rich and noble, although occasionally over-energetic gesture of the bow detract from its actual quality. Sometimes this is evident as a mannerism, for instance in her playing of the opening statement of the finale's theme, where she rips the bow off the final open A string at the end of the phrase with such force as to produce an unwanted bulging echo. One sees why Tortelier had tried to discipline her abandoned passionate approach, which made her occasionally force the sound.

In Jackie's supple left-hand usage, her idiosyncratic slides are already evident, although used with restraint. We can see her use of fourth-finger sliding down the semitone, an effect that became a du Pré hallmark. She already shows herself a remarkable master of the bow, and although by comparison with her later playing there was a certain rigidity, her seamless bow changes and capacity to distribute its length shows extraordinary control and flexibility. The fact that technique in itself was never a predetermined aspect of her playing is visible in her ability to achieve the same effect by different technical means. Her full sweeping bow strokes used for the syncopations in the second subject of the first movement exposition are replaced in the analogous passage in the recapitulation by employment of very small restricted strokes at the point of the bow.

It is interesting to compare this early filmed performance with one made seven years later by Christopher Nupen for Granada Television of the same Beethoven sonata played with Barenboim. Naturally, the later performance has a sophistication and refinement that were beyond Jackie's means at the age of eighteen. But despite her enormous development in terms of musical maturity and instrumental mastery, Jackie's basic interpretation of the sonata had already been conceived by 1963. This early film also gives us a valuable last glimpse of the adolescent Jackie, with short hair and puppy fat, before her sudden flowering into womanhood.

Around this time Jackie resumed her sessions with Joan Clwyd and picked up with her old London friends. Through Joan's daughter Alison she also started meeting a new circle of friends, many of whom were not musicians. One of them was George Debenham, who lived round the corner from the du Prés in Regent's Park. Jackie wanted to study maths, and Debenham offered to teach her. In his late twenties, well-read and with a wide range of interests, George was intense and inward-looking. He found Jackie to be very shy, but deeply curious and highly intelligent. Although her knowledge of maths was very basic, she possessed a natural curiosity about the physical world and wanted to know more about it in scientific terms. Debenham was aware that Jackie was undergoing a crisis caused by her uncertainty about accepting the responsibilities of a concert career, something that was clearly expected of her at home.

It was obvious to outsiders that Jackie desperately wanted to shake off the influence of her family and all they represented. She felt that she had missed out on learning things that other people knew and did not even have the basic O and A level qualifications needed to pursue a higher education at university level. Enrolling in a yoga class at London University was the nearest she got to entering university portals. As Alison Brown recalled: 'After her return from Paris Jackie wanted to give the whole thing up. My mother was very much responsible for encouraging her to go on. Jackie was frightened of the implications of a career and she passionately wanted just to be an ordinary girl; but so much was expected of her.'[3] The problem for Jackie was that she saw little alternative choice and felt stuck with being a cellist.

The maths tutorials with Debenham soon expanded from their original brief. As Alison realised, they had served as a pretext for Jackie and George to get to know each other better. Won over by her natural exuberance and carefree, teasing sense of humour, George was soon in love with his pupil. As Jackie grew out of adolescence into womanhood, her inherent sensuality, so evident in her music-making, needed an outlet in real life. She too was attracted to Debenham, and was more than ready to embark on a first serious relationship.

Alison Brown perceived George as solid, stable and dependable. 'He loved Jackie dearly and was very good to her. He was happy to support her in many ways, acting as chauffeur and carting her cello around for her.' Debenham was also a good amateur pianist and a sensitive musician, and Jackie was happy to play with him for fun.

Debenham's positive support over the next eighteen months, together with Joan Clwyd's encouragement, contributed enormously to Jackie overcoming her doubts and accepting the responsibility of a professional career.

Although in the summer of 1963 Jackie did not feel like playing concerts, chamber music was another matter. She was happy to go back to Sermoneta, where she would find sympathetic young colleagues with similar attitudes to music-making. This year the Sermoneta chamber music courses were extended into a festival, where teaching was combined with public concerts by outside artists. The Festival di Sermoneta (later renamed the Pontino Festival) nevertheless retained its atmosphere of informality and Lysy remained the driving force behind it. Among the artists who came and played there in the early years were Joseph Szigeti, Yehudi Menuhin, Gaspar Cassadó and Nikita Magaloff.

That year Jackie formed an important friendship with the talented Argentinian violinist, Ana Chumachenko. Six months younger than Jackie, Ana had come from Argentina to Europe to study with Arthur Grumiaux in Brussels. Menuhin had suggested to Ana's mother that she first go to Sermoneta, where she could work with Lysy, play chamber music and meet lots of talented young people – he mentioned Jackie's name among others.

Ana spoke no English and she and Jackie communicated in French. Ana recalls Jackie as 'a unique case' – a wonderful mixture of innocence and shyness, with a fantastic wildness and force of intuition.

When I met her Jackie was undergoing a crisis about the cello and was full of artistic doubts. She was always asking other people for their opinions, what she should do, how this should be played, how should the music be shaped. She listened to everybody, even to those who, by comparison with her, could hardly play two notes. But in the end her own playing was so naturally persuasive and had totally the right intuitive feel that all arguments and explanations were forgotten and everybody ended up by adopting her way of doing things. There was this strange conflict in her, but not once she was behind the cello and playing. Here she overruled everybody, no one else had a chance. The force of her intuition was incredible.

Jackie told Ana on more than one occasion that she wanted to quit playing and that she would like to go to university – through her friendship with George Debenham she had become very interested in Maths. 'Jackie almost seemed to have a complex about knowing so little. She was breaking away from her family and wanted to gain her independence.'

Ana also observed this contradiction in Jackie's everyday behaviour, where she was a curious mixture of shyness and *joie de vivre*. Many people were perplexed by the apparently contradictory signals, when sudden outbursts of loud laughter, often at what appeared inappropriate moments, might be followed by bouts of silence, when she would lock into her shyness and seeming lack of confidence. Jackie's high spirits did not resemble the extrovert openness of Latin or Southern people; rather, she had an air of Nordic mystery about her, powered by her rich inner world and spirit.

Alberto Lysy's former wife, Benedetta Origo, compared Jackie with an energetic lioness – with her adventurous spirit, her golden hair like a lion's mane, her tall, statuesque figure and her beautiful pale skin which tended to redness in the burning sun. Everything was fresh and fun. The musicians would play football in the castle keep and when Jackie got behind the ball everyone else had to move out of the way fast.

The level of music-making was high and the atmosphere very stimulating. One of the highlights of the festival for Alberto Lysy was performing Zoltán Kodály's Duo for Violin and Cello with Jackie. Alberto had first learnt the piece at the instigation of Gaspar Cassadó and they had played it for Kodály himself. He recounted to Jackie everything that Kodály had told them. The duo had been composed when the composer was deeply in love and he encouraged the performers to play the music with the utmost freedom and passion. Lysy recalled, 'Jackie was fascinated by these stories, and her imagination was fired. Of course she played the duo magnificently.'[4]

Benedetta Origo remembered that Jackie dominated the stage in performances of chamber music through her commanding presence, but at the same time she was never invasive. She was always responsive to the other musicians' playing, but fuelled it with her energy.[5] Ana, one of Jackie's favourite chamber music partners, remembered the tremendous power of her cello playing. 'Jackie was very wild and almost chaotic in the way she played, but at the same time there was always her own order in the way she did things and this inner order was totally compelling. She had absolutely everything in cellistic terms, a wonderful range of sound and colour, she could do what she wanted. If anything, I felt that she lost something over the years, as she became more thoughtful and aware. She started to filter her intuition through her intellect and I always felt that was a pity.'[6]

Jackie's friendship with Ana Chumachenko was strengthened when, at the beginning of August they found themselves going on with Alberto Lysy from Sermoneta to a summer festival at Taormina in Sicily. There the teachers and artists included Carlo Zecchi, Enrico Mainardi, Goffredo Petrassi, Nikita Magaloff, Remy Principe. Jackie was invited to play chamber music and Ana took part in master classes with Principe. They shared a room; but Ana's attention was soon distracted since during the course she met and fell in love with her future husband, the viola player Oscar Lysy.

The violinist Diana Cummings, who had played with Jackie in the short-lived Artemis Quartet, also attended the Taormina courses. Diana, who was now studying violin in Rome with Remy Principe, commented: 'Jackie had already acquired a reputation, her career had got off to a highly successful start. But we had heard that she was going through something of a crisis and that she wanted to give up the cello. She was certainly unhappy in herself.' Diana noticed that 'Jackie was always reluctant to go up and be with the "proper" artists. She would have been much happier mucking around with us, being part of our gang. She felt isolated and she minded.' Jackie had been invited to Taormina at the instigation of Mainardi, and she was expected not only to play with but to have her meals and mix with the teaching staff and other invited artists.

Compounding her feeling of social unease, she was much pre-occupied with her appearance. Diana recalled how Jackie '... used to walk into our room where there was a big wardrobe mirror. She would try to do something with her hair, which she was growing – but she was always dissatisfied with it. She was a rather gawky adolescent with a lot of puppy fat, and you would not have called her physically attractive. Yet she had terrific personality.'[7]

Franco Scala, a piano student of Zecchi, who became very friendly with Jackie during the courses, recalled that she had a complex about her looks. She longed to acquire elegance and dress sense that came to many other girls naturally. Franco, on the other hand, was much attracted by Jackie's vitality and physical exuberance. On the beach below the town, they would talk and swim, and have playful fights in the water.

Scala found Jackie simple and direct. As a colleague she was extremely helpful and knew how to offer constructive criticism with great gentleness. He was amazed at her phenomenal ability to sight-read and they played through many sonatas. Once he accompanied her playing the Lalo Cello Concerto, which Jackie sent up, treating it as a grand warhorse of the cello repertoire, in the same way as pianists regard the Grieg concerto.[8] Towards the end of her stay Jackie played a sonata programme with Carlo Zecchi, a concert that was a highlight of the courses. Zecchi himself was moved to tears by her playing.

On her return to London she performed her first professional concerto engagement since March. This was her second appearance at the Proms playing the Elgar concerto with Malcolm Sargent on 22 August. Her playing received accolades from the public and the critics alike, and Sargent was so moved that he came straight into Jackie's greenroom and announced, 'I have conducted all the great cellists, but never enjoyed a performance as much as tonight's.'[9]

In his enthusiastic review for the *Guardian*, Edward Greenfield wrote of Jackie's new confidence. 'This eighteen-year-old, walking on with the unassuming muscularity of a new champion hockey player, confirmed the mastery divined by all who have heard her. I cannot think of another young British artist who shows in quite the same way natural power to control a continuous musical argument, to make an audience of thousands hang in attention on a single phrase.' He was particularly impressed by her playing of the slow movement:

> Miss du Pré conveys an inner passion, rather than an external one. The speed [in the più mosso middle section] barely increases, the simple dignity of the rest of the movement remains and the appassionato marking is conveyed in a richer tone merely, a wider vibrato. It is not exactly what Elgar marked, but in Miss du Pré's hands it provides a flash of new insight. There were dozens of such points, and only the size of the Albert Hall prevented her full tones (though curiously not her half tones) from having a full effect.[10]

In this review Greenfield pointed for the first time to du Pré's superb understanding of soft playing. For her the dynamic marking of piano encompassed a large range of expression and sonority. It was through intensity rather than force that she made even the most hushed sounds tell in the hall. She understood the importance of making the 'little' notes speak, echoing Richard Wagner's exhortation to singers: 'The big notes come of themselves, it is the little notes that require attention.' More than any other player I know, Jackie was dedicated to the playing of each single note, and within its duration she knew how to use dynamic change and shading with the overall purpose of creating a connected single line.

It is very difficult to describe in words what musical sound means, since sound affects every one of us in a different way. Those moments of touching, almost painful beauty in Jackie's soft playing had to my mind a quality unique to her. The pianist Guthrie Luke remembered asking Jackie if she had ever been taught how to make such a telling pianissimo. 'At first she just replied, "Oh, I've never thought about it." But she then did address the question seriously and said that since Pleeth was a very intense man it was he who had instilled this quality in her, without her even realising it.'[11]

In fact, her Prom was an isolated engagement in an autumn notably empty of public concerts. Jackie was still tussling with those doubts that form an inherent part of a true artist's nature. As her future husband Daniel Barenboim rightly observes, 'the more talented the artist, the greater the doubts he suffers. In order for a musician to perform on stage and transmit his art, he needs to summon up enormous stores of positive energy. In the interim between concerts, he (or she) has to live with his demons – his doubts – and only after overcoming them is he able to give out freely in performance.'[12]

Jackie was also aware that she had outgrown her family. As her friend Christopher Nupen recalled, she did not expect more understanding than she already got from her parents. 'Iris had given her so much, but there were other difficulties, and by the time she was eighteen, both Derek and Iris had to accept that Jackie had gone past them, and they could no longer help her. Derek seemed continually astonished by his daughter's enormous gifts; indeed, they were both filled with wonder for her.'[13]

Apart from the fact that she had outstripped Iris in her musical development, she found her family's world hopelessly self-enclosed. Their private language seemed to Jackie embarrassingly childish and she would get irritated in particular by Derek's infantile pleading for a 'curzuppateseesles' or 'cuppoice' with 'suzugazoozles', meaning a cup of tea with sugar.[14] Iris had been a decisive and positive influence throughout her childhood, but it was one that Jackie now rejected. At this late stage Derek started to impose himself more on his daughter. He too fostered ambitions for her, although he was often shy of expressing them.

In his capacity as President of the Cosmopolitan Computation of Accountants, Derek arranged a private concert for the annual conference in Edinburgh on 10 September. The Scottish National Orchestra, conducted by Alexander Gibson, was hired to play at the Usher Hall a programme which included Brahms's First Symphony and Schumann's Cello Concerto with Jackie as soloist. The Scottish cellist Joan Dickson remembered Iris phoning her to ask if Jackie could come and practise in her Edinburgh flat during their stay.

Every morning Jackie was deposited with me while her father was out at meetings. The first day I was there, I put her into my spare room and went upstairs to practise myself. Each time I stopped and listened, I became aware that there was no sound of the cello being practised underneath. Finding this somewhat puzzling, I went down and knocked on the door, to find Jackie somewhat guiltily sitting and reading a book she had found in the room. She said, 'Please don't tell my parents that I wasn't practising. I get awfully bored with it.' I suggested that we took a break for a cup of coffee because I wanted to talk about a pupil of mine who was a school friend of hers. This girl had come up to study with me at the Royal Scottish Academy in Glasgow and was suddenly undergoing a crisis, and wondered whether she really wanted to do music. I asked Jackie about the girl's background and wanted to know her opinion. We talked for a while, then Jackie said rather dolefully, 'You know, that girl's lucky, she could give up music if she wants to. But I could never give it up because too many people have spent too much money on me.' At this young age she felt this burden bearing very heavily on her. I remember thinking at the time, she feels that she's in a trap. Later on, when she was ill, I heard her say similar things. I might have dismissed these remarks then, had I not already heard her speak like this all those years back.[15]

Jackie understood that throughout her childhood everything had been geared to her becoming a great cellist, but she resented the idea that her highly specialised musical education represented a commercial investment. One can only suppose that such a material concept was not foreign to Derek's way of thinking, versed as he was in the world of administration and accountancy management. But it reflected, too, the rationale behind Iris's ambitions and self-sacrifice.

Alison Brown also recalled the double-edged significance of all the effort put into Jackie's career by her family and well-wishers. 'The gift of a priceless Stradivarius cello was a wonderful thing for Jackie in a way, but it was also a blow in the guts – a tremendous psychological pressure to continue to play at the highest level.'

The cellist Moray Welsh, a pupil of Joan Dickson, recalled first meeting Jackie at a rehearsal with the Scottish National Orchestra. 'I remember going along to speak to her. Although I am only a couple of years younger than Jackie, she was a distant star to me. But I found her to be very open and friendly. At the time she was playing her first Strad and she asked if I wanted a go on it. I felt terribly self-conscious and embarrassed trying to play in front of her, but she was very sweet to me. Afterwards she allowed me to carry her cello back to the hotel and I felt very proud.'

On that visit Derek was in evidence rather than Iris. Moray recalled that, encouraged by Jackie's friendliness, he went to congratulate her after the concert. 'But to my astonishment Derek was standing at the door of the green-room like a sentry and refused admittance to everybody. I was most upset – it seemed unnatural and unfriendly to keep people out. Derek seemed very English and proper, and appeared completely to lack the ability to express himself. Jackie, of course, broke through all of this uptight inhibition with her playing – her depth of expression was a million years away from her background.'[16]

During the autumn Jackie's crisis came to a head and she was able to make some positive decisions. One was that she must move out of the family home; the other that she would return to her professional career. As Christopher Nupen perceived the matter, she was very concerned to honour the special gift that she had been given. 'For Jackie, performing meant giving no less than a hundred per cent of her full commitment.' Anything less than that would be an act of dishonesty on her part, and she worried that she could not always meet such high standards.[17] Three years later Iris du Pré confirmed this view when she spoke of her daughter's hesitations at this time: 'Jackie was always worried that she wasn't good enough. You've no ideas of the miseries she went through.'[18]

In her private life, Jackie's decision to gain her independence coincided with changes in her parents' life. Derek handed in his notice at the Institute of Costs and Works in January 1964, which meant vacating the Portland Place flat that belonged to the Institute. He then accepted a position as Secretary to the Chartered Accountants Students' Society and in the summer of 1964 he, Iris and Piers moved to a house in Gerrard's Cross within easy commuting distance of London.

Early in the new year of 1964 Jackie took up Nigel Finzi's (Kiffer's younger brother) offer to house-sit in his flat in Kensington Park Road. But living on her own did not suit her. By a piece of good fortune Alison Brown, having completed her studies at Cambridge, was searching for a new lodger to share her basement flat at 35 Ladbroke Grove. Alison recalls that, 'Jackie's brief experience living away from home in Nigel's flat had not been very satisfactory. She had a bit of a swither as to whether to come and live with me. But in the end we spent over two years as flat-mates, actually sharing two different flats near Notting Hill Gate.'

At the beginning of her time away from home Alison perceived Jackie as very vulnerable and insecure. 'I felt that there was some dark unresolved conflict still within her, a hidden element and a great uncertainty.' Alison, now working as a goldsmith's apprentice, was able to help Jackie gain social confidence by introducing her to a wide circle of friends. 'I took Jackie with me to the Study Society, of which I was a member, and I introduced her to my philosophical friends. It was an interesting circle and expanded Jackie's range. Even if she didn't join in the discussions, she liked being an observer – she tasted and tested out.'

But it was also a period of great excitement and discovery, and Alison saw enormous changes taking place in Jackie's life during the years they lived together. She had started to take an interest in her own appearance and was changing from being an over-sized gawky adolescent into an attractive woman, who knew how to make an asset of her tall stature. 'When we first met, Jackie used to wear clothes that were dull, childish and unimaginative. But she soon developed her own flamboyant dress sense – she started to become this sort of saucy French beach-girl, wearing skimpy busty jerseys that brought out her broad shoulders and emphasised her figure. I never thought her clothes were particularly glamorous, but they were always fun and sometimes they were out-rageously brash.'

Alison had taken one of her Study Society friends, Madeleine Dinkel, to hear Jackie at the Proms. Madeleine, a talented graphics designer and calligrapher, was horrified by the unflattering circular dresses that Jackie wore at concerts, which seemed to hide rather than enhance her figure. When Madeleine exclaimed, 'You can't go on wearing those dresses, I'll make you one,' Jackie was delighted and eagerly accepted her offer. For Madeleine, dressmaking was an extension of her artistic nature. She had had no training as a dressmaker, therefore she had no preconceptions about how a dress should be made. In Jackie's case she would construct the dress around her, lining and strengthening the bodice to withstand the strains and exertions of her energetic style of playing. Madeleine made a series of wonderful concert dresses for Jackie. For material she chose beautiful, bright-coloured raw silks that caught the lights on-stage, and like a sculptor draped them around Jackie, disguising the unflattering open-legged sitting posture that cellists must adopt. As time went on, Jackie relied more and more on Madeleine's skills. Not only was she thrilled to have clothes specially designed for her, but she came to value Madeleine as a friend and confidante, with whom she could relax at any time.

For Jackie, discovery involved testing out many new skills, often relating to the most ordinary things. Alison remembered her taking an almost childish pleasure in cooking: 'She had never had to cook before. I recall that she would write out recipes for me with great pride for what were probably rather ordinary meat stews.' The two girls didn't in fact see that much of each other. 'We had our own feeding arrangements. Jackie tended to eat sensible, swift things. Then, on one disastrous day when she was making herself a sandwich, my old bread-knife slipped. She cut her finger quite badly. Guthrie Luke was horrified and immediately went out and purchased the most grandiloquent bread-knife, telling Jackie that a sharp-bladed instrument is actually safer as it won't slip.' Guthrie recalled that this incident happened just before Jackie was going to play the Dvořák concerto with Jascha Horenstein at the Festival Hall in April 1965. Fortunately the injured finger was on the right bowing hand, and with a plaster in place, she went ahead and gave a superb performance.

At the beginning of the time they lived together Jackie was not overwhelmed by a busy concert schedule. Alison noted that even when she started playing more concerts, practising the cello was never a pressing need for her. It was the quality rather than the quantity of work that mattered. 'When Jackie got down to practise the cello she did so with such intensity that she could achieve a lot in a short time.'

To begin with, Jackie still had plenty of time for other activities. She and Alison often went away together for weekends, sometimes visiting the Clwyds' family home in North Wales to play chamber music.

Another time I took Jackie down to Bernard Robertson's music camp, which had been started some time in the 1920s in a Berkshire field. It became an annual gathering which rapidly developed into a place of excellence. We participated in some choral singing. Jackie had a nice untrained singing voice, but she stood out from the mass of voice because she sang as she played, with complete involvement and intensity. Ordinary choristers just sang the notes, whereas Jackie gave them this wonderful shape and expression, even getting to the top of a phrase a little bit earlier than the conductor if she felt like it.

In the first months of their flat sharing George Debenham was very much in evidence, often accompanying Jackie on her chamber music expeditions and ready with his car to drive her wherever she wanted. But as Alison noted,

During the time she lived with me she was learning about men. One could say that she enjoyed testing her powers of charisma. As she grew in confidence Jackie became more radiant and also more aware. She had a wonderful capacity for relating to men, but she could be quite provocative. As time went on, she had to learn to calculate more and more. Particularly when she was around twenty or twenty-one, when she was having a lot of 'men trouble', I noticed that she hardened up – or perhaps crystallised a bit more – as she came to terms with life.[19]

Jackie was catching up with life with a rapid intensity. Her independence gained, she entered into her twentieth year with growing confidence. As she realised her sexuality and flowered into womanhood she also matured as an artist. It was at this time that the musician and cellist that we know and love from recordings came into being.

II

To Be A Cellist

But God has a few of us whom he whispers in the ear.
The rest may reason and welcome; 'tis we musicians know.
                                        Robert Browning, 'ABT Vogler'

Jackie had not given another London recital since her Wigmore Hall début in March 1961. She owed her growing reputation largely to the enormous success of her Elgar concerto performances. After the interruption of her concert activity the du Pré comeback was signalled by two concerts with her new duo partner George Malcolm. The first of these, an all Bach programme, was given at Westminster Abbey on 7 January 1964, three weeks before her nineteenth birthday. Here Jackie performed Bach's Suite No.5 in C minor for unaccompanied Cello and the Gamba Sonatas No.2 in D and No.3 in G minor with Malcolm, who balanced out the programme performing the English Suite No.1 for Solo Keyboard. Although preferring the mixed sound of cello with piano, Malcolm felt that the harpsichord was more fitting to the acoustic and the occasion. Proceeds from the concert, sponsored by the British–Italian society, were to go to the Vincent Novello Memorial Fund with the aim of acquiring a new chamber organ.

As Edward Greenfield of the *Guardian* pointed out, Westminster Abbey was hardly the place one would choose for a cello and harpsichord recital: 'It said much for the playing of George Malcolm and Jacqueline du Pré that in spite of the inevitably tiny sound their presence filled the Abbey.' Greenfield was much impressed by Jackie's rendering of unaccompanied Bach, which for him provided the musical climax of the concert. In particular, he singled out her masterly playing of the central sarabande, where Bach compresses into a few bars a whole world of expression. The sorrowful melodic line made up of falling phrases has an enormous range of harmonic implication and in its emotional power is worthy of the lamentoso arias of Bach's passion music. Greenfield particularly admired the way du Pré differentiated the moods in the C minor sarabande and the adagio of the Third Gamba Sonata in G minor: 'For both Miss du Pré's tone was hushed and intense, but in the solo work she conveyed stark tragedy, and in the other a mood of yearning and wistfulness.'[1]

Interestingly enough, in this review Greenfield found du Pré's 'intense style of Bach playing [to be] very close to that of her master Tortelier'. This last comment evidently must have irritated Jackie considerably, since in a roundabout way her displeasure was brought to Greenfield's notice. This did not affect his opinion, however, since several months later, in his review of Jackie's 3 September Prom, he unrepentantly affirmed the notable influence of Tortelier: 'I was taken to task recently for underlining [Miss du Pré's] affinity as a player with Tortelier from whom she has taken lessons. Her English teachers, I was told, were more vital in her development. That may well be so, but the likeness in style with Tortelier is now even more striking than it was, and I cannot think it a coincidence that her maturing in the Elgar concerto had come at a time of study with the great French master.'[2]

Concluding his review of the Westminster Abbey recital, Greenfield declared: 'On the showing [du Pré's] interpretative judgement is unerring, and I can hardly wait for her to make records of this music.' One can only regret that EMI did not sit up and take note. However, this concert was relayed direct by the BBC Third Programme. I, for one, was introduced to the Gamba Sonatas thanks to this broadcast and I clearly remember my mother's thrilled reaction to this beautiful music in such a vibrant interpretation. Unfortunately, it would appear that the BBC tapes have been lost.

Jackie's next London concert took place at the Royal Festival Hall on 1 February at a Robert Mayer children's morning concert, where she performed the Saint-Saëns concerto with the LSO conducted by Trevor Harvey. This was the first of three Festival Hall dates in a space of as many months. On 25 March 1964 she was scheduled to play at the same hall the Brahms Double Concerto with the violinist Erich Gruenberg, but the performance was cancelled at the request of Antal Doráti, chief conductor BBC Symphony Orchestra, for reasons that I have been unable to establish. As the BBC agreed to pay Jackie her fee in full, it certainly meant that for her part she had been willing to honour the obligation.

On 17 March Jackie was back at the Festival hall performing a recital in aid of Central Tutorial School for Young Musicians with George

Malcolm at the piano. Their programme was made up of the Bach D major, the Beethoven A major and Debussy Sonatas, and finished with de Falla's *Suite Populaire*, which she had played at her Wigmore with such success.

The critic David Cairns used his review as an opportunity to draw attention to the 'grey mediocrity' of British musical education, pleading for the creation of better opportunities for young musicians. Du Pré was a 'lonely eminence', a notable exception who, at the age of nineteen could already fill the Festival Hall. 'She would of course be seen as a shining light anywhere, even in Moscow; but there she would be seen as the highest culmination of the system.' Cairns continued with an indictment of the English establishment. '[It] will instinctively try to stifle [du Pré] in that terrible atmosphere of cosy complacency and mediocrity. But she will surely resist it. She is such a wonderfully alive player. Almost every phrase she plays suggests a musician who knows where she is going yet would always be prepared to learn a different truth. Her rhythm is good, her phrasing generous and sensible, her attack reckless but controlled.'

Cairns's fears that Jackie would fall victim to the 'cosy complacency' of the musical establishment fortunately proved unjustified. She succeeded, rather, in being admired and accepted by it without losing a whit of her independence, vitality and commitment.

In the large space of the Festival Hall the acoustic was not always friendly to the cello. In Jackie's performance Cairns felt: 'Sometimes her splendid spirit outstrips her strength – we feel the sense and shape and fiery purpose of a scale passage or a rapid sequence of arpeggios rather than actually hear it.' His other critical comments concerned a lack of grandeur and tension in the Beethoven A major and an element of over-earnest intent in the second movement siciliana (adagio) of Bach's D major Sonata. Cairns felt that she played the de Falla 'with a touching seriousness which was beautiful and quite wide of the mark'. But he praised her admirable Debussy Sonata, where 'the smoothest phrases had the devil in them'. Her encore, Schubert's 'Wiegenlied', was exquisite: 'Only an artist of rare gifts and rarer attainment could have played it so.'[3]

Neville Cardus, already a convinced admirer of du Pré's talent, wrote a somewhat quirky review of the same concert, in which his main contention was the paucity of the cello repertoire. He, for one, would far rather have been listening to the Elgar concerto. He concluded his review with a wish that was to be granted within a year: 'Miss du Pré might look at the score of the forgotten Delius Cello Concerto. It isn't a masterpiece by any means. But there are passages in it which could well have been especially composed to emphasise Miss du Pré's gift for beautifully phrased poetic melody.'⁴

Cardus and other fans of du Pré's Elgar didn't have long to wait for her next performance of the concerto, which took place at the RFH on 7 April with John Pritchard conducting the London Philharmonic. This time the critics were in a less generous mood. *The Times* reviewer, while praising her 'almost impeccable' technique, felt the work required 'an interpretation of a degree of maturity which is beyond Miss du Pré's present achievement'. One might explain the critic's grumble by the apparent lack of sympathy between Jackie and the conductor John Pritchard.

It is certainly difficult to believe that that du Pré's interpretation of the Elgar at this concert was in any way lacking in maturity. It is true that the three extant BBC recordings of Jackie's Elgar performances between 1962 and 1965 provide evidence of the enormous qualitative growth and mellowing of her interpretation. Her 1963 version with Sargent already displays an extraordinarily complete vision of the music. Jackie herself never took much notice of what the critics said. She judged herself severely and knew full well if her playing had fallen short of her own high standards.

Whatever the critics may have thought, it was this work that the British public wanted to hear. Jackie explained that she played the Elgar so much because 'this is the work I am always asked to do. I like all the concertos – Dvořák, Schumann, Haydn, Saint-Saëns. They all reflect different moods.' At the same time she expressed her views on the responsibility of an interpreter: 'One can always associate oneself with the expression of the music, but one should not use the music for self-expression only. It's important to give what the music itself wants to say.'⁵

In fact, in the first six months of 1964 Jackie actually played very few concerts. Those she did were almost exclusively in London. This was partly due to choice and partly to the fact that her agents needed time to book her engagements. After her period of study in Paris and her subsequent time of uncertainty, Jackie will not have given the go-ahead to Mrs Tillett to make bookings for her until quite late in 1963. Bearing in mind the time factor involved in procuring engagements, which must be booked at least a year, if not two, in advance (nowadays top-class artists have to plan their concerts as much as four seasons in advance), Ibbs and Tillett was only able to start filling her diary in the latter half of 1964. Apart from two performances of the Elgar (one in April and her annual August Prom), orchestral engagements were notably absent in du Pré's schedule, whereas in the following 1964–5 season she was booked to play with most of the British provincial orchestras.

In early June 1964 Jackie returned for the last time to Sermoneta. This year, having established her own circle of friends in London, she was not quite so keen on spending the best part of two months away from home. She wrote to her parents the day after her arrival. 'Since having seen quite a lot of people I really like recently, the people here just seem so false I can't stand it.' Her remarks were directed at the predominantly Argentinian contingent of students at the course, followers of Alberto Lysy. Despite her 'throat-gripping reunion' with the Argentinians, she found their attitudes to life superficial: 'I have managed to meet insincerity with insincerity, which is quite fun as a game. When I arrived last night I set out to woo everyone with my sparkling humour and spontaneity (English inferiority complex), and judge my pleasure when I heard one Argentinian (married) say " *Quelle crétine*". However, that impression slightly deteriorated when I suddenly got bored and couldn't be bothered to act.' But the formal socialities also gave way to light-hearted entertainment. Once, dressed up as an Indian chief with toothpaste smeared on her face, Jackie strode up to Alberto Lysy, seated at the head of the dining-table, and 'with the excuse of my disguise, poured contempt on him in proud and unpardoning Indian fashion'.[6]

Her mood improved as the festival went on. Once again, there were the informal evening concerts in the outside piazzale of the Castle, where the musicians had to vie with the chirping of cicadas and the swarms of dancing fireflies in the languorous Mediterranean night. Jackie's friends Ana Chumachenko and Oscar Lysy had now become engaged. They decided to celebrate their marriage in the Castle of Sermoneta on 25 July 1964 and invited Jackie and Alberto Lysy to act as witnesses.

Ana had noticed changes in Jackie's life; she had matured considerably and gained much confidence in the course of this last year. But Jackie had also started to think about things more, and in Ana's view this increasing awareness obscured something of her natural spontaneity, not only in her everyday behaviour, but in her playing.[7]

For Jackie, the music-making included first performances of two favourite works by Schubert: the *Trout* Quintet D667, and the C major Quintet D956 (with two cellos). Ana and Oscar played in the groups with her, and in the latter the American cellist Daniel Domb played the second cello part. In a later BBC interview Jackie explained what it was that appealed to her about playing chamber music: 'One of the responsibilities of the cello as the lowest instrument in an ensemble is to support the weight of the other instruments. I am very proud of this role and enjoy it secretly. But I remember an occasion playing the *Trout* Quintet last summer in Italy's blazing sun when I suddenly became aware of the double-bass bursting in beneath me. I was thrilled, but my pride was sorely shaken and I felt my position had been usurped.'[8]

The highlight of the Sermoneta Festival that year was Yehudi Menuhin's participation in the chamber music concerts. Menuhin agreed to come to Sermoneta for a week as an opportunity to rehearse with Alberto Lysy in a relaxed atmosphere, before going on with him to Israel to play the two Brahms string sextets. Menuhin brought with him two of the other players: the viola-player Ernst Wallfisch and the cellist Maurice Gendron. But it was decided that in Sermoneta Jackie and Oscar Lysy, Alberto's viola-player brother, would substitute for the two local Israeli musicians booked to join the core group in Israel. Menuhin described the special quality of these Sermoneta performances of the Brahms sextets as 'that same natural, joyous music-making that is the dream of all musicians'.[9]

It was at Ninfa, as Menuhin recalled, that Jackie first confided in him about a problem of an 'ongoing, uncooperative right hand'. While at the time he thought it was nothing more than a passing discomfort, he later attributed 'this worrying sensation in her right arm [as] the first indication, I suppose, of the impending nightmare...'[10]

On her return to London Jackie was scheduled to play the Elgar for the third year running at the Proms. But this time William Glock, the Controller of Radio Three and Director of the Proms, suggested that she perform in the same programme a new concerto commissioned by the BBC from the South African-born woman composer Priaulx Rainier. This form of programming was representative of Glock's new policy of integrating contemporary music into popular programmes to guarantee audiences for new works. After a difficult new piece, the public was rewarded with a popular favourite. It was also Glock's way of gently undermining Malcolm Sargent's monopoly of conducting as many Prom concerts as possible. Younger, more enterprising conductors were able to take on the contemporary repertoire which lay outside Sargent's range of interests. In this instance Jackie played with two conductors – the Elgar concerto with Sargent and the Rainier with Norman Del Mar.

William Glock was a particular champion of Priaulx Rainier's music. In commissioning a cello concerto for du Pré, he hoped that Jackie's enormous popularity with the Promenaders would ensure that a large and predominantly young audience would come to listen to what they tended to regard as difficult, if not downright incomprehensible music.

Jackie's expressed interest in contemporary music was always minimal. Until this time, she had only performed a couple of twentieth-century pieces, including Bartók's First Rhapsody and Ibert's Concerto for Cello and Winds. Through her brother-in-law Kiffer, she must have been aware of Gerald Finzi and the national school of British composers. Kiffer was also responsible for an introduction to the young composer Jeremy Dale-Roberts, who was a student of Priaulx Rainier at the Royal College of Music. Jeremy remembers being recruited by Iris in her efforts to widen Jackie's horizons. Seeing in him a congenial and well-educated companion for her daughter, Iris asked him to take Jackie 'to see some paintings'. Although they did make at least one visit to the Tate Gallery, Jackie's friendship with Jeremy was centred on their common love of music. It is possible that he had introduced her to Priaulx and her music before she wrote the cello concerto for Jackie. Dale-Roberts recalled that 'Priaulx was rather thrilled that a young player – and a woman – was to perform the concerto, although she had a wee bit of misgiving as to whether Jackie's pronounced style might not accommodate itself to the music'.[11]

Despite Jackie's claims to have little interest in contemporary music, she brought to the new works she did learn the same commitment and enthusiasm as to anything else she played. The pianist Guthrie Luke remembered being impressed by how quickly she absorbed the music. 'I asked her at the time she was preparing the Rainier concerto if she needed time to get comfortable with the piece. She replied scornfully, "Of course I don't need to, I know it already." ' To others, like Hugh Maguire, Jackie complained how difficult it was to learn the notes. But she had an amazing gift of assimilation – Daniel Barenboim reckoned that she was capable of taking in about seventy per cent of a score at first sight.

Dale-Roberts remembered that Jackie had some preliminary rehearsals with Rainier where Tim Baxter, another of her composition students, played through the concerto on the piano. But as so often with first performances there was insufficient time for the orchestral rehearsals to prepare the new work thoroughly. As Jeremy recalled, 'Priaulx complained a bit about this. She could not tolerate any rhythmic untidiness. Her fast music is very nervous, Stravinskian and fragmentary. Precision, in this rhythmic sense, was probably not Jackie's strong point, although overall she played it incredibly well. But there was a rhetorical quality in the work which suited Jackie ideally. Even if it wasn't the kind of musical language that she was used to, her extraordinary instinct ensured that she did do a good job.'

In Rainier's own concert note provided for the première of the Cello Concerto she declared that 'in writing a concerted work for solo violoncello the approach was governed by the rhetorical nature and power of the instrument. The scoring is light with frequent use of solo wind instruments. String groups are employed in opposition to wind groups more frequently than in combination, and percussion is used to add sharpness or as extended resonance to the textures.' The concerto consists of three movements, performed without a break, where each movement's title conveys it character – Dialogue, Canto, Cadence and Epilogue.

The National Sound Archive holds a tape of the BBC recording, which vividly portrays du Pré's qualities as an interpreter of new music. In the opening movement the cello acts as a protagonist in a drama, while the orchestra's role is that of commentator rather than full partner of the Dialogue. The cello's extended line employs leaping intervals within a sustained cantilena, which is well served by the rich quality of Jackie's sostenuto sound. Indeed, she has that rhetorical speaking quality that befits a dialogue and she makes a confident orator. In contrast in the sparsely accompanied second movement, Canto, she conveys a sense of suspended time and space, where the rhapsodic meditation of the cello is cushioned against a static background of orchestral colour. Further contrast appears at the end of the movement, when the cello springs into a volatile cadenza punctuated by orchestral tutti episodes – this heralds the opening of the third movement. Jackie has just the right dynamic energy to stimulate these whimsical flourishes of dialogue, and she underlines the scherzo-like character of the first part of the finale.

This mood eventually dissolves into a Epilogue reminiscent of the meditative Canto, and the work ends in a mood of hushed calm.

Rainier's Cello Concerto is a difficult and fragmentary piece. Certainly it is not easy on the ears and at first hearing appears dissonant, although based on elements of tonal harmony. The cello is often used in its gruffer registers and in general, Jackie had to employ an intense level of forte in the fast music in order to project over the orchestra. Rostropovich, who has performed well over a hundred new concertos for cello and orchestra, attributes the success of a new work to a large extent to the ability of the composer to orchestrate suitably for the cello – with particular care not to obscure the lower and middle registers. Certainly some of the spiky orchestral textures in Rainier's Cello Concerto bring to mind an alleged comment of William Walton who, after a performance of Rainier's powerfully rhythmic *Sinfonia da Camera*, made a bet that the composer 'wore barbed-wire underwear'.

As Jeremy Dale-Roberts recalled, 'Jackie's rhetorical playing had a real function in the work, and especially in the central Canto movement. But by and large, it was a scrappy performance for a Prom. And it was a bitter grief to Priaulx that Jackie never played the concerto again after the première.'

Not that the critics commented on signs of insufficient preparation in the performance. Edward Greenfield wrote that despite the somewhat ungrateful material of Rainier's concerto, 'du Pré's playing almost convinced one that this was a great work. It is certainly a formidable one – the composer in as little need of feminine apology as the soloist . . .' But he expected that 'Miss du Pré will have more beautiful and rewarding concertos written for her before long, particularly if she continues to play with such committed artistry'.[12]

The *Daily Telegraph* critic sounded less convinced of the merits of the concerto, which he described as '[a work] of uncompromising austerity. Yet through the splendid advocacy of Miss du Pré and Norman Del Mar, one senses a tender, expressive lyricism.'[13]

It was, as always, Jackie's performance of the Elgar concerto that won her the highest accolades. David Cairns once more noted that du Pré showed 'more good intention than achievement in terms of sustained line, warmth of tone and power . . .' but commended the 'memorable mood of withdrawn, elegiac resignation and regret' in the first movement.[14] But Greenfield noted an ever-increasing authority in du Pré's interpretation: 'Her sense of repose is more intense than ever. The sweep of her bowing arm and the backward shake of her head more commanding – reminding one continually of Augustus John's portrait of Suggia. [. . .] If one has a reservation it is that when she tries to play really loudly then she loses the sweetness of tone and defeats her object.' Again, it was the magical quality of Jackie's sound in piano that left a lasting impression: 'It was the quiet lyrical playing, unforced and pure, that carried best and had the audience hanging on each note.'[15]

On this note of optimism, Jackie prepared herself for the 1964–5 season, her first complete one as a fully committed concert artist. It held much excitement in store, with dates with many orchestras outside London, the formation of a new duo partnership with Stephen Bishop, her first concerto recording in January 1965 and her USA début planned for May 1965. And, as if to reward her for her commitment to a full-scale international career, she was to receive as a gift one of the world's most renowned cellos.

Although already in possession of a Stradivarius, Jackie was becoming aware of its limitations. The fact that its loud sounds did not project in the hall had been picked up recently by the critics. The instrument dealer and expert Charles Beare, who had first met Jackie in December 1963, described the cello as 'a large-model early-period Stradivarius dating from the 1670s, without the original label inside it. The cello had been cut down in the nineteenth century in length but not in width, so it has the approximate proportions of a Montagnano cello. But it remains quite big and heavy. As it has been quite patched about on the inside, it doesn't have the response of a freshly preserved instrument. I always describe it as a bit of a brute, but in a sense it matched Jackie as she was such a forceful player.'[16]

While Jackie was studying in Paris, Tortelier had confirmed her doubts about the instrument, finding it to be over bass-orientated, with limited carrying power on the top strings. He suggested that a new bridge and other changes to the set-up might improve the sound. Jackie wrote to Iris from Paris in the autumn of 1962, explaining that: 'Tortelier also wants something done to the A string, because he is convinced that it is not my fault when I force. If nothing can be done having tried this, one can conclude that the cello will never be more open.'[17] Tortelier also suggested that Jackie should change to metal strings. While commending the great warmth and individual beauty of gut strings, he spoke of their technical disadvantages. 'The attack is problematic: the gut doesn't respond quickly to the bow and tends to be scratchy. It is also susceptible to changes in weather and intonation becomes variable. As gut is supple, it will not resist the pressure of the bow beyond a certain degree and so you must limit your power.'[18]

But even when the cello was set up with a new bridge, a hollow sound post, a curved end-spike and metal strings, Jackie felt her Strad had not improved sufficiently. She complained that she had to work very hard to get the best out of it and even so she could not project the sound.

Jackie had told Beare that she was looking for a spare cello and explained her reservations about her present Strad. 'What she liked about it was its robust strength – it travelled well. But she didn't like its restricted palette of colours – it didn't have the diversity of shades that a great Strad could obtain.'

At the time Beare had nothing in stock that was suitable for Jackie. 'Then, towards the end of 1964, she informed me that there was somebody who wanted to buy her a really fantastic cello and asked if I knew of one. It so happened that the "Davydov" Strad was for sale in New York, and I phoned up Rembert Wurlitzer, the instrument dealer who had been commissioned to sell it. I arranged with him for the cello to be brought to London for Jackie to try out.'

The instrument dates from Stradivarius's golden period, by which time the Cremonese master had established a slightly smaller sized cello as his standard model. From the late 1680s this model came to replace the larger Cremonese 'churchbass' cello. As Beare has remarked, the Davydov not only has a fantastic pedigree, but a very unusual story. 'We can trace its ownership back over 150 years, to the moment when in the mid-1800s Count Wielhorski acquired the cello from Count Apraxin in exchange for a Guarneri cello, a certain sum of roubles and the finest horse in his stable. On his seventieth birthday, in 1863, Count Wielhorski presented the cello to the great Russian cellist Karl Davydov who played on it until his death.'

According to the Hill book of 1902, the instrument was then taken to Paris, where it was sold to a wealthy amateur in 1900. It transferred hands again in 1928 and was sold to Herbert N. Straus, an American business executive. When he died his widow asked Rembert Wurlitzer to sell the instrument on her behalf. By this stage the cello was dubbed after its most illustrious owner the 'Davidoff' or more correctly the 'Davydov', with the accent on the middle syllable.

Beare recalled that when Jackie came to his shop to try out the Davydov, William Pleeth was also in the room. 'Jackie played it first, then handed it to Pleeth, who also tried it and was most enthusiastic. "It's a wonderful cello, one of the really great instruments of the world. The only thing is whether it suits you and that you must decide for yourself." Jackie played it for a few days, fell in love with it and agreed to take it.' She found that it responded in a completely different way from any other cello she had played before. She loved experimenting with the way it produced sound and found that with the right kind of gentle coaxing it could offer an incredibly fine palette of colours.

Once again, the generous benefactor was Mrs Holland who, as previously, insisted on her gift remaining anonymous. Through her solicitors Beare was instructed to acquire the Davydov on Jackie's behalf for the sum of $90,000, a vast amount of money at the time. Mrs Holland recalled that when she made this final gift to Jackie she decided to talk to her about its value as an investment. 'You know, dear child, this instrument is extremely valuable, very expensive. You must hang on to it as it's the only thing you've got. If anything happens to you [how strange that I should have said so] you've got this to sell.'

Jackie had abandoned her uncovered gut strings soon after she started playing concertos with orchestra. Then Tortelier had persuaded her to change to all-metal strings, but as Charles Beare recalled, when she acquired the Davydov she made a compromise about its set-up. Initially, she used covered gut on the bottom two strings and metal-wound strings on the top two – Beare specifies them as Eudoxa silver covered G & C and Prim Orchestra A & D. Only later did she switch over to all metal strings, choosing Prim Orchestra strings because they are hard and resistant.

A good bow is nearly as important to a player as a good instrument, and is responsible for approximately thirty per cent of the quality of sound. The quality of a bow is judged by its equilibrium and by the resilience and response of the stick, which is usually made from a hard but elastic Brazilian wood, pernambucco. As Beare recalled, Jackie liked heavy bows.

When I first knew her she was playing on Hill bows. Then I found her a really super Dodd, which she just adored. She preferred that to the Tourtes or Packards that she tried. When I showed her a bow and asked her what she thought of it, she would immediately play right next to the bridge, bending the bow in a curve with all the hair absolutely steady on the string. One day her mother was bringing the Dodd in for rehair and the bow got caught in the car door – it was such a strong stick it didn't break, but it bent round at an angle. That was the end of that bow. I cast around for another Dodd similar to that one and I came across a Palormo, so I gave that to Jackie who used it for the rest of her playing career. It was a very heavy bow.

To stop her thumb slipping on the stick, she added rubber tubing over the entire handle area of her bows. Beare recalled that with this addition the Palormo bow weighed in at 105 grams, which he believes to be a world record! Jackie would never consider using a bow by another maker and acquired a second Palormo to use as a spare.

When conditions were right the Davydov was a glorious instrument to play. In her recordings we can hear its golden, rounded sound, akin to the human voice in its emotional power, with wonderful shimmering colours in the softer range and a rich but unforced power in the louder. Ultimately, like all great players, du Pré brought her own individual sound to any instrument she played. There is tangible evidence of this from her recordings. Whether they were made in the studio or taken from direct broadcasts of concerts, whether a Stradivarius or a modern instrument was used, the idiosyncratic 'du Pré sound' is always identifiable. Nevertheless, in the recordings made between 1965 and early 1968, during the three years when Jackie played almost exclusively on the Davydov, we can hear an extra luminous sheen in the cello sound, a result of the combination of an outstanding player and an incomparable instrument.

12

A Budding Partnership

O youth! The strength of it, the faith of it, the imagination of it!
Joseph Conrad, *Youth*

'A wet election night might seem to offer poor prospects for the début of a youthful instrumental duo; but the Goldsmiths Hall was packed for the City Music Society's concert on Thursday. The two players concerned were Jacqueline du Pré and Stephen Bishop; each has built up within the last few years so big a reputation that curiosity about their association was only natural. The cellist and pianist make a well-matched pair, whose playing was consistently musical, if still occasionally tentative. Just now they are at a stage where mutual consideration is more noticeable than the strong corporate character which should develop with time.'[1]

As the critic of the *Sunday Times* pointed out, Jackie's newly formed partnership with Stephen Bishop came into being the same night that Harold Wilson's Labour Party was elected to power, on 15 October 1964.

It was originally Mrs Tillett's idea to put the two brightest young stars on her roster together. Stephen Bishop (now known as Stephen Kovacevich), an American of Croat origin, came to London originally to study with Myra Hess. Five years older than du Pré, he had given his début at the Wigmore Hall in 1961, the same year as she did, and soon made his name as one of the most exciting pianists of his generation and as a fine interpreter of the classics – notably Beethoven. He has always been an uncompromising artist and even today his playing can provoke in fellow musicians both the highest esteem and complete disagreement.

Stephen had heard Jackie's début recital. He recalled that 'I had the impression of a great flash of talent and I was completely bewildered and enraptured by it. I did think that Jackie played as if she was in love with the cello. She looked lovely on stage.'[2]

When Jackie went over to his house at Emmie Tillett's suggestion early in 1964 they read through some music and immediately decided that they wanted to play together. For Jackie it was a relief to be able to plan duo concerts, which would allow her to share with a like-minded colleague of her own age the habitual discomforts and loneliness of an itinerant concert artist's life.

At their Goldsmiths Hall début, Bishop and du Pré played four sonatas: Bach's Third Gamba Sonata in G minor, Beethoven's Op.5 No.2 (in the same key), Brahms's E minor and Britten's recently composed work. The *Sunday Times* critic praised the players' ability to shape and colour the phrases of the slower, more lyrical music, while finding that they sometimes lacked vigorous attack and definition in the faster movements. They were commended for their 'gallant shot' at Benjamin Britten's sonata (which was written for Rostropovich in 1961), although the reviewer felt – not surprisingly – that they were unable to emulate 'the surprise and wit and deceptively casual air with which the music is invested by Rostropovich and the composer'. According to this review, Bishop came over as the more decisive of the two players, although in terms of sound volume he seemed to be holding himself back.

Edward Greenfield, who had the highest regard for Bishop as a pianist (and still calls him 'one of my top favourites'), also expressed certain reservations about the balance between cello and piano in his review of a concert of the duo at Camden School on 11 March 1965. Greenfield recalled, 'They played Beethoven Op.69 and a Brahms sonata. Altogether I was a bit disappointed. Although Jackie was marvellously positive, Stephen didn't seem altogether sympathetic, he appeared rather over-compensating. I said as much when I reviewed the concert. It was through this that I got to know Stephen, as he wrote to me saying that he thought that I had been unfair.'[3]

In fact, Stephen had contacted Greenfield to explain that, due to the well-meaning interference of Iris du Pré, his playing had not represented his musical intentions. Iris had came round backstage in the interval and suggested that Stephen should close the lid of the piano, since the cello sound was being covered. Stephen agreed, one imagines with some reluctance, and recalls that he felt his playing was over-subdued as a result.

Generally speaking, Bishop would be the first to admit that it took him time to achieve a good balance in the duo, since he had had no previous experience of chamber music before playing with Jackie. In any case, it is notoriously hard to find the ideal balance with cello, particularly in those works where the piano-writing is thick and covers the same middle-bass register of the cello part.

The début recital at Goldsmiths Hall had also served as an audition for the BBC; a representative producer had gone, listened and noted his approval in a laconic message on the new duo's contract notes – 'Accept'. At the beginning of February 1965 they made their first recording for the BBC – a studio broadcast of Beethoven's G minor sonata Op.5 No.2 and the Britten sonata. The first movement of the former, and second and fourth movements of the latter, were also used to illustrate du Pré's sonata playing in the last of a series of four weekly radio programmes entitled *Artist of the Month*. Although the duo was thereafter extensively recorded in live concerts by the BBC, it would seem that only this extract of their first studio recording is extant.

Eleanor Warren, the BBC producer who worked on most of their performances, recalled that the BBC's policy about preserving tapes was fairly arbitrary and depended mostly on the producer's recommendation. 'But often other producers might want to use part of a recording for their programme before the original went out on the air, then they would wipe it because it had become part of another programme. Ultimately it was to do with economy of storage space – the old reel-to-reel tapes took up a lot of room and were costly to maintain in the right conditions.'

Eleanor Warren was not a committed admirer of the duo. For instance, she felt that at the second of two Royal Festival Hall recitals that she recorded on 7 November 1966 Stephen's sound was too harsh and tended to cover Jackie: 'It wasn't something I would have wanted to keep, because the balance wasn't good,' she said.

Finding a good balance between cello and piano in the conditions of a live concert is hard enough and the acoustic of the Festival Hall (particularly before it was revamped in the early 1970s) does not favour this combination. Warren's opinion reflected her personal taste, as well as the professional problems of a recording team, which has to achieve a good microphone balance. Many musicians who were present at that concert still have glowing memories of it and would have felt otherwise. Bishop recalls that at the time both he and Jackie had a very positive feeling about their performance.

Many of those who came to hear the duo were already acquainted with one of the players. As Vladimir Ashkenazy recalled, 'I knew and greatly admired Stephen's playing, but I had never heard Jackie. Then I went to one of the duo's London recitals and I was amazed, knocked off my feet by this combination. They played the *Fantasiestücke* by Schumann and the Beethoven A major Sonata. It was the first time I heard the Beethoven and I found it marvellous. They had a wonderful energy between them.'[4]

The composer, Jeremy Dale-Roberts, got to know Stephen through Jackie and was won over by their musical partnership:

> They had an extraordinary relationship, musical as well as human. I was in love with them both and it was incredible to see this chemistry going on between them when they performed. They were very different kinds of musicians and in many ways they were incompatible, as they operated on quite different tracks. Therefore the fusions – or rather the collisions – between them made for some extraordinary music-making – indeed, to my mind some of the most exciting duo playing I have ever heard.

Guthrie Luke, a long-standing admirer of Jackie's playing, also liked the duo's energy, although he expressed reservations about some of their interpretations. He attended a lunch-time concert for the Law Society at the Strand on 25 May 1965. 'They played the Brahms E minor Sonata, which I didn't like that much, as I found the first movement was *so* slow and the last movement was too fast for my taste. And I think that Stephen played somewhat too loudly for the hall.' The other work in the programme was the Britten sonata, of which, as Guthrie remembers, Jackie's mother expressed an emphatic dislike. Jackie was using her newly acquired Davydov Strad and asked Guthrie's opinion as to how it sounded in the hall. 'I remember telling her that the cello's bass was just out of this world. But I made a stupid comment about the higher register, saying it sounded like a tenor trying to be a soprano. Jackie just laughed and I was forgiven.'[5]

Dale-Roberts often wondered at the time how Stephen and Jackie negotiated their rehearsals. 'Jackie had this instantaneous grasp of the music – of the meaning of a one-line musical text. This might indicate that she would only want to do the music one way, that she would not cogitate – "maybe we could turn it this way". The intelligent way that an interpretation is built in collaboration with a partner would probably have been foreign to her.'

In fact, Jackie explained her approach to chamber music on the radio in the fourth of the BBC *Artist of the Month* programmes mentioned earlier. In a spoken introduction to the pieces she played with Bishop, she described duo playing as a 'thought-provoking combination of two artists. There are two different ways of looking at things which simply have to be reconciled. But it is enormously rewarding when they are fused.'

Jackie's words indicated a working process whereby each player had first established his own outlook, before moulding a mutually compatible and structured interpretation. Stephen recalled that in general he and Jackie were seldom at variance when playing together. Their rehearsal method involved playing through a movement, then sorting out questions about phrasing and breathing.

> Generally there wasn't much disagreement. In regard to tempi, we seemed to feel the same pulse. We did come to one conclusion, although not immediately, that should there be a basic disagreement, say about tempo, it was better to give one movement over to the other, rather than compromise. With compromise you have two miserable people; this way only one! And at least that movement had the conviction of somebody. In these cases we would say, 'OK, so you have this movement, and I'll get the next one!'

A successful performance is achieved through building an interpretation on the premise of mutual trust between the musicians involved. They must assume that they are listening out for the same things – the fine detail, which contributes to the shaping of each phrase and the basic elements that constitute the overall musical structure. Indeed, artists seem to possess a sixth sense, whereby they recognise and identify with the aims of their partners in the very act of playing. Should something in the phrasing or ensemble feel unconvincing during a play-through, it is usually sufficient to repeat the section once or twice for everything to fall into place naturally and to render discussion unnecessary. Ask any orchestral musician and he will tell you that words can waste time; an expressive gesture from the conductor and clarity of rhythm are far preferable to wordy explanations.

Stephen remembered one specific occasion when Jackie did ask him to adopt her ideas about the piano part and went to great lengths to explain them: 'During a rehearsal of the Debussy sonata, Jackie asked me to do the opening an inordinate amount of times so as to achieve a certain result. She wanted the initial declamation of the theme in the piano to be very spacious, while I felt it tighter and more classically. It's the only time I recall her working insistently on something with me; but I don't remember whether I got it or whether she gave up.'

As she matured, Jackie developed an extraordinarily acute ear which reinforced her natural intuition. Without being verbally articulate, she was extremely quick to perceive and assimilate another's ideas and this gave her great flexibility. Stephen had an enormous respect for her musicality and Jackie, on her part, was much impressed by the intellectual qualities in Stephen's playing (she particularly admired his *Diabelli Variations*, she once told me) and responded to the thrust and drive, and the taut structure of his music-making.

In the 1965–6 season, duo concerts formed a large part of Jackie's schedule. Ibbs and Tillett aimed at booking five a month, unless other work intervened in either of the artist's schedules. Hence, over the next three seasons, Stephen and Jackie played twenty-odd recitals during each season on the music-club circuit. Although most of their activity took place in Britain, the duo also performed in Germany, Portugal and the United States.

During the lifetime of the duo, Stephen and Jackie performed a dozen or so pieces from the mainstream repertoire: three of the five Beethoven sonatas, both the Brahms, Bach's Second Sonata for Viola da Gamba, Debussy and Franck sonatas and also Schumann's *Fantasiestücke*.

The classical cello repertoire is, of course, restricted and Stephen recalled that at one point they thought of commissioning a new piece. 'The Britten sonata was the most modern piece that we performed. We decided to approach Howard Ferguson, who adored Jackie's talent, to see if he would write something for us. Unfortunately, he never accepted our proposal, because by that time he had stopped composing music. To this day I regret it.'

In his earlier days Howard Ferguson had written some very fine chamber music and its intrinsically romantic style would have suited du Pré down to the ground. Ferguson already knew of Jackie through Mrs Holland and had first heard her play with Iris in the Hollands' Kensington house. But he recalled getting to know Jackie better when she and Stephen were visiting the Cotswold home of his friends Tony and Dorothy de Navarro. Stephen had played an afternoon recital in their house, and afterwards he and Jackie stayed on for supper and made music for their hosts. Ferguson vividly recalled that intimate occasion as 'a never-to-be-forgotten evening listening to the D major Cello Sonatas by Bach and Beethoven'.

When she later visited Howard Ferguson in his Hampstead home, Jackie complained that she had already played nearly all the important sonatas and concertos in the cello repertoire. Ferguson suggested that she should enlarge her musical perspective by playing more chamber music, which had virtually limitless possibilities.

In her introduction to the above-mentioned BBC *Artist of the Month* programme, Jackie talked about the superior pleasures of chamber music, explaining that greater rewards can be achieved by playing in small ensembles than with orchestra where, inevitably, rehearsal time is so limited. 'In chamber music, companionship and hard work are combined,' she declared, 'as long as the other players don't feel lazy.'[6] Indeed, Jackie came increasingly to enjoy exploring chamber music, not just for the wealth of repertoire *per se*, but as an opportunity to make music with friends informally.

She had gained her first important experiences of the genre in the summer festivals at Sermoneta. But in London, a city which attracted musicians from all over the world, there were now regular possibilities for informal music-making at a very high level. Not only Americans like Bishop came to London, but a large contingent of talented musicians from Eastern Europe (to mention a few important names among pianists only, Vladimir Ashkenazy, André Tchaikovsky, Tamás Vásáry, Peter Frankl and Fou Ts'ong were all resident in London at the time). As Zamira Menuhin (who was then married to Fou Ts'ong) noted, musicians in those days seemed to be in less of a hurry, performed fewer concerts and regarded music as something to be shared with friends and not just as a means of pursuing a career on the public platform.

Jackie's circle of musician friends was greatly extended through Stephen and she, like the rest of them, stayed up all night discussing life and music, listening to recordings or making chamber music for fun. Generally speaking, Jackie always much preferred making music than listening to it. But being an excellent and supportive colleague she would attend friends' concerts, and knew how to give advice and criticism in a very constructive way. Nevertheless, Stephen remembered that she rarely spoke about other musicians and, for instance, she never mentioned her studies with Casals or Tortelier.

Only on one occasion did Stephen recall her enthusing about another string player: 'She once phoned me and invited me over to listen to Jascha Heifetz's recording with Malcolm Sargent of the Bruch *Scottish Fantasy* and G minor Concerto. Jackie was in love with the recording and Heifetz at that moment was everything. She hated bad imitations in performance and she could not tolerate any form of mediocrity.'

Jackie benefited from the spirit of camaraderie that she encountered with Stephen and they seldom played concerts without musician friends in attendance. During a visit to Lisbon in November 1966 they were delighted to find a friend in town – the pianist Nelson Freire. Nelson offered to turn pages at their recital, perhaps not realising that page-turning requires particular skills of discretion. As Stephen recalled,

> When Nelson stood up to turn, he somehow always got in the way. Our arms got entangled and we started to get hysterical giggles. We found it very funny, although objectively it wasn't at all. I whispered to Nelson to leave the stage and he got up to do so, but realised he was laughing so much he couldn't move. He then sat down again and went on shaking with laughter. In all this my playing deteriorated considerably – I was playing fistfuls of wrong notes, making the music sound like Schoenberg rather than Brahms. I turned to Jackie to see what she was thinking, but she was playing, blissfully oblivious.

During her trip to the USA with the BBC SO in May 1965, Jackie struck up another important friendship with the orchestra's leader Hugh Maguire. She came to regard Hugh as a sort of partner in crime, who shared her passion for chamber music. She and Stephen played through piano trios with him and also with other violinists.

A lot of the music-making occurred in the home of the conductor Harry Blech who began his professional life as a violinist and in the late 1930s had formed a quartet with William Pleeth. During the war he discovered his true vocation when he started conducting, and founded the London Mozart Players in 1949 so as to explore the wealth of symphonic music by Haydn and Mozart. This, and the fact that he developed a problem with sensitive nerve-ends in the left-hand fingers, decided him to give up the violin professionally.

Harry recalled that Mrs Tillett rang him one day to say that Jackie was keen to play trios with him:

> I replied that I was very flattered, but I wouldn't recommend it, as I had virtually stopped playing the violin. However, Jackie came with Stephen

and in the next couple of years we played music quite frequently. Jackie and Stephen were very different kinds of musicians. I admired Stephen's playing and he was the first winner of the orchestra's Mozart memorial prize. He had a real feeling for Beethoven and was still close to Myra Hess. But I was less enthusiastic about his qualities as a chamber musician.[7]

As Hugh Maguire pointed out, most pianists needed to look at the notes beforehand, since the piano part is always much more complex than the single-line parts of the string players. 'Stephen was a very sweet person, very keen but he was not as relaxed as Jackie, who could sit down and play anything. Apart from Daniel Barenboim, the pianists we played with all needed to get to grips with the notes and to work it out beforehand.'

On one occasion when Stephen and Jackie were at Blech's house, the violinist Henryk Szeryng dropped by for some impromptu music-making. Blech recalled that the meeting was not entirely successful: 'The young artists had never met him before and reacted badly to his rather grand manner.'[8]

In fact, during this period both Stephen and Jackie appeared regularly as soloists with the London Mozart Players. In 1965, Jackie played three Festival Hall dates with Harry Blech and the LMP, performing both Haydn concertos and the Schumann. Gradually she grew beyond the range of the orchestra in terms of her international prestige and because of the steep rise in her fee – her last concert with them was in May 1967, playing Haydn and Boccherini's B flat major concerto (in Grütz-macher's arrangement). Harry Blech remembered these performances as very special. 'Her playing had this incredibly moving quality, which was quite unique. Once, when she played a concerto with us I noticed somebody in the orchestra crying – it was the only occasion I ever saw this. And she influenced the orchestral musicians and made them all play better.'

Guthrie Luke vividly recalled Jackie's first performance of the Haydn C major with Blech at the Royal Festival Hall on 23 June 1965. The concerto had recently been rediscovered and was taken up at once by Rostropovich, who was billed to play the first London performance. But Jackie actually pipped him to the post by a couple of weeks.

Before the concert Guthrie went backstage to wish Jackie luck and found her somewhat perplexed.

She showed me a telegram that Stephen had sent her with the message, 'Make Papa Haydn eat worms.' Jackie said, 'Whatever does he mean by it?' I replied that to my funny way of thinking Stephen was saying 'Bring the music back to life', because if Haydn himself were to return to life, he probably would be full of worms. Jackie laughed and accepted this suggestion. I remember asking her afterwards, 'When did Haydn write this concerto?' She had no idea and simply didn't care. There was no point in discussing such things with her. She played the work superbly, of course, without knowing anything about its background history.

As Stephen recalled they were serious about their music-making, but still very open-minded. 'Every concert was alive and different, we were very young. Jackie and I rarely entered into discussion after our performances, but if necessary we would set a few details right in the next rehearsal.' Jackie's natural exuberance and the freedom of her approach meant that she never repeated herself in music. For her, any fixed model of interpretation smacked of artifice.

In contrast, her free spirit and ingenuous naïvety could be quite disarming in everyday life. As Stephen recalled, she was totally unfettered by conventional education or social manners. Once, towards the beginning of their friendship, she revealed the extent of her ingenuousness. 'I was married at the time and my wife had a book by Freud on the kitchen table. Jackie wanted to give the impression that she was quite with it and said, "Oh, Freud, isn't he the one who invented the atomic bomb?" I couldn't believe my ears. Later, when she was ill, she was very much into psychoanalysis. I didn't know whether to remind her of that story, but then I decided that she would enjoy it. She roared with laughter and we would laugh about it many times thereafter.'

Guthrie Luke, too, remembered Jackie as sunny and open, and lots of fun to be with. She loved naughty stories and was a great tease. She enjoyed quoting a saying of Jean Cocteau's: 'Ordinary people go through life on a bus, an artist in a sports car.' When Guthrie acquired his first motor bike his friends thought he had taken leave of his senses. 'But Jackie didn't – she loved it. I took her for rides and I made her wear a helmet. On the first occasion I took her to Kew Gardens, where she had never been before; she loved the Gardens, but she liked the bike ride even more.'

Jackie took Guthrie to hear Stephen's Festival hall début.

It was the occasion when I first met Stephen. Jackie told me that Stephen was worried that people wouldn't know when the pieces were over and asked me to lead the clapping. He played the *Diabelli Variations* marvellously. Afterwards we went backstage, and Jackie asked me to go and talk to Stephen's wife. I asked Jackie quickly if she was a musician and she replied 'No'. We were duly introduced, and in order to make small chat I said, 'I hear that you are not a musician. I am sure that makes for greater harmony in the home.' My remark was met with dead silence. Jackie pulled me away quickly and whispered to me, 'You have just made a noise.' I started to protest and she interrupted, 'I think you'd better know that Stephen and I are having an affair.' I had really put my foot in it.

Coming from an American Catholic background, Stephen had married when he was only twenty years old and had children very early. When Jackie swept into his life with her dynamic musicality and her charismatic personality she was an irresistible force. Jackie, too, was attracted to Stephen, stimulated by his sharp, probing mind, his live musicality and his vivacious, if sometimes quirky, humour. Before long they became lovers.

For Jackie, entering into a complex adult world of entangled relationships was greatly exciting, but not always smooth sailing. She now had to extricate herself from her friendship with her first boy friend, George Debenham. George had provided her with support at a time she sorely needed it. While appreciating his devotion, Jackie had never reciprocated his deep feelings for her. When she broke off the relationship, Debenham was upset and didn't hide it. Perhaps for the first time in her life, Jackie had to cope with anger directed against her. But in the first flush of womanhood she was more concerned with moving through the adventure of life. Jackie relished her new-found confidence and enjoyed employing her considerable powers of fascination over people, and men in particular. Although her affair with Stephen was the first relationship of importance to Jackie and lasted for the better part of two years, it did not exclude other flirtations.

Stephen recalled that the idea of personal freedom was very important to Jackie at the time:

She felt that she should be free to have romances with whomsoever she wanted and she wished this for me as well. I didn't quite believe it at the time and I wasn't really free in this way. But Jackie put her feelings and action where her mouth was – she was very honest. This freedom was a

William Pleeth, Jacqueline's acknowledged 'cello Daddy', who taught her between the ages of 10 and 17.

Paul Tortelier. Jacqueline studied with the French cellist at the Paris Conservatoire for five months between October 1962 and March 1963.

Jacqueline with Mstislav Rostropovich, Moscow, April 1966. Jacqueline took half a year off her busy international career for lessons with the Russian cellist.

Jacqueline at a concert at Sermoneta, July 1963. Left to right: Alberto Lysy, Ana Chucmachenko, Jacqueline, Margaret Norris, Oscar Lysy.

Jacqueline on the beach near Sermoneta, 1964.

Jacqueline trying out a
double-bass, Sermoneta,
July 1964.

Jacqueline relaxing at the
castle in Sermoneta, 1964.

Steven Bishop and Jacqueline, featured in the 1965 BBC2 series 'In Rehearsal', preparin
for a performance of Beethoven's Seven Variations on a Theme from The Magic Flute.

Delius Concerto recording, January 1965. Listening to playback with Ronald Kinloch
Anderson and Sir Malcolm Sargent at the EMI studios.

Recording the Elgar Concerto with Sir John Barbirolli and the London Symphony Orchestra at Kingsway Hall, August 1965.

At the same recording, discussing a point with Sir John Barbirolli.

Jacqueline and the author standing by the banks of the Neva in Leningrad, May 1966.

A private lesson at Rostropovich's apartment, February 1966. Left to right: Mstislav Rostropovich, Stefan Kalyanov, Aza Amintaeva, the author and Jacqueline.

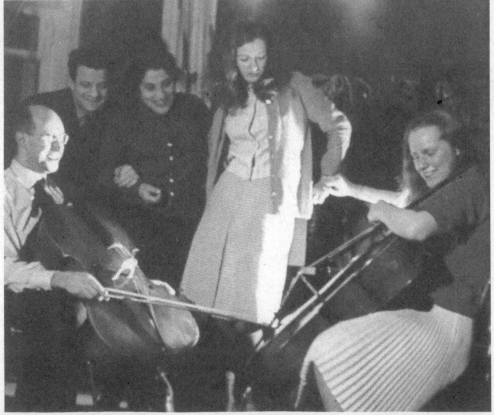

A lesson in Class 19 of the Moscow Conservatoire. Rostropovich makes a finer point to Jacqueline who turns to the author for a translation. Aza Amintaeva is at the piano and David Grigorian is turning the pages.

A still from the BBC2 programme 'An Evening with the Menuhins', 1966. Left to right: Yehudi Menuhin, Robert Masters, Walter Gerhardt, Jacqueline and Maurice Gendron.

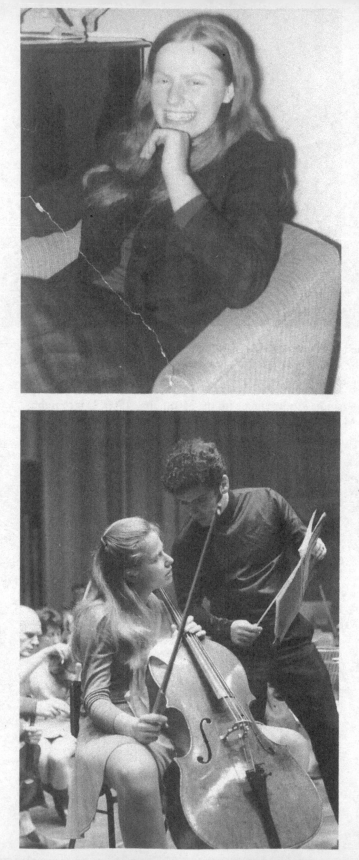

Jacqueline on the evening she met Daniel Barenboim, London, December 1966.

Jacqueline and Daniel rehearsing for their first concert together with the English Chamber Orchestra in London, April 1967.

philosophy of life she had developed consciously, and it was prompted from a great gush of talent and a great gush of love towards life and people. She wasn't trapped by laws, whereas as an ex-Catholic, I was all gummed up.

Stephen defined Jackie as the most generous person he has ever encountered. Her generosity manifested itself in her attitude to life and was the driving force behind her music-making.

Looking back on these times, Jeremy Dale-Roberts recalled them as very special, vivid and fantastic.

It was a marvellous time for all young musicians. Certain Proms and concerts are so clear in my memory. The way Jackie swung her hair around for instance. I remember that we played through the Rachmaninov sonata once or twice. It was then that I first realised that although an emotional player, Jackie was totally aware and almost manipulative in her ability to use emotion as an effect. Perhaps it was a sub-text of all her musical relationships that there should be some emotional traffic.

Her ability to combine spontaneity with the conscious and knowing gave an extra edge of excitement to Jackie's performances. She knew, in the way that a great singer knows, that the intrinsic emotional quality of the instrument (or voice) can be the most telling form of communication. Yet this physically sensuous aspect of her music-making never interfered with its integrity.

Jeremy remembered that Jackie and Stephen had cultivated their own term to describe their ability to manipulate the listeners' reactions.

They used to talk about the 'clit' factor in music, rather like film composers talking about a 'sting', when an effect has to be timed. Jackie knew exactly how to place things, she was very shrewd in her judgement of timing and this was what she meant by the 'clit' factor. It was something orgiastic on the one hand, but it also implied a conscious knowledge of when to press the button to exact a very particular frisson. An example of this in her marvellous playing of the repeated C transition into the Waltz in the recording of the Tchaikovsky Trio. Jackie's awareness of how to achieve a desired effect is absolutely there. In fact, I know of no other player who was so aware.

It would be a mistake to think that Jackie's ability to convey emotion through sound was limited to an expression of a palpable joy in life and music. At a deeper level it was born of a profound inner feeling; neither her intelligent awareness nor her physical exuberance ever interfered with this initial emotional impulse. It meant that her playing always seemed fresh and spontaneous, and she avoided the pitfalls of easy artistry whereby repetition means recreating formal patterns, and musical line means simply joining up points A and B.

Ultimately, the du Pré–Bishop duo will be remembered for the document they left in the form of their EMI recording of the Beethoven A major and D major Sonatas (Op.69 and Op.102 No.2), made in December 1965. It is a suitable tribute to their music-making, since it was with their Beethoven playing that the duo had made its mark at the time.

A few months before making their duo recording they each made their own solo records for EMI (Stephen a Beethoven solo recital and Jackie her two concerto recordings of Delius and Elgar). Their first recital disc was record on 19 and 21 December 1965 at Abbey Road Studios. Not long beforehand the du Pré–Bishop duo played a highly successful Royal Festival Hall concert on 21 November 1965. At the last minute they had decided to substitute Beethoven's D major Sonata Op.102 No.2 for the billed A major Op.69. The rest of their programme consisted of the Bach D major Gamba Sonata, the Franck Sonata and Schumann's *Fantasiestücke*.

The Beethoven D major Sonata was considered by critics and public alike to have been the highlight of the duo's Festival Hall concert. It was also the one with which Stephen and Jackie felt most secure. In the light of this they asked EMI if they could record it instead of the originally scheduled G minor Sonata Op.5 No.2; the change was agreed by Peter Andry. According to Stephen, the recording sessions went very smoothly from every point of view:

I remember driving to Abbey Road Studios with a very positive feeling. Although I had already made a solo record for EMI, I was still quite new to recording. So making a record was like climbing Everest and I came prepared to my last second. We had done both these two sonatas a number of times in concert and our last performances (in Harrogate and Tonbridge) a few days earlier had gone very well. The recording just had to be easier. This meant we would be able to 'get it in the can' and

I could look forward to the session. Jackie, on the other hand, was not at all anxious about it.

The critics both in Britain and America hailed the duo's first recording as a remarkable achievement. In the USA, Angel (the American counterpart of EMI) released du Pré's Elgar concerto recording simultaneously with the Beethoven sonatas and reviews often gave more space to the former. The *New York Times* critic Howard Klein wrote of du Pré's marvellous technical equipment and her vivid imagination: 'The music emerges a vital, living experience, not merely the result of youthful ardour, but also an extraordinary musical instinct. [...] It is impossible to avoid the fact that Jacqueline du Pré is one of the world's great cellists – at the age of twenty-two.' She was, in fact, twenty when she made the recordings.

In the *Philadelphia Inquirer,* David Webster praised the duo's 'unusual depth of feeling in the splendid playing [... Du Pré's] playing is expansive, her technique for its own sake. Bishop provides sparkling partnership. They see eye to eye on the spirit of the music and produce it as if playing were sheer joy.'[9]

The recording has survived the test of time very well, and exhibits a winning combination of mature understanding and youthful verve. Du Pré shares Bishop's classical poise, and in the slow movement of the D major Sonata they achieve their effect through an intense inner feeling which never obscures the simplicity of line. In this wonderful movement (which Casals likened to a funeral march) their playing is equally telling in the opening chorale-like theme and the grief-ridden arioso of the D minor section, as in the hushed inner expression of the D major section – with its associations of recalled distant happiness. The transition to the finale is performed with just the right sense of wonder and mystery, when Beethoven, leading us through a series of distant harmonic modulations, comes back to the dominant pedal point, a regaining of harmonic ground with an equivalent regaining of philosophical equilibrium. A whole range of human experience is elicited, from grief, hopelessness and total despair, to a rational acceptance, which in the finale-fugue is transformed into joy. Beethoven uses polyphony, as Bach did before him, to evoke eternal values; for the joy expressed here is one that follows on after suffering.

Perhaps the duo's performance of the A major Sonata is less convincing in its overall concept, but the lyrical sections of the first movement and the short adagio preceding the finale succeed marvellously. Here Jackie conveys a vibrant emotion through the warm, burnished sound of her cello, demonstrating a fabulous feeling for shade and colour. One is struck by the sureness yet subtlety with which she achieves her effects – a rubato here, a small slide there, a warming-up of the vibrato elsewhere. Throughout these sonatas she demonstrates her consummate artistry with her ability to touch and surprise.

Perhaps the best definition of the duo's special qualities came from Jeremy Dale-Roberts:

Stephen possessed a very individual classical style combining an Olympian cool with passion, whereas Jackie had this impulsiveness in her playing. To have these two aspects of Beethoven was very exciting. Stephen's intellectual approach and his ebullience were very marked in those days, and became synthesised with Jackie's dominant characteristics. It made for a single bracing personality. I remember when they did the D major (Op.102 No.2) the sense of competition in the last movement fugue was quite extraordinary, with Stephen's pointed syncopations sounding like very good jazz playing. They took it extremely fast, so that it sounded like a dare, a challenge.

The recording definitely captures that daredevil excitement, as the fugue rushes forward implacably like a rider galloping to the edge of a precipice. It is playing that makes you sit up in your seat and hold your breath.

The Beethoven record was culmination of the first year in the duo's life which was interrupted when Jackie left for Moscow in January 1966 for a five-month sabbatical to study with Rostropovich. Engagements were planned for the 1966–7 season after Jackie's return to London. These included another London recital at the Royal Festival Hall and a tour of the USA in early 1967. EMI were also negotiating for the two artists to complete the recording of the Beethoven cycle, as well as the two Brahms sonatas.

However, by the autumn of 1966 a sense of ambiguity was evident on both Stephen's and Jackie's part about a continued commitment to their duo and, for that matter, to their personal relationship. Jackie had much enjoyed playing with Richard Goode in Spoleto and wanted to form a trio with Fou Ts'ong and Hugh Maguire. But it was her meeting with Daniel Barenboim in December of 1966 which radically affected her professional as well as her private life. Barenboim was to replace all her other musical partners.

Jackie played her last recital with Stephen at Walthamstow Town Hall on 7 May 1967. Jeremy Dale-Roberts was one of those from their circle of shared friends who attended this concert. He remembered being overwhelmed by a great feeling of sadness, realising that Jackie was lost not just to Stephen, but to their coterie as she entered into a new and brilliant phase of her life and new friendships took her over.

After this, Stephen's and Jackie's paths did not cross for the next decade. Then, when Jackie became housebound through illness, Stephen picked up with her again. He became a regular and loyal visitor, and they could laugh about the past and discuss their musical partnership. Stephen recalled, 'Jackie and I were extremely proud of our Beethoven record at the time we made it, particularly of the D major, which was the sonata that we enjoyed playing most of all. And when I visited Jackie in the last years of her life we both agreed that the D major remained special. To this day, I cherish the slow movement. I had reservations about my own playing in the A major sonata, but none about hers.'

Stephen summed up Jackie's talent as an enormous generosity of spirit: 'Of all the musicians I have encountered she was the most generous and the most "musical". Her expressive talent was incomparable and she made most other string players sound as if they were playing the piano. Jackie's attitude to performing was characteristically generous and she described it in terms of having been privileged to receive a lovely gift, which she wanted to share and enjoy with her friends.'

One could add Jeremy Dale-Roberts's words as an epigraph to these times: 'All this was the elation of youth; it is the aroma of the memories which we are left with now.'

13

New Audiences

That's the wise thrush; he sings each song twice over,
Lest you should think he never could recapture
The first fine careless rapture!
                Robert Browning, 'Home Thoughts from Abroad'

Parallel to her duo activities with Stephen Bishop, the pace of Jackie's solo career was intensifying. During 1965 she played over a dozen concerto dates, which included débuts with the Royal Liverpool Philharmonic and the Hallé Orchestras. In both cases she played the Elgar concerto and established an important association with the orchestras' chief conductors – Charles Groves and John Barbirolli. On 9 February Jackie played the Dvořák concerto for the first time with the London Philharmonic Orchestra and Jascha Horenstein at the Festival Hall, replacing the indisposed Leonard Rose at short notice. She also added the Haydn C major Concerto to her repertoire, playing it twice in the space of six months at the Festival Hall with the London Mozart Players and Blech. With the same orchestra she performed the Schumann concerto in Croydon and London. The pinnacle of du Pré's achievement in 1965 lay in her two concerto recordings for EMI (to be discussed in the following chapter).

While the name of Jacqueline du Pré was already firmly imprinted on the British music scene, it was still little known abroad. Jackie had yet to be exposed to the international concert circuit. An important opportunity arose when she was invited to play the Elgar concerto in the USA with the BBC Orchestra in May 1965. The orchestra was making its very first tour abroad and William Glock was adamant that its programmes should represent a wide range of contemporary achievement, in part allied to British music and in part directed to the championship of avant-garde music. The concerts were to be divided between the Hungarian Antal Doráti, chief conductor of the BBC SO at the time, and the composer and conductor Pierre Boulez, who succeeded him in this position the following year. To counterbalance these non-British names, the soloists were chosen from native talent – Jacqueline du Pré, John Ogdon and Heather Harper.

The tour was arranged by the renowned American impresario Sol Hurok and was confined to New York State. At New York's Carnegie Hall, Hurok presented the BBC SO in six programmes of twentieth-century music (Elgar's Cello Concerto and Mahler's Fourth Symphony thereby being as eligible for inclusion as music by Gunther Schuller and Boulez).

Harold Shaw, who worked for Hurok's concert agency in New York, visited London in April 1965, just prior to the BBC SO tour. He recalls that Emmie Tillett called du Pré's name to his attention.

Jacqueline was playing with Stephen Bishop at the time, and I listened to some recordings and I though she was marvellous. So I decided that I would bring her into my section of the Hurok office and I signed her on. I hadn't heard her in the flesh. Within a few weeks of that conversation she came to New York and played the Elgar. It was quite marvellous and she was immediately an enormous success.

I think Hurok himself would never have put her on the list. The reason for this is nothing to do with Jackie herself, but with his attitude to women as instrumentalists. He always said – particularly about cellists – 'Why do you want to have a woman who plays the violin or the cello? You know that they are just going to get married and have children, and there is no money in that …' It was one of his favourite comments about lady artists, and he said it over and over again. Hurok was a businessman and regarded music as an industry where business came first.[1]

Six weeks prior to their departure for the USA, Jackie played the Elgar in a preliminary concert with Doráti and the BBC SO before an invited audience at Maida Vale Studios. The surviving BBC recording testifies to a performance that was very close to her interpretation on the EMI recording with Barbirolli, made only a few months later. The differences mainly stem from Doráti's somewhat Brahmsian approach to Elgar's music. Doráti favoured sharp attacks, a dense orchestral texture and a compact overall structure, rather than the mellow softness, spacious tempi and flexible manipulation of rubato that characterise Barbirolli's approach. Jackie could accept Doráti's understanding of the piece as intelligent and valid, without losing the integrity of her concept.

However, undoubtedly she had a far greater affinity with Barbirolli's perception of Elgar.

Jackie left for New York on 9 May. After playing two concerts with the BBC SO in up-state New York, she performed at the Carnegie Hall on 14 May. The Texan cellist Ralph Kirschbaum attended the concert quite by chance. He was a student at Yale University at the time.

> I had come to New York to have my cello adjusted. I saw the poster for Jackie's performance, and on the spur of the moment I bought a ticket and went in. I had not heard her play; neither had I ever heard the Elgar concerto for that matter. From the first note the effect was quite mesmerising, particularly because I had no template as to what my reaction ought to be – I knew nothing of Jackie's history. Her interpretation was almost classical in proportion and yet the life that sprang out from her represented an ideal balance between contained form and heart-felt passion. It was so harmonious in every aspect, so organic and spontaneous, that I was totally overwhelmed. What struck me most was the great purity of line throughout the whole performance and of course there was this wonderful emotional sense. It was quite exceptional.[2]

After Jackie's performance Ralph went backstage to congratulate her. 'I was a little bit shy, not knowing how she would react to the compliments of a complete stranger. To my surprise, she was on her own in the dressing-room – I suppose she knew nobody in New York. She was very friendly and we started talking; we ended up sitting on the steps of her dressing-room for the whole of the second half of the concert.'[3]

The New York audience received Jackie with great enthusiasm, giving her an ovation that lasted more than ten minutes. John Gruen, the critic of the *New York Herald Tribune* wrote: 'It has been many a moon that so extraordinary a sound has issued from a cello and one must go back to the heyday of Casals or to so singular an artist as Rostropovich for adequate comparisons.' He commended her technique as 'dazzling' and praised her for the quality and variety of tone that 'could be likened to a hand moving alternately from velvet to silk to damask'. The *New York Times* critic Raymond Ericson echoed Gruen's words: 'Miss du Pré and the concerto seemed made for each other, because her playing was so imbued with the romantic spirit.' Ericson compared Jackie's appearance to 'a cross between Lewis Carroll's Alice and one of those angelic instrumentalists in Renaissance paintings'. The angel analogy stuck with Jackie for a long time in the United States, where she fast became a favourite.

It was during this tour that Jackie got friendly with the leader of the orchestra, the violinist Hugh Maguire. He recalled seeing her sitting alone at a table at breakfast in Syracuse, where their first concert was given. 'I went and sat next to her and jollied her up. We talked a lot on that tour. When she first played with us a few years back, I was of course bowled over by her, but I felt too shy to speak to her. I was awestruck by her extraordinary talent and spontaneity of expression, and needed time to work out this phenomenon.'[4]

In New York, a reception was given at the Waldorf Astoria, where the Davydov cello was officially handed over to Jackie in front of the widow of its previous owner, Herbert N. Straus, and of Rembert Wurlitzer, the dealer who had organised the sale. In fact, Jackie had acquired the cello at the beginning of the year and had been using it in concerts since then. Maguire recalled that

> Charles Beare had come over from London. But somehow the whole thing was wrapped in secrecy and even Jackie didn't seem to know what was going on. She played some unaccompanied Bach, 'The Swan' and another slight but jolly little piece for this very smart, somewhat pretentious audience. Jackie was terribly naughty and one could see that she was sizing up her audience as she was playing to them. Assessing them rather accurately as grand people who didn't understand too much about music, she sent up the pieces quite deliberately, but in a way that was charming too. Although she was absolutely thrilled to have the Davydov, she could be quite skittish about it.

What struck Maguire about Jackie's playing was her great sense of musical understanding. 'When performing as soloist with orchestra, she was terribly aware of what I was doing as leader of the orchestra – to a far greater extent than anybody else I know of.' Maguire for his part was conscious of the extraordinary, direct communication she had with the orchestral players, which gave their performances an aspect of intimate chamber music-making. As he recalled, 'Jackie didn't pay too much attention to conductors most of the time. She had a great rapport with myself and various players, such as Norman Nelson, who sat beside me, and Trevor Connor – principal second violin. There was a wonderful crew in the BBC SO at the time, who were all very keen on chamber music, and Jackie soon joined in our sessions. We quickly discovered that we were kindred spirits.'[5]

Jackie came back to England full of her impressions of America. She told her friends, Stephen Bishop and Guthrie Luke among them, that she was thrilled by New York City and would like to go and live there. However, both Guthrie and Stephen, as expatriate Americans, weren't so sure that the excitement might not wear off. 'Yes, it's a wonderful place to visit, but I don't know how much you'd like it if you actually lived there,' Guthrie remembered telling her.[6]

But her enthusiasm did not wane so quickly. When next visiting the States in early 1967, Jackie told Charles Reid of the *New York Times* that her Carnegie Hall début was the best concert she had ever given. 'It was one of those occasions when everything seems just right.' To her mind New York was a breath-taking city: 'All those motor cars a mile long, all those buildings three miles high, all my New York friends, Carnegie Hall – I have great reverence for it.'[7]

In the wake of the enormous critical and popular success of her Carnegie hall début, Harold Shaw rang Terry Harrison at Ibbs and Tillett, who looked after Jackie's engagements outside Great Britain. Shaw announced to Harrison, 'I can book the hell out of that girl' and proceeded at relatively short notice to set up Jackie's next USA tour for the early months of 1967–8.[8]

Other engagements abroad in 1965 were few and far between – a duo concert with Bishop in Ettlingen on 11 June (which Jackie described as 'a fairy castle town on the Rhine'), a performance in Lübeck of the Schumann concerto with Gerd Albrecht conducting (4 October) and a recital with George Malcolm at the Lucerne Festival on 17 August.

Chamber music festivals were regarded by Ibbs and Tillett as outside the orbit of 'professional engagements' (not least because they tended to be paid very poorly, if at all). Thus an invitation to play at the Spoleto Festival dei Due Mondi in Italy in July 1965 was negotiated directly with Jackie. Whereas Sermoneta had, by association with a series of owners, acquired a somewhat English flavour and was directed by Lysy, an Argentinian, Spoleto was run by Americans and operated on a far grander scale. The Italian-born American composer Gian-Carlo Menotti had founded the festival in 1958. Opera performances and orchestral concerts have always been Menotti's chief concern at Spoleto, and when a chamber music element was added he entrusted the running of it to the pianist Charles Wadsworth. Many American music students from the Juilliard School and elsewhere were recruited to play in the orchestra, and Wadsworth brought over the very best young talent from the States to make chamber music together.

It was on the strength of hearing a tape of the Elgar concerto from one of Jackie's broadcast performances that Wadsworth issued his invitation for du Pré to spend a couple of weeks at Spoleto. As he recalled, 'I was very impressed by her extraordinary playing. My only hesitation was that there might be a risk that such a strong player would not adapt to the intimate style of chamber music.'

Wadsworth formed the musicians into groups, suggested the repertoire, then set them hard at work to get performances ready for the daily midday concerts held in the Teatro Caio Melisso. He had an uncanny flair for knowing which combinations of musicians would work best. Wadsworth had identified Richard Goode, a young American pianist still in his teens, as an exciting duo partner for Jackie.

However, in her first appearance in Spoleto, the day after her arrival, Jackie played unaccompanied Bach, since there would not have been sufficient time to rehearse any chamber music piece. Wadsworth recalled that both the Festival Director Menotti and Thomas Schippers, the conductor of the festival orchestra, upbraided him for his programming. 'They exclaimed in horror, "How awful, what could be worse than sitting through a Bach suite played by some unknown artist!" Jackie's appearance on stage wearing a country-style flowing skirt didn't help to reassure them, but the moment she put bow to strings, it was evident that here was genius at work. I remember Tom Schippers turning round and looking at me with astonishment.'

Richard Goode likewise had heard of Jackie's name before arriving in Spoleto without realising how celebrated she already was in Britain. Although he was told to expect something special, he was unprepared for his first impression: a robust, healthy-looking blonde girl who strode out and planted herself on the stage. 'She seemed immediately very firmly rooted, straddling her cello – there was something peasant-like about her. She attacked the C major Suite with total abandon and confidence. There's no doubt, this was her voice as well as Bach's. It was emotionally completed untrammelled, wonderful.'[9] Goode had been a regular visitor to the Marlboro Festivals and often attended Casals's master classes. He felt that Jackie's playing of Bach, while quite different in many ways, incorporated much of Casals's approach. Later, to his surprise, he learned that Jackie did not know Casals's famous Bach recordings.

Goode's first concert performance with Jackie was of Beethoven's D major Sonata Op.102 No.2 which, together with other performances, has been preserved on tape in the archives of the RAI (the Italian radio). Wadsworth found their duo to be immensely satisfying: 'Goode had intense musicality combined with deep musical intelligence and an ability to relate to everyday quotidian human life. He, like Jackie, was concerned with the human condition and connected to the emotions of others, while always remaining intellectually grounded.'

Their performance of the Beethoven D major Sonata shows the qualities of their partnership and the combined force of their temperaments is astonishing. Goode's grasp of the harmonic and polyphonic structure allowed him to create a skeleton framework under Jackie's breathing long lines, where the ebb and flow can sound free and spontaneous. His playing has the contained energy of a coiled spring, which can be released when needed – as, for instance, at the end of the first movement where an amazing crescendo in the semiquavers of the penultimate bar brings the music to a brilliant conclusion. In the slow movement the players achieve a sense of grief and anguish in the opening that seems allied to fervent prayer – a kind of Stabat Mater dolorosa. As the musical drama unfolds the emotional surging of Jackie's melodic line provokes stormy response from Goode. Her sound is at its most seductive in the D major section of the slow movement, where sometimes the inner feeling seems so intense that it almost chokes the vocal line. They take the fugue at a slower tempo than in her recorded performance with Bishop, but not at the expense of the excitement in the final build-up in the coda.

Jackie played more Beethoven in the following two concerts. On 14 July she and Richard Goode were joined by Michael Tree, the viola player from the Guarneri Quartet, in the E flat major Trio Op.70. No.2. (Tree, equally at home on violin or viola, of course played the violin on this occasion.) Their account of this most elusive of Beethoven's trios, although far from the maturity of vision in the recording made four and a half years later with the Barenboim–Zukerman–du Pré partnership, is very beautiful nevertheless. Jackie establishes a sense of mystery at the very start of the first movement introduction, and in the subsequent allegro the players combine energy and elegance. She is able to infect her partners with her innate ability to colour and match every innuendo of the music's varying moods. Those characteristic du Pré touches – a delicious, if unexpected, slide here, her subtle use of vibrato and the varied brushwork of the bow strokes – create a wonderful palette of colour. Sometimes the attack in the bow is on the rough side, when one hers a 'slapping' sound on the strings, or a somewhat rasping attack in the chords, as in the second movement variations. The dominant feature of this performance is its exuberance and vitality, in which Jackie acts as the driving spirit.

The following day Jackie played the A major Sonata Op.69, but this time she was partnered by another young American pianist Lawrence Smith. Their beautiful account is no less satisfying than her recording of it a few months later with Bishop. Smith has excellent ensemble instincts and a soft touch, although perhaps he was not ideally flexible in this performance. Their version of the scherzo, taken very fast indeed, is a fleeting, transcendental vision, which anxiously presses forward without quite rushing over the edge. Again the finale is taken as fast as its limits allow, and Smith sounds light and brilliant, and Jackie exuberantly virtuosic. Yet in the lyrical moments, particularly in the slow movement, she spins out the sound with a spaciousness that makes you wait on every note with baited breath.

Wadsworth recalled that 'Jackie was totally comfortable at Spoleto; she had a lovely friendship with Richard Goode, everything was very informal and warm; she was at ease. She complied totally with my suggestions, even though the schedule was very intense, with different programmes to be performed every day. All our spare time was spent eating and drinking wine in the lovely Italian hilltop town.'

It was at one of these relaxed Italian lunches that Jackie first met Arnold Steinhardt, the first violinist from the Guarneri Quartet. Steinhardt recalled that 'Charlie Wadsworth had given her a fantastic build-up. I was expecting to meet a kind of firebrand, somebody who would be brilliant, showy and urbane – the kind of person who Jackie obviously was *not*. Instead, she seemed a girl with a sweet, goofy smile, dressed in a very ordinary summer dress. There was a disarming simpleness to her, which was a shock to me. She was totally unaffected by celebrity and would always remain unaltered by success.'

Steinhardt recalled the fun they had together. 'Jackie had this wonderful low-key humour, not the kind one at all associates with somebody who is so much in the limelight. She enjoyed mimicking my accent: "Tell me Arnold, is it time for your Ba-aaath?" she would say, assuming an air of innocence. She would talk about her father's "Drott", a farm-machine like a caterpillar tractor. I and the other musicians, most of us city-slickers, had no idea what it was. She went on and on about this "Drott", an utterly useless topic to which none of the rest of us could contribute.'

Further hilarity (and a certain amount of concern) was caused when Jackie kept on leaving her newly acquired Davydov Strad behind in restaurants and public places, and was forever having to go back and retrieve it. The musicians also got a laugh from the ridiculous situation of a reluctant Menotti being pursued by a woman who was completely obsessed by him. As Steinhardt recalled, Menotti's admirer was dressed tragically and dramatically – à la Callas – constantly hovering in wait for her reluctant prey.

Jackie spent most of her time in the company of Richard Goode, with whom she 'palled around' (in Steinhardt's words) and with whom she continued a close friendship in London. Steinhardt, like Wadsworth, was amazed by the contrast between Jackie's off-stage and performing personae. 'She appeared to be a sweet, demure milkmaid, but with cello in hands she was like one possessed.' He was delighted to be asked to play the Mendelssohn D minor Trio with her and Tom Schippers. All the more so as Schippers, a young and very gifted conductor, had directed Steinhardt's performance of Wieniawski's Second Concerto at his Carnegie Hall début in 1958 with the New York Philharmonic.

Steinhardt hadn't realised that Schippers was also a pianist –

But when we started to rehearse I was shocked and mortified, because it turned out that Tommy Schippers could no longer play the piano. He was a very flamboyant player and in the concert he played fistfuls of wrong notes. It was embarrassing, even though there were some good things about the performance. In particular, I treasure a memory of one moment, so typical of Jackie. Before the coda, in the finale, the music finally goes from D minor to the major. Jackie and I had discussed how we would do it, but then in the concert something remarkable happened. Jackie stopped looking at the music, flashed her great smile at me, looking at me with utter joy and camaraderie, as if to say, 'Now just *look* at this, isn't it fantastic, here we are playing this glorious music.' It still brings tears to my eyes to think of it. That is the kind of enthusiasm that you have if you are very young, or if you were Jackie – she never lost it. It was a thrill to play with her.

In the same concert, on 18 July, Jackie and Richard Goode played Schumann's *Fantasiestücke* Op.73, which Wadsworth described as one of the most electrifying performances he had ever heard. 'Richard and Jackie had such enormous communication between them – you could call it the right chemistry. They shared the same vibrant and vital approach to music-making.' As Goode recalled, the spontaneity of this and all his other performances with Jackie was almost unavoidable, since the pressures of the schedule left hardly any time to rehearse from one concert to the next. In their performance of the Schumann pieces Goode had the sensation of being 'carried along by the current, sometimes turbulent, that she generated'.[10]

This concert was recorded, and the tapes of the Mendelssohn Trio and the Schumann pieces confirm the verdicts of the above-quoted musicians (the Mendelssohn Trio, incidentally, does have its marvellous moments and Schippers, while not an accurate pianist, has got absolutely the right instincts for Mendelssohn's music). The *Fantasiestücke* testify to a tender and intimate approach, especially in the first piece, where the players capture the inner-felt spirit so characteristic of Schumann's music. Not that the extrovert and dynamic side of Schumann is lacking, especially in the third piece, where Jackie leads in exuberant joy that is in danger of going over the top. Goode is able to rein in the music until the coda when, in response to Schumann's markings of *schneller* and again *schneller*, his playing flares up to match her fiery temperament. The audience were vocal in their wild enthusiasm – and also in their disappointment when no encore was forthcoming.

There was a tradition that the final chamber music concert of the festival should include a performance of the Schubert C major String Quintet D956 (with two cellos). That year, Wadsworth asked Jackie to play the second cello with the Guarneri Quartet. For Wadsworth, their performance attained a unique beauty and was never equalled by others before or since. He described Jackie as the galvanising force of the ensemble and was overwhelmed by her 'awesome' eloquence in the second movement: 'No one else spoke like that in their music-making. The dynamism she brought to the middle section of the second movement in particular was amazing – she made the triplet interjections sound ominous and threatening, creating just the appropriate contrast to the still outer sections.'¹¹ (One should add, to be fair, that for the space of about two bars Jackie actually got lost in the beginning of this middle section – which shows the minor importance of an error when the music-making is as powerful as it was on this occasion.)

In the RAI tape we can hear a performance that is distinguished by the cool elegance and sweetness of sound from the Guarneri Quartet. The second movement occupies its rightful place as the work's centre-piece, but the musicians' concentration seems to lapse in the following movements. Since one finds some of Schubert's most awkward and difficult string writing in the quintet's scherzo and the finale, it is not so surprising that there are the occasional untidy bits of ensemble and lapses of intonation. This was also the first time that the young Guarneri Quartet had performed the piece and, given the minimal rehearsing conditions at Spoleto, they achieved an amazingly high standard.

For Steinhardt, the most memorable feature of their performance was the utter abandon with which Jackie played:

> She was completely free, yet her playing was also flawless. With most flawless players, their preoccupation with perfection is governed by a need to calculate and nail down every note. And for this there is a price to be paid – a staidness and lack of excitement in the playing. Jackie's abandon was just on the edge of being too much, but it was so convincing that you had to accept it for what it was. This quality of her playing lent itself equally to solo repertoire and to chamber music. She had a won-derful sense of what was going on around her and knew how to fit in and give energy without imposing herself.'¹²

As Steinhardt remarked, Jackie individual style harked back to the great players of the early years of the twentieth century. 'In our age it's not easy to find great artists with individuality, nowadays so many people play "perfectly", but with surfaces and textures that are the same. Jackie was highly aware of texture, and in her use of slides and portamenti she was reminiscent of another age.'

Richard Goode realised that it was Jackie's total identification with the music that lent her playing such persuasive force. He had never heard the Elgar Cello Concerto before playing it through with Jackie. 'I was stunned by the piece and the overwhelming pathos of her performance, particularly the slow movement.' Through his musical contact with her, Goode developed an understanding of her creative response to life and art. He perceived a conflict in what he saw in her everyday conduct and what he heard in Jackie's outpouring of emotion on the cello: 'My predominant impressions of Jackie as a person were of her joyousness, as a musician of a tremendous pathos, a powerful sadness.'

These qualities of pathos and sadness are conspicuous features of Jackie's recording of the Elgar concerto made with Barbirolli only a month after leaving Spoleto. Everybody who knew her at this time remarked on the radiance of her personality. Few realised that there were still times when she struggled with depression. In September 1965, Dr Hatchick, the du Prés' family doctor, referred Jackie to the physician Sir Richard Bayliss. She had been suffering from headaches, nausea and recurrent cystitis, and had temporarily lost all interest in the cello. Bayliss wrote to inform Dr Hatchick that he could find no trace of any organic disease, apart from the cystitis, but remarked that Jacqueline was depressed and bored, and deplored the fact that she had had no holiday for four years. If she continued in this manner, he noted, 'then she is a candidate for a nervous breakdown'. Dr Hatchick was advised to talk to her agents, to ensure that Jacqueline did have time off for a holiday or a change as soon as her schedule allowed.[13] In the beginning of 1966 Jackie was indeed released from the pressures of concert life for a nine-month period. Going to study in Moscow could definitely be termed a change, but hardly a rest.

Thus we see in this first full year of concert engagements at international level that du Pré had problems in standing up to the pace. Sir Richard Bayliss's warning turned out to be prophetic.

14

Recordings

Music is in the air – you simply take as much of it as you want.
Attributed to Sir Edward Elgar

Jackie started her recording career in earnest in 1965. But her connection
with EMI dated back to 1962, when Peter Andry, then head of HMV,
invited her to make her first disc. Andry recalled that he originally
heard the name of Jacqueline du Pré from Yehudi Menuhin: 'Yehudi
called me one day and said, "You must come and hear this remarkable
girl. It was not often that he said things like that. So I went up to his
house in Highgate that afternoon. They were rehearsing trios in the
big music room – Yehudi, Hephzibah [Menuhin] and Jackie. Here was
this girl throwing her hair about and playing marvellously well. I
immediately thought that we should record her.'[1]

On Andry's initiative, Mrs Tillett was contacted and an initial contract was signed for Jackie's first recording to take place in July 1962.

In those days EMI had under its umbrella two catalogues – HMV
and Columbia. The former, divided into two categories of artists, international and local, was headed by Andry. Columbia was dominated by
Walter Legge, who recorded such exclusive names as Schwarzkopf, Klemperer and Karajan. Suvi Raj Grubb, who worked for four years as Legge's
assistant, recalled that 'it was a great jumble. Producers tended to find
themselves working for both outfits. Everybody took over everybody's
artists. I worked for Columbia, but for instance I also recorded the Melos
Ensemble, who were classified as local HMV artists.'[2]

Furthermore, the same repertoire was often recorded on both catalogues. Andry remembered that repertoire meetings used to be highly
competitive affairs: 'I had to leave the room when Legge discussed his
plans, because he thought that I might overhear and nab his repertoire.
In these cases Dave Bicknell acted as arbiter in his capacity as general
manager of the International Artistes Department.'

The situation was further complicated because the American sister company, Angel Records, although owned by EMI, also had a certain amount of autonomy. On the Pop music side, for instance, the American company Paramount, likewise owned by EMI, in the early 1960s initially refused to issue EMI's best-selling English group, the Beatles.

EMI handled a list of English artists on the HMV label, who were supposedly of purely local interest in England. Among them were Janet Baker (then newly 'discovered'), Heather Harper, Geraint Evans, Gerald Moore and Osian Ellis. The young Jacqueline du Pré was contracted originally as a 'local' HMV artist.

The picture only changed when Walter Legge left in 1964, and the HMV and Columbia lists were effectively amalgamated. Classical artists started to be contracted to EMI rather than the Gramophone Company (HMV label) or to the Columbia Gramophone Company (Columbia label). In the EMI hierarchy, Andry's position was consolidated and in 1969 he took over from David Bicknell as head of the International Artistes Department. Among his achievements was to persuade von Karajan to come back to EMI.

Recording in studio conditions is a completely different matter from performing concerts, particularly for a player like du Pré, whose artistry was motivated by a compelling need to communicate and interact with an audience. True, Jackie already had made a couple of BBC studio recordings, so she had a fair idea of the procedures involved. A studio recording is effected in isolation, in an acoustically sterile environment, where outside noises cannot cause interference. The only people with whom the artist has contact are the producer and the technicians. Thus the importance of the producer's role: while being supportive of and sympathetic to the artist's musical intentions, he must remain an objective judge of his playing.

Ronald Kinloch Anderson, a fine keyboard player with a great knowledge of chamber music, was assigned to Jackie and produced her first four EMI recordings. Kinloch Anderson had started working part-time for EMI in 1957, after a road accident forced him to cut back on his performing career. Peter Andry, who originally came to EMI as a sound producer and was now increasingly involved on the administrative side, asked Anderson to take over most of the HMV chamber music recordings.

Jackie's first record was made on a special format known as EPs. These were 7-inch, middle-length discs using 45 rather than 33 revolutions per minute and they were issued with the aim of introducing new artists to the public. The HMV label EPs were always popular and sold well. It was decided that Jackie's first recital record should be shared with the viola player Herbert Downes, with one side devoted to each artist playing a selection of short pieces.

What was unusual about Jackie's choice of pieces was not so much the repertoire, but the variety of accompanists and instruments that were involved. This meant that the studio work had to be spread over three days. On the morning of 15 July 1962 she recorded Bruch's *Kol Nidrei* and Mendelssohn's *Song Without Words* with Gerald Moore accompanying (on the piano). In the afternoon session on that day she recorded Bach's Adagio from the Toccata in C with the organist Roy Jesson, and the second movement allegro of Bach's Sonata for Viola da Gamba in D, with Ronald Kinloch Anderson playing the harpsichord. In another session with Gerald Moore on 16 July 1962 Jackie recorded the *Sicilienne* by von Paradis, the Sarabande and Allegro from Handel's Sonata in G minor (arr. Slater), and the first and third of Schumann's *Fantasiestücke*. (Another session was arranged in September 1962 to record the Schumann *Fantasiestücke* again in their entirety.)

On 21 July Jackie was in the studios again, this time with the guitarist John Williams and the harpist Osian Ellis, recording de Falla's 'Jota' from the *Popular Songs* with accompanying guitar, and Saint-Saëns's 'The Swan' from the *Carnival of Animals* with harp. The EP record was issued in mono in 1963, but for reasons of space not everything that Jackie had recorded was included on it (the von Paradis, Mendelssohn and Schumann pieces were left out).

Working in the studio was not an easy experience, as Jackie confessed in later years to Alan Blyth, 'At seventeen, [recording] seemed to me the very opposite of what music-making was about.'[3] In fact, du Pré at seventeen proved herself an artist in possession of an excellent technique and a genuine musicianship, which lacked any hint of the posturing of a precocious prodigy. It is true that in her later recordings she was able to display to a far greater extent a characteristic exuberance and freedom of music-making. Perhaps the quality of restraint detectable in these recorded performances also reflected a sense of inhibition in front of the microphone, something Jackie was later able to overcome.

For instance, in this 1962 interpretation of *Kol Nidrei*, Max Bruch's version of the Jewish prayer of atonement, her playing is beautifully shaped, but lacks the range of dynamic and colour, and notably the beautiful expressive slides, which were to become a du Pré hallmark. In later years Jackie declared that her youthful interpretation was a bit too straight – 'It's the "goyim" version,' she would explain. But she still liked it. In a televised extract from the same piece shown in Nupen's documentary film (recorded in BBC TV studios in September 1965 with Barbirolli conducting the Hallé) Jackie's performance has gained a greater dimension of inner emotional expression, as well as more security and colour in the instrumental playing. Unfortunately, it seems that the original television film of this version no longer exists.

When Jackie's EP was issued the critics took note of her exceptional talent. Edward Greenfield in his review for *The Gramophone* immediately nominated du Pré as a supreme artist on the strength of her playing in this recording.

After the enormous success of Jackie's performances of the Elgar concerto at the Festival Hall and Prom concerts in 1962, it was obvious that her interpretation of the piece should be recorded; the question only remained when J. K. R. Whittle, the Marketing Manager of Classical Repertoire at EMI, couldn't resist drawing comparisons with Yehudi Menuhin's successful championship of Elgar's Violin Concerto at a similarly young age. In an inter-departmental memorandum, entitled 'The Elgar Gimmick again', Whittle pointed out the extraordinary coincidence: 'We did it in 1934 – the boy Menuhin playing an inspired violin concerto. Now the girl Jacqueline du Pré doing the Cello Concerto. Her press notices read like Yehudi's all those years ago ... If she does on record what she did in the Festival Hall, we have about 7000 sales on our hands.' Whittle makes this estimate sound positively exciting; one wonders if he could ever have dreamt that, after thirty years on the market, du Pré's recording of the Elgar concerto with John Barbirolli would achieve sales of a quarter of a million!

In fact, Peter Andry, Kinloch Anderson and Mrs Tillett did not push for Jackie to record the Elgar concerto too soon. Neither was Jackie in a hurry. Waiting obviously provided time for her interpretation to mature and to gain in self-assurance. In the three years between her first performance of the concerto in London and her recording of it, her understanding of the music gained enormously in depth and sophistication. Naturally, she had also acquired a far greater command of her instrument.

But to the bewilderment of critics and fans alike, Jackie's first concerto recording turned out not to be Elgar's. In fact, it was of a relatively little-known work that she had to learn specially for the occasion – the

Cello Concerto by Frederick Delius, a work associated largely with another woman cellist, Beatrice Harrison. In fact, the world première of the Cello Concerto was given in Vienna by the cellist Serge Barjansky, but Delius insisted that Harrison give the first British performance on 23 July 1923 at the Queen's Hall – she had been the initial performer of two other Delius works: the Cello Sonata and the Double Concerto for Violin and Cello. After Harrison's death the concerto lay dormant, until taken up by du Pré for the recording.

It was commissioned by the Delius Trust, which invited Sir Malcolm Sargent to conduct several previously unrecorded Delius works. (The *Songs Before Sunrise*, and *Songs of Farewell* made up the rest of the record.) Sargent nominated du Pré as soloist in the Cello Concerto. The choice of the Royal Philharmonic Orchestra was apt, because of its long-standing Delian tradition through its association with Sir Thomas Beecham.

Jackie's first acquaintance with the music of Frederick Delius came through performing the Cello Sonata of 1917 with Ernest Lush at the composer's centenary celebration at Bradford in 1962. She was evidently an eloquent advocate for this attractive music. *The Times* critic claimed that 'only an implacable foe of the composer would not have been won over by her persuasive account.'

However, the Delius Cello Concerto is a much more substantial piece than the sonata and, as such, requires much more concentrated commitment. Stephen Bishop recalled that Jackie learned the concerto without ever seeing or referring to either the orchestral or piano score. It stretches credibility to think she could go into the recording studio having only studied the cello part. Sir Malcolm Sargent had written to Jackie suggesting they meet prior to the session to discuss the work[4] and one imagines that she will at least have played through the concerto with piano during this encounter. However, as Daniel Barenboim has emphasised, Jackie's intuitive gifts were so strong that she was capable of immediate assimilation, and could probably penetrate the core of a piece of music during a first reading and have a fairly accurate idea of what would be going on around her in the orchestra. In the case of the Delius concerto, where the cello plays almost continuously in an unbroken rhapsodic line, perhaps the one-line text of the cello part gave her the adequate clues.

Studio One at Abbey Road was booked for the recording of the concerto on 12 and 14 January 1965. In his capacity as reviewer for *The Gramophone* and for the American *High-Fidelity Magazine*, Edward

168

Greenfield was allowed to attend these sessions: 'I recall the first day of recording vividly, as it was then that I first met Jackie. Sargent, however, was in a funny mood during the sessions. I asked Jackie how she responded to hearing herself played back. Sargent was very annoyed with me as he thought it was an insulting question, but I thought it was fair enough. Jackie fortunately didn't mind at all and was just her natural self. It was impossible not to fall in love with her straight away.'

Greenfield recalled being slightly disappointed by the end result, but this was not in any way to criticise Jackie's playing: 'Sargent was not the most understanding or sympathetic conductor for Jackie, or indeed for Delius. For me, the Cello Concerto is one of Delius's greatest pieces; the themes are marvellous and despite the concerto's rhapsodic nature it is very tightly constructed.'[5]

Certainly Delius' musical structure is not the most evident feature of his composition. The casual listener would more easily identify with Elgar's description of it as 'a little intangible sometimes, but always very beautiful'. But the beautiful meanderings of the Cello Concerto in du Pré's rendering have the inbuilt logic of a slow-flowing stream which, however circuitously, follows its course from source to sea.

It is perhaps surprising to discover that Jackie had very ambivalent feelings about the Delius Cello Concerto. The pianist and broadcaster Jeremy Siepmann, who was a friend of hers during this period, recalled that Jackie 'vigorously disparaged it in conversation immediately before and after the recording was made'.[6] Nevertheless, as a true professional, Jackie gave the piece her total commitment. The rhapsodic quality of the music was perfectly suited to her and she achieved a level of technical security in her playing reminiscent of Heifetz, with a sound that is stunningly beautiful, particularly in the high registers.

Beatrice Harrison had written in regard to the Delius concerto that 'the artist must be inspired by a wealth of musical imagination to be able to interpret this music'.[7] Du Pré certainly seems to fulfil this edict. Not that Harrison's own rendering of the work should be discounted. Gerald Moore could still vividly recall her performance of it thirty years on: 'She sang on her instrument and had an infallible instinct for feeling where the muscle of the music slackened and where it tightened again, where it accumulated tension till the climax was reached.'[8] The qualities Moore praised in Harrison's performance of Delius were ones which were inherent in du Pré's musical nature and which characterised her own interpretation of the piece.

The recording commissioned by the Delius Trust was issued in early August to the highest accolades and the du Pré account of the Cello Concerto was singled out by the critics. In *The Gramophone*, praise was accorded both to 'Miss du Pré's warm and eloquent account of the Cello Concerto and the ravishingly beautiful orchestral sound which the RPO and Sir Malcolm provide to support her golden thread of Delian melody'.[9]

To coincide with the release of the Delius concerto, EMI's publicity department released an important, if somewhat verbose, press notice: 'Long ago EMI and Angel Records had resolved to give permanence to Miss du Pré's matchless reading of the Elgar, but wise counsels stayed the hands of the impetuous ones to await the day when one particular conductor, whose association with the Elgar concerto is unique, could join forces with Miss du Pré.'[10]

It did indeed prove good fortune that Jackie was able to make the record with John Barbirolli, the conductor who in his cello-playing days had been a member of the orchestra at the first performance and gave one of the next performances of the work as soloist in 1923. (He claimed it was the second, but Beatrice Harrison certainly played and recorded it before this.)

Elgar started writing his Cello Concerto in November 1918 and completed it in August of the following year. The tragic slaughter of the war years had thrown him into the deepest despair and he was unable to write any music of significance. But at the beginning of 1918 his depression gave way to intense creative activity, when at his Sussex retreat of Brinkwells he produced a series of wonderful chamber music works – the String Quartet, the Violin Sonata and the Piano Quintet. The Cello Concerto, the last work written in this period, has often been likened to a war requiem, but as Michael Kennedy, in his book *A Portrait of Elgar*, elucidates: 'the requiem here is not so much for the dead in Flanders fields as for the destruction of a way of life. With an artist's vision he saw that 1918 was the end of a civilisation.'[11] Elgar himself described the Cello Concerto as 'A man's attitude to life'. This statement, perhaps, is relevant to his own determination to use his art to overcome horror and tragedy. In the music of his Cello Concerto the composer's attempts to seek consolation in memories of a better past have the effect of making present reality appear all the more desolate. Thus, despite its lighter moments, the concerto is, in Kennedy's words, 'a musical expression of personal grief and bitterness'.

Elgar wrote in his catalogue after finishing the work 'Finis R.I.P.'; his words were loaded with a terrible significance, since the Cello Concerto was to be his last important work before entering into the musical silence of his declining years.

The première took place in October 1919, a few months after the composition was completed. Elgar entrusted this first performance to his cellist friend Felix Salmond and the conductor Albert Coates. But it proved to be one of the most shaming moments in British musical history, where Coates behaved with complete disregard for Elgar, with the excuse of promoting Scriabin's *Poème de l'Extase*. Barbirolli referred to the occasion as an 'utter disaster': 'Poor old Elgar, he was so upset! All the fault of that old rogue Coates. Pinched most of Elgar's rehearsal time for some Scriabin rubbish. Scandalous . . . Elgar only went on for Salmond's sake.'[12] For Salmond, the whole experience was so traumatic that he never again attempted to play the piece in public.

After this fiasco Elgar asked Beatrice Harrison to learn the piece specially for recording and in 1919 he conducted her in an abridged version of the concerto, adapted to the limitations of acoustical recording. Then, in 1928, Harrison recorded the complete concerto, again for HMV and with Elgar conducting. This version has historical value because one can assume that the tempi and dynamics corresponded to Elgar's wishes as marked in the score.

The next recording of importance was that of Casals made in 1945 with Sir Adrian Boult conducting. In England, Casals had performed the concerto both before and after the war; initially the British critics only grumbled about a foreigner's inability to 'catch Elgar's tone of voice'. But by the time Casals came to make the recording they had changed their tune. *The Times*, for instance, praised Casals's ability to render 'an Elgarian mood of wistfulness that few artists now understand'. (Yet when asked to define the differences in Casals's pre-and post-war performances, Boult said that there were none.)[13]

Other recordings of the concerto were made in the interim, but none that could match the version made by du Pré and Barbirolli in 1965. Barbirolli had the best possible credentials as an Elgar interpreter. No other living British conductor (with the exception, perhaps, of Boult) could claim such a close association with Elgar's music. Apart from performing the Cello Concerto himself, Barbirolli had subsequently conducted it with various illustrious soloists, including Pablo Casals, André Navarra and Armaryllis Fleming.

In his capacity of adjudicator of the Suggia Gift, Barbirolli had been keeping a close eye on Jackie's progress from the age of ten onwards. While aware of her astonishing rate of progress, he waited until du Pré reached maturity as an artist, some ten years later, before inviting her to perform with him. Significantly, the Elgar Cello Concerto was chosen for their first concert together with the Hallé Orchestra on 7 April 1965 at the Royal Festival Hall. Their performance received accolades from the public and critics alike. There was something touching in seeing a musician steeped in the Elgarian tradition responding with such empathy to the inspired artistry of one so young. That du Pré and Barbirolli should go on to record the Elgar concerto seemed an inescapable destiny.

Under Barbirolli's aegis Jackie become a frequent visitor to the Hallé in Manchester and she also played as his soloist with the London Symphony Orchestra and the BBC SO. With the latter orchestra they recorded for television Bruch's *Kol Nidrei* in September of 1965. Jackie's special association with Barbirolli was founded to a large extent on mutual respect. But another important factor of their relationship lay in the fact that he was the only conductor of those she played with whom Jackie could look up to as a teacher.

As the Hallé's General Manager Clive Smart recalled,

> Jackie had a wonderful rapport with JB [Barbirolli], who understood everything she wanted to achieve. Prior to performance, JB would talk through the work with his soloists at a piano rehearsal, but often the piano wasn't touched. JB's interpretations were very personal, as he would go with the feeling of the music at the moment. But they were carefully thought out and well prepared. Hence his performances of the same piece often varied quite a lot, although the basic concept was the same. He had a telepathic sympathy for Jackie and being a flexible accompanist, was able to bend with the music. This was important in the Elgar concerto, where Jackie was a law unto herself. Of course, JB was immersed in Elgar's musical world, and had very personal feelings for the Cello Concerto. Overall in Elgar his tempi were very fluid, but always spot on, however much rubato he used.[14]

Barbirolli's widow Evelyn Rothwell observed that Sir John had the highest respect for Jackie's musicianship and believed that she was far beyond her years in maturity:

> But I think that John did have a very great influence on Jackie's under-

standing of the Elgar, although perhaps in general terms rather than specific. He helped her to develop a sort of musical wisdom and tried to give her a little more tranquillity, to stop her giving out all the time. He was always on at her about that and also believed that her force of temperament sometimes caused her to use too much pressure. In the Elgar, they seemed to agree on tempi and the general feeling about the work. Sometimes he would also make specific suggestions, which she always tried to incorporate. He was rather touched that she took his advice so willingly – Jackie could be very stubborn if she wanted to, but never with John. As she had the most wonderful technical equipment, she could act on anything. After they had recorded the Elgar, I remember him saying that she was destined to be very great, he felt that she had the mark of genius.'[15]

Clive Smart recalled that it was a great disappointment to the Hallé Orchestra not to be invited to make the Elgar recording with du Pré and Barbirolli. 'It was because of economic reasons. EMI had an exclusive contract with Barbirolli and they disliked all the halls in Manchester, discounting both the Milton Hall, an old Baptist church, which was often used for recordings, and the Free Trade Hall. It transpired to be cheaper to book the LSO [London Symphony Orchestra] than pay the fares and overnight expenses for the Hallé to come to London.'[16] Although Barbirolli had a good working relationship with the LSO, he did not have the same flexibility and intimate rapport as with his own musicians of the Hallé.

The recording was anticipated within EMI as an event of artistic importance and potentially as a good seller. Ibbs and Tillett negotiated for du Pré a contract based on a small royalty percentage and cash advance. Her previous EMI recordings had been negotiated on a flat-fee basis.

The recording sessions were booked to take place at Kingsway Hall from 19 to 21 August. Edward Greenfield once again went along to listen:

I attended the morning session, where they recorded the first two movements. Barbirolli was in fine form, but the orchestra wasn't in the best of moods because of some internal dispute which had nothing to do with Jackie. They recorded the first movement and the scherzo almost in one go, and at the end of that, the LSO, forgetting their bad temper, broke out into spontaneous applause, something that is relatively rare in recording sessions. It was a great tribute to Jackie. At the lunch-break, as I was walking out of the hall, I bumped into Jackie putting on her old anorak. I asked her where she was going. 'Oh, to the chemist next door,' she said. 'I've got such a headache.' It was extraordinary, there was no one looking after her, seeing whether she needed anything, or asking whether she might want to rest. She told me that they didn't even send a car for her in the morning, she had had to go out and get a taxi. But despite the discomfort and the headache, she was able to convey the magic. I found it remarkable and in striking contrast to a recording session that I attended the following day with a certain prima donna. My goodness, what tantrums the singer threw because she couldn't get a bottle of Scotch in the middle of the afternoon (in those days everything was closed except during licensing hours). Jackie, on the other hand, was completely natural and totally undemanding.[17]

Evidently, quite an audience gathered for the final session. In a letter of congratulation, EMI's marketing manager informed Jackie: 'The staff do ask from time to time to attend recording sessions, but I have seen nothing quite like it the day you were doing this work with Sir John. The classical department here was almost devoid of people because they were all in the back row of the Kingsway Hall.'[18]

The record was finished with time in hand. Jackie herself must have been aware that she had given an exceptional performance. But reputedly, a few months later, on first hearing the completed record she burst into tears and said, 'This is not at all what I meant.'

When the record was released, in December 1965, the critics were unanimous in their praise of it. As Greenfield pointed out, Jackie's expressive personality was so great, that it was out of the question to apply the normal nit-picking critical criteria to her performance.

Jackie did play with much greater freedom maybe than Elgar envisaged, but she brought out something stronger and more intense than had ever been seen in this music before. A dedicated Elgarian like Jerrold Northrop Moore disparaged her performance, particular the later more expansive Philadelphia recording, because he looked at it from the purely Elgarian point of view. But I think the spirit of communication and her intuitive understanding of this music elevates it to another level. By the time of her EMI recording she had played the Elgar a great number of times and had gained enormous insight into the piece.[19]

But it was not only Jackie who was sometimes accused of being over-expansive in her interpretation of Elgar. As Daniel Barenboim observed,

> during his lifetime, people in England often criticised [Barbirolli's] musical personality in general and his Elgar in particular. They considered him too emotional and thought he took too many liberties. But I felt that he brought a dimension to Elgar's music which is so often lacking, a kind of nervous quality which he had in common with Mahler ... There is almost a certain over-sensitivity in some of Elgar's greater works, which is sometimes sacrificed for the conventional idea of Elgar as the perfect English gentleman.[20]

Most musicians would agree that du Pré's 1965 version set a new yardstick of interpretation for the Elgar Cello Concerto. Jackie demonstrated an uncanny ability to identify with the autumnal mood and pathos of the work, as if she had an instinctive understanding of the processes at work in the composer's mind. Thus she seems to capture ideally Elgar's varying moods of noble protest, whimsy, nostalgic regret, desolation and resignation.

It was du Pré championship of the Elgar concerto both in concert and on record that finally gained the piece recognition outside England as a major repertoire piece. In many places she gave local premières of the piece and she always played it with a dedication engendered by her understanding of it as a great piece of music. So much so that in 1968, as a token of appreciation of her role in popularising the work, the publishers of Elgar's music, Novellos, presented Jackie with a score of the concerto specially bound in blue leather with gold lettering.

Jacqueline's third EMI recording in 1965 was made with Stephen Bishop. Kinloch Anderson had been present at their début recital in October 1964 and immediately promoted the idea of recording this new partnership. Conveniently, Bishop was already signed up by EMI. Realising that their repertoire at the beginning was limited to the four sonatas they had played on that occasion, Anderson suggested a Brahms–Beethoven disc. On the promotional side there was concern that du Pré, with her strong public image 'would carry Stephen Bishop'. But this did not affect the company's decision to record the duo, rather, it was seen as a problem of conditions and the level of promotion.

Before each recording is made, an estimate is done of sales and costs. Du Pré's career was seen as climbing more rapidly than Bishop's. In drawing up an estimate of sales, the EMI marketing analysts predicted a maximum of 5500 copies sold (if labelled on the popular Concert

Classics series) which, according to EMI's classical music marketing manager J. K. R. Whittle, meant that '... studio charges will tend to kill the project'.²¹ But Whittle recognised that in the long term it was worth investing in these two artists as they would probably be 'the great ones of the future'.

David Bicknell, as Managing Director, did not think that the company was justified in supporting this 'encouraging young talent' through the International department of EMI. He wrote in a memorandum: 'If we need cellists, the greatest are at our beck and call and, therefore, this couple will stand or fall by their UK reputation, so if we cannot afford to finance them, a contract is not warranted.'²²

The view that cellists were an expendable commodity was a common one. Doubts about the wisdom of promoting another cellist were also expressed by Capitol Records, EMI's USA sister company: '... cellists have been legendary poor sellers on records and concert circuits. However, Jacqueline du Pré may prove an exception.'²³

If Bicknell's idea was originally to market the du Pré–Bishop duo as 'local' artists, their rapidly growing careers (both separately and as a duo) justified that within a year their duo should be upgraded to 'international' status within the internal mechanics of the EMI bureaucracy. They were contracted on a shared-royalty basis.

Their recording has already been discussed in chapter 12, but suffice it to say that even before its release, plans had been set in motion for du Pré and Bishop to continue recording together. A date was fixed to make both Brahms sonatas in May 1967; in view of Jackie's sabbatical studying in Moscow and her period away from the cello caused by glandular fever, it couldn't be arranged earlier.

As it was, events took a different course. In December 1966 Jackie met Daniel Barenboim, who soon became her principal recording partner, both in his capacity as conductor and as pianist. But even before that date Jackie no longer wanted to commit herself to playing duos exclusively with Bishop. In the autumn of 1966 she had spoken to Peter Andry about the possibility of recording the Chopin and Franck sonatas with the pianist Fou Ts'ong. Other projects discussed in 1966 included a recording of the Brahms Double Concerto (Jackie wished to play it with Hugh Maguire), as well as a definitely agreed plan to record the Schubert C major Quintet with Menuhin. Nothing came of these particular ideas, which were to be overtaken by another chapter in Jackie's life.

15

Moscow Interlude

... for in seeking a powerful master, they seek neither words,
nor information: they ask for an example, a fervent heart, hands
that make greatness.

Rainer Maria Rilke, Letter to Auguste Rodin dated 1 August 1902

In the autumn of 1965 Jackie became the first recipient of a newly
negotiated British Council exchange scholarship that allowed for British
music students to study in the USSR. The reciprocal quota stipulated
that the Soviets would send post-graduate students of science or tech-
nology to Britain in exchange for students of the humanities. The
British Council insisted on the placement of one or two musicians
among the 'art' students at Soviet Conservatoires. By awarding the first
scholarship to Jacqueline du Pré (as a prize, rather than through the
normal audition system) it ensured that, on the British side, the Cultural
Agreement got off to a prestigious start.

Since both Jackie and her assigned teacher, Rostropovich, had busy
concert schedules in the last months of 1965, it was agreed that she
would actually only take up the scholarship half-way through the
academic year. As it was, Ibbs and Tillett had to cancel or postpone
many of Jackie's engagements for the first nine months of 1966, on
the assumption that she would stay in Moscow from January until
September.

Rostropovich had first heard Jackie play when she was fourteen. As
a formality she played another 'audition' for him a few months before
coming out to Moscow. With Richard Goode as her accompanist, she
performed Bloch's *Schelomo* and Beethoven's D major Sonata Op.102
No.2. Jeremy Siepmann, at whose house this audition was held, recalls
that Rostropovich was not only impressed by Jackie's performance, but
was so struck by the energy and authority of Richard's playing in the
opening bars of the Beethoven that he nearly jumped out of his chair.[1]

Mstislav (Slava) Leopoldovich Rostropovich could trace his 'cellistic'
ancestry back to Karl Davydov, whose favourite student Alexander

Wierzbilowicz taught both of Rostropovich's teachers, his father Leopold and uncle Semyon Kozolupov. Rostropovich has often reiterated that his father, both as cellist and pianist, was a better player than himself. Slava started learning the cello with his father at an early age. Leopold not only gave his son a secure grounding in the cello, but encouraged him to compose. Slava also picked up from his father excellent skills on the piano and together they read through much of the musical literature.

On Leopold's early death, the sixteen-year-old Slava enrolled as a student of his uncle Semyon Kozolupov at the Moscow Conservatoire (at his dying father's express wish). The relationship was never a particularly happy one and Rostropovich maintains that his formation as a musician was due rather to his Conservatoire composition teachers Shebalin and Shostakovich. At the age of nineteen he won the coveted gold medal for graduate students. The previous year he had been awarded first prize in the cello section of the All-Union Competition for performers, where Shostakovich, as head of the jury, overruled his uncle's intrigues to withhold the prize from him. These prizes guaranteed Rostropovich a career in his own country, but he had to wait until the mid-1950s before the Soviet Union emerged from its isolation in the wake of Stalin's death to be able to travel and play abroad.

Rostropovich realised the importance of popularising his chosen instrument and was never above playing attractive virtuoso pieces, as well as the standard repertoire. In his early years as a performer he travelled all around the Soviet Union, playing for people who had never heard live classical music before, arriving in the most isolated corners of the country by river-boat or huskie-drawn sleigh.

But Rostropovich saw his real mission in life to be the creation of a new repertoire for the cello. Setting about his task with energy, he not only commissioned works by the most illustrious Soviet composers (Prokofiev and Shostakovich included), but besieged composers all over the world for new pieces. In the West, one of the first to respond to his remarkable gifts and his enthusiasm was Benjamin Britten, who wrote a series of works for him. With his exuberance, contagious energy and phenomenal memory, Rostropovich has always been an ideal champion for new music.

In the 1963–4 season he gave a cycle of concerts in Moscow and Leningrad, performing more than forty cello concertos covering the whole repertoire from the baroque to the present day. He repeated this concerto marathon in a reduced form in London in 1966, then condensed it further to a two-week cycle in New York in 1967.

Rostropovich started teaching at the Moscow Conservatoire while in his early twenties, and was soon promoted to become Head of the Cello Faculty at both the Moscow and Leningrad Conservatoires. To add to his accomplishments he was an excellent pianist and often accompanied his wife, the soprano Galina Vishnevskaya, in recital. He had also recently taken up conducting, to which he was to devote increasingly more time from the late 1960s onwards.

His whirlwind energy, and his uncompromising standards of artistry and instrumental virtuosity, had won him enormous popularity with audiences at home and abroad. He also brought these qualities to the classroom and was much sought after as a teacher.

In fact, Rostropovich had made a unique commitment to teaching for the first six months of 1966 in order to prepare the best Soviet students for the prestigious Tchaikovsky Competition, which was to take place in June 1966. Hence, apart from a few days away on brief concert tours, he remained stationed for a full five months in Moscow.

The preparations for the Tchaikovsky Competition started in early February in Moscow, when students were selected in a series of arduous trials on a national level. The top five prize-winners were rewarded with the chance to represent the Soviet Union in the Tchaikovsky Competition. Three of them were from Rostropovich's class and the youngest of them was the eighteen-year-old Mischa Maisky, currently studying in Leningrad.

It was, therefore, against a background of competition fever that Jackie arrived in Moscow on a bleak and cold winter afternoon in late January 1966 – just before her twenty-first birthday. She was met at the airport by the British Council representative and taken to the conservatoire hostel on Malaya Gruzinskaya street, where she was to stay.

I myself had arrived from England sixteen months earlier to study in Rostropovich's class and was likewise living in the hostel. I had, in fact, met Jackie briefly in England the previous summer. Knowing then that she was to come out to Moscow, my former teacher Anna Shuttleworth had taken me to a concert in Great Bedwyn Church where Jackie played the Rubbra *Soliloquy* and Leighton's *Veris Gratia* with the Newbury String Players. I still retain a clear image of her walking out of the church in the late afternoon with the sun streaming on her golden hair.

Rostropovich had instructed me to look after Jackie in Moscow. I vividly recall how impressed I was that, despite her tiring journey, Jackie's immediate wish on arrival was to go to her room and to play the cello. I later realised that this stemmed from the sense of security that Jackie achieved through doing the thing that was most familiar to her in such a strange and foreign place. It certainly did not reflect a desire to do any serious practice that evening.

Soon, Jackie had recovered her strength and we went round to meet Rostropovich at his flat in the centre of Moscow. He asked her what she wished to learn from him. I remember he seemed somewhat taken aback when Jackie replied without hesitation 'technique'. He suggested that in that case she might look at the instrumental study repertoire and I was delegated to get hold of some music for her. Within hours, I had managed to lay hands on a large pile of virtuoso pieces and concertos by such nineteenth-century cellistic luminaries as Romberg, Popper, Davydov and Goltermann. At the time, I often wondered if Jackie so much as glanced at them. My suspicions were confirmed when, years later, on looking through her music, I discovered these self-same scores in pristine condition, mostly with their pages still uncut. Certainly, she never played any of this music while in Moscow.

At this first meeting Rostropovich also suggested that Jackie should tackle Prokofiev's *Sinfonia Concertante* Op.125, an idea which met with her immediate approval. This work, in essence a rewriting of the Cello Concerto Op.58 of 1938, was created during 1951–2 with the partial collaboration of Rostropovich – its dedicatee and its first performer. At the time of writing, the *Sinfonia Concertante* was considered so technically challenging that for many years Rostropovich remained its only performer. But by the 1960s several young Soviet performers had taken it up, notably Natalia Gutman.

Jackie's arrival in Moscow coincided with the two-week winter break in the Russian academic year; the Conservatoire was closed from 25 January until 7 February. Many students (myself included) went home for this short winter holiday. I entrusted Jackie to the care of several students at the hostel, among them the cellist David Geringas, another Rostropovich student with whom she managed to communicate in broken German. Geringas lent Jackie his copy of the Prokofiev *Sinfonia Concertante* and was delighted when she in turn produced some cello duets by Offenbach and Couperin, which they played together.

Naturally, Jackie found immediate solace in the small English-speaking foreign community at the hostel. This contingent was far outnumbered by students from the Eastern European satellite countries, North Vietnam and Cuba. But among its members were two Mexican composers, a Brazilian composer, a Yugoslav pianist, a Norwegian pianist, an Australian violinist and myself. In her first weeks Jackie struck up a friendship with Rocio Sanz, a tall slim Mexican composer aged about twenty-six, who initially helped her adapt to Russian hostel life.

Foreigners found the most difficult adjustment lay in coping with the Russian diet, especially as fresh food and fruit were not readily available. Students usually either fed at the very basic hostel canteen or cooked themselves whatever they could procure in the meagrely stocked Soviet shops. Jackie used to cause amazement by buying up all the oranges at the canteen – for the Russian students oranges were a luxury, sold at an exorbitant price per piece.

As to her first impressions of student life, Jackie wrote to her friend Madeleine Dinkel, 'The atmosphere of the famous Conservatoire is all that one expected it to be – intensely earnest, hardworking and utterly professional, and for the talented ones a survival of the fittest (seeing that there is so much talent). I don't know many people as I do not come here [to the Conservatoire] frequently, but at my hostel I do not lack for friendly people with whom I hope to continue warmest possible friendship after I leave Moscow.'[2]

In the yellow brick five-storey hostel – newly built in 1964 – rooms were shared between two students, an unheard-of luxury by Russian standards. The rooms were in fact quite spacious, with large double-framed windows, simply furnished with couches, which also served as beds, a couple of chairs and a table. At the entrance were two cupboards for clothes and provisions; in winter, students simply hung food out of the window as a makeshift refrigerator. There was often a painfully embarrassing discrepancy between the contents of a foreign student's wardrobe and a Russian's. In Jackie's case all the more so, as she had arrived with several suitcases of clothes, including her gold concert gown made by Madeleine Dinkel, which seemed to the Russians to have come straight out of fairyland.

Each room also had an upright piano and there were other practice facilities in the basement. In these downstairs rooms the keenest musicians started their day at six-thirty in the morning. With what Jackie described as 'trumpets snarling, pianos scaling, and singers screeching',[3] sleeping in became difficult. On each floor there were also communal kitchens and bathrooms. But one had to traipse down to the ground floor to the showers, where hot water was not lacking, if other comforts were. For the girls, the greatest disturbance was caused by draughts of icy air and peeping toms spying on their washing activities. Even when the window cracks were boarded up with hardboard, the persistent peepers would drill holes in it from outside, before being chased away by an indignant concierge. The courtyard side of the hostel gave students a view of the basic realities of life – it was often used as an outdoor lavatory by passing drunks.

One of the concierges, Auntie Tonya, whose duties included reporting on the students' coming and goings, befriended us. She seemed wizened, toothless and old at forty, but for all that she was a great character and agreed to wash our floors and do our laundry for a small price; (Jackie delighted her by giving her a large quantity of her winter clothes when she left). Years later, when 'Tyotya Tonya' heard of Jackie's death, she implored an English student to put roses on her grave on her behalf.

Jackie's room-mate was a quiet girl called Tania, whom she described as 'a pianist from Lyubov (meaning love), small and chubby, because she cannot bear to eat anything other than pasta, bread and potatoes. We see little of each other and when we do communications are strictly limited.'[4] This lack of communication was due – at least initially – to Jackie's ignorance of Russian. But she attended the obligatory Russian lessons for foreigners at the Conservatoire and succeeded during her five months there in learning enough for survival purposes. What Russian she knew on arrival in Moscow was confined to some four-letter words and naughty phrases, which had little practical purpose beyond their shock value. All in all, it must have been a bewildering experience for Jackie to be thrown in at the deep end of Moscow student life, not least because, in the closed society of communist Russia, foreigners were simultaneously objects of suspicion and enormous curiosity.

During the first two or three weeks of her stay Jackie had her lessons privately with Rostropovich in his apartment in the very centre of Moscow. Thereafter, he taught her both in the Conservatoire class and at individual private lessons at home, a compromise that suited her very well. Mstislav Leopoldovich – as he was known to Russian students – allowed Jackie to call him by his diminutive name Slava. This in reality was a concession to a foreigner's difficulty in pronouncing his name and patronymic, for it would have been unthinkable for a Russian student to use this informal manner of address with a teacher or older person.

Early in the proceedings, Slava told Jackie that he was determined to give her fifty lessons in the five months of her stay. Effectively, it was an impossible aim, although he did give her a large amount of his time and they clocked up at least thirty lessons.

It was a memorable event at the Conservatoire when Rostropovich presented Jackie to the class for the first time. As the teacher with the greatest popular appeal, his classes were always packed out. His own students (sixteen in all) were expected to be present for as much of the day as possible, whether or not they were to play. But other conservatoire students and outside musicians would ask permission to listen in as well. And on some occasions the observers included such distinguished artists as David Oistrakh and Gennadi Rozhdestvensky.

An expectant crowd had gathered to hear the new English girl. Because the Russians were so cut off from what was happening outside their country they had little idea of Jackie's international reputation. In general, they had a very low opinion of Western musical training and the few other Western European students like myself whom they had met did little to change their prejudice. Thus, the moment Jackie started playing (she brought Prokofiev's *Sinfonia Concertante* to her first lesson) she created a sensation. Word spread with lightning speed that an extraordinary cellist and unique talent had arrived.

The general standard of playing in the class was, of course, very high and many of Rostropovich's students of that time went on to have successful performing careers; among them were Natalia Gutman, Karine Georgian, Victoria Yagling, Tamara Gabarashvili, Tatyana Remeinikova and David Geringas. Gutman and Georgian were among those who pointed to one particular feature in Jackie's make-up that they found quite extraordinary – namely, her complete freedom, both in her playing and in her everyday behaviour. That she was such a spontaneous child of nature, loving, generous and exuberant, was a self-evident truth. But for Russians who had grown up in the repressive society of Soviet communism, educated in a rigidly disciplinarian system and instilled with the idea of duty, whereby your work had value only if it brought glory to your country, Jackie seemed to come from another planet. She played with such a sunny radiance, yet there was no apparent trace of work or discipline behind what she did, rather a massive input of joy and energy.

It is almost a truism to say that the Moscow Conservatoire in those years was geared to train students to win international competitions. Without a prize under the belt, no Russian musician could think of beginning a career (or, for that matter, ever travel abroad). For Jackie, who had already achieved the pinnacle of an international career, there was something sad in this obsessive ambition to win competitions. She disliked the effect of pressure on the students' attitude to music-making.

Not surprisingly, by virtue not only of her extraordinary talent, but of her background and character, Jackie stood out from the rest of the students. The inspirational give and take between Rostropovich and Jackie created an electric atmosphere in the class, and little remained of the traditional pupil–teacher relationship. Soon, her lessons assumed the character of a dialogue between two equal figures and as such became the highlight of Rostropovich's classes.

On the whole, Jackie enjoyed the aspect of the class audience, knowing that she had the chance of more subdued teaching in the privacy of Rostropovich's flat. It was natural that Rostropovich did on occasion play to the gallery in the packed-out classroom and he some-times got a laugh at a student's expense. We were all in awe of his acute ear and his quick tongue, and knew that we could never get away with anything other than our most total effort. Overall, he tried to build up rather than destroy a student's confidence – but he sometimes put it mercilessly to the test.

Rostropovich's teaching reflected his exuberant character, his dynamic energy and his mercurial speed of thought. We were all spellbound by Jackie's ability to assimilate his suggestions instantly. Rigorous in his demands, he could be impatient when his students reacted slowly – and most of us needed time to digest new ideas or technical hints. Yet Jackie's instantaneous response never involved compromise and she always retained her own identity.

In general, Rostropovich was far more interested in communicating his insights into the music and his ideas about artistry than teaching instrumental technique. He rarely appeared with his cello in class, preferring to demonstrate on the piano. He claimed that this was because it would be wrong for his students to imitate him. It was expected that, after a rigorous training at specialist music schools, all students should be masters of the instrument.

However, imitation was effectively an unavoidable aspect of the class system, since all students were made to study their professor's 'edition' of any given work. Thus the initial learning process meant incorporating Rostropovich's bowings and fingerings from the start. In fact, the class assistant Stefan Kalyanov and the class pianist, a small, ferocious-looking but warm-hearted black-haired woman from Daghestan, Aza Magamedovna Amintaeva, were almost fanatical about adhering to the Rostropovich 'edition' (in regard to tempi and dynamics, as well as fingerings and bowings), and in this respect they were more catholic than the Pope himself.

Aza Amintaeva adored Jackie and made herself readily available for rehearsals when required. Rostropovich enjoyed teasing Aza and dubbed her 'Oysa' – the diminutive of Stalin's name, Iosif, noting that Aza's profile and somewhat evident moustache gave her an uncanny resemblance to the feared dictator.

Rostropovich, however, did not expect Jackie to copy his fingerings and bowings in the way his other students did. He often made suggestions about them or encouraged her to use less bow, to refrain from an open string or a slide, to use another string for a certain passage and so forth. For Jackie, there was no problem in changing these instrumental details instantaneously (or, if she wanted to, to change back to what she had been doing before). In general, Rostropovich aimed to help her harness and use her enormous energy to best effect. He worked on what sometimes appeared to be a weakness in bow strokes, trying to eliminate some of the occasional roughness in a middle-speed spiccato stroke and in attack.

Rostropovich drew on a rich world of associative ideas and images to convey the importance of creating atmosphere in music (and in particular of creating it in advance of the sound, before putting bow to string). Yet he remained insistent that one should never lose sight of the overall structure and form. He would frequently demand that Jackie sacrifice a particular moment of beauty (such as a luscious glissando, or an indulgent rubato) to benefit the whole.

Jackie herself used to recount that when she played for Casals she knew instinctively how he wanted the music to go and anticipated his corrections by playing it 'his way'. Although she tried to apply this rule up to a point in her lessons with Rostropovich, it was not always so easy. Perhaps he was a more unpredictable artist than Casals. Certainly his teaching, rooted as it was in the powers of his original imagination, had an intuitive, inspirational side.

Mischa Maisky, who became a student in the class the following year, still maintains that Rostropovich was often more inspiring as a teacher than as a player. As a young and impressionable eighteen-year-old, Maisky was in those days wildly enthusiastic about everything. He worshipped Rostropovich and was bowled over by Jackie.

Maisky recalled that Rostropovich exerted his enormous force of personality with an almost hypnotic power. 'Inevitably, Jackie was influenced by him at the time. No matter how much personality any of his students may have had, Rostropovich's was much more forceful. Jackie, of course, had more personality than the whole lot of the other students put together, but she too fell under Rostropovich's spell. Ultimately, because she had such a strong nature, she was also able to go back to doing her own thing.'[5]

Maisky was incredibly impressed by the ease of Jackie's playing:

> With her, you had no feeling of the instrument – the music flowed from her directly and spontaneously. One might say that certain cellists had a better technique than Jackie's – they could play cleaner and faster – but none of them possessed her quality of natural expression. I believe in the distinction between technique and virtuosity. Virtuosity emanates from technique, but goes way beyond it and undoubtedly Jackie possessed it. In her case she had overwhelming energy – it was almost scary – and this energy compensated for anything else she may have lacked. Jackie had that special technical prowess reminiscent of the spirit of virtuosity found in a Horowitz or a Heifetz.

Maisky remembers a particular lesson at Rostropovich's flat when Jackie played Tchaikovsky's *Rococo Variations*. 'I can still visualise Rostropovich showing her his elegant way of playing ricochet in the cadenza – down-bow and with a beautiful diminuendo. It was one of the few times when he actually demonstrated something on the cello. Jackie, of course, was able to reproduce it, she could do anything that anybody showed her.'

I was present at that lesson as usual in my capacity of interpreter and recall how Rostropovich helped Jackie develop a greater variety of spiccato bow strokes in the faster variations and urged her to use suave, cool colours in the expressive slow variations. He could not abide a facile 'heart-on-sleeve' type of expression in Tchaikovsky's music, where sensibility was mistaken for sensuality. For Rostropovich, Tchaikovsky's music was rarely an expression of a tangible reality, but rather a nostalgia for a lost world, or a yearning search for an unobtainable happiness. Emotional restraint and great sophistication were the prerequisites of Tchaikovsky interpretation.

It was natural that Jackie should be most open to Rostropovich's teaching in the repertoire that he was most closely associated with – Tchaikovsky, Shostakovich, Britten and Prokofiev. Unusually, she marked her music with his suggestions – something she only occasionally did for Pleeth and never for Tortelier or Casals. In the Britten Cello Sonata, for instance, Jackie wrote down as an epigram to the first movement Dialogue: 'Struggle between the world of unreal desire and the reality of what you are.' This corresponded to Rostropovich's understanding of Britten's sensitive and vulnerable nature, and of the conflict between his homosexuality and his wish for the warmth and security of a normal family life – actually not a million miles from Tchaikovsky's anguished inner world. Jackie's other written comments in the first movement concerned concrete technical effects. Rostropovich asked for stillness in the opening – the bow should remain stationary in the pauses where the piano plays in response to the cello, thereby creating an atmosphere of theatrical expectancy, a breathing silence. In the animato section he asked Jackie not to exert too much energy so as not to squash the sound, and to remain absolutely liquid in the syncopated quaver string crossings before Figure 2. In the second movement scherzo-pizzicato he demanded greater characterisation of the phraselets – Jackie marked 'petulant', 'fed-up' in the opening bars.

In April, Jackie played the first Shostakovich concerto for Rostropovich, both at his home and in class. Although she had acquired the music when it was first published in 1960, she got down to learning the concerto in Moscow. By coincidence, that very month Shostakovich was busily writing the score of his Second Cello Concerto, which was to be premièred by Rostropovich five months later, a secret which Rostropovich shared with Jackie.

In the First Shostakovich Concerto, Jackie marked up her copy with some detail on the technical side: 'use compact bow, heavy strokes – not brittle, don't force' and so on. Her other notes concerned the atmosphere of the music; for instance, the opening of the second movement is marked 'with inner intensity – don't muck up the line'.

And to create a suitable image in the opening statement of the theme in that movement, she wrote – 'A woman knitting and singing simply, without the emotion of tragedy'. Again, Rostropovich insisted on restraint, only building up the emotional tension as the music developed. The pizzicato chords near the beginning of the cadenza are likened to 'the chiming of a clock' and so on. At the end of the finale, Jackie analysed the repetitions of the final repeated G chord numerically, as an aid to memorising the last two pages.

Jackie covered a very large repertoire with Rostropovich. But as time went on, she spent more time 'reviewing' it than learning new works. Effectively, the only new pieces she did learn were by Prokofiev – the *Sinfonia Concertante*, the sonata, the Adagio from *Cinderella*, and she started learning the Concertina Op.132.

Perhaps her interest in Prokofiev was enhanced by meeting his widow Lina Ivanovna (the composer's first wife) and his son, Oleg. Her introduction came through acting as a messenger for her friend Camilla Gray, the English art historian. Camilla had visited Russia several times to research her book on early twentieth-century Russian art. She had met Oleg Prokofiev on her first visit and in 1963 they decided to marry. With a contrariness that was typical of the Soviet authorities in those years, the couple's plans were continuously thwarted as Camilla was refused a re-entry visa to the Soviet Union. Neither was Oleg permitted to leave the country. Thus they were destined for six years of separation, while 'messengers' from London and Moscow occasionally delivered news and letters from one to the other, thereby helping to keep the relationship alive.

Oleg remembered his first meeting with Jackie, likening her appearance to a Rubens painting of a florid young Flemish beauty. He spoke excellent French and good English, and was happy on occasion to act as a guide to Moscow. Jackie was thrilled, in particular by a visit to the beautiful churches at Kolomenskaya on the outskirts of Moscow, with their picturesque setting overlooking the ice-covered Moscow river. She and Oleg travelled out there on a sunny, cold winter's day by tram. Jackie attracted attention (and disgruntled mutterings from old ladies) with her freely flowing long blonde hair (for the older generation, untied long hair was a sign of a prostitute), her blue eyes and tall stature, and her obviously 'imported', if somewhat inadequate winter clothing. When she volunteered one of her few Russian phrases, Oleg was taken aback that it was full of four-letter words – however, the old ladies on the tram, already agog with curiosity, were even more amazed![6]

Oleg, like many other Russians, had no idea what an extraordinary musician Jackie was until he eventually heard her play in concert right at the end of her stay. His mother, Lina Ivanovna, a collector of celebrities, was genuinely very fond of Jackie without ever realising that she was dealing with a celebrity in her own right.

If Conservatoire discipline seemed somewhat grim to Jackie, there was plenty of fun and exuberant parties both at the hostel and outside it. Rostropovich invited the whole class to a couple of parties at his flat, one after a meeting of the Moscow Cello Club, where for some reason an Italian film (*Divorce Italian Style*) was shown. Food was plentiful, vodka flowed, there was much toasting – and of Jackie in particular. Rostropovich was in his element on these occasions with stories, jokes, exhortations and further entertained us by sitting down at the piano to play tangos. There was dancing, where Jackie excelled in a free improvisation. She enthused to her friend Madeleine Dinkel:

> What a marvellous drink vodka is! I've come to love it a lot and have learnt to drink it in true professional style – breath intake 1st, all the vodka knocked back 2nd (head thrust back extravagantly of course), exhalation 3rd, and finally inhalation with exotic fumes swirling up and down in and out of one! Mmmmm! Russians are pretty hot on the sort of party which has countless toasts, everyone gets up and expresses himself and gallons of vodka gets drunk by all. I have been to two great banquets in which Rostro has given me a formal big and warm welcome. Overwhelmed by this I have only been able to reply that I feel the warmth of the reception, I admire and love him and am intensely grateful that these five precious months have been possible.[7]

In the same letter she wrote to Madeleine of the problems of buckling down to work: 'But I am being spurred on by frequent lessons with a man I admire enormously and have come to love a lot. He has given me some wonderful tuition and has spent most of his time digging away at the hysteria and extravagance which are so firmly rooted in my playing. What relief!'

Similar sentiments were expressed in a letter to Guthrie Luke:

> My teacher is, in fact, doing me a great deal of good one way or another, and the basis of his musicianship feels very similar to mine which helps enormously to support me in the weakest places. Rostropovich is an

inspired teacher and a very definite one, which is both moving and invigorating. He hates a certain hysteria in my playing which has also bothered me a lot and he has been masterfully removing it (thank the Lord!) in the works that we have so far studied. As for the tempo of the last movement of the Schumann concerto, I agree with you that I have taken it too fast in the past. I think that you will find this changed when you next hear it.[8]

This last sentence was in reference to an earlier comment of Guthrie's that, at a recent London concert with the Mozart Players Jackie had taken the *sehr lebhaft* marking of the last movement of the Schumann concerto as almost a one in the bar presto, and that he wondered if this was what the composer meant.

In fact, Rostropovich's lessons with Jackie on the Schumann concerto were some of the most thrilling of all. Jackie performed the music with a touching beauty, with enormous poetry and inner feeling. But at Rostropovich's exhortation she contained her expression within a tighter structure. After they had finished working on the concerto Rostropovich exclaimed with enormous excitement. 'This is the most perfect Schumann I have ever heard; Jackusenka [his diminutive of her name], if you ever play it any differently I will come and burn your house down!'

Rostropovich's wife, Galina Visnevskaya, generally expressed little interest in his students. But once Slava insisted that she should listen to Jackie playing Bach's Third Unaccompanied Suite. Galina was much impressed, not least by the fact that a female could have such complete mastery of that 'masculine' instrument the cello. With this encouraging example Galina overcame her initial resistance and allowed their nine-year-old daughter Olga to take up the cello.

Jackie certainly made good use of her time in Russia, although she also suffered from homesickness, and missed her family and her musician friends. Once she remarked to Natasha Gutman that she could not understand why Russian musicians so rarely sat down to make music for fun. Natasha accepted this comment as a challenge and invited Jackie round to her flat for an evening of chamber music, where they played, among other things, Couperin duets and the Schubert two cello Quintet. (In fact, Natasha was later upbraided by her teachers for this forwardness in associating with foreigners.)

At the end of March, Rostropovich went to Switzerland for the best part of a week. To my delight he asked Jackie if, in his absence, she would work with me on the Lalo concerto; I was to profit from what he called her 'Spanish temperament'! I soon wrote home describing how Jackie had helped me enormously. I concluded: 'She could be a marvellous teacher – she is very inspiring.' My letter continued about our plans for that day: 'Tonight Jackie and I are to meet Natasha Gutman who will give us tickets to Richter's concert, where he is to perform (apparently the Shostakovich Quintet) with the Borodin Quartet. Jackie and I will shortly take our letters to the embassy, then walk to the Conservatoire (about forty minutes) for a horrible meeting where we will be told about the Twenty-third Party Congress and then, at last, to hear Richter.'[9] I doubt if either Jackie or I paid much attention to anything said about the Twenty-third Party Congress; it was one of the rare attempts by the Conservatoire authorities to indoctrinate us Western students.

We were lucky, because political indoctrination formed an inescapable part of a Soviet student's life. But, in the Soviet Union indoctrination did not necessarily apply only to politics; it was also evident in certain attitudes to music. Sviatoslav Richter was the undisputed idol of all Muscovite musicians and it was heresy to dare criticise his playing. Jackie was sceptical about any form of idolatry, but she also kept an open mind and went to several of his concerts.

As Jackie relaxed into the swing of being a student without the pressures of performance, she came to enjoy the less serious side of life more and more. We would walk around Moscow, visiting churches and museums, often in the company of Alice Waten, a violinist from Australia, and Liv Glaser, a pianist from Norway. In summer we once took a trip on a hovercraft from the Moscow Khimki river station, out on the river and canal complex to the beautiful birch and pine woods. We became friendly with a young couple from the British Embassy, Roderic and Jill Braithwaite – Roderic's father Warwick and brother Nick were both conductors. They often gave us meals and allowed us to use their flat as a haven, when we were tired of noisy hostel life. Jackie had a wickedly amusing gift of mimicry, and there was an inordinate amount of giggling and fun in the intervals between lessons and study.

When the long-awaited Moscow spring arrived it brought a change of spirit as well as season. In late March Jackie wrote to Madeleine Dinkel, 'it means months of snow and ice are being unwillingly melted into big brown steams and puddles. Water overflows from the gutter down one's neck and the beautiful brilliant sunshine and the blue, blue sky which go with the intense cold have given way to the greyness of the undecided season. Everyone waits, longs for the first glimpse of fresh green and from then on there will be no looking back and Moscow, with its plentiful trees and boulevards will be a really beautiful city.'[10]

A month later she wrote to Guthrie Luke, wondering whether spring had not got muddled with summer. 'It is hard to believe that what has been frozen, white, brown and bare all winter is now sweating with heat, green, brown and bursting with new life. Moscow is a silent city in winter as snow is an effective sound-proofing, but in the summer it rings with the cries of children playing in the street and with the usual city deafening noises. The change is really too sudden between the two seasons, and without the Easter holiday which we are used to, many of us are feeling Spring Fever!'[11]

Spring Fever culminated in a visit to Leningrad, 'land of my dreams' as Jackie called it. To make it a real holiday, at Rostropovich's suggestion, she left her cello behind. We travelled by the overnight 'Red Arrow' train. To her amusement, Jackie found herself sharing a compartment with a burly Red Army general – in Russia sleeper bookings are not arranged according to sex. We stayed at the European Hotel, across from the splendid Philharmonic Hall and did our sight-seeing on three sparkling sunny days. One afternoon we took a hovercraft out to Peterhoff, and walked in the gardens of the park where, after the pine and birch of the Moscow forests, the beautiful oak and beech trees reminded us of dear old England.

Jackie wrote about the whole marvellous experience to Madeleine Dinkel:

Today I arrived back from three sublime days in Leningrad. I don't think I have ever had a more perfect holiday; it consisted of looking at choice works from choicest painters and architects, of walking in the great fountain garden at Peterhoff (the country house, or rather the palace of Peter the Great), of picking wild flowers in the tender sunshine of spring (this after a spectacular thunderstorm the night before) and of listening to two of the world's greatest musicians in probably one of the most beautiful halls of the world. Can you imagine the drunken state I am in? Oh, my God the beauty and complete abundance of it, of the famous Hermitage. I drifted from room to room containing Rembrandts, stunning chandeliers, great crystal and precious stone vases, French impressionists, wide be-statued stairways, white, white dining halls, intricate patterned wooden-inlaid floors, big windows with views on to the Neva which was chock-a-block with great drifting cracking ice-lumps, pillars of every imaginable marble, precious stones inlaid in intricate flower, bird, geometrical designs & patterns in tables, gloriously painted & designed lofty ceilings, beautiful crockery, and ... and ... etc. But above all for me, the REMBRANDTS. I had no idea that they were there, and I just stood and wept as the force and emotion of it all charged into me.[12]

The cracking ice lumps on the Neva were a result of that St Petersburg phenomenon – the climatic clash between thawing winter and resplendent summer, as miles upstream, the ice on Lake Lagoda finally breaks up. When visiting the Petropavlovsky fortress we were much amused to see ordinary Soviet citizens in their very unglamorous underwear soaking in the sunshine under the fortress walls by the banks of the ice-loaded Neva.

Rostropovich's purpose in going to Leningrad was to perform a concert with the Leningrad Cello Club. Jackie and I attended some of the rehearsals, where the orchestra of cellos read through a large repertoire, including Karl Davydov's *Hymn*. She adored the sound of the hundred-strong massed cellos and was pleased, as the owner of the Strad named after Davydov, to hear his music in the city where he had lived and performed. In fact, Jackie had brought her other Strad with her to Russia, having been advised to leave the Davydov at home. There was the anxiety that the Soviets might reclaim the instrument as a national treasure, although it had been taken out of the country well before the 1917 revolution in circumstances that were totally legal. But both Mrs Holland and Charles Beare had advised against taking any risks.

A memorable moment at the rehearsals was when Rostropovich suggested to Jackie that she play the timpani in a read-through of Salmanov's *Triumphant Ode*. She was delighted to go and 'have a bash'. The Cello Club concert took place on the final evening of our visit at the beautiful Great Hall of the Leningrad Philharmonic. The first half of the programme consisted of duets played by various Leningrad cellists and students, while in the second half the orchestra of cellos played pieces by Salmanov, Golubyev and Glazunov (with harps, double-basses and trumpets added as required), finishing with Casals's *Sardana*. The penultimate item was Villa Lobos's *Bachianas Brasilieras* No.5 originally scored for eight cellos and solo soprano. 'Two of the world's greatest musicians' that Jackie referred to were of course Rostropovich and his wife Galina Vishnevskaya, who performed the solo cello and soprano voice parts in the *Bachianas* (but with a hundred cellos accompanying rather than the indicated eight). Jackie, seated in the front row box seats at the side of the hall, briefly caught Rostropovich's eye, causing him a momentarily lapse of concentration. He stumbled in the unison line with the singer – almost imperceptibly, but enough to be rewarded with a very black look from Vishnevskaya.

On return to Moscow, Jackie's lessons continued, but the intensity wore off as the Tchaikovsky Competition drew near. There was time for some relaxation as well. Rostropovich invited us several times to the Aragvi, a wonderful Georgian restaurant, where we were treated to caviare and vodka. Later in May Rostropovich took Jackie and me as his guests to the Moscow première of Britten's *War Requiem* at the Tchaikovsky Hall. I wrote home about the performance: 'the work speaks very deeply to the Russians. Kondrashin conducted and Vishnevskaya sang superbly. ... When we walked home after the concert Rostropovich told us that English audiences do not appreciate Britten enough, that he should be more loved and respected as he is the only musical genius we have or ever have had ... AND ... that in this country of musical geniuses such as Mussorgsky, Shostakovich and Prokofiev, Britten is better understood and loved than in England.'[13] I think the point was taken, put over as it was, in energetic Rostropovich style!

But Jackie never warmed sufficiently to Britten's music to tackle his Cello Symphony, although she was urged to do so by Rostropovich and others. While in Moscow she did study Britten's First Suite for Solo Cello (it was written the previous year) and I recall her delightedly observing a striking similarity between the themes of the fugue in that suite and Bach's C major Fugue from Book I of the *Well Tempered Clavier*.

Lessons came to a halt when the Tchaikovsky Competition opened on 31 May. The cello competition was held parallel to the violinists', between 1 and 17 June, with Rostropovich and Oistrakh heading the respective juries. The cellists' jury had an extraordinary line-up: Piatigorsky, Fournier, Cassadó, Sádlo and Pipkov, Khachaturian and

Shafran were among the members. The overall level at the 1966 cello competition was exceptionally high, with just under fifty cellists participating, including a strong contingent from the United States. Among the inscribed candidates were Piatigorsky's pupils Steven Kates, Larry Lesser and Nathaniel Rosen, Joel Krosnick, Tortelier's pupils Arto Noras and Raphael Sommer, Cassadó's pupils Johann Goritsky, Florian Kitt and Marco Scano, Fournier's pupils Rocco Filippini and Ken Yasuda. The Soviet team consisted of Tamara Gabarashvili, Karine Georgian, Marina Tchaikovskaya, Mischa Maisky and Eleanora Testelets. Stefan Popov represented Bulgaria.

Jackie had refused to participate, but she was a curious observer of the competition activities. She already knew several jury members and some of the participants, through her travels abroad and international festivals like Spoleto. We not only attended the cello auditions, but went to hear the violinists play the final round with orchestra. (I remember that she was very impressed at the time by Viktor Tretyakov's exhilarating rendering of the Tchaikovsky concerto and even more so by Oleg Kagan's beautiful performance of the Sibelius and Tchaikovsky concertos.)

But altogether Jackie had mixed feelings about the event, and was both repulsed and fascinated by the atmosphere of intense competition and inevitable intrigue. With the competition over and the participants and jury on their way home, Rostropovich had arranged for Jackie to play a public concert on 19 June. He felt that she couldn't leave for England without playing at least once for a Moscow audience. He collected a student orchestra to accompany her at the end-of-year graduation concert at the Grand Hall of the Conservatoire. They agreed on Haydn's C major Concerto and Rostropovich himself took up the conductor's baton. By chance, Karine Georgian, the winner of the Tchaikovsky Competition, had given an excellent virtuoso performance of the same concerto in the competition finals. She remembers seeing Jackie shortly before the concert, going off for a long striding walk to rid herself of her nerves. It came as a surprise to Karine to see Jackie nervous.[14]

The graduation concert, as Roderic Braithwaite remembered, seemed interminable, with conservatoire graduates trooping out one after the other to play substantial offerings from their diploma programme. Trombonists, singers and pianists were interspersed with violinists, flautists and double-bass players. By the time it came round to the final item – Jackie's performance with Rostropovich – the audience was feeling quite dazed and washed out. But only seconds into Haydn's concerto the whole hall was galvanised by the sheer energy of their extraordinary music-making.

Many Muscovites only ever heard Jackie on this one occasion, but remember it as though it had happened yesterday. Perhaps it seemed all the more remarkable, after the fortnight of cello trials at the Tchaikovsky Competition, to hear cello playing that possessed such completely different qualities. Many people burst into tears, others sat rigidly in their seats. Rostropovich inspired the student orchestra to play their best. The rapport between him and Jackie was electrifying. For those in attendance it was an unforgettable occasion.

Mischa Maisky identified the special qualities of Jackie's playing as her natural rapport with the instrument and her idiosyncratic sound: 'When a cellist is really great, as in Jackie's case, the sound emanates not from the instrument and not from the mind, but from something higher – the heart or the soul – and it is united with the instrument. In the same way that we each have individual fingerprints, each great cellist has a unique sound.'

Yet for some Russian musicians the wild elemental force of her playing was almost suspect and 'animal-like'. The physical movement and the hair-tossing went against their concept of the self-discipline and control that are a necessary part of artistry. As Mischa Maisky understood it, Jackie went for high stakes in her playing; but whatever risks she took, she was always saved by an inborn sense of taste. 'She could be refined and delicate, and she could also be totally wild. She walked a tightrope on the borderline of bad taste. If you try to imitate such playing it can easily sound vulgar. But with her hypnotic personality, Jackie managed to draw this fine line between the permissible and the impermissible. She always landed on the right side – it was quite unique.'

Jackie's two stays abroad studying were mixed experiences. She herself contributed to the confused perception of her studies with Tortelier and Rostropovich by saying very different things about them to different people at different times. Ana Chumachenko, a close friend of hers in those days, recalled that Jackie told her that she adored Tortelier, although she disliked his master classes. Similarly, she confided to her that Rostropovich had treated her very badly since he had forbidden her to compete in the Tchaikovsky Competition, which she had wanted to enter.[15] Yet this last statement was far from the truth; Rostropovich often expressed his regret, both before and after the competition, that Jackie did not wish to participate. His wife Galina reacted to the idea of Jackie needing a prize as ridiculous – 'What does she need it for? She has everything as an artist. What would she do with 2500 roubles – buy *matrioshki* [Russian dolls]?' It was clear to everyone that in her career Jackie was destined to reach the top.

The violinist Hugh Maguire recalled, however, that after her return from Moscow Jackie was extremely positive about Rostropovich's teaching and he noticed the influence.[16] His wife Susie remembered that Jackie told her she would always remember Rostropovich's lessons. She was less happy about feeling she was constantly under observation, something most foreigners were aware of in Moscow.

Another violinist friend, Arnold Steinhardt, recalled that he could clearly detect Rostropovich's influence on Jackie's playing directly after she returned from Moscow and he did not like what he heard – it was as if she were negating her own musical personality and assuming her teacher's. Much as he admired Rostropovich's artistry, Steinhardt felt that his style did not suit her and was relieved when this phase of 'unholy mimicry' was over.[17]

Overall, Jackie was careful about what she said, but she made it clear to most people that she had gained much more from Rostropovich's teaching than Tortelier's. She retained a healthy sense of humour about the hierarchical status of the world's great cellists. In private she would entertain friends with a devastating imitation of both her Masters. As time went on, she would emphasise the importance of Pleeth's influence; effectively he had given her not only a cellistic grounding, but had formed her as a musician. While this was a self-evident truth, her repeated statements to this effect in print could be interpreted as a dismissal of her more famous teachers. Benjamin Britten was one who felt deeply hurt on Rostropovich's behalf by what certain of his friends told him of Jackie's reported interviews in the press. Jackie's words seemed to him an expression of ingratitude and disloyalty, if not an actual snub.

Unfortunately, it is all too easy for a journalist to misrepresent or readers to misinterpret the words and ideas of another person. However, Jackie's description of Tortelier's and Rostropovich's teaching to David Pryce-Jones was consistent with what she said in private: 'both of them are so dramatic – they are cinerama.'[18]

Ultimately, as time and the very direction of her life took her further away from the experience, Jackie looked back on her Moscow stay in a negative light. To my mind, retrospective judgement coloured her memories; at the time of her stay there was obviously much that she did enjoy and she had an enormous admiration for Rostropovich. He involved himself with her on an artistic level as he had with no other pupil. Jackie had taken time off to study so as to overcome her doubts and she looked to Rostropovich as an experienced mentor. From his point of view, Rostropovich gave Jackie what he believed to be the right kind of guidance. He never lost sight of her identity and always admired her remarkable ability to translate music from her inner ear directly into sound without the instrument interfering in the process of communication. Towards the end of Jackie's stay in Moscow, Rostropovich paid tribute to her unique talent. While we were at lunch at his home after a lesson, he talked seriously about her role as a cellist and musician. 'There are many cellists who are better than me in the older generation,' he stated, 'but only you, Jackusenka, can play better than me in the younger generation.' He urged her to continue his work in popularising the cello and in creating new repertoire for it.

Ultimately, however, it was Daniel Barenboim who was to become Jackie's musical lodestar and give her the necessary frame of reference as an artist. In being able to identify so completely with him both musically and emotionally, she came as near as she ever could to finding a secure artistic 'home base'. From this viewpoint she re-evaluated her past endeavours and accomplishments, and to my mind it was through this criterion of judgement that she later assessed both her Paris and Moscow experiences in a critical light.

16

New Directions

O! there is – whom I could sit and hear whole days, – whose
talents lie in making what he fiddles to be felt, – who inspires
me with his joys and hopes, and puts the most hidden springs
of my heart into motion.

Laurence Sterne, *The Life and Opinions of Tristram Shandy*

It was while she was in Moscow that Jackie finally came to terms with
herself and her vocation. At last she was able to acknowledge her debt
of gratitude to Iris, to whom she wrote a touching letter of thanks.
'This is just a tiny private note to tell you that I have, finally, at last!
decided to be cellist. As you know I have been battling in the uncon-
scious for years against becoming one and against not becoming one
…' Jackie gave Rostropovich the credit for helping her to accept her
destiny. 'R[ostropovich] believes so totally in my talent. I can't tell you
what a relief it is to finally decide on what I want so much. It is largely
due to your ambition for me and your belief in my playing that has
kept me at it at all, despite everything. So here's a life-long "Thanks"
to you, old girl.'[1]

On arrival back in England, Jackie spent time at her parents' house
in Gerrards Cross, visited her sister and caught up with her London
friends. She needed time to rest and digest her impressions of the five-
month stay in Russia. Jackie had already expressed her reluctance about
returning to the rigorous life of a professional cellist in a letter to her
brother-in-law, Kiffer Finzi: 'I think of the approaching concert work
with horror and fright.'[2] But apart from a visit to the Spoleto Festival
in July for further chamber music, she had no professional concert
dates scheduled until September.

In the last days of June Jackie attended meetings with Mrs Tillett
and with Peter Andry at EMI to discuss next season's plans. A letter
dated 30 June from Peter Andry to Mrs Tillett described a fruitful
discussion with Jackie about proposals for recording. Jackie had agreed
to record Boccherini and Haydn concertos in October and Andry was

to look for a suitable chamber orchestra and conductor. Other projects for the coming season were defined as completing the Beethoven cycle and recording the two Brahms sonatas with Bishop, the Schubert C major Quintet with Menuhin and, with orchestra, Bloch's *Schelomo* and the Schumann concerto (on one LP) with the New Philharmonia. It was hoped that Barbirolli would conduct.³

One can detect Rostropovich's influence in Jackie's other suggestions: a coupling of Shostakovich and Prokofiev sonatas, and an orchestral record of Shostakovich's First Concerto and Prokofiev's Concertino. She also told Andry that she would like to record the Prokofiev *Sinfonia Concertante*, although not until after the following season at the earliest. Similarly, she was anxious to do the Brahms Double Concerto at some future date, although at the time no name was suggested for the solo violinist.

Jackie's second trip to Spoleto was shorter than the first, but she packed in a lot of playing. Once again she was partnered by Richard Goode; this time Brahms was at the centre of their repertoire, with performances of the E minor Sonata Op.38 and the C major Trio Op.87. In the Trio they were joined by the young American violinist James Buzwell who, as Wadsworth recalls, was regarded as the up-and-coming genius of his time.

In the radio recording of the Op 87 Trio from the 10 July concert one can hear how Goode's rock-solid discipline was counterbalanced by the string players' more extrovert temperament, creating an overall effect of drama and passion within a unified structure. Jackie's playing is perfectly integrated with Buzwell's, both in the themes in octave unisons – a device much favoured by Brahms – and in the dovetailing of phrases between the instruments. Throughout the work the players catch the varying moods characteristic of Brahms's music – whether it is the spaciousness of melodic line in the first movement or the elusive, dark melancholy of the second movement variations. The intimate dialogue achieved in the quieter music of the variations is in wonderful contrast to the proud heroic sections. Here it was Jackie, with her refined palette of colour, who set the atmosphere of yearning and world-weariness, heartache and nostalgia. In the following scherzo, the players captured the transcendental and dark character, presenting the music as a sort of Brahmsian version of a ghostly *vision fugitif*. The string players show their ensemble qualities in the integrated colour and bow stroke of the repeated semiquaver motif. Later this motif acquires a threatening, almost eerie quality in the cello's repeated bottom C, answered by the piano's downward arpeggio, where Jackie made her cello sound like an ominous drum beat. Relief from this shadowy sound world is provided when the trio erupts in a glorious singing major. In the finale the players achieve the right balance between the majestic and outgoing side of Brahms and his more elegant light-hearted music. Their communal sense of rhythm and youthful temperament make this altogether a wonderfully exciting performance.

In the Brahms E minor Cello Sonata, performed (and recorded by the RAI) at the midday concert on 13 July, Goode's classical approach comes into its own, as befits a work where the composer openly looks back to baroque and classical models for inspiration. Jackie plays with enormous temperament, indeed, there are moments when she appears to overcompensate for Goode's structured discipline, wanting to stretch the music to its full and forcing the sound almost beyond the limits of the instrument. In investing the long cantabile phrases with an almost sensual quality of parlando, Jackie makes the music speak with such urgency that the boundary between sound and words seems to be transcended. Every note is played with total dedication, and the arched perfection of her phrasing is achieved through Jackie's understanding of the interacting relationship between diminuendo and rallentando. Throughout the build-up of the development section, with its stormy F minor culmination, Goode keeps the reins taut and the rhythm steady, providing the necessary curbed tension to Jackie's passionate outpouring. The moment of real glory comes in the coda, where Jackie bestows her most radiant sound on the long blossoming of the phrase surging upwards in a triumphant E major, driving away all memory of earlier melancholy. The second movement is played with delicate tenderness, evoking the atmosphere of an eighteenth-century minuet. In the trio, taken a jot slower, the players succeed in keeping the rubato of the fluctuating phrases within the confines of the tempo. Goode sets off in a resolute frame of mind at the opening of the finale, showing a sound grasp of polyphonic structure, whereas Jackie claims more for the lyrical romantic episodes. Between them, they create a satisfying unity of vision.

Another of the du Pré–Goode team performances that has survived in the RAI recordings is that of Bach's D major Gamba Sonata. Their music-making in the fast movements is full of rhythmic verve and brilliant vitality, a contrast to the romantic expression of the central adagio, where Jackie's eloquent and free line is sung against Goode's unhurried walking quaver bass. Towards the end of the final allegro Jackie has a tiny memory slip, which she disguises by repeating semiquaver Ds instead of the written sequential passage. It was the kind of error caused by a momentary lack of concentration – something which rarely happened to her. But even if she was somewhat unnerved by this slip she did not show it and her assured exuberance made any such mistake seem of no consequence.

The performance from the 1966 festival that stuck most clearly in Charles Wadworth's memory was that of Beethoven's String Trio in G Op.9, given on 12 July. Wadsworth felt that here Jackie acted as a catalyst for the other two players, James Buzwell and the viola player Walter Trampler.[4] Certainly the surviving radio recording is testimony to her remarkable qualities as a chamber musician, particularly in her wonderful manipulation of the bass line. Even with a simple throbbing repeated quaver bass she could create the motor that drives the music and invests it with character – something that reflects Pleeth's understanding of the multifarious function of a bass line. The ensemble seems to be dominated by the soloistic virtuosity of the outer voices (Buzwell and du Pré), but it is the viola's middle voice, wedged between them, that helps maintain the necessary equilibrium. Walter Trampler's experience of chamber music was matched by Jackie's intuitive musical integrity and they achieve a real blend between them. Buzwell's playing occasionally has an aggressive edge, which actually becomes unpleasant in his harsh, spiky, fast spiccato stroke in the finale. Jackie could match his brilliance without roughness, and had in addition a capacity to be delicate and magically soft, and rhythmically buoyant in the accompanying figures.

In the finale Buzwell sets off at such a presto that the whole movement throbs with a knife-edge quality of excitement through to the end. Jackie achieves rhythmic elegance in her thrusting, dancing quavers accompaniments and remind us that the music should be dominated by rustic high spirits. The short coda shoots off at a hair-raising prestissimo, making the audience wonder whether the musicians will fall off the rails. Instead, they drive the music helter-skelter to a precipitous and triumphant finish – and brings the house down.

Jackie was in her element again at Spoleto and Wadsworth recalls her performances there as a revelation. The next player of a comparable talent to come to Spoleto was Pinchas Zukerman. But as Jackie did not return to the festival in 1967 when Zukerman first went there, she missed meeting her future trio partner until another year had passed.

Back in London, Jackie returned to the flat she shared with Alison Brown opposite the police station at the bottom of Ladbroke Grove. Having been starved of chamber music in Moscow, she was delighted to resume contact with musician friends, among them Hugh Maguire. Jackie used to bicycle up to the Maguires' house in Willesden Green on what Hugh recalled as 'a funny bike with small eighteen-inch wheels'.[5] It was a two-mile ride and uphill all the way. Jackie spent increasingly more time in their large house, enjoying the family atmosphere created by Susie (Hugh's wife in those years) and their five children. Susie was a homely mother figure and took to Jackie at once; the children, in Hugh's words, 'were gaga about her, regarding her as a kind of fairy-godmother.' Jackie loved spoiling them with surprises and presents, and entertaining them with her amazing whistle (she could even whistle in double-note trills). Indeed, the Maguires' six-year-old daughter Rachel took up the cello because of her.

Jackie obviously felt at home in a household which combined the warmth of a family and the possibilities of continuous music-making. Thus it seemed quite natural that one evening, after a long chamber music session, she stayed the night. At this point the Maguires felt that she might as well move in with them, a suggestion she accepted with alacrity. It was while staying with them, towards the middle of August, that Jackie contracted glandular fever, also known as hepatitis, or by its correct medical term, infectious mononucleosis.

Susie, who nursed her through three weeks of illness, recalled that Jackie was under doctor's orders to rest and stay in bed. 'Her fever was coming and going – shooting up and down. When she wasn't feeling too bad she would be very frustrated that she wasn't allowed to play. I remember once coming up the stairs and hearing her playing – I discovered her lying in bed with the cello on top of her.'[6]

During her illness Iris would come and collect and deliver Jackie's laundry – a task that she had assumed when Jackie first left home. One might add that the home laundry service had been carried out by post when Jackie was studying in Paris and that Iris continued to help out with menial tasks even when Jackie got married. Iris may well have been motivated in her wish to help Jackie with these practicalities so as to have a valid excuse for contact with her daughter. Now that she was ill, Jackie had made it clear that she would not come home to be nursed.

Iris was upset and offended. It was evident to the Maguires that, at heart, Jackie was very fond of her mother and acknowledged the influence that she had on her. But as Susie recalled,

> Jackie had deliberately cut her ties with home. She had obviously out-grown her parents. Iris, however, was hanging on and wanted so much to help. She was terribly earnest and found it difficult to communicate with her daughter. Derek was a remote figure. The one person in her family whom Jackie really loved was her maternal grandmother. She spoke of her Gran with great depth of feeling, telling me about her importance in her life. According to Jackie, her Gran was psychic and believed that she had lived in another life hundreds of years before and had been drowned. Jackie was also very attached to her sister Hilary and was considerably influenced by Hilary's husband Kiffer.

Derek and Iris had to content themselves with being on the sidelines of Jackie's life. They made their presence felt, however, in their role of advisers, not only in regard to household matters, but in managing her business affairs. Peter Andry had written in July, asking Jackie if, now that she was twenty-one, EMI royalty payments should still be sent to her father as previously. Further evidence of the family's involvement in her financial affairs can be garnered form the correspondence between Andry and Mrs Tillett. On 22 November Iris accompanied Jackie to a meeting in order to discuss her new contract with EMI with Andry. Iris wanted to know why Jackie's royalty payment for the Elgar concerto had been set at considerably lower a figure than the royalties normally contracted for big-name artists and indeed, lower than the shared royalty she had received for her duo recording with Bishop.

Jackie did not agree to sign the contract proposed by EMI on this occasion and Andry wrote in some agitation to Emmie Tillett, explaining that he felt 'the formality of a contract, rather than making Jacqueline feel restricted, would give her confidence that this Company would do everything in its power to help her career'. He defended the low royalty rate 'because, a) orchestral records are more expensive to make than solos. b) Jacqueline was being coupled with Sir John Bar-birolli, who is world famous. c) The work is in copyright.' He added that 'all payments are always a question of negotiation'.[7] Raising such questions on Jackie's behalf will have smoothed the path for the sub-sequent re-negotiation of her contract with EMI a few months later.

Towards the end of August, Iris and Derek were concerned that

Jackie was not making a quick enough recovery. In consultation with her doctor it was decided that she should be admitted to hospital for thorough tests. As Susie surmised, 'I wonder now, with hindsight, whether this perhaps was the beginning of MS. Jackie took a very long time to get over the hepatitis and I often felt she never completely recovered from it.' After a ten-day stay, Jackie was released from hospital on 3 September. Iris arranged for her to spend some time in France with Mary May. May, Iris's flat-mate from her students days, had a house near Toulon. Although advised to rest and gather her strength, Jackie took her cello and started practising. She also could not resist going for bathes in the Mediterranean, once in full view of the sailors and fishermen of Toulon harbour. On her return, Jackie stayed briefly with her parents, before going back to London (and the Maguires' house) to take up her October engagements, mostly scheduled duo recitals with Bishop. However, she still felt too tired to perform in public and cancelled most of her concerts until early November.

The Maguires welcomed Jackie back into their household, where she felt totally at home. Hugh recalled that 'there was a very happy atmosphere in my house at the time, with chamber music, children going to dancing lessons and very interested in music, and me coming in and out of symphony orchestras, trying to keep Jackie amused. During her convalescence I would try to stop her from practising, although we would also play together so as to keep her fingers going.' Jackie had never seemed to need to practise much, but as Susie observed, 'When she did get down to it, she did so with such intensity and energy that she would soon be drenched in sweat. Probably for this reason she wore summer dresses throughout the year.'

Susie found Jackie to be 'very perceptive, with an intuition for other people'. As she recalled, 'She never sat down for breakfast, but would stand at the table stuffing herself with toast, talking and eating all the time. It was all very jolly.' Jackie saw that Susie was overwhelmed by the demands of her children and her charming, if somewhat unreliable, husband and that she was increasingly allowing herself to become downtrodden. Jackie encouraged Susie to pamper herself by taking her along on shopping sprees. 'I remember going to Harrods with her when she egged me on to buy an expensive coat, something I would never have done without her. She herself acquired this striking emerald-green cape on that occasion and wore it to great effect. She was like a whirlwind with her big smile striding down the street with her hair and her green cape streaming in the wind. People stopped to look at her and stood back to let her pass.' Susie remarked, furthermore, that Jackie enjoyed the stir she caused; she liked male attention and holding court. 'Richard Goode used to come to the house to practise and he played with her a lot. He was obviously intensely attracted to her. Stephen Bishop was less on the scene in those months.'

Jackie had no shortage of admirers and for anyone who played with her, as both Hugh and Fou Ts'ong were to find, it was impossible not to be deeply affected by her music-making, which was such an integral part of her personality. Over these last two years, as Alison Brown noted, Jackie had been feeling her way in relationships with men, and this process of discovery was a vital and positive experience for her.

During the autumn Jackie played a couple of trio dates with Hugh and the pianist Antony Hopkins. One of them was arranged at a music club which Iris helped to run in the Chalfonts, near the du Prés' Buckinghamshire home. Hugh recalled,

> Tony and I drove out there in his sports car – I found it most alarming as he would speed round roundabouts as if he was driving at the Mons rally. When we arrived, Jackie immediately jumped into the car – 'Come on, Tony, do take me for a ride,' she said and off they went for a hair-raising spin. We also played a concert in Northampton – in a venue called the Carnegie Hall, which was a bit of a laugh. The concerts were organised by a delightful man, Joel Burgess, who put on Sunday concerts for people like me who were trapped in orchestras and needed to get out and express ourselves.

As Hopkins recalls, the Northampton concert was a happy occasion, where they performed Beethoven's Trio Op.1 No.1, the Mozart E major Trio and a Brahms cello sonata. 'Jackie still wasn't the really big star she became and was quite happy to play chamber music for the fun of it.' Hugh recalled Jackie's great delight in surprising him with unconventional bowings. 'They always turned out to have their own logic. For instance, in the finale of the Beethoven she played the first three notes of the second theme down down down and it worked wonderfully well.'

If her relationship with Stephen was on the wane, their duo continued to be much in demand. Jackie played some eight or nine concerts with Stephen in November and December, including their second Royal Festival Hall recital, and engagements in Dublin and Portugal.

But her heart was in a new venture, a trio she had formed with Fou Ts'ong and Hugh Maguire.

The Chinese pianist Fou Ts'ong was born in Shanghai and had studied in Poland after winning the Enescu Piano Competition. After completing his studies and winning second prize in the Chopin Competition (when Martha Argerich won first prize), he chose to stay in the West rather than go back to China, where he saw no future for his art in the worsening political climate. In London, he met and married Yehudi Menuhin's daughter Zamira.

Ts'ong remembers hearing Jackie for the first time at the Bath Festival in 1961, playing the Schubert Quintet in a team with Yehudi Menuhin and Gaspar Cassadó.

> I first talked to her when she came with her mother to hear me play a Mozart concerto at the same festival. Then, one day in Yehudi's studio, I heard an early recording of the Elgar, probably a Prom broadcast, and of course I was overwhelmed like everybody else. I next heard her play with Stephen at the Festival Hall. Then time passed and I heard that she had hepatitis. Soon after that, when I was at the BBC Maida Vale Studios doing some recordings, I happened to see Jackie as I was leaving. She smiled at me with great vibrancy, but we didn't speak. Shortly afterwards, Hugh telephoned me and said that Jackie wanted to play trios with me. I was delighted – it was the biggest compliment that could be paid me. And that same evening Jackie came to our house in Canfield Gardens with Hugh and her father, who helped her carry the cello. We sat down and read through lots of trios and had great fun. After that we met often, and soon decided to form a trio professionally.[8]

Ts'ong recalled that initially the rehearsals were simply play-throughs of the works. 'Perhaps we might play something through seven times in a row. When we did rehearse Jackie rarely used words – she just played, and the communication was easy and natural. Jackie might make some little practical suggestion like "don't go ahead quite so much here" or something to that effect. But the actual musical message was all there and we didn't need to discuss interpretation.'

On the other hand, Susie Maguire remembered, 'among the three players there were tremendous discussions as to how things should go. Jackie had a wonderful rapport with Hugh (although his playing was probably not up to hers). They were somewhat less voluble than Ts'ong, who was the most enthusiastic discusser of the group. Jackie tended to brush all talk aside and say, "Come on, let's play." ' As Hugh noted, 'Jackie didn't look at scores and had no academic interest in music – it had to be completely natural.'

Both Hugh and Ts'ong absolutely adored Jackie. Ts'ong had in common with her great imaginative gifts and a very emotional approach to music. As he recalled, 'My nature was in some ways too similar to Jackie's – sometimes when we played together, it was too much.' Ts'ong loved the freedom and the eloquent, speaking quality in Jackie's playing, and remembers a striking example in the way she spun out the big cello tune in the second movement of the C major Mozart Trio.

Hugh shared Jackie's intuitive sensitivity. He was much impressed by her command of the instrument.

Her approach to the instrument and to sound was entirely different from that of the great cellists of the moment – Tortelier and Fournier, for instance. I don't think that she played very much like Bill Pleeth either. It was not a case of pupil playing like teacher, in the way Menuhin played like Enescu, where in the recording of the Bach Double Concerto it is quite difficult to tell them apart. People seldom talk about Jackie's technical prowess, but it was considerable. In her highly original approach it seemed to me that she stepped back several generations. If she was going to do a slide or a portamento she really did it. Neither was she an innovator – in the way that Rostropovich could be regarded as cellist of the future.

That autumn Jackie had also resumed contact with Menuhin. He invited her to participate in two television programmes entitled *The Menuhins at Home*, made in late October. In a studio mock-up of the Menuhins' music room in their Highgate house they performed (with Robert Masters, Ernst Wallfisch and Maurice Gendron) the second movement from Schubert's C major Quintet D956 and a movement of the Brahms's C major Trio Op.87 (with Menuhin and Louis Kentner at the piano). The programmes ended with singsongs round the piano – something, as Christopher Nupen remembers, that most people (Jackie included) found somewhat embarrassing.[9]

Plans were made for Jackie's appearances with Menuhin at the 1967 Bath Festival in June and immediately afterwards they were to tour the USA (with the Festival orchestra) and perform at the Montreal EXPO. And in discussions with EMI in November, firm dates were set up to record the Schubert Quintet with Menuhin from 20 to 22 January

1967. A further commitment was made to record the Haydn C major and Boccherini B flat major Concertos with Daniel Barenboim and the English Chamber Orchestra (ECO) on 17 and 24 April. Sessions were also booked with Stephen Bishop between 9 and 15 May to continue the Beethoven Sonata cycle and to record the two Brahms sonatas.

On 5 November Jackie performed the Elgar concerto with Malcolm Sargent in Liverpool (with the RLPO) and was to appear with him again on 1 December, playing the Delius concerto at the Albert Hall. As Hugh Maguire recalled, 'She was cancelling a lot of dates. To begin with there was the valid excuse of glandular fever. But sometimes she was a little bit naughty about concerts, as if she couldn't be bothered with them. It was a bit like cancelling going to a party at the last minute. Once she "forgot" a date with the CBSO and Hugo Rignold in Birmingham.' The consternation of the manager and players of the CBSO when Jackie failed to arrive for the afternoon rehearsal on 8 December was reported in the *Evening Mail* – 'After frantic all-day efforts to get in touch with her in time for last night's symphony concert, a telegram arrived from Miss du Pré reading: "Most terribly, terribly sorry. Completely confused over the date. Thought it was Saturday." '[10]

Only a week earlier, Jackie had decided that she could not face resuscitating the Delius concerto for her Albert Hall concert. She had already postponed this date from March 1966, with the legitimate excuse of taking time off to study in Moscow. Despite having recorded the piece so successfully, Jackie was never able to overcome her hesitations about playing the Delius in public. Rather than pull out of the Albert Hall concert altogether, and with the excuse of her recent attack of glandular fever, Jackie asked Sargent if she could change the concerto to the Elgar. This last-minute swap considerably ruffled the feathers of many expectant Delius fans!

As these events show, there was an element of irreverence in Jackie's attitude to a serious concert career, rather as if she wished to ridicule the whole atmosphere of pomposity which surrounded the high priests of the music profession. Music-making was for her an opportunity to enjoy herself, not to prove anything. Not that she was without ambition – indeed, she took pride in her engagements with the world's best orchestras and conductors. But she clearly wanted to give rein to her youthful, carefree spirit and enjoy music as part of life. At the end of the day, she loved playing for people whether it was in a big concert hall or the intimacy of a friend's house.

As the autumn proceeded she was spending more and more time music-making in Ts'ong's and Zamira's house. According to Zamira:

> Our house was a cosmopolitan meeting ground, there was nothing particularly English about the household. We would get together in the evenings and play music, go out, perhaps to a concert, or see a film – or just sit and discuss things. There was a lot of talk about other people's performances – how such and such played this marvellously, and why so and so couldn't play this. These gatherings went through the night – I don't know how we survived. Although Ts'ong worked very hard, he always found time for his friends. I had a young child and found it exhausting. It was all right to be tired, just as long as you were interesting and capable of inventing a seven-letter word for scrabble at three in the morning! Jackie was like me – she didn't have that much stamina.[11]

Zamira kept an album which is a testimony to the number of interesting people who passed through their house. It included autographs from pianists such as Tamás Vásáry, Ilona Kabos, Vladimir Ashkenazy, Michel Blok, André Tchaikovsky, guitarists John Williams and George Harrison and other celebrities like Ravi Shankar, Jean-Louis Barrault, Jean Cocteau and Marcel Marceau.

Another frequent visitor to Ts'ong's and Zamira's house was Daniel Barenboim. The young Argentinian-born Israeli pianist was based at the time in London where, after having been one of the most prodigious of child prodigies, he was building up a highly successful 'adult' career as a pianist. In addition, he had just started conducting professionally and had already formed an important association with the English Chamber Orchestra. As Ts'ong stated, 'Of all my colleagues Daniel is the one I most admired. At that time I was very close to him and we used to discuss music every day. Despite the fact that he came from a Germanic tradition, where the construction and architecture of the music are all important, I found him incredibly open-minded – to a most unusual degree. Daniel had that absolute security, which allowed him to be flexible and meant that he could always see another point of view.'

Zamira, who had got to know Daniel through Ts'ong in 1963, found his social ease to be equal to his artistic security:

> Some people found his enormous confidence too much; but I don't

think he was over-confident, rather he was very positive and extrovert and had enormous energy. With lots and lots of friends and girl-friends in tow, there were continual outings to restaurants and talking through the night. He was very good-looking and absolutely charming, and many women seemed to be absolutely devastated by him. Daniel was always awake and lively – he never seemed to go to bed – but he was also very relaxed and laid back. If he had a recording the next day he would go on talking through the night, whereas any other pianist would have been practising like mad. Obviously, Daniel didn't have to practise as much as other musicians, but he was equally serious. Furthermore, he was a generous friend and could transmit his positive attitude to others.

Daniel Barenboim and Jacqueline du Pré had once been briefly introduced in recent months. But now it was their common affliction of glandular fever that aroused Daniel's interest in Jackie again. When Daniel complained to his friends about how ill he felt, they replied unsympathetically, 'Well, if you think you've got it bad, you should just see Jackie du Pré.' His curiosity thoroughly aroused, Daniel used an excuse of a professional engagement (they had been booked together to record Boccherini and Haydn concertos for EMI the following April) to obtain her telephone number from Ibbs and Tillett. Their first conversation was thus a comparison of notes on their symptoms.

Ts'ong, in the meantime, had been enthusing to everybody about Jackie and her incredible playing. 'Every time I saw Daniel I would say to him, "You've just got to hear this girl, you'll have to meet her."' Ts'ong remembered the occasion of their meeting on a late December evening vividly: 'When Daniel walked into the house we had just finished playing something and Jackie was lounging on a couch. I think the seeds of her sickness were already there. She would play with tremendous energy and passion, and afterwards she would collapse.'

As Susie Maguire recalled, 'Hugh and I were at Ts'ong's house the evening that Jackie met Daniel – they just gravitated towards each other immediately. If Jackie was still feeling the after-effects of glandular fever, Daniel, who was also just recovering from it, didn't seem to give into it at all and was full of energy.'

Zamira recalled that evening as 'an electrifying occasion. It started out as just another of our endless get-togethers. Jackie had arrived first with her cello. When Daniel walked in he took one look at her and said in a rather provocative manner, "Well, you don't look like a cellist."'

In her own account of this meeting Jackie would say that her inbuilt shyness about using words and an awareness of being somewhat over-weight 'from eating so many potatoes in Russia' prevented her from making any retort to this 'dark, dynamic person' – her only defence was to get out the cello and play. 'Instead of saying good-evening, we played Brahms,' was how she laconically summed up their first meeting.[12]

Ts'ong recalls the event somewhat differently. 'Jackie reacted to Daniel's remark by taking her cello and saying, "Come on Ts'ong, let's play." We played the Franck Sonata and out-vied each other in expression – it was just one big orgasm after another. After that, Daniel and she started playing, and that was it.'

As Zamira remarked, 'It was very much an evening for Jackie and Daniel, we might just as well not have been in the room. When they started playing they went on for about four hours. Not another word was said, they were speaking to each other in their own language. Afterwards I said to Ts'ong "that was quite something, wasn't it?" Ts'ong was probably feeling a little bit taken aback, although he wouldn't admit it, as he was extremely generous. But he realised that his days of playing with Jackie were numbered.'

Daniel and Jackie were obviously overwhelmed by each other and from that night onwards they spent as much time as possible together. Jackie did not hide from her friends that she was head over heels in love and Daniel, with characteristic pragmatism, identified Jackie as being totally special to him, both as a person and as a musician.

In 1966 Jackie had one more engagement to fulfil – a recital with Stephen Bishop at the Seckers Theatre in Rosehill on 30 December. Back in London, New Year's Eve was celebrated at Ts'ong's house, where the EMI producer Suvi Grubb first heard Jackie play (with Daniel) and immediately 'bagged' her for her next recording, remarking that nobody had yet caught her golden sound on tape. Grubb was amazed that even though the revelry lasted into the small hours, Daniel turned up as fresh as a daisy for his recording session on 1 January at the EMI Abbey Road Studios.[13]

The day after, Jackie took off on tour to Eastern Europe with the BBC SO and Barbirolli (Hugh Maguire, in his capacity as leader, also came on the trip). Thus, the new year commenced on a note of elation, a year that would bring to the brilliant young couple a whirlwind of musical activity, intense personal happiness and adventure.

17

The World At Her Feet

Art cannot be understood, but only experienced.
Wilhelm Furtwängler, *Notebooks*

Jackie's first concert in 1967 took place on 3 January in Prague where she played the Elgar concerto with Sir John Barbirolli and the BBC SO. It was relayed to UK listeners on Radio Three. Thanks to the existing BBC tape, we have an idea of the artistic licence that makes a performance so different from a studio recording. In this case the flaws of the performance are well compensated for by the display of a vivid musical imagination at work. It is in the slow movement in particular that du Pré and Barbirolli demonstrate a spellbinding freedom, where the most delicate hushed pianissimos are achieved through the art of suspense. Rubato is employed to make time seemingly stand still, while we wait with bated breath for an inevitable resolution. Yet the logical flow of the music is never interrupted. On the other side of the equation there are some moments of ragged ensemble, especially in the second movement, where Barbirolli sometimes appears slow off the mark in following his soloist.

After their concerts in Prague, the orchestra and soloists travelled by train to Warsaw, temporarily losing their tour manager, Anthony Phillips, at the border. Phillips had retrieved from the Prague hotel desk the 120-odd passports of the orchestra personnel, but his own was not among them. When discovered in a documentless state at the frontier, he was not allowed to travel on. Moved at the sight of a lone Englishman standing forlornly on the platform, Barbirolli thoughtfully threw him a bottle of brandy from the window of the departing train.

In Poland, it was the turn of the other two soloists – the soprano Heather Harper and the pianist John Ogdon – to perform with the orchestra. Two days later the musicians arrived in Moscow. Hugh Maguire recalled the lethal effect of the extremely cold weather they found there, where wind in temperatures of minus twenty celsius caused the eyes to water and the tears to freeze on the eyelashes – outside, Jackie appeared to have 'icicles' growing around her eyes.[1]

Artists and orchestras from the West had enormous rarity value in Soviet Russia. Apart from a previous visit by the English Touring Opera (with Benjamin Britten conducting his own works) and the National Youth Orchestra, the BBC SO was the first symphony orchestra from Britain to visit the Soviet Union. The chief attraction of their visit lay in the innovative programmes conducted by Pierre Boulez. Muscovite and Leningrad musicians, reared on socialist-realist dogma, had been taught to regard the New Viennese School and the post-war European avant-garde with the greatest suspicion – which, not unnaturally, only had the reverse effect of stimulating an enormous curiosity about such music. In his three Moscow concerts with the BBC SO, Boulez performed works by Schoenberg, Debussy, Stravinsky, Berg, Webern and also his own composition *Éclat*. In Leningrad, in a programme designed to last ninety minutes (where Boulez also conducted Bartók's *Miraculous Mandarin* Suite) the concert went on for nearly double that time due to the prolonged applause of an exhilarated audience clamouring loudly for encores.

Du Pré performed the Elgar concerto with Barbirolli in the beautiful Grand Hall of the Moscow Conservatoire on 7 January. They were also awarded a very warm reception by the Russian audience, but the music they played had less 'novelty' appeal. One wonders how much real interest there was in Elgar's music, even though, to Russian audiences, it was in fact as unfamiliar as Webern's. Rather, it was Jackie's emotional performance and its direct communicative quality that made an enormous impact on the listeners.

Apart from her Elgar performance, Jackie also played a recital with the pianist Naum Walter in Moscow's Tchaikovsky Hall on 12 January, where their programme included the Beethoven D major and Brahms F major Sonatas. Called back again and again by the audience's rhythmic clapping, Jackie played 'The Swan' (from Saint-Saëns's *Carnival of Animals*) as an encore. Again, du Pré made a great impression on the more 'general' public that tended to frequent the Tchaikovsky Hall, many of whom had never heard of her before.

Anthony Phillips recalled Jackie's enormously high spirits during the tour. At the station before departure for Leningrad, egged on by members of the BBC SO, she wrote out in cyrillic letters some rude English words and expressions, then asked an unsuspecting train guard to read out this apparent gibberish. She had the art of carrying out such pranks with charm and innocence, and without offending anyone.

Nobody could fail to notice that Jackie was bubbling over with love – as Phillips remembered, she spoke of nothing and nobody but Barenboim.[2] It was while she was behind the 'Iron Curtain' that the young couple first discovered how costly a relationship between two itinerant concert artists can be in phone bills! True, Jackie, who hadn't much practical sense of geography or understanding of time zones, was never deterred by expense from ringing friends around the world, sometimes waking them at the most unearthly hours of the night.

On her return to London Jackie was granted a couple of weeks' respite before setting out on tour to the USA. It was then that she moved in with Daniel and into his musical and social orbit. Although she always remained her own person, she submitted to his influence willingly, as if wishing in some way to discard her own background. Daniel observed that Jackie talked very little about her upbringing. When he met her family he found that in some ways he had more to talk about (in terms of 'piano shop' and so on) with Iris than Jackie had. 'She was close to her parents, but in a distant way. They no longer had much in common,' he recalled.[3]

Outside her music-making, perhaps the most wonderful and sur-prising thing about Jackie was her total lack of concern with the material side of life. As Daniel put it, 'the concept of career meant nothing to her. Before I had met her, I had heard a little about her from Harold Shaw, her American agent in New York. Shaw was having difficulty as she apparently did not want to come to the USA on a tour, and he asked if I would try and influence her. I said, "Well, I don't know her, although I can try, I suppose."'

Already at their first meeting, Daniel was deeply impressed by Jackie's strong individuality.

> She had what the French call *la force de la nature*. As far as music was concerned she was very alive. She lived totally inside the music and this meant that making music was a way for her to learn something about herself, not something outside herself. That was very obvious. It wasn't so much part of her – she was part of music. Most of her knowledge of music was instinctive and not derived from empirical knowledge. Yet without knowing the formal definitions, she was hyper-sensitive to everything in music, from modulations and harmony changes to struc-ture and form.

Barenboim acknowledged that Jackie sometimes wished that she knew more analytically, but as it was, by the time that he met her at the age of twenty-one she had already attained a very high level of musical development, with what Pleeth called 'endlessness' in her capacity to expand and develop.

Apart from the fascination with her musical personality, Daniel was won over by Jackie's integrity in everyday life, describing her as 'one of the most genuine people I have ever met'. And her sunny radiance was evident in her expression. As Christopher Nupen recalled, Jackie could not look at Daniel or himself without breaking into the most wonderful winning smile. Before long, Daniel and her close friends were calling her 'Smiley'.

When Daniel introduced her to his parents he immediately made it clear to his mother Aida that she was very special to him. Aida, a warm, intelligent and extrovert woman, welcomed Jackie as a member of her extended family and soon they formed a close rapport. Daniel's father, Enrique Barenboim, was a fine teacher and excellent musician. He had tutored his son from the age of five and was, in effect, his only piano teacher. Enrique and Aida Barenboim's cosmopolitan attitude to music and to the outside world contrasted sharply with that of Jackie's parents. They had emigrated from Argentina to Israel when their son was ten years old in 1952, fostering both his Latin roots (Spanish was spoken at home) and his Jewish culture. While remaining enthusiastically Zionist in their political ideals, Enrique and Aida were altogether European in their musical orientation. They insisted that their musically precocious son should attend school normally and, as far as possible, concentrate his concert activities during holiday times.

A man of wide cultural horizons, Enrique Barenboim transmitted to Daniel a wide-ranging knowledge of music and an understanding of the fundamental importance of the great Germanic musical tradition. He encouraged him to take up conducting, while continuing his piano studies with equal intensity, and brought about early contacts with such luminaries as Edwin Fischer and Wilhelm Furtwängler, two figures whose overwhelming influence Daniel has always acknowledged. Periods of study were also arranged with Igor Markevitch in Salzburg, Nadia Boulanger in Paris, and Carlo Zecchi in Rome and Siena.

Thus, in contrast to Jackie, Daniel was equipped with a good general knowledge outside music, had been taught to think analytically and had simultaneously developed a very strong practical sense of the world. Apart from anything, he became an excellent linguist and by the age of twenty he was already fluent in seven languages. Musically speaking, he was unique in his generation not only by virtue of his enormous talent, but through his ability to keep an open mind about all genres of music, combining an awareness of tradition with a forward-looking attitude. Equipped with a pragmatic sense of how the music 'business' operated, Daniel had developed a vision of the role of the interpreter which went far beyond the parameters of most of his contemporaries. His phenomenal memory and innate curiosity gave him a vast first-hand knowledge of music – something that many colleagues found somewhat intimidating.

Although Jackie might not have been as articulate or outwardly confident as Daniel, she could keep her end up when she had a cello in hand. Here her marvellous sight-reading and instantaneous grasp of music was on a par with his. Daniel later paid her the compliment of saying that he had never learnt so much from any other musician. When preparing orchestral scores he often asked her advice about how to achieve effects of sound and colour, and on bowings and fingerings of the string parts.

Daniel had suffered a 'lean' patch in his career in the mid-sixties, but at the time Jackie got to know him he was much in demand as a pianist and was embarking on a successful conducting career, based on his special relationship with the ECO. In the second half of January an important opportunity presented itself when he was asked to substitute at the last minute for an indisposed colleague conducting Mozart's *Requiem* with the New Philharmonia. Daniel's closest friend and confidant, the conductor Zubin Mehta, happened to be in London at the time: 'I went along to the chorus rehearsal and I saw Jackie sitting there. Daniel had mentioned her to me over the phone and spoke of her enormous musical talent. But I didn't know the friendship was that earnest. Then I looked at Daniel and said, "Aha, so there's something going on here." He acknowledged it straight away.'[4]

As Daniel described it, 'Our life was such a whirlwind, it was all music.' It was not just music on stage, either. In such spare time as they had they made chamber music, sometimes at Hugh Maguire's, or at Fou Ts'ong's new Chelsea house in Cheyne Walk. Ts'ong remembered: 'Before we moved in, I had a piano taken down to the huge studio, which had a wonderful rich acoustic. We used to go down there to enjoy ourselves, playing right through the evening and the night. There was no heating and it was absolutely freezing. Later, when we had moved in, we had musical parties there. By that time the only pianist Jackie would play with was Daniel.'[5]

Hugh Maguire recalled a special occasion when the couple came to his house to play chamber music.

Danny told me that he was expecting some friend. We sat down to play something or other, when a taxi drew up outside the house and the doorbell rang. I went to answer the door and saw a very beautiful girl holding a violin case. I said, 'Come on in.' She replied that she was waiting for her husband. Then out of the taxi appeared this crippled person, moving with great difficulty. We got him into the house, then I had to go upstairs for something. I suddenly heard this wonderful violin playing and I assumed it must be the beautiful girl. But of course it was her husband – Itzhak Perlman. They were playing the Mendelssohn C minor Trio – it was the first time I ever saw him and I was absolutely knocked backwards by his playing.[6]

In late January Jackie and Daniel played their first public recital together at Northampton's fortuitously named Carnegie Hall, where they performed both Brahms sonatas (the E minor Brahms Sonata had, in fact, been the first thing they ever played together at Ts'ong's house). Hugh Maguire recalls that to the dismay of the organisers they arrived inordinately late for the concert by taxi all the way from London.

Barenboim had never actually played in public before with a cellist, but was thoroughly familiar with the duo repertoire through his frequent chamber music 'jam' sessions. The composer he did discover through Jackie was Elgar; his previous knowledge was confined to the *Enigma Variations*. Through Jackie's ardent championship of the Cello Concerto, he came to love and perform Elgar's music.

Jackie's general knowledge of music was minimal compared with Daniel's, but with her extraordinary response and sensitivity she could assimilate what she heard instantaneously. Daniel recalled: 'A few weeks after we had met, I [played] a recording to Jacqueline of the 'Prelude' and 'Liebestod' from *Tristan und Isolde*. She had never heard a note of Wagner before, but when she listened to something for the first time it immediately became part of her. Whatever I showed her, or whatever she heard, seemed to bring out something that was already in her.'[7]

News of Jackie's romantic attachment soon spread around London's musical world. In a memorandum dated 6 January 1967 Peter Andry was already warning colleagues at EMI in strictest confidence of the 'du Pré–Bishop situation' – he might have been better advised to say 'the du Pré–Barenboim' situation. It would seem that nobody expected Jackie to honour her engagements with Stephen, now that she was going out with Daniel.

More urgently, there was the problem of her recording contract with EMI. Jackie took Daniel with her when she met with Andry to discuss the matter. The producer Suvi Grubb recalls that during this meeting Jackie kept shooting out of Andry's office, with the excuse that she must 'consult a friend'.[8] As Daniel observed, Jackie felt completely incompetent in practical matters. 'She had no interest in her contracts – and this was no pretence on her part. For instance, she couldn't cope with the idea of foreign currencies and wouldn't have known the difference between ten thousand and ten million lire in Italy. She was totally unconcerned with these practical things. But I felt that she had attained a degree of international stature which should enable her to negotiate better contracts.'

Andry later recalled that he had never had such a difficult time negotiating with anybody, because once Jackie had made up her mind (no doubt in this instance closely adhering to Daniel's advice), nothing would budge her. In this somewhat unorthodox manner Jackie was able to come to a satisfactory agreement and thus, on 3 February, Andry informed Mrs Tillett in writing that a two-year exclusive contract had been signed, on an increased royalty basis. A let-out clause was included, which permitted du Pré to record with another company in the second year of the contract, if EMI did not commit itself within six months to undertake a work proposed by her.[9]

At the time, not all of Jackie's suggestions were immediately accepted by EMI, although there was never any question of outright refusal. For instance, when she expressed a desire to record the Brahms Double Concerto with Hugh Maguire, gentle pressure was applied to dissuade her from her choice of soloist. EMI would undoubtedly have been happier with a 'big name', preferably Yehudi Menuhin or another violinist on their roster. In the meantime the January sessions planned to record the Schubert Quintet with Menuhin had been postponed.

On the other side of the Atlantic, Angel (also known formally as Capitol Records), EMI's American counterpart, released Jackie's recordings of the Elgar concerto and the Beethoven sonatas to coincide with her forthcoming two-month tour of the USA and set their publicity machines in motion. On 24 January Capitol's marketing director informed his London counterpart: 'Our du Pré campaign is under way; reviews of both discs have been excellent and I hope that [...] I shall [soon] have some kind of marketing success story to tell.' There was a postscript to the letter: 'Late breaking news! Hurok tells us that the Bishop recital aspect of the du Pré tour is suddenly off: romantic problems! Hurok is looking for an accompanist! Even the best marketing plans cannot foresee such developments!'[10]

In the event, Jackie and Stephen went on with their planned recitals in March, with four concerts in Ann Arbor, Pittsburgh, Fort Wayne and New York. Jackie left London on 1 February and started her gruelling tour with a concert on 4 February with the Columbus Orchestra in Ohio. She then proceeded to Oklahoma City for an orchestral concert on 9 February and made an enormous impression on her audience playing Bloch's *Schelomo* and the Elgar concerto with Guy Fraser Harrison conducting.

Fifteen years later, Jackie was to receive a fan letter from an 'Okie' student who had attended that concert. Recalling that occasion 'out in the cattle and oil country of Oklahoma', he confessed to her:

> it was not only your musical genius that worked the magic. You appeared on stage looking like a Botticelli angel, your long gold hair shooting fiery sparks of red light, your rich instrument glowing like one from a Vermeer painting, your body movements like a controlled, impassioned dance – perhaps the sort that ancient Greek dancers used in performances of Aeschylus or Euripides [...]. You captured us, mesmerised us by your genius – a genius made more disturbingly real by the juxtaposition of your beauty, vigor and lovely, lovely youth – [...] How you thrilled us. How you taught us things about music and the human soul we would remember a lifetime.[11]

I might add that this letter brought Jackie enormous pleasure and she would read it – with accompanying giggles, but not without pride – to her friends in the years when she was ill.

After Oklahoma, she flew to Dallas for concerts on 11 and 13 February, performing Elgar's concerto with the Dallas Symphony and Donald Johanos. As a result of the advance publicity her appearances were eagerly awaited – and nowhere did she disappoint. The *Dallas Morning News* praised du Pré's sense of drama and accomplishment. 'She plays with great waves of intensity and love, cradling her instrument to her body as if it were part of her. She is as dramatic to watch as she is to

hear, with her head held back high and her body swaying to the music.
. . .' wrote the enthralled critic. In another rave review in the *Dallas
Times Herald*, Eugene Lewis wrote that 'it is the bigness of the du Pré
sound which is the most instantly striking feature. When she moves
her long bow arm across the strings, she can draw a sound that flies to
every corner of a large hall and that burns darkly at the heart of it.'

From Texas she travelled to Los Angeles, where she appeared in four
concerts as soloist with the LA Philharmonic in Haydn's C major
Concerto. The conductor on that occasion, Lawrence Foster, recalled:
'A few days before Jackie arrived, Daniel called me up and said, "Treat
this soloist very well, but very deferentially – she is very important to
me." It was then that I had a strong premonition of what was happening
between them.' Foster recalls the concerts as an incredible experience.
'The orchestra were mad about her, so were the audience and the critics.
I was a young and inexperienced conductor. Although it is true that I
have always been a good accompanist, I had to be alert and on my toes
with Jackie, and flexible with the left hand. Her playing was very
spontaneous, improvised in the highest sense of the word, but it had
its own logic."[12]

A concert artist's life can be a lonely one and, without friends in a
particular city, a soloist is left much to his own devices. Jackie always
disliked going out to eat by herself and preferred to order room service,
so that she could read, watch TV or rest, accompanied by her mascot,
a toy koala bear called 'Doktor Wilhelm' (named after a fictitious
music-teacher), to give the appearance of home comfort to an anonymous hotel room. For the most part she did not have the energy or
curiosity to explore the cities she was in. The shorter a visit, the more
she needed to preserve her strength for the concert. On the longer stays
common in the larger American cities, where concerts are repeated
several times, she was dependent on friends and the musicians she was
playing with to provide company and entertainment. In general, she
was far more likely to spend time in clothes shops than in museums.

In Los Angeles she was fortunate in finding a congenial companion
in Larry Foster, who realised that Jackie craved company: 'I showed her
around Los Angeles during that week, and I found her to be simple,
straightforward and very friendly.'

After Los Angeles, Jackie travelled back east, and introduced the
Elgar concerto to Cleveland in performances with Louis Lane and the
renowned Cleveland Symphony Orchestra. She was hailed as a brilliant

and sensational cellist and the critic of the *Cleveland Press* wrote that du Pré played Elgar's music as though it had been written expressly for her. He was impressed, but also somewhat distracted both by her dramatic appearance and her playing mannerisms. 'Quite possibly the latter will slack off in a few years as she finds not all of them necessary. This is not a suggestion; if they help her music, then leave them alone.'

In the *Plain Dealer*, Robert Finn expressed some disappointment about the interpretation of the Elgar concerto, although laying the blame for this chiefly on the conductor. 'It did not make nearly the strong impression it does on the new Barbirolli recording.'

It was at one of these Cleveland concerts that Zubin Mehta first heard Jackie play and he was duly impressed. He commented that 'women usually have a small tone – they're all Mozart specialists. This girl plays like five men. No bar of the orchestra covers the tone. It's flabbergasting.'[13]

With a string of successes behind her, Jackie arrived in New York City, where she was to make her début with the New York Philharmonic and Leonard Bernstein in four concerts from 2 to 6 March. Coincidentally, Rostropovich was also in town, performing a marathon cycle of thirty cello concertos at Carnegie Hall with the London Symphony Orchestra.

Naturally the press had a field day, writing concurrently about these two extraordinary cellists, and in an article for *Newsweek*, each spoke about the other. 'Of course, just observing him is wonderful. He's so terribly dramatic ...' was how Jackie defined Rostropovich the teacher. The Russian Master in turn commented that 'coaching her was all pleasure. I am happy for her success. She is phenomenally talented.'

Despite these mutual compliments, the relationship between Master and ex-pupil had changed. In the same article Jackie emphasised that she was no longer taking lessons: 'I feel that I want to be entirely on my own now.' As Barenboim recalled, 'Jackie always got very annoyed when she was compared with Slava [Rostropovich] and, I think, so did he – the irritation was mutual. The similarity between them was very external. Other cellists were more subdued, even an extrovert like Tortelier, who was more of a "quixotic" extrovert. Whereas Slava and Jackie had this in common – they both had sheer unadulterated temperament. But that is where I think the similarity ended. For instance, Jackie certainly had a very different idea of sound.'

Photographers took pictures of a reunion between Slava Rostropovich and Jackie, sharing a joke and a bear hug in the Russian Tea Room, a restaurant round the corner from Carnegie Hall much frequented by musicians. Later Jackie told me that Rostropovich had heard rumours of a love story in her life and wanted to 'know all about it' – but wrongly identified her boy-friend as Zubin Mehta, who was in fact sitting with her at the table (and whom Rostropovich dubbed 'Apollo' for his irresistibly handsome face and figure).

The importance of her musical friendships was emphasised in the above-mentioned *Newsweek* article, where she was reported as saying: 'I belong to a group of young musicians, who share the spirit of music-making. It's wonderful, we're a clan, people like Vladimir Ashkenazy, John Williams, Itzhak Perlman, Fou Ts'ong, Stephen Bishop and Daniel Barenboim ... We keep together, go to each other's concerts and never miss a chance to play for ourselves. Aside from music, seeing friends like these is the most important thing in my life.'

In the same interview Jackie denied any conflict between being a woman and a musician, and defined her point of view quite explicitly. 'I can't see that being a woman limits my playing, technically, in any way. I may be less ambitious than a man but no less committed. I value my private life too much to continue such long and demanding tours. I hope eventually to limit my travelling. And I'd like to marry and have children. But I will never give up my career as a cellist.'[14]

It was undoubtedly Barenboim, with his dynamic personality, who exerted a magnetic force over the musical clan about which Jackie enthused. Behind the public statements, one senses her genuine happiness in at long last 'belonging' to a group of like-minded people. Despite the international spectrum of the musicians she named, for Jackie this 'clan' feeling was soon to be integrated with her identification with Jews, a people who, in the musical world she inhabited, seemed to have a monopoly on talent and, furthermore, appeared to have no inhibitions in displaying warmth and emotion. For Jackie, becoming part of Daniel's world was like finally sailing into a long-sought harbour.

In fact, for most of the tour she was separated from him. While keeping in regular touch by phone, she proved that she had little sense of geography. For instance, she might ring him in Switzerland from Dallas to announce that she had two days free in her schedule before going on to Los Angeles – should she fly over to meet him for the weekend? It didn't take long for Daniel to work out that – in those pre-

Concorde days – she would have to spend every minute of those two days on aeroplanes.

The most prestigious date of Jackie's US tour was undoubtedly her engagement to play the Schumann concerto with Leonard Bernstein and the New York Philharmonic. New Yorkers were left wondering if Jackie, with her extraordinary gift for rhetorical communication, was not 'upstaging Lenny'. (This became the editor's subtitle for Harold Schonberg's review of the concert in the *New York Times*.) Schonberg, the doyen of New York critics, reputedly had the power to make or break an artist's career. His review set the seal of approbation on Jackie's success, conceding that whatever the flaws or distracting mannerisms of her performances, they were all justified by a talent of such magnitude.

> For the last few years, everybody in music has been talking about the young British cellist Jacqueline du Pré, now twenty-one years old. She is the girl who is so talented, people rush to present her with Stradivarius instruments. ... She came out, tall, blonde, assured, in a red gown, listened attentively to the short introduction and launched into Schumann. Very fine: the tone, lyric approach, security of finger and bow arm. Also a set of gestures and physical movements that all but merged her body with the cello. ... Miss du Pré is a cellist in the modern vein. There is plenty of strength to her playing, and a good measure of romanticism without the romantic string mannerisms of portamento (sliding from note to note) and a fast, wide vibrato. [...] Her interpretation did show a few inaccuracies, though admittedly the Schumann is not an easy concerto to hold together. The slow movement, as Miss du Pré and Mr Bernstein conceived it, lacked natural, flowing simplicity. It was somewhat dragged and even a bit tricky. Too much lily-gilding here. There were spots, too, in the last movement where the performance sounded episodic, with Miss du Pré playing as though she did not know how to link the sequence with the following passage.

Schonberg concluded by identifying the particular feature of her formidable talent. 'Miss du Pré, like all young instrumentalists today, has tone and technique; in addition she has something rare, the ability to transmit. There might be reservations about this or that aspect of a given performance of hers, there can be no reservations at all about her personality and innate sensitivity.'

Harriet Johnson of the *New York Post* likewise was impressed by the communicative quality of Jackie's playing. 'She played with a strength that was far more than physical and with a direct communication and concentration that could only demonstrate the mystery of a phenomenal talent.' Johnson had noted that she performed the original version of Schumann's concerto, while Rostropovich had played it only a few days before at Carnegie Hall in Shostakovich's orchestration. Johnson, referring to Rostropovich as one of Jackie's mentors, observed that 'nobody could really teach Miss du Pré to play as she does with a mature emotional and intellectual grasp of the music that becomes incandescent the moment she begins to bow the string'. The review went on to describe Jackie's playing as 'white-hot, over-wrought at times, over-stated, with roughness of attack and sweep of head and shoulders, but with eloquence too'.

William Bender in the *World Journal Tribune* posed the question whether such great intensity justified the loss of quality:

> What one is left wondering about was the extent of her restraint and the nature of her sense of measure. ... She held nothing back. She played the Schumann as if it were the last concerto left on earth. She tore into her attacks, and she spun forth her rich sounds with a vibrato as wide as the English Channel. She phrased with a passion that probably even Casals could not have equalled. The trouble was that her passion was far in excess of what the work called for, and that her exuberance brought about a lot of buzzing, scraping, and clicking that no music needs. Obviously she misjudged the music at hand. That is permissible in one so young. She also misjudged the limits of her technique, and that is something she ought to attend to.

These various pronouncements in some way became the criteria for all future critical judgements in the USA on Jacqueline du Pré – she was labelled as an exciting, profound and highly communicative artist, whose excess of temperament and over-intensity tended to cause a loss of technical perfection, pushing her towards musical mannerism and physically distracting movements. Fortunately, the paying public had a greater capacity to accept and take to heart her artistry for what it was; Jackie was soon the darling of North American audiences in the same way as she had already become at home.

Having had an opportunity to listen to a surviving radio tape of her performance with Bernstein of the Schumann concerto, I can see the validity of some, but certainly not all, these criticisms. The first movement is conceived with an organic understanding of tempi and their relationships. Du Pré can be lyrical and reflective (as in the second-subject theme) as well as strong, but she never forces the drama. One feels that Bernstein helped to create a philosophically poetic conception of the work, with the element of struggle relegated to the orchestral tuttis, while the soloist conveys the rhetoric of a Werther-like hero, doubting and questioning rather than firm and decisive. Where Schonberg felt the second movement was dragged, I enjoyed the artists' wonderful ability to stretch the tempo without exaggerating the rubato. The enormous variety of colour and warmth in du Pré's sound never took away from the fundamentally inner-felt spirit and the shining luminosity of the music. The finale perhaps suffers from lack of shape and in this Bernstein does little to add direction to the music. Jackie achieves an enormous variety of stroke (both in weight and length) of the dotted quaver and semiquaver motifs, which make up an enormous amount of the cello part. Since this movement is not written 'cellistically' – for instance much of the arpeggiated passage work is written to fall under a pianist's hand – it is very hard for any cellist to avoid a certain gruffness or forcing (especially in the coda).

It is, of course, difficult to judge a recording where the orchestra is lamentably under-recorded, but there are moments when the orchestral ensemble leaves something to be desired (and on occasion sounds downright sloppy). But such flaws are acceptable as part and parcel of a concert performance. More important, what come over, even on an inadequate recording, are du Pré's wonderful sound quality and the fantastic spirit of her music-making – a spirit impervious to nit-picking criticism.

From New York Jackie went on to Canada, first for orchestral concerts in Winnipeg, then to Toronto, where on 14 and 15 March she performed Saint-Saëns's concerto with Seiji Ozawa and the Toronto Symphony. In Canada her début had been eagerly awaited, as John Kraglund of the *Globe and Mail* noted:

Advance publicity had suggested that one must think of her in terms of Pablo Casals and Mstislav Rostropovich, although it is difficult to understand the significance of such comparisons. It seems to me that Miss du Pré is remarkable enough in her own right.

That does not mean all her listeners were likely to consider hers a definitive performance, or even a flawless one, for she is an emotional performer and has a tendency, if not to sacrifice, at least to overlook more refined details.

The reviewer questioned whether the Saint-Saëns Cello Concerto was a fitting vehicle for such an 'emotional upheaval', especially in the first movement where '... a searing passion of almost orgiastic proportions, a passion as much physical as musical, [...] exhausted the listener as much as it must have exhausted the performer.' But he commended Jackie's remarkable ability to involve the listener 'even in the most relaxed moments'.

The last ten days of March were devoted to recitals with Stephen Bishop, with an intervening Elgar concerto scheduled in Montreal on the twenty-sixth of the month. And on 31 March Jackie played the final concert of her North American tour in New York, performing Brahms and Beethoven sonatas with Bishop. The whole tour was deemed an unparalleled success, both by the Hurok office in New York and by Angel Records.

Back in London, on 5 April du Pré gave her first concert with Daniel Barenboim conducting at the Royal Festival Hall, performing Haydn's C major Concerto with the English Chamber Orchestra for the Royal Philharmonic Society. (Daniel also played Mozart's D minor Concerto, directing from the keyboard, and conducted Haydn's Symphony No. 95 and Mozart's *Haffner* Symphony.) David Pryce-Jones, who interviewed Jackie on several occasions during April for a feature article in the *Weekend Telegraph Magazine*, questioned the slight foreign intonation in her voice and asked if this was linked to her name. 'The accent, she says, has been picked up from some Argentinians she is seeing a lot of ...' Soon it became clear to him that 'the Argentines ... prove to be the Barenboim family, and Daniel is her fiancé, a secret still'.

Pryce-Jones attended the Festival Hall rehearsal on 5 April and noted Jackie's informal and relaxed manner, something that became a characteristic of her new 'style' with Barenboim – although it never obscured the seriousness of their music-making. 'Very much at her ease throughout her Haydn concerto, Jacqueline smiles at friends, and mouths a greeting at Larry Foster, who in Los Angeles recently conducted her playing this piece. ... After the rehearsal, Daniel hugs her.'

For Jackie, this concert was to be the start of a happy association with the ECO, with whom she had played only one date previously. In contrast, Daniel had developed a very close relationship with the orchestra over the previous two years, conducting and playing from the keyboard. Indeed, as the 'owner' and manager of the orchestra, the viola player Quintin Ballardie, remembered, it was Daniel who had introduced the idea of conducting from the keyboard to England, following the example of the Swiss pianist, Edwin Fischer.

Although the orchestra had no chief conductor, effectively its work was now divided between three musicians – Benjamin Britten, Raymond Leppard and Daniel Barenboim. Soon Jackie, too, came to regard the ECO as a favourite orchestra, comprised of a group of friends, with whom she enjoyed a close professional rapport. With several of its musicians (such as Cecil Aronowitz, John Tunnell and José Luis García) she enjoyed playing chamber music for fun, while some of the ECO's members remained dear friends to her dying day.

Quin Ballardie recalled the first time Jackie came to play with the ECO. 'It was just after she had met up with Daniel and there was this incredible explosion of emotion when they played together. Hers was the kind of playing which is no longer trendy or popular, it was very highly charged and possessed this vibrant energy. I don't think such playing could happen now, because the whole ambience of musical culture has altered. It was a terribly exciting time.'[15] Or as another ECO member, the cellist Anita Lasker, put it: 'Jackie played as if it wasn't her doing it, rather as if she was performing in a trance. Everything happened so naturally.'[16]

This same feature of spontaneity was noted by *The Times* critic Joan Chissell. In an ecstatic review of du Pré's Haydn performance with Barenboim, Chissell reckoned that this concert would remain 'indelibly stamped' on the memories of the audience. 'It was as if each work was being created on the spot, instead of merely reproduced for the ten-thousandth time.' Evidently the performers' feeling of joy was contagious, at least in as sunny a work as the Haydn C major Cello Concerto. 'Miss Du Pré's playing exuded happiness in every bar, through tingling rhythm, radiantly lyrical tone and the keenest imaginable characterisation of every small detail. A few passing roughnesses of attack and bowing in the excitements of the finale were offset by some refined, intimate and meaningful streams of semiquavers that in other hands might have emerged as mere passagework. Again here the unanimity of phrasing between soloist and orchestra was a delight.'[17]

After their Festival Hall performance Daniel flew to Berlin for concerts and Jackie went along with him for 'a five-day rest'. From there she flew straight to Manchester on the evening of 11 April for concerts with the Hallé Orchestra and Barbirolli, to play the Elgar concerto. Jackie had come a long way since Sir John had first heard her as a small girl. The Barbirollis were delighted at the news of her engagement to Daniel, which by now was an open secret. They had an enormous affection and esteem for Barenboim, who had played regularly as soloist with Sir John and the Hallé.

Daniel flew in to Manchester on return from a concert in Venice, for a brief reunion with Jackie and to hear her performance with Barbirolli. While he returned to London the next day, Jackie went on to repeat the concert with the Hallé in Sheffield. In the afternoon she met up with her parents who were staying with their friends, Margot and Jack Pacey.

The giddy pace went on, as the day afterwards Jackie joined Daniel in Brighton, where he was performing at the new festival founded that year by Sir Ian Hunter. Two days later, on 17 April, she and Daniel were recording the Haydn C major and Boccherini B flat major Concerto (in the Grützmacher edition) at EMI's studios. The recordings went so smoothly that they were able to cancel one of the extra scheduled sessions a week later. As Quin Ballardie recalled, 'Jackie didn't seem to behave any differently in the studio than in the concert hall. She played the same, whether the red light was on or off.'[18]

Suvi Grubb was the producer on this occasion, and described how they worked together to overcome the difficulties of balance between solo cello and chamber orchestra. 'The groups of strings each out-number the solo cello by at least six to one, the woodwind all have greater carrying power and the cello's range lies within that of some of the heaviest of the orchestral artillery: horns, trombones, bassoons and timpani.'[19]

A cellist has a further disadvantage – he is seated, whereas a violinist, standing up, raises his instrument above the level of the seated orchestral musicians, thereby gaining in carrying power. Grubb offset this by placing du Pré on a rostrum some nine inches high, thus raising her clear of the orchestra. Then came the search for the ideal position for the solo cello in relation to the orchestra, starting with the conventional concert position, with cellist in front of the orchestra, to the left of the conductor, and facing away from it. Grubb said:

[Jackie] sounded marvellous but the leakage of the sound from the instruments [. . .] into her microphone made them go out of focus. I turned her around 180 degrees to face the orchestra. This sounded as if she and the English Chamber Orchestra were in, not two separate rooms, but two different towns. Then sideways, facing the conductor and so on till finally, by a happy accident [. . .] I found the best position. I sat her plumb in the centre of the orchestra, facing the conductor, with the other players in a rough horseshoe around her. The conductor could have stretched out his hand and touched her and, wondering whether her proximity would cramp his movements, I asked: 'Danny, is she too close?' His reply was a crisp: 'She can't ever be too close for me!'[20]

Grubb was impressed by Jackie's uncomplaining patience. She always played out as in a concert hall, with total commitment. 'She never had the attitude: "Oh well, if anything goes wrong we can always do it again." This is one reason for the immediacy and vibrancy of her performances on gramophone record.' Grubb recalled that once they had got the balance sorted out, the recording went very smoothly, although there was an unexpected hitch at one stage. 'She innocently changed her bow without telling anyone and drove us all to distraction trying to investigate all the possible causes of the sudden, inexplicable change in the sound of the cello before realising that the new bow might have something to do with it [. . .] This, the first of her records I produced, provides a perfect example of a sense of style – classical propriety for the Haydn and romantic indulgence for the Boccherini.'[21]

The sessions were attended by musician friends, Larry Foster and Itzhak Perlman among them. As Pryce-Jones noted in his interview, spirits were high, as fifteen friends accompanied Jackie and Daniel to a St John's Wood restaurant to celebrate – and with good cause, as the 'secret' of their forthcoming marriage had now been made public knowledge. Barenboim told reporters that their wedding would take place in September, since that was the earliest period when the couple had five free days. Jackie had confided to Pryce-Jones that she hoped to live in Israel. But, as he commented, 'for the moment their way of life must commit them to the world of airports, stages, hotels, and perhaps to piano–cello duos. Friends tease her that her sensitive projection of herself through her cello comes from her "Jewishness". She plans to convert to Judaism, but her knowledge so far is limited to such cries as "oi, oi, mamele", and a visit to a synagogue with Daniel.'[22]

A journalist for *The Times* Diary asked Jackie about her intended conversion. Her reply was uncompromising: 'I had no hesitation. I think it will be better for the children. My family are Protestant, but I never had any particular strong feelings about it.'

For agents and record companies, wedding bells between two star artists was something to exploit for all its worth. On 14 April John Coveney at Angel Records wrote an excited letter to Peter Andry at EMI reporting that Zubin Mehta had broken the news to him of the forthcoming marriage. 'Certainly, since they are both EMI exclusives, this is something for the international publicity mill. Their first USA album to be released after their marriage will be the Haydn–Boccherini concertos in November. Then later we can feature their first recording made after their marriage, and so forth. Think of how really big this news would be if Daniel were to marry the American Jacqueline!!²³' (This last reference, of course, being to Jacqueline Kennedy.)

After Daniel had announced his forthcoming marriage to the British Jacqueline the 'golden' young couple were constantly in the public eye. Over the following twelve months a large number of magazine and newspaper articles about them in the USA and Great Britain promoted the idea of Barenboim and du Pré as the embodiment of a success merited not only by their extraordinary talents, but by their youthful exuberance and self-confidence. Their talents were often compared with those of the most brilliant musical partnership of the previous century, Robert and Clara Schumann (one wonders, though, with how much thought for the vicissitudes of fate that the couple endured at the outset and close of their life together).

In public, Barenboim insisted: 'Our personal relationship and our professional one must remain separate [...] – this is the only way our life would be able to work.' But in practice, his musical rapport with Jackie was so close that inevitably they were drawn together increasingly on the platform – and audiences clamoured to hear them play together. In Barenboim's case, he had the energy, memory and stamina to combine 'extra' chamber music activity, while continuing to enlarge his scope as a conductor and play an enormously rich pianistic repertoire. Jackie welcomed the chance to play more chamber music. Since the solo repertoire for cello was comparatively limited, she regarded chamber music as her life-blood.

The last ten days of April saw a busy schedule for both artists. Jackie performed the Boccherini concerto with Daniel and the ECO at the Brighton Festival on 23 April. Four days later she played a duo recital with Bishop in the same town. She also completed her mini tour with the Hallé in Bradford, performing the Elgar again on 21 April. Then, on the thirtieth she played Shostakovich's First Cello Concerto with Hugo Rignold and the CBSO at King Edward's School, Selly Oak outside Birmingham. A BBC recording of the concert is in existence, testimony to her only public performance of the piece. Jackie claimed not to have enjoyed playing it and confessed to Pryce-Jones at the time that it was too much like hard work, which she didn't feel like. Certainly, the Shostakovich concerto requires enormous stamina of the soloist, particularly in the long third movement solo cadenza and the extremely demanding finale. Feel like it or not, she had no choice but to go through with the concert, after the embarrassment, only five months earlier, of 'forgetting' her date in the subscription series in Birmingham with Rignold and the CBSO.

Perhaps her ambiguous relationship with the Shostakovich was due to the fact that she was aware that the piece was so irrevocably associated with its dedicatee Rostropovich. In an interview given only a month previously, Jackie talked about the difficulty of accomplishing the mission with which she had been entrusted by the Russian Master – to continue his work propagating a new repertoire for cello. 'I would like to. The question is, can I? A woman cannot play as a man plays – she hasn't the physique and energy. A woman's hand is a limitation in itself. Rostropovich's hand is phenomenal. He can do anything with it.'

Jackie tended to dismiss most contemporary music, a fact she brought up almost apologetically in her interview with Pryce-Jones. 'I hate all this, it's so ugly, and it takes a lot of sorting out fingering-wise,' she had told him as she was preparing for her Shostakovich concert. In fact, the Birmingham evening remained her only performance of the work. One regrets that Jackie did not have a chance to play it again or record it, since whatever her complaints about its technical difficulties, she showed complete mastery of them. While the BBC Radio tape gives testimony of the dynamic energy she brought to this performance, it also shows up its defects, most notably some moments of imprecision in the orchestra. For her part, one might argue that du Pré did not always capture the pointed irony behind Shostakovich's music and that in some places she employed too extrovert an expression to convey the mood of melancholic contemplation and inner anguish in the slow movement.

During the first days of May, Jackie fulfilled three more recital engagements with Stephen Bishop, the last she played with him. Daniel Barenboim was in attendance in Oxford and Stephen recalled that they all had a cheerful dinner afterwards. Yet, after their final concert in Walthamstow Town Hall, some London musicians felt they had come to the end of an era, whereby Jackie finally cut her ties with a previous circle of friends, becoming part of a jet-setting world presided over by Barenboim.

A few days later, on 12 May, Jackie played a recital with the pianist Fou Ts'ong, one of several dates that had been set up – along with some trio concerts with Maguire. As Ts'ong recalled:

When Daniel appeared on the scene, our whole enterprise collapsed. In the end the only concert I played with Jackie was one that had already been arranged in Cambridge. I had chosen the programme – it was supposed to be Debussy and Franck sonatas in the second half, and Janáček's *Pohodka* [or *Fairy Tale*] and the Chopin Sonata in the first half. But as we rehearsed, it became evident that Jackie couldn't stand the Janáček piece. Janáček has to my mind a primitive and wild quality, somewhat like Mussorgsky. I am told that I am very domineering; perhaps that is why, when I kept telling Jackie what a wonderful piece it was, she would clam up more and more. Afterwards Daniel took me aside – 'But she just can't stand this piece – she's completely bewildered by you.' She had her rebellious side, and with my wild enthusiasm I just frightened her off. In the end we played the three sonatas without the Janáček – the programme was quite long enough. The Chopin Sonata nearly finished me – it's so difficult, and on top of it all, with Daniel there turning pages for me, the piece seemed twice as hard. The Debussy and Franck Sonatas always went well. Although I remember Daniel saying on that occasion about the Franck, 'How can you have two people having orgasms every bar?' I think temperamentally it was too much. Later the trio was supposed to play Beethoven's triple concerto with Barbirolli, but Hugh and I withdrew.

Ts'ong was a generous colleague, and realised, even from only hearing informal performances at his house, that Jackie's duo with Daniel had the ingredients of something quite remarkable.

I don't know any other musician who has the structure of the music so completely in control as Daniel. At the same time, as a musician he is not at all cold. So when he played Beethoven or Brahms the framework was rock solid, allowing Jackie to carry on with her eloquent passion. She was such a fantastic musician that she communicated and reacted to Daniel. In this way hers and Daniel's natures counterbalanced each other much better than mine and hers. Jackie also had a very great sense of natural balance within the musical phrase and form – the passion seemed to be almost overflowing, but it was always contained within the form.

Zamira was struck by the immediate contact of Jackie's whole way of expression. 'You were totally involved as a listener, because she was so much in the music.'[24] She likened Jackie's strength and beauty to that portrayed in the Pre-Raphaelite portraits of women. Ts'ong, too, was aware of a sort of primeval strength in Jackie's make-up.

There was so much earth in her. She had an inordinate appetite and gained a physical pleasure from eating! She went for her food like a tiger. ... And her big striding walk, her overall expression of vibrancy. It was such a strange combination – such seeming innocence with real earthiness. Daniel used to laugh at her apparent ignorance and disinterest in practical things. 'Where is Oslo?' he might ask her. 'Is it in Germany?' she would reply – she didn't seem to know anything ... But she didn't mind being teased like this. And at the same time there was such richness inside her; the fire and the temperament were unbelievable.[25]

In the middle of May Jackie once again performed Haydn's C major and the Boccherini B flat Concertos at the Royal Festival Hall with Harry Blech and the London Mozart Players. In a review for *The Times*, Stanley Sadie disparaged du Pré's approach to Haydn: 'It was a superb exhibition of cello playing, very much in the manner of Rostropovich ... The only trouble was that the concerto no longer sounded like a real piece of music. ... It was not a serious interpretation at all; the music was merely used, treated like a plaything.' While he appreciated her response to the Boccherini more, Sadie termed the inclusion of this 'phoney' piece by Grützmacher based on Boccherini's music as 'a blot on the London Mozart Players' record'.

On 18 May, the day after her Festival Hall concert, Jackie travelled to Berlin to give three performances of the Schumann concerto with Seiji Ozawa and the Berlin Radio Orchestra. On her return to London, she found her fiancé much preoccupied by the political situation in Israel. As Barenboim expressed it: 'In the spring of 1967, when Israel's very existence was at stake and Nasser had closed the straits of Tiran, one did not need to be a prophet to realise that war was imminent. [...] I could not stand the idea of being away from my family or my colleagues and friends in the Philharmonic. I decided to go back home. I arrived on one of the last normal commercial flights ... Jacqueline insisted on coming with me.'[26] In his concern for her safety, Daniel initially tried to dissuade Jackie from coming: 'I thought it could be dangerous. At the end of May the situation didn't look at all good and we didn't know what the outcome would be.' But Jackie was determined to be at Daniel's side and to share with him whatever fate had in store. With her stubborn insistence and her belief in a two hundred per cent commitment to whatever mattered at the moment – whether it was a piece of music or the man she loved – it is probable that nothing would have stopped her.

18

Love Triumphant

What is love? 'tis not hereafter;
Present mirth hath present laughter;
What's to come is still unsure:
William Shakespeare, *Twelfth Night*

On the evening of 28 May 1967, Jackie and Daniel boarded a flight from Heathrow to Tel Aviv. They arrived in the early morning hours of the twenty-ninth, to find the city still fully lit up and showing little evidence of the imminent hostilities. However, initial appearances were deceptive, as Israel was fully mobilised for the war which in fact broke out only a week later, on 5 June.

Both du Pré and Barenboim had cancelled engagements in Europe at the last minute in order to come to Israel. Jackie had disappeared so quickly from the scene that she had not had time to explain her hasty departure. She immediately sent a reassuring telegram to her mother and a few days later rang her friend Antony Hopkins to apologise for cancelling her dates with him at the Norwich Festival on 5 and 6 June. (Hopkins recalled her exhilaration, as she recounted how she and Daniel were playing for the Israeli troops.)

Furthermore, Jackie also had to pull out of two concerts in Germany with the Braunschweig Orchestra and could not honour her commitments at the Bath Festival (where she was due to play Haydn's D major Concerto and a recital with Fou Ts'ong). For Jackie there was no question but that it was right to be at Daniel's side and she gave no thought to her career, although she disliked letting people down. But at home her sudden cancellations were viewed with considerable annoyance, as if she had acted on a childish whim, in pursuit of adventure. Mrs Tillett believed in the sanctity of the 'professional date' and stated in public that 'Jacqueline is a naughty girl'. Yehudi Menuhin, Director of the Bath Festival, did not disguise his displeasure. Her non-appearance at the festival implied further cancellations of her concerts with him and the Bath Festival Orchestra in late June and July, when they were scheduled to play in North America and at the Montreal Expo.

Perhaps the irritation was heightened by the knowledge that Barenboim and du Pré were actually playing concerts in Israel. Immediately on arrival Daniel and Jackie offered their services to the Israel Philharmonic Orchestra, and on the evening of 29 May they played their first concert in Tel Aviv, where Daniel performed Beethoven's C minor Piano Concerto and also made his conducting début with the orchestra, accompanying Jackie in the Schumann concerto. 'Although the concert had a priori the hallmark of an improvised event (both soloists having arrived in Israel that same morning), it turned out to be an exciting experience,' wrote the critic of the *Jerusalem Post*. '... Miss du Pré is an outstanding cellist. Her treatment of the Schumann classic was full of subtlety, tonal suavity and exciting virtuosity ... An additional surprise was Daniel Barenboim's first appearance as conductor in the Schumann concerto. Judging from his accompanying, which was finely polished, with the orchestral interludes treated with a glowing exuberance, one can predict a conductor's career no less brilliant than the one he has achieved as a pianist.'[1]

The following three days saw further performances of the same works in Haifa, this time with Sergiu Comissiona conducting the IPO. (As concerts were not given on the Sabbath evening, there was a pause for 2 June.) On 3 June they played again at the Mann auditorium in Tel Aviv, and the following day gave two performances with Comissiona and the IPO in Beersheba, the first of which was for the Military. As Barenboim pointed out, Beersheba was about half-way between Tel Aviv and what was then the Egyptian border. 'Driving back to Tel Aviv that night, after the concert, we realised how close to war we were as we watched the tanks going along the road in the opposite direction.'[2] Sergiu Comissiona recalled that despite the tension in the first days of June, people had crowded into the concerts, many of them already in uniform. The male musicians performing were among the very few men under forty-six not eligible for call-up. Comissiona recalled feeling 'almost embarrassed to appear on the streets [...] It seemed that only children and cripples had not gone to the war.'[3]

In the meantime, Daniel's closest friend Zubin Mehta had left Puerto Rico for Tel Aviv. Getting there was no easy matter, but with the help of the Israeli ambassador in Rome he was able to board an El Al flight that was in fact carrying ammunition rather than passengers. He arrived in the early hours of 5 June and, in contrast to his friends, found the city in total black-out – the war had started. He was met by a representative of the IPO in pyjamas and was immediately taken to the Israel Philharmonic Guest House. As Mehta recalled, 'I was taken to sleep in the bunker downstairs. We were all on the floor in the cellar, which was being used as an air-raid shelter – Mr and Mrs Comissiona, the not-quite-yet Mr and Mrs Barenboim, and Daniel's parents Aida and Enrique.' Mehta pointed out the precaution was almost unnecessary, as the Israelis wiped out the Egyptian Air Force in the early hours of the first day of the war, thereby effectively winning it from the start.

Nobody was in the mood for sleep, though, and the night was given over to laughter. According to Mehta, 'Poor Comissiona was the chief butt of the fun. When he went to get a glass of water, I jumped into bed with his wife. The room was in darkness when he returned and the poor fellow was extremely perplexed. Affected by the tensions of a country at war, we played these childish pranks to retain some sense of normality.'[4]

As an Israeli victory became more apparent, normality gave way to high spirits and euphoria. Plans were made for celebrating in a newly reunited city of Jerusalem under Israeli control. Celebration was in the air and as Daniel said, 'As soon as the war ended, we decided to get married then and there, because of the exuberance of the moment. And getting married in Jerusalem was symbolic.'[5]

As there exists no form of civil marriage in Israel there was no question of anything but a religious ceremony. Effecting Jackie's immediate conversion to Judaism was the one obstacle to be overcome. From the start of their friendship Jackie had told Daniel that she wanted to be Jewish. 'We had intended to get married in London in a Jewish ceremony. Jackie had studied a bit and in normal circumstances she would have had to study much more. But because of the war and who she was, and what she had done, this didn't come into it. She was subjected to an exam by the Rabbinate, but they were lenient about that.'[6]

As Jacqueline's future friend and minister Rabbi Albert Friedlander observed, there was a feeling among some members of the Jewish community that she became a Jew too quickly and too easily. He explained: 'It was very natural for many Jews – particularly traditional Jews – to view this conversion with disdain: a one-day conversion and marriage the day after – in the face of all the Hallacha, the religious law. How could she claim to be Jewish?'[7]

But against this argument were others which proved more telling. As a liberal Jew, Rabbi Friedlander felt that in these circumstances it was not possible to measure the criteria which made a conversion more or less valid:

Daniel Barenboim and Jacqueline came to Israel to play for the troops. They were full of enthusiasm. They wanted to get married and Jacqueline was converted to Judaism – in a day! That's what she wanted. That's what Ben Gurion wanted. Usually it takes years of study to become a Jew – but the Rabbinate in Israel is a law to itself. One day, including immersion and an examination before the Rabbinic Court. As the story goes, the rabbis were flabbergasted: 'But one has to wait months after baptism,' they said, 'it would be a sin.' But clever Daniel, with his knowledge of the Talmud, is said to have remarked: 'which is the greater sin, to get married straight away or to live together straight away?' So they got married.[8]

Despite being busy organising their marriage and Jackie's conversion at a few days' notice, the two young musicians were also playing celebratory concerts every night. The first Victory concert was given in Jerusalem's Binyanei Ha'ooma on Saturday, 10 June – just after the cease-fire agreement was reached. Zubin Mehta conducted Daniel playing Beethoven's *Emperor* Concerto and Jackie in Schumann's Cello Concerto. The concert was billed in honour of Zahal (the Military) and all proceeds were given to the Defence Effort. As Mehta recalled, 'With at least half the audience in khaki, it was understandably an overwhelmingly emotional occasion, although I would concede it was not the greatest music the Israel Philharmonic had ever produced.'[9] The lawyer Y. Beinisch remarked that the euphoria was high, despite the deaths suffered during the war: 'To attend a concert like that was one of the highlights in a man's life – especially in the spirit and the atmosphere which existed.'[10]

These victory concerts were repeated in Jerusalem the following night, in Haifa on 12 June and in Tel Aviv on 13 and 14 June (this last was dedicated to Daniel and Jackie as a special farewell by the Israel Philharmonic).

The following day, Thursday, 15 June, was the day of their marriage in Jerusalem. Jackie had rung her mother on the Monday and asked if she could come to their wedding that very Thursday. Iris later wrote: 'It was not all that easy, as planes were not running to regular schedule, owing to the war. Anyway [Jackie's] father, her brother and I finally arrived, after making three changes, rather less than twenty-four hours before the wedding.'[11]

Among other friends who were able to be present – by fortuitous chance – were Sir John and Lady Barbirolli and Dame Janet Baker, who had just arrived in Israel to perform with the Israeli Philharmonic.

Janet Baker recorded: 'It was an unbelievable time to have chosen for a wedding, the very atmosphere seemed charged with wonder and rejoicing. Everywhere feelings ran high; Jerusalem was again a united city and the Wailing Wall of Solomon's Temple had been uncovered. Relief and happiness abounded; it seemed to be cascading through the ancient narrow streets and in the midst of it all was this radiant couple. Their sheer blissful elation was really something to have seen. It was such as to have left the deepest of impressions.'[12]

The wedding was to be performed according to strict Orthodox laws which included the ritual Mikvah, or purifying bath for the bride. Zubin Mehta contributed his services as 'chauffeur', largely as an excuse to involve himself more closely in the drama.

Being the only member of the wedding with transport, I had to drive the chief participants about in my borrowed car. I was absolutely determined to take part in the ceremony too, although Daniel said the rabbis would not allow me to be a witness and probably would not even ride in my car if they knew I was not a Jew. So Daniel decided upon a plan. He told the rabbi who was to perform the ceremony that I was a recently emigrated Persian Jew named Moshe Cohen. In those days I knew not a word of Hebrew, but most Persian Jews did not speak the ancient language either. Having collected a venerable rabbi, we drove him and Jackie to the Mikvah. As we sat quietly in the waiting-room, Daniel most unexpectedly became extremely excited and began shouting at some other rabbis who were gathered in the passageway outside the waiting-room. He had good reason to be incensed, for he had realised that what was concentrating their attention was that they were peeping into the room where Jackie was standing completely naked.

Order having been restored, we all got back in the car and I drove out to what is now the Jerusalem Music Centre. It was just on the border of what then was the 'no man's land' that used to divide the city. In a small house, just below the big windmill, Daniel and Jackie were married, and at the ceremony a certain 'Moshe Cohen' held one of the poles of the chupah, the canopy under which the bridal couple stand.'[13]

For Iris du Pré and her family the whole occasion must have seemed almost unreal: 'It was rather like a scene from the Old Testament. A large table was in the centre of the room around which the men sat. The women, as is customary, were obliged to sit back around the perimeter of the room. It was a charming and fully traditional ceremony, children and chickens wandered around, as the front door of the house was open to the street.'[14]

Jackie herself gave a detailed account of the ceremony to the journalist Maureen Cleave:

> I went to the conversion centre. I had to have an ordinary bath and wash my hair and nails and then, with no clothes on, I had to be totally submerged in this sort of mini swimming pool. A rabbi said a Hebrew prayer and I was given a Hebrew name, Shulamith (Salome). And so I came out with dripping hair and rushed off to the wedding. This was in a rabbi's little house. We had wine and nuts, and it was so exotic. We went out into the courtyard with the children all about, and under the canopy they married us. I think that when one gets married, one just thinks the same vows whatever the language. Then I had to drink wine from a glass and then Danny had to crush the glass completely. Then the rabbi's wife took us and put us into a little room and locked the door.[15]

This traditional gesture of uniting the two as man and wife was purely symbolic, and Daniel and Jackie were quickly released to go on to a celebratory wedding lunch at Jerusalem's King'David Hotel, where the guests included Israel's most important politicians – Ben Gurion, Teddy Kollek and General Moshe Dayan. Zubin Mehta, Janet Baker and Sir John and Lady Barbirolli represented the international music community. In fact, as Mehta recalled, discussion at the wedding table centred around a subject that had distinct political overtones: the organisation of a goodwill fund-raising tour of the United States and Canada by the Israel Philharmonic Orchestra. He and the Barenboim couple agreed to donate their services, and encouraged other colleagues to do likewise.

That evening in Tel Aviv, Barbirolli gave a performance of Beethoven's Ninth Symphony with Janet Baker as one of his soloists. (The scheduled Verdi *Requiem* had been deemed inappropriate in the circumstances and was substituted by Beethoven's celebrated work with its rousing 'Hymn to Joy'.) Afterwards the Barbirollis, Janet Baker and many other musicians from the orchestra arrived in force at the ongoing wedding reception given for Jackie and Daniel at the Philharmonic Guest House. Sir John proposed the toast to the young couple and Ben Gurion was the guest of honour. As Evelyn Barbirolli observed, 'It was a wonderful party, particularly so because we were celebrating not only the Barenboim wedding, but the fact that peace had once again returned to the troubled land of Israel.'[16] The couple were photographed with both the venerable guests – Ben Gurion, the founding father of the state of Israel, and John Barbirolli, Jackie's guiding musical spirit since the age of eleven.

Ben Gurion was no particular lover of music, as Daniel recalls, but he was a great admirer of Jackie's. 'There was that special significance of an English girl, and a gentile at that, who had come to Israel in 1967 when the country was at war. She became a sort of symbol in Israel and Ben Gurion was very aware of that.'[17]

As Rabbi Friedlander saw it, Jackie's conversion transcended the purely symbolic significance; it was also a tangible expression of her identification with her new family and musician friends: 'Jacqueline did not enter into a covenant of faith, but a covenant with Daniel, with Aida (her good mother-in-law whom she loved ardently), with Pinchas [Zukerman], Itzhak [Perlman] and all Israel. This covenant also counts.'[18] Friedlander emphasised that to his circle of progressive Jews hers was a very genuine conversion. 'It didn't necessarily mean Jackie became the clocking-in-each-day, observing Jew. But she felt quite relaxed to be part of the Jewish community and Israel, of course, helped a lot, particularly through what she gave to the country at the time of the Six Day War.'[19]

Perhaps there was more to it than that. I remember Jackie telling me that Judaism gave her a feeling of space and, in contrast to Christianity, a more abstract concept of God. Its teaching of an idealism that relates to our human existence and the practice of justice and love on a quotidian basis were qualities which she valued.

When she returned to London and announced her conversion to her friends, it did not always go down well. The cellist Anita Lasker remembers Jackie breezing into a rehearsal with ECO and telling her, 'I'm a Jew too, now.' Anita, who had lost many of her family in the Holocaust and had herself been incarcerated in Auschwitz, answered sharply, 'Try being born one.' Jackie was quick to take the point, and Anita was to become a beloved and respected friend, almost a mother figure for her.

Her own parents, Iris and Derek, were undoubtedly delighted to see Jackie's shining happiness, but as Daniel recalled, they did not voice any opinion of the lightning events of June 1967 and their lifelong implications. 'Jackie's parents never made any comments about the conversion or the marriage – but they were not very talkative on any level.'

However, it would appear that after Jackie had announced her engagement and forthcoming conversion in April, Iris and Derek had been receiving unpleasant letters from misguided friends and even from complete strangers, condemning their daughter's apostasy. According to Piers, his parents were completely ignorant of what Judaism was and had to call in their local vicar to enlighten them.[20] As practising Christians, they would probably have been more upset by the religious implications of the conversion than the racial issues. In fact, their elder daughter Hilary was married to a man with Jewish blood – Kiffer's father, Gerald Finzi, was born of Italian-Jewish stock.

The Barenboim couple left Israel the day after their wedding for a five-day holiday in Marbella, where they were the guests of Arthur Rubinstein. The great pianist was a sort of father figure for Daniel, who not only had an enormous admiration for Rubinstein's artistry and musicianship, but was captivated by his remarkable personality. Rubinstein had heard Daniel play as a boy and had always given him the greatest encouragement. In recent months he had heard Jackie's recordings and was equally impressed. Daniel recalled that when 'he invited us both to his house in Spain [...] he always made us play for him – he loved hearing Jackie – and there were innumerable occasions when we played until the early hours of the morning'.[21] Rubinstein welcomed the young couple as friends, and Daniel and Jackie came to feel 'almost like members of the family'.

After their short honeymoon the Barenboim couple returned to England, to face some rather disgruntled criticism of their 'unprofessional' behaviour in cancelling concerts at the last minute. As Daniel noted, in the space of less than a month there had been a drastic change of public opinion. 'When I returned to Europe a week or ten days after the war in June 1967, one could no longer talk about the Jewish underdog, but one had to tread very gently. The terrible events of the

Second World War appeared to have been suddenly forgotten, and at first there were veiled, and later more open allusions to Jewish imperialism. I realised again what a short memory we have. Within a matter of days the world had forgotten that the Arabs had initiated the war which they then lost.'[22]

One of the musical friendships sacrificed at the time was that with Menuhin. Barenboim recalled 'Yehudi was mad at us. He was in any case in sympathy with the Arab cause.'[23] Sadly, as a result, Jackie had no further musical contact with Menuhin, and their plans to play and record Schubert's Quintet and the Brahms Double Concerto were abandoned. However, later they were reconciled socially. Menuhin understood very well the impulse behind Jackie's actions: 'She was so enamoured of Danny and at that time so taken with the inebriating excitement of Israel, the wars, that she decided with her usual wonderful spontaneity that she and Danny had to be there in June 1967. It was as inevitable as falling in love.'[24] In the years of her illness, as Daniel said, the Menuhins were extremely supportive and kind to Jackie.

At the end of June the couple went to the Aldeburgh Festival to hear Sviatoslav Richter play Mozart's Piano Concerto K595, with Benjamin Britten conducting. Daniel remembered that when they saw Britten, 'he was highly unfriendly, probably partly because of the political aspect of our situation, and also because he regarded it as highly unprofessional to cancel engagements – Jackie had cancelled a concert at the Festival there.'[25]

Having had to give up her tour with the Bath Festival Orchestra to North America, Jackie was free during the month of July – apart from participating in a charity concert at the Queen Elizabeth Hall, playing the Brahms E minor Sonata with Daniel. At the end of the month the Barenboims left for the USA, where they joined the Israel Philharmonic Orchestra on the fund-raising 'Victory' tour that had originally been mooted at their wedding lunch party. The tour received the support of American Jewish musicians, and such celebrities as Bernstein, Heifetz, Piatigorsky and William Steinberg joined Mehta, Barenboim and du Pré in performing concerts with the IPO and donating their services to the Israel Emergency Fund. Thus, on 30 July, Jackie performed the Schumann concerto at New York's Philharmonic Hall with Zubin Mehta conducting, and played the same concerto under Daniel's baton in Toronto and Cleveland on 2 and 3 August.

Zubin Mehta remembered Jackie's happiness in those days; she appeared to be floating on a cloud. When she descended to earth, he was never sure what she picked up in the many discussions between him and Daniel:

> Her education in some things was so minimal that we didn't know what she followed in our conversations and what she didn't. Daniel had had a regular school education, as did I – something that parents of musically gifted children should really take care of. But Jackie, for instance, just did not understand the concept of distance – she had no idea that New York was far away from Seattle or how long it would take to get there. But she was very clever and she never let on what part of the conversation she was following – she sort of smiled and said 'Bless you' to everybody. She was just heaven.[26]

On the other hand, in Mehta's opinion Jackie had a healthy sense of balance unusual in young and gifted artists: 'She was much less devoted to her cello than to her life and to her home. And she was undoubtedly absolutely devoted to Daniel. It was he who had to coax her to practise and to learn new repertoire. It wasn't in her musical make-up to have a curiosity about today's creativity or to feel the urge to learn new things.'

Jackie loved playing with Zubin, finding in him a musician after her own heart, who possessed both the flexibility and ability to identify with his soloist. His own strong and deeply felt ideas about the music complemented Jackie's, and in this way she regarded him as an ideal accompanist. While Jackie grew to love Zubin as a brother, there was such a close spirit of camaraderie between him and Daniel that occasionally she almost got left out of things. Mehta quoted a particular instance which had her (and not only her) totally bewildered.

> Daniel was to play a concert in Pittsburg that August with Steinberg conducting. Prior to that, a reporter was sent to New York to interview him. He came to the Essex House, the hotel we were all staying in. I happened to be in their apartment, when the doorbell rang and I opened the door to find this man standing there. He greeted me, 'Oh Mr Barenboim – so nice to see you!' That was my cue – I couldn't miss such an opportunity. So I said, 'Please come in.' Danny and Jackie were in the other room and I called out to them, 'Zubin, you don't mind if I use your living-room? Jackie, won't you come and sit next to me?' Then Daniel came and sat right opposite me (I wished he wouldn't have) and I gave this entire interview posing as Daniel! Jackie had *no* idea what

was going on (she wasn't used to our little pranks) but she kept quiet. And I kept on putting my arm round her and kissing her cheek, and Daniel got increasingly furious. When the journalist said, 'You've just been in Israel for the Six Day War.' I answered by praising 'Zubin': 'Yes but that was a natural thing as I am Israeli. But it was Mr Mehta – a non-Israeli – who showed a real spirit of courage and generosity, as he went there, risking danger and cancelling all his appointments.' The man left for Pittsburg without knowing whom he had really interviewed. It must have been a shock to him when Daniel walked out on-stage to play the piano at Pittsburg.

Jackie was due back in the UK by the middle of August for further engagements. She performed the Schumann concerto at the Proms on 15 August with Sir Adrian Boult conducting, and later that month played a recital at the Harrogate Festival with Daniel. September was given over to recording and, once the concert season started again in mid-September, she plunged into a busy schedule of performances throughout Europe – many of them as soloist with orchestra, which meant being away from Daniel.

But as their musical rapport had proved so successful, Jackie's concert agents were now scheduling as many engagements as possible with Daniel, a lot of them centred round festivals such as Brighton and Edinburgh. And Barenboim had recently entered into negotiation with John Denison, Director of the Royal Festival Hall, to set up a summer festival in 1968 at London's South Bank complex, exploiting the fact that the newly built Queen Elizabeth Hall was unused outside the normal concert season. By the next season their schedules were so well dovetailed that the couple never needed to spend more than two or three days apart.

In fact, Jackie had strong views about restricting the number of her engagements and chose her concert dates carefully. This is evident from looking at the agency's artists' diary books, where her stated preferences about conductors and repertoire were recorded, and where she would block off sections of time so as to be with Daniel. It was noted from the summer of 1967 that the only pianist she would play recitals with was Barenboim, and that great discrimination should be displayed in booking her with regional British orchestras. Jackie told Terry Harrison to 'blacklist' the CBSO and the Bournemouth Symphony Orchestra, two groups with whom she had not enjoyed playing.

It was during the summer of 1967 that Christopher Nupen hatched a plan to make a documentary film about Jackie for BBC TV's *Omnibus*. Jackie enthusiastically supported his ideas and the film was shot during August and September.

Nupen had good credentials for making a film about a musician. South African-born, he had an unusual training both as a lawyer and musician, being a more than proficient guitarist. After a spell working in a merchant bank, he joined the BBC as a sound producer. While working at Radio Three, he became interested in making radio documentaries. Nupen had met Barenboim while recording a programme devoted to the summer music courses at the Accademia Chigiana in Siena. It was a natural step to move from radio to television, all the more so since Nupen was among the first broadcasters to realise the potential of television in popularising classical music. In 1965 he made his film, *Double Concerto*, for BBC TV about the two pianists Vladimir Ashkenazy and Daniel Barenboim – the first of a series of 'intimate' documentaries about musicians, which achieved great public success.

Television was initially used in the late 1950s as a means to bring classical music to larger audiences. Leonard Bernstein, an ardent believer in the popularisation of music, was particularly successful in bridging the gap between pop and classical music, and in stimulating the interest of the musically 'uneducated'. As musical director of the New York Philharmonic Orchestra, Bernstein felt it his obligation to woo new audiences, and his educational programmes on TV were designed in part to encourage people to leave their armchairs in front of the 'box' and to come into the concert hall to listen to live music. In contrast, the pianist Glenn Gould made no concessions to public taste in his use of TV as a radical means of transmitting musical knowledge and recording classical music. In his view, recording should substitute for live music in the concert hall.

Nupen had different aspirations, being interested in transmitting to a large public the vitality of live music-making and wishing to debunk the myths about 'great artists on pedestals'. He demonstrated that live performances of classical music could communicate to a wide range of people and saw that television in this way could now compete with radio in popularising classical music. As Nupen recalled, Jackie and Daniel were among the first classical musicians who understood the potential of TV and its capacity to reach large audiences:

In those days, we all perceived TV as a new medium of communication – it was a natural part of our discovery of things as young people. Now, TV tends to be seen as a way of making a career, which can spawn a new prodigy a month and discard them just as easily. At the time, we ourselves had no idea of the extent of TV's power. We knew it was a good thing, since we were interested in bringing music to a larger range of people. But we didn't realise that TV would make Daniel and Jackie as famous by the age of twenty-five as Rubinstein, Heifetz and Segovia were at forty-five.

Initially, many people did not take Nupen's efforts seriously. 'Why do you waste your time with home movies?' he was often asked. But as Christopher was aware, the time was right to put his ideas into practice, not least because the invention of the video-camera opened up new possibilities for documentary film-makers. 'The light-weight, noise-free 16-millimetre camera had originally been conceived for filming TV news items – a reporter could interview politicians on the street holding a camera on his shoulder. The old cameras were impossible to use when filming music unless you put them in a blimp. They made a noise like a machine-gun and this got on to the sound-track and spoilt the whole show.'

However, the 'blimp', an enormously bulky kind of cage made from rhinoceros steel, was heavy and unwieldy, requiring two men to lift it and at least thirty minutes to set it up; Nupen could now put the new camera at a metre's distance from his subject without intrusive noise. 'The film I made about Jackie started with her on a train – this was possible because we shot the sequence with a hand-held camera. This allowed me to create an intimate view of the artist and to show a side of a musician's life that had never been made public before.' As Nupen understood, Jackie was a natural on camera and by starting the film with her strumming her cello like a guitar, he hoped to intrigue his audience. He wanted to ensure that young viewers would not be put off by the idea of an 'art' film that would be above them.

As the critic Edward Greenfield observed in his review of the film after its first showing, the very title *Jacqueline* seemed to smack of a new 'pop' style:

One could almost hear the outraged snorts of the more conservative music-lover, tempted against habit to watch BBC 1 and a feature film on the cellist Jacqueline du Pré. Snorts continuing, no doubt, when in the very first shot the heroine was seen not in the concert hall but in a jolting railway carriage happily thrumming away on her precious Stradivarius as though it was a jazz bass and singing a French pop song. But then at once honour is satisfied with the exuberant girl replaced by the Great Artist playing her heart out in the Saint-Saëns concerto.[27]

Nupen was aware precisely why he wanted to make a documentary about Jackie. 'She had the ability to make me feel music with a depth and intensity that very few other musicians have. Her playing brought that extra dimension of meaning to the way our lives fit into the sorry scheme of things, something that defies description in words. Just through watching the "box" and seeing somebody with the level of communication that Jackie had was enough to penetrate all the mis-education, social prejudices and inhibition in the face of art and classical music that were so prevalent in our society.'

In his second film about her, *Remembering Jacqueline du Pré*, first shown in 1995, Nupen utilised many of the more informal sequences shot in 1967, which had been excluded from the first film *Jacqueline*. For instance, Jackie is shown in their basement flat in Upper Montagu Street playing a Kuhlau sonatina on the piano for Daniel and Zubin Mehta. Nupen recalled that this was something that happened more or less spontaneously – with some directional nudging from Barenboim. Mehta had just walked in and Daniel called to Jackie: 'Smiley, come and show Zubin how you play the piano.' Nupen acted on this cue and caught the scene on film without Jackie being aware that he was doing more than positioning his cameras for a subsequent interview. Incidentally, even those who were close to her were largely unaware of Jackie's skills as a pianist; William Pleeth, on seeing the new film in 1995, told Nupen: 'I had *no* idea she could play the piano so well.'

Another 'informal' scene shown only in this second film was set up in advance – a meeting with Jackie's dressmaker Madeleine Dinkel in her Hammersmith flat. Dinkel recalled that her home was taken over by technicians and cameramen, and when problems emerged with the power points, leads were connected to the mains in the street. The element of a 'surprise' meeting was created artificially, as Jackie was made to wait outside the door until the equipment was set up. But she proved to be a good actress – affecting surprise, she bursts through the door and warmly embraces Madeleine.

The filming of the musical episodes took place in various conditions during the end of August and in September. Jackie is shown at her most relaxed playing cello duets by Couperin and Offenbach with her teacher, Pleeth, in his music room. Here Nupen captures the spirit of home music-making, intimate and full of laughter and fun. The dynamic energy of Jackie's movement leaps out of the screen, almost seeming excessive in respect to the weight of the music. Although there is a considerable contrast between her instrumental style and Pleeth's apparently laid-back manner of playing, one is nevertheless made aware of the like-mindedness of their basic musical approach – visible evidence of how much Jackie owed to her teacher.

Nupen was also allowed to film sessions in the EMI studios when Barenboim and du Pré were recording the Brahms F major Sonata. One senses the relaxed atmosphere in the studio, helped along by Suvi Grubb's genial presence. The two artists are placed unconventionally facing each other, with du Pré raised on a platform, thereby enjoying a maximum visual contact. But once they start playing for the red light, we see an instant change, where their total concentration is directed on performing the music. The film seems to capture a tangible image of musicians in the process of translating musical ideas into the physical actions necessary to produce sound.

With the double purpose of showing Jackie's performance of the Saint-Saëns and Elgar Cello Concertos on TV, and of providing material for Nupen's documentary, BBC TV set up a concert in their Wood Lane studios for an invited audience. The New Philharmonia Orchestra was booked with Daniel Barenboim to accompany Jackie. The resulting filmed performance of the Elgar concerto undoubtedly has a lasting musical value through the added visual dimension, which makes one more aware than in any of her audio recordings of Jackie's complete freedom and originality as an instrumentalist.

What is even more amazing to discover, perhaps, is that this Elgar performance was recorded in concert without retaking a single note. Nupen explained:

> There was a rehearsal where the work was played through, giving the cameras a chance to see what was going on. Then the concert – which we recorded and filmed with six cameras. I cut it 'live', which meant that during the actual performance, I would say at a certain bar: 'Come in from camera 2 to camera 1' and so on. At the end of the day we had one sound-track and one picture track with the cuts already there, and

it was impossible to change anything. This was a spontaneous way of cutting and carried a high element of risk in it, since however good your material is, a film is made or broken through the cuts – they are its life-blood. Nowadays, I would have tried to make such a film with six picture tracks, as you can do a better job editing in the cutting room, provided that you can afford the money.

But in a certain way I was inspired by Jackie, and worked with a sort of intuition. How were we to know when she was going to look best on which camera, when would the eyebrow go up, when would the head go back, when would she turn, when would the glance come, when might she smile?

Interestingly enough, in the Elgar concerto performance, Jackie appears to be relatively static, belying the numerous descriptions of her large and vigorous movements when she played. Nupen explained that 'Jackie appeared to move less in the film than she did in live concert, but this is because you nearly always see close-up, or medium close-up, in film and rarely have a complete perspective – you do not see the whole. Furthermore, if you come in on camera at a certain moment to a certain image, when the music, the sound and the picture are all related, a movement will add something and doesn't strike you as distracting.'

Nupen recalled that his friend and mentor Andrés Segovia tried to persuade him to tell Jackie to move less. 'Of course, I never said anything. In Segovia's case he was determined to be still when playing and, for instance, disliked Rubinstein's flamboyance, saying "It's not my style". Jackie's movements were so deeply bound up, not just with the music, but with what she was trying to express, that they were completely natural and they never disturbed me. I thought at the time that those people who claimed to be deflected by her movements showed a shortcoming in their own perception.' (Segovia was not the only musician to have such reservations. Herbert von Karajan, reputedly, disliked Jackie's excessive temperament and vigorous body movements, and claimed it was a valid reason never to book her.)[28]

Nupen's documentary *Jacqueline* has become one of the most enduringly successful films about music and musicians. After Jackie developed multiple sclerosis he updated the original version in 1982, filming some new material showing her in a wheelchair, but still involved in music through teaching and editing the score of the Elgar concerto. For cellists in particular, the film provided a fascinating opportunity to observe du

Pré in action, and to see some of the idiosyncrasies of her technique in terms of fingerings and bow usage. For instance, few other cellists succeed in producing such a brilliant and controlled spiccato (bouncing bow stroke) as Jackie does in the second movement of the Elgar. But to see the unconventional way she produces the stroke (quite far up the bow towards the point) against the formulas of scholastic teaching is to believe in an alternative technical possibility.

Of course, it is not just the specialist musician who gains from observing Jackie in action. Nupen succeeded in translating her personality and the spirit behind her music-making into something immediately accessible to the man in the street. 'To have had the opportunity to put that on to the screen for an eventual audience of over fifty million people, many of whom had never been to a concert in their lives – this gave my life a real sense of purpose.'

Many people have praised this version of the Elgar concerto as the best film of a live performance yet. The cellist Lynn Harrell has pointed out that film is more accurate than audio recording, because you see the truth – and there is less possibility of editing an artificially perfect sound-track, through cutting and pasting the tape (or nowadays through digital editing). Yehudi Menuhin has stated: 'I think that Jackie will have had a great influence, if only for that unbelievably beautiful film of her playing the Elgar, with Danny conducting. This is perhaps the most successful musical film I know.'[29]

Certainly, the film testifies to Jackie's unique qualities of joyous spontaneity and profound intensity of musical expression. And some of the images of her in performance have a power greater than any words can express. Nupen refers in particular to the searing image of Jackie's face during her playing of the last movement coda as an icon that burns through to the heart. Here du Pré's facial expression seems a visual embodiment of the tragedy of Elgar's music, showing an age-old wisdom of inner spirit that cannot be derived from empirical knowledge or worldly experience.

The power of the imagery was so exceptional that after the film's showing some 'ordinary' viewers felt compelled to write to the *Radio Times* expressing their feelings. An example is a letter by a Mrs Joan Davis of Exeter: 'To see on [du Pré's] face such complete unselfconscious absorption in the beauty of the music and to witness the moments of intense joy and oneness with her husband as they shared in the miracle of music-making was indescribably moving.'

The critics, too, had nothing but praise for the film when it was first shown on BBC 1's *Omnibus* on 8 December 1967. Edward Greenfield of the *Guardian* called it 'the most vivid portrait of a musician I have yet seen on television',[30] and the *Daily Telegraph* critic expressed the grateful feeling that 'Jacqueline du Pré is one of those rare people whose public persona, and for all I know her private one as well, makes others feel good to be alive'[31] – a feeling echoed by so many who have seen and relished the film. Remarking that Nupen had given it an added human dimension, as Jackie was so palpably in love with her 'Romeo', the equally extrovert and exceptional Daniel Barenboim, the critic continued on a note of apprehension: 'The voltage of both their present relationship and their musical talents looked in the film so extravagant as to suggest that they must surely burn themselves out before their time, that this is the sort of thing which cannot last. Insofar as it can be preserved, perhaps Mr Nupen has done so.'

19

The Ideal Partnership

Like peas, music cannot be canned. It loses its flavour, scent, its life.

Sergiu Celibidache

Zubin Mehta once compared Jackie's career to the lightning passage of a comet which, with remarkable intensity – but all too briefly – illuminated our lives.[1] Her comet shone at its most luminous for the first two or three years following her marriage to Barenboim, as she travelled round the world (more often than not with her husband), bringing her art to a large range of people and leaving a legacy in her recordings.

EMI had originally booked their studios from 20 to 22 September for du Pré to record the Brahms Double Concerto with Maguire and Giulini, prior to their Festival Hall concert. But on 1 August, Peter Andry's assistant wrote to Jackie explaining that 'Maestro Giulini much regrets that it will not be possible to be in London [on those dates]'.[2] It was suggested that the Abbey Road Studio One be held for her and Barenboim instead. Thus, on 21 September, Jackie and Daniel started their recording of the two Brahms Cello Sonatas, Op.38 and Op.99. Christopher Nupen filmed part of the session, and in *Jacqueline* he included excerpts of the couple playing part of the first and second movements of the F major Sonata. We are given a glimpse of their working process when Daniel and Jackie correct a couple of minor ensemble problems in the final bars of the first movement, exchanging smiles and laughter but no words.

The following day Jackie felt unwell and withdrew from the sessions, since she needed to rest and prepare for her forthcoming performance of the Brahms Double. The studio time was put to good use by Barenboim and the clarinettist Gervase de Peyer, who recorded the Brahms clarinet sonatas for EMI. Sylvia Southcombe, who was married to de Peyer at the time, recalled, 'It was amazing as Gervase and Daniel just went to the studios, played and recorded straight away. Although they had talked about the music, I don't think that they had ever rehearsed or played together before. Afterwards we went out for a meal, and that's how my friendship started with Jackie and Daniel.' In fact, these Brahms cello sonata recordings were not completed until some months later. The whole of the E minor and the first two movements of the F major were made in two sessions on 20 May 1968, while the F major sonata was completed on 18 August.

There are so many marvellous fine points in the Brahms sonata recordings, all things which bring the dry page of the score to life. Barenboim and du Pré really present us with a recreation of Brahms's music, palpitating and alive, with blood coursing through its sinews and veins. As Suvi Grubb has commented, 'There is an eager spontaneity about these performances; du Pré and Barenboim were still in the process of discovering each other and this is reflected in their playing of these works.'[3]

The Barenboims capture the different sides of Brahms represented in the two sonatas, which were written with an interim of twenty years between them (in 1866 and 1886 respectively). The E minor is self-consciously 'backward-looking' and seems to follow on where Beethoven left off with his Op.102 sonatas (written forty-one years earlier). Yet the influences go back beyond Beethoven's sonata form and contrapuntal writing to an earlier ancestry, evident in the graceful 'eighteenth-century' minuet and in the third movement fugue, where the theme is derived from Bach's 'Contrapunctus 13' from the *Art of Fugue*.

In contrast, the tempestuous Second Cello Sonata (written in the characteristic Brahmsian key of F major/minor with long excursions to the remote key of F sharp major) is one of the composer's most concisely constructed works. It stretches the conventions of standard cellistic writing, with tremolos emulating orchestral textures, and daring and effective use of the cello's brighter upper registers (anticipating the dominant role of the cello in the ensuing Double Concerto). Brahms's contemporary, the critic Eduard Hanslick, observed on first hearing this work that it was ruled by a passion 'fiery to the point of vehemence, now defiantly challenging, now painfully lamenting!'. Despite the glorious long-spun song of the adagio's principal theme, and the almost childish innocence of the finale's opening theme, he deemed that 'pathos remains the determining psychological characteristic of the whole'.[4]

This quality of pathos and passion is admirably captured by du Pré in both works. Yet however much emotion she invests in her playing, her expression always has a natural function that is integral to the overall structure. Barenboim establishes this framework, which allows for flexibility while maintaining strength. For instance, the natural evolution of the tempi in the exposition of the E minor Sonata allows for the music to push through to a faster speed for the second subject and subside to a more relaxed pace for the closing section. A purist might object that these tempi fluctuations are not marked in the score; yet they have almost become a performing convention, logically derived from sonata form's built-in nature of contrast.

The spaciousness of line so essential to Brahms demands this ebb and flow within an organically unified tempo, representing what Bruno Walter called the 'apparent continuity' of tempo relationship through a sense of proportion. (This was something that Barenboim admired and emulated in Wilhelm Furtwängler's interpretations, where the inner logic was achieved through inter-relating the themes and through subtle changes of tempo, giving each movement the aspect of a single organic growth.) While able to sustain slow tempi, du Pré and Barenboim have a remarkable rhythmic vitality in the faster movements, but not because they opt for particularly fast speeds. Rather, they achieve the effect through attributing weight and intensity to each of the shorter notes, while investing the underlying pulse with a directive sense of urgency.

Jackie's lyricism always retains a speaking quality through the subtle use of enunciation and articulation even in the most legato phrases. In the E minor, she demonstrates the range of her palette of sound – dark and sombre in the opening theme, heroic in the second subject and luminous and warm in the closing theme. Her lyrical qualities are nowhere used to more touching effect than in the slow movement of the F major Sonata. Similarly, she brings a marvellous speaking eloquence to the rhetorical opening of the first movement of the same work. Her attention to detail is evident in the subtle differentiation of the semiquaver up-beats in the opening theme, which can seem to rush forward impulsively or linger a little wistfully depending on the direction of the phrase.

In both works Brahms treats the cello and piano as equal partners in his allocation of the musical material. Yet, as du Pré's recording producer Suvi Raj Grubb noted, 'You cannot find two more incompatible instruments than the piano and cello; besides, the cello's entire range lies within the compass of the piano's weightiest and most sonorous section, and so when both are required to play loudly the pianist has to take special care not to swamp the cello. Brahms, of course, made no concessions as far as the piano part is concerned, for it is as heavy and as full as in a piano concerto.'⁵

Yet Grubb found that in balancing du Pré's cello, there was no need to make concessions, for instance by 'miking her up' too prominently. Jackie had an amply large sound, where intensity and strength were never used at the expense of force, and thus had no difficulty in holding her own. She was furthermore helped by Barenboim's precise understanding of the nature of instrumental balance.

As Daniel has frequently repeated, a pianist must be a master of illusion to make one forget the inherent defects of the piano, which Ferrucio Busoni termed 'its impermanent sound and its implacable division into semitones'. The pianoforte is, for better or for worse, a mechanical instrument. It is through illusion that a pianist overcomes the instrument's percussive nature to create the impression of sustained legato, colour and texture. And while the piano's system of tempered tuning renders the effect of universal 'correctness', it necessarily compromises the tensions and pulls inherent in the traditional harmonic system. A great pianist like Barenboim not only governs the musical structure in chamber music, but through using transparent textures and careful voicing (based on an understanding of harmonic overtones), creates the further illusion of 'expressive intonation' that is natural to singers and string players.

Grubb, in his capacity as producer, found that the usual problems of the recording process were minimal, since Jackie knew exactly what she wanted to achieve musically, and Daniel always played with the right degree of weight to support the cello and not to drown it. 'I marvelled at the musicianship of the two and the understanding between them, which made each adjust the volume of sound to allow the important lines to come through.'⁶

As Grubb recalls, Jackie showed endless patience at recording sessions in the knowledge that everybody in the studio was working for her. 'She never complained that she wanted to get on with things. After recording, Jackie would come back and listen very attentively in the control room, and always had very precise suggestions to make.'⁷ As Daniel observed: 'Jackie found recording easy, since she was oblivious of the external conditions. She was not interested in the editing process, although she was concerned that the sound and the balance were right.'⁸

From the number of times that she brought up the subject with Peter Andry, it is obvious that Jackie greatly looked forward not only to performing, but to recording the Brahms Double Concerto – one of her favourite works. Her first public performance of the piece was on 24 September with Hugh Maguire at the New Philharmonia Orchestra's opening concert of the season, with Carlo Maria Giulini conducting. There are mixed accounts of the concert. Lord Harewood, who was at the time working with the New Philharmonia Orchestra as General Manager, remembered it as 'not so successful', implying that the soloists were not well suited to each other.[9]

Hugh Maguire, however, recalls the concert as an inspiring occasion:

> I was immensely nervous, but once we started it was fine. I must say I have never ever played so well in my life, because Jackie lifted me right up. She was magnificent and absolutely in her element when she was performing. We had rehearsed the piece a lot. In our discussions on bowing and fingering, Jackie influenced me considerably. For instance, she compelled me not to go up the G string in the opening theme of the second movement as is the convention. She thought that the phrase and colour were better achieved by crossing strings, and convinced me that this was the right choice.[10]

Christopher Nupen vividly remembers the concert as an example of some of du Pré's very best playing.

> When I heard Jackie perform the Brahms Double with Hugh, I nearly died. I went back afterwards and couldn't speak, the tears were rolling down my face. And Jackie said, 'Kitty, Kitty, why are you always crying?' And I stumbled out, 'because of the way you play.' I will never forget her face when I said these words – she understood what I was trying to express. She was in a way conscious of her powers and the effect she had, except it was a consciousness about something you cannot possibly explain.[11]

Only ten days later, on 3 October, Jackie appeared again at the Festival Hall with the same orchestra and Norman Del Mar for a performance of Elgar's concerto, which Lord Harewood recalls (in contrast to the Brahms Double) as 'such stuff as dreams are made on'.[12] Two days earlier Jackie had been booked to perform the same work with Yehudi Menuhin at the Royal Albert Hall in a concert in aid of his newly opened music school. But because of the temporary deterioration of her relationship with Menuhin, her place was taken by Maurice Gendron.

Jackie's next engagements took her to Edinburgh and Glasgow, where she performed the Dvořák concerto with Sir Alexander Gibson and the SNO (on 6 and 12 October respectively). She had a good relationship with Gibson (they had first played together four years earlier at a private concert in Edinburgh), and enjoyed his vivacious Scottish wit off-stage and his warmth and musicality on it. In fact, these two concerts were a prelude to a two-week tour with the SNO of Austria and Germany, where she and Janet Baker were the alternating soloists (representing the very best of young British talent). Jackie performed Dvořák, Schumann and Elgar concertos, making her début in Vienna in the beautiful Grosses Musikvereinsaal with the Schumann.

In the middle of the tour she flew back to London to play the same work at the Festival Hall with Daniel conducting the ECO. *The Times* critic, Mosco Carner, described her performance as 'eloquent and ardent, and completely at one with the spirit of the music'. Jackie's deeply felt response to Schumann's poetic romanticism retained the necessary spontaneity '... to say nothing of her vital and mellow tone and her immaculate passage work'. He deemed that the kiss awarded her by Daniel on stage after the performance 'was more than deserved'.[13]

Jackie's tour with the SNO finished with a single performance in Holland, in Rotterdam's De Doelen Hall, where she played the Elgar on 29 October to a delighted and enthusiastic audience. After a week's respite in London she was off again, this time to Italy, a country she loved to visit. Her tour lasted between 6 and 20 November, and was all the more enjoyable because she was partnered by Daniel. On 7 November they played for Milan's prestigious Società del Quartetto in the Verdi Hall of the Conservatoire. A week later she performed in Naples with the Scarlatti Orchestra, and she completed the tour with two more recitals with Barenboim, in Rome and Perugia on 17 and 19 November.

From Italy she travelled straight on to Sweden for two performances of the Dvořák concerto with the Swedish Radio Orchestra and Sergiu Celibidache in Västerås and Stockholm. Daniel, who was present at the first of these concerts on 24 November, recalled it as one of her most extraordinary performances. 'She had a really wonderful rapport with Celibidache. He insisted that she come early for rehearsals – they had one piano rehearsal, then about three or four with orchestra. I heard their first concert in Västerås and it was quite wonderful.'

In a surviving radio tape,[14] one certainly hears music-making of the first order, with du Pré giving a full-blooded account of this well-loved romantic concerto. The deeply emotional and outgoing spirit of her performance is shared by Celibidache, whose orchestral accompaniment matches du Pré's playing in intensity of sustained sound. Through particular attention to the voicing, Celibidache has at his command a rich palette of colour and creates textures which blend with the solo cello, yet are sufficiently transparent to allow it to come through. Not that he had to hold back the orchestra that much, as Jackie's sound was exceptionally large and well-focused.

Very occasionally her highly charged emotional approach pushes the sound beyond the capacity of her instrument. Thus, at the end of the exposition of the first movement, the heroic ascending triplet arpeggios tend towards forcing, and the final low B flat before the resolution into D major is invested with so much energy and pressure that the note is in danger of distortion. Indeed, the fermato pause over the note is ferociously held until near breaking point. Overall, the music is infused with a marvellous sense of luminosity and enormous space, something that is achieved without recourse to slow tempi, but rather through the weight of expression. In fact, the tempi of the first movement are largely consistent with those of Jackie's EMI recording with Barenboim, although, as is appropriate to the dictates of live performance (where the space and acoustic of a hall must be taken into account) the speeds incline towards their outer extremes.

The slow movement, on the other hand, is taken at a more leisurely pace than in the EMI recording with Barenboim. Here the emphasis is on flexibility and contrast, whereas in the recording the artists are more concerned to maintain unified tempi in the interests of the whole. Thus, in the Swedish Radio Orchestra performance the drama of the G minor section is achieved by a faster, more driven speed, while after the cadenza the basic pulse slows down to below the indicated 'Tempo I' for the recapitulation. Here, against the throbbing heartbeat pulse of the violas and cellos, Jackie squeezes every ounce of expression from the long singing line.

In the last movement du Pré's basic tempo is just a jot slower than in the EMI recording, while in the meno mosso section (in the cello and clarinet dialogue) she and Celibidache slow up far more. Yet du Pré always transforms these fluctuations of speed into something organic to the structure. Phrases, which in lesser hands could sound slow and indulgent, have an intensity and naturalness of expression in hers, and the driving force of her temperament gives plenty of bite and excitement to the faster music.

Right through the work the opulence of Jackie's sound is staggering and nowhere more poignantly than in the final bars of the last movement coda. Through the transfiguration of his material in the coda Dvořák consciously aimed at creating a sense of nostalgia – recollection in the face of loss. Great interpreters show that the effect can be achieved in more than one way. Du Pré's sound glows with warmth and emotion as she sings her way down from the trill on high B, riding over the fleeting reference to the first movement opening theme. In observing the composer's marking of forte right through this final melodic descent, she evokes an atmosphere of raw emotion in the face of grief, rather than the exalted contemplation born of suffering as favoured, for instance, by Rostropovich, who plays the same passage in a fabulous cool pianissimo.

Jackie's next engagements were in Munich at the end of November, where she performed the Elgar concerto with the Munich Philharmonic and John Pritchard. During the first ten days of December she took time off to accompany Daniel to the USA, returning to London to participate in the fortieth anniversary concert of John Barbirolli's conducting début with the LSO on 12 December. The programme of works by Haydn and Elgar was a replica of the one he had conducted forty years earlier, and Barbirolli asked that Jackie should be his soloist in Haydn's D major Concerto. This delightful piece has always been regarded with a certain ambiguity by critics since, until relatively recently, there were doubts as to its authenticity (musicologists attributed it to Antonin Kraft). Perhaps for this reason, *The Times* critic noted in a somewhat condescending tone of voice: '[du Pré's] honeyed tone, winsome ways and little displays of temperament were in themselves delicious, and in this concerto almost justified, for it is by no means great or strong Haydn. She played the last paragraph of the adagio exquisitely. Unfortunately, the same could be said about the opening of the final allegro, which could do with sturdier treatment.'[15]

We are almost in a position to judge for ourselves whether this is fair comment, since du Pré's and Barbirolli's recording of the piece was made the following day at EMI's Abbey Road Studio One. While agreeing with *The Times* critic about the exquisite phrasing in the second movement (which is altogether remarkable for its golden radiance of sound), I find that Jackie's playing of the opening theme of the rondo-finale has just the right touch of insouciant nonchalance and good humour. Her unhurried tempo (a comfortable 6/8) serves to illuminate the elegance of the rococo side of Haydn, rather than emphasising the rustic character favoured by Casals. Here in particular her choice of tempo is very much at variance with today's fashions – for instance, in Yo-Yo Ma's recording with the English Chamber Orchestra the finale is played at nearly twice the speed. But to my mind, Jackie's approach is so eloquent and convincing that it overrules the dictates of fashion, or the dogma laid down by pundits of 'authentic' historical performance in regard to tempi.

Jackie had especially asked for Suvi Grubb to record the EMI sessions. This initially caused some offence to Kinloch Anderson, who had worked with du Pré in her three 1965 recordings and furthermore was usually assigned to Barbirolli. Anderson had written Jackie a warm and courteous letter on 29 November, proposing that he should do the sessions and hoping she would not object.[16] But although Jackie respected his musicianship and his gentlemanly manner, she had come to rely on Grubb not just for his excellent ear, but for his warm and encouraging presence. She felt far less comfortable on the occasions when, for one reason or another, he could not direct her studio recordings.

Barbirolli, it seems, had no strong feelings on the matter. In any case he was totally at one with Jackie's interpretation and, according to his widow Evelyn, his impulsive vocal participation in the music was a sign of his approval – he was 'having a whale of a time'! Evelyn had felt bound to reprimand JB for singing along during the actual recording, at which he responded indignantly, 'Oh no, I wasn't singing – it's far too high for me!' 'But you're singing it an octave down!' she corrected him.[17] If one listens very carefully to the original recording of the concerto, one can even hear – very faintly – Barbirolli's voice singing along under Jackie's cello line.

And one can sympathise with him. Jackie is irresistible in her expressive approach to Haydn's music, where she treats the simplicity of ideas in the work (such as its apparently 'innocent' themes) with great sophistication. Haydn was ahead of his time in utilising both the cello's expressive quality and its virtuosic capacity, for instance, in the extremely effective use of the instrument's high register. And in du Pré's hands the filigree arabesque passage work never loses its cantabile quality – virtuosity always plays handmaiden to the overall expression.

Immediately after completing her Haydn recording Jackie returned to the USA to join Daniel in Philadelphia, where he was performing Beethoven's *Emperor* Concerto with Eugene Ormandy. His last concert with the Philadelphia Orchestra was given in New York on 19 December. As Daniel recalled,

> That night the hall was full of violinists – Oistrakh, Stern, Ricci, Milstein were all there. Ormandy said to me rather sardonically, 'Why is it that pianists don't come to hear you play?' Isaac Stern brought Pinchas Zukerman backstage – he was only a kid of nineteen. (I was twenty-five at the time, and from that great age one looks down on a nineteen-year-old as a kid.) Immediately Pinky announced in front of everyone, 'I want to play with you.' I didn't even know who he was. I remember there was general laughter and Oistrakh, who hadn't understood what he had said, had to wait for Isaac to translate – then he too roared with laughter. Jackie and I were leaving the next evening for Israel. But we said, 'All right, come along tomorrow to our hotel, bring some music and some music stands.'[18]

Zukerman remembered the whole occasion vividly. He had met Barenboim very briefly in Israel some years earlier, and he had heard of Jackie's name from Charles Wadsworth and Arnold Steinhardt. 'She had been in Spoleto the two years before I first went there. Steinhardt talked of this blonde girl who played like a wild stallion and nearly ripped the cello apart performing second cello in Schubert's Quintet. While Wadsworth had told me that if we ever played together it would be a match made in heaven.'[19]

The next morning Pinky turned up as agreed at the Essex House with his wife (at the time he was married to the flautist Eugenia or Genie Rich). Immediately Daniel and Jackie sat down to play with him. 'We read through as much music as possible – as much as I had been able to bring with me. From the start it was a complete fit – like playing hand in glove. It seemed to me that we just started playing and never stopped – it was the start of a four to five-year whirlwind relationship.' Genie recalled that after playing through the first movement of a Beethoven trio they all stopped, looked at each other and burst into happy laughter. There was no need to formulate in words what was self-evident – that this was a perfect trio team.

The success of a good piano trio depends on several vital elements –

the ability of the pianist to lead and create the framework within which the violinist and cellist operate as a unit, with a common approach and mutual understanding. What made this first meeting so exciting, as Daniel observed, was that 'There was a kind of instant empathy from the very beginning between the two string players. It just clicked ...'[20] Zukerman was a musician after Jackie's heart. Although he had undergone a rigorous formal training at the Juilliard School with Galamian, his rich intuitive gifts were akin to Jackie's, and he played with the same physical exuberance, energy and spontaneity. As Pinky recalled:

> It was an amazing time altogether. Playing with other people like that when you are so young was extraordinary, because you have not yet acquired that inherent 'excess' baggage that comes with the years. I mean by that the idiosyncrasies you develop, the studied, conscious knowledge and just the sheer experience of having played the music so often before, of having gone through that address so many times. But then it was all so fresh. I had played trios, sonatas, quartets since I was ten years old, so I knew the repertoire, I knew the notes. But it was unbelievable to play with two people like that – there was never any question of what to do, just how to do it – give a little bit there or take there. We never wrote things down – we never put in bowings – we never discussed tempi – things changed spontaneously from performance to performance and it was remarkable – it just fitted.[21]

By the end of the day it was clear to all three of them that they would form a trio. When Jackie and Daniel boarded a plane that night for Israel they were already wondering when to plan their first performances together. Given that they had by then booked Itzhak Perlman to play chamber music with them at the South Bank Festival, it had to be worked out carefully.

In Israel, Daniel and Jackie were greeted like old friends and heroes – and they were after all 'coming home'. Not that it was anything of a holiday, as within the space of a fortnight they performed thirteen concerts with the Israel Philharmonic in two full subscription series. Daniel conducted all the concerts and Jackie introduced the Elgar concerto to Israeli audiences and also played Haydn's C major Concerto.

On their return to London Jackie fulfilled engagements in and around the city (a recital at the Guildhall with Daniel and a concert with the ECO at Mill Hill). Between late January and April 1968 she shuttled back and forth between North America and the UK. Increasingly, she liked to restrict the number of her own concerts and was happy to spend some time being 'Mrs Barenboim'. Thus, on her first visit she herself only played three concerts – performances of the Schumann concerto with Lorin Maazel and the Philadelphia Orchestra on 16 and 17 February in Philadelphia, repeated on 20 February in Baltimore. She then flew back to London for the last week of February, before setting off again for North America.

Jackie initially played in Vancouver on 3 and 4 March, where she gave her first performance of Strauss's *Don Quixote*. She was booked to go on to Honolulu for concerts on 10 and 12 March, but she cancelled these dates at the last minute, with the excuse of an unspecified accident. However, she honoured engagements with the Denver Symphony Orchestra on 18 and 20 March. She interrupted her North American tour for five days, going back to England to perform with Barenboim and the Hallé Orchestra. In their three concerts in Leeds, Manchester and Huddersfield (on 23, 24 and 25 March respectively), she again performed the Schumann concerto.

Back in the USA she played the Elgar concerto with the Detroit Symphony Orchestra on 28 and 30 March, followed by recitals with Daniel in Princeton on 1 and 2 April and at a sold-out Carnegie Hall in New York on the fifth. In the *New York Times* review of the recital Jackie's technical prowess was praised: 'Her bowing technique . . . is a model of flexibility and sensitivity, and the reason for her greatness.' But the critic was unhappy with the mismatch of balance in the first-half offering of Beethoven (one of the sets of Variations from *The Magic Flute*) and the A major Sonata, where the piano sound seemed to overwhelm the cello; he felt that the balance was better for the Brahms F major Sonata, where '. . . they did manage to arrive at a nearer semblance of musical unity'.[22] One can be sure from the ovations accorded to the players that the audience was left with far stronger impressions of their music-making. Over the coming years, Jackie and Daniel were to play in New York more regularly than any other city apart from London.

As if all the travelling were not enough, Jackie was under extra pressure, having undertaken commitments to expand her repertoire and to record Richard Strauss's Symphonic Poem *Don Quixote* with the New Philharmonia Orchestra. The conductor was to be the illustrious octogenarian Dr Otto Klemperer. Jackie had first met Klemperer the previous year at a rehearsal when Daniel was performing Berg's *Kammerkonzert* with Pierre Boulez. Klemperer, an admirer of both Boulez and Barenboim, told Jackie (perhaps to test her out) to go and turn pages for Barenboim. As Daniel recalled, 'She had no difficulty in doing so, although she didn't like the piece.'[23]

On another occasion, when Daniel was recording the Beethoven piano concertos with Klemperer, Jackie came to the recording sessions. In the interval, Klemperer decided to see if her ear was indeed as phenomenally sharp as he had been told. Suvi Grubb recalled, 'He sat down at the piano and played what could not possibly be described as a chord, but was a weird combination of notes. "Miss du Pré, what notes am I playing?" he challenged, and without even having to think about it, she replied, "A, B, C sharp, D sharp, F." Klemperer himself had to look down at the keyboard to confirm that she was right, and having done that he said in admiration: "So!" – a monosyllable he could invest with greater meaning than most with an oration.'[24]

Contrary to the generally accepted convention, Klemperer always liked to make a recording before a concert, feeling that players benefit from the scrutiny of the microphone prior to performance. The first rehearsal and session that du Pré was asked to attend was held at Abbey Road Studios on 7 April (Klemperer had rehearsed the orchestra on the preceding two days).

Despite Klemperer's early association with Mahler and Richard Strauss, he was by no means an indiscriminate advocate of their music. The conductor's daughter, Lotte Klemperer, recalled that her father did not have a high regard for *Don Quixote*, 'which in reality he did not want to do, but was persuaded into by EMI and the Barenboims. (He had performed it only once thirty years earlier.)' The first viola from the NPO, Herbert Downes, played the prominent solo part characterising the Don's faithful squire, Sancho Panza. Of the abortive recording of *Don Quixote*, Downes has been quoted as saying, 'Klemperer didn't like the way [du Pré] played it ... you know how she used to throw herself about ... We had one session and went right through. She played all the notes, in fact she played very well, but I think Klemperer wasn't happy.'[25]

Lotte Klemperer contradicts this notion, saying that his subsequent withdrawal had nothing to do with du Pré's playing.

My father had the highest regard for her – as for Daniel Barenboim – as musician, soloist and person. They were friends and we often got together. The basic reason was his dislike of this particular piece of Strauss ... We had been in London since 9 February, where my father had a very heavy schedule to absolve [*sic*] ... By April he was quite exhausted, and during the *Don Quixote* session on 7[26] April he twice dozed off during a playback and claimed to be unwell. So we cancelled the recording as well as the concert. Mark Brunswick, the American composer and a good friend, also happened to be present on this occasion, and he and I both agreed that had it been better music, OK would not have been so overcome by fatigue.[27]

Left without a conductor for the forthcoming Festival Hall concert on 11 April, the NPO invited Barenboim to take over. As he did not know the score well, and in any case was playing the piano in the same concert, he declined the offer. At that point the orchestra turned to another distinguished octogenarian conductor, Sir Adrian Boult, who agreed to step in. On Tuesday, 9 April he rehearsed *Don Quixote* in the EMI studios, since that space had been booked and the Festival Hall was not available. Without anyone realising it, the sound engineer, Christopher Parker, turned on the microphones and recorded the whole rehearsal–play-through in the studios.

For a variety of reasons, the project for du Pré to record *Don Quixote* was subsequently abandoned. These tapes from the session and rehearsals on 7 and 9 April lay forgotten for over twenty years, gathering dust on EMI's storage shelves. When rediscovered, it was questionable whether they were of acceptable standard for commercial release. Certainly, had there been the chance to record the work again in the studio, we would have been given a performance of more refinement and precision in both the orchestral and solo playing. As the producer of the recently issued CD, Andrew Keener, has noted, 'Judging by the sundry noises – pencils dropping, even talking at one point – Boult's single take was probably made with the recording light off and it may have been simply a whim to switch on the recorder.'[28] Given that du Pré was incapable of compromising her standards for a 'mere' rehearsal, her committed vision of the music has been captured in that recorded play-through. As Keener says, 'The intensity throughout is unmistakable and characteristic.'

The sudden withdrawal of Klemperer could have been extremely awkward for EMI, since the New Philharmonia Orchestra had been contracted for four days for the *Don Quixote* rehearsals and recording. Barenboim and du Pré saved the situation by agreeing to use the 'dark' studio on the intervening day, Monday 8 April, to do the Schumann Cello Concerto. The work had already been scheduled as their next recording together later that spring, in a coupling with the Saint-Saëns Cello Concerto and the Fauré *Élégie*. At the same time Peter Andry had proposed that Jackie make with the Israel Philharmonic Orchestra a second LP consisting of Bloch's *Schelomo*, Bruch's *Kol Nidrei* and the Lalo concerto.[29]

Although Jackie wanted to oblige EMI by using the time to record the Schumann, she did not find it easy to adapt her mood to Schumann's intimate world of expression, having immersed herself so thoroughly in the drama of the fantastical character of Don Quixote. An understanding of theatrical drama is indeed essential to the interpretation of all Strauss's tone poems, which represent a departure from the aesthetic system of his predecessors. Earlier classical and romantic composers meant their programme works to be 'rather expressive of the feeling than tone painting', as Beethoven remarked about his *Pastoral* Symphony. In his tone poems Strauss conveys the dramatic programme through vivid orchestral illustration of his subject, which in *Don Quixote* achieves the effect of a kind of sonic cinerama, where we can almost visualise the hero's actions and feel his emotions.

Strauss was by no means the first musician to have attempted to depict the adventures of Cervantes's knight with the sad countenance, but he did so in a completely new way, devising the form of variations on a composite theme. In the elaborate orchestral introduction, the composer presents all the musical motifs that characterise Don Quixote and his servant Sancho Panza, then dedicates each variation to one of his imaginary adventures. The solo cellist, sometimes aided by a solo violin, represents the hero and as such is an active protagonist of the drama. It is this aspect of playing a role on stage which has proved irresistibly attractive to so many great cellists, many of whom claim that their version is *the* definitive one. This notion certainly guarantees performances of enormous commitment, yet results in a surprising variety of interpretations.

Jackie's reading of *Don Quixote* showed her close identification with the character of the chivalrous knight and the emotion behind the drama. Those who attended her Festival Hall concert remember the extraordinary intensity of her playing, something that the critics did not necessarily respond to favourably. Hugo Cole of the *Guardian*, while praising Jackie's assurance and passion, felt that she remained too much in her own character: 'It is not often that one wishes a soloist to show less intensity, less involvement; but how else to discover the sort of divine ease that exists in Don Quixote's maddest fantasies – the ease of a man who can fit the world around his own illusions?' To his mind, the performance, was neither 'eloquent or transparent enough to allow easy sorting out of essential from inessential. As a result, we were made over-aware of the works' complexity, of its episodic nature, of the multiplicity of composing and performing skills involved, and we were never led to read through the thousand musical surface-signs to the mad, unifying logic in Don Quixote's mind.'[30]

William Mann, while commending the inspired solo contributions of both Barenboim (who performed Beethoven's Fourth Piano Concerto) and du Pré in the concert, wrote in *The Times* with feigned consternation:

> The female Don Quixote seemed a curious notion – but only for a short space: once Miss du Pré got into her stride the sex of the solo cellist [...] became completely irrelevant. She gave us a flamboyant, earnest, dynamic portrait of the man from La Mancha, especially eloquent in the third variation, where Quixote expands the ideal of knight-errantry in rose-tinted F sharp major, and in the epilogue where poignant regret clears his mind as he lies dying – Miss du Pré coloured the final downward glissando with a heavy vibrato suggestive of quivering sobs, astonishing and most moving.[31]

While we are fortunate to have du Pré's version of the work in the CD released by EMI in 1996, we must remember that the recording was made without the knowledge or permission of either conductor or soloist. The minor ensemble problems and roughnesses in the orchestral reading would not have been passed if the aim had been to set down a recorded performance. One wonders how much du Pré herself would have wanted to change or correct this rendering. But for want of a better one, the recording serves to document du Pré's approach to the work in collaboration with Boult; for overall, *Don Quixote* is governed more by the conductor's vision than by the very substantial solo offerings.

Yet Boult's and du Pré's interpretation can certainly stand up to comparison with some of the finest. Their approach is in extreme contrast to that of Rostropovich with von Karajan and the Berlin Philharmonic, whose reading fosters an almost ponderously philosophical concept of the work. Boult's orchestra sounds somewhat rough by comparison with Karajan's suave and rich orchestral textures, which are a model of clarity. In contrast to Karajan, Boult tends to concentrate on the narrative drama and creates living personalities out of the protagonist. Naturally the conductors' approaches influence the interpretations of the two cello soloists. Rostropovich's Don is a dreamer, reluctant to leave the meanderings of his deranged fantasy to take part in adventure. Du Pré's Don is ardent and passionate, driven to impetuous actions by his afflicted condition. The differences are most notable in the two big showpieces for solo cello – the fifth and tenth (and final) variations. In the fifth variation (a description of the Don's lonely night vigil before being formally knighted) du Pré's monologue has enormous pathos: it is a portrait of a man consumed by intense anguish and burning passions. In contrast, Rostropovich is initially intent on the context – he evokes an atmosphere of nocturnal mystery, where the Don's contemplatative fantasy can rove undisturbed; thus, his elicited image of Dulcinea hovers so far in the distance as to be surely unattainable. The two soloists' different concepts are evident also in the final variation. When the principal motif is stated for the last time in a slow, wistful D major, Rostropovich uses it as a device to portray a dying man ethereally looking back over his lifetime. In contrast, Du Pré's version is invested with eloquent sunset passion, a picture of a man leaving his life full of poignant regrets.

Fou Ts'ong remembers discussing some of these features of Strauss's *Don Quixote* with Jackie after hearing her play it in Vancouver. He disagreed with her over-passionate version of the final variation and suggested a less earth-bound Don, who had achieved, if not Nirvana, then at least acceptance in a Buddhist sense of his vision of oncoming death. But it was not in Jackie's nature (at least at the age of twenty-three) to divorce feeling and emotion from her characterisation of Cervantes's hero.

Du Pré only performed *Don Quixote* a couple of times; although she did not have time to develop her views about the piece, the compelling ardour of her portrayal of the Don in the surviving recording is perhaps unmatched. In this sense her interpretation has something in common with Gregor Piatigorsky's reading in his recording with the Boston Symphony and Charles Munch. It also shares something of the impulsive drive behind Tortelier's highly individual rendering of the piece with Rudolf Kempe.

Strauss himself never came down in preference between a cello soloist playing the solo part concerto style (sitting in front of the orchestra) or the lead cellist of the orchestra playing it from the front of the section (the composer conducted it in both situations). Toscanini's authoritative interpretation, with Frank Miller as the solo cellist played from the ranks of the orchestra, is a successful example of the latter approach.

Evidently for Jackie the association with Boult was a happy one. She had enormous respect for his musicianship and also for his practical wisdom. Boult always told his pupils that in accompanying a soloist a conductor should take into account the player's requests and ideas, because a soloist has perforce spent far more time studying the music than the conductor. If it is true that Boult was willing to adapt his concept to Jackie's, one would like to think that their interpretation of *Don Quixote* was arrived at through a mutual understanding and respect.

In later years Jackie liked recounting how, in one of her performances over the years with Sir Adrian, she had a small memory slip. Afterwards, when she apologised to him, he replied without hesitation, 'But never mind, my dear, nobody listens for mistakes.' She recorded this incident in a notebook she kept from the mid-1970s, describing Boult's response as 'one of the most humane and constructive things I have ever heard'.

If circumstances beyond her control forced Jackie to abandon the project to complete the *Don Quixote* for EMI, it was she who wished to veto the other recording made that month. As Suvi Grubb recalled,

> It had been arranged for Jackie to record the Schumann concerto, when I was in hospital recovering from a severe heart attack. She was very reluctant to go ahead, but the orchestra had been booked. The recording was then edited and put together. By the beginning of May I had been discharged from hospital and had resumed work. One day Jackie appeared with Daniel. She wanted to tell me something, but was very shy about it. Daniel urged her to give voice to her thoughts: 'Come on, Smiley, out with it – you're talking to Suvi'. It transpired that she was unhappy with her Schumann recording. She never said why. I said, 'Well, if you're unhappy, we'll have to do it again.'

EMI, as one of the most prestigious recording companies, were ready to respect the wishes of their top international artists, even though cancelling a performance with orchestra involved a great deal of expense and the costs of re-recording were high. But no one doubted du Pré's integrity in observing the most stringent professional standards, or her high degree of preparation for recordings, so it was difficult to refuse her request. Both Barenboim and Grubb totally supported Jackie in using her right of veto on this occasion. Peter Andry, who had replaced Grubb in the April sessions, also gave his approval to the re-recording.

On 11 May, Jackie and Daniel were back in the Abbey Road Studios with the New Philharmonia Orchestra for their second recording of the Schumann Cello Concerto. The result was one of du Pré's most inspired interpretations on record.

Schumann wrote his Cello Concerto in 1850, by which time his unstable mental state was causing him terrible anguish. Clara Schumann described the pathetic scene of her husband in an asylum correcting the score of the new Cello Concerto and explaining that he hoped that such work would distract him from the perpetual torment of hallucinatory voices. The music of the first movement in particular is full of dark apprehension, although it by no means excludes those two essential features of Schumann's creative expressive personality: the introverted and gentle, and the ardent and impetuous. Jackie catches the spirit of the music, spinning long rhapsodic lines, where the expression can be alternatively contemplative, dramatic and poetically tender. She and Barenboim opt for unhurried tempi, where a great sense of spaciousness and freedom is achieved within an underlying unity of form. Jackie's playing is distinguished by great beauty of sound, impassioned and eloquent, with the full spectrum of dynamic from explosive fortes to the most yearning pianissimos. The slow movement is played with a luminous intensity that captures the essential Schumannesque quality to transform inner experience into heartfelt musical expression. In contrast, the finale is played with verve and concise rhythmic energy, without any of the accompanying roughness in the passage work that so often blights performances.

It may be true that Jackie's EMI recording of the Schumann concerto differs from her concert performances (as far as we can judge them from existing radio tapes) in having less impulsive passion and spontaneity and a more philosophical approach. But it is because the overall vision is so complete and logically structured that the recording stands up to frequent hearing and can be regarded as an enduring document. Towards the end of Jackie's life, when she had long since stopped playing the cello, it became one of her favourite recordings. Although in the intervening years she had thought a lot about the music, she never once remarked that she would have done things differently now. The fact that she so cherished the interpretation she laid down at the age of twenty-three makes one wonder if in her intuitive identification with the outpourings of the tormented and ailing Schumann there was some presentiment of the suffering and anguish she was to endure when struck down by illness.

The second side of the record was to be Saint-Saëns's First Cello Concerto. Jackie and Daniel had already recorded it with the New Philharmonia for BBC TV in September 1967 and played it again with the same orchestra at the Festival Hall on 14 May. Although the recording was originally scheduled for the spring months of 1968, the sessions booked were probably the ones used to re-record the Schumann. It was not until September that a session could be set up for the Barenboim couple and the New Philharmonia. The recording resulted in an elegant performance of this most classically proportioned composition, where a beautiful balance is achieved between passion, vitality and graceful lightness. In later years Jackie would remind her pupils of the importance of form, where the expression is built into the music. 'Too much expressive indulgence will distort the musical structure,' she warned.[32] Du Pré proved able to resist the temptation to overload the expression in Saint-Saëns's music, without depriving it of an ounce of her impassioned commitment.

This second orchestral record with Barenboim was released parallel with du Pré's second concerto recording with Sir John Barbirolli. For the latter record, the 'filler' for the Haydn D major Concerto was the little-known concerto of the Austrian composer, Matthias Georg Monn (1717–50). She learnt the work specially for the recording in September 1968. Evelyn Barbirolli recalled that Jackie arrived at the Abbey Road Studios with a 'stinking' cold: 'John afterwards said that he thought it was quite a good thing in the end as it calmed her down.' Monn's concerto is an excellent, if not inspired, example of the transitional style between the late baroque and the early classical. It has characteristics that are reminiscent both of Handel and Monn's own contemporary C. P. E. Bach. Although one could regard the G minor Concerto as an antecedent to Haydn's cello concertos, Monn's work does not pretend to the range of expression or instrumental virtuoso writing that we find in Haydn's two concertos. Nevertheless Arnold

Schoenberg, for one, had been sufficiently impressed by this concerto to write a harpsichord part for it and later composed a cello concerto based on a free transcription of a keyboard concerto by Monn.

Barbirolli and du Pré made convincing advocates for Monn's music. They chose measured tempi for the outer movements, imparting to the music a spaciousness and dignity without ever becoming ponderous. The slow movement makes a beautifully expressive centre-piece to the work. Jackie never lost the rhythmic buoyancy that is the essential key to performance of this music, and her passage work was well articulated and eloquent. She might have won popularity for Monn's concerto had she performed it in concert. Apart from a single occasion with the Newbury String Players, it was a piece that she only played in the studio.

In the meantime, in July of 1968 Jackie was awarded the prestigious Académie Charles Cros 'Grand Prix du Disque' for her recording with Barenboim of the Haydn C major and Boccherini B flat Concertos. Now, after completing three records in the 1967–8 season, there then followed a substantial pause in her recording activity, since plans were temporarily blocked because of a burgeoning contractual dispute with EMI. With hindsight one can say that it was a tremendous waste that for the remainder of her career du Pré only went back to the recording studio twice, once in 1970 to do the Dvořák concerto, and lastly in 1971 when she recorded Chopin and Franck sonatas with Barenboim. All Jackie's other discs were derived from concert performances that were broadcast on radio. The special feature of every concert performance is its transience. The artist is intent on conveying an immediate truth to a particular audience, and his interpretation is influenced by both subjective and objective factors, such as the rapport between conductor and orchestra, and the hall's acoustic. Thus a live performance that is recorded does not possess the same aura of a permanent document that is inherent to studio recording.

The pity of it is the greater since du Pré was one of the few recording artists who actually succeeded in communicating on record at almost the same level of intensity as in the concert hall. She certainly never changed her basic approach to playing when a microphone was placed in front of her. Perhaps it is the very immediacy of expression captured in her recordings which allows her influence to persist. Indeed, many of today's cellists started their careers inspired by Jackie's playing and recording. Alexander Bailey, aged twelve, immediately abandoned the violin in favour of the cello on hearing her recording of Haydn's C major Concerto and thereafter attended every one of Jackie's London concerts, sitting in the front row whenever possible. Steven Isserlis was given her Elgar concerto recording as a young boy by his first teacher, which, as hoped, proved an enormous stimulus to him.

The American cellist Yo-Yo Ma got to know Jackie's playing exclusively from recordings and recalled, 'When I started listening to them in my late teens, I fell for them head over heels. ... Her playing had a way of jumping out at you. Some artists' recordings are perfect almost to the point of being sterile. But Jackie had such an appeal ... her vitality and the tactile quality of her playing were so exciting, she seemed such a spontaneous and expressionistic player. And this made each playing of a recording a musical experience.'[33]

In common with such great performers of an earlier generation as Furtwängler, Schnabel and Huberman, Jackie's spirit of spontaneity lives on in recordings. She was not interested at the time in laying down her interpretations for posterity, and perhaps for this reason her music-making continues to remain fresh and appealing.

20

The Festive Season

There is an art to not playing in tempo, an art which one has
to learn, one has to feel.

Pablo Casals*

Since her official début in 1961, Jackie's affairs had been looked after by
the Ibbs and Tillett concert agency. Their style of management was old-
fashioned, and the relationship cultivated between artist and manager
inclined towards formality. By today's standards, there was a tendency
to undersell younger artists, in a climate where there was perhaps an
exaggerated reverence for age and experience.

Ibbs and Tilletts did little to build up the artists' careers in a systematic way and divided the responsibility of selling each single artist
between several members of the office – a method that was inefficient
to say the least. For instance, Jackie's affairs were managed by no less
than four or five people: Miss Lereculey and Beryl Ball looked after
music club dates within the UK, Martin Campbell-White was in
charged of BBC dates, Mrs Tillett herself took care of what she regarded
as the holiest of holies – British festivals (including the Proms), while
two new recruits to her office, Terry Harrison and Jasper Parrott saw
to the business of co-ordinating with foreign agents or directly booking
artists' dates outside Great Britain.

Jackie was little interested in the business side of her career and she
seldom raised questions about practical matters. In the mid to late
sixties, cellists usually did not command large fees – not, at least,
until the appearance of such highly charismatic figures as du Pré and
Rostropovich. The latter, after he left the Soviet Union in 1974, learnt
to quantify his own market value in terms of demand and could ask
for some of the highest fees available to any musician working in the
field of classical music.

When Jackie met Daniel things started to change in the management

---

* From David Blum, *Casals and the Art of Interpretation*.

of her professional life. Appreciating her popular appeal, as well as her stature as an artist, Barenboim insisted that she should receive the highest fees available. After their marriage it seemed a logical step for a couple whose professional schedules were so closely linked to share an agent. Because of the complex nature of Daniel's multiple musical activities this was not so easily achieved.

In Great Britain, Barenboim's affairs were managed by Harold Holt's office and in the USA by Sol Hurok's. But as Daniel started to develop his conducting career he had to seek other solutions, since his agents wanted to sell him exclusively as a pianist. Sol Hurok, for instance, believed that Daniel should stick to the piano and refused to contemplate his having a parallel career as a conductor. Not for a moment daunted by such apparent lack of faith in his abilities, Barenboim decided to manage his own engagements as a conductor in the United States. Elsewhere, he also set up contacts with orchestras without intermediaries.

As Daniel admitted, 'At the time I was not certain whether I should give up the piano in favour of conducting, or vice versa, and many people I worked with could not see how I could combine the two. [...] I fought against this rather blinkered way of thinking, I wanted to keep my options open.'¹ One person who certainly had complete faith in everything Daniel did was Jackie, who realised the enormous extent of his gifts and valued his capacity to organise them to maximum effect.

Daniel decided that it would relieve some of the pressure on him to ask Terry Harrison to look after his (as well as Jackie's) bookings outside Britain, excluding only the USA, where both Barenboim and du Pré were under the management of Harold Shaw. Terry, as a member of Ibbs and Tillett, was in a good position to co-ordinate Jackie's schedule, acting as a link between the various agents involved.

In fact, some dissatisfaction had been voiced at the way Emmie Tillett ran Jackie's affairs. Tillett was capable of taking rather arbitrary decisions on behalf of her artists. Peter Diamand, who in 1966 inherited the running of the Edinburgh Festival from George Harewood, recalled a specific instance. He had first heard of du Pré and Barenboim from his friend Hans Keller, who had unhesitatingly pointed to these two names – independently – as the most interesting artists of the up-and-coming generation. Diamand recalled,

I had never heard Jackie play, but what Hans Keller had to say about her was reason enough for me to issue her an invitation. But my attempts to book her for my first Edinburgh Festival were unsuccessful – whereas Daniel did play a recital for me. Emmie Tillett told me she was unavailable. I then asked for Jackie to come to the 1967 Festival and Emmie was doubtful about that too. She refused to make any promises and that annoyed me. Later, while talking to Daniel, I discovered that Jackie didn't know anything about these invitations since Emmie hadn't passed them on. Naturally, Jackie was quite upset. I then arranged directly with Daniel for him and Jackie to come to the 1968 Edinburgh Festival. This in turn upset Emmie Tillett, who had proved to be somewhat disloyal to her artist, and indeed to the Edinburgh Festival.[2]

Daniel was probably the only person who really had a grasp of his and Jackie's independent concert schedules, and with his incredible memory for logistics (as well as music) he could find solutions that allowed the couple to spend as much time as possible together. But their life moved at such a whirlwind pace, and between concerts, rehearsals, and recordings time was needed to plan and sort out their domestic needs, as well as the business of their careers. It soon became obvious to Daniel that they needed some help to deal with their growing correspondence.

For the last year the Barenboim couple had been renting a two-roomed basement flat at 27 Upper Montagu Place. Despite its cramped space (Jackie confessed to sometimes having to practise in the bathroom), this was a real home to them during the periods spent in London. Jackie was at heart a homely creature, and she came to enjoy cooking and entertaining friends in their flat. Eleanor Warren, who lived round the corner, remembered meeting her at the local butcher's and giving her advice on which cuts of meat to buy. She was more surprised to discover that Jackie had an aptitude for carpentry and was not above wielding a hammer to put up a shelf.

From the start of their life together the Barenboims proved to have the capacity to build up a nucleus of loyal friends. After concerts they always took a large party out with them to restaurants, enjoying good food and stimulating talk. It was a natural step to find somebody to help them with their organisational problems from within this core of friends. Christopher Nupen (known to his friends as Kitty) introduced his future wife, Diana Baikie (nicknamed Pukety), to the Barenboims. With her shy humour and lovable nature, she soon became Jackie's closest confidante. Diana possessed excellent secretarial skills and offered to sort out some of the Barenboims' paperwork until other commitments (a job at the ECO and her active involvement in helping Christopher in his projects) prevented her from continuing. At this stage Sylvia Southcombe (who was at the time getting divorced from Gervase de Peyer) took over as a sort of unofficial secretary. From 1973, when illness caused Jackie to withdraw from the concert platform, Sylvia was to become very important to Jackie – almost an amanuensis – and dealt with her correspondence and helped to co-ordinate the running of the household.

Sylvia recalled that when she took over things were in a terrible mess.

> They hadn't got a general manager and effectively Daniel was doing everything himself. He had all these letters from agents and recording companies which needed sorting out. I turned up without secretarial skills, without shorthand and without knowing languages. But I attacked this enormous pile of papers and Daniel started dictating letters, which I would take down in an abbreviated longhand, which seemed incomprehensible to an outside eye. But Daniel is so incredibly gifted – to my amazement he could read it at a glance. It wasn't only the professional work side that needed sorting out, they were in a mess with paying household bills. Eventually Daniel found Rixie (Diana Rix) at Harold Holt and that proved to be the answer for their professional affairs. It evolved that I would take care of the household side of things. Later, when they moved up to Hampstead, I looked after the correspondence and kept the house running when they were away – to make sure the gas wasn't cut off and so on.[3]

Daniel's connection with Harold Holt's Concert Agency went back to 1956, the year when he gave his London début. Ian Hunter, as director of Holt, recalls that this was probably the only occasion in his life when Daniel actually had to audition for an agent. Hunter immediately understood the quality of his talent and was responsible for promoting Barenboim's early career in Britain. Diana Rix joined Harold Holt in 1966, having previously gained experience in the managerial music world working for George Harewood at the Edinburgh Festival. Ian Hunter soon assigned her the job of looking after Barenboim's affairs in the UK.

Both Daniel and Jackie quickly found that the sympathetic 'Rixie', as they dubbed Diana, had the ideal combination of efficiency, wry humour and firmness, which made for an easy and friendly relationship between manager and artist. Having decided in the beginning of 1968 that du Pré should leave Ibbs and Tillett, there was nevertheless a time-lag between booking concert engagements and executing them. Although Jackie had officially transferred her affairs to Harold Holt from July 1969, many of her contracted dates were still effectively looked after by Ibbs well into 1970. And by the time Harold Holt started contracting her engagements, Jackie's professional career was already fraught with health problems. This meant that during the remaining three years of Jackie's playing life Diana Rix had to spend nearly as much time cancelling as booking dates for her.

Harold Holt's management was dominated by the personality of its director, Ian Hunter, a figure of far greater vision than the normal concert impresario. His real interest lay in creating new opportunities for artists and music, and he was responsible for setting up some of the most successful music festivals. As a young man he had made his mark working as assistant to Rudolf Bing, the founder of the Edinburgh Festival, at a time when the very concept of a music festival was still new and exciting. Before the war, Salzburg, Bayreuth and Lucerne were the only festivals of international standing in Europe. Founded in 1946, the Edinburgh Festival soon became as well established as its European predecessors.

When Bing left Edinburgh in 1949 to go to the Met in New York, Ian Hunter succeeded him, remaining as Festival Director until 1955. The first of Hunter's own creations was the Bath Festival in 1948, which at the time was distinguished by its pioneering spirit. Hunter went on to found the City of London Festival in 1962 (where Jackie performed while still a student of the Guildhall), the Brighton Festival in 1967 and the Hong Kong Festival in 1973. As he admitted, 'I enjoyed getting these things started and then handing them on.'[4]

From the start, Hunter decided to involve Barenboim as fully as possible in the Brighton Festival, regarding him as definitely the most dynamic and interesting artist of his generation. Furthermore, Hunter determined to make the new festival into a go-ahead enterprise, in keeping with the innovative spirit of the sixties. As the composer Alexander Goehr recalled, 'It was Hunter's ambition to create a trendy festival, which included all kinds of surrealist, over-the-top ideas. On the one hand, to keep the public happy, he booked the Menuhins and Barenboims, the cream of the classical music world. But Hunter also wanted to dye the sea red and to create happenings, something which was in the nature of those wild times.' With this aim in mind, Hunter set up a conference during the first festival in 1967, which served as a forum for radical ideas. Goehr was among those invited to participate. As he said, 'All the discussion resulted in a lot of hot air. But as I myself got on quite well with Ian Hunter, he saw the possibility of working with me. It was his idea to find the money to commission me to write a piece for Jackie and Daniel to perform together.'[5]

The second Brighton Festival promoted as its theme 'A New Look at the Arts', with special reference to 'the young artist'. Asking one of Britain's most talented composers (still young enough at thirty-five) to write for her best young string player certainly put the emphasis both on Youth and on the New.

Goehr had started making a reputation for himself in the late 1950s, when, together with fellow students from the Royal Manchester College of Music – John Ogdon, Peter Maxwell Davies and Harrison Birt-wistle – he emerged at the forefront of the younger generation of composers. This loosely knit group, known as the Manchester School, was united chiefly by its rejection of the traditional scholastic approach to composition. Their music incorporated many ideas of the New Viennese School and the radical avant-garde, without being tied down to any fixed programme. Even when the Manchester School composers started diverging in their ways the name stuck for some time, probably because of the convenience of the label.

Goehr continued his studies with Olivier Messiaen in Paris and on return to London worked at the BBC as a radio producer to supplement his living as a composer. As his reputation as a composer grew, he went on to make a brilliant career in the academic music world, becoming Professor of Music at Leeds, then Cambridge, Universities.

Sandy had first met Daniel in the years preceding his marriage to Jackie. As he recalled, 'We got on very well. Daniel knew little about contemporary music and he liked talking to me, as I told him things he didn't know.'[6]

Goehr viewed the commission to write his Romanza for Cello and Orchestra as 'an externalisation of what had become a personal friend-ship'. He was very aware that in writing a piece for Jackie he should take into account what she could best do and the kind of music that she would most enjoy performing. Adapting his style to the nature of a commission was for him something of a challenge and in no way involved compromise. As he recalled, 'The gap between the kind of music I wanted to write then and what Jackie would be able to play was even bigger then than it would be today – for instance, I have now accepted the notion of longer lines. Realising that she would pick up on the gestural aspect of the piece more than the structural, I wrote a declaiming piece, like a sort of operatic aria.' In an explanatory programme note written immediately after composing the piece Goehr was more explicit in unfolding his aims:

A Romanza is an instrumental aria, and I decided to use this form of composition rather than the more conventional concerto form which poses special, wellnigh insoluble problems for the composer of our time. My composition is in one continuous movement, although other types of movement such as a Scherzo for the orchestra alone, and later a Lento – which is a cello cadenza accompanied only by cellos, basses and harp – are incorporated within it. The opening melody, twenty-six bars long, forms the basic material for the whole composition. It is developed in a variety of ways and returns in the final section of the composition in a heavily ornamented manner which was influenced by the ornamentation in some of Chopin's Nocturnes.[7]

At heart, Goehr was intent on writing a rhetorical showpiece for du Pré: 'Basically once the cello started to play, it never stopped. In the circumstances I felt that there was no point in creating an ensemble type of dialogue, where there was a complex relationship between soloist and orchestra.'

In fact, the title Romanza did seem to confuse the critics, who expected from Goehr something that was structurally more concise and stringent. As Stephen Walsh of the *Observer* wrote, 'Perhaps the unexpected title has something to do with Goehr's idea of Miss du Pré's style of playing. It certainly gives a very inadequate picture of the piece he has written, which is long and intense, if possibly of lesser stature than the recent chamber works to which it supposedly relates.'[8]

Goehr completed the score in February 1968 and Jackie had two months to learn the piece, in the midst of a heavy schedule. Sylvia Southcombe recalled that she was often a reluctant student.

In mid-April 1968 I accompanied Gervase [de Peyer] and Jackie and Daniel to New York. Daniel had stepped in at the last minute for István Kertész to conduct the LSO (Gervase was principal clarinet in the orchestra at the time). It was Daniel's first big conducting job with the orchestra and the boys in the LSO gave him a hard time. Jackie was not performing during that visit, but she had taken her cello with her because she was meant to be learning Sandy Goehr's new piece. But she didn't seem too keen on practising it. Daniel would press her, 'Smiley, now don't forget to do some Goehr today.' 'Oh, yes,' she would say quizzically. She always rebelled against any pressure. We were only in New York for four days and hardly ever went to bed. We just stayed up all night talking and making music, we were all full of youthful high spirits.

In fact, these concerts proved to be Daniel's conducting début in the USA and their success helped him earn his spurs as a 'symphonic' conductor, something that had an important positive influence on the managers of many of the American symphony orchestras. Jackie knew that her support was of utmost importance to Daniel at this time. She did not hesitate about undertaking yet another tiring trip across the Atlantic (her third in as many months) to be with him. Most artists learning a new piece would have regarded such an extra commitment as a foolhardy interruption to their study schedule.

Jackie's learning methods were somewhat unorthodox, as she later explained to Alan Blyth: 'I charge at [the new piece] and send everything flying. I like to make a big impact and not tackle it at first bar by bar. Then I come down to ground and look at it more carefully, or perhaps you could say that out of the chaos I put the bits together again.'9

The première of Goehr's Romanza took place at the Brighton Festival on 28 April, with Barenboim conducting the New Philharmonia Orchestra. The piece certainly engaged Jackie's imagination as well as her fingers, and gave scope to a drama where lyrical singing co-existed with gritty conflict. That it was a marvellous performance vehicle was evident already in the opening statement, which Desmond Shawe-Taylor described as '... an impassioned, extended, self-generating melody for the soloist, speaking strongly to my ears of a nostalgically tinged D minor, even though the composer informs us that it is based on a segment of a 12-note row'. Perhaps it was the force of du Pré's personality that initially put into Shawe-Taylor's mind an evocation of the spirit of Elgar's Cello Concerto. However, the association faded as the piece unfolded and the atmosphere changed to one of '... prolonged struggle, [with] the dour and fierce soloist refusing to give ground before the strong and shrill thrusts of the orchestra, and both parties indulging in repeated sforzando attacks which made an impression of constant bar-by-bar effort, at times almost of flogging a reluctant horse'. The critic defined the Romanza as 'a tough nut to crack', but nevertheless concluded that it might come to rank among the best of Goehr's works.[10]

That Goehr succeeded in encapsulating du Pré's interpretative personality was affirmed by William Mann of *The Times*. Whatever the complexities of the score, he declared, '... when Miss du Pré is there to play the solo part, all this is effectively an elaborate and appropriate setting for the scene in which the particular qualities of her art seems to have been comprehensively captured – portrayed if you like – by the composer.'

Goehr certainly admitted that he had Jackie's qualities in mind while writing the piece and he recalls her performance of it as very striking. 'It was like a great actor declaiming – an Olivier-like performance. But as the Romanza is a declaiming piece and Jackie possessed the art of rhetoric, it was just right.' He felt that her interpretation was influenced by Barenboim's understanding of the music's gestures and his ability to realise the detail. 'Daniel was very spontaneous and open, and he was immediately able to explain this gestural aspect to Jackie. I think it did work as a performance. Other people may have subsequently given more precise performances; certainly Jackie's performance did not bear imitation. She only played the Romanza a couple of times, probably because no one would have asked her to play it, since the people who "bought" Jackie as a commodity would not have "bought" me. They wanted to hear her perform Elgar or Dvořák.'

After the Brighton première, Jackie's only further performance of the work was given in London's Royal Festival Hall on 22 October of that year. This concert, again with Barenboim conducting the New Philharmonia Orchestra, was recorded by the BBC. (It was issued as a commercial CD in 1993 – apparently as a pirate recording on the Intaglio label.)

Despite Jackie's public expressions of dislike for most contemporary music, Barenboim recalled that she enjoyed playing Goehr's piece. 'She had an emotional and sensual relationship to sound in itself, quite independent of the composition. In a C major scale, for instance, just the C, E and G that make up the tonic triad already had magic for her. You have to try and imagine that she lived in a world that breathed not through ordinary air, but through the world of sound.'

Back in London, Jackie devoted most of the month of May to

recording. Apart from re-recording the Schumann Cello Concerto and continuing her Brahms Sonatas recording for EMI, she and Daniel teamed up with the clarinettist Gervase de Peyer for a BBC TV cycle devoted to Brahms. For studio audiences they performed both the cello sonatas and clarinet sonatas, and the Trio Op.114. At the end of the month the Barenboim couple gave two recitals in Lisbon where they included Prokofiev's sonata in their programme – the only time they ever played it. Retrospectively they would joke about having lost their way in the finale, where the music tends to go round in circles and a wrong modulation can land you in a lot of trouble. It was most probably a momentary lapse that would have gone unnoticed by the majority of the audience.

Back in London in early June, Daniel and Jackie joined forces with the visiting Israel Philharmonic Orchestra. On 3 June Jackie recorded Bruch's *Kol Nidrei* with the IPO and Barenboim for BBC TV, and the following day she performed the Schumann concerto at the Festival Hall with Mehta conducting – this concert was transmitted live by BBC Radio Three. An extant radio tape testifies to a performance dominated by the excitement of the occasion, where the passion was sometimes almost dangerously unrestrained. Occasionally, in an excess of energy Jackie would finish a phrase by ripping the bow out of the string and producing a distorting bulge. Yet this quality of excitement made for a thrilling performance.

Only a few weeks before, Jackie had recorded her 'definitive' version of this concerto for EMI, a beautifully poetic and well-structured interpretation. This live performance offers a different perspective of her qualities as an artist, proving that her concept of a work was never fixed and static. Indeed, the idea of a definitive interpretation was alien to her. In a radio interview she talked of how each concert is different and how the various audiences affect the artist. 'The audience is made up of different people and is never the same – it gives off an essence – an audience feeds back to an artist.' Her idea of communication definitely implied give and take.

For Jackie, the ability to be flexible and take risks on the night was part of the very nature of her art. Such passionate playing as is demonstrated in her performance with the IPO seduced any listener willing to be carried away by the music. But it was not to everybody's taste.

In his review of the concert, the distinguished scholar and critic

Stanley Sadie – sometimes dubbed 'Dr Sadisticus' by victims of his rigorous criticism – admitted that du Pré played very beautifully with

> ... a gorgeous sound, and an open-hearted response to every phrase. But it was disastrously self-indulgent: there was no basic pulse, no framework within which rubato could be significant. I found myself sighing with relief, at every orchestral tutti, for the joy of a few seconds' music where the rhythm was not like warm plasticine. Perhaps a sturdier structure could better stand up to such unending rhapsody; this lovable piece crumpled pathetically. Miss du Pré's playing was the playing of an innate musician, but complete musicianship comprehends intellectual and emotional discipline too.

Sadie, to my mind, was far too severe in his attack on du Pré's lack of rhythmic and emotional discipline. This may not have been one of Jackie's more refined performances, but it was one where the musical expression was given all its worth within a defined structure. While Jackie observes the first movement's tempo marking of '*nicht zu schnell*', it was Mehta – following a time-honoured tradition – who moved it on in the tuttis. Invoking Toscanini's maxim *tradizione è tradimento* (Tradition is Betrayal), one can say that performing traditions are indeed full of pitfalls. Given the contrasting nature of the cello's chiefly rhetorical role and the dramatic function of the orchestral tuttis, a certain elasticity of tempo (provided it is related to the unity of the whole) is perfectly justified. Schumann expressed his views about the subjective nature of musical time-keeping: 'You know how I dislike quarrelling about tempo, and how for me the inner measure of the movement is the sole distinguishing feature. Thus the faster adagio of a cold performer always sounds lazier than the slowest adagio of a warm-blooded interpreter.'[11]

It is possible that the slight element of discomfort noted by the critics in Jackie's playing might have been due to problems with her Davydov Stradivarius. The cello was sensitive to climatic changes and reacted badly to forcing. A player like du Pré, who felt her instrument was not producing the necessary quality or volume of sound, can easily employ a compensating force. With a Strad, any volume gained in this way tends to be illusory, existing only under the ear; in reality, the sound gets suffocated and diminishes as it travels towards the audience. As Yo-Yo Ma, the present owner of the cello, has remarked, 'Jackie's unbridled dark qualities went against the Davydov. You have to coax the instrument. The more you attack it, the less it returns.'[12]

Charles Beare felt that Jackie became disenchanted with the Davydov partly because she wasn't prepared to play it in the way it demanded, and partly because Daniel didn't like it (although Barenboim himself denies this, saying that it was Jackie's discomfort that influenced his view of the instrument). Beare surmised that on-stage, under the conductor's or pianist's ear, the instrument gave the illusion of relatively small power and projection, since the Davydov (as indeed most Strad cellos) transmitted its sound through a narrow corridor which radiated out towards the hall.[13]

Be that as it may, Jackie rang up Beare in the middle of June in desperation, telling him that the Davydov was unplayable. As he recalled, 'She asked me, "Have you got anything I could borrow? I'm playing at La Scala tomorrow." I just happened to have in stock a cello by Francesco Gofriller, which I was able to lend her. She felt that it had most of the qualities which she needed and in addition it withstood travelling better than the Davydov. She discovered that she could press harder with the bow and still get sound. So she bought it from us. Her affair with the Gofriller lasted until the end of 1970.'[14]

Again, one must stress that Jackie had her own idiosyncratic sound, whatever cello she was playing on. I wonder how many people who listened to the original couplings on LP of her two concerto records made that season – the Schumann–Saint-Saëns and the Haydn D major–G. M. Monn – realised that in both cases the two concertos were played on different cellos (for the Schumann and Haydn Jackie still used the Davydov).

Armed with the Gofriller cello, Jackie left for Milan to perform the Dvořák concerto on 17 and 18 June, with Zubin Mehta conducting La Filarmonica della Scala. Genie Zukerman, who attended these concerts at the magnificent La Scala theatre, recalls them as extraordinary occasions, where Jackie's rapture in the music swept the listeners away, creating an unforgettable atmosphere. Not only was her interpretation magnificent, but there was that extra dimension in her playing – both sensual and ecstatic – which generated an aura of excitement. As Genie observed, those people who found Jackie's playing 'self-indulgent' were largely unable to cope with this physical aspect of her music-making, which seemed to them almost threateningly direct and provocative.[15] But in Italy directness of communication is not regarded with the same suspicion as it is in the Anglo-Saxon ethic. Jackie had a sensational success with the Milanese audience and critics, and was immediately engaged to come back.

At the end of June, the Barenboim couple travelled across the Atlantic by boat with the English Chamber Orchestra. This was the ECO's first tour of the United States, and consolidated Barenboim's flourishing relationship with the group. They gave over half a dozen concerts, mostly on the east coast, of which four took place (on 5, 9, 11 and 12 July) in New York's Lincoln Centre. Jackie's contribution as soloist was with performances of both Haydn concertos. She won critical accolades for her two New York appearances. Allen Hughes of the *New York Times*, for instance, was enchanted by the way she 'breezed through' the notorious difficulties of the D major Concerto: 'Her ease of performance made it possible for her to achieve the loveliest and most natural-sounding of expressive effects.'

From New York the couple travelled to Los Angeles, where on 18 July Jackie played the Saint-Saëns A minor Concerto in the Hollywood Bowl. Jackie always responded with enthusiasm to such events, finding large and predominantly youthful audiences an inspiration. Daniel conducted the Los Angeles Symphony Orchestra, with which he and Jackie developed a close association, not least because Zubin Mehta, as the orchestra's Music Director, had complete faith in their talents, quite apart from their close friendship.

Before returning to London the Barenboims stopped off in Caracas, where they gave a recital on 27 July. Back in Europe, as the festival season got into full swing, their relentless schedule continued. The most prestigious of Jackie's summer dates was at the Salzburg Festival, where she played the Dvořák concerto with the Berlin Philharmonic and Zubin Mehta on 4 August. Peter Andry remembers this as one of her most flamboyant and physical performances, which many found exhilarating and inspiring. But for others, like the Berlin Philharmonic's lead cellist Ottomar Borwitzky, her playing was over the top, and it was the external quality of excitement that dominated the music. Borwitzky was not speaking from a position of bias, as in general he admired Jackie's emotional style of playing, her large and noble, richly vibrated sound, and the enormous energy with which she invested her performances.

Zubin Mehta also maintained that no cellist had a larger or more opulent tone than Jackie in her prime. Her cello could carry across an orchestra, even such a rich powerhouse of sound as the Berlin

Philharmonic. Mehta recalled that Leonard Bernstein, who was present at this Salzburg concert, afterwards exclaimed to him in mock horror 'But you never put up your left hand' – the conductor's gesture to make an orchestra play down and let the soloist through. Given that the Dvořák concerto is renowned for the difficulties of balance, this was a big tribute to Jackie.

Perhaps more surprising – and equally refreshing to Mehta – was Jackie's spontaneity and her ability to introduce changes (musical and instrumental) during a performance. 'Now, few instrumentalists would dare to sit down in front of the Berlin Philharmonic at a Salzburg Festival concert and suddenly introduce a little divergence of interpretation. Many are the soloists who work eight hours a day to perfect their playing of a concerto correctly in one particular way. But Jackie possessed this flair, control and imagination, plus this magnetism for the audience.'[16]

Back in England, Jackie and Daniel paid a brief visit to their former stamping ground of Dartington Summer School, giving a recital on 6 August. Within only a few years of their last visits there (independently of each other) they had crossed that threshold that divides the young, up-and-coming artist from the celebrity.

Riding on the crest of a wave, they returned to London for the inauguration of Barenboim's new brain-child, the South Bank Festival, on 10 August. Since the Festival Hall was occupied by a summer ballet season and was only available on Sundays, the new festival was centred on the use of the Queen Elizabeth Hall, which dictated the chamber dimensions of the enterprise. Daniel, with his multi-faceted gifts, proved an ideal artistic director. He had organisational flair, and knew what made programming attractive and interesting, combining the new and the familiar, drawing unexpected connections between various pieces and composers, and ensuring quality of interpretation. The ECO was used as orchestra in residence (and many of its members played in small chamber groups) and Barenboim himself, as pianist and conductor, acted as the force and stimulus behind the performers that he gathered together. His eclecticism was evident in the choice of themes and repertoire for the three South Bank Festivals for which he acted as artistic director from 1968 to 1970.

The rise of Barenboim had been irresistible in the last year and he had become a vital and prominent force on London's musical horizon. In the last season Daniel had enthralled audiences with his performances of the cycle of the complete Beethoven sonatas, and had embarked on a project to play and conduct from the keyboard all the Mozart piano concertos and the mature period symphonies with the ECO. All these works, and others, were being recorded for EMI. At the same time Barenboim was making his mark as a conductor of symphonic repertoire, particularly of the Austro-German classics. At the South Bank Festival he was able to show off another facet of his gifts – those of a natural chamber music player. Here he combined musical exuberance with sensitive mastery of ensemble, where his conductor's authority stood him in good stead.

The opening concert of the 1968 festival was devoted to chamber music by Schubert and gave Barenboim ample scope to display these qualities. The first half consisted of the B flat major Piano Trio Op.99, where Daniel and Jackie were joined by the violinist Itzhak Perlman. The single offering in the second half was the *Trout* Quintet, where the three musicians were joined by two distinguished members of the ECO, the viola player Cecil Aronowitz and the double-bass player, Adrian Beers.

Geoffrey Crankshaw in *Music and Musicians*, while hailing this concert as a glorious start to the festival, expressed doubts about the balance in the piano trio, feeling that the cello was over-dominant: 'Of course, Miss du Pré's tone was generally glorious but this was not sufficient in purely musical terms to offset her excess of vigour in the more strenuous movements, especially the first.' The second movement's marvellous opening tune on the cello, the critic conceded, 'was lit with wonderful lyrical repose and the sheer poignancy of Schubert's conception was magically communicated'.

As for the *Trout* Quintet, it was Barenboim who was the dominating force. 'So often one hears this work played with a kind of dreamy inconsequence: not so on this occasion. The scherzo, especially, had tremendous impetus. There were times when the sheer rippling clarity of the piano playing brought revelations of Schubertian grace.' The critic felt that du Pré was more relaxed in the quintet – 'I hope that she will bring this quality to the many further chamber music performances, which I feel sure she and her husband have in store for us.'[17]

A year later Daniel, Itzhak and Jackie, this time aided by Pinchas Zukerman and Zubin Mehta, played the *Trout* Quintet again at the South Bank Festival, a performance that has been preserved for us in Christopher Nupen's film. Not only was the quality of the playing superb, but it showed music-making that was relaxed and informal on the one hand and totally exuberant on the other. It is difficult to imagine du Pré ever lacking these qualities when she was playing music she loved with like-minded musicians.

The next concert in which Jackie participated at this first South Bank Festival on 17 August, was devoted to Brahms's chamber music. Here, together with Barenboim and the clarinettist Gervase de Peyer, they played pieces that they had already recorded for BBC TV in May – the F major Cello Sonata Op.99, the Clarinet Sonata Op.120 No.2 and the Trio for Clarinet, Cello and Piano Op.114. *The Times* critic, Max Harrison, was particularly impressed by the trio, which '... received the most satisfying performance. [...] Jacqueline du Pré and Gervase de Peyer showed the greatest sensitivity in the adagio, and there was never the slightest danger of the first movement's highly compressed development section sounding as dry as it often does.'

Again it was Jackie's 'excess of vigour' which disturbed the critic in her performance of the F major Cello Sonata: 'Miss du Pré attacked with too unrelenting an intensity; when everything is so much emphasised – and the tempi so unsettled – there is no room for the degrees of contrast that are essential in what is perhaps the tersest of Brahms's chamber pieces.'[18]

Three days later Barenboim and du Pré were joined by Itzhak Perlman for a programme of piano trios, consisting of Beethoven's *Kakadu* Variations, the Brahms C major Trio Op.87 and Mendelssohn's D minor Trio. Those who attended the concert remembered wonderful playing. Yet this formation, which only a few months ago seemed to hold out such promise, was destined to go no further. Daniel's and Jackie's instant musical empathy with Zukerman was the decisive factor in choosing him as their permanent trio partner after the summer of 1968. Fortunately, there was no sense of rivalry between these musicians, rather, there existed a sense of mutual admiration, of shared fun and friendship. As it was, Barenboim found plenty of other opportunities to play chamber music with Perlman in the future (and does so to this day). As they themselves were aware, people spoke of this close-knit group of talented (and predominantly Israeli) musicians as the 'Barenboim' clan, or the 'Israeli Mafia'.

In the meantime, world events during the summer of 1968 had lasting repercussions on the lives of many people. When, on 8 August, Soviet troops invaded Czechoslovakia, public opinion and the international press (notably the British) reacted strongly in protest against this violation of a nation's sovereignty and found ways to express its solidarity with the oppressed people of Czechoslovakia.

In London, the night after the news of the invasion broke, Rostropovich was scheduled to play the Dvořák Cello Concerto at the Proms with a visiting Soviet orchestra. The Russian cellist, who had always held the Czechs in great affection, was mortified to have to perform in the Albert Hall in these circumstances and to be playing, of all pieces, the Dvořák concerto, which was so closely associated with Czech nationalist aspirations. Rostropovich said at the time he would not have been surprised to be booed off the stage. But the British public (despite the vocal protests made in demonstrations outside the hall) only had a moment's hesitation before breaking into warm applause for such a great favourite, a gesture which signified that music must triumph over politics.

The visiting Soviet artists – the Moscow Philharmonic, David Oistrakh, Sviatoslav Richter and Rostropovich – proceeded to the Edinburgh Festival, where larger demonstrations against the Soviet intervention were organised outside concert halls and sometimes inside them – during a Beethoven recital given by Richter and Rostropovich, two members of the audience ran through the hall shouting 'Viva Casals'.

Immediately after the South Bank Festival was over Jackie and Daniel also went up to Edinburgh, where they gave performances, both separately with orchestra, and together in a sonata recital at the Leith Town Hall. The Barenboims took pains to express their personal support of Rostropovich and visited him in his hotel. (An occasion which the Russian cellist remembers with mixed pleasure, since Daniel, referring to his New York marathon cycle of a few months back, made what appeared a deliberate slip of the tongue, substituting the German word *Zirkus* – circus – for *Ziklus* – cycle.)

Jackie also played the Dvořák concerto with the LSO and István Kertész at the Usher Hall on 26 August. It was a radiant and highly emotional performance, where she broke a string during the first movement. While staying in Edinburgh, Barenboim accepted a proposal to do a televised United Nations concert in aid of Czechoslovakia at the Albert Hall in the first days of September. Daniel was to conduct the LSO and Jackie was to play the Dvořák concerto again.

The couple were busy both off- and on-stage, and had rented a house in Edinburgh's Georgian New Town, which was full of friends coming and going. Pinky and Genie Zukerman and Daniel's parents were staying, and Daniel's mother Aida was often called upon to cook large meals. Music was made in every available free minute, particularly playing through trios with Zukerman. If Jackie had an hour or two free, she would rush out and take a walk in the hills surrounding Edinburgh. (I remember how, the day after her recital at Leith Town Hall, she took me up to the top of Arthur's Seat at a very brisk pace.)

A few months earlier Jackie had set her heart on a holiday on one of the Hebridean islands with Daniel and a group of eight friends. Wishing to follow in Mendelssohn's footsteps, they hoped to visit Fingal's Cave on the small island of Staffa, off the west coast of Mull. In fact, they undertook the trip to Mull accompanied only by the Zukerman couple. Genie vividly remembers this short holiday. They flew to the island in a private plane and on arrival, discovered the hotel where they were booked to stay had burnt down. Luckily they found a comfortable farmhouse, which offered bed and breakfast. Daniel and Pinky played football and they went riding. (At least, legend says that they each got as far as mounting a horse.) In the evenings they listened to music in the home of a congenial stranger they had met by chance. Jackie took Genie on long walks, striding over the purple hills, eyes skinned for a 'good-luck' piece of white heather. To their disappointment the inclement weather did not permit a visit to Fingal's Cave, which can only be approached by boat when the sea is calm. Genie was impressed by Jackie's enormous energy and her intense joy in the spacious freedom of the Highland landscape. Daniel, however, was on the phone much of the time organising the Czech concert and Jackie was terribly disappointed that this extra engagement meant having to cut short their holiday.

The concert in question was to take place in London's Albert Hall on 2 September and had been highly publicised. Early that same morning Barenboim had been woken in their basement flat at Upper Montagu Street by a threatening phone call. An anonymous voice told him, 'If you go on stage today we will shoot you.' Barenboim recalled that he took the threat seriously, but was not going to be intimidated by it. Wishing to protect her, he decided not to tell Jackie about it, but instead informed the Israeli embassy and requested special security at the hall. Later he admitted to journalists that initially he had had to resist the temptation to look over his shoulder as he conducted, but as he immersed himself in the music he stopped worrying.

The hall was packed. According to the *Daily Telegraph*, apart from the 7000 people who listened inside, there were over a thousand people left ticketless outside, who tuned in to the performance on their transistor radios. 'The atmosphere was electric with emotion. [...] Tears rolled down a thousand cheeks as the conductor raised his baton, turned and said, "This concert you are about to hear is dedicated to the very brave effort of a very brave nation." '[19]

In fact, goodwill messages had poured in from all over the world, some of which Barenboim read out. But he emphasised that the concert was not to be seen as a protest – a view not necessarily shared by the many listeners, some of whom had been actively demonstrating outside the Soviet embassy. Rather, he added, it was for a cause (to help Czech students). The actor John Clements added some appropriate readings before the main musical fare – the Dvořák concerto and Beethoven's *Eroica* Symphony.

For *The Times* critic, Joan Chissell, the Dvořák Cello Concerto was indeed the highlight of the occasion and spoke to the audience more potently than any words.

> Miss du Pré gave what must have been one of the greatest performances of her life – passionately felt, yet controlled in every minute detail, a flood of glorious evocative song. The spell was momentarily broken at the start of the finale when a string snapped, but not for long. Yet the most enjoyable feature was the oneness of the performance as a whole: the orchestra was an equal partner, discoursing, embroidering and upholding at every turn. From the LSO there were far too many telling individual contributions to list.[20]

The concert was relayed both on radio and television. When Jackie had to leave the stage for a few minutes to change her string, the BBC commentator was left to fill in the silence. Improvising his 'chat', he informed viewers that only a couple of weeks back, the Soviet artist Rostropovich had played the same piece in the same hall, but now, fortunately Miss du Pré was 'exorcising his ghost from the Albert Hall'. It so happened that Rostropovich was watching the broadcast and, not unnaturally, took great exception to this comment. A few months later, when he was teaching the Dvořák concerto in his Moscow class, he indirectly expressed his disapproval of what he felt to be the over-emotionalised aspect of Jackie's performance. Unexpectedly, he asked his student to play the upward octave scale that resolves into the B major second-subject recapitulation (bar 266) absolutely in tempo. 'I used to do some ritardando myself here,' he explained, 'but when I heard how terribly long and drawn-out that bar became in Jackie's recent London performance, it made me want to do it strictly in time.'

Yet Jackie's impassioned performance of the Dvořák concerto remained in the minds of many people for a long time as the most glorious music-making and the outpouring of a generous and loving spirit. Certainly, on that evening one particular member of the audience, a Czech lady called Olga Rejman, was moved to tears. In 1974, after Jackie's illness was diagnosed and when Daniel was desperately looking for help, Olga unexpectedly came into their lives as an important force. Daniel, in the company of the violinist Rodney Friend, had eaten dinner in a restaurant where she was working. He started talking to Olga, who had recognised him and approached him to express her gratitude for his music and her sorrow about Jackie's illness. Feeling the warmth of her sympathy, Daniel, acting on a sudden impulse, asked if she would come to their house and cook dinner for guests next evening. She did so and stayed on for six years as the Barenboims' dearly beloved housekeeper. Surely the seeds of her affection for Daniel and Jackie were sown at the Albert Hall Concert.

21

Belonging To The World

The proper function of the critic is to save the tale from the artist who created it.

D. H. Lawrence, *Studies in Classic American Literature*

For Jackie, the new autumn season of 1968–9 followed a continuing pattern, with engagements spread between Britain, Scandinavia, Germany, the United States and Canada. The quality of these engagements reflected her growing reputation, which allowed her to select only the most prestigious dates. Her staple repertoire was confined to the three great romantic concertos – Schumann, Dvořák and Elgar, with the addition of the two classical Haydn concertos. Occasionally she gave an airing to other works, but in this season added no new ones to her repertoire. Thus, without too many learning commitments and no real wish to play very frequently, Jackie could concentrate her activity in given periods, often reserving time simply to be with Daniel. As she reported in a newspaper interview, 'If we are both to perform in America, for instance Daniel performs in the first week while I accompany him and in the second week I work while he accompanies me. As a general rule we have never been separated for more than two days in one month.'

The fact that their schedules were so well dovetailed was due to careful planning and in particular to Barenboim's exceptional organisational talents. Increasingly, Daniel acted as adviser to Jackie and helped her not only to plan her schedule, but to choose her repertoire. Agents tended to find themselves talking to him about Jackie's dates. By and large, she was content with this passive role. Her choices – insofar as she made them – were governed by her wish to be with or near her husband and when not playing with him, by strong feelings in her preferences of conductor.

As it was, Barenboim was making his conducting début with several of North America's most prestigious orchestras in this and the following season, and most orchestras concerned were only too pleased for Jackie to appear as soloist in his programmes. With this increasing commitment to a conducting career on top of his obligations as solo pianist, Daniel had little time left to play with Jackie in recital. In actual fact, not only their limited availability, but the joint fees of two star artists put duo concerts by the Barenboim–du Pré team out of the range of many music societies. However, to compensate for their rarity value, their appearances together on the platform as a duo were imbued with a real sense of festive occasion and were highly sought after.

In the middle of 1968 Daniel had the idea of contacting the South African-born pianist Lamar Crowson to play as Jackie's accompanist in the periods when he himself was unavailable. Crowson, a fine pianist in his own right, had considerable experience as a chamber musician and over the years had accompanied many cellists, Pierre Fournier, Zara Nelsova and Amaryllis Fleming among them. He recalls being flabbergasted at Daniel's invitation musically to 'chaperon' Jackie and accepted with alacrity. This new 'alternative' partnership operated on and off from the autumn of 1968 for the rest of du Pré's playing career.

Jackie commenced her activities that autumn in Birmingham on 22 September with a performance of the Elgar concerto with the New Philharmonia Orchestra. This was followed by a tour with the English Chamber Orchestra, performing Schumann's concerto in Chichester, Bournemouth, Peterborough and Cleethorpes. During a trip to Belfast in late September Jackie caught up with her childhood friend, the cellist Winifred (Freddie) Beeston, who was now playing in the Ulster orchestra. Freddie recalled her vital, glowing account of Haydn's C major Concerto, but more important was her discovery that Jackie had remained open and friendly, completely unspoilt by celebrity.

In October, concerts took her to Scandinavia, where she performed to sold-out halls with resident orchestras (and resident conductors) in Oslo, Bergen and Copenhagen. Her accounts of the Schumann concerto (in Oslo and Bergen) and the Haydn C major (in Copenhagen) were hailed by the press and public alike. Indeed, according to the *Oslo Dagbladet*, the audience in that city greeted du Pré not just with stormy applause, but an ovation of 'hurricane' force. The same newspaper praised the brilliance and palpitating sensitivity of her cello playing and her 'burning musical intensity'. Another Oslo paper, the *Morgenbladet* reckoned that the Schumann was 'a pretty boring piece', but that du

Pré had made the best imaginable showing for it and herself had made a lasting impact on the Oslo audience.

On return to London later that month, Jackie performed Goehr's Romanza for the second time at the Royal Festival Hall, again with Barenboim conducting the NPO. A few days later she was playing the Saint-Saëns A minor Concerto and Bloch's *Schelomo* at the Festival Hall with the London Symphony Orchestra conducted by André Previn. The cellist Sandy Bailey was at the concert and his impressions of Jackie's performance were so strong that thirty years later he still remembers it vividly: 'I was at the Sunday afternoon repeat concert. Jackie's playing of *Schelomo* stuck in my mind because I had never heard anyone play so quietly. She also was able to make the orchestra play even more quietly than her. Being very young and inexperienced I had no idea about projection and did not realise that her sound was also reaching the very back of the hall.'

The more seasoned *Times* critic also praised du Pré's fine form, noting that she always contained her expression within a balanced framework: 'Saint-Saëns's Cello Concerto enjoyed the benefit of Jacqueline du Pré's judiciously affectionate advocacy: she rightly realised that its emotions are not white hot, and did not tear it to bits. The Schumannesque episode was particularly sensitive and beautiful. Bloch's *Schelomo*, subtitled 'a Hebraic Rhapsody', gave her more chance for that freely rhapsodic, ultra-expressive kind of playing much after her own heart at the moment, though again here she did not allow her feelings to run away with her.'[2]

In early November Jackie cancelled her engagements with the Residentie Orchestra in The Hague due to an unspecified 'accident', but a week later she had recovered enough to fulfil an engagement with Barenboim in Berlin, performing Brahms's F major Sonata for ZDF television. Jackie's opening attack – she plays the semiquaver upbeat on a down-bow at the point of the bow, and the strong downbeat F is given a whole up-bow – had so much impetuosity that the cameras have to veer backwards so as to be able to frame her broad, sweeping gestures. It continued as a performance of enormous spirit and energy, although perhaps somewhat at the expense of accuracy, particularly in the piano part.

The following week Jackie set off for the United States in the company of Lamar Crowson. The day after their arrival on 17 November, they launched into a recital tour of eight concerts, which was largely confined to East Coast cities, such as Philadelphia and Baltimore, although they had reached the mid-West by early December.

Crowson had first met Jackie at Dartington Summer School in 1964. Bill Pleeth had already approached him suggesting that he should work with his most talented student, but Crowson had to turn down this first offer to perform with Jackie because he was then about to move back to South Africa. But while at Dartington, he had a first 'exhilarating experience' of making music with her, playing through Beethoven's *Archduke* Trio. Both Jackie and their third partner, a young French violinist, were sight-reading. But it was Jackie's musical and personal magnetism which provided the inspiration and driving force. Lamar felt that the 'kids' were really putting him through his paces; he had never played the final presto so quickly.

Now, four years later, Jackie and Lamar were quick to find a common approach in their music-making and to make any necessary adjustments. Rehearsals, such as they were, were mostly devoted to righting minor problems of ensemble or balance. As Lamar defined it, 'Our individual concepts were expressed in sound and not words. Every concert was an adventure – no performances were ever the same (and rightly so). We would react to each other's statements – and not always tonally. Jackie always giggled when I played the descending scale in the second bar of the last movement of Beethoven's G minor Sonata [Op.5 No.2].' Mutual respect allowed for diversity of opinion and as long as the personal message was never eclipsed their partnership thrived on the individual expression of each player. Or, as Lamar put it succinctly: 'Jackie's exuberant spontaneity balanced my perhaps too academic attitude.'

Again, Daniel often helped to plan their programmes. Apart from the staple repertoire of sonatas by Beethoven (they played the second, third and fourth), Brahms and Franck, Barenboim suggested that they include the cello sonatas of Rachmaninov, Shostakovich and Britten – works that he himself did not play. Lamar recalled Jackie's first exposure to the Rachmaninov sonata in rehearsal. 'In the first movement there is a troublesome entry for the cello. She didn't miss it and I was full of praise. Then the confession – she had asked my wife (who was turning pages) to signal!' (In fact Jackie had certainly read through the work before, for instance, with her composer friend Jeremy Dale-Roberts.)

Jackie and Lamar soon established an excellent rapport both on and off the platform, and their relationship was teasing and affectionate at the same time. Lamar, like other close friends in the Barenboim circle, called Jackie 'Smiley', while she dubbed him 'Padre'. Evidently she felt totally comfortable with the paternalistic role she allocated him and accepted with wry humour such gestures of parental concern as Lamar polishing her shoes. He confessed that as a 'father' he adored her: 'As an older musician I was constantly inspired by her zest for life, which was so much a part of her approach to music. I never thought of her as just a cellist – she was a music-maker. Her life was music. In our musical relationship there was never a question of youth against maturity. She made me young and I hope that I didn't make her old. We approached performances as equals.'[3]

Being at least in the same continent as Daniel, they were able to meet up quite frequently and Daniel was present at several of their concerts. Christopher Nupen was also often in attendance and sometimes volunteered his services as 'chauffeur'. Lamar has a particularly vivid memory of a late-night reunion in the unlikely venue of a highway transport café, when he, Christopher, Daniel (wearing his 'teddy-bear' coat) and Jackie ('in fur coat, short skirt and boots, looking like she had stepped off the cover of *Vogue*!') had made an appointment with the guitarist John Williams and his glamorous girlfriend: 'I'll always remember the look on the truck drivers' faces as they watched our seemingly extra-terrestrial group.'[4]

After her last recital with Lamar on 4 December in Iowa City Jackie proceeded to Oklahoma for concerts on 8 and 10 December, performing the Dvořák concerto with the Oklahoma City Orchestra and Guy Fraser Harrison. On this occasion she was joined not only by Daniel but her friends Genie and Pinky Zukerman (the latter was in town performing a recital with Charles Wadsworth). It was here, in a hotel room in Oklahoma, that Genie recalled Jackie complaining for the first time of weakness and fatigue. While there was nothing that could be termed a symptom of any specific illness, she felt she didn't have the strength in her hands to open her cello case or to close a window. Yet when it came to performing she showed not one ounce less energy or commitment.

Wadsworth recalled the hilarity of the friends, when at an after-concert reception, Barenboim (present this time merely in his capacity as spouse) was addressed condescendingly by one of the hosts: 'And you, Mr du Pré, are you also in the music business?'[5] Attending such receptions in the USA is almost an obligatory duty for artists, who must be aware that American concert life is largely dependent on private funding from rich local sponsors. On the one hand, these parties can be a demonstration of the best of American hospitality, but sometimes they can be little short of torture for the artist. Crowson recalled one particularly embarrassing occasion, when the host – a member of an amateur cello–piano duo – insisted that Jackie should play with the pianist and Lamar with the cellist of their ensemble – just after they had performed a concert. Daniel's agony was all too visible and he barely controlled himself from giving vent to his anger.

Jackie's next engagements took her to Los Angeles to perform the Elgar concerto with Zubin Mehta and the Los Angeles Philharmonic, on 12, 13 and 15 December. Jackie immensely enjoyed her musical rapport with Mehta and needed little persuasion to remain in Los Angeles while performing her next engagements in the relatively nearby town of San Diego on 19 and 20 December. Mehta had arranged to book Daniel as soloist immediately after her concerts, so that the three friends could spend more time together.

Elgar's Cello Concerto was still regarded as a rarity with US audiences and Jackie's committed performance made the critics wonder why such an excellent piece was apparently ignored by cellists, who have such a small standard repertoire. Henry L. Roth in the *California Jewish Voice* defined du Pré as 'one of the most exciting instrumental personalities currently before the public. The dynamic scope of her playing – alternating the most intense emotion with relaxed introspection – is staggering.' But Roth was one of the critics who also found the physical aspect of her performance mannered and distorting. 'In her zeal to outdo her own and her instrument's normal physical limitations, she resorted to abrasive bow pressings on phrase-end tones and was guilty of more than a few inelegant, "over-ripe" finger slides. Yet she can be a joy to behold, as she looks toward the conductor with a gleam of devilish glee in her eye, as she applies maximum visceral exhortation to her cello.'

Just as Jackie's uninhibited delight in the music was totally genuine, so were her gestures spontaneous and totally lacking in artifice. She was far more interested in communicating the spirit and emotion behind the music than presenting a totally 'clean' instrumentally perfect performance. The critics may have complained about her performance mannerisms, but audiences tended to enjoy such tangible demonstrations of rapture as her head-throwings and body-language, because they were allied so naturally to the musical expression.

Zubin observed that the physical joy evident in Jackie's music-making was no less intense in her identification with nature. Once he took her up to a spectacular viewing point on a hillside outside Los Angeles where he owned some land. He recalled Jackie's immense exhilaration in the beauty of the scene as she rushed off and threw herself in the grass 'like a young mustang'.[6] Jackie herself confessed in an interview that nature had an equally powerful effect on her as music: 'I love the physical thing of being on the earth that bore you, the longing to get in touch with something that's more infinite. I have the same feeling when I walk in a very beautiful place that I have when I play and it goes right. Playing lifts you out of yourself into a delirious plane where you feel abandoned and very happy – like being drunk.'[7]

Jackie had to learn to accept that her passion for the elemental forces of nature was something that she could not share with Daniel. While she loved 'the rain and all the things that Danny can't stand', Daniel remained a committed sun-lover. And heat was something she barely tolerated. Yet it was the positive, sunny quality of Jackie's personality and her force as a sort of earth figure which exercised a magnetic attraction not just for Daniel, but for all admirers of her art.

In the event, the Barenboims exchanged sunny California for the dull grey drizzle of English winter when they travelled home to London for a brief respite from concerts over the Christmas season. The coming year was to be a particularly busy one, and the couple were to travel the world, bringing their art as far afield as Australia. One thing, however, that was notably absent in Jackie's schedule for 1969 was any recording plans. Her two-year contract with EMI ran out in January and while EMI was very anxious to renew it on a continuing basis of exclusivity, the two parties found themselves in dispute over the terms. A major stumbling block was EMI's demand that, in addition to sound recording rights, the company should hold exclusive rights to produce music films with her participation, whether made for television, cinema release, or to be marketed as videos. This latter point was, of course, a recent problem, since video had only been in existence a couple of years, and so far 'the magic box' (or 'EVR' – Electronic Video Recording – to give videos their correct reference term) had yet to be marketed for the general public. Although EMI was still to enter the EVR field, the market for music videos had a potential that could not be ignored and the company saw it as imperative to insist on contractual rights permitting the exploitation of signed-up artists in the visual as well as the audio medium.

The significance of filmed performances of music had been understood first and foremost by von Karajan, who soon made it a policy to film most of his recordings with the Berlin Philharmonic (often taking on the multiple role of conductor, editor, director and producer). Von Karajan, in contrast to most music film directors, was not interested in music-making on film as a spontaneous process, and often resorted to artifice through 'miming' his own and the orchestra's performance for camera to the play-back of a pre-existing audio recording.

Barenboim and du Pré were not attracted by such narcissistic attitudes, rather believing in the communicative power of film as a means to transmit to large audiences the live element of performance. Their friend Christopher Nupen had recreated the fresh energy and the extemporaneous quality in their music-making with remarkable success in his films *Double Concerto* and *Jacqueline*, made for BBC TV. It was a natural step for Nupen to promote other ventures with the Barenboim couple and indeed, their next project – a film devoted to the informal preparation and a concert performance of Schubert's *Trout* Quintet – was to prove the most successful of its kind.

In their refusal to be committed to EMI over the matter of EVR rights the Barenboims were partly influenced by Nupen's decision to leave the BBC to work as a freelance. Nupen had found the strictures imposed through working within an institution immensely limiting and saw no advantage in exchanging the control of one large institution for another, and therefore in seeing his friends committed to an institutionalised company the size of EMI. At the time, the BBC represented a real threat to the large record companies like EMI, since it had at its disposal an enormous range of both audio and filmed recordings from their radio and television archives, which could be issued commercially. EMI regarded any music film made with one of its listed artists for an outside company as trespassing on its property, since inevitably there was a strong probability that repertoire already recorded on gramophone records would be duplicated. Effectively it was an argument as to whether the term 'exclusivity' should apply to an artist's repertoire in the two different mediums of film and audio recording. The artists feared that by remaining within the company for film and EVR rights they would be deprived of an important element of choice. As Nupen reminded his friends, it was precisely in this visual field that the choice of director had an enormous bearing on the end product, for the simple reason that a film is shaped in the editing process. Whereas a record or a sound-track is, relatively speaking, a fixed entity, the visual aspect of a film can be cut in an infinite number of ways. And there were other factors that influenced the outcome of music films, not least the enormous cost of making them.

Thus, the negotiations over Jackie's recording contract dragged on through the first nine months of 1969 until matters came to a head and a meeting was convoked on 8 October specifically to discuss the EVR clause. Peter Andry represented EMI, while the Barenboim couple insisted that their lawyer, Louis Courts, and Christopher Nupen (in a consultative capacity) should also be in attendance. The meeting did not solve the problem, since neither side was prepared to make sufficient concessions to agree on conditions for a further contract. In the end, as a temporary measure Louis Courts suggested leaving the EVR clause of the contract 'in limbo', suspended until such time as the two parties could reach agreement. This would allow other projects for sound recording to continue. By that time, indeed, there was a certain urgency in finding some kind of compromise solution since the planned recording of Beethoven's piano trios (with Pinchas Zukerman) was looming on the horizon.

In the meantime, Jackie started playing again after the Christmas break in mid-January 1969, performing concerts in Göteborg, Stockholm and Rotterdam. After spending a few days with Daniel and the ECO in Switzerland, she travelled to Hannover, where on 24 January she played the Schumann concerto with Eugen Jochum conducting. At the end of the month the Barenboim couple were together again in Rome to play two concerts under the auspices of the Academy of Santa Cecilia.

While in Rome, Jackie met up with a friend from Croydon High School days, Parthenope Bion, who had come to greet her backstage after hearing her performance of the Schumann concerto. Bion had followed in her father's footsteps and become a psychiatrist, and was now married to an Italian musician and living in Rome. She was disconcerted by the feeling that the Barenboim circle of family and friends not only excluded outsiders like herself, but seemed to pay scant attention to Jackie, treating her more like a wonderful ornament. The next day, Parthenope met Jackie at the grand Rome hotel where she was staying, and found her tired and depressed. Parthenope recalled,

'I got the impression that the marriage was not going so well, although Jackie was trying to give out that everything was absolutely marvellous – but one could pick up from various signals that she was feeling troubled. I remember her telling me on that occasion how she was looking forward to having children and bringing them up in Israel, and how thrilled she was by the kibbutz system. This, indeed, had been one of the reasons she had converted.'

Parthenope was not the only one of Jackie's former friends who felt excluded by the Barenboim circle, or observed that Jackie was sometimes peripheral to it herself and was 'talked down to'. Alison Brown, who remained a lifelong friend to Jackie, was another who felt uneasy with what she saw as an imposed duality in Jackie's social situation. Diplomat friends from Moscow days, Roderic and Gill Braithwaite, now posted to Rome, found Jackie more distant, but also more sophisticated and totally under the cosmopolitan influence of Daniel; the most obvious change in her was the adoption of an indefinable 'mid-Atlantic' accent.

In fact, when the time and place were right, Daniel enjoyed socialising, and was always warm and welcoming to a large variety of people. But he did so on his own terms and could be quick to show signs of boredom. Not unnaturally, with his mercurial talents, he disliked wasting time. Indeed, one could say that egocentricity has always been a necessary prerequisite for artists wishing to achieve the maximum in their creative life. While his positive confidence could be interpreted as arrogance, or even Olympian disdain, his attitudes rather reflected his total engrossment in his professional life, his need to maximise his energies and his time to enable him to accomplish his manifold aims. With their existence so much under public scrutiny, Daniel was perhaps quicker than Jackie to realise the vital necessity of guarding the emotional core of their life together with the utmost privacy.

Nevertheless, while on tour together, Jackie was often left to her own devices, and would use her time to see friends, walk and shop, while Daniel rehearsed the orchestras he was conducting or prepared orchestral scores, a process which entailed analytical procedures, as well as such practicalities as marking in bowings, and sorting out problems of orchestral balance and colour. As Barenboim emphasises, 'The manipulation of sound is very hard to learn and particularly difficult for a conductor who [unlike an instrumentalist] has no physical contact with the sound.' But a conductor must come to his first rehearsal completely prepared for his job of 'organising the sound of an orchestra'.

In fact, Daniel often sought advice from Jackie about the technical aspects of string playing. As the violinist Rodney Friend remarked, he also learnt a lot simply by observing her. 'Daniel was very quick to pick up an incredible feel for bowing from Jackie. His understanding of natural bow distribution, the feeling for the colour of each string, for certain expressive fingerings, these were all a mark of Jackie's influence.'

Her influence also extended to the interpretation of music. Many musicians, first and foremost Daniel, had an implicit faith in the truth of Jackie's intuition. She seemed to come closer than most other great performers to the initial creative impulse behind a particular work. Fou Ts'ong recalled having problems in understanding a Chopin piano piece. 'Ask Jackie,' suggested Daniel, and he did. Jackie, without knowing that particular piece, had such an immediate intuitive reaction to it that she was able to identify Ts'ong's problem and help him resolve it. Plácido Domingo was another artist who was amazed at the insights she showed through her reactions to listening to opera. Once, when he was recording Berlioz's *La Damnation de Faust*, Domingo wanted her opinion, at Daniel's suggestion, on whether to sing an A flat softly rather than in mezzo-forte. In this instance she preferred the soft version, explaining that '... she could never make herself accept anything that sacrificed musicality to theatricality'.[8]

But Barenboim warns against the over-simplified view of du Pré as a totally intuitive artist: 'Intuition without the rational side is incomplete, and rationality without the intuition is no artist! But Jackie was highly intelligent and as the years went by she acquired a lot of conscious knowledge through experience.'

At the beginning of his conducting career, Daniel had to overcome the prevalent prejudice that he was primarily a pianist and thus not automatically licensed to pick up the conductor's baton. In this respect he had more to prove than other young conductors who had not won their colours, as he had, as a brilliant instrumentalist. Barenboim's facility almost worked against him and probably there were those at the time who failed to realise how thoroughly serious he was in his mission to become a conductor.

The 1968–9 season was the first where Barenboim devoted about half of his engagements to guest-conducting some of the most important symphony orchestras in the USA and Europe. Initially, some reviewers were quite dismissive of his efforts and he had to show a steady persistence to disprove such attitudes. Fortunately, the unswerving faith of many notable musicians (Jackie among them) and of several important orchestral managers and musical administrators, in addition to his popularity with the public, helped him to overcome any doubts he may have experienced at the time.

Certainly the Rome critics were some of the rudest and also probably the least qualified to make judgements. After their first concert on 29 January, a symphonic programme with the Santa Cecilia Orchestra, one reviewer went as far as to call Barenboim's conducting 'opportunistic', with the hardly veiled implication that he was making his career in this field on the strength of his wife's reputation. On the other hand, the newspaper *Il Popolo* praised him for the clarity of his ideas, the security of his large linear gestures and the vigour of his rhythm in performances of Beethoven's Eighth and Tchaikovsky's Fourth Symphonies. Yet another publication, *l'Unità*, considered his interpretations to be superficial and its critic expressed doubts about the couple's forthcoming duo concert of 'pseudo-cello music' (a reference to Schumann's *Fantasiestücke* and the Franck sonata, both originally scored for other instruments), asking why the Academy of Santa Cecilia had accepted such a programme and when the artists were going to start taking music more seriously. Du Pré's performance of Schumann's concerto also came in for a knock, being considered too nervous and too 'physical', only gaining moments of touching beauty and luminosity in the second movement. Another Rome newspaper *Momento Sera*, remarked that the 'qualifications' of being both an excellent pianist and Jacqueline du Pré's husband were insufficient for Barenboim to become a good conductor.

The critics overall were more generous in their praise of du Pré, both for her rendering of the Schumann concerto and for her performance in recital of Beethoven's G minor Sonata, as well as the Schumann pieces and the Franck. The critic Corrado Atzeri was charmed by Jackie's 'Melisande'-like mane of blonde hair and her altogether 'Debussyian' figure, and no less by the Debussyian range of soft shades and mellow colours that she achieved in the Schumann concerto.

The public were probably more discriminating than the gentlemen of the press and expressed genuine appreciation of the couple's talents by noisily demanding more – they were rewarded with two encores. One musician who understood and appreciated the merits of the Barenboims' Rome recital was the great singer Dietrich Fischer-

Dieskau, who wrote a touching letter of thanks to them afterwards. This initial contact helped to smooth the path for Fischer-Dieskau's long-standing musical collaboration with Barenboim and potentially also with du Pré although, sadly, illness struck before she could play, as planned, as his soloist in the autumn of 1973, at the time when the singer was starting his own conducting activities.

Jackie's next concerts took her to Berlin, where she performed the Dvořák concerto once again with the Berlin Philharmonic and Zubin Mehta at the Philharmonie on 5 and 6 February. By mid-February Jackie was back in the USA, where she started her month's tour in Minneapolis. She played the Elgar concerto with the Minnesota Orchestra conducted by Stanislaw Skrowaczewski, once again introducing the work to another American city. Immediately afterwards she travelled on to Chicago to join Daniel, who was Pierre Boulez's soloist in Bartók's First Piano Concerto with the Chicago Symphony Orchestra. On 28 February it was Jackie's turn to play with this great orchestra conducted by Boulez (in fact, it was her début with them). There were to be three performances of the same programme in which a first half of Haydn and Schumann was designed to appease the more traditional members of the subscription audience before a more exacting second half, devoted to Boulez's own piece *Livres pour Cordes* and Berg's *Three Pieces for Orchestra*. Boulez recalled Jackie's rendering of the Schumann concerto as an 'extraordinary extrovert performance – not that she imposed anything extrovert on the work, but she brought out the romanticism inherent in it. I think that this piece can bring out different approaches. It was not a question of her playing as a gutsy extrovert; rather her performance had enormous energy and outward-going expression. For me there were no difficulties in identifying with her. What she did was intuitive, but hers was an intuition which had its own logic.'[9]

Daniel remembers the occasion as an interesting exercise in rapprochement of two utterly different musical starting points – Boulez's precise and cerebral concept and du Pré's emotional and intuitive one. There was respect on both sides for the other's point of view and it took only very little time for the necessary adjustments to be made to meet in the middle ground.

Yet the Chicago critics were not necessarily impressed by the unity of their interpretation. In the *Tribune* Thomas Willis spoke of a discrepancy of approach, while praising Jackie's enormous gifts:

Miss du Pré plays for keeps all the time. Each note has maximum persuasive power. There is a total commitment of both physiological and musical resources. [...] When she is not playing she is often reacting to the orchestral dialogue. Sometimes the reaction is akin to petulance. Last night she seemed to be urging the first violins and cellos to 'get in there and fight'. This, as you might suspect, was not in Mr Boulez's plan. Keeping in mind the score's tricky balances and the clear distinction Schumann made between the contrapuntal dialogue and the accompaniment, he kept both dynamic and rhythmic intensity low. As a result Miss du Pré's vigorous approach became shadow boxing.[10]

The critic of the *Daily News* found that there was some disturbing evidence of du Pré forcing the cello, especially on the top string, although by the second movement, she relaxed into a fine performance. Strangely, considering that Jackie had only once before played in the vicinity of Chicago (in Ravinia the previous summer with the ECO) he expressed the hope that 'this glimpse of Miss du Pré's old mastery is a sign of her returning confidence'. A more illuminating comment was made by Kathleen Morner in the *Sunday Times* (28 February 1969) who wrote that du Pré's gloriously impetuous singing performance reminded her of the 'bewitching way Lotte Lehmann used to flirt with meter in [Schumann's] *Frauenliebe und Leben*'.

From Chicago the Barenboims moved on to New York, where they gave a recital on 2 March in Philharmonic Hall, playing the Brahms E minor Sonata, Schumann's *Fantasiestücke* and Franck's sonata. Donal Henahan, in his review of the concert for the *New York Times*, valued the quality of spontaneous re-creation of the music. Presenting the score as 'a living, breathing extension of their personalities' was far harder than trotting out the same pre-conceived 'bronze cast' model of a performance, he commented – which is usually what one hears in the concert hall. He described their playing as extremely personal, even at times 'peculiar', but 'always musically absorbing'. The Brahms E minor Sonata set the tone of the evening's music-making in the 'dreamlike, rather improvisatory style' of interpretation. As a quibble, the critic questioned du Pré's somewhat obvious portamenti, which distracted from the cello's legato line. But he had nothing but praise for Barenboim, whom he described as 'a virtuoso who dares to be non-assertive' when playing chamber music.

The next day the Barenboims left for Toronto, where Daniel was to

make his conducting début. Jackie, as his soloist, gave performances of
Elgar's Cello Concerto on 4 and 5 March, which were rapturously
received by the public and the press. The critics' reactions to Barenboim's conducting were altogether more cautious. John Kraglund
wrote, '[Elgar's] concerto might well have been written for Miss du Pré,
for the opening cello recitative, despite its brevity, was sufficient to
inform the listener of the cellist's interpretative power and virtuoso
technique.' He continued: 'Barenboim obviously deserved credit for
the excellence of the accompaniment, but one is inclined to modify
enthusiasm for his contribution after hearing the purely orchestral
portions of the programme' – namely Mendelssohn's *Ruy Blas* Overture
and Beethoven's *Eroica* Symphony. William Littler, on the other hand,
felt that Barenboim was developing by leaps and bounds. Whereas in
his concert over a year earlier with the Israel Philharmonic Barenboim
had 'conducted like a pianist who had found a baton in his soup. Now
he conducts like a conductor.' But, he noted, the Barenboim couple

> keep going from strength to strength as performing musicians. They
> have talent, bushels of it.... Until recently, I firmly believed du Pré's to
> be the more deeply rooted. Barenboim has tended to behave like a
> playboy with a limitless chequing account, presuming to do everything
> [...] and not getting to the heart of anything. Now I am less certain.
> Du Pré still communicates more urgently as well as more profoundly.
> [...] But Barenboim has come to share his wife's capacity for growth.
> He gave us a reading of Beethoven's Third Symphony that was light years
> more thoughtful and probing than the one he slapped over Beethoven's
> Seventh a year and a half ago with the Israel Philharmonic.

And finally Littler observed that 'du Pré had become a more refined
artist than her physical mannerisms on stage might suggest' and he
praised in particular the beautiful pianissimo playing and the poignancy
of her instrumental voice.

A week later Jackie was back in England – her first engagement
was to perform the Haydn D major Concerto with the Liverpool
Philharmonic and Sir Adrian Boult, followed by a number of concerts
with Daniel and the Hallé Orchestra in and around the Manchester
area.

Barenboim's association with the Hallé went back many years and
was now being consolidated as he started to conduct the orchestra on
a regular basis. Daniel particularly enjoyed their ability for making

music. 'All the qualities I respected and admired so much in Barbirolli were in evidence there.'[10]

Clive Smart, the Hallé's Manager, was aware that Daniel valued his dates with the orchestra as an opportunity to learn his craft and try out repertoire: 'The orchestra recognised Barenboim as a great musician and in those days as a good but not great conductor. Nevertheless he did much better than others who had more conducting skill and experience.' Indeed, when Barbirolli died in 1970 it was to Barenboim that the Hallé first turned to replace him as Music Director, an offer that Barenboim declined, feeling himself insufficiently equipped and unready for the responsibility. Clive Smart recalled that 'Danny always liked to have Jackie with him when he was working – he would come up for two weeks at a time. Naturally, he liked to book her as soloist – but the limitations of the cello repertoire precluded this from always happening.' Certainly, whether as individuals or as a team, they were favourites with Manchester audiences.

In the event, of the nine concerts that Barenboim conducted in eleven days, Jackie only performed in the last one. As Daniel recalled, it was during the second half of March that Jackie suffered from one of those strange, elusive symptoms that with hindsight could be seen as an early manifestation of multiple sclerosis. One morning she woke up with numbness affecting one side of her body. At the time, no explanation was found for this lack of sensation. It was thought that the cause might be psychosomatic and could be blamed on the stress of concert life. Yet within a few days the symptom had disappeared as mysteriously as it had come and Jackie was able to resume her concert life. She fulfilled her last engagement with the Hallé on 30 March, playing the Saint-Saëns concerto, again with Daniel conducting.

Back in London the following day, Daniel and Jackie contributed separately to a celebration record to be released for Gerald Moore's seventieth birthday in July of that year. Jackie had enthusiastically responded to Suvi Grubb's idea to gather together on one record performances by EMI's top artists, all playing with the veteran accompanist himself. As Edward Greenfield reported in *High Fidelity Magazine*, 'tight studio schedules were stretched to fit in such artists as Victoria de Los Angeles, Yehudi Menuhin, Janet Baker, Nicolai Gedda, and Gervase de Peyer. EMI's Number One Studio was signed up like a busy squash court ... in order to have the record ready by the July deadline.'

Grubb termed the final session on 1 April one of the most enjoyable recording sessions he ever had produced and Greenfield, who attended it, wrote about the cheerful, relaxed atmosphere:

> Jacqueline was playing the Fauré *Élégie* – a sentimental selection by the young cellist, for this *Élégie* was the first piece she had ever played with orchestra, as a student at the Guildhall School. [...] On playback, Jackie winced at one note. 'It sounds like a racing car –' she commented, giving a good imitation of a racing car and a barely recognisable one of a whining cello. Daniel Barenboim had already shown his appreciation by chortling out loud when his wife had topped a climax with that sudden 'give' of emotion that marks her best playing.

Moore had only rarely played with Jackie, but he had the greatest admiration for her artistry, claiming that 'she inspires everyone who comes into contact with her'. He recalled his surprise on that occasion to discover that Barenboim was hearing the Fauré *Élégie* for the first time.[11] (This perhaps compensated in some measure for Barenboim's amazement at discovering Jackie's ignorance of Tchaikovsky's First Piano Concerto – all the more surprising considering she had been present in Moscow during the 1966 Tchaikovsky Competition.)

As a fitting conclusion to the birthday tribute it was suggested that Moore should record the last item (Dvořák's G minor Slavonic Dance) as a four-hand piano duet with Daniel. This was done immediately after Jackie had completed her contribution. Greenfield explained that 'Barenboim made only one condition: in any piano duet Moore should play primo to his secondo, so that for once the unashamed accompanist would be able to take the tune. ... At the end of the first run-through Barenboim seized the opportunity he had been waiting for. Exploding in laughter on the final chord, he turned to his partner and flung at him the very question that Moore had made famous: "Am I too loud?" '[12]

By the time he arrived at the recording studio, Daniel had already spent six hours in rehearsal with the English Chamber Orchestra and yet, to Moore's amazement, he showed not a suspicion of tiredness, and still had plenty of energy to work and play pranks. Such a day was typical of Daniel's tornado-like pace of activity.

The following day, just prior to departure on the tour which was to take them round the world, Daniel conducted the English Chamber Orchestra in a programme with Jackie performing the Haydn D major Concerto in the Festival Hall. The critic of the *Financial Times* was delighted by the refinement of her performance, admitting to having wrongly anticipated that the passion and intensity of her playing might threaten 'to spill over and blur the shapeliness of Haydn's writing'.[13]

Jackie had decided that the tour would be a holiday; she was happy to come along 'for the ride' to be with Daniel. She did not perform any further concerts with the ECO until the last week of the tour in mid-May.

The musicians arrived in Australia on 10 April, after having given a few concerts *en route* in the USA. The Barenboims held a press conference immediately on arrival at Sydney. The Australian journalists were intrigued and disappointed by Jackie's wish not to perform – she explained she was having a holiday and intended to do some swimming. It was noted that she had nevertheless brought her Gofriller cello with her (misspelt, and no doubt pronounced, to rhyme with 'Gorilla') – even though she claimed to do very little practice.

It was while in Australia that Jackie experienced some other minor health problems. The co-leader of the orchestra, José Luis García and his wife, the cellist Jo Milholland, recalled how these difficulties started. 'We had a day off which we spent together and in the evening we were all invited to a party. During the course of the day Jackie began to lose her voice and by the time she got to the party she could hardly speak. This kind of thing can be perfectly normal, if you get your voice back in a few days. But we still had three weeks of the tour to go and when at the end of that time she still hadn't recovered her voice, it seemed rather unusual.'

This seemingly insignificant malaise was another of those myriad tell-tale symptoms, which taken by itself was innocent enough. Only in retrospect could it be attributed to multiple sclerosis, an illness which is notoriously difficult to diagnose in the early stages, since it manifests itself through signs that could also be regarded as unimportant everyday complaints. As García explained, 'Rather than being physically tired or run down, Jackie regarded this laryngitis as a nuisance and went on living her life normally.' Quin Ballardie of the ECO also noticed other things that didn't seem right with Jackie during the tour: 'It was the beginning of a strange kind of physical unsteadiness. We were worried – it was as if she had drunk three gins and tonics; but she hadn't. In fact, Jackie hardly ever drank and never excessively. Once she slipped down some stairs in the foyer of a hall and fell heavily – I had to pick her up.

She thought she had just tripped on the carpet and was more surprised than upset.'

While in Australia, Jackie did seek medical advice for these various complaints. Her laryngitis, in the meantime, did not respond to any normal treatment. One of the doctors she consulted, instead of reassuring her or seeking to get to the bottom of the problem, to Jackie's fury dismissed her troubles as 'adolescent trauma'.

Nevertheless, by the time they had come back to Europe via Israel, Jackie had recovered her strength. She gave two performances of Haydn's C major Concerto in Florence on 12 and 13 May, and a further one the day after in Milan as her contribution to the ECO world tour. Back in London, with her mini-sabbatical now over, she resumed her concert activities at an almost feverish pace. Health problems were put to the back of her mind as she got back into the swing of things. Only in retrospect could doctors view this episode of ill health, followed by a longer period of remission, as pointing to a pattern typical of the early stages of multiple sclerosis.

22

Belonging To The Clan

Freedom is the antithesis of arbitrariness, the enemy of anarchy.
Heinrich Neuhaus, *The Art of Piano Playing*

No sooner were they back in England than the Barenboim couple launched into the festival season. For the third year running they were much involved in the Brighton Festival, where, on 17 May, Jackie performed the Haydn C major Concerto with the ECO. The following day she played the Brahms Double Concerto with Pinchas Zukerman (their first performance together). Barenboim, who was conducting the New Philharmonia Orchestra on this occasion, recalls the wonderful empathy between the two players which made for an inspired interpretation of the work. He has always regretted that there is no extant recording from any of their various performances to testify to the special quality of their understanding of this piece.

The following day, Monday 19 May, Jackie and Daniel were back in London to play the first of two concerts devoted to the complete Beethoven cello works, comprising the five sonatas and three sets of variations, at the Festival Hall. The whole of musical London came to hear the cycle, a fact noted by Edward Greenfield of the *Guardian*, who enthused, 'I don't know whether any other duo today could pack the Royal Festival Hall twice over for such intimate, undemonstrative music. Undemonstrative, but in the hands of these young players intensely expressive. [...] You would have concluded, had you just heard and not seen the performers, that they were mature in years as well as in musical experience.'

The duo opened the cycle with a performance of the early F major Sonata Op.5 No.1. As Joan Chissell commentated in *The Times*,

It took no more than a dozen bars to disclose the nature of the playing we were in for – individually flawless, finely balanced and hyper-sensitive in musical response. In this work the pianist has the lion's share, but with his fleetness of finger and translucent tone and texture Mr Barenboim never allowed the cello to sound a mere passenger. Nor, with her way of giving life and character to any kind of note, could Miss du Pré have emerged as a passenger anyway. She supported him like a tigress in several of the finale's climaxes, albeit with nothing thematic to say.

The first two Cello Sonatas Op.5 Nos 1 and 2, pose considerable problems for performers in terms of balance. Beethoven wrote the works to perform with Pierre Duport, the cellist to the Prussian Court, during a visit to Berlin in 1796. No doubt anxious to show off his pianistic skills, the composer conceived these sonatas very much for piano with cello. Chissell felt that Barenboim and du Pré overcame the inherent difficulties in the first F major Sonata, something which Nicholas Kenyon (writing in the *Daily Telegraph*) believed to be a near impossibility: 'In spite of Daniel Barenboim's evident concern, there were moments when the piano's cumulative sonority swamped the cello tone.'

The critics continued to disagree in their assessment of the two other sonatas presented in the first concert (the C major Op.102 No.1 and the A major Op.69). While Chissell was emphatic that '... the mercurial responsiveness and darting brilliance of these two young artists suited the younger music best', Kenyon insisted that it was in the C major that '... the performers produced some of the best playing of the evening.'

Beethoven commentators often lament the lack of slow movements in the cello sonatas, where the cello's singing qualities could be put to best advantage. Greenfield observed that du Pré and Barenboim compensated for such oversights in their treatment of the introduction of the early G minor Sonata. 'The opening adagio sostenuto of the Op.5 No.2, taken intensely slowly, had a weight and depth such as you find only rarely in early Beethoven.' Yet for the *Financial Times* critic, Max Harrison, the same slow intensity of this opening movement was highly irritating: 'The long adagio introduction [was taken] at such a funeral lento, with the rests so disturbingly prolonged, that the dark brooding line lost much of its essential coherence, and all but fell apart. Fortunately with the dotted semiquaver movement both players quickened to a more realistic tempo.' Neither was Harrison convinced by their rendering of the last D major Sonata, Op.102 No.2: 'Miss du Pré gives us a rather disconcerting mixture of plain vulgarity (the allegro first movement) and inspired intensity (the wonderful adagio ...)'. He concluded somewhat witheringly that 'unfortunately, a great artist is not merely one who plays a single movement of a sonata extremely beautifully'.

Yet the Barenboim–du Pré team evoked eulogies from Greenfield for their handling of this very sonata, in particular for the central adagio: 'How glorious it is when artists have the stature to meditate untroubled, to "play through the pauses", to let one appreciate Beethoven's emotions in their full expansiveness.' Chissell echoed these sentiments: 'Miss du Pré's restrained use of vibrato [which] doubled the music's eloquence. And the merging of the slow movement into the finale and the gradual build-up of the fugal argument was supremely well done.'

The critics all seemed to agree that Barenboim and du Pré were particularly successful in their interpretation of the three sets of variations, works which, compared with the sonatas, could seem insubstantial, mere 'pot-boilers'. But here Beethoven had other aims than in the sonatas. The very charm of the cello variations (two sets on themes from Mozart's *Magic Flute* and one on Handel's *Judas Maccabaeus*) lies in the way he treated and sometimes transformed tunes that would have been familiar to Viennese audiences, sifting his predecessors' music through his own perceptions. An obvious example of this is the way he introduced change into Mozart's 'Ein Mädchen oder Weibchen' theme, where he turns the original quaver triplets of the second part into a dotted quaver/semiquaver rhythm, completely changing the emphasis and making for a more angular rhythmic pattern. Obviously Beethoven needed the device for its unifying effect, but it was also a way of dissociating himself from Mozart's magical glockenspiel world.

Again in the audience on both occasions was the thirteen-year-old Alexander Bailey, who unfailingly attended every one of Jackie's London concerts.

> I remember hearing Jackie's Beethoven cycle at the Festival Hall with Barenboim. As usual I was sitting in the front row (called row B, since row A doesn't exist). Although Daniel was very charismatic and powerful, nevertheless it was Jackie who led and dominated the performances. It seemed as if the whole of Daniel's attention was intent on establishing contact and responding to her, whereas Jackie was content to let herself be followed. The effect was of two people playing in very different ways, yet producing a very strong result.

As Bailey recalled, the most remarkable thing about these concerts, and many of those at the South Bank festivals, was the quality of audience reaction. 'The silence and attention were incredible, you would have heard a pin drop. Jackie's presence was so powerful and she communicated in an electrifying way even when she was playing chamber music works like *Verklärte Nacht.*'

Bailey, now one of Britain's leading cellists, confessed: 'At the time I was completely besotted and star-struck by Jackie. I used to get told off at school for writing Jackie's name in enormous letters on the blackboard.' Similarly, the cellist Stephen Isserlis recalled that his viola-playing sister Rachel had her bedroom decorated with pin-up pictures of Daniel and Jackie. Their enthusiastic response was indicative of the excitement generated by these interpretative artists, whose combination of youth, vitality and artistic brilliance was irresistible.

This Beethoven cycle was prepared in anticipation of the bicentenary of Beethoven's birth the following year; Daniel and Jackie not only were to perform the sonatas and variations many times throughout the following eighteen months, but with Zukerman were to play and record all the music for piano trio. In addition, Barenboim planned to repeat the cycle of the thirty-two Beethoven piano sonatas in London and New York. In fact, by 1970 he had completed his project of recording all of Beethoven's piano sonatas and concertos (with Otto Klemperer) for EMI.

Barenboim also conceived another project for the Beethoven jamboree, which brought his insights on the composer to a far wider audience. During the summer months of 1969 he prepared a series of thirteen television programmes on the composer to be transmitted by Granada Television the following year. Christopher Nupen, now working freelance, directed the programmes in which Daniel not only played some of Beethoven's seminal works, but spoke about them. Among the chosen works was the A major Cello Sonata (Op.69), which Jackie and Daniel recorded in the studio. Nupen's filmed account shows us the serious side of the art of performance, and the camera did not catch the smiles and backstage jokes which helped to create the informal, joyful spirit of his musical documentaries.

The first week of June found Jackie and Daniel on their travels again. They had been invited to perform at the Puerto Rico Festival, of which the ninety-three-year-old Casals was Director. In that year the veteran cellist gave his last performance at the festival as a cellist in a chamber music concert with Menuhin. Whereas two years earlier he had conducted Piatigorsky in the Schumann concerto, on this occasion he preferred to leave the direction of the Festival Orchestra to others, and it was Barenboim who conducted Jackie's performance of the Elgar concerto in San Juan. Casals most certainly would have been totally won over by her interpretation, however much it may have differed from his own concept of Elgar's masterpiece. Indeed, he was reportedly moved to tears by her playing. Henry Raymont wrote of Jackie's enormous personal success in his review in the *New York Times*: 'Miss du Pré ... was called back to the stage six times by a standing ovation. Backstage, after the concert, the two young artists were embraced by Casals, who had listened to the performance from a high-backed chair placed in the wings. "I always said you can't be English with such a temperament," he told the beaming Miss du Pré. "Of course, it must come from your father's French ancestors. It was beautiful. Every note in its place and every emphasis so right." '[1]

In the second half of June the Barenboims travelled to Tel Aviv, where they both performed at the Israel Festival, in a special concert commemorating the second anniversary of the Israeli victory in the Six Day War. They were joined by Zubin Mehta and the Israel Philharmonic, so that the line-up of artists repeated that of the original Victory concert in 1967. Jackie played Bloch's *Schelomo* and Barenboim Brahms's Second Piano Concerto in the beautiful Roman amphitheatre of Caesarea which, apart from boasting a remarkable acoustic, has the most suggestive setting. The tenor Plácido Domingo attended the concert. Although he already knew of Jackie by reputation he admitted that he was certainly not prepared for what he heard: 'From the moment she began to play, I found myself hypnotised by her. Immediately I was aware of the artistry, concentration and power that was being marshalled to make her cello sing in a way I had never heard a cello sound before.'[2] Some years later, in London, Domingo told Jackie that the cello was his favourite instrument and he liked to imitate its sound in legato passages. (Usually it is the other way round – cellists want to imitate great singers.) Jackie took his compliment to its logical conclusion and immediately suggested that he should start learning the cello – she undertook to teach him and gave him several lessons.

Back in London, Jackie played Schumann's concerto on 3 July with Lawrence Foster and the RPO. On 10 July she participated in a celebrity recital at the Cheltenham Festival with Lamar Crowson, which was shared with Heinz Holliger (oboist and a distinguished composer in his own right) and his wife the harpist Ursula. The composer John Manduell, Director of the Cheltenham Festival at the time, had some interesting ideas of radical programming, but this particular concert he recalled as 'a dreadful mistake'. Instead of confining each of the duos and their very different offerings to two separate halves of the concert, he decided on a 'sort of quadruple sandwich'. As he recalled,

> The interesting thing was that the audience which had come to hear Jacqueline du Pré play Beethoven and Debussy found the extreme modernity of Heinz Holliger's part absolutely offensive, and some of them, indeed, got very angry. We've had a few riots in Cheltenham, and this is one of the riots that I remember with particular pleasure, because it got to the point in the second half where the traditional audience was leaving the hall for the next fifteen minutes and colliding with the adventurous half which was coming back from the bar across the way for another vigorous dose of Stockhausen.[3]

It was interesting to note in this collision of tastes that du Pré's 'traditional' followers could cope with the Britten Cello Sonata, if not with Stockhausen. Whereas the avant-gardists rejected Britten, but relegated the composer Jolivet (who was eight years older than the English composer) to their camp. Stanley Sadie, writing in *The Times* of the mixture of jeers and clapping in this divided audience, had nothing but praise for du Pré's and Crowson's contribution: 'They caught the fleeting, shadowy colours of Britten's Sonata to perfection; and in Beethoven's G minor Sonata the intellectual and rhythmic control of Mr Crowson's pianism brought out the best in Miss du Pré. I specially admired the finale, done rather deliberately with just the right tone of serious, tigerish playfulness.'[4]

On 25 July Jackie played Dvořák's Cello Concerto at the Proms with Sir Charles Groves conducting the RLPO. Jackie had a strong affection for Groves, a paternalistic figure on the English music scene who had worked hard to bring a more adventurous repertoire and higher standards to the provincial English orchestras. While not necessarily a brilliant or charismatic conductor, Groves's integrity as a musician and his innate modesty made him one of the best accompanists and most popular figures in the British musical world.

The extant radio tape from this Prom performance (which was to prove to be her last ever at this unique English festival) shows Jackie in great form, accompanied somewhat stolidly, but always musically, by

Groves. The Royal Liverpool Philharmonic displayed many of the typical defects of a provincial English orchestra, with a rough edge to the ensemble and some dubious intonation, but their strength lay in their empathy with and enjoyment of Dvořák's music. Jackie's heartfelt rendering of the piece was conveyed through her characteristically rich sound, which mostly seemed more than sufficient to fill the cavernous spaces of the Albert Hall. Occasionally, the excitement of the performance caused some flaws – a distorting bulge or a raucous attack – in the melodic flow. One can detect in her performance an obsessive insistence on volume of sound, something that increased over the remainder of Jackie's playing years in proportion to her diminishing strength. Sometimes she paid the price for this in loss of tone quality.

Certain features of her playing, her stretching the phrases, indulgent slides and somewhat exaggerated rubato, were often perceived as mannered and distracting, and for some critics they obscured the quality of the music's message. It is difficult to know how much the changes in Jackie's musical personality were a result of a wish to compensate for her decreasing control as illness gradually encroached on her physical powers. Or whether, as Jeremy Siepmann suggested, Jackie's unselfconsciousness as a performer was being overlaid by a growing awareness, resulting in her 'imposing a quasi-analytical vision on the music'. Siepmann speculated that while earlier she had seemed a medium to transmit the musical message with complete spontaneity, in the last years of her playing career 'the medium began to be replaced by the manipulator'.[5]

In this concert performance of the Dvořák, other du Pré idiosyncrasies – the beautiful variety of glissandi and portamento – were used to wonderful effect, as were her magical pianissimi, coloured by a gorgeous vibrato and singing warmth and legato of the bow. Yet Jackie had the courage to dispense with vibrato altogether when she needed to achieve dark or icy cold colours. There are some marvellous moments of inspired dialogue in this performance, where Groves allows his wind soloists the freedom to 'rhapsodise' with the soloist without imposing constraints.

Spaciousness was the keynote to this interpretation, and here again we can hear many instances of Jackie's innate ability to spin out the sound and suspend time, or hover deliciously at the end of a phrase. Her intuitive understanding of the contours of the score is reflected in her response to harmonic change. Even on a long suspended note, she was able to modify the colour so as to suggest or anticipate a significant harmony change or modulation.

In this recording one is always aware that Jackie was playing for the occasion and completely disregarded the presence of microphones. In the coda of the finale the intonation suffers both in the solo and orchestral voices, problems which were no doubt partly due to the difficulties of maintaining the tuning of both string and wind instruments in a very hot and overcrowded hall. Yet, in Jackie's case, it seems not a matter of misplacing the fingers of the left hand, but rather an exertion of too much pressure of the bow which caused distortion.

After the Prom, Jackie and Daniel spent the first ten days of August in the USA, performing the Elgar concerto at Tanglewood on 3 August, where they both were making their début with the Boston Symphony Orchestra. On 7 August they performed the Saint-Saëns concerto with the Philadelphia Orchestra at Saratoga Springs, the orchestra's summer festival venue. Before returning home, they flew out to California, where Daniel and Jackie played as soloists in separate concerts at the Hollywood Bowl with Zubin Mehta and the Los Angeles Philharmonic.

Back in Europe, they paid a flying visit to the Lucerne Festival, where on 18 August Jackie performed Haydn's D major Concerto with the ECO – Daniel again conducted. The violinist Rodney Friend and his wife Cynthia were at the festival by chance. As Cynthia recalled, 'During those couple of days I got to know Jackie quite well. I was shocked by how tired she was, we were all so young then. She played absolutely beautifully, but afterwards she was so very weary that we took her straight back to the hotel, without waiting till the end of the concert.'

With such a strenuous pace of activity, let alone the flying mileage clocked up in the preceding few weeks, it was no wonder that Jackie felt tired. But her tiredness was not the kind which goes away with a few days' extra sleep. Fatigue on its own is rarely thought of as a symptom of illness – sometimes it can just seem a convenient excuse for someone who wishes to escape from unwelcome obligations. Since a concert artist has to fulfil duties that have been contracted long in advance, it was not surprising if Jackie sometimes found them to be onerous. On days when she felt full of strength, she still thoroughly enjoyed the music-making that was at the centre of her high-flying career. But on others, when she suffered from a peculiar sensation of fatigue that left her feeling weak and dazed, it was hard for her to get up in front of an audience and play. It was difficult to explain this to herself, let alone justify it to others. In fact, as she was later to learn, this type of fatigue is one of the commonest symptoms of multiple sclerosis. But as portents of this elusive illness in its initial stages can disappear as quickly and inexplicably as they have come, their effect is extremely disarming.

Certainly if Jackie was tired at this stage of the summer, there was little respite awaiting her in London. She and Daniel threw themselves into the second South Bank Festival which, as in the previous year, had been planned by Barenboim in his capacity as Artistic Director. This year, building on a basis of classical and romantic works, Barenboim took the music both forward into the twentieth century – with a particular emphasis on Schoenberg and the New Viennese School – and back into the baroque period – with offerings by Bach, Handel and Couperin. Barenboim's decision to focus on the chamber music of the New Viennese School was partly dictated by his own tastes and interests, but also as a means of anticipating another anniversary – the centenary of Anton Webern's birth in 1970. A further dimension to this year's ten-day festival was the inclusion of master classes and seminars, in which Barenboim also found time to participate, as well as both conducting the ECO and playing chamber music.

Jackie, too, was busy playing – she participated in no less than six of the concerts. She preferred not to involve herself with the organisational side of Daniel's life and to some people her passivity seemed tantamount to a lack of interest or support. But Daniel sees this view as a misconception.

> While Jackie wasn't really interested in the planning of the festival or in helping me with ideas, she contributed by performing and was willing to learn a lot of new works, particularly during the 1969 festival. In that respect she was as docile as a child – 'Will you learn *Verklärte Nacht...?*' 'Yes.' 'Would you like to play this or that?' 'Yes.' She didn't say 'no' because I think for better or for worse she had complete faith in my artistic judgement and followed my suggestions. She was totally unintellectual and therefore she had no intellectual curiosity.

Daniel was able to encourage Jackie to learn new repertoire most particularly in the context of chamber music, where the learning process was enlivened by the presence of other musicians. One suspects that Jackie, with her ability for instant assimilation, did most of her learning in rehearsal. She certainly adored every minute of music-making with

Daniel and their friends, as is obvious from the glimpses we get of high-spirited fun at the rehearsals of Schubert's *Trout* Quintet and the 'behind the scenes' warming up before the *Ghost* Trio in Nupen's films. One should add that seeing Jackie on screen, she shows no sign of the fatigue that she had complained of at other times during that year.

The opening chamber concert of the festival on 22 August, given by the Barenboim couple and Gervase de Peyer, was a model of how the inherent fascination of a concert can be shaped by its programming. It was planned with two shorter pieces in each half to framework the main offerings of the clarinet trios of Beethoven and Brahms. The mirror construction was achieved by two performances of Schumann's *Fantasiestücke* Op.73 – in the first half of the concert the original version for clarinet and piano, in the second the cello version. Two additional offerings from the New Viennese School made up the rest of the programme – Berg's Four Pieces for Clarinet and Piano Op.5 in the first half and Webern's *Three Little Pieces* for cello and piano in the second.

The English Chamber Orchestra was again at the centre of the music-making. As Quin Ballardie recalled, 'It was a period of great music-making with Barenboim, and they were wonderful times to have lived through together. We were all affected by the generous spirit of the Barenboim Trio, and of the fourth musician of their team, Itzhak Perlman. It gave us something quite unique.'

The orchestra's co-leader, José Luis García, cited as an example of this spirit a fantastic performance of Schoenberg's sextet *Verklärte Nacht*:

Pinky and I played violins, Peter Schidlof and Cecil Aronowitz violas, with Jackie and Bill Pleeth on cellos – it was quite an event. Jackie loved playing it – it was music very much up her street. In fact, she already knew the piece inside out from hearing the orchestral version, which we often played with Daniel. She would have assimilated it through hearing it just a couple of times. While she never seemed to spend time studying scores, she knew them and could sing all the orchestral parts of the concertos she played. In the rehearsals she contributed as much as anybody, and in particular was a great master in working out the sonorities and colours, through the use (or non-use) of vibrato, and so on. Her suggestions were very sound, since she had a marvellous ear and a wonderful sense of balance, and was immediately aware if one instrument was too loud or another not prominent enough. She was very accom-

modating about bowings and was always happy to try out any suggestions. In these rehearsals we all felt as equals because we could express
our opinions freely and remain in harmony. Pinky was a marvellous
leader without being over-assertive.

As Itzhak Perlman recalled, chamber music was an integral part of their
lives, since they played it whenever and wherever they met. Therefore
it felt totally natural to extend their private sessions into public concerts
so as to share their zest and enjoyment. Barenboim, of course, was the
moving spirit in all the performances: 'Daniel was the one who took
the initiative and would come up with phenomenal programmes. He
made us play things we would never have thought of. "How about this,
how about that?" he would suggest and, in fact, he still does that. It
made it easy for things like the *Trout* film to come about within the
context of the festival.'

Christopher Nupen's documentary film of a performance of Schubert's Piano Quintet D667, the *Trout*, was created not least because of
the happy coincidence of being in the right place at the right time. In
the week before the concert informal shots of the players were filmed
and the cameras eavesdropped at rehearsals. We see Zubin Mehta
arriving at Heathrow with his new wife, Nancy, and his double-bass
(an anxious moment as the huge instrument in its soft case lurches
through the airport conveyor belt into the luggage hall), Perlman
relaxing in a Hampstead garden with his family and Zukerman trying
out a viola at Charles Beare's Wardour Street shop. The cameras pick
up on the laughter of the rehearsals, as well as testifying to the musicians'
sharp ears and critical spirit. The first glimpse of the rehearsal is
Barenboim's horrified reaction to the opening chord: 'That was awful,'
he grimaces and suggests that Perlman should spread it more. No
sooner said than done and the artists move on, playing with an ease
and intimacy which suggests that they had been performing together
for years.

It seemed to prove what Zukerman felt about it: 'We'd all been there
before.' With two conductors in the group, there is much teasing about
how to give the leads to the other players. But Barenboim and Mehta
keep a low profile, leaving Perlman to assert himself as leader. He is
every now and then upstaged by Zukerman, who at one point gives an
imitation of the explosive downbeat of Casals. Even in the last few
minutes before going on stage the pranks go on, as the players swap

instruments; Perlman gives a rendering of *The Flight of the Bumble Bee* on the cello, where his energy camouflages the approximity of the notes, and somehow he conveys the overall effect of immense virtuosity. Jackie holds Perlman's violin vertically like a cello and produces a mellifluous rendering of the opening bars of Mendelssohn's Violin Concerto. Daniel, an equal participant in the larking around, nevertheless has to exercise his authority to get the players out on to the stage – after all, he is director of the show. The miracle happens when the performance starts and the players are instantly transformed into serious musicians. Fortunately their seriousness never affects their youthful verve and joy, for it is youthful music that they play, Schubert was himself only twenty-one when he wrote the piece.

At the time, none of the participants thought of the film as having any special significance; nor were they aware of its enormous potential success. Rather, for them, it was sharing some fun with 'Kitty' Nupen while he filmed their music-making. As Perlman observed, while Jackie participated no less than the others in the 'fooling around', her music-making retained complete integrity whatever the situation. 'I'll never forget the couple of little thematic bits for cello in the *Trout.* Listening to anybody else – however well they play it – spoils it for me, because what Jackie did was so incredible. The principal thing about her music-making was the sheer pleasure she got from playing.' It was a pleasure that was infectious, and one that reflected the complete bond between her playing and her personality.

For Perlman, the speaking quality in Jackie's artistry and her predilection for slides were in themselves an expression of her personality. 'Sometimes if she did a particularly obvious slide, it made me feel I wanted to slide less – one had a reaction as in a game.' As Perlman noted, Jackie's inner impulse was inextricably linked to the conviction of her music-making. 'Her technique was derived from the inner ear and was not something imposed from outside. If something didn't come to her immediately and naturally, it might have felt like a lack of technique to the outsider. Occasionally, Jackie herself might experience the need to do five minutes' practice, so as to overcome a technical flaw. But as I recall it she could do everything, and in a totally uncalculated way. Yet the placement of her bow and fingers was so secure.'

The film of the *Trout* enjoyed an unprecedented success and now, nearly thirty years after its first showing, it remains the most popular classical music documentary ever made. One might ask, what was so special about it? Nupen himself gave the answer to this rhetorical question in his introductory leaflet to the video. 'First and foremost it was the time when five young musicians were forming exceptional musical partnerships and personal friendships. Second, it was the time when they were making the transition to world stardom. Indeed the film contributed a great deal to that transition and the speed of it.' As Nupen pointed out, they were of a generation who had grown up with television and were not camera shy. The excellent quality of the performance is self-evident, but it is filmed in such a way as to give the viewer the impression of being right in the middle of the music-making. Nupen himself certainly deserves much credit for the film's success through capturing so powerfully the spontaneous spirit of fun.

One can only regret that he didn't keep the cameras running for the second half of the concert – a performance of Schoenberg's *Pierrot Lunaire*, where Mehta resumed his baton. His small band consisted of Zukerman on violin and viola, Jackie on cello, Richard Adeney on flute and piccolo, Gervase de Peyer on clarinet (but he passed on the responsibility of the double part of bass clarinet to Stephen Trier) and Daniel at the piano. The soprano Jane Manning, the speaker (or *Sangsprächerin*) in this performance, recalls that Jackie had the perfect quality of dramatic intensity necessary for the music.

Once the cellist Jenny Ward-Clarke stepped in for Jackie at one of the *Pierrot* rehearsals. Being very familiar with the music (she was an original member of the Pierrot Players formed to play this particular piece and other contemporary music for the same formation), she had the impression that, at rehearsal at least, accuracy was not top of the list of the group's priorities.

Another of Schoenberg's works that Jackie played in this festival was the Second String Quartet, a performance that Perlman led, with Ken Sillito and Cecil Aronowitz playing second violin and viola. The additional soprano part in the third and fourth movements was sung by Heather Harper. All this, as Perlman pointed out, '. . . was Daniel's idea, and boy, was it hard. We rehearsed long hours and I cursed Daniel. But we had good working rehearsals, although some of the time it felt like we were swimming.'

The conductor Larry Foster was present at many of these concerts and can be seen turning pages for Daniel during the performance of the *Trout*. He recalled that Jackie had no problems in playing *Pierrot* or the other pieces and that she could easily have held her own in any contemporary music group. Since Jackie is so much associated with the central cello repertoire, this may seem surprising, all the more so because she always disclaimed interest in contemporary music. As Zukerman recalled, 'Jackie had an amazing ability to read any kind of music without any difficulty. But don't forget, she lived with someone who knew more about music than anyone else of his generation. Daniel can sit down at his instrument and read anything without putting a foot wrong.' As he saw it, there was an enormous gap between Daniel's conscious empirical knowledge and analytical approach, and Jackie's instantaneous intuitive grasp of music, which seemed to bypass the conscious process.

> In Jackie's case the fascination was enormous. When people argue about whether the musical imagination or the musical structure is more important, I find as I get older that there is no answer. I can sit with the score and explain in detail why the music should be played like this, but, I then ask myself, why should anybody need to analyse music, because if the harmony doesn't draw you to an emotional state – a high or a low of some sort – or give you some association, provoke some recollection or stimulate a futuristic thought process, then you shouldn't be doing it – give it up. With Jackie what I remember most of all was that all the qualities in her music-making were so completely unified.

Other works that Jackie performed during the festival included Bach's Second Suite for Unaccompanied Cello, Beethoven's G major String Trio Op.9 (with Zukerman and Schidlof) and Ibert's Concerto for Cello and Winds, which she had recorded for the BBC seven years earlier. This year Jackie was twice partnered by her teacher William Pleeth – in one concert they performed duets by Defesch and in the final concert, on 31 August, they played Handel's Concerto for Two Cellos – an arrangement by Ronchini of an original concerto for two violins.

We have been left testimony of the distinguished teacher and his favourite pupil both in an early BBC recording of duos by Couperin and, more important, in Christopher Nupen's two documentaries about Jackie. Even when reading through light-weight pieces by Offenbach, one can relish their shared enthusiasm and their ability to invest music that can hardly be called first-rate with enormous character. One time, for instance they play through a slow movement with an almost over-the-top sentimentality. 'This music makes us get slower and slower, we'll grind to a halt,' Jackie splutters out, overpowered by merriment. 'Well, let's try it twice as fast – just for fun,' responds Pleeth – and they do, transforming something that is sugary and sentimental into a piece of dancing elegance.

The ability to connect and interplay with other musicians was one of Jackie's most distinct and endearing qualities. It is particularly touching to see the interaction between her and Pleeth, even if by now in her unfettered approach to music-making Jackie has far transcended the influence of her teacher. Similarly, this musical interplay worked particularly well with Daniel and with Pinky. The tangible complicity between Zukerman and du Pré even in their playing of simple accompanying figures is very much in evidence in the filmed performance of the *Trout* Quintet.

When the South Bank Festival came to an end, Barenboim's reputation in London was at a new peak. It was no wonder that Edward Greenfield divided London musical life in those years into two categories – concerts with Barenboim and concerts without him. Wits among London's orchestral musicians dubbed him 'Mr Music', demonstrating a typical British combination of grudging admiration and irony. More to the point, this teasing nickname implied a real appreciation of the vast scope of Daniel's creative activities, his positive energy and the enormous quality of his talent.

23

Celebrating Beethoven

There is a vast difference between doing something intellectually, wilfully, deliberately, and as it were being acted upon.
When we play music, the process is as much creatively passive
as it is active.

Yehudi Menuhin*

It is sometimes hard to remember that Jacqueline du Pré's entire career
at international level spanned only six years and that all she achieved
with Barenboim (both in terms of concert activities and recordings)
was condensed into fewer than four years. Yet within this time du Pré
not only made an enormous mark on the general public, but exerted a
lasting influence on the musicians with whom she came into contact
and inspired a younger generation of cellists by her example.

In the 1969–70 season an extra dimension was added to Jackie's
schedule by the inclusion of trio concerts with Pinchas Zukerman, as
well as performances of the Brahms Double Concerto. Otherwise she
performed the majority of her dates with Daniel, either in his capacity
as conductor or pianist.

After the strenuous South Bank Festival, the Barenboim couple had
only a few days' respite before resuming their concert activities with a
two-week visit to Copenhagen, where Daniel was booked to conduct
the Danish Radio Orchestra. Jackie appeared with him as soloist in the
Elgar concerto on 10 and 11 September, and immediately afterwards
they were joined by Zukerman, performing all the Beethoven piano
trios. During this period Jackie and Daniel crossed over to Sweden
twice – once for a duo recital in Göteborg and finally for a concerto
performance in Malmö.

Their itinerary took them next to the island of Jersey, a venue
somewhat off the normal circuit. On 24 September Daniel and Jackie

* Robin Daniels, *Conversations with Yehudi Menuhin*, Futura Publications, London, 1980,
p. 48.

played a duo recital in St Helier, whence the du Pré family originated. Jackie had last spent time in Jersey on holiday when she was twelve. Now she was greeted like a conquering hero.

From Jersey the couple proceeded to Germany, where on 26 September they played at the Berlin Festival, performing both sets of Beethoven's *Magic Flute* variations and the two Brahms cello sonatas. Before returning home, Jackie fulfilled concerto engagements in Brussels on 28 and 29 September; then, back in England, she gave further recitals with Daniel in early October. At her next orchestral engagement in Manchester on 16 October, she performed the Brahms Double Concerto with Zukerman and the Hallé directed by Barenboim. Three days later she was playing the Elgar concerto with the New Philharmonia at the Royal Albert Hall, with John Pritchard replacing the indisposed Barenboim. *The Times* critic expressed disappointment at having been deprived of Barenboim's participation, especially since he was to have conducted *The Dream of Gerontius* for the first time, but du Pré's 'marvellous wistful performance' of the concerto was a compensation.

After further recitals in Germany and Naples in the last days of October, Jackie was back with the Hallé Orchestra in Coventry and Manchester on 4 and 6 November respectively, performing the Dvořák concerto with Maurice Handford.

Then, following the pattern of previous years, the Barenboims left for North America for a six-week visit. Whereas her popularity with her North American audiences was never in question, it was during this period that she started receiving many less than complimentary notices. One has to ask if there were objective reasons for this, or if saturation point had been reached in her spiralling critical acclaim. An artist at the pinnacle of success is always vulnerable to re-evaluation and it is all too easy for the critic to become a willing accomplice in the act of destroying the very thing he has helped to create.

Nevertheless, when the only record of a concert remains in the notices, one cannot discount repeated observations by independent reviewers that du Pré was forcing the sound and experiencing problems of intonation. It would seem that during this autumn she was not always functioning at her best.

The tour started with the USA début of the Barenboim–Zukerman–du Pré Trio at Carnegie Hall in New York on 16 November. From there, Jackie travelled to Montreal, where she performed the Dvořák concerto on 18 and 19 November with Zubin Mehta. On the twenty-third, she and Daniel played a recital at New York's Metropolitan Museum of Art, where the novelty aspect of their programme lay in the inclusion of Webern's *Three Little Pieces* and Schumann's *Stücke in Volkston*.

In contrast to what he deprecatingly referred to as 'the worshipping throng', Harold Schonberg of the *New York Times* was not inclined to praise. While finding the content of their programme interesting, he voiced doubts about the qualities of its execution, criticising du Pré's forced tone and faulty intonation in the high positions. Beauty of sound was sacrificed, he claimed, 'In striving for a quality of drama and volume that is neither in her bow arm nor, one suspects, in her temperament. There was too much wood against wood, rather than string against string in her playing – the big sweep of her bow coming down with consequent buzzing, rattling and actual ugliness of sound.' Indeed, in Beethoven's F major Sonata she tried too hard for bigness and Schonberg wondered why: 'The music is not that monumental a statement,' he reminded his readers.

While Schonberg conceded that Barenboim's playing was 'immensely authoritative' in Beethoven, he paid him some double-edged compliments for the execution of the piano part of the Chopin sonata. On the one hand Barenboim performed 'an amazing feat. [...] He went through the music with a minimum of pedal, hardly any color, hardly a single metrical displacement. It was impressive, even formidable, for its easy solution. But it was not Chopin,' the critic concluded. He preferred du Pré's natural lyricism in the Chopin sonata (in the largo movement in particular) and praised her ability to spin out long cantabile lines. Grudgingly enough, he conceded that Webern's miniatures were well played, as were the 'pleasant' Schumann pieces.

The day after this recital the Barenboims proceeded to Chicago, where Jackie once again played Dvořák's concerto. She was the soloist for Sir Georg Solti's first concerts in his official capacity as Music Director of the Chicago Symphony Orchestra. The three performances on 27, 28 and 29 November, as Barenboim recalled, were not Jackie's most satisfactory, partly because she was not in sympathy with Solti's approach to the music. 'Jackie felt that he was too rigid and found him over-emphatic, almost too hard. I remember them having a discussion about the end of the concerto. Solti tried to put the music into a frame, something which Jackie refused to go into.' The critics, on this occasion, were far kinder to Solti than to du Pré. In the *Daily News*, Bernard

Jacobson wrote in bewilderment, 'Four or five years ago Jacqueline du Pré, who is still only twenty-four, was one of the world's great cellists. Something sad and baffling has happened to her playing since then. When she played the Dvořák concerto on Thursday night there were beautiful things in the adagio, and intermittently in the outer movements too. But there was also far too much out-of-tune playing and far too much super-expressive distortion of the music's shape.'

In another unidentified paper she was accused of attempts to 'defy a decree of nature' in her pursuit of large tone: 'Jacqueline du Pré's search for expressive bigness led her repeatedly into rhetoric, far too much of it vulgar. Simply enough, her tone is small – Victor Aitay's powerful violin unison in the finale confirmed that fact.' (Although one should point out that the solo cello should be subordinate to the solo violin line.)

Thomas Willis in the *Sun Times* was more positive in his appreciation. He believed that her individual account owed a lot to Rostropovich, with whom she shared 'an outspoken expressivity and dash. But, at twenty-four, Miss du Pré takes her own time – a little too much now and then – and fashions her own concept.' Praising her technical command and her use of colour, he concluded, 'Few performers at any age can keep listeners as engrossed, even when she steps over the limit of portamento line into pure corn.'

It was du Pré's ability to engross and involve her audience that made such an indelible imprint on people's minds. Her flamboyant personality on stage, with her blonde hair flying, her swaying figure draped in flowing, strong-coloured raw silks – all this was part of a striking stage presence that was stylish yet never pretentious. The communication of the musical expression was all the more potent, since it derived from the visibly external joy in music-making together with an intense interior concentration, a combination which excluded superficiality.

It was at this time that negotiations commenced for the Barenboims to record the Dvořák Cello Concerto with the Chicago Symphony Orchestra. The absence of this piece in Jackie's recorded repertory was glaringly conspicuous, and it was the obvious candidate for her next orchestral recording. EMI were persuaded to make an exception to its rule to make concerto recordings in London, where studio costs and the hire of the best London orchestras were considerably lower than the equivalent in the United States. Dates were set up for the sessions in November 1970, when Barenboims were next booked to play in the Chicago Symphony Orchestra's season. Ironically, by the time Jackie was prepared to commit herself to recording the Dvořák she was beginning to find it problematic for totally different reasons. She no longer had the sheer energy and physical power needed to sustain her concept of the piece as a grandiose structure of symphonic proportions. At the time, however, these problems of fatigue appeared to be only temporary and there was no reason to believe that they would not disappear.

From Chicago, Jackie flew west for concerto dates in Portland, while Daniel went directly to Los Angeles for three weeks of engagements with the Los Angeles Symphony Orchestra. Jackie's next concerts were in Hawaii, where she had an outstanding obligation to the Honolulu Symphony Orchestra, having cancelled dates with them in the spring of 1968. Here, in concerts on 7 and 9 December, she played two concertos – Bloch's *Schelomo* and Tchaikovsky's *Rococo* Variations. The latter was one of the repertoire works that Jackie avoided playing, as she found certain passages in it very awkward. With its beautifully transparent orchestration, the *Rococo* Variations represents one of the most exposed scores for cellists and in this way its difficulties are not dissimilar to those of the Haydn D major Concerto. Yet Jackie never found the Haydn problematic and all those who ever heard her play the *Rococo* Variations can vouch for her virtuosity and her ability to combine a filigree delicacy with just the right degree of fervent expression.

From Hawaii, Jackie returned to Los Angeles for four performances of the Schumann concerto with the LA Philharmonic under Daniel's direction between 17 and 21 December. In contrast to their colleagues in New York and Chicago, the critics were full of praise. They found that du Pré had cut back on her stage mannerisms and had gained deeper musical insights since her first appearance in Los Angeles. Walter Arlen wrote that her performance '... displayed little false pathos or ostentatious drama. The tone was silken and perfectly focused, the interpretation understated and quietly romantic, and somewhat small-scaled.' Orrin Howard noted the happy collaboration between soloist and conductor, who did not 'exploit the romanticism' of their marital status: 'Miss du Pré's lovely, buoyant energies, and Barenboim's serious, brisk vitality were directed, totally without affectation, to the business of bringing off a glowingly burnished performance.' The critic found that du Pré was a marvellous champion for a piece which was far from being one of Schumann's most successful: 'Yet, under the spell of du Pré's ravishing, unerringly musical impulses, the work unfolded with stunning conviction.'[2]

Returning to London for what the agent's diaries referred to as a 'holiday', the Barenboims spent the last week of the month preparing to record the complete Beethoven trios with Zukerman for EMI. Their first sessions at Studio One in Abbey Road were scheduled for 29 and 30 December. During these last days of the year they also found the time to rehearse and perform a celebratory New Year's Eve concert with the English Chamber Orchestra at the Queen Elizabeth Hall. Here du Pré's contribution was confined to two Dvořák pieces, the Rondo and *Waldesruhe* (*Silent Woods*) which she learnt for the occasion. Looking to the future, they were designed as a good coupling for her projected recording of the Dvořák concerto. The cellist Sandy Bailey attended the concert and has a vivid recollection of du Pré's playing: 'The way that Jackie began the *Waldesruhe* has stayed in my mind like a brain pattern. One sensed in her an incredible coiled-up energy just before playing, then a very, very smooth, soft, small-gestured upbeat, which at the same time was immensely powerful, then the sound coming immediately (in an up-bow at the very point of the bow), a sound that was so soft, warm, gentle yet intense and strong. It was thrilling.'

In fact, this seeming combination of contradictions in one sound was something Jackie was very conscious of and would use to achieve a special effect. In the finale of the Elgar concerto there is a passage at the end of the coda (the very last reminiscence of the slow movement theme marked lento) which had a special significance for her – she likened it to a tear-drop. 'It's very inward, very intense, very passionate and very flamboyant, and at the same time very soft,' Jackie once explained on a BBC Radio interview. 'It's difficult to play in the sense that one has to be well aware of the kind of sound one is making and know exactly how to achieve this.'

In the New Year concert, though, there were also fireworks and fun, the former produced by Zukerman in Wieniawski's *Polonaise de Concert*, while the more comic side of the concert was left to Barenboim, revealing extra-musical skills in the playing, acting and miming of Francis Chagrin's Concerto for Conductor and Orchestra (a piece originally commissioned by Gerard Hoffnung in 1958). The concert finished with Haydn's *Farewell* Symphony, with its famous finale where the musicians steal off the stage one by one (in this instance hurrying off to celebrate rather than in protest).

The Beethoven piano trio recordings were resumed on New Year's Day and finished on 3 January. In all, there were eight sessions scheduled (each usually lasting three hours), which meant completing one record side in each session (the full boxed set consisted of four LPs). This was a rare instance of inter-company co-operation, which allowed Zukerman to be released from his newly signed exclusive contract with CBS so as to join Barenboim and du Pré in this EMI recording. In exchange, du Pré and Barenboim were to be released from exclusivity to record the Elgar concerto for CBS with the Philadelphia Orchestra (from live concert), and Barenboim also was to conduct the Mozart violin concertos with Zukerman for the same company.

There is a marvellous repertoire for piano trio, but it is not an easy combination. Hans Keller wrote of the problematic textures inherent in all chamber music for piano and strings, indicating that the two different categories of sound do not readily mix: 'You either mitigate the contrast in sound or you don't. If you don't, you have to make a textural virtue of the contrast, renouncing blend and throwing the heterogeneous sonorities into relief against each other.'[3] Yet a piano trio, far more than the combinations of piano and larger string groups, allows the different components of the formation to retain their individual characteristics.

Barenboim has always maintained that a piano trio should, ideally, be formed by three soloists with an understanding of chamber music. Certainly Zukerman, du Pré and Barenboim all had larger-than-life stage personalities, yet they were matched not only in their ebullience, but in their ability to reveal the interior expression of the music. The string players had that special rapport in everything from the unity of attack to the understanding of sound, where the slightest gesture or glance evoked an instant response. Barenboim relished his role of authority, but also possessed a conductor's ability to listen and accompany.

As the pianist Charles Wadsworth observed, Zukerman, the incomer into the established Barenboim–du Pré duo, acted as the catalyst for the trio. Wadsworth noted that Pinky's instinctive approach allowed him to relate immediately to Jackie, but that he stood back somewhat in awe of Daniel's enormous gifts. By comparison, Barenboim retained a kind of Olympian detachment, which might have inhibited lesser talents, yet served to discipline and restrain the wilder side of the string players.[4] Certainly, Daniel's total security allowed him to be giving and flexible, and never to impose his concepts rigidly.

The flexibility in their performances is, of course, most evident in the matter of tempo, although tempo modifications are related to the overall structure. In Barenboim's perception, 'Although tempo helps in creating the outward form of the music, tempo doesn't make expression, it is only the box into which you put the contents, where the phrasing and the articulation make the expression. In other words, the different elements of tempo, volume and articulation are all interdependent, in the same way as the juxtaposition of harmony, melody and rhythm.' This was something that both the string players understood instinctively. As Daniel pointed out, 'Jackie was among that category of intelligent creative artists who sought and found the relationships between the notes and in the harmonies, and this led her to accentuate certain aspects. Hers was never just a capricious, instinctive, wilful reaction to the printed score, but rather a creative reaction to a composer's code of combinations. With relationships of this nature, the artist creates different degrees of accentuation, of leaning on, pushing or pulling.'

Daniel emphasised that even if she rarely articulated her thoughts, Jackie understood these compositional processes: 'Jackie had a fantastic instinct for these things. It wasn't as if she thought about them consciously so much, or we discussed them. But if you so much as mentioned something in rehearsal she was so quick to pick up on it that you didn't need to finish the sentence, she already knew what you were going to suggest and how to do it. While Jackie could not intellectualise her instincts, she had a fantastic instinct for intellectual and rational thoughts.'

Inevitably, in a piano trio it is the pianist who controls the structure of the music more than the other players. However, the cohesive approach of the string players is also a necessity, and in Zukerman and du Pré's music-making there was a kind of unspoken complicity. They shared intuitive flair, overwhelming musical energy and, most important, an imaginative perception of sound and colour. Indeed the Barenboim–Zukerman–du Pré Trio had all the ingredients necessary for a great trio, and despite its short existence we are fortunate that its one recording legacy (apart from a concert performance of the Tchaikovsky trio) is that most central to the repertoire – the complete Beethoven trios and variations.

Edward Greenfield, an avid fan of the Barenboim couple and of the young Zukerman, was once again privileged to attend some of their Beethoven trio recording sessions. He arrived on the morning of 2 January, while the three artists were discussing what they should record next. They had, in fact, got half of the great B flat Trio Op.97 'in the can' during the previous session. Greenfield was amazed by the team's spontaneity and total lack of inhibition in front of the microphone:

'Let's do the *Archduke*,' they said, like children about to enjoy a treat, and the *Archduke* it was. The scherzo came first (they had always already done one run-through at the previous session), followed by a couple of takes for the first movement with minimal patching and then – literally within ten seconds after completing the last 'insert' – the biggest test of all: the slow, lengthy variation movement and the finale. This they completed in a single break, and it is that first flush of concentrated intensity that will appear on the finished record. Again, the number of 'inserts' was negligible and the only major interruption came when another musician friend, the clarinettist Gervase de Peyer, decided to pay a visit. Barenboim greeted him with a piano version of the Brahms E flat Clarinet Sonata, daring him to phrase it any better on the clarinet.

In fact, as Greenfield noted, it was de Peyer who questioned a discrepancy of tempo in the slow movement during the playback of the *Archduke*:

After the sublime adagio variation, the basic andante was not precisely restored, and [de Peyer] was not convinced when I suggested that this was something of a Schnabel trick. What Barenboim realised – and he was seconded not only by his fellow players but also by Suvi Grubb – was that a gradual rather than a sudden restoration of the andante was essential to the kind of performance that the trio was aiming for: a spontaneous and concentrated reading that would be remarkable enough if heard live in the concert hall, but even doubly so when captured in the recording studio.

This concentration is, if anything, even more astonishing in the slow movement of the *Ghost* Trio (Op.70 No.1) where the players succeed in sustaining an extremely slow speed, without ever seeming static. The string players in particular have an amazing ability to vary the colour

The victory concert in Jerusalem, June 1967. Left to right: the President of Israel and his wife, Daniel, Jacqueline and Zubin Mehta.

Jacqueline and Aida Barenboim in Israel, June 1967.

Jacqueline and
Daniel get married
in Jerusalem, June
1967

Iris du Pré, Aida
Barenboim and
Jacqueline at
her wedding in
Jerusalem, June
1967.

Jacqueline and Daniel
outside the EMI studios,
London, circa 1968.

Jacqueline and Daniel
relaxing during recording
at the EMI studios,
circa 1968.

Jacqueline and Pinchas Zukerman in Paris, June 1970.

Recording the Beethoven Trios with Daniel Barenboim and Pinchas Zukerman, EMI studios, January 1970.

The lighter and darker sides of Beethoven. Jacqueline rehearsing in August 1970.

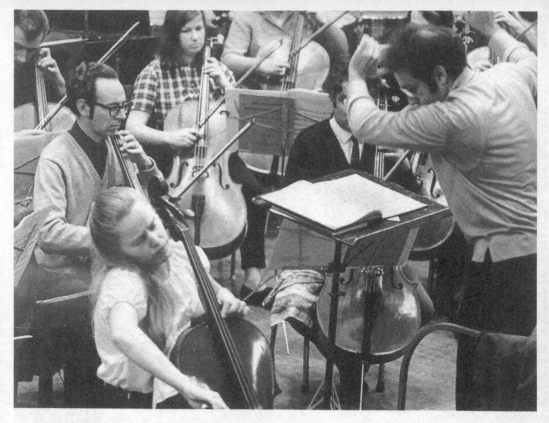

Jacqueline rehearsing the Dvorak Concerto with the NZBCO and Lawrence Foster, Wellington September 1970.

Left to right: Itzhak Perlman, Arthur Rubinstein and Jacqueline playing trios on New Year's Eve in New York, 31 December 1970. Daniel is turning the pages.

Jacqueline arriving with Daniel at the Royal Festival Hall, where he was conducting the London Philharmonic Orchestra on the day that news of her illness was made public, 6 November 1973.

Jacqueline and Daniel leaving Buckingham Palace on 24 February 1976 after the investiture ceremony in which she received the OBE.

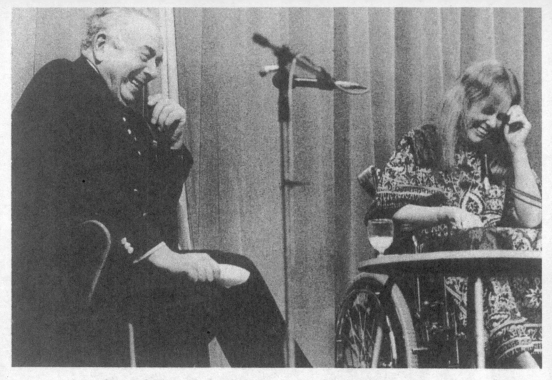

Jacqueline and Harry Blech collapse in giggles while listening to Jackie's choice of record (Victor Borge's Punctuation) at a Haydn-Mozart Society Members' evening.

Jacqueline and Daniel after a rehearsal of Peter and the Wolf, London 1978.

within piano from a muted, vibratoless sul tasto in pianissimo to intense gritty fortes, achieving a range of expression from hushed whispers to anguished cries from the heart. Not that Barenboim has a lesser palette at his disposal; he can equally well recreate on the piano a mass of orchestral sound, sometimes imitating a whole double-bass section (an important factor in this music where the bass line is mostly relegated to the piano's left hand), or conjure up woodwind textures in his voicing. At other times he seems to add a third solo string line to merge with the violin and cello.

It is this central movement that best demonstrates the Barenboim Trio's predilection for slow tempi, intensity and spaciousness. Among the other fine performances of the work by some of the 'great' trios of the past, one could identify at the opposite extreme with the Busch Trio's interpretation of the slow movement of the *Ghost*, which lasts three and a half minutes less than the Barenboim group (9'30" as opposed to 13"). Here Rudolf Serkin's compelling need to drive the music on means that achieving the goal, rather than the process of quest, is the governing force of the performance. This is not to say that one approach is necessarily more valid than the other – in either case the thing that counts is the performers' total dedication to the interpretative concept.

Whereas it is the *Ghost* Trio that perhaps best allows the Barenboim Trio's qualities for the drama of expression, their approach to the E flat Trio of Op.70 No.2 shows another side of their abilities. Here, Beethoven's tonic key does not convey the heroic, triumphant spirit of the *Eroica* Symphony or the Fifth Piano Concerto, but, instead, a quality of intimate philosophical meditation, where the players cast their glance forward to the world of Beethoven's late quartets. This mood of wistful contemplation is already evident in the quiet restraint of the cello's opening phrase in the first movement. The players capture no less the unhurried charm and humour of the allegretto variations, and the elusive Schubertian lyricism of the scherzo, whose reflective spirit transcends the here and now. This juxtaposes admirably with the finale's declamatory character, where du Pré in particular comes into her own, especially in the big heroic cello solo in the recapitulation (starting at bar 312) which she plays with an exhilaration at her own prowess, arriving in triumph on the two dominant B flats before passing the phrase over to the piano.

It was a remarkable thing that when they played together du Pré and Zukerman virtually never marked bowings into their parts. Indeed, on the rare occasions when they did, the bowings tended to be Barenboim's suggestions. Pinky cited a specific instance: 'I remember Daniel saying just as we were about to play the opening of the *Ghost* Trio, "Try starting it up-bow." I think most people would say why – but I said why not? If you have this ability to be flexible it allows you to do anything at any time.' But, as he recalled, 'Sometimes in a performance, Jackie and I would find we had reached the spot with a marked-in bowing and we were both doing the exact opposite – this was totally intuitive, we never discussed or planned it.' Zukerman concedes that it was largely through Jackie's influence that he started to use up-bow more readily than down: 'On a down-bow – when started near the nut of the bow – you can have too hard a weight; whereas the up-bow is a natural departure point, since the sound commences easily at the point of the bow.' In fact, the two players were also quite capable of using different bowings to achieve the same effect, even when this would normally go against conventional thinking. The opening of the second movement of the *Ghost* Trio in the filmed performance is an instance in question – Jackie plays the opening unison motif in down-bow and Pinky in an up.

Zukerman recalls that intonation – another difficult aspect of string playing – held no problems for him and du Pré:

> Jackie had just the right feeling for where the note should be placed: she heard in harmonic and not tempered intonation. When playing with piano, string players should use harmonic intonation to bring out the overtones, which help to give the piano a sustaining power. The pianist helps by voicing the music properly and using the pedal expressively. Daniel, of course, knew all this, but in those days I was fresh to these ideas. It was remarkable, though, because with Daniel and Jackie I never had to think about intonation – it was easy and always worked for us.

Such a natural, apparently unthinking approach might have led one to believe that this was not a trio suited to Beethoven's profoundest concepts. Indeed, as Greenfield noted, 'Playfulness, practical joking, fits of uncontrollable giggles – these are some of the hallmarks of the Barenboim, du Pré and Zukerman team.' But Zukerman observed rightly that such high spirits were only the other side of the coin to the intensity and seriousness of the musical experience. 'There was such an incredible contrast between the euphoric music-making and the rest of our life – there was this whole other personality. I think that most performers have this duality – there was, after all, a childish animal in all of us. An artist can be terribly naïve and childlike, and then have this ability to garner so much profound information into one performance and communicate it to others. And Jackie was the arch leader in this apparent contradiction.'[5]

Greenfield recalled the session after the monumental day's recording on 2 January, where the *Archduke* was completed, the whole of the *Ghost* recorded as well as the charming one-movement trio, the Allegretto in B flat [WoO 39] and the *Kakadu* Variations Op.121:

> I arrived the following morning to find them preparing to hear the playback. After something like seven hours of concentrated recording, could it have been anything but a tired performance of *Kakadu*, I wondered, particularly when reheard in the dispassionate light of the morning after. Not a bit of it. The exhilaration was still unmistakably evident in the long slow introduction which was given really weighty, intense treatment. Then, with Zukerman at his jauntiest, came the perky *Kakadu* theme that Beethoven took from Wenzel Müller's long-forgotten opera, *Die Schwestern von Prag*. I laughed out loud at the sheer effrontery of Zukerman's phrasing. Suspiciously he turned round and asked: 'What are you laughing at?' It hardly seemed convincing to answer that I was musically ticklish, and playing like that always makes me laugh.[6]

There are many such instances where the team's music-making elicits a smile or makes one wish to laugh out loud – an example being the beautiful playing of the cello theme in the C major trio of the minuetto of the C minor Trio, where the piano's rippling descending scales are played with just the right degree of accentuation and delicacy – yet, like a good narrator, Daniel subtly differentiates them each time.

The high spirits observed by Greenfield had indeed been real at the time. Zukerman recalled, 'When we were doing the *Kakadu* Variations, and it came to the violin and cello variation, I remember that Daniel went stomping around the studio – he was actually dancing. After three attempts to record it we had to ask him, "Will you please stop, go and sit down."'

Beethoven's early set of Op.1 trios undoubtedly benefit from the players' youthful exuberance. The music is played with dynamic verve and energy, and also with singing lyricism. Humour is amply evident in the finales of the E flat major and G major Trios, as is the veritable *Sturm und Drang* drama of the C minor Trio – a key which was associated with tragedy in both Mozart's and Beethoven's world. And the beautifully performed largo con espressione movement from the G major Trio has a profound expression, worthy of mature Beethoven at his best. The players also make a wonderful case for the lesser known E flat Variations Op.44, the little E flat Trio and for the two small allegretto movements [WoO39 and Hess 48].

But the team's real achievement lies in their interpretative solutions to the more challenging later trios (the Op.70 Nos 1 and 2 and the Op.97), and these bear comparison with all the 'greats'. The *Archduke*, for instance, was recorded before the war by two of the most famous formations of all time – the Cortot–Thibaud–Casals Trio and the Rubinstein–Heifetz–Feuermann Trio. In fact the Barenboim–Zukerman–du Pré team set down their interpretation on record at a relatively much younger age, but this does not in any way detract from the depth of their musical perception. While their performances remain open to discussion, their statements about these great repertoire pieces are deeply considered and illuminating.

Eleanor Warren, who recorded them on occasion for the BBC, was an ardent fan of the Barenboim–Zukerman–du Pré Trio. She defined their outstanding quality in the concert hall: 'They played as if they were making music for the first time, with a marvellous spontaneity – it seemed unrehearsed, but I mean that as a compliment.'

Certainly the Barenboim Trio's legacy in these Beethoven recordings has stood up remarkably well to the test of time. Jackie's contribution is superb throughout and shows her playing at top form. Indeed, if one were allowed to separate it from the whole, one could say that the cello playing in these recordings is one of du Pré's greatest achievements.

After completing the trio recordings, Beethoven's music remained on the agenda for the rest of the month. For the second time Barenboim performed the cycle of the composer's thirty-two piano sonatas, in five concerts at the Queen Elizabeth Hall in London. No sooner was this marathon over, than he embarked on a Bartók cycle with the Hallé Orchestra in Manchester.

Jackie, in the meantime, spent January playing recitals with Lamar Crowson, in Glasgow, Croydon and Wales, and also gave concerts at The Hague, where she performed the Schumann concerto on 23 and 24 January with the Residentie Orchestra conducted by Willem van Otterloo. At the beginning of February the Barenboim couple returned to North America, where they opened their tour with a Beethoven recital in Toronto's Massey Hall. Jackie gave further recitals with Crowson, and on 18, 20 and 21 February she performed the Haydn C major Concerto with the San Francisco Symphony Orchestra and Seiji Ozawa – Daniel had been the orchestra's soloist the previous week.

On 4 March she played two concertos – the Haydn C major and the Dvořák – in New York's Carnegie Hall with the Philadelphia Orchestra conducted by Eugene Ormandy. Daniel recalled that these were performances that Jackie was particularly happy with, since she felt in total sympathy with Ormandy's musical understanding and warmth, and she adored the superb playing of the orchestra with its 'sumptuous' rich string sound, as she liked to describe it.

In contrast, she never established more than a formal musical rapport with Claudio Abbado, who conducted her four performances of the Saint-Saëns A minor Concerto with the New York Philharmonic at the Lincoln Centre between 5 and 10 March. Nevertheless, their joint appearance was greeted enthusiastically by the critics. Alan Hughes wrote that du Pré and Abbado 'together brought extraordinary vivacity and grace to the interpretation of the Saint-Saëns Cello Concerto in A minor. [...] Miss du Pré scaled her natural strength and dynamism down to the non-heroic sentiments of the music, and Mr Abbado made the reduced orchestra a perfect partner in the solo–ensemble relationship.'[7]

Harriet Johnson wrote ecstatically of du Pré's interpretation. She perceived that the unique quality in her performances lay in her ability to transmit her irrepressible joy in the music, playing as 'if she were conquering a mountain with many peaks'. Johnson concluded: 'With Miss du Pré one cannot speak of technique or gorgeous tone or any single facet of her incredible art. She makes everything culminate in the drama of the music. She is dramatic in gesture, too, as if she couldn't contain her intensity and her love. Everything fits her and her style. Everything adds up to the glory of the music.'[8]

From New York Jackie, flew back to England. On 15 March she participated in a 'special' benefit concert with the Hallé Orchestra, conceived by Barenboim as a means to help the Hallé Concert Society raise funds to refurbish their rehearsal rooms in an old and dilapidated Victorian congregational church. The concert featured Zukerman playing Bruch's First Violin Concerto and Jackie delighted her Manchester fans with another marvellous performance of the Elgar concerto.

Like all great artists, Jackie often got requests to play for charity and she liked to include one or two benefit concerts in her schedule. In addition, she sought to oblige various of her old friends and was sad not to be able to keep a promise to Sybil Eaton to play in aid of rural music schools. One obligation she did fulfil was to Jim Ede, who had recently donated his unique collection of twentieth-century paintings and sculpture to Cambridge University, housed in his home Kettle's Yard.

Having played for Jim Ede in the old days, Jackie had now agreed to give the opening concert of the Kettle's Yard extension. Ede's stated aim 'to foster the arts as one of the most important manifestations of living' may have seemed an ambitious one; yet he succeeded in creating a living ambience at Kettle's Yard, where people could not only visit his home and view his collection, but were encouraged to touch the sculpture or just to sit and contemplate. Undergraduates were even given the opportunity to borrow some of his paintings. To hear music played by first-rate musicians in an intimate setting was the extra dimension needed to realise Ede's concept.

As Diana Rix recalled, the organisation of this one charity concert was far more taxing than arranging a dozen professional engagements; Ede was a compulsive letter writer, and over-anxious about every detail, from the last cup of coffee to the changing facilities. Since the Prince of Wales, the City Fathers and the University authorities were all to be present, the protocol was further complicated. But on 5 May, despite all the previous anxieties, the opening concert took place, with Barenboim and du Pré performing sonatas by Brahms and Franck.

Whereas Jackie spent April playing recitals with Daniel, performing in Birmingham, Windsor, Munich and Stockholm, the month of May was largely devoted to trio performances. In preparation for their complete cycle of Beethoven Piano trios at the Brighton Festival in three concerts at the Dome on 9, 10 and 16 May, the Barenboim–Zukerman–du Pré Trio gave a few 'try-through' concerts earlier in the month. Christopher Nupen vividly recalled hearing one of these performances at the Oxford Town Hall, where they played both the *Ghost* and the *Archduke*. 'It was the first time I had ever heard the *Ghost* and I was absolutely flabbergasted. I did not know the piece before and I remember thinking that it was an even bigger piece than the better-known *Archduke*. Then I heard them perform the *Ghost* again in Brighton and, although to my mind it was wonderful playing, it was

344

not quite so special as the earlier performance – perhaps this was due to objective reasons like the acoustic.'

A few days later Nupen was scheduled to film Segovia, who was already in England and also playing at the Brighton Festival.

For the filming I had booked St John's Smith Square in London for Thursday, 14 May. But Sol Hurok got in the way of the project and forced Segovia to withdraw. Suddenly I found that I had an empty hall on my hands, with all the technicians and lighting men booked. I rang Daniel in Brighton and said, 'Listen, what are you doing on Thursday?' He replied, 'Nothing, as it so happens.' I persuaded the trio to come up. They took the first train from Brighton, recorded the *Ghost* Trio for me in St John's, then took the last train back there at night.

As Nupen recalled, they played the work with the same intensity of communication as they had done in the two previous concerts. 'None of us conceived it as a studio recording. For Jackie, Pinky and Daniel it was going to London to play for Kitty because Segovia had dropped me in a spot of bother. There was a lot of horsing around and fun before the performance started – a bit is shown on the film I made about Zukerman. In fact, from that point of view it was even more carefree and spontaneous than the backstage shots during the filming of the *Trout.*'

In the filmed performance we see playing that is totally dedicated and serious, yet as Nupen has stressed, it retains the characteristic qualities of freedom and intensity which illuminated the trio's concert performances.

Only the day before, Barenboim had been conducting the LPO in Brighton with Arthur Rubinstein as his soloist in Brahms's Second Piano. Ian Hunter remembered the wonderful meal that followed the concert at Wheeler's restaurant on the sea front, where Barenboim and Rubinstein outvied each other in telling stories and jokes late into the night. Needless to say, Daniel's energies were in no way diminished at the filming session. Back in Brighton, the trio finished their cycle and Barenboim conducted the NPO in an all-Beethoven programme with the Choral Fantasy (where Alfred Brendel was the piano soloist) and the Ninth Symphony.

The following month the trio performed more Beethoven concerts in Paris, but the preceding week the Barenboims were in Milan at La Scala on 11, 12 and 13 June with La Filarmonica della Scala in a programme consisting of the Schumann Cello Concerto followed by Bruckner's Seventh Symphony.

In Paris, the Barenboims met up with Zukerman again for two concerts dedicated to Beethoven trios. A recently acquired friend was the Barenboims' new GP in London, Dr Len Selby, who attended their concert on 15 June – the day of Jackie's and Daniel's third wedding anniversary. Dr Selby recalled, 'Just before the concert I visited Marlene Dietrich who was my patient. I said to Marlene, "Why don't you come to the concert?" and I remember her replying that she would have loved to, but that she would have needed forty-eight hours to get her make-up on and get herself ready. It was a beautiful concert and afterwards we went to the flautist Michel Debost's house – there were four flautists there and they made music all through the night.'

As usual, the summer months were dedicated to the festival rounds. The last week of June found Jackie and Daniel in Iceland as guests at Vladimir (Vova) Ashkenazy's newly founded festival in Reykjavík. The Barenboims played a recital which Ashkenazy found very satisfying: 'They made a wonderful combination and I particularly remember their beautiful Brahms E minor Sonata.' It was here that Jackie had her first rehearsal with Vova for a concert they were to play together at the South Bank Festival. He recalled that afterwards Jackie told him, 'Well there won't be any problem, it's as if we've been playing together for years' – the biggest compliment one musician can pay another.

It was in Iceland that the American banker and music lover James (Jim) Wolfensohn and his wife Elaine first met the Barenboims. They had already become friendly with Ashkenazy and through him had got to know many musicians. Wolfensohn was working in London at the time and, in 1969, initiated one of his first acts of patronage to music, through helping the young agents Terry Harrison and Jasper Parrott to set up their own agency after leaving Ibbs and Tillett in the wake of some bitter disagreements.

Jim and Elaine recalled how thrilled they had been by the Barenboims' Beethoven recitals in London and were delighted now to meet them in a relaxed setting. Although Daniel seemed to be the dynamic force at the centre of this close circle of musicians, they perceived that it was actually Jackie, with her integrity and great humanity, who exercised in an undemonstrative way an even greater authority on the group.

Back in London by the beginning of July, Jackie embarked for the first time in her professional career on recitals devoted to the unaccompanied Bach suites – hallowed ground for cellists. Although she often included one Bach suite in a mixed recital with piano, she had not yet summoned up the courage to devote a whole concert to playing unaccompanied music. There is, after all, a totally different concentration in playing a string instrument solo; and for the audience, too, the intimate experience of listening to a single voice implies a different type of involvement.

It was Sir Ian Hunter who had invited Jackie to give the opening concert of the City of London Festival at the Church of the Holy Sepulchre in Holborn with a programme of three unaccompanied Bach suites. The previous day, 5 July, Jackie tried out her programme at the Cathedral of Bury St Edmunds. She performed the First, Second and Fifth Suites, but rather than play them in chronological order, she chose to separate the two minor-keyed suites with the luminous G major. The concert was part of the Bury St Edmunds Festival, run that year by the Marchioness of Bristol; proceeds from the concert were given to the Malcolm Sargent Cancer Fund for Children. I recall meeting Jackie late that evening at her flat in Upper Montagu Street after her return from Bury. Although she was obviously tired, she entertained us with imitations of the Church dignitary who had accompanied her in the car and a hilarious description of the somewhat stuffy dinner afterwards.

Obviously, she had recovered her strength by the next day, since her concert at the Church of the Holy Sepulchre is recalled by those who attended it as a remarkable occasion. Jackie's special ability to communicate was self-evident in the more extrovert works of the romantic repertoire, but she also knew how to draw her listeners into the intensely private world of solo Bach. As Sir Ian Hunter pointed out, 'Of course, she had a wonderful tone and a very special sound. Although you cannot compare a singer to a string player, Jackie had the sort of quality of sound that Kathleen Ferrier had in her voice, which touched you in a special way.'[9]

Following what was becoming an annual tradition, the Barenboims spent the rest of July in Israel, where together they performed the Beethoven Cello Sonatas and Variations at the festival. Here the couple always hoped to combine work with rest. Certainly Daniel (whose schedule was always far busier than Jackie's) enjoyed the hot Mediterranean sunshine, whereas Jackie complained that the heat affected both her cello and her fair skin adversely. But she was always much moved by the beauty of the country and of the city of Jerusalem in particular.

Back in London by the end of July, the Barenboims prepared for the third South Bank Festival. At the opening press conference Barenboim announced that he was to retire from his position of Artistic Director. Having launched the festival into the world, he was happy to let others continue, while he himself gained some time to pursue his many other interests, notably opera. (He was to make his début as an opera conductor at the 1972 Edinburgh Festival.)

The opening concert on Sunday, 2 August at the Royal Festival Hall featured the Barenboim–Zukerman–du Pré Trio playing Beethoven's two best-known trios – the *Ghost* and the *Archduke*. Max Harrison of *The Times* admonished the musicians for pulling the music in contrary directions. It would seem that the trio 'had not given time to developing a common view of the pieces. Accomplishment on one's own instrument is a beginning not an end ... one could not help feeling that we were being offered adept run-throughs instead of the fruit of long and loving consideration which music of this stature demands.'

Quin Ballardie of the ECO, who heard all the trio's performances at the South Bank, interpreted this quality of extemporary music-making differently:

> Pinky, Jackie and Danny were a true chamber music trio, so spontaneous and yet such equal partners. They appeared to play without ever rehearsing, but when they performed it was explosive. I have never heard any other group of players who had such communication with an audience. You could hear a pin drop before they started, they created such atmosphere just as they walked on stage. The style of playing that they epitomised doesn't exist any more; nowadays a cooler intellectual playing is in fashion. But it doesn't mean that their playing was superficial or without thought; it was very moving in its passionate outpouring.[10]

Two days later, at the Queen Elizabeth Hall, Jackie participated in an all-Bach programme, playing four transcribed duets from the *Clavierübung* with Zukerman and the D major Gamba Sonata with the harpsichordist Rafael Puyana. This latter item, according to the critic Stephen Walsh, was the highlight of the evening: 'Miss du Pré gave a bold sweeping performance, marvellously controlled, and her playing seemed to add a dimension to her partner's, which suddenly took on new vitality and involvement.'[11]

The following Sunday, again at the Festival Hall, the trio performed Beethoven's Triple Concerto with Zubin Mehta conducting the ECO. On 12 August, back in the smaller hall, Barenboim made a concession to public demand by programming twice in the same evening a chamber concert with the participation of Dietrich Fischer-Dieskau. Here the trio was in action accompanying the singer in Beethoven's arrangements of Scottish and Irish songs (five from the Op.108 set and three from Op.255 and Op.233). The rest of the programme consisted of Beethoven's Trio in E flat major (Op.70 No.2), and four Webern songs. Christopher Nupen passionately wanted to film the concert, but Fischer-Dieskau vetoed the presence of cameras in the hall. Nupen bitterly regretted that he was unable at least to film the Beethoven folk songs, since the performance (as he had foreseen) had such calibre and spirit that a film of it would have rivalled the success of the *Trout*. Fischer-Dieskau's musical intensity and the force of his communication found an instant response in Zukerman, du Pré and Barenboim. As Nupen understood the matter, the singer's refusal was proof that even the greatest artists can suffer from nerves; in addition Fischer-Dieskau's need to concentrate on the performance without distractions was also a sign of his humility as an interpreter.[12]

Two days later, on 14 August, Jackie gave a duo recital with Vladimir Ashkenazy. They had rehearsed their programme of sonatas by Beethoven, Shostakovich and Franck six weeks earlier in Iceland. As Vova recalled, 'At the concert, everything went very well, although I remember that both Daniel and his father Enrique came backstage to tell me that I played too loudly in the Beethoven F major (Op.5 No.1). But thereafter everything went fine as I toned down the sound somewhat for the Shostakovich and the Franck. It was, alas, the only concert we played together and it was a fantastic experience for me.'[13]

For Stephen Walsh, the Franck sonata was the highlight of the evening. 'Miss du Pré, always a marvellous player of French music, brought to the sonata an intensity and warmth of line which few violinists could expect to equal, and with Ashkenazy also in superlative form, it was comfortably the most enjoyable performance in the recital.'

The critic was less generous when it came to their playing of Beethoven: 'Miss du Pré, who sets a lot of store by linear tension and not so much by sheer intellectual stamina, was guilty of some messy over-phrasing. . . . Ashkenazy's masculine strongly drawn playing dominated the music excessively.' After finding much to praise in their rendering of the Shostakovich sonata, Walsh concluded that 'a feature of these performances was the rapport between two players whose temperaments one would have thought rather contrasted'.[14]

Certainly Ashkenazy and du Pré were matched in their total dedication to their art. As Vova recalled, 'Jackie was so absolutely true to music, she was absolutely sincere in a way that is very rare. There was nothing contrived or done for show in her playing.' In fact, at least one more concert was scheduled for the du Pré–Ashkenazy partnership at Hunter College, New York in the autumn of 1973, where they were to have played the Rachmaninov sonata, in anticipation of a fixture to record the work for Decca in June 1974.

The final concert of the South Bank Festival on 15 August was given by the Guarneri Quartet, who were joined by Pinky and Jackie in a performance of Tchaikovsky's sextet, *Le Souvenir de Florence*. Max Harrison in *The Times* described the work as 'the composer's most completely satisfying chamber work, not least in its highly skilled use of the medium. For the extra strings have a proper role and never merely thicken a basically quartet-styled texture.' He deemed this performance as 'splendid', while being more critical of the Guarneri Quartet's offerings in the first half.[15]

This year Jackie opted not to participate in any of the North American festivals; whereas Daniel wanted to fulfil his commitment to the Philadelphia Orchestra and made a flying visit to the Saratoga Springs Summer Festival. Recently Jackie had again started to feel unaccountably weary – something beyond the tiredness caused by travel and a demanding concert schedule. To make matters worse, she was often plagued by insomnia and was unable to recuperate energy through sleeping. The glamour of being a star was wearing thin and the music-making which she so enjoyed was becoming an increasing physical effort. Hence, with a few free days on her hands, rather than accompany Daniel as she might have done in the past, Jackie decided to take a short holiday with her sister Hilary's family in their mountain home in France. She was always particularly happy to see her three small nieces and nephew, and to enjoy the relaxed family atmosphere and the simple pleasures of rural French cooking and the unspoilt countryside.

By the end of August she was back with Daniel at the Edinburgh Festival to give two recitals of the complete Beethoven works for cello and piano on 25 and 26 August. Fortunately, these concerts were recorded by the BBC. When Jackie's illness put paid to plans to record the Beethoven cycle in the studio, EMI acquired the rights from the BBC and issued these performances on record, allowing us to have du Pré's interpretations on these key repertoire pieces.

Eleanor Warren was the BBC's producer at the concerts and recalled that at the time she was worried by some moments of exaggeration in Jackie's playing. Eleanor, who had an immense admiration for Daniel's genuine musicianship, said: 'When we were recording, Daniel advised me not to tell Jackie that something might be better done another way. "Leave it," he would say, "she must do things her own way. You can tell me afterwards if anything needs changing." He felt that the whole genius of her talent lay in her spontaneity. While he was able to influence her, he realised that it was better not to interfere. As he pointed out, she would do it differently the next time anyway.'

Now, as Jackie became increasingly worn down by fatigue she needed to muster all her physical and mental resources to play in public, and she tended to find advice and suggestions upsetting. Daniel recognised the aspect of rebelliousness in her. If anybody suggested she should tone down a 'mannerism' she was more likely to re-introduce it emphatically at the concert performance with a note of triumphant glee. Suvi Grubb recalled that at one of the Edinburgh concerts this is exactly what happened.

Indeed, those who attended the Edinburgh Beethoven recitals remembered that the intimate rapport between the players was so intense that they seemed to be enjoying a series of 'in-jokes', sometimes making the audience feel like eavesdroppers on a private discourse. Yet, as Gerald Moore remarked, Jackie's performances were completely without artifice: 'Jackie was simply obsessed by the music and flung herself into it with utter lack of self-consciousness. I nearly wrote "fierce concentration", but I have seen her and Daniel Barenboim at public performances exchange smiles or ecstatic glances during the course of some inspired dialogue between cello and piano.'[16]

Peter Diamand, Director of the Edinburgh Festival at the time, retains clear memories of Jackie's concerts with Daniel. 'I had heard her play with other pianists and conductors and I was amazed by how much her playing changed and was influenced when performing with Daniel. That reflected well on both of them.' The critics often argued about the validity of some of the things that Jackie did in performance, defining them as mannerisms or even a misunderstanding of the musical text. But Diamand felt their judgements were out of place.

She belonged to those artists of whom a professional musician, qualified to judge in these matters, might say that lots of the things she did were wrong. But in her hands they sounded completely right. I had the same reactions to de Sabata's conducting and to Slava Rostropovich's playing. To copy them exactly would sound dreadful. The rights or wrongs of performances by such artists are totally irrelevant, because they are unique musicians who possess such an overwhelming conviction. I found the spontaneity of Jackie's playing was immensely impressive. Put together with Daniel's qualities, their duo was quite extraordinary in the dialogue and the marvellous aspect of giving and taking.[17]

Among the many musicians who would have endorsed Diamand's views was the cellist Joan Dickson, who had known Jackie's playing since she was sixteen. Joan never doubted Daniel's beneficial influence on Jackie as a musician. But as Diamand observed, du Pré's and Barenboim's approach to music-making was not to everybody's taste. David Harper, writing in the *Scotsman* (28 August), found that du Pré tended to force the tone and applied more weight to the bow than the string could support. The following day Conrad Wilson, in the same paper, was almost dismissive of the duo's interpretations, calling them 'sound, decent, sensitive but uncompelling'. While he found du Pré's playing 'firmer, more relaxed and less self-indulgent' than her partner's, the overall impressions of their music-making remained superficial. There was, he complained, little sign of the 'spontaneous combustion' and fervour that made their Leith Town Hall recital in the 1968 festival so exciting.

In fact, as one can tell from listening to the du Pré–Barenboim recordings, these Beethoven concerts from the 1970 Edinburgh Festival display different approaches in operation within the cycle. Some of their interpretations seem to strive for an idealised conception, while others give the impression of being shaped in the heat of the moment. This spontaneity is particularly evident in their account of the G minor Sonata (Op.5 No.2) and especially in their highly characterised account of the rondo finale.

This movement lends itself to many different opinions just in regard to its basic speed. Certain players invest the 2/4 allegro with such brilliance as to turn it effectively into a one-in-the-bar presto; one of the fastest performances on record is that of Mischa Maisky and Martha Argerich, whose reading almost seems a caricature version of the already very fast account of Rostropovich and Richter. Du Pré and Barenboim approach the music from the other extreme, and their interpretation has far more in common with that of Pablo Casals, especially in his recording with Rudolf Serkin taken from a live concert at the 1951 Casals Festival in Perpignan. Considering that Casals was nearly seventy-five years old at the time, it is not surprising that his rendering is more reflective and lacks the youthful vigour of the du Pré–Barenboim team. But the younger musicians share with him the same approach to articulation and phrasing. Whereas Maisky–Argerich play the finale of the G minor in 7'33", Casals–Serkin stretch their version to 10'22". Du Pré and Barenboim play it in a moderate and spacious 9'19", imbuing the music with a mixture of sardonic humour, graceful flourishes and elements of a stomping rusticity. They succeed in making the music sound both fast and relaxed, and maintain the two-in-a-bar feeling through the clarity of the articulation and by giving enough weight to the smaller notes.

Jackie did not have fixed views on tempo; certainly on some occasions she herself played this movement faster – but then that was in response to different subjective factors and, more important, to a different kind of piano playing.

In the case of the most popular A major Cello Sonata, we are lucky to have two versions of Barenboim's and du Pré's interpretation – a studio performance filmed for Granada Television (directed in 1969 by Nupen) and the Edinburgh Festival concert performance. While their basic approach is similar in the two recorded performances, the most notable differences involved the tempi, which in the concert hall tended to be slower. In live performance, for instance, du Pré and Barenboim offered a more deliberate and reflective characterisation of the scherzo, although, strangely enough it is the studio performance that seems to have greater *élan* throughout. In general, du Pré's qualities are much suited to this work, where the lyrical first movement and the short adagio introduction to the finale are played with a touching beauty. But she can equally well be heroic or humorous, wistful or dramatic.

In the first movement the duo eschew the exposition repeat, whereas in the D major Sonata (Op.102 No.2) they always observed it. As Barenboim explains,

I have no scholastic feeling about whether it is necessary to do repeats. Each case has to be judged on its own merits; for me the key lies in the build-up and proportions of the music. I have to ask if by repeating I can create a new dimension either for the exposition or the development. Unless I find this reason I don't do the repeat. In the opening of the Beethoven A major Cello Sonata, the stopping and restarting and the fermatos give a surge to the impetus of the music. Therefore, to come back to the surge only serves to lower the psychological temperature of the music – you lose the tension and also the element of surprise. Indeed in the recapitulation Beethoven extends the idea, rather than repeating it exactly. In the finale, however, the repeat is essential for the build-up of the movement.

In the televised recording Barenboim explained something of his attitude to the A major Sonata in a spoken introduction. Beethoven's inscription on the presentation copy of the score '*Inter lacrima et luctus*', created much speculation about the content of the work and the biographical circumstances behind its creation. But, as Daniel pointed out, there is little evidence of tears and sorrow in this sonata, one of Beethoven's most confident and radiant middle-period pieces. 'Beethoven's genius penetrated to the depths of human existence ... He would have written tragic music even if he himself had not had to endure such sufferings and he wrote his happiest music because he understood human aspirations.' Certainly, in the A major Sonata du Pré and Barenboim capture something of the spirit of Arcadian joy which permeates the *Pastoral* Symphony, the work's direct predecessor.

In the Edinburgh Festival concert recordings, Du Pré and Barenboim perhaps succeed less well in their presentation of the last two sonatas (Op.102 Nos 1 and 2), where the tension in the fast movements has a tendency to slacken. But they penetrate to the heart of the matter in the slower movements and particularly in the great adagio con molto sentimento d'affetto of the D major Sonata, where they seem to stretch the expressive meaning of the music to its limits, following its evolution from fervent contemplative prayer, through transfigured recollection, to the abyss of despair.

As for the lighter-weight sets of variations, du Pré and Barenboim make persuasive champions of this music in their capacity for humorous conversational exchange and their ability to contain the expression to suit the conventions of variation form. While each individual variation is beautifully characterised, they find a satisfying solution to the tempo inter-relationships within the whole.

Sonically, these Beethoven recordings from the Edinburgh Festival performances are far from being perfect; this, then, is the minus side of a concert performance, together with the audience's contribution of coughs and splutters. In recompense, there is a tangible sense of the music being recreated in the heat of the moment, where the performers display a freedom that is usually absent in the studio.

It is a terrible shame that du Pré was deprived of the opportunity of recording works which she knew so intimately in studio conditions. But we must be grateful for these recorded concert performances, since they make one understand what it was that got the critics arguing about du Pré's interpretations.

24

Playing Against The Odds

> Since a musician cannot move unless he is moved, he must be
> able to project himself into all the emotions which he wants to
> arouse in the listeners: he makes them understand his passions
> and moves them thereby most fully to compassion.
>
> Carl Philipp Emanuel Bach

The Barenboims set out for Australia directly after their Edinburgh concerts, arriving on 1 September. Despite the long and tiring journey the couple were expected to appear at a press conference that very same day. The Australian Broadcasting Commission who hosted the tour had scheduled fourteen concerts for Barenboim and four for du Pré in the space of four weeks. The principal offering was once again Beethoven – Daniel played the complete piano sonata cycle, as well as the five concertos, while together they performed all the cello sonatas and variations; these cycles were divided between the two cities of Sydney and Melbourne, and were broadcast directly from concert.

Jackie's two orchestral performances (both under Daniel's direction) were also divided between the two cities. The critic Eva Wagner waxed lyrical over the accomplishments of both players and described Barenboim as 'brimming over with the joys of life and of being able to make music, which for him seems to amount to the same thing'.

Du Pré's performance of the Elgar concerto in Sydney on 15 September was praised for its musical integrity: 'Theirs is an essentially young, uninhibited, almost wild approach, entirely honest and therefore arguably right. ... To me [their] concerts were an exhilarating experience, one that made me feel that the world is not such a bad place to live in. And this, I think, is the fundamental purpose of music.'[1] While Daniel continued with his cycle of Beethoven piano sonatas in Sydney, Jackie flew to New Zealand, where she performed two concertos on 19 September in Wellington with the NZBC SO conducted by Lawrence (Larry) Foster. The orchestral musicians' impression of du Pré's performance was so intense that it is still remembered after thirty years as one of the highlights of New Zealand's musical life – indeed, one of the orchestra's cellists even named his daughter after her. Another of the musicians, John Gray, recalled, 'She strode on with this cello and simply tore into the Haydn Cello Concerto in C [...] She came back after the interval and threw herself into the big Dvořák concerto. It was a big emotional occasion...'[2]

Even if its standards were well below those of the first-class American and European orchestras with which Jackie was now used to playing, the NZBC Orchestra rose to the occasion, inspired by her music-making, as well as by Foster's excellent and 'fiery' direction. As Larry observed, Jackie was always a helpful colleague, as long as she had the necessary support: 'The one thing she could not abide was indifference in a conductor and in an orchestra. She could forgive a lot if she saw you cared and were trying.'

Their performance of the Dvořák has been preserved on a radio tape and shows Jackie to be on very top form. As the concerto unfolds, so does the orchestra's confidence, and Foster injects the right kind of enthusiasm and structured direction into the performance. It is interesting to observe how Jackie adapted to the limitations in the orchestral playing where, for instance, problems in spinning out the big woodwind solos or sustaining a full string sound made her adopt slightly faster tempi and keep the music moving.

The day after the concert Jackie flew back to join Daniel and they spent the rest of September in Melbourne. During some of her free days there, Jackie was entertained by the writer Judah Waten and his wife (parents of her 'Moscow' violinist friend Alice). They found her more subdued than in the past, but always ready to respond with humour to the vicissitudes of the concert artist's life. Jackie played two concerts in Melbourne: on 23 September she performed Dvořák's concerto with the Melbourne Symphony Orchestra under Barenboim's direction, and just prior to their departure the couple gave their second Beethoven recital.

Back in London on 1 October, Jackie enjoyed a three-week respite from playing, but was kept busy with domestic concerns. She and Daniel had recently purchased a small detached house in a quiet road in Hampstead within walking distance of the shops and of the Heath – two things that made it attractive to Jackie. They were now in the process of having the house redecorated and altered; the garage was to be converted into a sound-proofed studio, where they hoped to make music at will without disturbing their neighbours. Effectively, the Barenboims would only start living in their new home in Pilgrim's Lane at the end of January, when they had planned a three-month sabbatical, their first real break from concert life in four and a half years. The rest would provide a much-needed opportunity to take stock, a chance to take a real holiday and also to study music without the pressures of performances.

At the end of October Jackie started her North American autumn season in Toronto, with two performances of the Schumann concerto conducted by Karel Ančerl on 27 and 28 October. The critic John Kraglund praised both du Pré's and Ančerl's inspired music-making, but conceded that 'for sheer musicality and ability to command the listener's attention, it was Schumann and Miss du Pré who took top honours'. He summed up her achievement as 'great cello playing by one of today's leading cellists'.[3]

Jackie proceeded to New York for two performances with Zubin Mehta and the Los Angeles Philharmonic at Carnegie Hall. On 30 October she played the Schumann concerto and on the 31st, together with Barenboim and Zukerman, gave a performance of Beethoven's Triple Concerto.

The following day the trio (without Mehta) moved on to the mid-West, where Barenboim was booked for two weeks to guest-conduct the Chicago Symphony Orchestra. Their first five concerts were given 'out of town', at Michigan State University, East Lansing, where a small Beethoven bicentennial festival had been organised around the Barenboims, Zukerman and the Chicago Symphony. The music of the festival was not confined to Beethoven.

In the opening recital concert on 2 November, given by Jackie and Daniel, the first half was devoted to two Beethoven sonatas (in F and C); after the interval they performed Brahms's E minor Sonata and Dvořák's *Waldesruhe* Op.68 and the Rondo Op.94, the latter pieces as a try-out for their Dvořák recording scheduled for the following week.

Three days later, Daniel conducted Jackie in a performance of the Dvořák concerto with the Chicago Symphony Orchestra. It was the auspicious occasion of Barenboim's conducting début with the orchestra and he won his spurs with the contribution in the second half of the programme of Beethoven's *Eroica* Symphony, a piece which is a hard test of any conductor's skills and musicianship. The reviews concentrated on what was immediately perceived to be a special rapport between the Chicago Symphony and Barenboim. Bernard Jacobson, writing in the *Chicago Daily News*, prophesied that the twenty-eight-year-old Barenboim 'will one day be spoken of in the terms we now reserve for conductors like Weingartner, Nikisch and Furtwängler. It is that kind of talent, and it is already ripe.' He concluded that 'there are no bounds to this extraordinary artist's gifts. Everything he does is interesting [...] and he has made music I know by heart come alive again for me with the intensity of first acquaintance.'[4] Jacobson was certainly not mistaken when he claimed that 'Barenboim's performances will go down in Chicago's musical annals'; this special rapport had its logical conclusion when Daniel succeeded Sir Georg Solti as Music Director of the Chicago Symphony Orchestra in 1991.

Although he devoted less space to her performances, Jacobson noted that 'Jacqueline du Pré had much more assurance and security than on the occasion of her Orchestra Hall appearance last season' when she had played the same concerto with Solti. Jackie's performances were also acclaimed elsewhere in the press; the *Lansing State Journal* of 11 November wrote that 'Miss du Pré must be heard and seen to be believed. Her beautiful playing of the Dvořák concerto enthralled a capacity audience.' The critic urged those who had missed the concert to hurry to acquire tickets for the repeat performance in Chicago.

In the final concert of the series in East Lansing on 6 November Jackie played the Saint-Saëns A minor Concerto with Daniel. One of the reviewers described Barenboim as 'a conductor with few equals', but emphasised, 'It was Miss du Pré that stole the audience's hearts with her unique rendering of the Saint-Saëns concerto. . . . While she played she seemed to go into a trance . . . she broke the spell only twice to watch her husband for a cue, and smile triumphantly at the concertmaster.'[5]

While Jackie captivated her listeners with her heartfelt performances, few people can have suspected how much effort every concert cost her. Kate Beare, a cellist and the former wife of Charles Beare, recalled: 'Before Jackie knew what was wrong with her, I remember her telling me, "Nobody will believe me when I say how difficult I find it to play the cello."' Kate, who herself contracted multiple sclerosis in the early 1980s, explained, 'The fatigue you suffer with MS is bewildering. Yet it is impossible to communicate your feeling of weakness to others, who see nothing on the surface. Because Jackie did manage to play the cello, and wonderfully at that, it was difficult to comprehend that there might be some kind of problem.'[6]

Daniel was undoubtedly aware that something was not right, and was concerned about Jackie's frequent complaints of exhaustion and of cold, sometimes numb hands during their autumn tour of North America. He remembered: 'When Jackie picked up something, she had no idea of its weight, whether it was fifty grams or five kilos.' Undoubtedly, this strange lack of sensation would have been disturbing at any time, but in playing the cello it would have acted as a massive handicap, since the weight of the bow on the string is one of the main factors in creating the expression of sound.

Zukerman recalls the tumultuous pace of their activities: 'Usually we would arrive at the concert hall and just go out and play, there was no time to warm up.' Jackie normally had never needed to practise, but now she was finding it impossible to operate in these conditions. She had to get to a hall several hours early, armed with gloves, and play for a long time so as to heat her hands sufficiently to perform. As Zukerman observed, it was not a question of her being nervous about the music, since her warm-up practice often only consisted in playing the little tunes her mother had written for her as a child. He recalled that

> Jackie had no feeling of time in the normal way. She had an inner clock that told her what she had to do. It was interrupted only when she had to go on-stage, and sometimes this inner clock wasn't ready. 'Why go on-stage now?' she might ask. In such cases, she seemed always to be disturbed and she often got very nervous. There was a kind of reluctance in her body. But I'll never forget walking on-stage behind her – the minute she stepped out on the stage and the lights were on her she was propelled forward. She always walked very erect, very outwardly full of energy. She had a sense of concentration that was very unusual, this extraordinary magnetic quality which one associates with the greatest actors.'[7]

Charles Wadsworth, who was in East Lansing to give a duo recital with Zukerman, noticed that Jackie wasn't herself: 'After the concerts Pinky and Danny wanted to "party", but Jackie always seemed very tired and asked to be taken back to the hotel.' For Daniel and their friends all this was perplexing. People remembered him musing out loud: 'I don't understand it, my mother is more than twice Jackie's age, but has far more energy than her.' The Jackie whom Daniel had first met and known, full of energy, joy and seemingly always smiling, was undergoing a character change.

Although her schedule was far less demanding than Barenboim's, after concerts she just wanted to collapse in bed, whereas Daniel needed to go out with friends to eat and 'unwind'. In the last months she had come to resent him as the figure responsible for imposing on her a programme of travelling, playing and socialising, which she could barely cope with. As Daniel recalled, Jackie was no longer enjoying this lifestyle, but did not know what she wanted instead. The couple felt increasingly helpless in this situation, from which it was difficult to exclude feelings of resentment and guilt, and for which there seemed no obvious solution.

To compound her anxiety about her own physical condition, Jackie received worrying news from home about her father's health. What appeared to be an attack of jaundice soon needed further investigation; liver cancer was suspected and Derek was hospitalised in mid-December and a biopsy was performed. Much as Jackie would have liked to pack her bags and be near her parents, she had to wait until her professional commitments were fulfilled. She kept in touch with her family regularly by phone and suggested that her own doctor, Len Selby, should examine and treat her father.

Jackie's intense schedule in early November was in part geared to help her prepare for the recording of the Dvořák concerto. Her second performance of the work on 7 November in Chicago's Orchestra Hall, outside the normal subscription series, served as an extra rehearsal, as well as being a highly publicised event. Daniel in the meantime was also busy rehearsing the programme for the following week's subscription concerts, where Zukerman was to make his solo début with the orchestra.

EMI–Angel had booked Medinah Temple, a large, resonant Victorian-style hall, for two sessions on 11 November. To Jackie's great regret, Suvi Grubb was unable to produce the recording because of ill health and Peter Andry came out from London in his place. Daniel recalled that from the start there were problems in getting the correct balance between the solo cello and orchestra – the cello sounded either too far back, or too far forward. The sound of a recording is not only dependent on the acoustic of the hall, but to a certain extent is created artificially by the placing of the microphones and manipulation of balance. Photographs show the unusual positioning adopted for the concerto recording, where the solo cello was actually placed on a podium behind the conductor facing the orchestra. But in this particular recording it was Jackie who insisted that the cello be miked up. Undoubtedly she did not want to compromise her concept of the grand scale of this concerto, almost a symphony in its own right. Her request to bring forward the cello sound implied an unstated admission that now she lacked sufficient sonority to ride over the sumptuously sustained sound of the Chicago Symphony Orchestra.

Despite its wealth of colour and beautiful solo woodwind writing, Dvořák's orchestration in the B minor Cello Concerto sometimes lacks transparency, making it difficult for the solo cello voice to cut through the thicker textures. Nevertheless, in the Chicago recording, from the very first *quasi improvisando* cello entry, Jackie plays with enormous force and density of sound, pitting herself as the sole combatant against the symphonic forces. She is appropriately resolute rather than wilful in this improvisatory opening, which she was often known to attack on a sweeping up-bow so as to achieve the maximum weight at the heel of the bow for the rhetorical semiquavers. In her desire to emphasise the declamatory aspect of the dialogue Jackie strove for nobility of sound and sought to stretch out the phrases to the maximum.

It is evident from the subsequent correspondence between Robert Myers, General Manager of Angel Records, and Peter Andry that the editing of the tapes of the Dvořák concerto caused considerable problems. (Naturally we are speaking about the pre-digital era, when tapes were still physically cut and glued together.) Myers complained that some takes were recorded at different levels of sound because monitoring levels were changed during recording. He also pointed out that the takes began exactly at an indicated spot, not a few bars earlier as is usual, making it virtually impossible to achieve good joins. Furthermore, he criticised Barenboim's tempi, 'which varied considerably from take to take'.[8] Andry's reply showed that he had also been aware of these problems. In regard to the slow tempi he wrote, 'I pointed this out many times to Barenboim in the sessions, but he said that he would stand by his performance and his wife's.' Andry disclaimed responsibility for the recording levels – this lay with the engineering department, although he admitted that he had to change the monitoring level from 'the unbearable to the just bearable'. The letter ends on a somewhat sad note: 'Clearly what we need is a good producer, as, obviously, I am no longer up to the job!'[9] It was, in fact, to be Andry's last sortie into the studios in his capacity as sound producer.

Whatever the problems of balance may have been, one cannot judge the matter of tempo as an independent component of music, since it is so closely allied to the emotional expression. Certainly, the somewhat leisurely speeds taken in this recorded performance with Barenboim achieve a feeling of spaciousness, giving ample scope to the luxuriant resonance of the Chicago Symphony Orchestra in the big tuttis. Du Pré's response to Dvořák's music has undoubtedly matured and gains from an element of restraint, reflecting the nobility of an older man's world of recollected emotion, rather than the striving of youthful passions. The flamboyant spate of emotion that distinguishes her earlier performances (notably her 1967 interpretation with Celibidache) is replaced by an expression of intense vulnerability, even in the most highly charged episodes. Few cellists can ever have attained such tenderness and beauty in the first hearing of the heartachingly soulful second subject, where Jackie was careful to observe the composer's indication of pianissimo. The element of nostalgic recollection and the pain of lost happiness are never far from mind and serve to heighten the expressive power of her music-making.

The filler for the LP was originally to have consisted of two Dvořák pieces – the *Waldesruhe* and the Rondo. Barenboim recalled that although they recorded the former quite quickly, they ran out of time for the Rondo. 'Jackie was not particularly keen to record it since she felt ill at ease with the piece. As it was, there was more than enough music to fill the record without it.' Yet it would have been marvellous to have had du Pré's interpretation of this characteristic piece, so close to the world of the popular *Slavonic Dances*, with its wistful G minor theme contrasting with the carefree episodes based on folk modes and rhythms. However, we are fortunate that Jackie's gloriously expressive view of *Waldesruhe* is preserved. It was a piece which she saved from unjust neglect and her recording of it became one of her personal favourites.

While Daniel went on to do a fortnight's guest-conducting in Philadelphia, Jackie travelled to Minneapolis, where she performed the Lalo concerto on 19 and 20 November, accompanied by Stanislaw Skrowaczewski and the Minnesota Symphony Orchestra. It was the first time she had played this work since her early teens and its re-introduction into her concert repertoire heralded plans for a recording in the not too distant future.

On 21 November Jackie joined Daniel in Philadelphia. She was scheduled to play four concerts with the orchestra under his direction performing the Elgar concerto. The first two concerts on 27 and 28 November would be recorded by CBS, fulfilling the exchange part of the deal for Zukerman's release to record the Beethoven trios for EMI. Despite the enormous success of du Pré's Elgar recording with Barbirolli, it was felt that there was room on the market for another interpretation from her. Undoubtedly, Jackie had developed new insights into the piece over the last four years, especially in her many performances with Daniel, and a recording taken from a live concert would benefit from the direct impact of approach.

On the morning of 27 November the violin-maker Sergio Peresson arrived at the Elgar concerto rehearsal bearing a gift for Jackie – a new cello he had just completed. Jackie was so impressed by the speaking quality of the instrument and its easy response that she decided there and then to use it for that night's concert.

The story had its genesis the previous August, when Barenboim met Peresson almost by chance. As Daniel recalled:

> I was giving concerts at Saratoga Springs Festival with the Philadelphia Orchestra. One day Zubin Mehta told me that, as he wanted to acquire some instruments for the Israel Philharmonic, he had arranged to see Sergio Peresson in Philadelphia. I went along with him and the violinist Ivry Gitlis. Peresson, a very charming man, told me that it was his dream to make a cello for Jackie. I said, 'Well, she's coming in November, so you'll be able to talk to her then.' The next thing I knew he had turned up at our rehearsal with the new cello already completed.

Mehta, in turn, had heard of Peresson's name through Zukerman, who had acquired an instrument from him in the spring of 1969. Charles Beare recalls that Pinky absolutely adored the instrument. 'But I was somewhat sceptical when he showed it to me in London, knowing that many new instruments have a large open sound when they are first played, but thereafter do not develop any further. I said to Pinky, "Let's see if you still like it by Christmas." ' Beare was right in his prediction that Zukerman's love affair with his new violin would not last. But Jackie's allegiance to her new instrument was unswerving; she never wanted to play her precious old Italian cellos again.

While acknowledging that Peresson's instruments were beautifully crafted, Zukerman attributed part of the reason for Jackie's enthusiasm for the new cello to her physical condition. 'The Peresson was easy to play. Jackie was probably already in pain, because in her last performing years she had no power in her arms. One was beginning to see the effect in her playing – for instance in the left hand, it was sometimes difficult for her to get up into the higher positions – her arms wouldn't co-operate to do the large shifts.'

Daniel confirmed that Jackie needed less effort to play the new cello. 'The Peresson had a more open, more penetrating sound and it was easier to balance in the big moments of the Dvořák concerto – much more so than with the Strads or Gofriller. Jackie was still playing the Gofriller for the Chicago recording of the Dvořák and she found it hard work to produce the sound she wanted.' In fact, as Barenboim points out, 'Jackie had her own idiosyncratic sound which was not dependent on the instrument she played. I remember that within a few weeks of the Philadelphia recording, she played the Elgar again with me and the Berlin Philharmonic. Ottomar Borowitzky, one of the two solo cellists of the orchestra, had the evening off and went to listen to the performance in the hall. Afterwards he came back saying he had never heard the Davydov sound so good – he did not realise that she was playing a brand-new cello.'

Not everybody felt that Jackie's new instrument could do justice to her enormous range of shade and colour. Certainly Charles Beare could never understand her preference for the more direct, superficial sound of the Peresson. Yet as Daniel recalled, many other string players did like the instrument, among them Piatigorsky. 'When he came to London he loved to play on it. Even though he owned two Strad cellos (one of them the renowned Bata), Piatigorsky held it was very important that people should play on modern instruments, otherwise the making of them would stop.' In recent years Barenboim has lent out the cello and is convinced it has retained its excellent sound qualities.

The gift of the new instrument came at just the right time and gave Jackie a new burst of energy to help her through the next month of concerts. She felt elated to be able to produce the sound she wanted so much more easily with the new cello, and anybody who listens to the Philadelphia recording of the Elgar will remain impressed by the spectrum of colours and the sheer volume of sound she produced with it.

It is also true that Elgar's Cello Concerto poses lesser problems than the Dvořák in terms of balance, because of the exemplary economy of the orchestration. The beauties in Elgar's score are perhaps less conspicuous than in Dvořák's; the latter's Cello Concerto abounds in gloriously colourful solos in the woodwind and imaginative use of the brass. But Jackie identified totally with Elgar's restraint as well as his inner passion. She could well have subscribed to Ralph Vaughan Williams's words: 'Elgar has that peculiar kind of beauty which gives us, his fellow countrymen, a sense of our own fields and lanes; not the aloof and unsympathetic beauty of glaciers and coral reefs and tropical forests.' Vaughan Williams felt that it was not the bombastic pieces where Elgar deliberately tried to be popular (such as *Cockaigne* or 'Land of Hope and Glory') that had become part of the English national consciousness, 'but at those moments when [Elgar] seems to have retired into the solitude of his own sanctuary'.¹⁰ Nowhere did he achieve this more tellingly than in the Cello Concerto where, to quote the musicologist Jerrold Northrop Moore, 'The cello traces its lonely path through a wide but largely empty landscape, discoursing music which seeks its tonic home again and again through sub-dominant shapes of melody.'¹¹

Du Pré's and Barenboim's recorded account of the Elgar Cello Concerto from Philadelphia is the result of the editing of two concert performances and conveys the immediacy of the concert hall, including disturbing audience coughs and splutters. Jackie's concept had certainly matured over the years, diverging in many small details from her earlier televised performances with Barenboim and her 1965 recording with Barbirolli. But it had not changed in essence. The most obvious difference lies in the adoption of somewhat slower tempi, which Daniel justified for various reasons:

> Jackie was playing on a new cello which had a wonderful sustaining power and she was experimenting with it. She was making music with the Philadelphia Orchestra which had a very rich sustained sound and this allowed for slower tempi. The English orchestral string players didn't produce this kind of sound and therefore when you played with them you couldn't afford to take quite so much time. Jackie was very sensitive to questions of time and space, and was well aware that tempo is dependent on such variable factors as the acoustic, and the intensity, volume and continuity of the sound.

In fact, in the Philadelphia performance she spins out the first movement to a duration of 8'43", some forty-five seconds longer than in the recording with Barbirolli. Barenboim claims some of the responsibility for this slower speed. It derived from a basic need to wring out the maximum expression in the music, where the tempo is closely related to the musical substance of the work in question. It is through the build-up and relaxation of tension, using natural flux in the tempo, that the structure of the music is created. Barenboim admits that his interpretations initially tend towards spaciousness, so that he can highlight the expression of the music. 'However, when I do consecutive performances of a work with the same orchestra I tend to get more and more compact. Jackie's approach was close to mine in this.'

Barenboim observed that Jackie possessed a fantastic sense of rhythm. He sees a clear distinction between musicians who have a good sense of rhythm and those with a good sense of tempo (two qualities which actually rarely come together). 'By rhythm I mean the inner pulse rhythm, and by tempo I mean metronomical tempo. Rubato was a natural thing to Jackie. If you want to be very philosophical about it, she was subconsciously living in her own world – and rubato meant going against the conventional, against the accepted dogma, against pre-defined and pre-determined time. There was something rebel-like about her idea of rubato; it was as if she enjoyed being naughty and cheating the clock.'

It is arguable that in the Philadelphia performance du Pré occasionally pushes the musical expression beyond the restraints of the musical form. She uses rubato extensively and with extraordinary effect, at times in the slow movement almost drawing out the music 'for eternity' (a favourite expression of hers when teaching). A telling example is her slow reaching for the octave D in the two bars after figure 39. Having magically gained the top note (with the indicated fermato) she suspends it in a ravishing pianissimo over the 'false' dominant seventh, before the music subsides into the B flat tonic. Jackie was free to take such liberties in this movement in the knowledge that she was supported throughout by a cushion of warm, yet hushed, sustained string sound.

While du Pré had a unique ability to 'stop the clock' in her music-making, she also knew how to play with time. It is through the emotional force generated that she governs the rhythmic flux. For instance, in the first movement's ascending semiquaver scale which connects the cello's original singing of the theme in the real E minor with the full orchestral statement, Jackie conveys the sensation of individual striving and eventual conquest. This was something she used to demand of her pupils: 'When you eventually achieve the top E and you are overtaken by the huge orchestral sound, you must make the audience feel that you have moved the universe,' she once said to Sandy Bailey.[12]

Overall, the freedom she plays with in this Philadelphia recording reflects not only the depth of du Pré's experience of Elgar's music, but her highly developed conscious ability to use and even manipulate her interpretative powers. There are times when Jackie seems nearly over-emphatic in her communication of the musical message in the pointing of an accent, or the holding of a tenuto; it is perhaps this element of her playing that people have in mind when they talk about it being indulgent or exaggerated. But taken as a whole, the Philadelphia recording of the Elgar concerto is extraordinary for its confessional quality and the emotional outpouring which exposes the raw pain and heartache of the music to an almost unbearable extent.

As the violinist Rodney Friend observed, in du Pré's open vulnerability there was an undeniable element of exaggeration, which not every listener could cope with.

> It got to the point when Jackie almost felt it was expected of her to be over the top, although this would have been her subconscious reaction and never a deliberately imposed mannerism. Those who preferred the more contained expression of her early recordings do not take into account that her life experience, with all the emotional changes and problems, was bound to leave its mark on her as a performer. And she would have continued changing and developing if she had gone on playing. Having said that, Jackie was in any case by far the best player around in those years.

The guitarist John Williams perceived signs of an unresolvable conflict within Jackie, of which she herself was unaware.

> There comes a point when a very creative personality cannot contain its genius. If it is not given enough rein for expression, it expresses itself through a kind of indulgence. One can see this with certain great pop stars. When taken to extremes, they destroy themselves, as they simply cannot contain their creative dynamism within the form they are working. Jimi Hendrix is an obvious example. But in Jackie's case, I think that as the indulgence grew more and more expressed, it was a reflection of a creative conflict within the personality.

Williams ventured this hypothesis, while emphasising that it was not a musical judgement: 'Those who said that Jackie was over-indulgent in her playing were wrong, and neither understood the music nor her. I think that everything she did musically was fantastic.'

Nevertheless, there were critics of du Pré's playing who viewed this expression of her deeply emotional musicality not only as self-indulgence, but as a lack of fidelity to the composer's score. Barenboim refutes this suggestion:

Without entering into the philosophical aspects of whether you sin by commission or omission, the business about being faithful to the score is an objective impossibility in any case. Of course you are unfaithful to the score if you misread the rhythm or the notes, or if you play forte when piano is indicated. But there are those who, by being apparently faithful to the text, commit great sins of omission. For instance, Jackie was extremely particular about the articulation, which many 'faithful-to-the-score' players are not. She was extremely particular about colour – which is also an essential part of the music. As for the much discussed question of tempo, a composer's metronome marking is only one type of indication, but there are further implicit aspects of tempo which are equally important, above all its actual character, let alone the ebb and flow which exists in linear music.

To follow Jackie's Philadelphia recording of the Elgar concerto with a score allows one to see how she interprets every small accent, how accurately she articulates and phrases. She may take the dynamic or tempo markings to further extremes than other interpreters, but this is because such a deeply felt concept of the music needs extra spatial dimensions.[13]

As Barenboim notes, the process of bringing the music into the physical world takes it a stage beyond that of the composer's initial imaginative vision, something which creates a continual challenge to the performer:

As long as the work only exists in a composer's imagination it is subject to whatever laws that they invent in their own head in terms of tempo, intensity, transparency and volume. The moment a composer puts it down on paper it ceases to be subject only to that. In fact, many composers' metronome markings are too fast because the one thing that they lack in their inner hearing is the mass and weight of sound. That is why in piano rehearsals the tempi are always faster than in orchestral rehearsals. The orchestra lends the sound another weight. Nowadays it is fêted as an act of great moral courage if you are totally 'faithful' to the composer's tempo markings, but you risk being cowardly because you are leaving out the inspirational and imaginative aspects of music, which are the very essence of interpretative creativity.

The problem of bringing the written score into the world of real sound holds an endless fascination for performers and composers alike. As the English composer Ralph Vaughan Williams confessed: 'Musical notation ... is notoriously inadequate, so that those who translate these symbols into music are bound by their personal equation and each performs slightly differently. Thus come about what we call the different renderings by great performers or conductors of the same music.' Vaughan Williams concluded that the interpreter is an essential factor in bringing a composer's vision to life: 'Ulysses [would not] have been obliged to be tied to the mast if the Sirens, instead of singing to him, had given him a presentation copy of the full score.'[14]

It would be simplistic to suggest that there can ever be only one solution to the interpretation of a composer's score. Barenboim strongly believes that every great piece of music has two faces – one directed towards its own time and one towards the future, or the *Zeitgeist*. In the case of Elgar, his own recordings serve as documentation of his views on interpretation. Yet Jackie's various recorded performances of the cello concerto (from broadcast concerts as well as the two commercially made records) offer profound, almost visionary insights into the music, which were not available to the interpreters who tackled the score during Elgar's lifetime. And she undoubtedly revealed aspects that quite possibly went deeper than Elgar's original imaginative vision. In this work more than any other du Pré seemed to act as a vessel transmitting a message that came from outside her or, perhaps, as Daniel put it, came from a deep hidden source within.

Indeed, by the age of twenty-five du Pré had recorded most of the standard cello repertoire and was showing signs of being bored by its limitations. In the near future, she had committed herself to learn Carl Maria von Weber's little-known Concerto Fantasy Op.20 and to resuscitate Richard Strauss's *Don Quixote* for a date at the Festival Hall with Mehta and the RPO on 10 June 1971.

Du Pré continued to show a strong identification with English composers, and already as far back as the autumn of 1969 she had asked her agents to programme both the Delius and Walton Cello Concertos during the 1971–2 season. The latter was to be a new addition to her repertoire, and it was a work which would certainly have suited her lyrical and rhetorical gifts. But her performances of the Delius scheduled with Charles Groves for the spring of 1972 (with the RPO in London and the RLPO in Liverpool) and of the Walton concerto with the Hallé and Liverpool Philharmonic Orchestras in the autumn of 1972 all had to be cancelled. Just before Jackie made her short-lived come-back to the concert platform, she agreed again to include the Walton concerto in her repertoire for the season. What would have been her first performance of the work was scheduled with the Guildford Philharmonic in June 1973.

At various times in her career Jackie received proposals to perform or record such pivotal twentieth-century works as Britten's Cello Symphony, Hindemith's concerto of 1940 and the Prokofiev *Sinfonia Concertante*. But these were all works for which she showed little enthusiasm and which, apart from the Prokofiev, she never learnt. When the Northern Sinfonia suggested she should perform Shostakovich's First Cello Concerto (which, of course, she did know) in a series of four concerts in April 1972 she refused outright. Interestingly enough, she put forward the idea of Prokofiev's Concertino as a counter-proposal.

Among the new pieces that did attract Jackie's attention was the richly romantic score of Hugh Wood's new Cello Concerto. She had been invited to give its first performance, but had not found time to do so; it was Zara Nelsova who gave the world première at the 1969 Proms. But when Robert Ponsonby, the manager of the Scottish National Orchestra, invited Jackie to open their season on 1 October 1971 with Wood's Cello Concerto, she agreed without hesitation. The original dates were put forward to March 1972, then postponed again. Once more, it was Ponsonby, now in the position of controller of BBC Radio Three, who suggested early in 1973 that du Pré should première Arnold Cooke's Cello Concerto at the Proms in September 1974. Jackie immediately turned down the proposal with the excuse of ill health, but it is probable that Cooke's music did not hold much appeal for her.

Other new works that Jackie was aware of included cello concertos by Dutilleux and Lutoslawski (both pieces that had been written for Rostropovich). In early 1973 Jackie was sent the score of Dutilleux's *Tout un Monde Lontain* from the publishers. It is unknown whether she had a chance to consider it, but it would certainly have been intriguing to hear her play this suggestively sensual score, inspired by fragments of Baudelaire's poetry. Later that year Rostropovich presented her with a score of the Lutoslawski concerto. Hoping that illness was only momentarily preventing her from playing, he suggested that she learnt the music 'with her eyes and ears' away from the cello.

All this was not to be, and one can only echo Bill Pleeth's lament that Jackie was deprived of the opportunity to play so much more wonderful music.

25

Crisis

Music discloses to man an unknown realm, a world that has
nothing in common with the external sensual world that sur-
rounds him, a world in which he leaves behind him all definite
feelings, to surrender himself to inexpressible longing.

E. T. A. Hoffmann, Essay on Beethoven

Even at the time, Jackie's emotional performance of the Elgar concerto
in Philadelphia seemed to some people to convey a note of desperation,
and with hindsight we can listen to the recording and imagine we hear
a plea for help. Certainly the tension and anxiety had been building up
in her and pointed to something being seriously wrong. They were to
snap a few months later, but in the meantime she continued to perform,
evidently still giving the best of herself in concert. She was able to fulfil
her schedule until the beginning of February 1971, when her long-
planned three-month sabbatical was to start.

Before returning to London she and Daniel gave a final performance
of the Elgar concerto with the Philadelphia Symphony Orchestra in
New York on 1 December, followed by two further recitals at Man-
hattan's Philharmonic Hall, their last Beethoven cycle of the bicentenary
year. In the meantime, Daniel had spread his own cycle of Beethoven
piano sonatas at Alice Tully Hall over the autumn months, completing
it by mid-December.

Back in London, Jackie played Dvořák's concerto with the London
Philharmonic Orchestra under Daniel's direction at the Royal Festival
Hall on 17 December. The critics wrote enthusiastically of their performance and Peter Stadlen noted that du Pré's resplendent interpretation of Dvořák's concerto sometimes gained from her being 'unfaithful'
to the score: 'By ignoring a primo tempo [indication] with enchanting
results she would have been qualified for the medal the Habsburgs used
to give away when disobeying an order led to success in the field.'

Rodney Friend, leader of the LPO, recalled the inspiration that

Jackie communicated not only on her audiences, but to the orchestral musicians.

> When one was playing with Jackie one always felt motivated. If I looked around in the orchestra, I could see that the players were highly enthusiastic and wanted to give of their best. It was easy for the whole orchestra to fit into what she was doing, because her musicianship was so natural and because she inter-related with all the players. Indeed, I would go so far as to say that through the sheer excellence of her playing Jackie had the ability to carry an orchestra to a level that hardly any conductor can do.

In this particular Festival Hall concert du Pré underlined the rapture and pathos of Dvořák's music. Rodney recalled his duet with Jackie (violin solo and cello) in the third movement as an exhilarating experience. 'It was like being whisked away in a Rolls-Royce or a Ferrari. She was so full of energy and the great joy of making music.' He observed that while Jackie's approach to the instrument was never conventional, she could achieve anything she wanted through having enormous reserves to draw on. 'For instance, Jackie could sustain sound for an incredible amount of time, drawing out these incredibly long bows with seamless changes. And within the bow length she had an extraordinary range of dynamic, textures and colour. She could lock the hair into any sound she imagined.'

The next day the Barenboims left for Berlin, for performances with the Berlin Philharmonic Orchestra on 20 and 21 December. In these final concerts of the year Jackie played the Elgar concerto once more. Her performance under Daniel's direction made an indelible impression on the audience and orchestral musicians alike. It turned out to be the last time that they played the piece together.

Back in London, Jackie devoted much of her time and energy to helping Iris. Derek's jaundice had not responded to treatment and he was admitted to the Prince of Wales Hospital for investigations, including a biopsy. Daniel was due back in New York by the end of December for four weeks of engagements as guest conductor of the New York Philharmonic Orchestra and Jackie was committed to going with him, although she only had one scheduled concert during this period. She left home reluctantly, still anxious about her father. It was not until the middle of January that Derek was discharged from hospital. It had been discovered that he had chronic hepatitis and now needed a long period of convalescence.

The Barenboims celebrated New Year's Eve in New York in the company of their closest musician friends – the Zukermans, the Perlmans and Arthur Rubinstein. After dining at Trader Vick's, they proceeded to the Zukermans' apartment on Riverside Drive for an informal session of music-making, which lasted into the small hours. In a photograph taken that evening Jackie is seen playing piano trios with Perlman and Rubinstein, with Barenboim in the passive role of page turner. Her pale, tense face could just be a reflection of the ordinary fatigue of too many late nights; but another detail, her bare feet, tells a story – Jackie had discarded her shoes to counteract the effects of numbness in her feet.

On 23 January she played the Saint-Saëns concerto with the Philadelphia Orchestra under Daniel's direction at a gala concert in Philadelphia in celebration of the 125th anniversary of the orchestra's foundation. At the end of the month the Barenboims flew back t‑ London, ready to settle into their house in Pilgrim's Lane for their sabbatical, which they had been looking forward to for over a year. Yet, as this period of free time approached, Jackie began to dread it. Although she would be resting from the strains of the itinerant concert artist's life, she had started to realise that her problems were not all due to external pressures and that they might have a deeper cause.

It was already evident to those close to her that Jackie was suffering from a severe inner crisis in the last months of 1970, intensified by a build-up of fatigue and anxiety. As Daniel recalled, 'It was obviously not just a question of physical tiredness. I didn't know whether Jackie's problems were mental. Certainly, neither of us had any idea that she was suffering from a physical illness. She had already experienced strange symptoms like numbness in her limbs back in 1969. But it took four and a half years from the appearance of that first symptom until the diagnosis of multiple sclerosis was made. And that was the hardest time for her and for me.'

A few months back, Jackie had consulted her GP, Dr Selby, about some skin moles on her body. He had advised her to have them excised, although they were not dangerous. She was booked to have this routine minor surgery at University College Hospital in London on 26 February; the operation required a general anaesthetic and a couple of nights' stay in hospital. After Jackie was discharged Dr Selby visited her at home on 28 February. He found her very depressed and she complained to him of feeling numb. By the next day this lack of sensation had affected the whole left side of her body. Dr Selby recognised the symptom as hemi hypoalgesia, a unilateral loss of feeling on one side of the body, which is often associated with hysteria (particularly in female patients), but can have other causes. The numbness cleared up after a day or two as inexplicably as it had come.

Jackie was not given to grumble about her ailments, but she found it distressing to have her complaints dismissed as psychosomatic or a product of stress. As there was no apparent cause for this specific physical disorder, even her own doctor started to wonder if she was suffering from hysterical symptoms. Dr Selby was well aware of Jackie's anxiety and told her gently that this loss of sensation was probably a stress-related symptom.

As Dr Leo Lange, the neurologist who later treated Jackie, explained, 'Certain things are known to trigger symptoms or relapse in MS patients, including certain forms of surgical or emotional trauma.' He also observed that musicians are often willing to accept psychological causes for any small disorder: 'There's a lot of emotion involved in making music and I think that artists are more susceptible than others to such explanations.' But it would seem that Jackie fought against the notion that this strange and frightening numbness was either stress-related or psychosomatic. Yet the very idea of this possibility was enough to throw her into confusion and lead her to wonder whether she might be heading for a nervous breakdown.

Multiple sclerosis (commonly abbreviated to MS), an illness that affects the central nervous system, can manifest itself in many, often seemingly insignificant ways in its early stages. Some of these early symptoms are so bizarre as to defy description, whether they are twitches in the legs, a sensation of pins and needles or a feeling of queasy unsteadiness. One constant aspect of MS is its unpredictability – the tell-tale symptoms of an attack can recede as mysteriously as they come and the patient is often granted long periods of respite (termed remission). The causes of the illness are unknown; at one time it was thought to be triggered by viral infection, but now it is believed to be an auto-immune disease, in which possibly external, environmental factors also play an important role. Individual cases range from a 'benign' form of MS, where after a single attack there is no recurrence, to the other end of the spectrum, where patients can suffer from a severely progressive form of the illness.

Multiple sclerosis causes specific damage to the myelin sheath, which protects the nerve fibres and cells. In Dr Lange's words, 'The initial thing in MS, the demyelination, is an inflammatory response to the damage to the myelin sheath, and that may be so severe as to damage the nerve fibres so that they stop passing impulses. Or it may be relatively flat, so that they can recover completely, leaving no residual damage.'[2] Demyelination causes interference with transmission of the electrical messages along the nerves and may affect the motory, sensory or optic nerves. After an attack there can sometimes be regeneration of the affected cells, allowing for partial or total recovery, but in other cases the nerve tissue is scarred, causing permanent damage. In this latter case remission can only be partial.

A clinical diagnosis of multiple sclerosis is made initially by a process of deduction, through eliminating other possibilities. There must be neurological evidence of a minimum of two or three parts of the central nervous system having been affected within certain typical time patterns. Once the disease is suspected, laboratory tests of one kind or another can be used to confirm the findings.

After the illness was diagnosed, doctors could point to Jackie having developed it as far back as 1969, possibly already in the autumn of 1968. The du Pré family's GP, Dr Hatchick, had examined Jackie early in the summer of 1969 after her return from Australia for complaints of recurrent cystitis. As he wondered if this was a neurological disorder rather than an infection, he referred her to a neurologist, Dr Anthony Wolf. Wolf's findings confirmed his suspicion, but did not as yet point to MS, perhaps because Jackie did not inform him of certain other symptoms that she had already experienced in the previous months.

Looking back over her medical history Jackie could recall various signs which might have been connected with multiple sclerosis. The earliest instance of any disorder could be traced back to the age of sixteen, when she experienced some moments of blurred or double vision. In fact, retrobulbar neuritis or diplopia, to give these symptoms their medical names, can be among the first manifestations of the illness, although they often clear up completely.

Alison Brown recalled that Jackie not only occasionally suffered problems with vision while they lived together in Ladbroke Grove, but that she often complained of icy hands or cold feet. At the time, Alison attributed this in part to the effect of the damp English winter weather and in part to problems of poor circulation. Jackie's friend, the eye specialist and amateur musician John Anderson, had examined her after her return from Moscow in the summer of 1966, when she told him that in the previous months she had suffered problems with her vision. But he found nothing wrong; evidently by the time she consulted him her symptoms had disappeared.

Other observers pointed to Jackie's prolonged attack of glandular fever in the early autumn of 1966 as a possible starting point for the illness. Already a year before that, in September 1965, when she had consulted Dr Hatchick and Sir Richard Bayliss, she had been complaining not only of physical indispositions such as headaches and cystitis, but of apathy and depression following a particularly busy schedule. She was warned then that her intense activity could bring on a nervous breakdown.

More recently, Jackie had occasionally experienced other strange symptoms: attacks of laryngitis, an unaccountable unsteadiness which could make her lose her balance or stagger with the ataxic gait associated with drunkenness. Likewise, her co-ordination could be suddenly affected, her knees might 'cave in', causing a fall. Once in Moscow (in the spring of 1966) I saw her stumble all at once and hurtle down the Conservatoire staircase – nobody knew whether to be more anxious for her or her precious Strad cello. Jackie seemed shaken and complained of a sore wrist. (I remember taking her to the Botkin Hospital to have her right hand X-rayed to check that nothing was wrong.)

Dr Lange, however, felt it was dangerous to attribute too great a significance to these signals: 'It is easy to look back and see milestones. I can't believe anyone with a neurological disturbance could use their co-ordination and play the cello as well as Jackie did. There are some people who are by nature clumsy – they stumble more often than others, but it doesn't mean they have MS.'

Certainly, had Jackie and Daniel known then that the various symptoms that had been accumulating over the last two years signalled a physical illness, they would have been saved a lot of agony and uncertainty. With hindsight, Daniel could summarise Jackie's dilemma as follows: 'I think in a deeper and longer sense, it was like having stayed up too late at a party where she had been enjoying herself no end. At a certain point it became too much and she couldn't cope.'

Other people were quick to assume that Jackie was exhausted by her life-style, the travelling, the 'world-schlepping' and the strains of concert life. The implication was that she could not keep up with Daniel's demanding pace. Such accusations were quite unjust, since Daniel went out of his way to protect Jackie and always checked her diary very carefully, making sure that she really wished to do an engagement. In fact, she had more rest periods programmed into her schedule than many concert artists of her age and one must never forget how much she herself enjoyed playing.

Yet, as Jackie lived so completely in the present, it was an imposition for her to be tied to obligations planned so far ahead. As physical exhaustion rendered playing concerts an unwanted task, she came to resent having to adjust her inner clock to go on-stage when she didn't feel like it. The trappings of a musician's life might have seemed glamorous to outsiders, but anything that smacked of artifice had no appeal for Jackie. While observing these exterior aspects with a keen wit, she abhorred the false adulation and small chat at receptions. Giving interviews or talking 'shop' with impresarios and managers was always just a chore, which she preferred to leave to Daniel. Barenboim was well-equipped to look after the practicalities and deal with the outside world, endowed as he was with a magnetic personality, dynamic force and the power to regenerate his energy with two or three minutes of intense sleep, seemingly taken at will even in a crowded and noisy room.

As the then Director of the Edinburgh Festival, Peter Diamand, commented, 'People on the fringe of the Barenboim circle (but not those who belonged to it) used to say before the illness was diagnosed that Daniel had pulled Jackie into a rhythm of life that was too much for her. That it was all Daniel's fault. I never had the feeling that she was forced into things. Rather, I always felt that Jackie was a full partner to everything that Daniel undertook and enjoyed this side of their partnership.'

But now, as the very things that mattered most to her – her playing and her relationship with Daniel – were called into doubt, Jackie started to retreat into her own world. Diamand recalled that during this difficult period of her life her behaviour could seem quite impulsive, if not downright eccentric: 'At receptions in London or Edinburgh, Jackie seemed withdrawn and hardly talked. Then she would suddenly get up and say, "Excuse me, I must go out and walk around the block two or three times." And off she went. Of course it was only a trivial detail, but it made one ask if there was something wrong. And in discussing things that were relevant to her programmes, I was struck by the strange impassivity with which she approached even minor decisions, not to talk of major ones.'

When she was on form, Jackie loved nothing more than the company of friends. But now, beset with misgivings, she withdrew into herself. Evidently there was a growing dichotomy between the public and private persona, and it was to the latter that Jackie needed to devote herself at this stage. Some years later she noted in her diary that she had only known how to speak through music: 'An artist can be at his loneliest in company; and at his fullest, most replete and expansive when alone with his art.' Having laid aside the cello from the beginning of 1971 (apart from her one concert in Philadelphia), she now felt deprived of her natural means of expression and could hardly muster the inner resources to confront a crisis. Depressed and anxious, with her sense of self-esteem at its lowest ebb, it was all too easy to project her feelings of anger and frustration on to the person closest to her. Jackie had come to regard Daniel as the one who stood between her and her true identity. In a situation where bewilderment was mixed with anger, it was not surprising that their relationship suffered and communication between them began to break down.

No sooner were they back in London for the start of their sabbatical than Jackie decided on a temporary separation from Daniel. While deeply upset by her decision, he was aware of her need for space of her own and did not impede her departure. No less than she, he was overwhelmed by a sense of powerlessness and anxiety as to what was happening between them: 'Jackie said that she felt terribly confused and didn't know how to deal with the feeling that things were over-coming her. When people suggested that these were hysterical symp-toms or overtiredness, it didn't help; it just upset her further. I was heart-broken that she wanted to go, but I could not stop her.'

Jackie's first instinct was to turn to her family for help. While Iris had always been a support in practical ways (she would still help out with Jackie's laundry, for instance), the ties of the mother–daughter relationship had slackened. Jackie felt unable to confide in her parents, since she did not believe they could respond with the necessary under-standing. In any case, Iris was now almost entirely occupied with her husband's poor state of health and convalescence. Thus it was that Jackie turned to her sister Hilary and her husband Christopher (Kiffer)

Finzi, seeking refuge at their farmhouse in Ashmansworth. Here, in the hub of family life and far removed from the public eye, Jackie hoped she would find the necessary peace of mind to solve her problems. She and Hilary shared many interests, and their protected childhood had left them naïve and unfettered by outward conventions. Whereas Jackie had more than fulfilled her enormous gifts, Hilary had been side-tracked from a professional career in music, which her considerable talents merited, and had opted for domestic happiness. Now, after ten years of marriage and with four young children, Hilary seemed to have the things that Jackie hankered after – a stable base and a young family to love.

Kiffer undoubtedly had far wider horizons than the du Pré girls and through the force of his personality was able to stimulate Jackie's interest in other disciplines, from poetry to philosophy, as well as giving her a different perspective on life and music. An unorthodox figure, some-where between a gentleman farmer and a 1970s hippy, he achieved some measure of success in carrying on his father Gerald Finzi's work with the Newbury String Players (much more than with the cello, which he had studied formally). His aspirations were those of a well-informed amateur, radically opposed to the assertive super-pro-fessionalism of Barenboim's and du Pré's world careers. Whether con-sciously or not, Kiffer certainly fostered Jackie's rebellious attitude towards Daniel and the professional 'music business'.

Kiffer's espousal of amateurism in music as a way of life in some respects echoed his father's (and other of the national school composers') attitudes towards Benjamin Britten as an establishment figure, intent on promoting his own interests in achieving an international career. Gerald Finzi regarded Britten as a shallow and superficial composer, and condemned his association with the 'professional racket'. In turn, Britten deplored the amateur standards of the Newbury String Players and could not stomach Finzi's enthusiasm, which he defined facetiously as a ' "I prefer this to those horrible professionals" sort of thing'.[3]

Despite being welcomed and comforted by her sister's family, Jackie's depression deepened during her sabbatical. While her mental state was all too evident, she did not confide in her family the extent of her physical symptoms, but she did consult her doctor again. On 6 April Dr Selby referred her to a psychiatrist, Dr Mezey, who latter confirmed his diagnosis of depression, and prescribed anti-depressants and tran-quillisers. A month later Jackie went back to Selby with complaints of headaches, nausea and numbness. Although he attributed these disorders partly to anxiety, Len informed Daniel that he was suspicious that there was something seriously wrong. The turn that events were taking, however, deflected them from reading the signals correctly. Jackie's affliction soon appeared to be a full-scale nervous breakdown.

In the meanwhile, shortly after Easter Hilary and Kiffer had taken Jackie to their mountain home in France, hoping that she could rest and be revitalised through contact with the wild, unspoilt landscape. Daniel, who had kept in touch with Jackie throughout this period, decided to join them for a few days. But the time spent together did not establish a reconciliation between them. Instead of restoring her peace of mind, the holiday drove Jackie deeper into dejection. Having lost faith in her marriage, she now sought male protection elsewhere.

She was becoming increasingly dependent on Kiffer. She had always sought mentors in life and now, in an extremely fragile emotional state, she was perhaps too ready to submit to his influence. By the end of the sabbatical her relationship with Kiffer had changed from that of trusted friend to lover. There can be no doubt that both parties must have known that embarking on an affair would be hurtful towards their respective spouses. The fact that they conducted it without hiding it from Hilary more or less obliged her to condone it.

In Finzi's self-confessed fascination with the work of R. D. Laing, the maverick Scots psychiatrist, there perhaps lies a key to his logic. Laing's belief that the fetters of the conventional family should be broken and allow for wider relationships certainly influenced Finzi in the future, when he turned Church Farm in Ashmansworth into a commune.

More recently, Kiffer has stated that feelings of guilt never came into the picture, since the du Pré sisters completed trusted each other and did not experience any form of jealousy. 'I think Jackie paid Hilary a tremendous compliment, because when she was desperately looking for someone to latch on to she chose Hil.'[4] It would seem, however, that for a few months it was Kiffer whom Jackie latched on to. Hilary later justified her husband's behaviour as a means of seeing Jackie through a profound crisis, almost as a form of therapy.[5] But this excludes another obvious truth – that for a while her sister and husband were highly attracted to each other; oblivious of anything but the here and now, they did not consider the consequences of what essentially can be described as very selfish behaviour. At the time, for Jackie the duality of the experience had its exhilarating as well as confusing side. But within a year she was to see the situation in another light, and came to regard her brother-in-law as a man who wielded his authority in a manipulative way and who had taken advantage of a woman in a distraught state.

By the beginning of May the Barenboims' sabbatical had come to an end and Jackie was due to resume her concerts which, as usual, were programmed in conjunction with Daniel's. Going ahead with her schedule implied a decision on Jackie's part to go back to Daniel, perhaps even an initial gesture to reconstructing the marriage. The first of their collaborations took place on 13 May in Manchester's Free Trade Hall with the Hallé Orchestra. Here Jackie performed Weber's Concerto Fantasy Op.20, a work rarely heard on concert platforms and which she had learnt for the occasion. Plans had been made to record it, together with Tchaikovsky's *Rococo Variations* with the ECO that coming July.

The following week the Barenboims left for the USA, where they were engaged to perform with the Philadelphia Orchestra in a coast-to-coast tour. In her highly vulnerable state it was perhaps unwise for Jackie to embark on a concert tour that took her thousands of miles from home. In the event, she only fulfilled the first of the scheduled engagements on 24 May, playing the Dvořák concerto under Daniel's direction at Newport Beach, California.

If Jackie found it difficult being back with Barenboim, she could cope no better with her return to professional life. Her confusion was all too visible to Daniel and he could see she was close to breaking point. The entangled web of relationships that she had left at Ashmansworth weighed on her mind. Since she was constitutionally incapable of hiding the truth, she soon confessed the situation to Daniel, but her state of fatigue and confusion rendered her explanations almost incoherent. In a state of intense emotional distress she felt drained of all remaining energy.

Cynthia Benz, in her sensitive and informative book on multiple sclerosis, vividly describes the feeling of weariness which can accompany the early stages of the illness: 'Sometimes fatigue is a permanent symptom that drags around with you. At other times it creeps up unnoticed. The typical pattern is to start on a project [...] and perform quite normally until suddenly energy goes and you seize up or flop. The energy loss can be so immediate that you are taken quite by surprise. It is frequently accompanied by a dazed feeling and an inability to communicate through excessive weakness. The fatigued person with MS is unable to enter into arguments or work out reasons.'[6]

However much Daniel tried to reason with Jackie, she was adamant that she could not continue with the tour. It remained for him to placate the concert organisers, agents and orchestral managers whom she was letting down. Daniel realised that further persuasion was pointless, and he could only suggest that she consult a local doctor to find some short-term remedy for her distress and acquire the medical certificate required to protect her from breach of contract. Having cancelled the next month's concerts, she flew home to her sister's family in England, leaving Daniel, hurt and no less confused, to finish his tour in the USA.

After her hasty retreat, Jackie's initial relief gave way to agitation at the thought of an imminent return to the concert platform for the summer festival season. Matters were not eased by the fact that the press had scented rumours that du Pré was suffering from a nervous breakdown and that her marriage to Barenboim was on the rocks. It was the task of Diana Rix to fend off journalists and to placate concert organisers. She firmly attributed du Pré's health problems to tenosynovitis (inflammation of the tendon of the wrist) and was able to deflect journalists by suggesting that it would be best to call the Barenboims' lawyer, Louis Courts, who represented both Jackie and Daniel. This fact in itself was enough to put paid to rumours regarding alleged marital problems. Indeed, it would seem that, in private, Jackie did give some substance to these rumours. In the early summer she informed some of her close friends (either directly or by letter) that a separation from Daniel was imminent; she was anxious lest they might learn of this from press reports.

As the summer wore on and her anxieties did not abate, she came to realise that even the best intentions of her family could not substitute for the professional help she needed to deal with her problems. Indeed, the peculiar and potentially explosive situation of a ménage-à-trois at the Finzis' home was hardly helpful to the recovery of her mental or emotional equilibrium. She was aware of the disapproval of those few trusted friends who knew of the situation. By the beginning of July a solution was found when Jackie was put in touch with a Freudian psychoanalyst, Dr Walter Joffe. She met him and liked him, and it was agreed that she should start some treatment with him. The initial course of psychotherapy almost immediately turned into a commitment to full-scale psychoanalysis. To allow this to happen, one of the first things that Dr Joffe did was to provide Jackie with a medical certificate, stating that she was suffering from nervous exhaustion and needed at least one year's rest from the concert platform. She passed Joffe's letter, dated 12 July 1971, to Diana Rix, who was then faced with the unpleasant duty of cancelling all her concerts. Du Pré's engagement book was put on hold until 1973, when a come-back was cautiously planned.

In the meantime Jackie was too depressed to want to make music. Her new Peresson cello mostly remained in its case. As for the Davydov, she lent it to her cellist friend, Anna Shuttleworth, with whom she occasionally played duets. But on a couple of occasions she was persuaded to make exceptions to her rule of silence by playing 'unofficially' with the Newbury Players, hidden in the back desk of the orchestral cellos. She even went so far as to perform the Monn G minor Concerto with this orchestra on 18 July, only a few days after all her professional engagements had been cancelled in the wake of Joffe's certifying her state of nervous exhaustion. Although this concert took place in the small Hampshire village of Inkpen and was effectively an amateur event, Jackie was taking an unwarranted risk that her performance might be noticed. Indeed, her occasional appearances in public during her extended sabbatical sometimes prompted disgruntled complaints that she was shirking her duties as a performer.

A misunderstanding of this nature provoked a BBC producer to write to Jackie at the beginning of February 1972 with an invitation to play at the Basingstoke Carnival festivities. The opening sentence of his letter was almost an accusation: 'Since you were seen at the Wigmore Hall a few evenings ago I expect that you have now recovered from your illness and that your retirement from the concert platform was only temporary.' Jackie wrote to Diana Rix, asking her to reply to the letter and to explain her situation; she commented, 'Perhaps I should go round disguised as Fournier! . . . From the sound of the first sentence it would seem that Scotland Yard should be interested in me, not Basingstoke Carnival Committee.'

In fact, throughout the time she was staying with the Finzi family Jackie kept in touch with Daniel, her London friends and with Diana Rix at Harold Holt. During the spring and early summer, Rixie continued to plan next season's concerts and recordings in consultation with Barenboim, who helped to choose the repertoire and to establish fee levels. Plans made that year with EMI included a definite date to record the *Trout* Quintet in Munich during August 1971 with the same formation as appeared in Nupen's film. Other recording projects under discussion were the complete Mozart piano trios, the Brahms Double Concerto with Zukerman and a Chopin recital record, consisting of the Cello Sonata Op.65, the Polonaise Brillante Op.3 and the rarely heard Grand Duo on themes from *Robert le Diable* composed in collaboration with the cellist Auguste Franchomme. All these proposals were approved, having met the required target figures of the sales estimates put forward by EMI's financial department.

Eleanor Warren recalls inviting Jackie to lunch during the early autumn and suggesting to her that she might like to record some unaccompanied Bach, and that this could be arranged very informally at the BBC. Eleanor explained that apart from two of them, nobody would be informed, nor would there be any pressure to release a radio recording. It was an offer for which Jackie was grateful, implying, as it did, an understanding of her predicament and continued faith in her talents, but unfortunately one she never took up.

As the number of her intensive sessions with Joffe increased to sometimes as many as five a week, it was natural that Jackie should move her base back to London and in doing so she reestablished her contact with Daniel. Often she would walk the two miles from the house in Pilgrim's Lane across Hampstead Heath to Joffe's studio in Burgess Hill; on the way back she would pop in on various of her North London friends. Dr Joffe noted that Jackie's psychological disturbances went back as far as the age of four, when she had been sent to hospital to have her tonsils removed and was separated from her family without explanation. Four was also the age when she took up the cello.

In the course of her psychoanalysis, Jackie would sometimes turn against one or other member of her family while a specific relationship was under scrutiny, feeling unable simultaneously to face that person in real life. It would seem that Joffe initially did not discourage Jackie from holding Daniel responsible for her troubles. But this was only a prelude to making her accept responsibility for herself, and for understanding the deeper implications of a recurring pattern in her life of dependence and submission followed by rebellion.

Daniel, in the meantime, continued with his busy concert commitments, which more often than not took him away from London. He sought elegant solutions to problems caused by Jackie's withdrawal from concerts, based on his understanding that an artist has an obligation towards his audiences. Jackie's place in a performance of the *Trout* Quintet at the Israel Festival was taken by Uzi Wiesel, cellist of the Tel Aviv Quartet. At the Proms the Barenboim–Zukerman–du Pré Trio's scheduled performance of the *Archduke* Trio was substituted by Beethoven's C minor Violin Sonata played by Zukerman and Barenboim.

Knowing how resistant she could be to any kind of influence, Daniel exerted no pressure on Jackie. For a man who could often seem impatient, he proved to possess remarkable resources of patience. His rationality will have dictated that time would be the most effective medicine and he probably had a strong intuition that Jackie would need him before long. Now dividing her time between London and Ashmansworth, it was natural for her to resume contact with Daniel at their shared Pilgrim's Lane house when he was at home from touring.

Over six months had passed since Jackie had played in public, when she woke up one December morning in her Hampstead home feeling immeasurably better. She got out her cello and started making music with Daniel, as had been their wont in the good old days. Delighted at the unimpaired quality and complete ease of Jackie's playing, Daniel rang Suvi Grubb to see if there was a studio free at EMI. He felt that an unscheduled and unpublicised recording session would not put undue pressure on Jackie; if, for some reason, it didn't work out, nobody would be the wiser. In total sympathy with the situation, Suvi was able to oblige and found a free Abbey Road studio for 10 and 11 December. Instead of playing the three Chopin works that formed their original recital proposal, Jackie and Daniel opted to record only the sonata, together with another sonata that they had often performed – that of César Franck. In any case Jackie had never learnt the two Chopin pieces in question and according to Daniel was uneasy about one or two passages in the Polonaise Brillante. This is surprising, since the virtuosic difficulties belong almost exclusively to the piano writing.

Certainly, listening to the recordings one could never suspect that Jackie had been away from the cello for so long, or that as a duo the Barenboims had been out of action for a year. Du Pré's playing of these romantic sonatas favours a refined intimacy rather than full-blooded passion. Through the music she speaks from the heart with a vulnerable sensibility which transcends the restraints of the instrument and touches the listener directly. Jackie evidently was not using the authoritative

Polish edition of the Fryderyk Chopin Institute, since in the first movement there are some discrepancies in register (on two occasions she puts the music up an octave), and one and a half bars of the slow movement (bars 8 and 9) have a completely different reading. Such details, of course, in no way detract from the intrinsic quality of her interpretation.

The Barenboims' account of the Chopin Sonata illuminates the composer's world of inner melancholy, which seems to draw its inspiration from Schubert. There are striking similarities between the melody of the opening theme of the first movement and the first song, 'Gute Nacht', from Schubert's despairing song cycle *Winterreise*; another common feature of the two works lies in the emphatic dotted quaver motif of an ascending and descending semitone.[7]

In the outer movements of the sonata Jackie invests the declamatory rhetoric with great nobility, while her touching account of the largo absolutely avoids artifice or cellistic indulgence. Barenboim, a sensitive partner, provides passion and drive, while never allowing the piano figuration to obscure the cello line; both he and Jackie treat the virtuoso passagework as an expressive feature of the music. Through articulation and rhythmic character, the artists underline the scherzo's kinship to the mazurka and link the last-movement theme to a Polish dance. Barenboim and du Pré maintain the classical proportions of the sonata, yet their flexible phrasing shows an understanding of the Chopinesque rubato which Liszt likened to a breeze rustling in the branches of trees, stirring the leaves to life, while the actual tree remained itself rooted in the ground.

The Franck sonata poses different problems for a cello–piano duo, not least in that it was originally written for violin, even if initially conceived for cello. Yet this version benefits from the contrast in the registers of the cello, encompassing a range from baritone to soprano. Perhaps the weakest point comes in the last movement, where the cello's canonic imitation of the piano's opening theme duplicates the register of the piano's left hand, whereas the violin's response soars an octave above the pianist's right hand.

There are so many things to admire in the Barenboim–du Pré account of the sonata – whether it is the element of improvisatory fantasy or the careful observance of the composer's repeated indications of molto dolce and dolcissimo (which all too often are mistaken for an outward form of expression). Du Pré's soft yearning sound is ideally suited to the musings of the first movement, and to the rhapsodic improvisations of the third movement recitativo–fantasia, where she and Barenboim seem to capture the very essence of the creative impulse. Similarly, they invest the second movement with passion and drama, while maintaining clarity of texture and a feeling for the rhythmic flux without losing drive. Jackie's use of portamento and glissando add weight of expression and drama, particularly in the great leaping theme of the third movement (in the original version for violin it seems to me impossible to capture the same feeling of conquering space). It is here and in the finale that Jackie sometimes stretches the phrases almost beyond the acceptable boundaries of taste and form; in this her playing does not bear imitation, although she justifies any extravagance through the intensity of feeling. Throughout, du Pré benefits from Barenboim's support and ability to mould the form so as to contain her passion.

Many have commented on the immediacy of Jackie's playing in these recordings. In the words of the cellist Sandy Bailey, 'In these accounts of the Chopin and Franck sonatas Jackie's level of sincerity is almost confrontational. She seems completely un-earthbound in her playing.' It would also be fair to say that in terms of pure cello sound, this recording shows up the Peresson cello as having lesser depth or refinement of sound (particularly on the C string) than the Italian cellos that du Pré previously played. The feel of how the instrument responded was far more important to Jackie than its latent capacity for sound, and her idiosyncratic tone and enormous range of colour were not dependent on the cello she played. One only notices the discrepancy of tone quality through making a direct comparison with earlier recordings where du Pré uses the Gofriller or Davydov cello.

Suvi Grubb states that Jackie played as superbly as ever during the two-day recording sessions. 'When we had finished she said that she would like to start on the Beethoven sonatas. Barenboim and I were concerned, for she looked tired, but we recorded the first movement of Op.5 No.1. At the end of it she placed her cello back in its case with "That is that" and did not even want to listen to what we had taped. That was Jacqueline du Pré's last appearance in the recording studio.'[8]

26

A Short-lived Comeback

We possess art lest we perish of the Truth.

Friedrich Nietzsche

By the new year Jackie's confidence had returned to such an extent that she felt ready to confront the world. Her sessions with Joffe were producing positive results. Now, with Daniel's support and participation, she could work on the rebuilding of their relationship. While still not performing, Jackie kept in touch with the cello through playing duets with her cellist friends. Often these sessions turned into impromptu lessons, a mark of Jackie's generous and sharing spirit. There was something touchingly naïve about her desire to teach the cello to people she liked, even to complete beginners. Not only did she help professional cellists like Jo Milholland, Kate Beare and myself, but she encouraged Sylvia Southcombe to get back to the instrument after neglecting her playing while bringing up young children. She even persuaded her closest friend Diana Nupen to take up the cello and insisted on teaching her from the start. Later on, when she became ill, she volunteered to give lessons to two complete beginners from very different walks of life: the banker James Wolfensohn and the singer Plácido Domingo.

Jackie also enjoyed going out to concerts, and visiting and entertaining friends. Daniel recalled, 'We had some very nice evenings in Pilgrim's Lane when Jackie would prepare dinner. Walter Legge came to visit, Arthur Rubinstein, Shura Cherkassky, Clifford Curzon and many others. Jackie may not have been a cordon bleu cook, but she produced very good meals and enjoyed cooking.'

In the meantime dates for du Pré's 'come-back' were being set up. It was thought better to wait until the beginning of 1973 before accepting concerto engagements; in any case, duo or trio recitals could be planned at shorter notice. By the beginning of the summer Jackie was feeling so much stronger that she felt ready to start performing. It was arranged for her to participate in chamber music concerts, the first of which took place at the Israel Festival on 31 July 1972. Here, with Zukerman and Barenboim, she performed Beethoven's *Ghost* Trio and the Tchaikovsky Trio in A minor, Op.50. Fortuitously, this concert was recorded by Israeli Radio; some ten years later Suvi Grubb arranged for the tape to be acquired by EMI and issued commercially. It had, as Daniel recalled, enormous significance for Jackie: 'She adored playing the Tchaikovsky and felt emotionally close to this music. Coming back to performing after a period of silence represented a rebirth for her.' This successful come-back to the stage symbolised a renewed confidence in her powers and the rediscovery of happiness with Daniel.

Tchaikovsky dedicated his piano trio to the memory of his friend, Nicholas Rubinstein, founder of the Moscow Conservatoire. In the first movement, written on a grandiose scale, pathos alternates with nostalgic lyricism. In the recording we hear how du Pré and Zukerman immediately capture the essential mood of elegiac lament, while Barenboim shows enormous flamboyance in the virtuoso piano writing, a tribute by Tchaikovsky to the school of Russian pianism which both Nicholas and his brother Anton Rubinstein did so much to develop. By contrast, in the predominantly sunny and light-hearted second movement variations, the trio capture the varying moods of the imaginative (if over-lengthy) transformations of the simple Russian folk-song theme. As in a ballet with changing scenes, we are entertained by a characteristic mazurka, a lilting waltz (played by Jackie with a deliciously enticing charm), a mournful lament (where Zukerman tugs exquisitely at the heartstrings), not to mention a full-scale fugue, where Tchaikovsky pays homage to the ideals that Rubinstein fostered in helping to create a national school of composition. The exuberance of the team draws on their calibre as individual soloists and allows them to present this trio as music of epic proportions, which owes little to the more intimate traditions of Austro-German chamber music.

When the performance was eventually released on record by EMI, Jackie would listen to it over and over again, saying, 'You can tell from the playing that I must have been in love with Pinky!' This joking confession in a way perfectly describes Jackie's complete musical symbiosis with the violinist in music where the string players' eloquent partnership is designed to contrast with the concerto-like dimensions of the piano writing.

Indeed, when she was ill, Jackie was able to derive an almost vicarious pleasure from connecting to the excitement of this recorded live performance. But she was equally merciless in her attitude to the occasional dropped note in the piano part, which had initially made Barenboim reluctant to allow the recording to be released. One suspects she would not have forgiven him if he had withheld permission. Certainly, note perfection had never been a preoccupation in her playing days; rather, she recoiled from music-making which was sterile and lacking in spirit.

For the rest of the summer Jackie rested from performing, spending most of August at the Edinburgh Festival with Daniel, who was making his début in opera, conducting Mozart's *Don Giovanni*. Years later, when chosen to participate in *Desert Island Discs* for BBC Radio, Jackie told of the 'happy time I had going to all the rehearsals and getting to know the cast'. Soon she knew the opera by heart and would be quick to note errors not only in the musical text, but in the sung libretto. One small (and repeated) mispronunciation in the trio of Don Giovanni, Zerlina and Masetto (scene 18) from the closing section of Act 1 led to much laughter between her and Daniel, and gave rise to pet names for each other. Altogether this first-hand experience of Mozart opera whetted Jackie's appetite for both music and dramatic theatre, something she was able to indulge when illness forced her to stop playing altogether.

Du Pré's next public appearance was once more with the trio at the Festival Hall in London on 22 September, repeating the programme they had played in Israel. The occasion was a tense one for extra-musical reasons; in the aftermath of the massacre of Israeli athletes at the Olympic Village in Munich there was fear of world-wide reprisals and further attacks. As Daniel recalled, 'Although there had been no actual threat to us, it was decided to take precautionary measures.' Eleanor Warren, who was responsible for the direct transmission of the concert for BBC Radio, remembered that the hall was abuzz with detectives:

All the news boards proclaimed 'Arab killers in London'. Each of the artists had a detective assigned to them. They reacted very differently to the situation: Pinky took a fatalistic attitude, saying, 'If you're going to get shot, so you're going to get shot.' Daniel insisted on being able to see his detective all the time, whereas Jackie was wandering around backstage, seemingly oblivious, although I think she had been told what was going on. I got friendly with the private detective allocated to Daniel that evening, and asked him if there was any real danger that we would get blown up. He replied, 'I doubt it, since nearly everybody in the audience has a gun in their pockets.'

Fortunately, the concert passed without incident. *The Times* critic Max Harrison, never a great admirer of the Barenboim circle of musicians, wrote a barbed review in which he expressed extreme irritation for 'two superficial' performances. 'In contrast with the misconception of classical purity and restraint visited on Beethoven, Tchaikovsky's rarely heard trio Op.50 suffered from a complementary misreading of romantic passion ... for much of the time it was like hearing somebody talk at the top of their voice with maximum expressiveness from the very first bar...'[1]

A week later, on 29 September, Jackie and Daniel played a recital at the Albert Hall, performing the Brahms E minor, Beethoven A major and Franck Sonatas. The *Daily Telegraph* critic had the highest praise for the actual performances, only regretting that they were held in the ungrateful acoustic of the Albert Hall. 'A splendid concert wrongly placed,' he concluded. Friends, including the photographer Clive Barda and his wife Rosie, remembered the strong emotional impact of the concert. To them it seemed that Jackie was putting her whole self into her playing without reserve and that she transcended the restrictions of the instrument through her heartfelt outpouring of the music.[2] As the cellist Sandy Bailey recalled, 'In these last concerts the charisma with which she projected and the actual way she played the cello were sometimes two separate things. In other words, occasionally the gesture became louder than the actual sound produced. But it didn't matter because the musical message was so strongly communicated that it superseded any flaw such as bow surface noise.'

Perhaps because the physical process of playing was no longer something which Jackie could rely on automatically, other features came into play. One was an increased freedom to take risks on impulse, without worrying about instrumental difficulties or defects. But, there was also the development of a conscious awareness, necessitating the use of the eyes to place the fingers and bow. This analytical process served as a back-up when her natural technique failed her. That Jackie sometimes had to resort to such artifice was seldom evident to her fellow musicians, let alone to audiences. As Bailey observed, 'To hear Jackie miss a note was as exciting as to hear her get it. If she suddenly felt like going up the G string to a harmonic and missed it, the audience got nearly the same impact as if she had hit the note spot on.'

Meantime, the publicity machine was being set in motion for the du Pré 'come-back' to concert life. Jackie was to start her engagements with orchestra in early January 1973 in the USA and Canada, playing the Lalo concerto. This piece had been on her agenda for recording as far back as June 1971, when plans were made to perform it with Fauré's *Élégie* and Saint-Saëns's *Allegro Appassionata* with the Orchestre de Paris and Barenboim. The recording had been rescheduled for December 1972, then postponed again until June 1973 so as to coincide with du Pré's first concert appearances with the Orchestre de Paris. Daniel and Jackie now requested EMI to couple the Lalo concerto with Ibert's Concerto for Cello and Wind Instruments, since Jackie had programmed it for her Paris concerts.

However, EMI were no longer happy about the venture, since their financial department questioned the 'profitability' of recording Lalo's Cello Concerto in the first place; the idea of adding a work by Ibert made it even less attractive. Apart from the surprisingly low sales estimate and the high cost of engaging the Orchestre de Paris, Ibert's works were still under copyright. Influenced by these findings, EMI's financial department rejected the proposal. Suvi Grubb now asked Peter Andry to reconsider the matter, reminding him of the limited popular repertoire for cello and orchestra. As he pointed out, apart from Tchaikovsky's *Rococo Variations*, Jackie had recorded almost all the well-known cello concertos.[3]

It is evident from the correspondence that Andry would have preferred to scrap the whole project, but in order to maintain good relations with du Pré and Barenboim, he offered a compromise – namely recording the Lalo concerto and substituting the Ibert concerto with some César Franck pieces, a solution which avoided copyright charges. He also suggested using a 'less expensive' London orchestra.[4]

It was ironic that while Jackie was undergoing a final crisis on the concert platform in New York in February, Grubb was pressing insistently for her recording of the Lalo to be made in Paris. He also was setting up chamber music recordings in Israel, to include Schubert's *Trout* Quintet and Mozart's piano quartets, this time with Perlman as the violinist and Zukerman playing the viola. All these projects had to be postponed once more in the spring of 1973, but were only finally abandoned when it was evident that du Pré's illness had put paid to her ever performing in public again.

It is no less paradoxical that over twenty years later EMI finally issued a posthumous recording of du Pré's interpretation of the Lalo concerto. This was due to the good fortune that her first dates in 1973 (on 4 and 6 January) with Barenboim and the Cleveland Symphony Orchestra were both recorded by a local Cleveland radio station. The recent CD version is in fact edited from the two performances, but the editing is unable to disguise some tangible evidence of Jackie's physical difficulties in playing the cello. Not that these small defects detract from the eloquence of Jackie's rhetoric, or her overall vision of the concerto. They can be detected in a lack of security in some of the left-hand shifts, the occasional roughness of bow attack and the clumsy spikiness of some of her bow strokes (as, for instance, in the main theme of the last movement). Because of her diminished strength du Pré found it difficult to control the bow and sustain the sound in fortissimo, which caused her to force the tone in the loudest passages.

By issuing Strauss's *Don Quixote* on the same CD, recorded five years earlier, EMI unwittingly underlined the discrepancy between du Pré's playing at the top of her form in 1968 and in the last struggling month of her career. In the Strauss we can hear Jackie's total instrumental security, and one cannot but be impressed by the enormously rich and powerful sound that she was able to produce.

Nevertheless, we should be grateful that du Pré's interpretation of this underrated concerto has been preserved. Jackie admirably captures the declaiming character of Lalo's work, and invests even the most awkward passagework in the murkiest regions of the cello with a nobility and well-defined sense of purpose. In the first movement she can be lyrical or heroic by turns, mischievously teasing in the hispanic rhythmic syncopations of the second movement intermezzo, and rhapsodic and flamboyant in the finale. Barenboim's accompaniment emphasises the Latin character of the piece, whether in the short, sharp accompanying orchestral chords of the first movement, the dark, dramatic introduction to the finale, or in the elegant rhythmic patterns of the intermezzo. He always creates the necessary tension to help the music move forward, without ever covering the passagework of the cello.

At the time, Robert Finn wrote enthusiastically of the Cleveland performances, praising du Pré's 'defiant' brilliance, and her preferred emphasis of 'strong, gutsy articulation to beauty of tone or stylistic niceties'.[5]

After their concerts in Cleveland, Daniel and Jackie proceeded to Toronto to play the same concerto on 9 and 10 January. The critic in the *Globe and Mail,* an admirer of du Pré's immense gifts, was left wondering why her performances with the Toronto Symphony Orchestra lacked the accustomed fire and vitality: 'The quality of the sound seemed surprisingly small for this artist,' he observed. By normal criteria of judgement her cello playing remained musically and technically 'outstanding'. But, he concluded, the concert 'was just not great du Pré'.

While Daniel returned to Cleveland for a further week's work with the Cleveland Symphony Orchestra, Jackie gave two recitals with Lamar Crowson at the Kennedy Centre, Washington DC and in Brooklyn. On 15 January she was joined by Daniel for what proved to be their last recital together at New York's Philharmonic Hall. Billed as 'Jacqueline du Pré's return to New York after two years' absence', the concert hardly achieved the effect of a triumphant come-back.

The programme consisted of the Brahms E minor, the Debussy and Chopin Sonatas, all works which Jackie knew inside out. The critic of the *New York Times* admitted that du Pré was a performer of marked individuality. 'But on this occasion her work veered dizzily from the extraordinarily good through the questionable to the downright inadmissible.' In the last category the critic complained of wailing shifts, wide vibrato and notes that were 'pounced on' and sometimes missed. While Barenboim received praise for his calming influence and lucid, focused playing, du Pré was offered advice: 'Through the technical lapses and interpretational eccentricities, one can still discern a musician of great talent and a personality of communicative vitality. Perhaps Miss du Pré should consider tempering self-indulgent abandon with a little hard thinking about the notes and where they are headed.'[6]

Not only the critics, but many of Jackie's friends and admirers were also bewildered by the changes in her playing. Those who knew her, refrained from voicing their doubts, since Jackie was visibly distressed. She had always been her own severest judge and there was no reason to call her musical integrity into question now.

From New York Jackie flew back to London for a couple of weeks' rest then, on 8 and 11 February, she gave two concerts in the Festival Hall, playing the Elgar concerto with Zubin Mehta and the NPO.

Originally du Pré had been booked to perform *Don Quixote*, but as she became increasingly anxious about her diminishing strength, she opted to play concertos that she felt completely secure with. As Mehta recalled,

> We decided on the Elgar; it could even be possible that Jackie had a premonition that this was going to be her last concert in London. She had been experiencing problems with the right hand for some time, and for this reason she changed her bow and chose to play the Peresson cello – it gave her a superficial big tone. Even so, she was unable to produce the big sound that we remembered. And as the sound kept diminishing, she started to exaggerate musically. I remember at the rehearsal of the Elgar many of the cellists from the New Philharmonia came up to me and begged me to intercede with her and dissuade her from some of her more excessive indulgences.[7]

Mehta knew better than to interfere; despite his powerful sense that something was wrong, he realised that his best course was to provide Jackie with comfort and encouragement. She clearly needed moral support and insisted that her psychoanalyst Walter Joffe should attend one of the concerts. Joffe had a clinical interest in seeing whether Jackie's complaints about the physical difficulties of playing corresponded to his objective observations. He also wanted to know exactly how she felt about her performance.

For Jackie evidently it was a highly emotional occasion and the many memories of her triumphs with this particular piece in this particular hall must have come flooding back. She certainly never gave more of herself than she did in these two sold-out concerts and those who attended them knew that they were witnessing something quite out of the ordinary. Coloured by our retrospective knowledge of events, it is tempting to recall her playing as a foreboding of disaster worthy of Greek tragedy.

At the time, Peter Stadlen wrote, 'Her profoundly felt performance ... held the audience spellbound ... Thinking back over the years since this superb young artist's first appearance we may well marvel at the distance travelled from a certain discreet reticence towards the unconditional surrender to the music we witness today.'[8]

Neville Cardus's review in the *Guardian* goes one step further, reading almost like a poignant epitaph to du Pré's achievement. He noted that although 'time and poor health have momentarily taken something from her art of technical certainty, much has been returned to her in maturity of understanding and inwardness of thought as she goes through this most private and troubled music Elgar ever composed'.

Few can have written with such honest appreciation of du Pré's visionary powers and interpretation as Cardus did in his finely perceived assessment:

. . . Jacqueline went to the heart of the matter with a devotion remarkable in so young an artist, so that we did not appear so much to be hearing, as overhearing, music which has the sunset touch on it, telling the end of an epoch in our island story and, also, telling of Elgar's acceptance of the end. The bright day is done, and he is for the dark. Towards the close of the concerto Elgar recalls a theme from the slow movement and the falling cadences are even self-pitying. Jacqueline du Pré got the wounding juice out of this self-revealing passage; her tone came from her sensitively quivering fingers.

Cardus concluded by recalling how 'Years ago I described Miss du Pré in these columns as the most precious gift to English interpretative music since Kathleen Ferrier. After last night's benediction I repeat the description and compliment with some emphasis.'[9]

At the Thursday night concert which I attended there were already small signals of alarm, when a shift was nearly missed, or there was a slight hiccup in the co-ordination of passagework. For some people, the slow tempi in the slow movement was almost too much. Here Gillian Widdicombe complained of 'finger slides so extravagant that one could have said "portamento" several times before she arrived at the final note'.[10]

But the effect of her musical message was so irresistibly strong that it obscured any such flaws and mannerisms. Rodney Friend was completely overwhelmed by Jackie's performance at the Thursday night concert: 'I just sat in my chair for ten minutes afterwards in tears; I found the effect of Jackie's highly emotional playing quite exhausting. I think it is true to say that I have never before or since experienced such absolute giving in music, without any trace of artificiality or superficiality. The pain and suffering in her playing were almost tangible and it is something for which there is no explanation.'[11]

Sandy Bailey recalled that there were more dicey moments in the second concert on Sunday afternoon. 'Jackie's final performance of the Elgar was to me both wonderful and awful. I could tell that cellistically she was having problems with the bow control, although I had no idea why. She was so uncomfortable that she seemed to have almost to stand up out of the seat in the third movement. Not that any of this impeded the communication – it was still a fantastic performance. The Elgar was so deeply in her, she couldn't play it badly.'

Immediately after the concert, Jackie was taken to Heathrow Airport, where she caught an evening flight to New York, to join Daniel for another performance of the Lalo concerto with the Cleveland Orchestra in New York's Carnegie Hall on 14 February. To judge by the reviews, she was back on relatively good form. Harriet Johnson praised du Pré's 'tongue-in-cheek perception' of Lalo's music: 'Always exuberant in despatch once she begins to play ... du Pré had something of a Devil's charm last night not only in her playing as she slid to a high position only to leave breath-takingly to another climate on the instrument, but also in the intermittent sly smiles she gave Barenboim and others in the front line orchestra. She played as if engaged for the night on a dare and the attitude suited the work's insouciant character.'[12]

After what transpired to be her final concert with Barenboim, Jackie was scheduled to play the Brahms Double Concerto with Pinchas Zukerman and the New York Philharmonic under Leonard Bernstein. As usual, the concerts were to be repeated four times in the subscription series at Philharmonic Hall, between 22 and 27 February. Already at rehearsal Jackie's disturbing symptoms had intensified: her fingers were so weak that she could hardly open the cello case, and the strange sensation of pins and needles and a spreading numbness had returned. She had been telling friends recently that at each concert she didn't know if she would last through a performance. Her arms felt like lead and she was worried lest she drop the bow, as she could no longer assess its weight. Genie Zukerman recalled that Jackie consulted a doctor before the first New York concert who dismissed her symptoms as hysterical. This only served to increase her agitation, making her feel that everything was her own fault.

Bernstein initially assumed that du Pré was suffering from nerves and cajoled her to play. Jackie managed three of the four dates. But the third of these was a nightmare experience for her. She walked on to the stage as if on to a scaffold, knowing that she could no longer feel the strings under her fingers. In this final performance Jackie had to rely exclusively on her eyes so as to know where to place her fingers. Later she confessed 'it was not good playing'.[13] Genie Zukerman described Jackie's playing that night as wild and scratchy.

Arnold Steinhardt who also attended this last concert, recalled that there was already some controversy among New York musicians because Jackie was playing her new Peresson cello:

> People were shocked that she preferred a brand-new cello to her old Italian instruments. But I was shocked at her playing. I remember saying to myself, 'How sad that she allows herself such sloppy playing, it sounds as if she's not practising. How can a person of her gifts not honour her talent?' When I found out what the matter was I felt so badly that I had accused her like that, even though I had kept my thoughts to myself. Later Jackie told me how she had struggled and what she had gone through to play that concert.[14]

After the third concert Jackie explained to Bernstein that she would have to cancel the last on 27 February. As Pinky recalled, 'She just couldn't manage it; emotionally she had struck rock bottom and she simply did not have the energy to play any more.' Bernstein, having been initially sceptical of Jackie's complaints, now took them seriously and went out of his way to be helpful and to soothe her. Jackie called Daniel (who was in Los Angeles) and told him she was going back to London and was cancelling all her engagements. As he said, 'Jackie was highly distressed, she did not know what was happening to her. I recall she was very touched by Bernstein's concern and attention. He personally took her to see a doctor. She was well aware of the extrovert public side of Lenny, but here she saw and experienced the personal caring side as well.'

The *New York Times* reported that du Pré's sudden cancellation was due to paraesthesia of the right arm, a disorder of the nerve endings. Back at home, Dr Selby tried to be reassuring. While taking her complaints seriously, he could find nothing specifically wrong, although by now he was beginning to suspect that she was suffering from a neurological rather than a psychological disorder. Rather than upset Jackie at this point, he preferred to wait for more definite evidence before sending her on for clinical tests, which would lead to a diagnosis. As Cynthia Benz writes in her book on MS, 'Diagnosis is a pivotal point. [...] It is devastating to be given it too soon, and infuriating to be held out on.'[15]

In the meantime Diana Rix wrote letters cancelling all Jackie's engagements for the foreseeable future, explaining that du Pré was suffering from tenosynovitis. Dr Joffe tried to shore up Jackie's shaken confidence, but he too could not explain this disappointing recurrence of her disorders. It was now more than ever that Jackie came to rely on Daniel's support. Rather than be separated from him, she accompanied him on tour in the following months, travelling to Japan, Paris, Israel and in August to the Edinburgh Festival – in every place she had had to cancel her own engagements.

Jackie's continuing agitation about her health left her more and more immersed in herself. People often found her absent and distracted. By now, Daniel was highly concerned about her condition. He recalled several worrying incidents: 'While we were in Japan, Jackie fell down the stairs a couple of times for no reason. People didn't know what to think, neither did I.' Later that summer, friends were sometimes bewildered to find Jackie wandering aimlessly on the streets of Hampstead. Sandy Goehr recalls once seeing her stranded on a traffic island, apparently immobilised. It turned out that she was on her way back from a session with Dr Joffe; Goehr gave her a lift and took her to his mother's house to calm her down.

Jackie tried to keep up an appearance of normality, but sometimes it was hard to disguise her own fears. Yet she did not want to be a cause of anxiety and often hid her symptoms from Daniel. If she turned up late at home, he would wonder if anything were wrong; Jackie was likely to answer him reassuringly, saying she had visited a friend or had got caught up doing some shopping. Later it might transpire that she had fallen down in the street and had not been able to pick herself up.

On the night of 5 October Jackie and Daniel entertained friends to dinner at Pilgrim's Lane. It was the eve of Yom Kippur and the tense situation in Israel threatened war. Daniel was anxious to go to Tel Aviv as quickly as possible, as he had done in May 1967. Much of the evening was spent telephoning his parents and making arrangements to leave London and cancel his engagements. Jackie had cooked an excellent dinner, but seemed strangely truculent when Daniel asked her to fetch an address book from their upstairs bedroom. In fact, she successfully hid from her husband and her guests the fact that that her legs were too weak to take her up the staircase.

Daniel arrived in Israel the next day, in circumstances that were much bleaker than they had been in the spring of 1967. There was to be no clear-cut victory as in the Six Day War. Jackie's presence with Daniel in Israel during that war had served as a symbol of hope and generosity, and as a couple they had shared the euphoric spirit of a nation in victory in the consummation of their personal happiness. Now their brightest hopes were crumbling around them as forces greater than them overtook their destiny.

Daniel was aware that he had left Jackie in a disturbed state of mind and health. After another fall in a Hampstead street she returned to her doctor. On 8 October Dr Selby examined Jackie and decided to refer her to a neurologist. 'I realised that these local symptoms could no longer be described as psychosomatic. There was obviously something seriously wrong. I saw some of her reflexes were not what they should be and this made me fairly certain that there was some neurological condition.'[16] The following day Jackie visited the consultant neurologist Dr Leo Lange at the London Clinic, who observed that 'although Jackie had no gross physical signs, there were enough of them to make me think that there was something structurally wrong'. It was decided that Jackie should be admitted to St Mary's Hospital, Paddington, where various tests were performed.

As Dr Lange recalled, 'In those days the diagnosis had to be deductive. There were no MRI scans, which would have clinched the diagnosis. As a routine investigation, I performed a lumbar puncture, where the cerebrospinal fluid is extracted for analysis. An MS patient will have abnormal proteins or a high level of antibodies in the spinal fluid.' Since the medical history is as important as the physical examination, Dr Lange needed to talk to Dr Selby so as to establish the diagnosis with certainty. He recalled that he tried to speak out of Jackie's hearing. 'But this made her very anxious. Daniel was in Israel and Isaac Stern's wife had come to the hospital to visit. I could not say too much in front of someone who was not a relative.'[17] Dr Lange's clinical diagnosis of multiple sclerosis was confirmed by the consultant neurologist at St Mary's Hospital, Dr Harold Edwards, on 16 October.

Her doctors broke the news to Jackie as gently as possible. She reacted with a mixture of shocked disbelief and understandable relief. Rather than alarm Daniel while he was in Israel, she decided to await his return to tell him the truth. But this was easier said than done. Zubin Mehta, who was in Israel performing concerts with Barenboim, recalled that Daniel phoned Jackie every day: 'One day, when he called their home . . . he was told she had gone to hospital for a check-up. He asked what was wrong. The answer he received, from an obviously uncomprehending housekeeper, was that the doctor suspected multiple sclerosis – just like that.'

In the 1960s and early 1970s MS was an illness with a low public profile – most people had never heard of it and neither had Barenboim or Mehta. As Zubin put it, 'Because of our ignorance of this wretched illness ... we did not react to the enormity of what we had been told on the telephone. But of course we had to find out as soon as possible, so I telephoned a doctor friend of mine to ask for an explanation. As there was only one telephone in the room, Danny came close to the instrument so that he could hear what the doctor said. That was how he first learnt of the tragedy which was to come into his life.'

27

Fortitude Under Affliction

A robin redbreast in a cage
Puts all Heaven in a rage.
William Blake

It probably took quite a few days, if not weeks, for Jackie to grasp the full implications of the diagnosis of multiple sclerosis. But its immediate effect was to put the distressing events of the past years into perspective. As Dr Selby put it, 'Now, at least, Jackie knew that it wasn't all in the mind.' The definite knowledge that she was physically and not psychologically ill unleashed in her a myriad pent-up emotions, ranging from exhilarated relief to anguished sorrow.

On discovering that Jackie was in hospital, Daniel took the first flight available to London out of war-ridden Israel. He was determined to confront the situation with his wife, lending her the full strength of his loving support. Undoubtedly the diagnosis was initially more shocking for Daniel than for Jackie. Not wanting to alarm her unnecessarily, her doctors softened their explanations, pointing to the fact that in the usual course of the sickness, attacks were followed by long remissions. But nobody tried to delude Daniel about the bleaker prospects of the illness. From a position of total ignorance he had to learn some stark facts about multiple sclerosis, as well as listening to conflicting advice about treatments.

Daniel recalls that it was he who insisted on being given a realistic prognosis of Jackie's case: 'Dr Edwards (the senior consultant neurologist at St Mary's) described to me the various ways the illness could manifest itself and develop, with the possibility of long remissions in certain cases. In fact, the worst scenario he painted – of a rapidly progressive form of MS, with a life expectancy of about fifteen years – turned out to be a rather accurate picture of what actually happened. Jackie died fourteen years after the diagnosis was made.'

Such a cruel possibility must have been dreadfully shocking to a man of barely thirty, who himself possessed a fundamental vitality and robust health. As Daniel admitted, 'When you are young it is almost impossible to imagine what fifteen years of such an illness and its nightmare developments could be like.'

The doctors did their best to be reassuring to Jackie. Len Selby, a close friend of the Barenboims, always showed a gentle humour in his dealings with her; she was as grateful for his warmth and humanity as for his medical care. As he recalled, 'At the beginning Jackie hoped to get back to normal life and perform concerts. She was able to put on a brave face for the world – she was a very great actress. But I did also see the other side of things and I suspect that deep down she was terrified.'

Everyone prayed that the disease would take a gentle course and that Jackie might be granted long remissions (which is the pattern experienced by eighty-five per cent of MS patients). Both Daniel and Jackie lived with the hope that she would play the cello again and perhaps recover sufficiently to have children, a prospect that would give them a sense of normality. Having overcome a recent crisis, Jackie and Daniel felt their marriage was stronger than ever. Now that it was being subjected to another cruel blow of fortune it must have been very difficult for the couple to maintain their optimism.

While still in hospital, Jackie phoned a large circle of friends and family with the news of the diagnosis. I remember her trying to soothe my horrified reaction by patiently explaining the nature of the illness and confessing her own relief at having a tangible cause for her troubles. It was typical of her thoughtfulness that she wanted to reassure people that she was all right and was worried lest anyone learn the alarming news of her condition through press reports.

Her prudence was well justified, since not long after she was discharged from hospital the *Daily Mail* printed on its front page the sensational headline 'Du Pré will never play again'. Daniel was infuriated at the insensitivity of this speculative report, which was reprinted in most of the national press, and broadcast on TV and radio. He interrupted a morning rehearsal with the LPO to give an impromptu press conference that same day (6 November). Denying that Jackie was seriously ill, he explained that 'she is leading a normal life at home and doing some cooking and tidying up the house'. She was also coming to hear his concert that night. His final words were a reprimand: 'It is no help at all to say she is gravely ill.' Barenboim asked his lawyer to issue an official press statement to the effect that there was no truth in the rumour that du Pré would not play again – she was only suffering from a 'mild' attack of multiple sclerosis.

After coming home, Jackie initially enjoyed having the licence to rest as much as she wanted and not to have to think about long- or short-term engagements. But while indulging her invalid status she was left with a lot of time to ponder the cruel nature of a debilitating disease which could cause so many levels of disability. She also had to cope with her feelings of guilt, wondering how her illness would affect those closest to her.

And indeed, having to confront the issue of an illness for which there was no guaranteed cure had a highly unsettling effect on Daniel. His first instinct was to cancel most of his concert engagements. This was not only because Jackie needed him in the house, but because coping with the shock temporarily extinguished the kind of extrovert confidence an artist needs to walk on-stage to perform. Daniel now found himself in charge of a host of administrative problems, from discussing and agreeing to doctors' treatments and getting planning permission to redesign the house where a staircase represented a major hurdle for Jackie, to domestic administration. His friends could see the tangible effects not only of his very real grief, but of the mounting pressures on him. While unfailingly sweet to Jackie, away from her Daniel was a dark and troubled man. The laughing, almost childishly joking side of his personality now often gave way to a dour seriousness.

Ultimately he succeeded in taking various pragmatic decisions for himself and on Jackie's behalf. The first was that she should live at home, be able to entertain friends and be free to go out as much as she wanted. This entailed finding a live-in housekeeper; before too long she was to need a resident nurse as well. Later still, Daniel bought a car which could accommodate the wheelchair and employed a part-time chauffeur to take Jackie out and about.

The second no less important decision regarded his continuing career. Len Selby recalled that in those early days Daniel expressed the wish to stay at home to look after Jackie. Len dissuaded him from the idea, pointing out that the illness would be very costly, especially if she were to be kept at home. His friends, too, were in agreement that one life sacrificed to multiple sclerosis was enough and that Barenboim should be encouraged to fulfil his talents by pursuing the career for which he was destined.

A realist at heart, Daniel needed to summon up all his resources to find positive solutions to such a difficult situation. He has acknowledged the importance of Spinoza's philosophy in teaching him that reason must be used in everyday life: 'Reason can show us the difference between what is temporary and what is permanent. In a desperate situation, unless you are able to apply reason, the logical conclusion can only be suicide, or, at the very least anguish.'[1]

In the new year of 1974 Daniel started playing concerts again, although he cancelled engagements that took him away from London for any length of time. During the remainder of the 1970s he drastically reduced all touring in North America, even though this involved severing some flourishing relationships with top American orchestras. Daniel soon realised that he needed a stable base, which would allow him to spend regular intervals of free time with Jackie, without having to confront the problems of her care on a daily basis. Rather than continue guest-conducting, he decided to seek a position of music director. In view of the distance, he did not even consider any proposal made by orchestras in the United States. As he recalled, 'I was offered jobs with the LPO and then the Philharmonia as chief conductor. The main reason I didn't accept a London orchestra, though, was that Jackie was already sick and I wouldn't have been able to cope with a position which obliged me to live in London. In 1974, I was offered the position of Music Director of the Orchestre de Paris, which I accepted. When the job started in September 1975, I transferred my base from London to Paris.'

After the initial euphoria following diagnosis, Jackie sank into lethargy and depression. Later she was able to talk about what she had been through in these first months: 'There were long periods of being encompassed by four walls, time to feel very lonely, time to analyse each symptom with great intensity and watch its progress as if under a microscope. Those times were horrible and I managed them very poorly. When things are hard and one is not well, one is very conscious of the effect this has on those who are close to one; of the enormous resources it calls for in them.'[2]

Jackie was well aware that Daniel faced a huge conflict of interests and she encouraged him to take up the job in Paris. But she was very dependent on him and when he was away she missed him. Daniel made a habit of ringing her every day to check that all was well and these daily calls were a highlight in her routine.

In the months following the diagnosis her close friends visited her regularly. Diana Rix remembered going to Pilgrim's Lane several times when Daniel was not there to find Jackie lying disconsolately in bed in her room upstairs. Often Iris was in the house, cooking and helping out, but Jackie appeared not to want to talk to her or anybody else. She had lost all interest in the outside world and would reject any positive suggestion, whether to listen to music, read books or brighten up her room with pictures. Evidently just coming to terms with the illness was taking a momentous effort on her part and demanded every ounce of her mental energy.

To begin with, her cello remained firmly locked away. Occasionally, Jackie would listen to and advise her cellist friends, although at this stage she had no desire to teach professionally. She did not have the strength to face the world with her disability. Kate Beare was one of Jackie's first visitors on her return from hospital and, at Jackie's request, she brought her cello with her. Kate remembered that 'Jackie was lying on her bed upstairs, looking tired and lackadaisical. She was quite unlike her old self and didn't appear to care about anything. I felt, "Oh God, the last thing she wants is to listen to me play the cello." But as soon as I played the opening of the Schumann concerto, she came to life, sat bolt upright and was transformed. It was very inspiring and deeply moving.' With the help of her friends, Jackie gradually emerged from this initial depression.

Although both Iris and Aida Barenboim made themselves available during the first few months to help in the house, Daniel realised the urgent need for a permanent live-in housekeeper. Neither he nor Jackie could cope with cooking, especially when there were so many friends and visitors coming in and out of the house. By chance, he discovered the perfect solution in Olga Rejman, a warm-hearted Czech woman in her early sixties, who had been living in London since 1964. She was a music-lover and had attended several of Barenboim's performances, including the benefit concert for Czechoslovakia at the Albert Hall given by him and du Pré.

Rodney Friend was with Daniel when, in February 1974, they walked into a small London restaurant where Olga worked as a chef:

For some reason Olga was standing outside the kitchen and she saw us walk in. The moment she recognised Daniel she flipped – here was the saviour of Czechoslovakia in person! Daniel was desperate to find someone not only to look after Jackie, but also him. He had the whole musical élite of the world coming to the house and he could not cope with entertaining. Daniel started talking to Olga, and was touched by her kindliness and compassion. 'Why don't you come and see us?' he asked. 'Perhaps you could come tonight and cook dinner – Isaac Stern's coming.' Olga came, and she ended up by staying for six years.'[3]

Olga showered Jackie with love and attention, although she reserved her absolute devotion for Daniel. Being a witness to their daily life, she saw better than anyone how much he cared about Jackie and tried to bring comfort into her life. Olga was soon accepted as a member of their family. She was an excellent cook and prepared meals untiringly for a seemingly unending stream of friends. Every now and then she would protest that it was too much for her, and the Barenboims would curtail the entertaining. But it was against Olga's nature as well as theirs to withhold hospitality to their guests, who continued to come in droves.

If Jackie made light of her difficulties in front of her family and friends, it was all the more essential to have an outlet for her fears and anxieties. To begin with she relied on her sessions with Walter Joffe to be able to give voice to them. His sudden death from a heart attack in the early summer of 1974 came as a horrible shock. Joffe's wife, realising that Jackie could not be abandoned, immediately arranged for her to be referred to another psychoanalyst, Dr Adam Limentani. They met and Limentani instantly won her trust. He soon became indispensable to her and remained so for the rest of her life. Jackie developed a great affection for him, dubbing him Amadeo to his face and 'the Lemon' or 'Lemondrops' to her friends.

In Jackie's situation there was little choice but to adopt a philosophical attitude to the vicissitudes of life. She usually managed to look on the bright side of things and acknowledged that she was fortunate in her misfortune. Daniel could not have been more attentive; when he was away he ensured that a rota of friends came to visit her. Jackie discovered new interests, principally a love of literature and theatre. She took up typing and bombarded her friends with missives.

While she was able to exercise enough physical co-ordination she would still play the cello, even though the sounds she produced were far from what she intended. Despite the frustrations involved, playing kept her actively involved in music and was a useful form of physiotherapy. As she wrote to Maggie Cowan, her violinist friend from the

ECO, 'Oh dear, why are some things that are simple to say difficult to say? It's all so much easier on my new-old cello! This friend now keeps me company upstairs & every now and then I try "Baa Baa Black Sheep" and other useful exercises of that ilk. Very edifying.'[4]

She was encouraged in these exercises by friends and colleagues. When Gregor Piatigorsky came to London in the summer of 1974, to take Jackie's place in concerts with Daniel and Pinky at the City of London Festival, he made a point of visiting daily and playing duets with her. Daniel was always happy to play through things with Jackie and sometimes they were joined by others of their close circle. On one such occasion Itzhak Perlman played the Schubert B flat Piano Trio with them. 'Amazing as it may seem,' he recalled, 'Jackie's technical security was all there inside her and she made no concessions to her disability, she never tried to adapt to her physical limitations. The gestures, the placement of the bow and fingers were all done with the same panache and risk as in her best playing days, although now she would miss the shifts and couldn't control the sound.'[5]

Pleeth, a frequent visitor, recalled Jackie once phoning to invite him for a duet session. She apologised in advance for her playing, warning him that unless she used her eyes to guide her she had no idea which side of the bridge she was playing on. 'But we'll cross that bridge when we come to it,' she quipped. Pleeth appreciated Jackie's courage and humour in this situation, and was amazed that she succeeded in transcending her physical limitations on the cello. The rough, scratchy sounds lost their relevance in the face of a spiritual communication so strong that it seemed directly related to the initial impulse, or what Pleeth described as 'the music of the inner ear'.

Jackie always knew how to turn music-making into a special occasion. I remember her coming to my house with her cello and a present of the de Fesch cello duos. Having discovered that I didn't know them she had taken the trouble to procure the scores and proceeded to play the pieces with me, illuminating the music in an unforgettable manner.

For the first year and a half Jackie retained enough mobility to cope with walking. Attempts to have the house modified for a disabled person by putting in a lift were thwarted when planning permission was refused. But Jackie determinedly managed the stairs at the Pilgrim's Lane house, even if she sometimes had to slide down them on her bottom. When she felt up to it she went out to concerts, and enjoyed shopping and cooking.

Since there is no specific treatment for multiple sclerosis, doctors talk of the 'management' of the illness. Dr Selby recalled that in Jackie's case every remedy was tried from diet to strong drugs, but nothing had any noticeable effect. It very quickly became apparent that her co-ordination was deteriorating and that the pattern of relapses was not compensated by any significant remission. In other words, she rarely regained the ground she had lost. This fact in itself pointed to the progressive nature of the illness.

Apart from the evident physical symptoms, multiple sclerosis often produces wide mood swings in patients which, in Jackie's case, were exacerbated by the use of steroids – she tended to be euphoric rather than depressed. Dr Lange had prescribed steroids early in his treatment, hoping they would contain, if not cure, the existing symptoms. Initially they had the required holding effect, but it soon became evident that they were making no great impact on the progress of the disease. Yet when Jackie stopped taking them she experienced further small relapses. Steroids also produced unwanted physical side-effects: weight gain, hair loss and fluid retention. She was mortified at the changes in her appearance, as her face became swollen and puffy.

Since her illness was now public knowledge, Jackie received many letters from well-wishers suggesting cures. Some of them were medically valid, others involved diet and 'alternative' treatment, and a few were so crankish as to be dismissed out of hand as ridiculous if not grotesque. Jackie did try some of the suggested diets. One she persisted with for some time (Dr Grier's diet) included a prohibition of salt; Jackie would point out with wry humour that in certain religious orders eating without salt was prescribed as a penance.

Any letter containing a serious medical suggestion was passed on to Len Selby. He also scanned the international journals for information about new treatments. As Len observed, 'The trouble with MS is you can never know if a patient has had a natural remission, or if he is responding to some form of treatment or diet. I wrote around the world from Moscow to Los Angeles in search of a cure. One day I read about research being done into the connection between measles and multiple sclerosis by Dr Zabriska at the Rockefeller Institute in New York.' On further investigation, it was agreed that this therapy was worth serious thought. Jackie did not expect miracles, but hoped that Zabriska's treatment would at least contain the progress of the illness and allow her to recover some of her movement. Dr Lange explained:

The research into the transfer factor and its connection with MS is a long-standing theory, still unproven today. It is based on the fact that elevated levels of measles antibodies are found in the blood and spinal fluid of MS patients. Normally there are no cells in that fluid, but in periods of inflammation, antibodies from all previous infections (even a common flu virus) are present in elevated levels. This has bedevilled research. It is further complicated by the fact that it is not known whether MS itself is caused by a virus.

The six weeks that Jackie spent at the Rockefeller Institute Hospital in the spring of 1975 proved to be an unhappy experience and medically it failed to meet her expectations. Yet she had arrived in New York at the end of April with optimism and hope, as is evident in one of the first letters she wrote to Rodney and Cynthia Friend: 'I have a lovely view of the river, and everybody is extra nice and pleasant. Dr Zabriska is a cellist, Dr Espinoga(!) a great music lover and a lot of other [doctors] have music in their lives.' The day before, she had gone to a concert at Philharmonic Hall where Rostropovich played with Bernstein. 'We had lots of fun backstage. I tried the Duport Strad [Rostropovich had just acquired this cello], which left me speechless because of its sound and strength. Beautiful.'[6]

A couple of weeks later she typed another basically cheerful letter to the Friends, where she described her daily routine: 'A tough schedule has been drawn up, which I feel would give you both many a laugh. It consists of – wait for it – one hour's piano, one hour's cello, one hour's PT, one hour's typing, and things like knitting and crotcheeing (however you spell the damned thing) are encouraged in one's spare time.'[7]

Daniel in fact spent the whole of May in the States and came to visit when he could. Jackie told Rodney and Cynthia that she had been able to attend some of his New York concerts, and she had particularly enjoyed the 'magical best' of Clifford Curzon's performance as Barenboim's soloist. Her reticence about medical symptoms perhaps was a façade for her increasing fears. A passing reference to the doctor's statement that her walking 'will not return for months' is almost brushed aside and it seems that she was more concerned about being weaned off steroids which, she hoped, would mean that her hair would grow back. 'So it's not so schwer zu sein a Yid,' she concluded with an appropriate joke about her Jewishness directed to Cynthia, like herself a convert to Judaism.[8]

Yet during her stay at the Rockefeller Institute Hospital Jackie could not have failed to realise that far from improving, her condition was worsening. However, it was not the treatment (which principally involved injecting transfer factor) that caused her distress. Dr Limentani was unhappy not to have been consulted about the decision for Jackie to go to New York. He had predicted that the withdrawal of psychological support for such a long period might have dire results and believed in retrospect that his fears were justified: 'Jackie walked on to the plane when she left London – but she arrived back in a wheelchair. That's difficult to account for. One must recognise that despite the slow erosion of physical functions which was part of the illness, medical stress also had an effect. In Jackie's case it was caused by the doctors making her more fully aware of the seriousness of the illness. The realisation that she probably wouldn't get better was highly distressing.'[9]

In later years Jackie would often talk vitriolicly of the cruel doctors at the Rockefeller Institute Hospital who, without mincing words, had painted a dire picture of how the illness might affect her. She had been told that she would probably not walk or play again, and to add insult to injury there was a strong possibility that her mind would be affected and, worse still, her hearing impaired. She never forgave a certain Doctor Meli for telling her she would go mad.

Yet several of her New York friends who visited her in those weeks recalled that Jackie did not seem outwardly unhappy at the time. She was well looked after and was even able to enjoy some of the occupational therapy which was devised as useful exercise for her hands. Later she came to regard these activities as a humiliating reminder that she was no longer capable of handling a cello. But at the time her innate creativity came to the fore and she made several gifts for friends, including two leather belts on which she had punched musical quotations. For James Wolfensohn she inscribed the opening bars of Bach's G major Prelude from the First Cello Suite and for Dr Limentani the passage from the coda of the Elgar concerto which she referred to as the 'tear-drop'.

Genie Zukerman, another of her regular visitors, remembered that Jackie became interested in both the psychological and medical aspects of illness and read books by Oliver Sacks. Genie perceived that the stay at the Rockefeller Institute Hospital was a crucial experience for Jackie, as it made her realise that there was no cure for her disease and that the doctors were basically only grasping at straws.

Jackie was immensely relieved to return to London on 20 June. Before going home, she was admitted to St Mary's Hospital, Paddington, for medical checks. It was here that she first met the nurse Ruth Ann Cannings, a young black woman from Guyana. During her stay at St Mary's, Jackie warmed to Ruth Ann's cheerful disposition and dubbed her with her own nickname 'Smiley'. She was impressed by her nursing skills, particularly the ease with which Ruth Ann could lift her, all the more so after the 'manhandling' she had experienced at the hands of the male nurses at the Rockefeller Institute Hospital.

During her six weeks' absence from London the deterioration in Jackie's walking was so great that it was obvious she would no longer be able to cope with the stairs at Pilgrim's Lane. Fortuitously, the ballerina Dame Margot Fonteyn had come up with a timely proposal to rent out to the Barenboims her mews house in Knightsbridge. It had been adapted for wheelchair use, since Fonteyn's husband, Dr Roberto (Tito) Arias had become a paraplegic as a result of an assassination attempt.

Thus, at the beginning of July the Barenboims moved into Rutland Garden Mews, a quiet cul-de-sac on the south side of Hyde Park. The walls of the large downstairs sitting-room were decorated with carved wooden panelling, removed intact from a church in Panama. At the other end of the room was the dining area, giving on to a large patio window, which Olga filled with beautiful plants. A lift which just accommodated a small wheelchair, its occupant and a 'pusher', connected the hallway with the upstairs bedrooms, which were sufficient in number to allow the Barenboims to employ a live-in nurse as well as a resident housekeeper. Jackie might have missed Hampstead, but she appreciated being in wheeling distance of Hyde Park and the Serpentine, as well as Knightsbridge's smart shops, which included the 'local drugstore', as she referred to Harrods.

Moving into Rutland Garden Mews meant accepting a new level of disability, which necessitated using a wheelchair to give Jackie mobility. It became for her a symbol of her dependence and the associated frustration and guilt. For Daniel the wheelchair was a stark reminder of the reality of Jackie's invalid status, if not a reproach for his continuing life in music.

Rodney Friend recalled helping Daniel acquire Jackie's first wheel-chair at the end of 1974.

> When we walked into the shop, it was a serious moment – a horrible confrontation; Jackie was going into that chair and not coming out. The silly part of the story was trying to get the empty wheelchair back to the car. I ended up by wheeling Daniel, which would have been fine had I known how to negotiate a roadside kerb, steps or a lift. Getting back to the multi-storey car-park became a farce, since we were pursued by a well-meaning gentleman who kept offering his assistance. This in turn forced us to keep up our pretence, although we were by now convulsed by giggles. The whole situation was so tragic, yet we found ourselves using this façade so as to make this awful moment into a gag.'

A disabled person may feel lonely, but seldom gets a chance of being alone. Jackie found herself being looked after by a veritable army of people: Olga, a live-in nurse, a relief nurse, doctors and specialists, and her psychiatrist Limentani. To these were added her old friend Sylvia Southcombe, who came every Friday afternoon to deal with cor-respondence and settlement of household bills and nurses' salaries. Jackie also started having weekly sessions with the physiotherapist, Sonia Corderay, whom she quickly adopted as a friend.

Sonia recalled that at their first meeting she had suggested that there should be some trial sessions to see how they got on. 'Jackie roared with laughter and said, "Oh I think we'll like each other." I was struck immediately by her loving personality.' Sonia explained to Jackie that physiotherapy cannot stop the progress of the condition, but would help her maintain her general level of health through exercising unused and weak muscles. She insisted that Jackie should start some walking with a zimmer frame. Jackie was initially enthusiastic, but once, when over-anxious to show off her skills, she took a tumble in her bedroom. 'Daniel and Ruth Ann were downstairs, and on hearing a loud bang, they rushed upstairs. We lifted her up. She was a bit shocked, but basically unhurt. I went away that night feeling awful. But the next day I got a card from Jackie with a typically humorous message: "What's a fall amongst friends! See you on Thursday." That illustrated her concern for me and her wonderful human understanding.'

As well as walking exercises, Sonia arranged for Jackie to go swim-ming at a pool in Notting Hill Gate, where an experienced teacher of the Halliwick technique enabled her to get in and out of the water with slings. 'Jackie still had quite strong arms and she loved the swimming as it gave her freedom. But, after four or five months we had to stop because Jackie fell out of one of the special chairs and got quite a fright.' It was not so long before walking with a zimmer frame was also abandoned.

As Sonia recalled, Jackie did not suffer fools gladly and would expect honest answers to direct questions about her health. 'Sometimes I didn't have the answers, but when she asked if she would walk again, I told her gently, "No, Jackie, I don't think you will." Like everybody in that situation she still entertained hopes.'

In fact, the failure of the transfer factor treatment in New York had dashed these hopes and severely dented Jackie's confidence. It was very hard to accept the medical evidence that she might not get better. Soon after her return Jackie underwent a crisis. As Dr Limentani perceived it, she had decided to give up. Indeed, her physical condition deteriorated so fast that the doctors gave her only two months to live. She was put on to further heavy doses of steroids and in November Daniel was called back to London. Dr Limentani was convinced that it was the love and support of Daniel and her closest friends that saw her though the crisis. Jackie also had to exercise an overwhelming mental and spiritual effort to recover the will to live and overcome her own considerable revulsion for an invalid's life.

In addition, public recognition played a large part in providing Jackie with an impetus beyond the confines of her wheelchair. It helped her to regain her self-esteem. Through understanding what she represented in the eyes of the world, she learnt to value herself. In April 1974 du Pré was appointed an Honorary Member of the Royal Academy of Music and she was also elected a Fellow of both the Guildhall and the Royal College of Music. In subsequent years, she was to receive further honours from the musical establishment, and collected honorary doctorates (Hon.Mus.D.) from seven British universities. The last of these was conferred on her by the University of Oxford; at the same time she was elected Honorary Fellow of St Hilda's College, Oxford.

In January 1976 Jackie was awarded the OBE in the New Year's Honours List. She was particularly delighted by this. The national press printed pictures of her accompanied by Daniel going to Buckingham Palace to receive the medal from the Duke of Edinburgh. This renewed public attention helped Jackie to find the courage to break a silence that she had maintained since her withdrawal from the concert platform. At the end of January she agreed to be interviewed for BBC TV's *Tonight* programme, where she talked of her illness and how it had affected her life. This signalled du Pré's re-emergence into public life.

One of her first 'public' acts was to join the MS Society. Soon the name of Jacqueline du Pré became a symbol of dignity and courage for MS sufferers. On the occasion of the launch of CRACK, a splinter association of the MS Society set up in early 1976 to give hope to younger sufferers, Jackie addressed a capacity audience at the Royal Festival Hall. For the first time she was on-stage using words instead of her beloved cello.

The creation of the Jacqueline du Pré Research Fund (the brain-child of James Wolfensohn and Barenboim) within the umbrella of the International Federation of Multiple Sclerosis Societies in January 1978 was a further important step in contributing to public awareness of the illness through use of her name. At the launch of the Research Fund, it was announced that several world-class musicians (including Barenboim, Zukerman, Perlman, Fischer-Dieskau and others) would each donate four benefit concerts a year to raise money for research. Daniel explained that the genesis of the Research Fund came through an increased awareness of the suffering that multiple sclerosis brought to the lives of so many people. 'We thought that something had to be done to encourage research, rather than to help individual cases who lacked money. Jackie was interested in the project, but it was not something in which she became actively involved, or which gave her motivation.'

Ultimately, she gained far more satisfaction from recognition of her musical achievement than for her services in the cause of MS. In 1976 EMI finally sorted out du Pré's contract, which had remained in limbo since 1969. This allowed for the release of the Beethoven cello sonatas, taken from the 1970 Edinburgh Festival concerts. Until this point she had never shown much interest in her own recordings – listening to them was far too painful a reminder of what she no longer could achieve.

Jackie's life soon settled into a routine of doctors' visits in the morning, seeing a friend for lunch, resting in the afternoon, then either teaching or being read to in the early evenings. When not going out to the theatre or a concert, she had guests for supper. The highlights were the weekends when Daniel came back from Paris. He might arrive with flowers or some thoughtful gift, then take her out to eat at a favourite restaurant. Or they would entertain friends, more often than not musicians, in which case there was almost always some impromptu music-making. Even if Daniel spent relatively little time with Jackie consecutively, he compensated for this by the quality of attention he gave her. He took endless trouble in trying to bring her out of herself and to stimulate her interest in projects such as learning Italian or listening to Beethoven quartets.

A year after her illness was diagnosed, Daniel had suggested to Jackie that teaching would be a way of remaining in active contact with music. Even if she could no longer play, Jackie never stopped being a cellist and her musical memory remained unimpaired by illness until the end of her life. In the spring of 1975 her friend Jim Wolfensohn added his voice to Daniel's and immediately volunteered to become Jackie's first regular pupil. Although a complete beginner, he possessed the necessary background knowledge of music. Jim recalled that at his very first lesson Jackie launched him without further preliminaries into repertoire pieces: Bach's prelude from the G major Unaccompanied Cello Suite and Saint-Saëns's 'The Swan'. Despite the fact that he hardly knew how to tune the cello or hold the bow, this instant immersion proved to be effective for Jim. His Sunday afternoon lessons at Rutland Garden Mews soon turned into sessions that were therapeutic for both of them. When Jim's cello lesson was over, Jackie would unburden herself, frequently calling on his sympathy to voice her worries and troubles.

Now, with Jackie's return to the arena of public life, Daniel urged her again to dedicate more time to teaching, reminding her that it was a valuable professional activity. Jackie herself recognised that it was important at all costs to keep the mind active – as she wrote in her notebook, 'Working hard does not kill. Sloth, non-activity and boredom can.' Word passed round musical circles in London that Jacqueline du Pré was willing to teach privately. Soon cellists of every nationality were coming to her for consultation lessons or for longer periods of study. In the spring of 1976 it was suggested that her lessons could be extended into master classes. Erica Goddard was asked to organise Saturday afternoon sessions at her home.

Over the next few years an enormous number of cellists of all ages and stages had contact with du Pré. They ranged from the young and inexperienced – the youngest, ten-year-old Jane Godwin, travelled down from Perth for fortnightly lessons – to musicians of international calibre. Ralph Kirshbaum, Rafael Wallfisch, Steven Isserlis and Yo-Yo

Ma were among those who on occasion played for Jackie.

Seeing that the Saturday afternoon classes at her home proved so successful, Sir Ian Hunter suggested that Jackie should give public master classes at festivals. After some initial hesitation she accepted. Her first appearance in public as a teacher took place at the Brighton Festival in 1977, and was followed by others at the Malvern and South Bank Festivals in June and August 1978 respectively, and at Dartington Summer School and the Pears–Britten School in Aldeburgh in August 1979. Jackie was immensely grateful for Hunter's encouragement and wrote to thank him for his continuing faith in her. She told him how much the realisation meant to her 'that [teaching] is possible, and that perhaps I can say something instead of feeling useless and just sitting on my arse'.[10]

Although the public master classes gave Jackie satisfaction, they were also an undoubted strain. It had been no easy task to face an audience in a wheelchair; given the unpredictable nature of her sickness, there remained the anxiety that on the day itself she would not feel up to it. As Dr Limentani commented, 'It cost Jackie an enormous amount of courage, interest, energy, concentration to go out and do those master classes. She was very very brave, many in her place wouldn't have done it, but it was a challenge that she accepted. Yet it did satisfy her need for the public, one of the things she found hardest to give up.'

Sir Ian has left a moving description of du Pré's first master class at the Brighton Festival. On the morning 9 July 1977 he drove Jackie and Daniel down to Brighton. They lunched at Wheeler's, the scene of so many happy celebrations after their concerts in previous festivals. 'Jackie seemed in fine form and we had lobster and wine – I think I had something stronger to steady my nerves because neither Daniel nor I was at all sure how Jackie would react to appearing before the public again. As she was wheeled on to the platform of the Polytechnic Theatre there was a great wave of applause and the artist in her immediately responded.'

Peter Thomas's parents were also present sitting in the front row. Jackie saw them and beckoned them to come backstage. While embracing Mona Thomas, Jackie commented, 'You were the only ones at my Prom début, and you are the only ones at my master class début.' Mona was moved to tears by the occasion, saddened not only by Jackie's condition, but at seeing her so forlorn. Although Daniel was there, none of her own family had come to support her.[11]

Jackie's master class at the South Bank Festival the following year was even more successful. Bryce Morrison suggested his review in *The Times* could be summarised in the words 'In Praise of Eloquence'. He commented on du Pré's ability to 'persuade' students gently but firmly to clarify and strengthen their existing ideas. 'How wonderful to watch her guide [them] ... with such quiet authority, combining a remarkable variety of constructive suggestions with beautifully apt verbal analogies.'[12]

Earlier in the spring of 1979 it was arranged that the BBC televise two sessions of public master classes at the Guildhall. By that time Jackie had started to have problems with her short-term memory. Her students were aware of her difficulties, but the remarkable camaraderie of the occasion made them fade into insignificance. As one of the participants, Sandy Bailey recalled, 'We were like partners in crime. Jackie was almost bubbling over with a kind of euphoric giggling, because at that stage she couldn't really remember what anyone had played as little as five seconds ago. She would say, "Would you like to play that again?" to give herself time to formulate things she wanted to say. No one watching the class would have known that her energy was focused in thinking in the "right now". Her eyes would widen and she displayed the same charisma when listening that she had when she played.'

Jackie hated any dogmatism and never believed in foisting her view of the music on a pupil. Rather, it had to come from a convinced inner response. She had no time for the pomposity and self-importance of artists who set themselves up in the role of a grand *maître*. Her pupils were grateful that she avoided any hint of the hyped-up atmosphere of public master classes and through her encouragement helped build up their confidence. She would make her suggestions almost apologetically: 'Would you mind trying that again?' or 'Have you ever thought of starting on an up-bow?' But her courteous approach did not work with everybody. Jackie recalled with amusement how a certain American student reacted to her with dismay: 'Tell me, don't ask me.'

As another ex-student, Melissa Phelps, observed, Jackie was well aware of her pupils' anxieties, and could dispel their nerves with a radiant and understanding smile. Yet as she wrote in her notebooks, 'Not to be keyed up or even scared before a performance can loosen the sense of adventure, daring, and I think, even timing.'

Teaching forced Jackie not only to think about the cello but to verbalise the processes of performing. Considering her own diffidence in using words, she acquired remarkable fluency in articulating her musical ideas and technical suggestions. She succeeded in analysing very precisely the way she reproduced sound and used the bow and fingers, and was able to convey the actual physical feeling of playing. It seemed astonishing that a person who had lost all feeling in her limbs could so vividly recall the physical sensations involved in playing the cello. Anyone who saw Jackie teaching would have been convinced that, had she been restored the use of her hands, she could have immediately sat down and played everything in the repertoire from memory and with no loss of quality.

All Jackie's students would agree that the one thing that was always demanded of them was *more* – more expression, more intensity and more projection. Lowry Blake, one of Jackie's most talented students, noted that Jackie not only taught how to project the big momentous climaxes, but also the quietest, most tender moments in the music.[13] Although she could no longer demonstrate on the cello, she would sing the music, using wide sweeping movements of her arms to convey the joyous expression. To indicate a climax the whole upper torso of her body seemed involved in the gesture, led by arms flailing over her head. Some cellistic movements could still be indicated with her hands and to convey a specific fingering, she would sometimes sing it to the notes of a given passage.

Moray Welsh remembered such an occasion at Dartington Summer School in 1979 – Jackie was there teaching master classes and he was playing concerts. On learning that Moray had been rehearsing the Brahms C minor Piano Quartet, Jackie asked him how he fingered the big opening cello tune of the slow movement:

> Her response to my fingering was quite scornful: 'That's no good at all.' When we met at mealtimes she would sing me various possibilities – '4–1–2' or whatever. The first time she suggested a fingering I thought, 'That's very interesting, I must try it.' Then at the next mealtime, she told me, 'Forget about that fingering, try this one.' This happened about three times. The more she thought about them the more eccentric and idiosyncratic the fingerings became, as if they were getting away from the simple quality of the melody. I was fascinated because the more Jackie thought about this phrase, the closer I began to feel how she herself would have played it. I remember that she used an open A on

the fourth note, which gave the semitone A natural–G sharp a particular tension. It was a daring fingering, which would have worked for her. In general, it was dangerous to copy her fingerings because they involved little glissandos between the notes, which in her hands would sound marvellous, but tended to sound absolutely dreadful in the hands of lesser talents.

Certainly Jackie never thought of fingerings in terms of convenience. She often used several shifts for a passage where other players would stay in one position. As she explained to Kate Beare, when you shift a lot, your movement up and down the fingerboard gives you greater freedom – and movement, after all, is the opposite of tension. Du Pré's use of slides and glissandi were a hallmark of her playing. There existed an enormous variety of them, slow, fast, with or without vibrato, light or heavy, within the bow, or after the bow change. It is an intriguing exercise to listen very carefully to her Elgar recordings to see exactly where she uses expressive fingerings and slides.

Jackie was fascinated by correlations between notes, remarking, 'A note or chord in isolation says nothing, is lifeless. Next to another it immediately speaks, has contour, geographic significance and expression.'[14] She sometimes demanded from her students an extra expressive slide within a very small interval. As Sandy Bailey recalled, this could appear to be a contradiction in terms.

> There is a place in the Dvořák concerto when the music goes wistfully back from the minor into the major. Jackie spent a lot of time getting me to slide from an F natural to F sharp and to vibrate the note at the same time. I wasn't succeeding in doing what she wanted, and at a certain point I stopped and said, 'But there isn't enough room to slide, it's only a semitone.' Jackie replied with astonishment, 'But those two notes are a million miles from each other.' It made me realise that it was the intensity of the emotion which conditioned her idea of sliding, never the geographical distance.

Similarly, Jackie's understanding of how phrasing works was governed by her emotional response to the music. As Moray Welsh commented, 'She always knew where the axis of the phrase was, the moment of maximum tension. Jackie would often say, "In this phrase, there is only one place where you could possibly slide." It wasn't obvious to me but she knew that *this* was the place that mattered, even if she couldn't necessarily explain why.'

Jackie was equally inventive in her approach to fingering in fast passagework. She would often use the left thumb as a pedal or a lever, giving her hand a greatly extended range. She used this technique in a striking manner in the upward semiquaver arpeggio passage near the beginning of the Schumann concerto where, by placing the thumb on the harmonic D and disguising the shift with a bow change, she could articulate the top note with immense clarity and power. Similarly, in the recitative introduction to the second movement of the Elgar concerto, rather than use a slide, she negotiated a leap through substituting the thumb on the A harmonic (actually a chord – the A–C sixth – where the bottom note is briefly released to leave the harmonic) to pounce like a tiger on the top F sharp, a virtuoso effect that is astoundingly dramatic.

It was probably easier for students to learn from Jackie's left-hand technique, since many aspects of her bowing, like her spiccato or sautillé strokes, were so totally individual. It was almost impossible to convey the techniques involved without being able to demonstrate them. But in discussing the general feeling for sound, Jackie would explain in detail how to use the weight and placement of the bow, as well as the specific bow speed. In fact Jackie's approach to bowing started from the premise of how the note should sound and not how it should be bowed. Sandy Bailey recalled once asking Jackie how she negotiated bow changes: 'I'll never forget her answer – "Bow changes?" she said. "There is no such thing. There is only the link between one note and the next." '

Jackie disliked talking about any technical point in isolation, since everything was born of and connected with the music. Indeed, it was unusual for her to talk about the bow without pointing to the accompanying left-hand colour. This might be done in specific instructions to use no vibrato or a wide vibrato, but more often than not through a verbal image – 'Here the colour is icy', or, 'Wait for the dark note, that's the one that really hurts.'

Du Pré's preoccupation with the colour and shade of each note was a notable feature of her teaching. Melissa Phelps observed, 'Jackie thought almost in terms of a painter applying a myriad of shades within the colour, which influenced the emotional direction of a note. The facet of one colour could also change within the note, and she could use this device with devastating effect.'¹⁵ This was achieved in part through the rich variety of vibrato that Jackie had at her disposal, but also from the idea of sculpting sound textures with the bow.

The sixteen-year-old Robert Cohen came to Jackie for a brief but intense period of study. Like her, he had studied with Pleeth since the age of ten. Robert recalled that the single most important thing he learnt from Jackie was her absolute and complete dedication to every note of the phrase. 'Living for every single note was something I already knew about from Pleeth, but until I went to Jackie I had never experienced it to such a degree. Jackie taught me that with each note, your awareness of your level at that precise moment is absolutely crucial. If you are finishing a phrase that tails away, it is vital that each note in the diminuendo right through to the last is played in a particular way to create that feeling.'

Jackie's musical conviction evidently carried its own implacable logic. Cohen was surprised to discover that du Pré was an incredibly aware player:

> My impression, from hearing and seeing her play, was that the music just poured out of her, as a natural and unthought process. Soon I realised that she had always known precisely what she was doing – you understand this when you listen to the records. In fact, she had a conscious intellectual grasp of the processes of playing and she was utterly aware despite the impression she gave of complete intuitive freedom. Many people assumed that it was an awareness that she acquired, because she had been forced to analyse things away from the cello when she became ill. But this had happened years earlier.¹⁶

Jackie seemed to sense what each student needed. For Gillian Thoday and Andrea Hess her teaching was an antidote to the very analytical French school, and gave them the freedom to explore their musical individuality. Andrea remembers being amazed to discover that Jackie observed no rules: 'To begin with I was taken aback by the "illegal" things she did to negotiate instrumental problems. She threw any scholastic approach out of the window and taught me that it was all right to do anything as long as it worked. The most valuable thing that Jackie offered her students was the permission to be themselves. In this she was the total opposite of all the grand maestros I ever encountered.'¹⁷

Perhaps it was more difficult for those pupils who had never heard Jackie's playing to grasp the essential freedom of her approach. Among them was Tim Hugh, who started having lessons with her in 1980. He found inspiration in his contact with her and from the knowledge that she had reached the top and within such a short time achieved so much. 'But it was like entering a time warp to find this great artist, still very much alive but no longer functioning as a cellist. I remember Jackie crying when listening to her Elgar recording with Barbirolli. There was a poignancy in seeing her living in the past with no prospect of a future.'[18]

It would be impossible to categorise du Pré as a teacher, any more than it is as a player. She eschewed any dogma and for this reason one cannot point to a school or even to a code in her approach to playing. As her former pupils will testify, it was the strong interpretative feel for a piece that Jackie communicated so well, and all her technical suggestions were subordinate to the musical context. Jackie herself often complained that none of her students could really play the cello. As Daniel reminded her, a student is like a patient in search of a doctor; he only comes when he knows he has problems. Even when her arms were virtually paralysed, Jackie would answer the question 'Who can play the cello well?' by stating emphatically 'Me'. Probably the cellist who learnt most from her style and sound was Moray Welsh, who became a close friend. Jackie always disliked using the term 'pupil'. 'No,' she insisted. 'They are not pupils, they are my friends.'

Parallel to her teaching activities, Jackie tried her hand at making editions of the established cello repertoire. Her first commission came from Chester Music to edit the six Bach Suites for Unaccompanied Cello. While preparing her edition, Jackie studied those of other cellists and she acknowledged the particular influence of Enrico Mainardi, whose edition of the Bach Suites Daniel had bought for her. Through her friend Tony Pleeth she also became aware of developments in authentic baroque performance. But Jackie preferred to emulate Mainardi's method and, for instance, initially indicated her musical intentions by marking the harmonic pedal or the chords that should be arpeggiated or spread. It was important in this single-voiced music to keep the implied fundamental harmony in mind, since 'it dictates the direction and therefore the musical expression'. Jackie also suggested that 'the music be thought geographically ... as a helpful guide to a true resolution in areas where it is easy to meander musically.'[19] In the event, these indications were not used in the published edition, which unfortunately suffers from some careless misprints and errors. The biggest area of doubt concerns the fingerings. Despite the fact that her fingering systems were highly original, I very much doubt if the marked fingerings always represented what she meant. (It would seem that the edition was not checked through by someone with a working knowledge of the cello.) Certainly there is a notable difference in the approach to the four Suites that Jackie played and the two (the Fourth and the Sixth) she never performed in public. In the latter the fingerings are sometimes arbitrary and her markings lack a thought-out confidence.

Bill Pleeth has claimed that the ideas on bowing and articulation in du Pré's edition echo his. While it is true that Jackie assimilated Pleeth's approach to Bach, his claim does not account for her musical development. If one listens to the early BBC recordings of the First and Second Suites while following Jackie's edition, one will notice many discrepancies between her playing and the markings in it. It is unlikely that Jackie herself ever would have adhered to one set of bowings and fingerings from one performance to the next. But there are several striking things to be discovered from studying du Pré's Bach editions: her insistence for the original scordaratura (the A string tuned down to a G) in the Fifth Suite, and her idiosyncratic fingering system, involving many semitone slides on the fourth finger and abundant use of open strings, sometimes necessitating awkward jumps across two or three strings.

Jackie was probably discouraged when she later asked cellist friends to play through the Bach Suites with her printed fingerings and bowings. It proved a pointless exercise, since nobody could reproduce what she herself would have done and no amount of indications in the score would have helped. Perhaps for this reason her heart was not in the task when late in 1979 she accepted a proposal to edit the Elgar concerto, a project for which she was eminently suited. Jackie asked Moray Welsh to help with her work on the Elgar. As by then she found it difficult to write, he was to act as an amanuensis. Moray vividly recalled their first working session:

> The first thing that Jackie said was, 'We'll get rid of the *nobilmente* at the beginning.' 'But Jackie, you can't just get rid of it, that's what Elgar wrote,' I replied in consternation. 'And in any case that's how you played it.' 'No, it isn't,' she replied and insisted that we scrapped Elgar's indication. Jackie seemed to have had the idea that she could change just about everything apart from the notes and she might have done that

as well. She rubbed out of all Elgar's instructions. It soon became evident that this was not going to make a viable edition and that it would be unpublishable. I don't think we got beyond the first movement.

Jackie's deteriorating health was beginning to take its toll and she no longer felt up to completing the task.

The Legacy Lives On

No wheelchair can interrupt the journeys of the mind.
Jacqueline du Pré, notebooks

In July 1976, Jackie was in the audience to hear Barenboim conduct Beethoven's Ninth Symphony on the steps of St Paul's Cathedral as the opening concert of the City of London Festival. Ruth Ann Cannings was also present and came to say hello to her after the performance. Daniel caught sight of her as she was walking away: 'Isn't that the nice nurse from St Mary's?' he asked and immediately sent his mother in pursuit. Aida Barenboim caught up with Ruth Ann and invited her there and then to come and nurse Jackie privately. There had been a succession of unsatisfactory agency nurses and the Barenboims were desperate for a reliable professional to live in.

After overcoming her initial hesitations, Cannings accepted the proposal and stayed with Jackie for the rest of her life. For Ruth Ann, nursing Jackie was a vocation and in this she was aided by her profound evangelical belief. Jackie, who was not religious by nature and hated anything that smacked of any kind of fanaticism, nevertheless respected Ruth Ann's spiritual commitment. Whatever their differences, they tacitly agreed not to interfere with each other's way of thinking.

Ruth Ann's first concern was to ensure that Jackie could live as full a life as possible. She completely understood that her job meant more than simply catering to an invalid's needs and ensured that Jackie was involved in all decisions concerning her care. She did her best to make Jackie feel and look good, and took an immense amount of trouble to see to it that she was beautifully turned out, dressed with matching accessories and well-groomed hair. Similarly, Ruth Ann decked out Jackie's room with bright colours and hid from sight all the accoutrements of her invalid condition. She proved to be more than a devoted nurse, providing love and comfort, and gradually taking on more and more responsibility for running the household.

Having overcome a major health crisis in the late autumn of 1975, Jackie's appetite for entertainment returned, and she started going to the theatre and to visit friends. She soon discovered that not all London theatres are negotiable in a wheelchair and on occasion, arrangements were made for her to be lifted from a car into a box so that she could see a particular play. Her godfather Lord Harewood, then Director of English National Opera, encouraged her to discover a new love in opera. However, her interest in music focused largely on performances by friends within her intimate circle. Nearly every time Daniel, Pinky, Itzhak or Zubin performed in London Jackie was in the audience. At the Festival Hall, a special dispensation overruling fire regulations was made so that she could use a private box on the left-hand side of the hall, reached through a labyrinthine route via the backstage entrance. Wheelchair users are normally put in the front row of the stalls, a vulnerable position for a celebrity like du Pré.

As Sonia Corderay recalled, 'Jackie disliked feeling that people noticed her disability. But she managed to find humour in the situation. She recounted how well-meaning strangers would approach her and in an effort to say something comforting would do the opposite. "Do you know, my auntie had just the same thing. She had quite a good life although she died so young," they might say, before realising that they had made a dreadful gaffe.'[1]

One of Daniel's happiest ideas gave Jackie the chance to satisfy her love of performing on stage. In the summer of 1976 she appeared at a special concert at the Albert Hall playing a small drum in the *Toy Symphony* (attributed to Haydn). The occasion was in honour of the anniversary of the foundation of Harold Holt, many of whose artists performed in the concert under Rafael Kubelik. (Years ago, as a small child, Jackie had thumped her toy drum so enthusiastically in a television recording of the same piece that she split it.) In 1979, Daniel arranged for her to do the narration of Prokofiev's *Peter and the Wolf* with the ECO under his direction. Apart from a public performance, they made a studio recording of the work, issued by Deutsche Grammophon. Jackie revelled in being back on-stage and in using words. Her considerable artistry came into play during her recitation, not least in her sense of timing and puckish humour.

A year later, she recited Ogden Nash's verses to the *Carnival of Animals*, with the ECO and Charles Mackeras, but by now her diction was getting blurred and she was on the verge of collapsing into euphoric giggles during the performance. (Something one hears on the radio tape from the Upottery Festival in her recitation of Nash's poem the Fossils.) Suvi Grubb suggested to Peter Andry that EMI record this work. But Andry disliked the idea of superimposing Nash's poems on Saint-Saëns's music, pointing out that they had already refused to record the recitation of Menuhin's wife Diana in the same work.

It was hard for Daniel to accept the bitter truth of Jackie's musical silence and he initially refused to perform with other cellists, although he made an exception for Piatigorsky. Even though he eventually overcame this resistance, there were certain works like the Elgar Cello Concerto and Schubert's *Trout* Quintet, which were so closely associated with Jackie that he never wanted to perform or record them again.

Daniel often debated about how to lead his life, but he was never in doubt that Jackie should be protected in every way. When his doctors suggested that she might be better off living in a hospital or home, which could cater more expertly for her paraplegic condition, he was not convinced it was the right solution. Nevertheless, he went to see the Putney Home for Incurables, the only institution in London that at the time could have taken care of patients with the type of chronic condition from which Jackie suffered. This only confirmed his conviction that his wife must be looked after at home, whatever the difficulties. He never told her of his visit to the home with such a depressing name.

In the early years of her disease Jackie showed considerable concern for Daniel. She told Dr Selby that she thought he should be free to divorce her and have a family with children. At the same time, as she told her friends, after coming through so many difficulties they were now closer than they ever had been and could talk freely at length, and make considered decisions together.

But as Daniel became more immersed in his work as Music Director of the Orchestre de Paris he had to compartmentalise his life to a greater extent. The effort of travelling with nurses and the paraphernalia of illness discouraged Jackie from coming to see him in Paris, although on one occasion in 1976 she went for a week's visit. Inevitably, Daniel had to realise his need for company in Paris and Jackie was essentially excluded from his new circle of friends. Whereas he continued to share in her life in London, she expressed less and less outward interest in his. On the one hand, this implied an instinctive need for self-protection, but also the necessity to focus increasingly on herself, as her horizons narrowed.

As Jackie's condition deteriorated and she became increasingly self-engrossed, it was inevitable that Daniel should withdraw somewhat from her emotionally. In the 1980s he started to reduce his visits to London. By then, he had entirely given up hope of her recovery. She did not ask questions, but at heart would not have been surprised to learn that, having reached the age of forty, Daniel felt the need to settle down with a woman who could give him children. In his decision to split his life in two, he had the understanding and sympathy of his friends and his partner, Elena Bashkirova. Those who knew the 'secrets' of his private situation would never have dreamt of divulging them, and in this sense they proved their loyalty to both Daniel and Jackie. That Daniel exercised a full sense of responsibility towards her and that it was motivated by his continuing love for her was also never in question.

While Jackie's friends saw a role for themselves in distracting her from her problems, stimulating her interests and sustaining her with sympathy, they realised that most of all she required love and reassurance. For male friends this could sometimes be difficult. Jackie was explicit in her need to be reassured of her femininity. She might have been an invalid, but her emotions and her sexuality were very much alive and not to be ignored.

Jackie had always been someone who needed to give; deprived of the opportunity to do this through her music, she could still give of herself generously in friendship. Even when she was very ill she knew how to be a compassionate listener. Another capacity that she never lost was her gift for laughter and it took a lot to suppress her sense of humour, whether it touched on the odd, the ridiculous, or the plain bawdy.

Consolation and support also came from a spiritual source. The Westminster Reform Synagogue was just round the corner from Rutland Garden Mews. Out for a walk one day in the wheelchair Jackie and Daniel met Rabbi Albert Friedlander by chance. They took to each other and he soon became a regular visitor to the house. In his meetings with Jackie their talk ranged through a large variety of subjects, from literature to Judaism. Rabbi Friedlander introduced Jackie to several writers and musicians, including Donald Swann, Dannie Abse and Alan Sillitoe. He helped her prepare her choice for the radio programme *Desert Island Discs* and the narration of *Peter and the Wolf*. 'I went to the performance, which was very moving, since one could feel the love for Jacqueline in the warmth of the audience's reception. I also heard her recite Ogden Nash's verses for the *Carnival of Animals*, her last stage appearance. Jackie so enjoyed performing and it was a very bitter thing to have to accept that she couldn't do it any more.'²

Rabbi Friedlander tried to avoid making their encounters into religious meetings. As he observed, 'There was never a feeling that she was being visited by the minister. We sometimes talked about prayer and she liked reading some of the Psalms for me. Her Judaism certainly was not the traditional Judaism, but there was a very simple faith and belief that she was Jewish. She did come to synagogue on some occasions. We used to listen to her recording of *Kol Nidrei* at Yom Kippur – Jackie's way of observing it was through music.'

For both Daniel and Jackie there was nothing dogmatic about their Judaism, and they were tolerant of the beliefs of others. As Zubin Mehta recalled, there were no objections when one year he and his wife Nancy decided to make a big Christmas celebration at Rutland Garden Mews. They knew how much pleasure Jackie derived from the old traditions, and arranged for an enormous decorated tree and a real Christmas dinner.

In Jackie's case, Judaism was linked to Daniel and the predominantly Israeli circle of musician friends with whom she had loved to perform. It was also connected with a close feeling for her Jewish friends who rallied round at the time of need. In contrast to Iris, Daniel's mother Aida was always willing to leave her home and pupils in Tel Aviv at a moment's notice if she was needed. Aida's practical intelligence and her warm-hearted good cheer made her a pillar of strength, and as Jackie's illness progressed, she was a regular presence in Rutland Garden Mews.

Nevertheless every time there was a crisis, whether it involved a relief nurse walking out, the sickness of the housekeeper, or a sudden relapse in Jackie's condition, the responsibility to sort it out fell on Daniel. At Rutland Garden Mews the household was run between Ruth Ann and Olga relatively smoothly, but after a few years their relationship started to deteriorate. It seemed almost a quirk of destiny that the two women who had come into the Barenboims' life by chance should be unable to get on with each other. Olga had a generous heart, but coming from Eastern Europe she had not been exposed to living in mixed racial communities. Her inability to accept Ruth Ann's colour led to a confrontation. In 1980 Barenboim was forced to choose between the two live-in helps. Reluctantly, he had to ask Olga to leave. Ruth Ann was irreplaceable.

This was only one of the many crises that forced Daniel to cancel engagements and fly back to London. While he could rely on his mother for support, he was always bewildered that at such times Jackie's family seemed to evaporate into thin air. 'I never understood it. Perhaps, because I was young, I didn't do enough to shake the du Prés up and I should have been more direct in asking them to help.'

Yet however much they might have cared for Jackie, it was not in Iris's or Derek's nature to search for a dialogue or volunteer their help. They suffered from the restrictions of their backgrounds and what appeared to outsiders as a rather 'English' sense of inhibition. Iris's real grief at Jackie's incapacity was also a grief for her loss. She had devoted a large part of her life to helping Jackie become a great musician; to see all she had invested in crumble before her eyes was bitter indeed. Jackie in turn felt deeply hurt by what appeared to be her mother's withdrawal of love and interest. At a certain point, through friends in the ECO, Jackie's godmother Isména Holland was contacted with a mission to persuade Iris to visit Jackie more frequently. As Mrs Holland recalled, Iris and Derek did indeed react and started paying fortnightly visits to London, invariably coming on a Friday to lunch with Jackie and afterwards take tea with her.[3] Yet Iris confessed to her friend Margot Pacey that she no longer knew how to make contact with her daughter and on both sides there was a lingering sense of rejection.[4] All this served to reduce the value of these routine visits into a formality. Jackie managed a couple of trips to her parents' home in Curridge, outside Newbury. Ruth Ann recalled that Jackie always felt cold and uncomfortable because their house was not equipped for her disabilities. She also undoubtedly craved a warmer demonstration of love from her family.

The problem was exacerbated when in 1979 Jackie's brother Piers and both Iris and Derek became born-again Christians. Jackie had little sympathy for what she regarded as the naïve, almost simplistic nature of her family's belief. Her claims that Iris thought that her illness had been caused by her abandoning Christianity to convert to Judaism were certainly exaggerated. But they had some foundation in an inverted perception of Iris's real belief that she had been saved by Jesus. As Rabbi Friedlander recalled, 'Jackie was quite clear that her mother thought that she was being punished because she had deserted Jesus. It was spelt out. Jesus had become central to her mother's life. This only had the effect of making Jackie more certain that she was Jewish rather than Christian, and it antagonised her against her mother and her siblings.'

Maybe the only person who ever told Jackie to her face that she should reconsider her conversion was Rostropovich's wife Galina Vish-nevskaya, who was stating a personal belief that each person should practise the religion he or she was born into. Vishnevskaya was always very direct in saying what was uppermost in her mind and she certainly was not motivated by missionary zeal. Jackie did not hold it against her, whereas she resented innuendoes and heavy-handed hints from militant Christians, whether they came from her family or Ruth Ann's circle of friends.

At one level the question of religion was almost an irrelevance, but at another it was used to fuel antagonisms on both sides. There is no doubt that Jackie felt let down by her family. She always retained a very real affection for her sister and, as Dr Limentani recalled, was delighted when she found time to visit. Jackie knew that Hilary's life was not easy and that she was dedicated to looking after her extended family. Jackie was always interested in her Finzi nieces and nephew, whom she had grown to love during her stay at Ashmansworth. But she had little but contempt left for Kiffer. As for her brother, she often suspected that Piers was more interested in being taken out to exclusive restaurants and ordering the most expensive bottle of wine than in coming to see her.

Jackie confessed on several occasions to being troubled by the idea of having to pay recompense for her gifts, of being in some way guilty for her own suffering. Rabbi Friedlander offered her consolation by explaining that, as far as Judasim is concerned, suffering is never a punishment for sins. 'All suffering is a terrible misfortune and a burden to carry. But hers was not a suffering about which she had to feel at all guilty. The illness at times brought out in her a sort of determined cheerfulness, which was partly psychological. She feared that a lack of cheerfulness would drive others away.'

Certainly, Jackie's stoic good cheer stood her in excellent stead. She had acquired a large circle of friends, including royalty. She was thrilled when Prince Charles visited her at home and treasured the two or three letters that he wrote to her. Jackie also became an intimate friend of the Duchess of Kent. But she was never a snob and was equally happy to spend time with her driver Doug Rockall, whom she appreciated for his loyal, warm-hearted kindness.

One of the highlights of those years was her invitation to Prince Charles's wedding with Diana Spencer. In Daniel's absence, Ruth Ann suggested that Moray Welsh should escort her. Moray recalled Jackie's horror at finding herself placed in a row of wheelchair invalids at the ceremony in St Paul's Cathedral. She demanded that Moray wheel her to the front to get a better view of the proceedings and he had a difficult time convincing her that protocol on royal occasions is sacred.

Through Moray, Jackie also found a way to put her love of words to professional use. He introduced her to the actress Penelope Lee, who invited du Pré to present a programme of readings for the Upottery Festival in Devon, which was recorded by BBC Radio Four for their series *With Great Pleasure*. Moray recalled that Jackie greatly enjoyed the preparations for the programme and that it served to focus her attention for the best part of six months beforehand. 'During that time Penelope, the actor John Carlson and I used to go along and read poetry to Jackie. We set aside what she liked in a pile as possible readings. In the last year or two it had become increasingly difficult to spend time with her, but now that we had found something positive to do and a way of involving Jackie in a real goal, it was easier for all concerned.'[5]

During this time Moray noticed a considerable deterioration in Jackie's physical condition. 'At the beginning she could still read, but by the end of those six months she was really unable to see properly. So we had to enlarge the print and put the poems on to big cards so that she could read them out.' It was agreed that the two actors would do most of the readings, but that Jackie should introduce them and recite one or two poems. At the last minute there was a scare that Jackie's health would not stand up to the strain of the event. However, she managed to go ahead and the occasion was deemed a great success, with Jackie's courage and enormous stage presence winning through. She transmitted her own enjoyment and presented the evening with great style. As Moray recalled, 'Jackie's main problem when reading the poems at home was that she would dissolve into giggles, so we were a bit nervous as to whether this would happen on-stage. But she got through it all right, although you can hear on the tape that she was just on the edge of total disintegration.'

While in Upottery, Jackie met two other actors, Edward Fox and Joanna David. They became friends and often came to read poetry to her, and invited her down for weekends to their Dorset home. Jackie had always suffered from a complex that her minimal schooling had left her ignorant of everything outside music. Janet Suzman, another actress friend who helped her prepare the *Peter and the Wolf* narration, later wrote of this ignorance as a positive asset: 'What a relief it is to a person whose daily business is words, words, and more words, to talk to someone whose response is so immediate and fresh and uncluttered by boring old education. She has no prejudices of a literary kind, no half-formed ideas, she is exhilaratingly unread, a tabula positively rasa.'[6] But it is easy to exaggerate Jackie's lack of education. She relished words and if she was not widely read, she was quick to acquire a real understanding of the literature that she did come across. She especially identified with the music of poetry and remained fascinated by Shakespeare. To Jackie's disappointment, a promised visit from Paul Scofield to read the Bard's sonnets never materialised.

From about 1981 Jackie started suffering a decline which was manifested not only physically but mentally. On the one hand her speech became blurred, her limbs grew weaker and she had difficulties in swallowing. To stop the tremors in her arms, she would often keep them folded. The illness was now also affecting certain areas of the brain. As Dr Lange explained, 'When you have physical and chemical changes in the brain, you also have changes in your emotions, your memory, your reasoning ability and behaviour. When the conditioning reflex (which has its seat in the frontal lobes of the cerebral cortex) is affected, your personality undergoes change and your socialisation alters.'[7]

Many people did not recognise that these changes in Jackie's personality were due to a physical effect. Dr Limentani observed, 'Many things Jackie said when she was extremely ill should be taken with a large pinch of salt, although far too many people took them for the truth. Her use of scatalogical words and her demands on men were due to the lack of self-control – known as the inhibiting factor, or conditioning reflex – which is related to the illness and can make a person either seem euphoric or manic. All this had its roots in the restrictions of her childhood. She used to think it was great fun to shock people.'[8]

It was around this time that Dr Limentani felt it his duty to inform Barenboim that he could no longer carry out analysis in the formal sense. 'The only reason I continued to see Jackie was that I gave her something to hang on to – somebody with whom she could have an outburst of rage. With me, she could give vent to her anger when she could no longer feed herself or she had to ring a bell. She hated everything to do with her dependence.'

Friends noticed that, uncharacteristically, Jackie's stoicism was beginning to crumble. In giving voice to her bitterness and frustration she now started complaining about the people around her. Her principal butts, apart from her own family, were the two people on whom she was most dependent: Ruth Ann and Daniel. It was perhaps a natural consequence of her illness that, as she became locked into her dependence, Jackie came to regard Ruth Ann as something of a jailer. Her resentment and anger emerged in a mockery of Ruth Ann's religious faith. Friends could help in various ways, either by listening to her outbursts, by putting forward the other side of the argument or by distracting her from the subject. Yet for the casual visitor her invective could be highly upsetting.

It did not need much imagination to recognise that the angry words were a façade, a much-needed outlet for her frustration. Every time Daniel came to the house or phoned, Jackie's eyes would light up and her voice would soften. And in the lonely hours of the long nights it was Ruth Ann who sustained Jackie with her comradeship, good cheer and love.

Dr Limentani believed that these calls for sympathy were in part due to the fact that Jackie was incapable of feeling sorry for herself. 'She wanted her friends to do what she couldn't do for herself. Many of the things she said were done to provoke pity. Yet she was doing exactly the opposite of what she intended to do, because at the same time she did not want this pity. This isn't unusual in such a situation.'

In the summer of 1983 Jackie moved to a new home better suited to her increased disability. Barenboim had acquired two adjoining flats on one level in a new conversion at Chepstow Villas near Notting Hill Gate, and they were adapted to Ruth Ann's and Jackie's specifications. Nevertheless, the Chepstow Villas flat lacked the bright warmth of the house in Rutland Garden Mews. Even though Ruth Ann did her best to disguise it, there was something sterile about a home that was geared principally to managing the final stages of Jackie's illness. When Daniel came, he brought comfort and light and vitality to the house, but increasingly his visits were devoted to sorting out problems.

From the medical point of view, 1983 marked the beginning of the end for Jackie. As her condition deteriorated visibly, almost day by day, she could no longer feed herself or hold things. Her speech became so blurred that she could hardly make herself understood. While the illness encroached on her mental and physical powers, her feeling of isolation and rejection intensified, and it became next to impossible to retain any optimism. Jackie's anxiety that she would be abandoned by her friends turned into a fixation about keeping her diary filled with engagements. No sooner would she greet a visitor than she was already arranging for their next visit. There was all the more reason to be grateful for the faithful circle of friends who continued to come and always had something positive to offer in terms of comfort. Many of her oldest friends – Zamira Menuhin, Stephen Bishop, Cynthia and Rodney Friend, Charles Beare, Ian and Mercedes Stoutzker, Toby and Itzhak Perlman, Bill and Tony Pleeth, as well as her 'ECO buddies', Jo Milholland, Maggie Cowan and Anita Lasker – were among those in her close circle who made themselves available.

There was also comfort from the cheerful presence of a new part-time French housekeeper, Ann-Marie Morin, who brought light relief into Jackie's life. As Jackie weakened, Ruth Ann took on all the nursing and caring, feeling unable to trust anybody else for more than a few hours in case of a crisis. On at least two occasions she had saved Jackie's life by taking the right steps to stop her from choking. Ruth Ann could rely on the support of a few valued friends such as Jo Milholland and Cynthia Friend to stay with Jackie, allowing her the time to go to church and refuel her energies.

Ruth Ann also knew how to help Jackie at times of intense depression. When Diana Nupen was dying of cancer she arranged to take Jackie for a weekend to Brighton. Sylvia Southcombe who accompanied them, recalled that Jackie was unable to cry or give vent to her bitter grief on learning of Diana's death. This was in part due to physiological reasons, since the illness affected the tear ducts and Jackie was no longer able to indulge in what she termed 'the great gift and merciful medicine' of crying.

But it also represented a hardening in her, a refusal to countenance pity for others or for herself. When her father contracted Parkinson's disease in the mid-1980s, Jackie shocked many people by her patent lack of sympathy. Yet when she learnt that Iris was terminally ill with cancer she could not hide her anxiety. Ruth Ann knew that whatever Jackie might say to the contrary, it was important to arrange a farewell visit and took Jackie down to see her mother at Newbury Hospital in September 1985. It turned out to be a final family reunion.

Within a few months not only had Iris died, but Jackie learnt that Aida, her mother-in-law, was terminally ill. But by now she was too absorbed in her own struggle to grieve fully for these two women who each in her own way had contributed so much to her life. Words to express her sorrow did not come easily at the best of times and by now Jackie's speech was so poor she could hardly make herself understood.

In the last years of her life one of the few pleasures left to her were her own recordings. Listening to them was a way of sharing the best of herself with her friends, some of whom had never heard her play in concert. It also gave Jackie the opportunity to relive her performances. But as her need became more and more obsessive, friends found these listening sessions more of an ordeal than a pleasure. It was heart-rending, almost unbearably so, to try and relate the two conflicting images: the audible evidence of du Pré, the great artist with the sad picture of her decline. At the time I was surprised that she would invariably ask me, as each record came to an end, 'Was it good?' It was never difficult to give her the necessary reassurance, any more than to respond to her generous and loving spirit. It became apparent that her own recorded music-making was the only form of reality that mattered to her and the one thing the illness could not take away from her.

Zamira Menuhin recalled a poignant meeting just a week before Jackie died. 'Jackie knew that she couldn't last much longer – every time she got ill she got that much weaker, she could no longer speak. She was not bitter, but the writing was on the wall. I remember saying to her "It's obvious that we all have to die one day. But in a hundred years from now most of us will be forgotten, but you will still be around, because there will be always great interest in your art." I know this sounds banal, but it really pleased her to hear it.'⁹

Patients with chronic illnesses like multiple sclerosis very often die from secondary infections and this was so in Jackie's case. In December 1986 she developed pneumonia, but responded to antibiotics. The writing was on the wall, though, and when she came down with a chest infection in early October 1987 it again turned into pneumonia. This time she was too weak to fight it. Daniel kept in touch with Len Selby, who reported on Jackie's progress. On Sunday, 18 October Len telephoned to inform him that the end was very near. Cynthia Friend moved into the flat to help Ruth Ann and many of Jackie's friends and her brother and sister came to make their farewells; even if she was past speech, she seemed to recognise them all. But, as Ruth Ann observed,

Jackie was holding out until Daniel arrived early in the afternoon of Monday, 19 October. Having waited for him, she was free to let go of life and find her final peace in death.

During the weekend of Saturday, 17 and Sunday, 18 October the south of England was ravaged by hurricane-force winds which wrought terrible destruction. Enormous numbers of trees were damaged and uprooted, including some of the rarest species at Kew Gardens. There was something strangely fitting in Jackie's exit from life happening in the lull following the aftermath of such a storm. Daniel had always compared Jackie to a force of nature. She had deployed her meteoric talents with the positive energy of sunshine. The years of her wretched suffering had caused tempestuous havoc not only in her own life, but in those of the people close to her.

Jacqueline du Pré touched the lives of all who had contact with her, through her music and her personality, which radiated the same warm generosity and joy in the beauties of the world, yet equally could communicate deep sadness and enormous compassion. In his funeral address Rabbi Friedlander recalled Jackie's much-quoted words in the face of the calamity of illness: 'I was so fortunate to have achieved everything while I was young. I have recorded the full repertoire. . . . I have no regrets.'

'Dare we say that she was right – and that she was wrong?' he asked. As he wrote elsewhere, the song does not cease with the singer. The real truth cannot be found in texts but lives on in the music.

Notes

1   *The Birth Of Talent*
1   Robin Daniel, *Conversations with Menuhin*, Futura Publications, London, 1991, p. 25.
2   Mrs Derek du Pré in William Wordsworth (ed.), *Jacqueline du Pré: Impressions*, Grafton Books, London, 1983–9, p. 22.
3   George Malcolm in interview with EW, June 1994.
4   Mrs Derek du Pré in op. cit., p. 25.
5   Quoted in *A Record of the London School of Dalcroze Eurhythmics 1913–73* (compiled by Nathalie Tingey), p. 17.
6   This and other quotes in this chapter from taped interview with Mary May, December 1995.
7   Margot Pacey in interview with EW, May 1993.
8   Ronald Smith in interview with EW, December 1995.
9   In interview with EW.
10   In interview with EW.
11   In interview with EW, London, May 1996.

2   *Early Musical Discoveries*
1   *BBC Music Magazine*, January 1995.
2   Ibid.
3   In conversation with EW.
4   Margaret Campbell, *The Great Cellists*, Victor Gollancz, 1988, p. 128.
5   In interview with EW.
6   In interview with EW.
7   In interview with EW.
8   Interview with Christopher Nupen in his documentary film *Jacqueline*, 1967.
9   In interview with EW, London, March 1995.
10   Interview with Winifred Beeston, August, 1993.
11   Ibid.
12   Ibid.
13   BBC Radio programme *With Great Pleasure*, 1980.

3   *Recognition*
1   From letter to EW, November 1995.
2   In interview, September 1993.
3   In interview with EW, Collegno, May 1995.
4   In telephone interview with EW, August 1995.
5   Foreword to William Pleeth, *Cello*, Yehudi Menuhin Music Guide, Macdonald & Co., 1982.
6   In interview with EW, Collegno, May 1995.
7   Robert Baldock, *Pablo Casals*, Victor Gollancz, London, 1992, p. 71.
8   Eugene Goossens, *Overture and Beginners*, Methuen, 1951, p. 99.
9   Gerald Moore, *Am I too Loud?*, Hamish Hamilton, 1962, pp. 108–9.
10 In interview with EW.
11 Harold Atkins and Peter Cotes, *The Barbirollis, A Musical Marriage*, Robson Books, London, 1992, p. 130.
12 In interview with EW, London, June 1993.

4   *Studies With Pleeth*
1   This and all subsequent quotes in interview with EW, London, June 1993.
2   In interview with EW, London, March 1995.
3   This and all subsequent quotes in interview with EW, London, June 1993.
4   Hilary du Pré and Piers du Pré, *A Genius in the Family*, Chatto & Windus, London, 1997, p. 80.
5   Quoted (as all above extracts) from interview with EW, London, December 1995.
6   Ibid.

5   *Emerging Into The Public Eye*
1   In interview with EW, Hove, June 1993.
2   This and all further quotes of Peter Thomas from interview with EW, London, March 1994.
3   From letter to EW from Mona Thomas, December 1994.
4   From Jacqueline du Pré's notebooks, written in the late 1970s.
5   From letter to EW from Mona Thomas, December 1994.
6   Letter in archive of Queen's College.
7   Ibid.
8   In BBC radio interview, 1976.
9   In interview with Maureen Cleave entitled 'Triangle: Daniel and Jacque-

line Barenboim and the cello', *New York Times Magazine*, 16 March 1969.

10   In BBC Radio 3 interview in programme for Jacqueline du Pré's fortieth birthday (1985).

11   From a letter to Miss Kynaston dated 8 April 1959, Queen's College archive.

12   From letter in Queen's College archive.

13   Ibid.

14   Robin Daniels, op. cit., p. 38.

15   In interview with EW, May 1996.

16   From interview with Patsy Kumm, *New York Times*, August 1968.

6   *Wigmore Hall Début*

1   In interview with EW, London, June 1993.

2   Yehudi Menuhin, 'Sharing a Language' in Wordsworth (ed.), op. cit., p. 68.

3   Harold Atkins and Peter Cotes, op. cit., p. 130.

4   David Blum, *Casals and the Art of Interpretation*, University of California Press, 1977, p. 4.

5   Quotes here and above from an interview with EW, London, June 1994.

6   'Reflections' by Jacqueline du Pré, published in *Crescendo – A Magazine for young Concert-goers*, No. 132, February 1964.

7   David Blum, op. cit., pp. 50–1.

8   Letter of thanks to the Suggia Trust dated 17 September 1960 addressed to Miss Tatham at the Arts Council.

9   This and other quotes from interview with EW, May 1993.

10   Jacqueline du Pré, op. cit.

11   From a letter to EW from Howard Ferguson, May 1994.

12   In interview with EW, March 1995.

13   In interview with EW, May 1993.

14   In interview with EW, June 1994.

7   *Widening Horizons*

1   In interview with EW, May 1993.

2   BBC Radio 3 tribute with Jacqueline du Pré's fortieth birthday, 1985.

3   In interview with EW, London, June 1993.

4   Interview in BBC Radio 3 tribute for Jacqueline du Pré's fortieth birthday.

5   In telephone interview with EW, August 1994.

6 Yehudi Menuhin, 'Sharing a Language', in Wordsworth (ed.), op. cit., p. 70.
7 In a faxed letter to EW, 15 December 1994.
8 Ibid.
9 This and all further quotes by Alberto Lysy from a recorded interview with EW, Sermoneta, June 1996.
10 Harold Atkins and Peter Cotes, op. cit., pp. 130–1. Unfortunately there is no reference in the book to which piece Barbirolli is referring to in his first comments.
11 Initially the directors of the Guildhall School insisted that all du Pré's BBC recording engagements should be referred to them and be strictly limited. The proviso became invalid when du Pré's connection with the school terminated in the spring of 1962.
12 From a letter from Susan Bradshaw to EW, dated 23 October 1994.
13 This and above quotes from an interview with EW, London, June 1994.

8 *Orchestral Début*

1 Letter from Mona Thomas to EW, 28 May 1995.
2 In interview, Milton-Keynes, August 1993.
3 In interview with EW, London, June 1993.
4 In interview with EW, London, March 1995.
5 Harold Atkins and Peter Cotes, op. cit., p. 131.
6 In interview with EW, June 1994.
7 Ibid.
8 From two letters from Mona Thomas to EW, December 1994 and May 1995.
9 In interview with EW, December 1995.
10 In interview with EW, London, June 1994.
11 Paul Tortelier and David Blum, *Paul Tortelier: A Self-Portrait*, Heinemann, London, 1984, pp. 213–14.
12 EMI CDM 7 631662, Early BBC Recordings, Vol. 2.

9 *Paris Interlude*

1 Daniel Barenboim, *A Life in Music*, Weidenfeld & Nicolson, London, 1991, p. 105.
2 David Blum and Paul Tortelier, op. cit., p. 100.
3 David Blum, op. cit., p. 102.
4 Ibid.
5 Ibid., p. 101.

6   Ibid., p. 110.
7   Arthur Rubinstein, *Autobiografia – gli anni della maturità*, Flavia Pagano Editore, Napoli, 1991, p. 545.
8   This and all further quotes in this chapter from recorded interview with EW, Turin, September 1995.
9   This and all further quotes in this chapter from recorded interview with EW, London, December 1995.
10 Quoted in recorded interview with EW, June 1994.
11 From letter from Maud Tortelier to EW, 4 July 1994.
12 From BBC Radio programme, fortieth birthday tribute to Jacqueline du Pré.
13 David Blum and Paul Tortelier, op. cit., p. 209.
14 *The Gramophone*, January 1969, 'Jacqueline du Pré talks to Alan Blyth'.
15 Hilary du Pré and Piers du Pré, op. cit., p. 139.
16 Ibid., p. 140.
17 Ibid., p. 140.
18 Ibid., p. 141.
19 Ibid., p. 141.
20 From BBC TV master class filmed at RNCM Manchester.
21 BBC Radio programme, fortieth birthday tribute to Jacqueline du Pré.
22 David Blum and Paul Tortelier, op. cit., p. 214.
23 Ibid., p. 213.

10 *Overcoming Doubts*
1   In interview with EW, London, June 1994.
2   In interview with Anna Wilson, August 1993.
3   Interview with EW, Glasgow, August 1995.
4   In interview with EW, Sermoneta, June 1996.
5   In a telephonic interview with EW, January 1997.
6   Ibid.
7   In interview with EW, London, April 1995.
8   In a telephonic interview with EW, 1995.
9   Charles Reid, *New York Times*, 26 February 1967
10 *Guardian*, 23 August 1963.
11 Interview with EW, London, June 1995.
12 In interview with EW, Berlin, December 1993.
13 Ibid.
14 Hilary du Pré and Piers du Pré, op. cit., pp. 126ff.
15 Interview with EW, London, June 1994.

16   Interview with EW, London, May 1993.
17   In interview with EW, London, January 1997.
18   David Pryce-Jones, 'The girl with the most famous cello in the world', *Sunday Times Magazine*, June 1967.
19   Interview with EW, Glasgow, August 1995.

11   *To Be a Cellist*
1   *Guardian*, 8 January 1964.
2   *Guardian*, 4 September 1964.
3   *Financial Times*, 18 March 1964.
4   *Guardian*, 18 March 1964.
5   *Evening Standard*, January 1964.
6   Hilary du Pré and Piers du Pré, op. cit., pp. 152–3.
7   In telephone interview with EW, January 1997.
8   From BBC Radio programme *Artist of the Month*, February 1965.
9   In Yehudi Menuhin, 'Sharing a Language', in Wordsworth (ed.), op. cit., p. 70.
10   Ibid. and from faxed letter to EW, 15 December 1994.
11   In interview with EW, London, November 1995.
12   *Guardian*, 4 September 1964.
13   *Daily Telegraph*, 4 September 1964.
14   *Financial Times*, 4 September 1964.
15   *Guardian*, 4 September 1964.
16   In interview with EW, May 1993.
17   Hilary du Pré and Piers du Pré, op. cit., p. 138.
18   Paul Tortelier and David Blum, op. cit., p. 138.

12   *A Budding Partnership*
1   *Sunday Times*, 18 October 1964.
2   These and all further quotes in this chapter from a recorded interview with EW, London, June 1993.
3   From recorded interview with EW, London, December 1995.
4   Ibid.
5   From recorded interview with EW, August 1994.
6   From BBC programme for radio *Artist of the Month*, February 1965.
7   From a recorded interview with EW, June 1994.
8   H. Blech, 'Forty years of the London Mozart Players', *Recollections without Chronology*, p. 42.
9   *Philadelphia Inquirer*, 19 February 1967.

13 *New Audiences*
 1 Interview with EW, New York, February 1994.
 2 In interview with EW, London, November 1995.
 3 Interview with EW, London, December 1995.
 4 Interview with EW, Aldeburgh, June 1995.
 5 Interview with Hugh Maguire, Aldeburgh, June 1995.
 6 Interview with EW, London, December 1995.
 7 *New York Times*, Sunday 26 February 1967.
 8 Terry Harrison in interview with EW, May 1993.
 9 From faxed letter to EW, November 1997.
10 Ibid.
11 Interview by phone, June 1996.
12 This and all above quotes from interview with EW, Milan, January 1997.
13 Sir Richard Bayliss's letter, 23 September 1965, quoted in Dr Len Selby's medical notes.

14 *Recordings*
 1 In interview with EW, London, November 1995.
 2 In interview with Anna Wilson, September 1993.
 3 *The Gramophone*, January 1969.
 4 In a letter dated 30 November 1964.
 5 In interview with EW, London, November 1995.
 6 In an article for EMI CD box '*Les introuvables de Jacqueline du Pré*'.
 7 Margaret Campbell, *The Great Cellists*, Victor Gollancz, London, 1988, p. 208.
 8 Ibid.
 9 Review by F. A. in *The Gramophone*, August 1965.
10 EMI publicity department's 'An Eyewitness report'.
11 Michael Kennedy, *Portrait of Elgar*, Clarendon Press, Oxford, 1993, p. 283.
12 Ibid.
13 Robert Baldock, *Pablo Casals*, Victor Gollancz, London, 1992, pp. 171–2.
14 In telephone interview with EW, August 1996.
15 In interview with EW, London, May 1993.
16 In interview with EW, May 1996.
17 Interview with EW, November 1995.
18 In a letter to Jacqueline du Pré from J. K. R. Whittle, December 1965.
19 Interview with EW, November 1995.

20   Daniel Barenboim, op. cit., pp. 65–6.
21   Internal EMI memorandum letter signed by J. K. R. Whittle, 16 October 1964.
22   Internal EMI memorandum letter of 26 October 1964.
23   Capitol Records memo, 29 April 1966.

15   *Moscow Interlude*
1   From an interview with EW, Oxford, December 1995.
2   Letter from Jacqueline du Pré to Madeleine Dinkel, 26 March 1966.
3   Postcard from Jacqueline du Pré to Madeleine Dinkel, postmarked 25 April 1966.
4   Letter from Jacqueline du Pré to Madeleine Dinkel, 26 March 1966.
5   Interview with EW, Turin, 1994.
6   Interview with EW, August 1966.
7   Letter from Jacqueline du Pré to Madeleine Dinkel, 26 March 1966.
8   Letter from Jacqueline du Pré to Guthrie Luke, 20 April 1966.
9   Letter from EW to her parents, 31 March 1966.
10   Letter from Jacqueline du Pré to Madeleine Dinkel, 26 March 1966.
11   Letter from Jacqueline du Pré to Guthrie Luke, 20 April 1966.
12   Letter from Jacqueline du Pré to Madeleine Dinkel, 10 May 1966.
13   Letter from EW to her parents, 1 May 1966.
14   Interview with EW, May 1966.
15   Interview with EW, September 1997.
16   Interview with EW, Aldeburgh, June 1995.
17   Interview with EW, Milan, January 1997.
18   Article in Weekend *Telegraph* Magazine, June 1967.

16   *New Directions*
1   Letter quoted in Hilary du Pré and Piers du Pré, op. cit., p. 179.
2   Ibid., p. 178.
3   From notes and letters in EMI archive.
4   Telephone interview with EW, June 1966.
5   This and all further quotes from interview with EW, Aldeburgh, June 1994.
6   This and all further quotes from an interview with EW by phone, August 1994.
7   Letter dated November 1966 in EMI archive.
8   This and all further quotes from interview with EW, London, June 1995.
9   Interview with EW, London, 1 January 1997.

10 *Birmingham Evening Mail*, 9 December 1966.
11 This and all further quotes from interview with EW, London, June 1993.
12 Interview recorded for BBC Radio. Quoted in programme dedicated to Jacqueline du Pré's fortieth birthday.
13 Suvi Raj Grubb, *A Genius On Record* in Wordsworth (ed.), op. cit., p. 96 and in interview with Anna Wilson, September 1993.

17 *The World At Her Feet*
 1 In interview with EW, Aldeburgh, June 1994.
 2 In telephone interview with EW, May 1996.
 3 This and all further quotes (unless otherwise acknowledged) from interviews with EW, Berlin, December 1993, London, June 1994 and Paris, April 1995.
 4 In interview with EW, Turin, 1994.
 5 In interview with EW, June 1993.
 6 In interview with EW, Aldeburgh, June 1995.
 7 Daniel Barenboim, *A Life in Music*, p. 78.
 8 In interview with Anna Wilson, London, September 1993.
 9 Document in EMI archive – quoted by courtesy of EMI.
10 Document in EMI archive.
11 Letter to Jacqueline du Pré from Larry Taylor, 1980.
12 In telephone interview with EW, January 1997.
13 *Newsweek*, 13 March 1967.
14 Ibid.
15 In interview with EW, London, June 1994.
16 Ibid.
17 *The Times*, 6 April 1967.
18 In interview with EW, Bath, May 1993.
19 Suvi Raj Grubb, op. cit., p. 96.
20 Ibid., pp. 96, 97.
21 Ibid.
22 *Weekend Telegraph Magazine*, June 1967.
23 EMI archives.
24 In interview with EW, London, June 1993.
25 Ibid.
26 Daniel Barenboim, op. cit., p. 109.

18 *Love Triumphant*

1 AVIDOM Musical Diary, 20 June 1967.

2 Daniel Barenboim, op. cit., p. 109.

3 *Belfast Telegraph*, 14 June 1967.

4 Zubin Mehta, 'Fun and Laughter', in Wordsworth (ed.), op. cit., p. 88.

5 Daniel Barenboim in interview with EW, Paris, April 1995.

6 Ibid.

7 In interview with EW, London, June 1994.

8 Rabbi Albert Friedlander, *A Thread of Gold*, p. 77.

9 Zubin Mehta, op. cit., pp. 89–90.

10 Letter addressed to Teddy Kollek by Y. Beinisch. Courtesy of Teddy Kollek.

11 Mrs Derek du Pré, 'Born for the Cello', in Wordsworth (ed.), op. cit., p. 30.

12 Dame Janet Baker, 'The Bolt of Cupid', in Wordsworth (ed.), op. cit., pp. 73, 74.

13 Zubin Mehta, op. cit., pp. 88–90.

14 Mrs Derek du Pré, op. cit., p. 30.

15 Maureen Cleave, *New York Times Magazine*, 16 March 1969.

16 Evelyn Barbirolli, 'From Evelyn, Con Amore', in Wordsworth (ed.), op. cit., p. 50.

17 Daniel Barenboim, op. cit., p. 78.

18 Rabbi Albert Friedlander, op. cit., p. 78.

19 In interview with EW, June 1994.

20 Hilary du Pré and Piers du Pré, op. cit., pp. 195–6.

21 Daniel Barenboim, op. cit., p. 44.

22 Ibid., pp. 112–13.

23 In conversation with EW, Berlin, December 1993.

24 From faxed letter to EW, December 1994.

25 In conversation with EW, Berlin, December 1993.

26 This and further quotes from interview with EW, Turin, February 1994.

27 *Guardian*, 9 December 1967.

28 In letter to EW from Ottomar Borwitzky, 11 July 1994.

29 From faxed letter to EW, December 1994.

30 *Guardian*, 9 December 1967.

31 *Daily Telegraph*, 9 December 1967.

19   *The Ideal Partnership*

1   In his speech at the Memorial Thanksgiving Concert for Jacqueline du Pré, Westminster Hall, London, January 1988.

2   EMI archive.

3   Suvi Raj Grubb, op. cit., pp. 97, 98.

4   Eduard Hanslick, *Musikalische und Literarische Kritiken und Schilderungen der Modernen Oper*, Berlin, 1899, pp. 1949–56.

5   Suvi Raj Grubb, op. cit., pp. 97, 98.

6   Ibid.

7   In interview with Anna Wilson, London, September 1993.

8   In interview with EW, Paris, April 1995.

9   Lord Harewood, 'My Goddaughter', in Wordsworth (ed.), op. cit., p. 33.

10   In interview with EW, Aldeburgh, June 1994.

11   Christopher Nupen in interview with EW, London, January 1997.

12   Lord Harewood, op. cit., p. 33.

13   *The Times*, 21 October 1967.

14   Kindly provided to me by Swedish Radio for study purposes only. In view of Celibidache's total veto of making commercial recordings, the beginnings of each movement were cut.

15   *The Times*, 13 December 1967.

16   EMI archive.

17   In interview with EW, London, June 1993.

18   In interview with EW, Paris, April 1995.

19   In interview with EW, Turin, September 1993.

20   In interview with EW, Paris, April 1995.

21   In interview with EW, Turin, September 1993.

22   *New York Times*, 7 April 1968.

23   In interview with EW, Berlin, December 1993.

24   Suvi Raj Grubb, op. cit., p. 98.

25   Tully Porter, 'Don Quixote Rediscovered', *Strad Mag*, December 1995.

26   Lotte Klemperer gives this date as the seventh, as opposed to the sixth which is the date quoted by Andrew Keener in his commentary to the recording in the notes for the EMI CD.

27   Letter to EW, 27 March 1996.

28   Notes to the EMI CD C 5 55528 2 1995.

29   Letter dated 22 December 1967 (EMI archive).

30   *Guardian*, 13 April 1968.

31   *The Times*, 13 April 1968.

32 From BBC Radio programme *With Great Pleasure*, 1980.
33 Faxed letter to EW, 5 May 1994.

20 *The Festive Season*
1   Daniel Barenboim, op. cit., p. 100.
2   In interview with EW, London, June 1994.
3   In interview with EW, London, November 1995.
4   In interview with EW, November 1994.
5   In interview with EW, Cambridge, June 1995.
6   Ibid.
7   *Radio Times*, May 1968.
8   *Observer*, 5 May 1968.
9   *The Gramophone*, January 1969.
10 *Sunday Times*, 5 May 1968.
11 Blum, op. cit., p. 91.
12 In a faxed letter to EW, April 1994.
13 In interview with EW, London, May 1993.
14 Ibid.
15 In interview with EW by telephone, November 1996.
16 Zubin Mehta, op. cit., p. 91.
17 *Music and Musicians*, October 1968.
18 *The Times*, 19 August 1969.
19 *Daily Telegraph*, 6 September 1968.
20 *The Times*, 2 September 1968.

21 *Belonging To The World*
1   *Daily Telegraph* (Australia), 11 April 1969.
2   *The Times*, 1 November 1968.
3   From Lamar Crowson's letter to EW, 21 June 1994.
4   Ibid.
5   Interview with Charles Wadsworth (on telephone), June 1996.
6   In interview with EW, Turin, January 1994.
7   Maureen Cleave, 'Triangle: Daniel and Jacqueline Barenboim and the Cello', *New York Times Magazine*, 16 March 1968.
8   Plácido Domingo, 'Musicality Comes First', in Wordsworth (ed.), op. cit., p. 82.
9   Interview with EW, London, June 1993.
10 *Tribune*, 28 February 1969.

11 Gerald Moore, *Farewell Recital – Further Memoirs*, Penguin Books, London, 1979, p. 109.
12 Edward Greenfield, 'Behind the Scenes', *High Fidelity Magazine*, July 1969.
13 G. W., *Financial Times*, 3 April 1969.

22 *Belonging To The Clan*
1 *New York Times*, 8 June 1969.
2 Plácido Domingo, op. cit., p. 79.
3 Cheltenham Festival of Music 1945–94: Reminiscences of Sir John Manduell (taken from a radio interview in 1982).
4 *The Times*, 11 July 1969.
5 Article written for CD album *Les Introuvables de Jacqueline du Pré*, EMI CZS 5 68132 2.

23 *Celebrity Beethoven*
1 *LA Times*, 20 December 1969.
2 *Citizen News*, 20 December 1969.
3 From an article in the concert programme for the South Bank Festival, 2 August 1970.
4 In telephone interview with EW, June 1995.
5 In interview with EW, Turin, September 1993.
6 *High Fidelity Magazine*, July 1970.
7 Alan Hughes, *New York Times*, 7 March 1970.
8 *New York Post*, 6 March 1970.
9 In interview with EW, London 1994.
10 In interview with EW, London, June 1994.
11 *The Times*, 5 August 1970.
12 In interview with EW, London, 1 January 1997.
13 In interview with EW, Milan, September 1994.
14 *The Times*, 15 August 1970.
15 *The Times*, 17 August 1970.
16 Gerald Moore, op. cit., p. 114.
17 In interview with EW, London, June 1993.

24 *Playing Against The Odds*
1 *The Australian*, 21 September 1970.
2 Joy Tonks, *New Zealand Symphony Orchestra, The First Forty Years*, p. 191.

3   *Toronto Globe and Mail,* 28 October 1970.

4   *Chicago Daily News,* 10 November 1970.

5   *Lansing State Journal,* 11 November 1970.

6   In interview with EW, London, 1993.

7   In interview with EW, Turin, September 1993.

8   Letter from Robert Myers to Peter Andry, 16 December 1970. EMI archive.

9   Letter from Peter Andry to Robert Myers, 22 December 1970, EMI archive.

10   Ralph Vaughan Williams, 'What have we learnt from Elgar?', from *National Music and Other Essays,* Clarendon Press, Oxford, 1996, pp. 251–2.

11   From leaflet for Jacqueline du Pré's 1970 CBS recording of the Elgar concerto MK76529.

12   From an interview with EW, London, November 1994.

13   In the CD version of the recording there is a concrete error, probably due to an oversight in the editorial stage – namely a gap in the sound at figure 13 of the first movement, where the cello's long tied B is not held over into the woodwind's 12/8 theme – the small pause is evidence of an editing splice. It is inconceivable to me that Jackie would not have held this note through at a performance.

14   Ralph Vaughan Williams, 'How do we make music', op. cit., p. 216.

25   *Crisis*

1   *Daily Telegraph,* 18 December 1970.

2   In interview with EW, London, June 1995.

3   Stephen Banfield, *Gerald Finzi, An English Composer,* Faber & Faber, London, 1997, p. 285.

4   Interview with Christopher Finzi, *The Times,* Wednesday, 8 October 1997.

5   Hilary du Pré and Piers du Pré, op. cit., chapter 37ff.

6   Cynthia Benz, *Coping With Multiple Sclerosis,* Macdonald Optima, London, 1988, p. 25.

7   From Anatole Leikin, 'The Sonatas', in Jim Samson (ed.), *The Cambridge Companion to Chopin,* Cambridge University Press, 1992, p. 185.

8   Suvi Raj Grubb, op. cit., p. 100.

26 *A Short-lived Comeback*

1   *The Times*, 25 September 1972.
2   Interview with EW, London, June 1993.
3   EMI archive. Note to Peter Andry from Suvi Raj Grubb dated 20 February 1973.
4   EMI archive. Note to Suvi Raj Grubb from Peter Andry dated 28 February 1973.
5   *Plain Dealer*, 6 January 1973.
6   Peter Davis, *New York Times*, 17 January 1973.
7   In interview with EW, Turin, February 1994.
8   *Daily Telegraph*, 9 February 1973.
9   *Guardian*, 9 February 1973.
10 *Financial Times*, 9 February 1973.
11 In interview with EW, June 1993.
12 *New York Post*, 17 February 1973.
13 BBC Radio 4 tribute for Jacqueline du Pré's fortieth birthday.
14 In interview with EW, Milan, January 1997.
15 Cynthia Benz, op. cit., p. 32.
16 In interview with EW, London, June 1993.
17 In interview with EW.
18 Zubin Mehta, op. cit., pp. 92, 93.

27 *Fortitude Under Affliction*

1   Daniel Barenboim, op. cit., p. 172.
2   From Jacqueline du Pré's BBC Radio interview *I Really Am a Very Lucky Person*.
3   In interview with EW, London, June 1993.
4   Letter from Jacqueline du Pré to Maggie Cohen, 17 December 1974.
5   In interview with EW, New York, February 1994.
6   Postcard from Jacqueline du Pré to Cynthia and Rodney Friend postmarked 30 April 1975.
7   Undated letter of Jacqueline du Pré to Cynthia and Rodney Friend, May 1975.
8   Ibid.
9   In interview with EW, London, May 1993.
10 Jacqueline du Pré's letter to Sir Ian Hunter, 17 July 1977.
11 From Mona Thomas's letter to EW, December 1994.
12 *The Times*, 21 August 1978.
13 From her letter to EW.

14 From Jacqueline du Pré's notebooks.
15 In interview with EW, June 1993.
16 In interview with EW, London, November 1995.
17 In interview with EW, London, 1995.
18 In telephone interview with EW.
19 Jacqueline du Pré, unpublished notebooks.

28 *The Legacy Lives On*
1 Interview with EW, London, November 1994.
2 This and all further quotes in this chapter in interview with EW, London, June 1994.
3 Interview with EW, Hythe, June 1993.
4 Interview with EW, Bath, May 1993.
5 This and all further quotes in this chapter from interview with EW, London, May 1993.
6 Janet Suzman's article 'Jackie and the Wolf' in Wordsworth, op. cit., p. 127.
7 Interview with EW, London.
8 This and all further quotes in this chapter from interview with EW, London, June 1993.
9 Interview with EW, London, June 1993.

Index